INTRODUCTION TO POLITICAL THINKERS

SECOND EDITION

INTRODUCTION TO POLITICAL THINKERS

SECOND EDITION

William Ebenstein
(1910–1976)

*University of Wisconsin at Madison, Princeton University,
and University of California at Santa Barbara*

Alan Ebenstein

THOMSON
™
WADSWORTH

Australia • Canada • Mexico • Singapore • Spain • United Kingdom • United States

Publisher	Earl McPeek
Executive Editor	David C. Tatom
Project Editor	Claudia Gravier
Art Director	Susan Journey
Production Manager	Diane Gray

ISBN-13: 978-0-15-506666-3
ISBN-10: 0-15-506666-8
Library of Congress Catalog Card Number: 2001092711

Wadsworth Group/Thomson Learning
10 Davis Drive
Belmont CA 94002-3098
USA

For information about our products, contact us:
Thomson Learning Academic Resource Center
1-800-423-0563
http://www.wadsworth.com

For permission to use material from this text, contact us by
Web: http://www.thomsonrights.com
Fax: 1-800-730-2215
Phone: 1-800-730-2214

Printed in Canada
10 9 8 7

To Joe Atwill

A.E.

Works by WILLIAM EBENSTEIN

FASCISM AT WORK

REINE RECHTSLEHRE

FASCIST ITALY

THE LAW OF PUBLIC HOUSING

THE NAZI STATE

THE GERMAN RECORD
A Political Portrait

THE PURE THEORY OF LAW

MAN AND THE STATE
Modern Political Ideas

GREAT POLITICAL THINKERS
Plato to the Present, Sixth Edition (co-author)

INTRODUCTION TO POLITICAL PHILOSOPHY

MODERN POLITICAL THOUGHT
The Great Issues, Second Edition

TODAY'S ISMS
Socialism, Capitalism, Fascism, Communism, Libertarianism, Eleventh Edition (co-author)

POLITICAL THOUGHT IN PERSPECTIVE

CHURCH AND STATE IN FRANCO SPAIN

TWO WAYS OF LIFE
The Communist Challenge to Democracy, Second Edition

TOTALITARIANISM
New Perspectives

COMMUNISM IN THEORY AND PRACTICE

AMERICAN GOVERNMENT IN THE TWENTIETH CENTURY
Third Edition (co-author)

AMERICAN DEMOCRACY IN WORLD PERSPECTIVE
Fifth Edition (co-author)

INTRODUCTION TO POLITICAL THINKERS
(co-author)

Works by ALAN EBENSTEIN

THE GREATEST HAPPINESS PRINCIPLE
An Examination of Utilitarianism

GREAT POLITICAL THINKERS
Plato to the Present, Sixth Edition (co-author)

INTRODUCTION TO POLITICAL THINKERS
(co-author)

TODAY'S ISMS
Socialism, Capitalism, Fascism, Communism, Libertarianism, Eleventh Edition (co-author)

EDWIN CANNAN
Liberal Doyen

FRIEDRICH HAYEK
A Biography

PREFACE

Introduction to Political Thinkers is an abridgment of *Great Political Thinkers* (sixth edition, 2000). Many reviewers during the revision process of *Great Political Thinkers* requested an abridged version. Not all instructors teach courses for which the more comprehensive treatment of *Great Political Thinkers* is required. Forty-six thinkers are covered in the larger book; twelve are contained here. The chapters here (with minor exceptions) are exactly as they appear in *Great Political Thinkers*. Only the number of chapters is abridged.

The purpose of *Introduction to Political Thinkers* is to present the most significant political philosophers from Plato forward. Each thinker is critically analyzed and placed in his historical context, and a key reading is then presented. This approach combines the strengths of commentary and original readings.

There are several changes to this second edition of *Introduction to Political Thinkers*. The introduction and chapter on Hayek are new. There are significant revisions to the chapters on Mill and Rawls and lesser changes elsewhere. The bibliographical notes have been updated.

This book—as its title states—is an introduction. After the reader is finished, he is encouraged to study other political philosophers in *Great Political Thinkers*.

Alan Ebenstein
Santa Barbara, California
2001

CONTENTS

INTRODUCTION

The history of political thought is the history of human society. The question of how men should organize their societies is the stuff of political thought. Political thought concerns groups, not individuals. It is primarily concerned with the Ought not the Is of societal life. In its broadest sense, political thought concerns how men should live together.

Political thought is typically based on empirical foundations—what societies are possible. But its fundamental issue is not empirical but ethical. Political thought is not primarily about how men and women do live with one another, but how they should. As such, it is a branch of morality or ethics.

Politics does not arise in the situation of an isolated individual. Politics occurs in the circumstance of groups. It is largely forward-looking: How should society be ordered or organized? Its fundamental concern with morality and ethics stems from the situation that political thought guides individuals in how they lead their collective lives. No activity that concerns how men should live together can be anything other than fundamentally moral in nature.

How ought men to live together? This is the fundamental question of political thought. The question of how men and women should live together has been answered differently by the thinkers introduced here. Plato, Aristotle, St. Augustine, St. Thomas Aquinas, Machiavelli, Hobbes, Locke, Rousseau, Mill, Marx, Hayek, and Rawls are among the leading political philosophers through the ages. They answer the "Ought" question of society in different ways.

For Plato, at least in his explicit philosophy, there is an ideal world of forms that is eternal and unchanging of which this world is only a shadowy representation. He puts forward an ideal threefold class system composed of societal governors (guardians), soldiers (auxiliaries), and the masses, based on the Spartan system of government, ideally led by a philosopher-king. Plato advocates a communal lifestyle for guardians. Women members of the guardian class would have rights with men. Children would be raised in common. There would be significant thought control.

Though from Athens, Plato is no democrat. His mentor is Socrates, in whose name he largely speaks. Aristotle has a more practical outlook than his teacher Plato. Socrates, Plato, and Aristotle are part—toward the end—of the great intellectual flowering in Greece half a millennium before Jesus' birth.

The Greeks were never able to unify politically, and Aristotle's is the last great Greek voice to instruct future centuries. Though Aristotle is thoroughly informed by the city-state in his conceptions of optimal political order, he identifies lasting strands in political organization in societies—rule by the one, rule by the few, and rule by the many. Aristotle prefers rule by the wise one, as Plato does, but he does not think that this is very likely. Aristotle distinguishes between true and corrupt forms of rule by the one, few, and many and, in their corrupt forms, favors rule by the many over either the corrupt few or one. He sanctions slavery and has a strong sense of community, including political community. He supports a predominantly middle-class society and mixed forms of governance, the latter of which became a prevailing theme during constitutional theorizing and making during the seventeenth through twentieth centuries.

Few deities last through the ages. No one (or almost no one) now worships Zeus or Jupiter. But the ancient Hebrews' god remains God for around two billion Christians and Jews. Jewish monotheistic consciousness has spread over much of mankind. In the oldest sense of the term, the west—in the sense of the Occident distinguished from the Orient—and the realm of Jewish monotheistic consciousness are one.

St. Augustine is a transitional figure between the classical world and European Christendom. He was reared in the thought of the classical world but his outlook is different. While the classical writers emphasized this life, Augustine focuses on what he believes is the life to come. The City of God, not the earthly city, is Augustine's goal.

The Middle Ages are traditionally considered to be a period of falling away in which mankind lost much of the knowledge it previously held, a millennium during which civilization quickly degenerated and remained at a lower level. From a technical sense this is surely true. Perhaps nothing better symbolizes it as it practically reflected the decline of civilization during the Middle Ages than the fate of the great Roman roads made of stone that connected an empire throughout the Mediterranean world during antiquity. These were literally ripped up and their stones utilized as a source for buildings in the semi-independent castle states of the Middle Ages. Roads connecting humanity with each other were turned into castles protecting them from each other.

The Middle Ages were a period of contrast in which philosophical and religious unity accompanied great political disunity. The order of things that existed during the Roman era completely reversed—Rome had great political unity and great philosophical and religious diversity. The Roman Catholic Church became the most important European societal institution during the Middle Ages as nation-states embryonically grew.

St. Thomas Aquinas was the single most important Catholic writer following Augustine. Aquinas, who lived during the thirteenth century, furthered the rediscovery of Aristotle's more practical thought to the more mystical, supernal approach found in Augustine through the tradition of Plato. Aquinas is a rationalist who thinks this world, as well as the next, vital. Aquinas thus paves the way for the modern, tentative approach to knowledge and truth that came into existence during the Renaissance and Enlightenment. Aquinas, as does Aristotle, has a communitarian conception of the good society, though more catholic-universal.

The late Middle Ages are a period whose interpretation has shifted during recent decades as the ever-changing present changes conceptions of the past. Whereas the thirteenth through fifteenth centuries were once considered more an adjunct to the high medievalism of the ninth through twelfth centuries, they are now more likely to be considered a precursor of the modern age, roughly from the sixteenth through twentieth centuries.

An even more accurate analysis of the development of European civilization might be to consider the fifteenth and sixteenth centuries, the 1400s and 1500s, essential transitional centuries from the ancient-medieval world to the modern world. The world was a very different place—substantively, in outlook—and in direction, in 1399 and 1600. During the 1600s, the first real outcroppings of institutional forms and political ideas that guided and continue to guide first European and now world civilization appeared.

So significant was the change in outlook during the sixteenth century that the 1500s are even more appropriately considered Europe's crucial transformative century, when antiquity was rediscovered and embraced—and yet separated from the past—when the printing press for the first time allowed the mass distribution of information, when gun powder revolutionized political relations, and when the discovery of a New World in the Americas changed mankind's temporal outlook in myriad ways. Machiavelli of Florence is a leading representative of the new conception of man that emerged in politics. No more tied to a God-centered conception of the world nor possessed of the communal spirit of antiquity, man in Machiavelli's view is a being without eternal or spiritual significance. Machiavelli focuses strictly on this life, and his political thought reflects a bifurcation between the ends and means of politics that existed in his time and place. Typically, when there are no limits on the means of politics, both politics' ends and means deteriorate.

There were competing intellectual, spiritual, and national strains during the seventeenth through nineteenth centuries. The Protestant Reformation was the greatest change in how men viewed the political and spiritual worlds. The Protestant Reformation to some extent returned to the mystic individualism of Plato through Augustine in contrast to the contemporaneous Aristotlean emphasis of the Roman Catholic Church in part through the influence of Aquinas. Men and women may be saved, according to the Protestant conception, through God's grace alone. There is a law higher than the law of men.

The most significant nations in Europe during the next several centuries to emerge during the late Middle Ages and early modern ages are England, Germany, and France. While the Germanic Holy Roman Empire was the pretended successor to the ancient Roman Empire, England was where and whence the most significant action in European civilization occurred during the modern age.

The political right of rebellion or revolution finds its spiritual justification in and practical inspiration from Protestant individualism and its material impetus from changes in technology. Seventeenth century England was a hotbed of political agitation. First came the Puritan Revolution and then the Glorious Revolution. Hobbes' complex thought is difficult to summarize. He is most famous for the statement that in a philosophical state of nature man's life is "solitary, poor, nasty, brutish, and short." Though Hobbes politically tends toward absolutism, he emphasizes contract and the positive role of the state to establish a safe and materially productive society.

Locke was philosopher of the English Glorious Revolution of 1688 through which parliament became supreme. The seventeenth through twentieth centuries experienced the expansion of democracy throughout much of the world. It was through the United States Revolution of 1776 that democracy really took root as the foundation of a state system. Concomitant with democracy typically have come institutional safeguards of individual rights—freedom of expression, the rule of law, and private property. The American Revolution was largely Lockean in inspiration; Locke justified the right to rebellion.

English-speaking areas' role in the world was predominant almost throughout the modern age. England was perhaps the preeminent European nation from the seventeenth through nineteenth centuries, and the United States was preeminent during the twentieth century. In addition to emphasizing constitutional government Locke puts forward the labor theory of value—that goods have value as a result of the labor that goes into producing them. This idea influenced future socialists as much as capitalists.

During the seventeenth through nineteenth centuries France played a larger role than it did during the twentieth. The French Revolution was the dominant political event in Europe during the eighteenth century. Although it should not be maintained that Rousseau was responsible for the French Revolution, the romantic element in his thought and his stress on human and material equality were an important part of the intellectual background that formed a number of revolutionaries.

Britain produced a string of great thinkers and writers on politics during the seventeenth through nineteenth centuries, including, in addition to Hobbes and Locke, David Hume, Adam Smith, Edmund Burke, Jeremy Bentham, and John Stuart Mill. Mill was the greatest British political philosopher of the nineteenth century. His most well known work is *On Liberty* (1859), which classically defends freedom of thought and expression. Mill was both a liberal and evolutionary socialist, but his decisive commitment was to liberalism, not at all state socialism. He philosophically paved the way for much of the welfare-state expansion of government during the twentieth century.

Marx became a much greater figure in the twentieth century than he was in the nineteenth, as a result of the 1917 Russian Revolution. Since the demise of the Soviet Union in 1991, and as a result of the brutality of the political systems that called and call themselves "Marxist," the great intrinsic intellectual significance that was ascribed to him a few decades ago has diminished. *The Communist Manifesto* remains a work of historical importance.

Hayek is the most important libertarian philosopher. His thought grows out of the socialist calculation debate on the practical possibilities of socialism. He puts forward the idea of spontaneous order, that it is possible to reach a world society in which law, not man, rules. He sees private property as the most important institutional safeguard of a free society and prices as necessary to efficient economic calculation. His accomplishment is to turn the question of socialism from an ethical to empirical one.

Rawls is perhaps the most important philosopher of the welfare state. While there is much in his thought that appears contradictory, his idea of "maximin"—to maximize the circumstances of the least well off (minimum) group in a society—may remain as an enduring contribution to political thought. While the principle of maximin may be implemented in ways entirely different than Rawls conceives (in very inegalitarian societies rather than very egalitarian ones), the idea itself is a noble ethical conception and one that a good society should consider if not fully embrace.

In the history of political thought, the works of philosophers may as much represent an era as form one. The value in studying political thought includes that this can enlighten moral understanding or clarify moral understandings of the way societal life should be. As the twenty-first century begins and a new human circumstance emerges, the thoughts of the greatest political philosophers from the past may become less relevant because the situation humanity faces is so new and different compared to the human condition through the ages. Political thought will continue to be about how men ought to live together, however, and the thought of such great political philosophers as Plato, Aristotle, Augustine, Aquinas, Machiavelli, Hobbes, Locke, Rousseau, Marx, Mill, Hayek, and Rawls may continue to enlighten historical understanding of how the fundamental question of political thought has been answered and provide enduring insight into the human soul that will influence new political thought.

So profound are the changes that may occur in the human circumstance, as well as that have occurred during the past century, that it may become accurate to consider the whole period before the twenty-first century as one age compared to the new age or ages that may lie in the twenty-first century and beyond. Answers to the question of how men ought to live together may change as the human circumstance revolutionizes, but the question should continue.

CHAPTER ONE

PLATO

The imperishable contribution of the Greeks to western civilization lies in the taming of man and nature through reason. In the pre-Greek world, advanced peoples had learned to live with nature by wresting from it, through patient observation, some of its secrets, and by applying them to gainful purposes. But such practical knowledge never lost its close association with demons and myths, fears and hopes, punishments and rewards; and the pre-Greek conception of nature viewed physical phenomena as essentially individual, unique, and incalculable rather than as general, universal, and predictable. The Greeks were not the first to think about recurrent regularities of inanimate events; but they were the first to develop—going beyond observation and knowledge—the *scientific attitude,* a new approach to the world that constitutes to this day one of the distinctive elements of western life.

In the field of human relations, too, Greek inventiveness and originality lay, not in this or that political theory, but in the discovery of the scientific study of politics. The Greeks were not the first to think about the problem of a well-ordered society. But pre-Greek political thought had been a mixture of legend, myth, theology, and allegory, and if there was an element of independent reasoning, it served as a means to a higher end, usually to be found in the tenets of a supernatural system, such as religion. Thus the contribution of Jewish thought to the political heritage of the world has been seminal: The idea of the brotherhood of man, of "one world," is deeply rooted in the conception of monotheism as transmitted through the Bible. By contrast, polytheism made it difficult for the Greeks to see the basic oneness of mankind, and their religious pluralism reflected their inability to transcend, intellectually and institutionally, the confines of the city-state.

From a social viewpoint, the Bible was opposed to slavery on principle—a unique phenomenon in antiquity—established a weekly day of rest (still unknown in some parts of the earth), and contained a host of protective rules in favor of workers, debtors, women, children, and the poor. The concept of "covenant," first appearing in the agreement between God and Abraham, is a frequent theme in the Bible whenever momentous decisions are to be made; it becomes again an inspiration centuries later when the Puritans attempt to build a new religion and civil society, or, still later, when President Wilson, a devout Presbyterian, names the constitution of the League of Nations a "Covenant." But, significant as these contributions to western civilization have been, they never were, nor were they meant to be, political science. They were political and social *ethics* rather than science, and as such constitute one of the three chief tributaries to the mainstream of

1

western civilization, the other two being the Christian principle of *love* and the Greek principle of *rationalism.*

The first work that deserves to be called political science, in that it applies systematic reasoning and critical inquiry to political ideas and institutions, is Plato's *Republic.* After almost twenty-four hundred years it is still matchless as an introduction to the basic issues that confront human beings as citizens. No other writer on politics has equaled Plato (427–347 B.C.) in combining penetrating and dialectical reasoning with poetic imagery and symbolism.

One of the main (and most revolutionary) assumptions of the *Republic* is that the right kind of government and politics can be the legitimate object of rigorous, rational analysis, rather than the inevitable product of muddling through fear and faith, indolence and improvisation. This Platonic assumption of the applicability of reason to social relations is as hotly debated in the twentieth century as it was in Plato's own time, and it is one of the key elements that go into the making of our political outlook and temperament. To the extent that we believe in the possibility of applying reason and critical analysis to the solution of political and social issues we are all Plato's spiritual heirs, although we may heartily disagree with any or all of his specific teachings. By seeking to disprove Plato on a point of political doctrine or practice, the anti-Platonist has already conceded to Plato the most important single point: that political and social issues can be clarified by argument rather than by force and dogma.

Socrates, Plato's teacher and the chief figure in the *Republic,* has been contemptuously called the "first Social Democrat" by some modern totalitarians; what they hate in him above all is his irritating habit of endlessly searching, through argument, for the reason that lies behind accepted ideas and institutions. Other totalitarians, penetrating less deeply into Plato's thought, have usurped him as their first intellectual ancestor because there is so much in the *Republic* that is explicitly undemocratic, or outright antidemocratic. Yet, implicit in Plato's and Socrates' rationalism is the assumption, incompatible with the cult of violence, that man's intellect can discover the nature of the good life and the means of attaining it by philosophical inquiry.

In one basic point, modern political analysis would gain in insight and understanding if it followed Plato more closely: Plato never starts out with the hypothesis of a *homo politicus,* an abstract "political man" unrelated to the richness and complexity of individual selves or of society as a whole. Today Plato's psychology may seem naive in its analogies and presumed facts, but what is of timeless significance is his conviction that no theory of politics can be sound unless based on the study of man. Modern psychology has taught us enough about neurotic persons to make us realize that a healthy society cannot be composed of men and women who are haunted by fear and insecurity.

Plato's political thought also introduced the concept of the "public" as distinct from the "private" in the context of governmental relations. As a Greek, Plato could not be clearly aware of the opposing ideas of the individual and (or, sometimes, versus) the state because the city-state was a spiritual and religious unity, as well as a social, economic, and political one. The Jewish and Christian religions separated man's soul from his quality as a citizen and established the notion of an inalienable and indestructible human spirit outside the domain and jurisdiction of government, a philosophy that was unknown and unknowable to Plato. In the polytheistic religions of the city-states, the gods were community gods, and there could be no question of the individual's being in one respect a member of his community, and in another not. Yet, if Plato was unaware of the opposition of the individual versus the state—since the seventeenth century the dominant leitmotiv of western political speculation—he was keenly aware of the *res publica,* the "common thing" in the mutual relations of human beings.

Before Greek experience and analysis, the only major dichotomy known to man, consciously or unconsciously, was that between the "sacred" and the profane." Its evolution into that of "public" and "private" is part of western secularism that goes back directly to Greek life and thought. Medieval feudalism abandoned the distinction between private and public relations in political and economic institutions; from the king downward there was no clear-cut division between the private and public property or authority of the lords and their vassals. In such a system the color and intensity of personal relations between the ruler and the ruled make rational discussion of political issues and true constitutionalism difficult; this fact can still be observed today in countries in which (as in some parts of the third world) impersonal government is an ideal rather than a reality.

Even when the concept of the modern sovereign state first developed in sixteenth-century Italy, *lo stato* meant essentially the ruler and the "machine" that he had built up for himself, and it was a long time before "the state" assumed the anonymous and impersonal character with which it was later endowed. In some modern authoritarian and totalitarian regimes, rulers tend again to mingle inextricably the domains of the public and the private, "borrowing" castles and picture galleries that belong to the state, "acquiring" vast industrial empires for their brothers and nephews, and building up private, and often personal, military forces competing with those of the state. The inevitable growth of corruption in such regimes is the price paid for the dissolution of the clear separation between public and private authority.

One of the hallmarks of genius is that it can enrich each generation anew. In the heyday of *laissez faire,* Plato's ideal of a highly trained administrative and political class, dedicated to public service without consideration of personal happiness or financial gain, exercised relatively less appeal because society was assumed to be an automatic and self-regulating piece of machinery, and political wisdom could well be summarized in the succinct formula of "the less government, the better." Plato's conception of government as the highest moral and practical task to which men of knowledge and virtue ought to devote themselves seemed out of date in the days in which doing nothing was deemed to be the noblest function of a political association. The force of circumstances, accelerated by wars and depressions, has necessarily enlarged, in recent times, the scope and function of government, and in Plato we rediscover the ideal of public service as second to none. Democrats are bound to reject Plato's own solution of this problem, the rule of those who know over those who do not, regardless of the latter's consent, but they will have to grasp, if democracy is to survive in a tough and dangerous world of competing skills, that there is no substitute for high-minded and efficient government in solving tensions and conflicts within and between nations.

We also increasingly practice Plato's teaching that the road to better government and public service is through an appropriately conceived system of education. In fact, the ultramodern and rapidly growing realization of education as a never-ending process, embracing adults as well as the young, goes back directly to Plato: he clearly saw that education was more than the acquiring of basic facts and ideas in one's childhood and adolescence, and he was the first to propose an elaborate system of adult training and education.

Democrats differ with Plato's system of education on two scores: first, Plato reserved educational opportunities of prolonged duration and intensity for future rulers only, whereas the democrat looks on education as a means to the good life that should be available to all. Second, Plato believed that the selection of rulers could best be made through the prolonged training of men and women, generally those born into the ruling class or picked, in exceptional situations, from the lower classes of the workers, farmers, and merchants. Democrats reject such a scheme and insist that political rulers be selected by popular voting. This democratic theory is valid as long as voters have enough judgment and discrimination to elect the best to public office. When they freely choose to put knaves and fools into high positions of public trust and authority, the democratic theory of selecting rulers is quickly swept away by demagogues and dictators. Whereas democracy will continue to reject Plato's scheme of training an elite of political *rulers,* it will view more sympathetically the possibility and desirability of training *public servants.* On that point, democracies are more and more abandoning the older doctrine that the spoils system, or government by crony, can be a substitute for honest and efficient administration.

One of the main causes of Plato's pervasive and persuasive influence throughout history is that he is the ablest exponent of the aristocracy theory of the state, and the acutest critic of the democratic way of life. In the evolution of mankind the extent of democratic experience is infinitesimally small, compared with its ignorance of democratic living, and putting the one on top of the other is like putting a postage stamp on top of a tall skyscraper. If history has been largely the history of inequality, it is no wonder that Plato's philosophy of inequality, mellowed by the accretion of prestige and sweetened by the reasonableness of its argument, should have been the most venerated and idealized political philosophy of the ages. Its relative moderation has immensely added to the influence of the *Republic.* Though in general in favor of a hierarchical society that, once set up, is closed rather than open, the *Republic* must seem repugnant to some conservatives on several grounds: The idea of rational inquiry into the foundations of society, that is, going to the roots of social institutions, must seem too radical, because the conservative likes to behold them as a product of natural growth with which one must not willfully, by intelligence or other means, interfere.

In describing the "first city," before the "feverish condition" sets in that necessitates the formation of the two classes of the rulers (guardians) and soldier-administrators (auxiliaries), Plato portrays a pattern of natural growth of social institutions, untampered by conscious reason, that would appeal to the conservative. But the first city, whose sole *raison d'être* lies in the satisfaction of material wants through the principle of the division of labor, is, as Glaucon puts it, a "community of pigs," lacking as yet the conscious direction of a ruling class whose specific excellence is reason. The growth of the simple first city into a condition of fever is caused, according to Plato, by the expansion and refinement of human wants, that is, by luxury. The inability of the community to fill the newly developing luxurious needs out of the existing resources (land, labor, skills) is the cause of war, either aggressive or defensive war.

The feverish condition is, however, not limited to the threat of external war but also implies the possibility of the disruption or dissolution of the health and balance of the first city through internal unrest. In order to safeguard or, rather, restore the original balance of the community, a special class of fighters is needed. Yet, if the new fighting class is not to degenerate into a class of praetorians, drunk with power and quarreling continuously among themselves and with the members of the producing class, it must receive a training that will make its members "gentle to their own people and dangerous only to enemies," instill them with courage to defend the city against internal and external enemies, and at the same time imbue them with an understanding of the principles that make the city worth defending.

The class of the fighters (auxiliaries) thus makes the existence of a still higher class necessary, the guardians, or rulers, who pick and train the auxiliaries as well as the future guardians. The characteristic quality of the rulers is *wisdom,* just as *courage* (tempered by understanding) is the characteristic quality of the fighters and *appetite* (or the desire to satisfy material wants) is the distinctive trait of the working population (workers, farmers, merchants, doctors, nurses, actors). Just as the first city was the product of unconscious growth, the "second," or "ideal," city of the *Republic* is the product of rational direction.

The Platonic community is the first example of a planned state; but it must be borne in mind that the planned sector of this state applies only to the guardians and auxiliaries, whereas the producing class is left to itself as far as its economic activities go. Plato was an aristocrat who exhibited the bias against labor and business so characteristic of aristocrats in all ages, and the lack of regulations of the economic order of the producing class in the *Republic* indicates the contempt of the nobleman for the prosaic existence of those who must work for a living.

The life of the guardians and auxiliaries excludes individual interests, whether in property, love, or the family, but this community of absolute sharing is not socialism. The outlook of socialism is hedonistic: Its objective is the increase of human happiness through the abolition of want and misery. The goal of socialism is not the realization of a preconceived just ideal of society but the attainment of maximum *happiness* for the maximum number of people *here and now.* The sharing of the guardians and auxiliaries in the *Republic* is based on a principle that is almost diametrically opposed to that of socialism: the principle of *austerity,* which puts little, if any, value on material wants and their satisfaction. Not happiness of human beings with varying and unique personalities, but the realization of a predetermined social ideal of justice is the purpose of the political community as described in the *Republic.*

Though the analogy to the communal life of the guardians and auxiliaries is not to be found in the socialist state (in which all citizens share in the amenities of life) nor in socialist communities within a nonsocialist state, it can be found in armies, monastic orders, and the clergy of churches who are denied marriage or private property. In all such groups the ruling class shares with the Platonic guardians the certainty of knowing what is best for the ruled, without asking for their consent, as well as the relative disregard for property, sex, family, or other forms of personal happiness. Plato's "socialism" of the guardians was authoritarian service rather than the sharing of happiness and enjoyment, and as such the exact antithesis of western socialism.

The *Republic* is opposed to democracy on two levels of argument: a more obvious explicit level and a less obvious implicit level. The explicit opposition of the *Republic* to democracy rests on the threefold division of the population into rulers, fighters, and producers (farmers, artisans, traders). A numerically small aristocracy of rulers, in command of a well-trained body of soldiers and administrators, governs the third class, or producers, which constitutes four-fifths or more of the total population. Plato claims that the threefold class division of the second city is but an extension of the principle of the division of labor, characteristic of the first city. Ruling or defending a state, Plato argues, is just as much a *specialized craft* as shoemaking; and if the principle of the division of labor forbids the shoemaker from making furniture, he is equally excluded from ruling, or defending and administering, the city—functions that constitute special, and specialized, crafts.

There is one objection to Plato's reasoning here (and this objection is fundamental to the whole edifice of the *Republic*): If the nature of ruling and administering a state is a specialized craft no different from shoemaking or farming, it is difficult to see why he does not simply add the two new crafts of the second city to the already existing number of crafts of the first city. In it, we may recall, there were no special crafts of ruling and administering, because the harmony of society was maintained naturally, growing out of the division of labor and without conscious guidance or rule. If, for example, the number of crafts in the first city was one hundred, the addition of two new crafts of ruling and fighting in the second city should produce one hundred and two crafts, if the second city were still based, as before, on the principle of division of labor. Instead, Plato presents us with the concept of *three classes* in the second city: first, the class of rulers (guardians in the narrower sense); second, the class of military and civilian executive aides (auxiliaries); third, the class of producers or handworkers. This last class composed, in the first city, the entire population, organized on the principle of division of labor; now, in the second city, the working part makes up only from eighty to ninety percent.

The principle of the division of labor can produce only more and more specialized crafts, as the needs and skills of society proliferate, but it can never lead to a class system based on hierarchical values. If Plato nevertheless introduces the concept of the threefold class division into the second city, a new principle, different from that of the division of labor, must be found to distinguish the functions of ruling and administering the state from all other crafts. The main difference between the ruler-philosophers and the producers in the *Republic* is the difference between *political wisdom* and *technical knowledge*. Only the philosophers have insight into *human* problems, insight that is more than highly specialized learning. The craftsman, by contrast, has no all-comprehensive understanding of the phenomena of nature and society of which he is a part, only *limited* knowledge of a *technical* nature. Even where such knowledge, as in medicine, applies to human beings, it is still only technical knowledge and not higher philosophical understanding and insight, because the physician is interested in human beings as parts of the psychophysical world, and not of the world of values and ideas.

The Platonic craftsman is thus inferior, in two ways, to the philosopher: First, his material is limited and finite, and subject to causal or esthetical laws, the knowledge of which is relatively easy, compared with the material of the philosopher—mankind and the cosmos, the laws of which are most difficult to discover and grasp. Second, the knowledge of the craftsman never attains the height of wisdom and understanding that the philosopher reaches in his study of ultimate values, intrinsic forms, and cosmic laws. The knowledge of the craftsman is only an intermediary stage, raw material that goes into the process of learning and acquiring wisdom to which the philosopher is subjected in the *Republic*.

The democratic theory of politics challenges Plato not only in his basic assumption that the capacity to govern is possessed by only a small class, but that such capacity can be transmitted, in general (Plato admits occasional exceptions), by selective breeding. This Platonic concept of a hereditary aristocratic ruling class, not too hermetically closed to talent from below, is rejected by the democratic theory of man and the state on grounds of historical evidence and rational reflection. The democratic view of man is less pessimistic than Plato's and assumes hopefully that wisdom and understanding may be found in the most unexpected places, in log cabins as well as in stately mansions.

If the explicit opposition of the *Republic* to the democratic way of life is serious enough, the implicit opposition is even more fundamental and irreconcilable. Plato assumes (in the *Republic* as in his other writings) that Truth is something eternal, unchanging and unchangeable, and that it can be made accessible to a select few through an ingeniously devised training reserved for the future fighters and rulers. The preparation of the rulers begins before they are born, as the very pairing of the parents is arranged by a preconceived plan that is to insure the highest physical and mental qualities of the offspring to be bred. Nothing is left to personal whim or accident from infancy on, and the process of education, both theoretical and practical, continues until the age of fifty. Literature, music, physical and military instruction, elementary and advanced mathematics, philosophy and metaphysics, and subordinate military and civilian-service assignments are the stages of the planned program of training philosopher-rulers:

> Then when they are fifty, those who have come safely through and proved the best in all points in action and in study must be brought at last to the goal. They must lift up the eye of the soul to gaze on that which sheds light on all things; and when they have seen the Good itself, take it as a pattern for the right ordering of the state and the individual, themselves included. For the rest of their lives, most of their time will be spent in study; but they will all take their turn at the troublesome duties of public life and act as Rulers for their country's sake, not regarding it as a distinction but as an unavoidable task.

Plato thus regarded the training in literary, mathematical, and philosophical knowledge as a mere preparation for the "ascent to the vision of Goodness," the "highest object of knowledge," which final stage cannot be mastered by mere rational instruction or comprehension, but partakes of the nature of *revelation,* a mystical and socially incommunicable experience.

Plato nowhere defines the nature of the Good in verifiable or rational terms; it is a secret, "something beyond truth and knowledge, and, precious as these both are, of still higher worth," as he says in the *Republic.* The only approach to it is through vision and revelation, and few are blessed with the capacity to "climb the ascent" to such visions. The Platonic philosopher-ruler thus bases his rule over the people, not on superior character and rational knowledge alone, as it might appear from a hasty reading of the *Republic,* but on a personal and unique innermost experience that is mystical and incommunicable in rational terms. To know is to "contemplate the realities themselves as they are for ever in the same unchanging state," and because the ruler *knows,* as the result of his vision of the Good, he has the right to rule the people; they can never hope to attain similar summits of insight and vision and can only *believe* in, but not rationally understand, a social order built on intuitions that are, in the ultimate, mysterious and inaccessible to common-sense experience.

The nature and scope of the authority of the rulers in the *Republic* are intimately related to its foundation. Just as the knowledge of the rulers that gives them title to rule is directed to the absolute, so is their authority, which is morally based on their training and wisdom, absolute and unconditional. The rulers have the moral right to constrain the ruled if they show any sign of defection from the established order. Plato assumes that, in general, such compulsion will not be necessary. The people will be brought up to believe in the existing class system by means of myths and allegories, because they are incapable of rigorous scientific and philosophical thinking.

But if the use of force in the *Republic* raises serious critical considerations, the recommended use of censorship and the "medicinal lie" for the upbringing of the ruling and military-executive classes is no less alarming. Plato often compares the rulers to doctors, and the ruled to patients, and he says that "for a private person to mislead the Rulers we shall declare to be a worse offense than for a patient to mislead his doctor"; and he goes on to attack such crimes as "fatal" and "subversive" in a state. Though the ruled are under no circumstances permitted to deviate from truth, particularly in their relations with the rulers, the latter may lie "in the way of a medicine." Just as a medicine may be handled only by a doctor, "if anyone, then, is to practice deception, either on the country's enemies or on its citizens, it must be the Rulers of the commonwealth, acting for its benefit; no one else may meddle with this privilege."

An illustration of such a "medicinal lie" is the fable of the origins of the class system, according to which God put gold into those who are fit to rule, silver into the auxiliaries, and iron and brass into the farmers and craftsmen. "I shall try to convince," Socrates says, "first the Rulers and the soldiers, and then the whole community," and if they accept this fable, all three classes will think of each other as "brothers born of the same soil" and will be ready to defend their land, which they will eventually think of as "mother and nurse." It is significant that Plato's example of a "medicinal lie" relates, not to a matter of subordinate expediency and convenience, but to the root of his ideal political community, namely, the inequality of the threefold class system.

As to censorship, Plato frequently expresses in the *Republic* hostility toward artists. His hostility arises from his apprehension that art appeals to feeling and passion rather than to reason and intellect. Specifically, poets must write in a way that will further the objectives of the future rulers' training (it may be recalled that only the rulers and the military-executive, but not the ruled population, are to be educated). Negatively, the poet must not, for example, present the gods in an unattractive and "all-too-human" light; if he does, "we shall be angry and refuse him the means to produce his play." Positively, the poets will be told by the rulers what elements to stress in their stories and "the limits beyond which they must not be allowed to go." The main, perhaps only, value of art is moral education, particularly self-control: "And for the mass of mankind that chiefly means obeying their governors, and themselves governing their appetite for the pleasure of eating and drinking and sex."

Plato finds Homer, Hesiod, and the other masters of Greek literature opprobrious and corrupting. Toward the end of the *Republic* the conclusion is presented that "all poetry, from Homer onwards, consists in representing a semblance of its subject, whatever it may be, including any kind of human excellence, with no grasp of the reality." In fact, the artist is assigned a place below the shoemaker or smith, because the latter have at least a limited *direct* knowledge of reality, that of their craft, whereas the artist "knows nothing worth mentioning, about the subjects he represents"; art, therefore, "is a form of play, not to be taken seriously." Because the poet, by appealing to sentiment rather than reason, "sets up a vicious form of government" in the individual soul, "We shall be justified in not admitting him into a well-ordered commonwealth." Like Plato, modern authoritarian rulers are also keenly aware that poetry, fiction, and other kinds of imaginative literature can be more dangerous than factual historical, political, or economic analyses. In the twentieth century, four of the most influential books against totalitarian government have been novels: Arthur Koestler's *Darkness at Noon,* George Orwell's *1984,* Bores Pasternak's *Dr. Zhivago,* and Aleksandr Solzhenitsyn's *One Day in the Life of Ivan Denisovich.*

In accepting the "medicinal lie" and the regulation, positive and negative, of the arts, Plato started a line of thought that has been enthusiastically accepted by those who base their right to rule on superior and exclusive knowledge rather than on the freely expressed consent of the ruled. Those who adhere to the creed of certainty are eventually driven to use, as a means of governing, medicinal lies, censorship, thought control, and physical compulsion.

The Platonic conception of Truth is challenged by the modern view. Modern philosophers insist that truth is intimately, related to experience, that it can never be fully grasped, that it is an *endless process* of testing new hypotheses against new experiences, that it is not something that exists prior to man, but that it is constantly made and remade in *doing,* rather than discovered in intellectual speculation or in a flash of mystical insight. Plato's concept of Truth is more *absolute* and *individual-aristocratic:* Truth is eternally the same and unchangeable, and it can be perceived by the use of the speculative and intuitive faculties of the philosophical person, who therefore has the right to rule those who do not possess these capacities. The modern view of truth is more *relative, empirical,* and *social-cooperative:* Truth is not eternally the same, is changeable and changing, is never attainable more than in a proximate and practical way, and—what is perhaps most important of all—it is not the product of brilliant individual intellects but of the cooperative effort of many individuals and social groups.

To take a practical illustration, according to Plato the concept of social justice is one that can be discovered and defined through illuminated reasoning. The more modern empirical and relative view holds that social justice is not a preexisting reality logically or intuitively *discovered* by speculation or revelation, but that *temporary approximations* to justice can be worked out in a socially satisfactory fashion through negotiation and bargaining of interested groups and classes. This *dynamic* concept of truth is more modest than the *static* one of Plato, inasmuch as it appreciates the limitations of human capacity and disinterestedness in the face of a constantly, changing world of circumstances; but at the same time, it is also more optimistic than Plato's concept, because it holds that the process of working out approximations to truth is *open to all,* and that, in fact, such approximations are likely to be more accurate if related to the widest possible range of ascertainable experience. By contrast, Plato's view of the possibility of finding truth is more pessimistic in the sense that it is conceived as a form of intellectual insight that is open, because of its final and absolute value, to only a *few select* minds. If antidemocratic and authoritarian political systems throughout history have looked back sympathetically to Plato, the reason has been less the explicit opposition of the *Republic* to democracy than the implicit view of the world in which truth—social, philosophical, metaphysical, religious—is the prerogative of a small elect class, endowed with special and exclusive capacities to apprehend it in a regime of formal training, and enabled to translate it into reality in a preconceived framework of society in which the few govern and the many obey and conform.

Yet even more deeply than Plato's conception of Truth, his conception of an is not compatible with democracy. In Plato's three-class society, the rulers have the right, and duty, to rule all because they possess the highest quality—rational wisdom. The class of civilian-military administrators (auxiliaries) is characterized by courage, or the ability to face reality, to serve as an intermediary between the ruling class and the third, lowest, class, the mass of the people whose dominant psychological trait is the desire to satisfy their crude material and instinctual desires. According to Plato, this threefold division of society merely reflects the threefold division of the individual soul: It, too, is made up of three elements: the *rational,* which is the highest; the *spirited,* which has the capacity to follow and assert the claims of reason; and the *appetitive,* the lowest in rank, which harbors man's desires and emotions. Plato assumes that in these three elements of the soul, the rational is the highest and has the duty to keep the other two elements in line. In society, too, the class that is characterized by superior rational endowment is therefore the natural ruler over the other two subordinate classes. The case against Plato's three-class society in which one small superior class rules over the rest can thus be greatly strengthened if his psychological premise is wrong or at least open to serious challenge.

Modern psychological thought often divides the human mind into several components. Freud, for example, divides the human mind into three elements which bear a striking resemblance to Plato's three parts of the soul: First, there is, according to Freud, the *id*—the seat of man's undirected and unconscious instinctual drives. Then, there is the *ego,* which is in the conscious level of the mind and adjusts *id* drives and primitive desires to reality, that is, to the rules of morals and society. Finally, there is in the human mind the *superego,* the civilized rational conscience which directs the *ego* in dealing with the claims of the *id.* However, in Freud's view—and this is a fundamental rejection of Plato—the three elements of the mind are not ranked hierarchically as superior and inferior, but are coordinate. In particular, Freud pointed to the psychic dangers of repressing *id* drives too harshly rather than channeling them off for purposes that cause no harm to either the individual or society.

Following Freud's pioneering work, modern psychological thinking holds that mental health and stability depends on the balance between intellectual and emotional interests and activities, and that neither are inferior or superior to the other. In modern psychological thought, repression of the so-called lower emotional elements of the mind by the so-called higher intellectual element has been largely replaced by the concept of balance and integration, in which each element of the human personality has its rightful place. Following Plato's example and projecting the relations of the different elements of the mind on the larger social canvas, the modern conception of the human personality would seem to lead to a democratic conception of society in which each group and class has a rightful place of recognition and respect, being neither naturally superior or inferior to any other group or class.

The *Republic* is not a utopia but the work of a thinker passionately interested in practical politics. Rejecting the doctrine that man must fatally and inextricably remain a prisoner of natural or social circumstances, Plato has faith in man's ability to create a community that will correspond to the ideal of knowledge and, therefore, justice. If philosophy and the vision of the Good are the highest forms of human activity, "there can be no rest from troubles" for states or for all mankind, "unless either philosophers become kings in their countries or those who are now called kings and rulers come to be sufficiently inspired with a genuine desire for wisdom; unless, that is to say, political power and philosophy meet together." This passage, probably the most famous in the *Republic,* summarizes Plato's conception of a society in which the best rule, and it makes little difference to him whether this rule is monarchy ("when there is one man who stands out above the rest of the rulers") or aristocracy ("when there are more than one"). The plan of such a perfect constitution and of a "perfect man" might be difficult, "but not impossible."

Nevertheless, Plato anticipated the eventual decline of the best state and its degeneration into progressively lower types of constitution. The first of these forms of state is timocracy, based on ambition and love of honor and war, as represented by Crete and Sparta, "so commonly admired." The second is oligarchy or plutocracy, the rule of the wealthy; the third is democracy, the rule of the people; the fourth, and most imperfect, is despotism, which develops inevitably out of the anarchy of the democratic state. In each instance, Plato correlates a type of human character with the form of government in which it is most commonly reflected: "Constitutions cannot come out of sticks and stones; they must result from the preponderance of certain characters which draw the rest of the community in their wake."

This penetrating insight of Plato, that government is more than a piece of machinery, that its essence is ultimately determined by the quality of the men and women who compose it, is still not fully grasped today. The twentieth century, in particular, has been strewn with the wreckage of constitutions that failed dismally, not because they were imperfect in themselves, but because they were not suited to the "preponderant characters" in the societies for which they were devised, whether these individuals were the rulers or the ruled.

In his classification of forms of state, Plato considered democracy the second worst type of government. His description of life in a democratic society may be overdrawn, but it remains to this day the most incisive critique of democracy. Unless democrats assume that democracy is an exception to all human creations, and thus free from imperfections, they must be aware of its intrinsic as well as its incidental weaknesses. If Plato maintains that democracy is "an agreeable form of anarchy with plenty and variety and an equality of a peculiar kind for equals and unequals alike," who can say that his thesis is completely wrong? The buoyant diversity and creative pluralism of the democratic society are its glory, but they are often the path to dissolution and disintegration when its members forget that they are not merely individuals with rights and liberties but also social beings with duties and obligations. Similarly, the unwillingness of democratic citizens to be led is one of the mainsprings of democratic vitality; but if carried too far, if the honest and able leaders are prevented from governing, the dishonest demagogues will take their place.

The fate of democracies in the twentieth century, in particular, has demonstrated that Plato's critique of democracy and the democratic man, far from being an unrealistic caricature of democratic life, is full of sound warnings that no democrat should miss. Nazi, fascist, and communist criticisms of democracy were and are relatively ephemeral and superficial, compared with the enduring and fundamental objections that Plato raises. The answer to Plato's apprehensions about the possibility of democracy lies not in the arguments of democrats but in their lives. The experience of history is harder to disprove than a theoretical argument. If Plato makes democrats more keenly conscious how difficult the life of freedom and fellowship is, he has, perhaps unwittingly, performed a major service to the cause of democracy.

The literary form of the *Republic* is the dialogue, in which Socrates is both the narrator and chief figure. In fact, as the dialogue proceeds, it becomes virtually a monologue, for the other participants increasingly confine their dialectical contributions to nods, monosyllabic expressions of consent, and brief rhetorical assertions that merely give Socrates a cue to go on with his argument. The conversation starts in the house of Cephalus, a retired wealthy businessman. The company includes Cephalus' son, Polemarchus, Plato's two elder brothers, Glaucon and Adeimantus, and a sophist, Thrasymachus, who is represented as a cynic. The discussion soon turns to the central question in the *Republic,* What is justice? In the discussion of justice, all elements of Plato's political philosophy are contained. In his theory of justice the relations of man to nature, to the *polis,* and to his fellow men form an architectonic whole.

Cephalus states the view, based on a long life of practical experience, that justice means honesty and rendering what is due to gods and men. Socrates sees some merit in this approach but is not satisfied with it. Polemarchus next suggests that justice means helping one's friends and harming one's enemies. Socrates is again not satisfied, as such a definition befits more the moral standards of a despot than those of a just man. At this point Thrasymachus breaks into the discussion and puts forward the view that "just" or "right" means nothing but "what is to the interest of the stronger party."

PLATO

*The Republic**

JUSTICE AS THE INTEREST OF THE STRONGER

All this time Thrasymachus had been trying more than once to break in upon our conversation; but his neighbours had restrained him, wishing to hear the argument to the end. In the pause after my last words he could keep quiet no longer; but gathering himself up like a wild beast he sprang at us as if he would tear us in pieces. Polemarchus and I were frightened out of our wits, when he burst out to the whole company:

What is the matter with you two, Socrates? Why do you go on in this imbecile way, politely deferring to each other's nonsense? If you really want to know what justice means, stop asking questions and scoring off the answers you get. You know very well it is easier to ask questions than to answer them. Answer yourself, and tell us what you think justice means. I won't have you telling us it is the same as what is obligatory or useful or advantageous or profitable or expedient; I want a clear and precise statement; I won't put up with that sort of verbiage.

I was amazed by this onslaught and looked at him in terror. If I had not seen this wolf before he saw me, I really believe I should have been struck dumb;[1] but fortunately I had looked at him earlier, when he was beginning to get exasperated with our argument; so I was able to reply, though rather tremulously:

---

*From *The Republic of Plato* (trans. F. M. Cornford, Oxford University Press, 1945). By permission.

[1] A popular superstition, that if a wolf sees you first, you become dumb.

Don't be hard on us, Thrasymachus. If Polemarchus and I have gone astray in our search, you may be quite sure the mistake was not intentional. If we had been looking for a piece of gold, we should never have deliberately allowed politeness to spoil our chance of finding it; and now when we are looking for justice, a thing much more precious than gold, you cannot imagine we should defer to each other in that foolish way and not do our best to bring it to light. You must believe we are in earnest, my friend; but I am afraid the task is beyond our powers, and we might expect a man of your ability to pity us instead of being so severe.

Thrasymachus replied with a burst of sardonic laughter.

Good Lord, he said; Socrates at his old trick of shamming ignorance! I knew it; I told the others you would refuse to commit yourself and do anything sooner than answer a question.

Yes, Thrasymachus, I replied; because you are clever enough to know that if you asked someone what are the factors of the number twelve, and at the same time warned him: "Look here, you are not to tell me that 12 is twice 6, or 3 times 4, or 6 times 2, or 4 times 3; I won't put up with any such nonsense"—you must surely see that no one would answer a question put like that. He would say: "What do you mean, Thrasymachus? Am I forbidden to give any of these answers, even if one happens to be right? Do you want me to give a wrong one?" What would you say to that?

Humph! said he. As if that were a fair analogy!

I don't see why it is not, said I; but in any case, do you suppose our barring a certain answer would prevent the man from giving it, if he thought it was the truth?

Do you mean that you are going to give me one of those answers I barred?

I should not be surprised, if it seemed to me true, on reflection.

And what if I give you another definition of justice, better than any of those? What penalty are you prepared to pay?[2]

The penalty deserved by ignorance, which must surely be to receive instruction from the wise. So I would suggest that as a suitable punishment.

I like your notion of a penalty! he said; but you must pay the costs as well.

I will, when I have any money.

That will be all right, said Glaucon; we will all subscribe for Socrates. So let us have your definition, Thrasymachus.

Oh yes, he said; so that Socrates may play the old game of questioning and refuting someone else, instead of giving an answer himself!

But really, I protested, what can you expect from a man who does not know the answer or profess to know it, and, besides that, has been forbidden by no mean authority to put forward any notions he may have? Surely the definition should naturally come from you, who say you do know the answer and can tell it us. Please do not disappoint us. I should take it as a kindness, and I hope you will not be chary of giving Glaucon and the rest of us the advantage of your instruction.

Glaucon and the others added their entreaties to mine. Thrasymachus was evidently longing to win credit, for he was sure he had an admirable answer ready, though he made a show of insisting that I should be the one to reply. In the end he gave way and exclaimed:

So this is what Socrates' wisdom comes to! He refuses to teach, and goes about learning from others without offering so much as thanks in return.

I do learn from others, Thrasymachus; that is quite true; but you are wrong to call me ungrateful. I give in return all I can—

praise; for I have no money. And how ready I am to applaud any idea that seems to me sound, you will see in a moment, when you have stated your own; for I am sure that will be sound.

Listen then, Thrasymachus began. What I say is that "just" or "right" means nothing but what is to the interest of the stronger party. Well, where is your applause? You don't mean to give it me.

I will, as soon as I understand, I said. I don't see yet what you mean by right being the interest of the stronger party. For instance, Polydamas, the athlete, is stronger than we are, and it is to his interest to eat beef for the sake of his muscles; but surely you don't mean that the same diet would be good for weaker men and therefore be right for us?

You are trying to be funny, Socrates. It's a low trick to take my words in the sense you think will be most damaging.

No, no, I protested; but you must explain.

Don't you know, then, that a state may be ruled by a despot, or a democracy, or an aristocracy?

Of course.

And that the ruling element is always the strongest?

Yes.

Well then, in every case the laws are made by the ruling party in its own interest; a democracy makes democratic laws, a despot autocratic ones, and so on. By making these laws they define as "right" for their subjects whatever is for their own interest, and they call anyone who breaks them a "wrongdoer" and punish him accordingly. That is what I mean: in all states alike "right" has the same meaning, namely what is for the interest of the party established in power, and that is the strongest. So the sound conclusion is that what is "right" is the same everywhere: the interest of the stronger party.

Now I see what you mean, said I; whether it is true or not, I must try to make out. When you define right in terms of interest, you are yourself giving one of those answers you forbade to me; though, to be sure, you add "to the stronger party."

An insignificant addition, perhaps!

Its importance is not clear yet; what is clear is that we must find out whether your

---

[2] In certain lawsuits the defendant, if found guilty, was allowed to propose a penalty alternative to that demanded by the prosecution. The judges then decided which should be inflicted. The "costs" here means the fee which the sophist, unlike Socrates, expected from his pupils.

definition is true. I agree myself that right is in a sense a matter of interest; but when you add "to the stronger party," I don't know about that. I must consider.

Go ahead, then.

I will. Tell me this. No doubt you also think it is right to obey the men in power?

I do.

Are they infallible in every type of state, or can they sometimes make a mistake?

Of course they can make a mistake.

In framing laws, then, they may do their work well or badly?

No doubt.

Well, that is to say, when the laws they make are to their own interest; badly, when they are not?

Yes.

But the subjects are to obey any law they lay down, and they will then be doing right?

Of course.

If so, by your account, it will be right to do what is not to the interest of the stronger party, as well as what is so.

What's that you are saying?

Just what you said, I believe; but let us look again. Haven't you admitted that the rulers, when they enjoin certain acts on their subjects, sometimes mistake their own best interests, and at the same time that it is right for the subjects to obey, whatever they may enjoin?

Yes, I suppose so.

Well, that amounts to admitting that it is right to do what is not to the interest of the rulers or the stronger party. They may unwittingly enjoin what is to their own disadvantage; and you say it is right for the others to do as they are told. In that case, their duty must be the opposite of what you said, because the weaker will have been ordered to do what is against the interest of the stronger. You with your intelligence must see how that follows.

Yes, Socrates, said Polemarchus, that is undeniable.

No doubt, Cleitophon broke in, if you are to be a witness on Socrates' side.

No witness is needed, replied Polemarchus; Thrasymachus himself admits that rulers sometimes ordain acts that are to their own disadvantage, and that it is the subjects' duty to do them.

That is because Thrasymachus said it was right to do what you are told by the men in power.

Yes, but he also said that what is to the interest of the stronger party is right; and, after making both these assertions, he admitted that the stronger sometimes command the weaker subjects to act against their interests. From all which it follows that what is in the stronger's interest is no more right than what is not.

No, said Cleitophon; he meant whatever the stronger *believes* to be in his own interest. That is what the subject must do, and what Thrasymachus meant to define as right.

That was not what he said, rejoined Polemarchus.

No matter, Polemarchus, said I; if Thrasymachus says so now, let us take him in that sense. Now, Thrasymachus, tell me, was that what you intended to say—that right means what the stronger thinks is to his interest, whether it really is so or not?

Most certainly not, he replied. Do you suppose I should speak of a man as "stronger" or "superior" at the very moment when he is making a mistake?

I did think you said as much when you admitted that rulers are not always infallible.

That is because you are a quibbler, Socrates. Would you say a man deserves to be called a physician at the moment when he makes a mistake in treating his patient and just in respect of that mistake; or a mathematician, when he does a sum wrong and just in so far as he gets a wrong result? Of course we do commonly speak of a physician or a mathematician or a scholar having made a mistake; but really none of these, I should say, is ever mistaken, in so far as he is worthy of the name we give him. So strictly speaking—and you are all for being precise—no one who practises a craft makes mistakes. A man is mistaken when his knowledge fails him; and at that moment he is no craftsman. And what is true of craftsmanship or any sort of skill is true of the ruler: he is never mistaken so long as he is acting as a ruler; though anyone might speak of a ruler making a mistake, just as he might of a physician. You must understand that I was talking in that loose way when I answered your question just now; but the precise statement is this. The ruler, in so far as he is acting as a ruler, makes no mistakes and consequently enjoins what is best for himself; and that is what the subject is to do. So, as I said at first, "right" means doing what is to the interest of the stronger.

Very well, Thrasymachus, said I. So you think I am quibbling?

I am sure you are.

You believe my questions were maliciously designed to damage your position?

I know it. But you will gain nothing by that. You cannot outwit me by cunning, and you are not the man to crush me in the open.

Bless your soul, I answered, I should not think of trying. But, to prevent any more misunderstanding, when you speak of that ruler or stronger party whose interest the weaker ought to serve, please make it clear whether you are using the words in the ordinary way or in that strict sense you have just defined.

I mean a ruler in the strictest possible sense. Now quibble away and be as malicious as you can. I want no mercy. But you are no match for me.

Do you think me mad enough to beard a lion or try to outwit a Thrasymachus?

You did try just now, he retorted, but it wasn't a success.

RULING AS AN ART

Enough of this, said I. Now tell me about the physician in that strict sense you spoke of: is it his business to earn money or to treat his patients? Remember, I mean your physician who is worthy of the name.

To treat his patients.

And what of the ship's captain in the true sense? Is he a mere seaman or the commander of the crew?

The commander.

Yes, we shall not speak of him as a seaman just because he is on board a ship. That is not the point. He is called captain because of his skill and authority over the crew.

Quite true.

And each of these people has some special interest?[3]

No doubt.

And the craft in question exists for the very purpose of discovering that interest and providing for it?

Yes.

Can it equally be said of any craft that it has an interest, other than its own greatest possible perfection?

What do you mean by that?

Here is an illustration. If you ask me whether it is sufficient for the human body just to be itself, with no need of help from without, I should say, Certainly not; it has weaknesses and defects, and its condition is not all that it might be. That is precisely why the art of medicine was invented: it was designed to help the body and provide for its interests. Would not that be true?

It would.

But now take the art of medicine itself. Has that any defects or weaknesses? Does any art stand in need of some further perfection, as the eye would be imperfect without the power of vision or the ear without hearing, so that in their case an art is required that will study their interests and provide for their carrying out those functions? Has the art itself any corresponding need of some further art to remedy its defects and look after its interests; and will that further art require yet another, and so on for ever? Or will every art look after its own interests? Or, finally, is it not true that no art needs to have its weaknesses remedied or its interests studied either by another art or by itself, because no art has in itself any weakness or fault, and the only interest it is required to serve is that of its subject-matter? In itself, an art is sound and flawless, so long as it is entirely true to its own nature as an art in the strictest sense— and it is the strict sense that I want you to keep in view. Is not that true?

So it appears.

Then, said I, the art of medicine does not study its own interest, but the needs of the body, just as a groom shows his skill by caring for horses, not for the art of grooming. And so every art seeks, not its own advantage—for it has no deficiencies—but the interest of the subject on which it is exercised.

It appears so.

But surely, Thrasymachus, every art has authority and superior power over its subject.

To this he agreed, though very reluctantly.

So far as arts are concerned, then, no art ever studies or enjoins the interest of the superior or stronger party, but always that of the weaker over which it has authority.

---

[3] All the persons mentioned have some interest. The craftsman *qua* craftsman has an interest in doing his work as well as possible, which is the same thing as serving the interest of the subjects on whom his craft is exercised; and the subjects have their interest, which the craftsman is there to promote.

Thrasymachus assented to this at last, though he tried to put up a fight. I then went on:

So the physician, as such, studies only the patient's interest, not his own. For as we agreed the business of the physician, in the strict sense, is not to make money for himself, but to exercise his power over the patient's body; and the ship's captain, again, considered strictly as no mere sailor, but in command of the crew, will study and enjoin the interest of his subordinates, not his own.

He agreed reluctantly.

And so with government of any kind: no ruler, in so far as he is acting as ruler, will study or enjoin what is for his own interest. All that he says and does will be said and done with a view to what is good and proper for the subject for whom he practises his art.

At this point, when everyone could see that Thrasymachus' definition of justice had been turned inside out, instead of making any reply, he said:

Socrates, have you a nurse?

Why do you ask such a question as that? I said. Wouldn't it be better to answer mine?

Because she lets you go about sniffling like a child whose nose wants wiping. She hasn't even taught you to know a shepherd when you see one, or his sheep either.

What makes you say that?

Why, you imagine that a herdsman studies the interests of his flocks or cattle, tending and fattening them up with some other end in view than his master's profit or his own: and so you don't see that, in politics, the genuine ruler regards his subjects exactly like sheep, and thinks of nothing else, night and day, but the good he can get out of them for himself. You are so far out in your notions of right and wrong, justice and injustice, as not to know that "right" actually means what is good for someone else, and to be "just" means serving the interest of the stronger who rules, at the cost of the subject who obeys; whereas injustice is just the reverse, asserting its authority over those innocents who are called just, so that they minister solely to their master's advantage and happiness, and not in the least degree to their own. Innocent as you are yourself, Socrates, you must see that a just man always has the worst of it. Take a private business: when a partnership is wound up, you will never find that the more honest of two

partners comes off with the larger share; and in their relations to the state, when there are taxes to be paid, the honest man will pay more than the other on the same amount of property; or if there is money to be distributed, the dishonest will get it all. When either of them hold some public office, even if the just man loses in no other way, his private affairs at any rate will suffer from neglect, while his principles will not allow him to help himself from the public funds; not to mention the offence he will give to his friends and relations by refusing to sacrifice those principles to do them a good turn. Injustice has all the opposite advantages. I am speaking of the type I described just now, the man who can get the better of other people on a large scale: you must fix your eye on him, if you want to judge how much it is to one's own interest not to be just. You can see that best in the most consummate form of injustice, which rewards wrongdoing with supreme welfare and happiness and reduces its victims, if they won't retaliate in kind, to misery. That form is despotism, which uses force or fraud to plunder the goods of others, public or private, sacred or profane, and to do it in a wholesale way. If you are caught committing any one of these crimes on a small scale, you are punished and disgraced; they call it sacrilege, kidnapping, burglary, theft and brigandage. But if, besides taking their property, you turn all your countrymen into slaves, you will hear no more of those ugly names; your countrymen themselves will call you the happiest of men and bless your name, and so will everyone who hears of such a complete triumph of injustice; for when people denounce injustice, it is because they are afraid of suffering wrong, not of doing it. So true is it, Socrates, that injustice, on a grand enough scale, is superior to justice in strength and freedom and autocratic power; and "right," as I said at first, means simply what serves the interest of the stronger party; "wrong" means what is for the interest and profit of oneself.

Having deluged our ears with this torrent of words, as the man at the baths might empty a bucket over one's head, Thrasymachus meant to take himself off; but the company obliged him to stay and defend his position. I was specially urgent in my entreaties.

My good Thrasymachus, said I, do you propose to fling a doctrine like that at our heads and then go away without explaining it properly or letting us point out to you whether it is true or not? Is it so small a matter in your eyes to determine the whole course of conduct which every one of us must follow to get the best of life?

Don't I realize it is a serious matter? he retorted.

Apparently not, said I; or else you have no consideration for us, and do not care whether we shall lead better or worse lives for being ignorant of this truth you profess to know. Do take the trouble to let us into your secret; if you treat us handsomely, you may be sure it will be a good investment; there are so many of us to show our gratitude. I will make no secret of my own conviction, which is that injustice is not more profitable than justice, even when left free to work its will unchecked. No; let your unjust man have full power to do wrong, whether by successful violence or by escaping detection; all the same he will not convince me that he will gain more than he would by being just. There may be others here who feel as I do, and set justice above injustice. It is for you to convince us that we are not well advised.

How can I he replied. If you are not convinced by what I have just said, what more can I do for you? Do you want to be fed with my ideas out of a spoon?

God forbid! I exclaimed; not that. But I do want you to stand by your own words; or, if you shift your ground, shift it openly and stop trying to hoodwink us as you are doing now. You see, Thrasymachus, to go back to your earlier argument, in speaking of the shepherd you did not think it necessary to keep to that strict sense you laid down when you defined the genuine physician. You represent him, in his character of shepherd, as feeding up his flock, not for their own sake but for the table or the market, as if he were out to make money as a caterer or a cattle-dealer, rather than a shepherd. Surely the sole concern of the shepherd's art is to do the best for the charges put under its care; its own best interest is sufficiently provided for, so long as it does not fall short of all that shepherding should imply. On that principle it followed, I thought, that any kind of authority, in the state or in private life,

must, in its character of authority consider solely what is best for those under its care. Now what is your opinion? Do you think that the men who govern states—I mean rulers in the strict sense—have no reluctance to hold office?

I don't think so, he replied; I know it.

Well, but haven't you noticed, Thrasymachus, that in other positions of authority no one is willing to act unless he is paid wages, which he demands on the assumption that all the benefit of his action will go to his charges? Tell me: Don't we always distinguish one form of skill from another by its power to effect some particular result? Do say what you really think, so that we may get on.

Yes, that is the distinction.

And also each brings us some benefit that is peculiar to it: medicine gives health, for example; the art of navigation, safety at sea; and so on.

Yes.

And wage-earning brings us wages; that is its distinctive product. Now, speaking with that precision which you proposed, you would not say that the art of navigation is the same as the art of medicine, merely on the ground that a ship's captain regained his health on a voyage, because the sea air was good for him. No more would you identify the practice of medicine with wage-earning because a man may keep his health while earning wages, or a physician attending a case may receive a fee.

No.

And, since we agreed that the benefit obtained by each form of skill is peculiar to it, any common benefit enjoyed alike by all these practitioners must come from some further practice common to them all?

It would seem so.

Yes, we must say that if they all earn wages, they get that benefit in so far as they are engaged in wage-earning as well as in practising their several arts.

He agreed reluctantly.

This benefit, then—the receipt of wages—does not come to a man from his special art. If we are to speak strictly, the physician, as such, produces health; the builder, a house; and then each, in his further capacity of wage-earner, gets his pay. Thus every art has its own function and benefits its proper subject. But suppose the practitioner is not paid; does he then get any benefit from his art?

Clearly not.

And is he doing no good to anyone either, when he works for nothing?

No, I suppose he does some good.

Well then, Thrasymachus, it is now clear that no form of skill or authority provides for its own benefit. As we were saying some time ago, it always studies and prescribes what is good for its subject—the interest of the weaker party, not of the stronger. And that, my friend, is why I said that no one is willing to be in a position of authority and undertake to set straight other men's troubles, without demanding to be paid; because, if he is to do his work well, he will never, in his capacity of ruler, do, or command others to do, what is best for himself, but only what is best for the subject. For that reason, if he is to consent, he must have his recompense, in the shape of money or honour, or of punishment in case of refusal.

What do you mean, Socrates? asked Glaucon. I recognize two of your three kinds of reward; but I don't understand what you mean by speaking of punishment as a recompense.

Then you don't understand the recompense required by the best type of men, or their motive for accepting authority when they do consent. You surely know that a passion for honours or for money is rightly regarded as something to be ashamed of.

Yes, I do.

For that reason, I said, good men are unwilling to rule, either for money's sake or for honour. They have no wish to be called mercenary for demanding to be paid, or thieves for making a secret profit out of their office; nor yet will honours tempt them, for they are not ambitious. So they must be forced to consent under threat of penalty; that may be why a readiness to accept power under no such constraint is thought discreditable. And the heaviest penalty for declining to rule is to be ruled by someone inferior to yourself. That is the fear, I believe, that makes decent people accept power; and when they do, they face the prospect of authority with no idea that they are coming into the enjoyment of a comfortable berth; it is forced upon them because they can find no one better than themselves, or even as good, to be entrusted with power.

If there could ever be a society of perfect men, there might well be as much competition to evade office as there now is to gain it; and it would then be clearly seen that the genuine ruler's nature is to seek only the advantage of the subject, with the consequence that any man of understanding would sooner have another to do the best for him than be at the pains to do the best for that other himself. On this point, then, I entirely disagree with Thrasymachus' doctrine that right means what is to the interest of the stronger.

THE RUDIMENTS OF SOCIAL ORGANIZATION

I was delighted with these speeches from Glaucon and Adeimantus, whose gifts I had always admired. How right, I exclaimed, was Glaucon's lover to begin that poem of his on your exploits at the battle of Megara by describing you two as the

sons divine
of Ariston's noble line!

Like father, like sons: there must indeed be some divine quality in your nature, if you can plead the cause of injustice so eloquently and still not be convinced yourselves that it is better than justice. That you are not really convinced I am sure from all I know of your dispositions, though your words might well have left me in doubt. But the more I trust you, the harder I find it to reply. How can I come to the rescue? I have no faith in my own powers, when I remember that you were not satisfied with the proof I thought I had given to Thrasymachus that it is better to be just. And yet I cannot stand by and hear justice reviled without lifting a finger. I am afraid to commit a sin by holding aloof while I have breath and strength to say a word in its defence. So there is nothing for it but to do the best I can.

Glaucon and the others begged me to step into the breach and carry through our inquiry into the real nature of justice and injustice, and the truth about their respective advantages. So I told them what I thought. This is a very obscure question, I said, and we shall need keen sight to see our way. Now, as we are not remarkably clever, I will make a suggestion as to how we should proceed. Imagine a rather short-sighted person told to read an inscription in small letters from some way off. He would think it a godsend if someone pointed out that the same inscription was written up elsewhere on a bigger scale, so that he could first read the larger characters and then make out whether the smaller ones were the same.

No doubt, said Adeimantus; but what analogy do you see in that to our inquiry?

I will tell you. We think of justice as a quality that may exist in a whole community as well as in an individual, and the community is the bigger of the two. Possibly, then, we may find justice there in larger proportions, easier to make out. So I suggest that we should begin by inquiring what justice means in a state. Then we can go on to look for its counterpart on a smaller scale in the individual.

That seems a good plan, he agreed.

Well then, I continued, suppose we imagine a state coming into being before our eyes. We might then be able to watch the growth of justice or of injustice within it. When that is done, we may hope it will be easier to find what we are looking for.

Much easier.

Shall we try, then, to carry out this scheme? I fancy it will be no light undertaking; so you had better think twice.

No need for that, said Adeimantus. Don't waste any more time.

My notion is, said I, that a state comes into existence because no individual is self-sufficing; we all have many needs. But perhaps you can suggest some different origin for the foundation of a community?

No, I agree with you.

So, having all these needs, we call in one another's help to satisfy our various requirements; and when we have collected a number of helpers and associates to live together in one place, we call that settlement a state.

Yes.

So if one man gives another what he has to give in exchange for what he can get, it is because each finds that to do so is for his own advantage.

Certainly.

Very well, said I. Now let us build up our imaginary state from the beginning. Apparently, it will owe its existence to our needs, the first and greatest need being the provision of food to keep us alive. Next we shall want a house; and thirdly, such things as clothing.

True.

How will our state be able to supply all these demands? We shall need at least one man to be a farmer, another a builder, and a third a weaver. Will that do, or shall we add a shoemaker and one or two more to provide for our personal wants?

By all means.

The minimum state, then, will consist of four or five men.

Apparently.

Now here is a further point. Is each one of them to bring the product of his work into a common stock? Should our one farmer, for example, provide food enough for four people and spend the whole of his working time in producing corn, so as to share with the rest; or should he take no notice of them and spend only a quarter of his time on growing just enough corn for himself, and divide the other three-quarters between building his house, weaving his clothes, and making his shoes, so as to save the trouble of sharing with others and attend himself to all his own concerns?

The first plan might be the easier, replied Adeimantus.

That may very well be so, said I; for, as you spoke, it occurred to me, for one thing, that no two people are born exactly alike. There are innate differences which fit them for different occupations.

I agree.

And will a man do better working at many trades, or keeping to one only?

Keeping to one.

And there is another point: obviously work may be ruined, if you let the right time go by. The workman must wait upon the work; it will not wait upon his leisure and allow itself to be done in a spare moment. So the conclusion is that more things will be produced and the work be more easily and better done, when every man is set free from all other occupations to do, at the right time, the one thing for which he is naturally fitted.

That is certainly true.

We shall need more than four citizens, then, to supply all those necessaries we mentioned. You see, Adeimantus, if the farmer is to have a good plough and spade and other tools, he will not make them himself. No more will the builder and weaver and shoe-maker make all the many implements they need. So quite a number of carpenters and smiths and other craftsmen must be enlisted. Our miniature state is beginning to grow.

It is.

Still, it will not be very large, even when we have added cowherds and shepherds to provide the farmers with oxen for the plough, and the builders as well as the farmers with draught-animals, and the weavers and shoe-makers with wool and leather.

No; but it will not be so very small either.

And yet, again, it will be next to impossible to plant our city in a territory where it will need no imports. So there will have to be still another set of people, to fetch what it needs from other countries.

There will.

Moreover, if these agents take with them nothing that those other countries require in exchange, they will return as empty-handed as they went. So, besides everything wanted for consumption at home, we must produce enough goods of the right kind for the foreigners whom we depend on to supply us. That will mean increasing the number of farmers and craftsmen.

Yes.

And then, there are these agents who are to import and export all kinds of goods—merchants, as we call them. We must have them; and if they are to do business overseas, we shall need quite a number of shipowners and others who know about that branch of trading.

We shall.

Again, in the city itself how are the various sets of producers to exchange their products? That was our object, you will remember, in forming a community and so laying the foundation of our state.

Obviously, they must buy and sell.

That will mean having a market-place, and a currency to serve as a token for purposes of exchange.

Certainly.

Now suppose a farmer, or an artisan, brings some of his produce to market at a time when no one is there who wants to exchange with him. Is he to sit there idle, when he might be at work?

No, he replied; there are people who have seen an opening here for their services. In well-ordered communities they are generally men not strong enough to be of use in any other occupation. They have to stay where they are in the market-place and take goods for money from those who want to sell, and money for goods from those who want to buy.

That, then, is the reason why our city must include a class of shopkeepers—so we call these people who sit still in the market-place to buy and sell, in contrast with merchants who travel to other countries.

Quite so.

There are also the services of yet another class, who have the physical strength for heavy work, though on intellectual grounds they are hardly worth including in our society—hired labourers, as we call them, because they sell the use of their strength for wages. They will go to make up our population.

Yes.

Well, Adeimantus, has our state now grown to its full size?

Perhaps.

Then, where in it shall we find justice or injustice? If they have come in with one of the elements we have been considering, can you say with which one?

I have no idea, Socrates; unless it be somewhere in their dealings with one another.

You may be right, I answered. Anyhow, it is a question which we shall have to face.

THE LUXURIOUS STATE

Let us begin, then, with a picture of our citizens' manner of life, with the provision we have made for them. They will be producing corn and wine, and making clothes and shoes. When they have built their houses, they will mostly work without their coats or shoes in summer, and in winter be well shod and clothed. For their food, they will prepare flour and barley-meal for kneading and baking, and set out a grand spread of loaves and cakes on rushes or fresh leaves. Then they will lie on beds of myrtle-boughs and byrony and make merry with their children, drinking their wine after the feast with garlands on their beads and singing the praises of the gods. So they will live pleasantly together; and a prudent fear of poverty or war will keep them from begetting children beyond their means.

Here Glaucon interrupted me: You seem to expect your citizens to feast on dry bread.

True, I said; I forgot that they will have something to give it a relish, salt, no doubt, and olives, and cheese, and country stews of roots and vegetables. And for dessert we will give them figs and peas and beans; and they shall roast myrtle-berries and acorns at the fire, while they sip their wine. Leading such a healthy life in peace, they will naturally come to a good old age, and leave their children to live after them in the same manner.

That is just the sort of provender you would supply, Socrates, if you were founding a community of pigs.

Well, how are they to live, then, Glaucon?

With the ordinary comforts. Let them lie on couches and dine off tables on such dishes and sweets as we have nowadays.

Ah, I see, said I; we are to study the growth, not just of a state, but of a luxurious one. Well, there may be no harm in that; the consideration of luxury may help us to discover how justice and injustice take root in society. The community I have described seems to me the ideal one, in sound health as it were: but if you want to see one suffering from inflammation, there is nothing to hinder us. So some people, it seems, will not be satisfied to live in this simple way; they must have couches and tables and furniture of all sorts; and delicacies too, perfumes, unguents, courtesans, sweetmeats, all in plentiful variety. And besides, we must not limit ourselves now to those bare necessaries of house and clothes and shoes; we shall have to set going the arts of embroidery and painting, and collect rich materials, like gold and ivory.

Yes.

Then we must once more enlarge our community. The healthy one will not be big enough now; it must be swollen up with a whole multitude of callings not ministering to any bare necessity: hunters and fishermen, for instance; artists in sculpture, painting, and music; poets with their attendant train of professional reciters, actors, dancers, producers; and makers of all sorts of household gear, including everything for women's adornment. And we shall want more servants: children's nurses and attendants, lady's maids, barbers, cooks and confectioners. And then swineherds—there was no need for them in our original state, but we shall want them now; and a great quantity of sheep and cattle too, if people are going to live on meat.

Of course.

And with this manner of life physicians will be in much greater request.

No doubt.

The country, too, which was large enough to support the original inhabitants, will now be too small. If we are to have enough pasture and plough land, we shall have to cut off a slice of our neighbours' territory; and if they too are not content with necessaries, but give themselves up to getting unlimited wealth, they will want a slice of ours.

That is inevitable, Socrates.

So the next thing will be, Glaucon, that we shall be at war.

No doubt.

We need not say yet whether war does good or harm, but only that we have discovered its origin in desires which are the most fruitful source of evils both to individuals and to states.[4]

Quite true.

This will mean a considerable addition to our community—a whole army, to go out to battle with any invader, in defence of all this property and of the citizens we have been describing.

Why so? Can't they defend themselves?

Not if the principle was right, which we all accepted in framing our society. You remember we agreed that no one man can practice many trades or arts satisfactorily.

True.

Well, is not the conduct of war an art, quite as important as shoemaking?

Yes.

But we would not allow our shoemaker to try to be also a farmer or weaver or builder, because we wanted our shoes well made. We gave each man one trade, for which he was naturally fitted; he would do good work, if he confined himself to that all his life, never letting the right moment slip by. Now in no

---

[4] "All wars are made for the sake of getting money," *Phaedo* 66 c.

form of work is efficiency so important as in war; and fighting is not so easy a business that a man can follow another trade, such as farming or shoemaking, and also be an efficient soldier. Why, even a game like draughts or dice must be studied from childhood; no one can become a fine player in his spare moments. Just taking up a shield or other weapon will not make a man capable of fighting that very day in any sort of warfare, any more than taking up a tool or implement of some kind will make a man a craftsman or an athlete, if he does not understand its use and has never been properly trained to handle it.

No; if that were so, tools would indeed be worth having

These guardians of our state, then, inasmuch as their work is the most important of all, will need the most complete freedom from other occupations and the greatest amount of skill and practice.

I quite agree.

And also a native aptitude for their calling.

Certainly.

So it is our business to define, if we can, the natural gifts that fit men to be guardians of a commonwealth, and to select them accordingly. It will certainly be a formidable task; but we must grapple with it to the best of our power.

Yes.

THE GUARDIANS'
TEMPERAMENT

Don't you think then, said I, that, for the purpose of keeping guard, a young man should have much the same temperament and qualities as a well-bred watch-dog? I mean, for instance, that both must have quick sense to detect an enemy, swiftness in pursuing him, and strength, if they have to fight when they have caught him.

Yes, they will need all those qualities.

And also courage, if they are to fight well.

Of course.

And courage, in dog or horse or any other creature, implies a spirited disposition. You must have noticed that a high spirit is unconquerable. Every soul possessed of it is fearless and indomitable in the face of any danger.

Yes, I have noticed that.

So now we know what physical qualities our Guardian must have, and also that he must be of a spirited temper.

Yes.

Then, Glaucon, how are men of that natural disposition to be kept from behaving pugnaciously to one another and to the rest of their countrymen?

It is not at all easy to see.

And yet they must be gentle to their own people and dangerous only to enemies; otherwise they will destroy themselves without waiting till others destroy them.

True.

What are we to do, then? If gentleness and a higher temper are contraries, where shall we find a character to combine them? Both are necessary to make a good Guardian, but it seems they are incompatible. So we shall never have a good Guardian.

It looks like it.

Here I was perplexed, but on thinking over what we had been saying, I remarked that we deserved to be puzzled, because we had not followed up the comparison we had just drawn.

What do you mean? he asked.

We never noticed that, after all, there are natures in which these contraries are combined. They are to be found in animals, and not least in the kind we compared to our Guardian. Well-bred dogs, as you know, are by instinct perfectly gentle to people whom they know and are accustomed to, and fierce to strangers. So the combination of qualities we require for our Guardian is, after all, possible and not against nature.

Evidently.

Do you further agree that, besides this spirited temper, he must have a philosophical element in his nature?

I don't see what you mean.

This is another trait you will see in the dog. It is really remarkable how the creature gets angry at the mere sight of a stranger and welcomes anyone he knows, though he may never have been treated unkindly by the one or kindly by the other. Did that never strike you as curious?

I had not thought of it before; but that certainly is how a dog behaves.

Well, but that shows a fine instinct, which is philosophic in the true sense.

How so?

Because the only mark by which he distinguishes a friendly and an unfriendly face is that he knows the one and does not know the other; and if a creature makes that the test of what it finds congenial or otherwise, how can you deny that it has a passion for knowledge and understanding?

Of course, I cannot.

And that passion is the same thing as philosophy—the love of wisdom.[5]

Yes.

Shall we boldly say, then, that the same is true of human beings? If a man is to be gentle towards his own people whom he knows, he must have an instinctive love of wisdom and understanding.

Agreed.

So the nature required to make a really noble Guardian of our commonwealth will be swift and strong, spirited, and philosophic.

Quite so.

Given those natural qualities, then, how are these Guardians to be brought up and educated? First, will the answer to that question help the purpose of our whole inquiry, which is to make out how justice and injustice grow up in a state? We want to be thorough, but not to draw out this discussion to a needless length.

Glaucon's brother answered: I certainly think it will help.

If so, I said, we must not think of dropping it, though it may be rather a long business.

I agree.

Come on then. We will take our time and educate our imaginary citizens.

Yes, let us do so.

PRIMARY EDUCATION OF THE GUARDIANS: CENSORSHIP OF LITERATURE

What is this education to be, then? Perhaps we shall hardly invent a system better than the one which long experience has worked out, with its two branches for the cultivation of the mind and of the body. And I suppose we shall begin with the mind, before we start physical training.

Naturally.

Under that head will come stories,[6] and of these there are two kinds: some are true, others fictitious. Both must come in, but we shall begin our education with the fictitious kind.

I don't understand, he said.

Don't you understand, I replied, that we begin by telling children stories, which, taken as a whole, are fiction, though they contain some truth? Such story-telling begins at an earlier age than physical training; that is why I said we should start with the mind.

You are right.

And the beginning, as you know, is always the most important part, especially in dealing with anything young and tender. That is the time when the character is being moulded and easily takes any impress one may wish to stamp on it.

Quite true.

Then shall we simply allow our children to listen to any stories that anyone happens to make up, and so receive into their minds ideas often the very opposite of those we shall think they ought to have when they are grown up?

No, certainly not.

It seems, then, our first business will be to supervise the making of fables and legends, rejecting all which are unsatisfactory; and we shall induce nurses and mothers to tell their children only those which we have approved, and to think more of moulding their souls with these stories than they now do of rubbing their limbs to make them strong and shapely. Most of the stories now in use must be discarded.

What kind do you mean?

If we take the great ones, we shall see in them the pattern of all the rest, which are bound to be of the same stamp and to have the same effect.

---

[5] The ascription of a philosophic element to dogs is not seriously meant. We might regard man's love of knowledge as rooted in an instinct of curiosity to be found in animals; but curiosity has no connexion with gentleness, and for Plato reason is an independent faculty, existing only in man and not developed from any animal instinct.

---

[6] In a wide sense, tales, legends, myths, narratives in poetry or prose.

No doubt; but which do you mean by the great ones?

The stories in Hesiod and Homer and the poets in general, who have at all times composed fictitious tales and told them to mankind.

Which kind are you thinking of, and what fault do you find in them?

The worst of all faults, especially if the story is ugly and immoral as well as false—misrepresenting the nature of gods and heroes, like an artist whose picture is utterly unlike the object he sets out to draw.

That is certainly a serious fault; but give me an example.

A single instance of false invention about the highest matters is that foul story, which Hesiod repeats, of the deeds of Uranus and the vengeance of Cronos;[7] and then there is the tale of Cronos's doings and of his son's treatment of him. Even if such tales were true, I should not have supposed they should be lightly told to thoughtless young people. If they cannot be altogether suppressed, they should only be revealed in a mystery, to which access should be as far as possible restricted by requiring the sacrifice, not of a pig, but of some victim such as very few could afford.[8]

It is true: those stories are objectionable.

Yes, and not to be repeated in our commonwealth, Adeimantus. We shall not tell a child that, if he commits the foulest crimes or goes to any length in punishing his father's misdeeds, he will be doing nothing out of the way, but only what the first and greatest of the gods have done before him.

I agree; such stories are not fit to be repeated.

Nor yet any tales of warfare and intrigues and battles of gods against gods, which are equally untrue. If our future Guardians are to think it a disgrace to quarrel lightly with one another, we shall not let them embroider robes with the Battle of the Giants[9] or tell them of all the other feuds of gods and heroes with their kith and kin. If by any means we can make them believe that no one has ever had a quarrel with a fellow citizen and it is a sin to have one, that is the sort of thing our old men and women should tell children from the first; and as they grow older, we must make the poets write for them in the same strain. Stories like those of Hera being bound by her son, or of Hephaestus flung from heaven by his father for taking his mother's part when she was beaten, and all those battles of the gods in Homer, must not be admitted into our state, whether they be allegorical or not. A child cannot distinguish the allegorical sense from the literal, and the ideas he takes in at that age are likely to become indelibly fixed; hence the great importance of seeing that the first stories he hears shall be designed to produce the best possible effect on his character.

Yes, that is reasonable. But if we were asked which of these stories in particular are of the right quality, what should we answer?

I replied: You and I, Adeimantus, are not, for the moment, poets, but founders of a commonwealth. As such, it is not our business to invent stories ourselves, but only to be clear as to the main outlines to be followed by the poets in making their stories and the limits beyond which they must not be allowed to go.

True; but what are these outlines for any account they may give of the gods?

Of this sort, said I. A poet, whether he is writing epic, lyric, or drama, surely ought always to represent the divine nature as it really is. And the truth is that nature is good and must be described as such.

Unquestionably.

Well, nothing that is good can be harmful; and if it cannot do harm, it can do no evil; and so it cannot be responsible for any evil.

I agree.

Again, goodness is beneficent, and hence the cause of well-being.

---

[7] Hesiod, *Theogony,* 154 ff. A primitive myth of the forcing apart of Sky (Uranus) and Earth (Gaia) by their son Cronos, who mutilated his father. Zeus, again, took vengeance on his father Cronos for trying to destroy his children. These stories were sometimes cited to justify ill-treatment of parents.

[8] The usual sacrifice at the Eleusinian Mysteries was a pig, which was cheap. In a mystery unedifying legends might be given an allegorical interpretation, a method which had been applied to Homer since the end of the sixth century B.C.

---

[9] Such a robe was woven by maidens for the statue of Athena at the Great Panathenaea.

Yes.

Goodness, then, is not responsible for everything, but only for what is as it should be. It is not responsible for evil.

Quite true.

It follows, then, that the divine, being good, is not, as most people say, responsible for everything that happens to mankind, but only for a small part; for the good things in human life are far fewer than the evil, and, whereas the good must be ascribed to heaven only, we must look elsewhere for the cause of evils.

I think that is perfectly true.

So we shall condemn as a foolish error Homer's description of Zeus as the "dispenser of both good and ill." We shall disapprove when Pandarus' violation of oaths and treaties it said to be the work of Zeus and Athena, or when Themis and Zeus are said to have caused strife among the gods. Nor must we allow our young people to be told by Aeschylus that "Heaven implants guilt in man, when his will is to destroy a house utterly." If a poet writes of the sorrows of Niobe or the calamities of the house of Pelops or of the Trojan war, either he must not speak of them as the work of a god, or, if he does so, he must devise some such explanation as we are now requiring: he must say that what the god did was just and good, and the sufferers were the better for being chastised. One who pays a just penalty must not be called miserable, and his misery then laid at heaven's door. The poet will only be allowed to say that the wicked were miserable because they needed chastisement, and the punishment of heaven did them good. If our commonwealth is to be well-ordered, we must fight to the last against any member of it being suffered to speak of the divine, which is good, being responsible for evil. Neither young nor old must listen to such tales, in prose or verse. Such doctrine would be impious, self-contradictory, and disastrous to our commonwealth.

I agree, he said, and I would vote for a law to that effect.

Well then, that shall be one of our laws about religion. The first principle to which all must conform in speech or writing is that heaven is not responsible for everything, but only for what is good.

I am quite satisfied.

If anyone, then, is to practise deception, either on the country's enemies or on its citizens, it must be the Rulers of the commonwealth, acting for its benefit; no one else may meddle with this privilege. For a private person to mislead such Rulers we shall declare to be a worse offence than for a patient to mislead his doctor or an athlete his trainer about his bodily condition, or for a seaman to misinform his captain about the state of the ship or of the crew. So, if anyone else in our commonwealth "of all that practise crafts, physician, seer, or carpenter," is caught not telling the truth, the Rulers will punish him for introducing a practice as fatal and subversive in a state as it would be in a ship.

SELECTION OF RULERS: THE GUARDIANS' MANNER OF LIVING

Good, said I; and what is the next point to he settled? Is it not the question, which of these Guardians are to be rulers and which are to obey?

No doubt.

Well, it is obvious that the elder must have authority over the young, and that the rulers must be the best.

Yes.

And as among farmers the best are those with a natural turn for farming, so, if we want the best among our Guardians, we must take those naturally fitted to watch over a commonwealth. They must have the right sort of intelligence and ability; and also they must look upon the commonwealth as their special concern—the sort of concern that is felt for something so closely bound up with oneself that its interests and fortunes, for good or ill, are held to be identical with one's own.

Exactly.

So the kind of men we must choose from among the Guardians will be those who, when we look at the whole course of their lives, are found to be full of zeal to do whatever they believe is for the good of the commonwealth and never willing to act against its interest.

Yes, they will be the men we want.

We must watch them, I think, at every age and see whether they are capable of preserving this conviction that they must do what is best for the community, never forgetting it or allowing themselves to be either forced or bewitched into throwing it over.

How does this throwing over come about?

I will explain. When a belief passes out of the mind, a man may be willing to part with it, if it is false and he has learnt better, or unwilling, if it is true.

I see how he might be willing to let it go; but you must explain how he can be unwilling.

Where is your difficulty? Don't you agree that men are unwilling to be deprived of good, though ready enough to part with evil? Or that to be deceived about the truth is evil, to possess it good? Or don't you think that possessing truth means thinking of things as they really are?

You are right. I do agree that men are unwilling to be robbed of a true belief.

When that happens to them, then, it must be by theft, or violence, or bewitchment.

Again I do not understand.

Perhaps my metaphors are too high-flown. I call it theft when one is persuaded out of one's belief or forgets it. Argument in the one case, and time in the other, steal it away without one's knowing what is happening. You understand now?

Yes.

And by violence I mean being driven to change one's mind by pain or suffering.

That too I understand, and you are right.

And bewitchment, as I think you would agree, occurs when a man is beguiled out of his opinion by the allurements of pleasure or scared out of it under the spell of panic.

Yes, all delusions are like a sort of bewitchment.

As I said just now, then, we must find out who are the best guardians of this inward conviction that they must always do what they believe to be best for the commonwealth. We shall have to watch them from earliest childhood and set them tasks in which they would be most likely to forget or to be beguiled out of this duty. We shall then choose only those whose memory holds firm and who are proof against delusion.

Yes.

We must also subject them to ordeals of toil and pain and watch for the same qualities there. And we must observe them when exposed to the test of yet a third kind of bewitchment. As people lead colts up to

alarming noises to see whether they are timid, so these young men must be brought into terrifying situations and then into scenes of pleasure, which will put them to severer proof than gold tried in the furnace. If we find one bearing himself well in all these trials and resisting every enchantment, a true guardian of himself, preserving always that perfect rhythm and harmony of being which he has acquired from his training in music and poetry, such a one will be of the greatest service to the commonwealth as well as to himself. Whenever we find one who has come unscathed through every test in childhood, youth, and manhood, we shall set him as a Ruler to watch over the commonwealth; he will be honoured in life, and after death receive the highest tribute of funeral rites and other memorials. All who do not reach this standard we must reject. And that, I think, my dear Glaucon, may be taken as an outline of the way in which we shall select Guardians to be set in authority as Rulers.

I am very much of your mind.

These, then, may properly be called Guardians in the fullest sense, who will ensure that neither foes without shall have the power, nor friends within the wish, to do harm. Those young men whom up to now we have been speaking of as Guardians, will be better described as Auxiliaries, who will enforce the decisions of the Rulers.

I agree.

Now, said I, can we devise something in the way of those convenient fictions we spoke of earlier, a single bold flight of invention,[10] which we may induce the community in general, and if possible the Rulers themselves, to accept?

What kind of fiction?

Nothing new; something like an Eastern tale of what, according to the poets, has happened before now in more than one part of the world. The poets have been believed; but the thing has not happened in our day,

---

[10] This phrase is commonly rendered by "noble lie" a self-contradictory expression no more applicable to Plato's harmless allegory than to a New Testament parable or the Pilgrim's Progress, and liable to suggest that he would countenance the lies, for the most part ignoble, now called propaganda.

and it would be hard to persuade anyone that it could ever happen again.

You seem rather shy of telling this story of yours.

With good reason, as you will see when I have told it.

Out with it; don't be afraid.

Well, here it is; though I hardly know how to find the courage or the words to express it. I shall try to convince, first the Rulers and the soldiers,[11] and then the whole community, that all that nurture and education which we gave them was only something they seemed to experience as it were in a dream. In reality they were the whole time down inside the earth, being moulded and fostered while their arms and all their equipment were being fashioned also; and at last, when they were complete, the earth sent them up from her womb into the light of day. So now they must think of the land they dwell in as a mother and nurse, whom they must take thought for and defend against any attack, and of their fellow citizens as brothers born of the same soil.

You might well be bashful about coming out with your fiction.

No doubt; but still you must hear the rest of the story. It is true, we shall tell our people in this fable, that all of you in this land are brothers; but the god who fashioned you mixed gold in the composition of those among you who are fit to rule, so that they are of the most precious quality; and he put silver in the Auxiliaries, and iron and brass in the farmers and craftsmen. Now, since you are all of one stock, although your children will generally be like their parents, sometimes a golden parent may have a silver child or a silver parent a golden one, and so on with all the other combinations. So the first and chief injunction laid by heaven upon the Rulers is that, among all the things of which they must show themselves good guardians, there is none that needs to be so carefully watched as the mixture of metals in the souls of the children. If a child of their own is born with an alloy of iron or brass, they must, without the smallest pity, assign him the station

proper to his nature and thrust him out among the craftsmen or the farmers. If, on the contrary, these classes produce a child with gold or silver in his composition, they will promote him, according to his value, to be a Guardian or an Auxiliary. They will appeal to a prophecy that ruin will come upon the state when it passes into the keeping of a man of iron or brass. Such is the story; can you think of any device to make them believe it?

Not in the first generation; but their sons and descendants might believe it, and finally the rest of mankind.[12]

Well, said I, even so it might have a good effect in making them care more for the commonwealth and for one another; for I think I see what you mean.

So, I continued, we will leave the success of our story to the care of popular tradition; and now let us arm these sons of Earth and lead them, under the command of their Rulers, to the site of our city. There let them look round for the best place to fix their camp, from which they will be able to control any rebellion against the laws from within and to beat off enemies who may come from without like wolves to attack the fold. When they have pitched their camp and offered sacrifice to the proper divinities, they must arrange their sleeping quarters; and these must be sufficient to shelter them from winter cold and summer heat.

Naturally. You mean they are going to live there?

Yes, said I; but live like soldiers, not like men of business.

What is the difference?

I will try to explain. It would be very strange if a shepherd were to disgrace himself by keeping, for the protection of his flock, dogs who were so ill-bred and badly trained that hunger or unruliness or some bad habit or other would set them worrying the sheep and behaving no better than wolves. We must take every precaution against our Auxiliaries treating the citizens

---

[11] Note that the Guardians themselves are to accept this allegory, if possible. It is not "propaganda" foisted on the masses by the Rulers.

[12] Just as the tradition that the Athenians were "autochthonous" in a literal sense was popularly believed, though Plato would suppose it to have been originally invented by some myth-making poet.

in any such way and, because they are stronger, turning into savage tyrants instead of friendly allies; and they will have been furnished with the best of safeguards, if they have really been educated in the right way.

But surely there is nothing wrong with their education.

We must not be too positive about that, my dear Glaucon; but we can be sure of what we said not long ago, that if they are to have the best chance of being gentle and humane to one another and to their charges, they must have the right education, whatever that may be.

We were certainly right there.

Then besides that education, it is only common sense to say that the dwellings and other belongings provided for them must be such as will neither make them less perfect Guardians nor encourage them to maltreat their fellow citizens.

True.

With that end in view, let us consider how they should live and be housed. First, none of them must possess any private property beyond the barest necessaries. Next, no one is to have any dwelling or store-house that is not open for all to enter at will. Their food, in the quantities required by men of temperance and courage who are in training for war, they will receive from the other citizens as the wages of their guardianship, fixed so that there shall be just enough for the year with nothing over; and they will have meals in common and all live together like soldiers in a camp. Gold and silver, we shall tell them, they will not need, having the divine counterparts of those metals always in their souls as a god-given possession, whose purity it is not lawful to sully by the acquisition of that mortal dross, current among mankind, which has been the occasion of so many unholy deeds. They alone of all the citizens are forbidden to touch and handle silver or gold, or to come under the same roof with them, or wear them as ornaments, or drink from vessels made of them. This manner of life will be their salvation and make them the saviours of the commonwealth. If ever they should come to possess land of their own and houses and money, they will give up their guardianship for the management of their farms and households

and become tyrants at enmity with their fellow citizens instead of allies. And so they will pass all their lives in hating and being hated, plotting and being plotted against, in much greater fear of their enemies at home than of any foreign foe, and fast heading for the destruction that will soon overwhelm their country with themselves. For all these reasons let us say that this is how our Guardians are to be housed and otherwise provided for, and let us make laws accordingly.

By all means, said Glaucon.

Here Adeimantus interposed. Socrates, he said, how would you meet the objection that you are not making these people particularly happy? it is their own fault too, if they are not; for they are really masters of the state, and yet they get no good out of it as other rulers do, who own lands, build themselves fine houses with handsome furniture, offer private sacrifices to the gods, and entertain visitors from abroad; who possess, in fact, that gold and silver you spoke of, with everything else that is usually thought necessary for happiness. These people seem like nothing so much as a garrison of mercenaries posted in the city and perpetually mounting guard.

Yes, I said, and what is more they will serve for their food only without getting a mercenary's pay, so that they will not be able to travel on their own account or to make presents to a mistress or to spend as they please in other ways, like the people who are commonly thought happy. You have forgotten to include these counts in your indictment, and many more to the same effect.

Well, take them as included now.

And you want to hear the answer?

Yes.

We shall find one, I think, by keeping to the line we have followed so far. We shall say that, though it would not be surprising if even these people were perfectly happy under such conditions, our aim in founding the commonwealth was not to make any one class specially happy, but to secure the greatest possible happiness for the community as a whole. We thought we should have the best chance of finding justice in a state so constituted, just as we should find injustice where the constitution was of the worst possible type; we could then decide the question which has been before us all this time. For the moment, we are constructing, as we believe, the state which will be happy as a whole, not trying to secure the well-being of a select few; we shall study a state of the opposite kind presently. It is as if we were colouring a statue and someone came up and blamed us for not putting the most beautiful colours on the noblest parts of the figure; the eyes, for instance, should be painted crimson, but we had made them black. We should think it a fair answer to say: Really, you must not expect us to paint eyes so handsome as not to look like eyes at all. This applies to all the parts: the question is whether, by giving each its proper colour, we make the whole beautiful. So too, in the present case, you must not press us to endow our Guardians with a happiness that will make them anything rather than guardians. We could quite easily clothe our farmers in gorgeous robes, crown them with gold, and invite them to till the soil at their pleasure; or we might set our potters to lie on couches by their fire, passing round the wine and making merry, with their wheel at hand to work at whenever they felt so inclined. We could make all the rest happy in the same sort of way, and so spread this well-being through the whole community. But you must not put that idea into our heads; if we take your advice, the farmer will be no farmer, the potter no longer a potter; none of the elements that make up the community will keep its character. In many cases this does not matter so much: if a cobbler goes to the bad and pretends to be what he is not, he is not a danger to the state; but, as you must surely see, men who make only a vain show of being guardians of the laws and of the commonwealth bring the whole state to utter ruin, just as, on the other hand, its good government and well-being depend entirely on them. We, in fact, are making genuine Guardians who will be the last to bring harm upon the commonwealth; if our critic aims rather at producing a happiness like that of a party of peasants feasting at a fair, what he has in mind is something other than a civic community. So we must consider whether our aim in establishing Guardians is to secure the greatest possible happiness for them, or happiness is something of which we should watch the development in the whole commonwealth. If so, we must compel these Guardians and Auxiliaries of ours to second our efforts; and they, and all the rest with them, must be induced to make themselves perfect masters each of his own craft. In that way, as the community grows into a well-ordered whole, the several classes may be allowed such measure of happiness as their nature will compass.

I think that is an admirable reply.

THE VIRTUES IN THE STATE

So now at last, son of Ariston, said I, your commonwealth is established. The next thing is to bring to bear upon it all the light you can get from any quarter, with the help of your brother and Polemarchus and all the rest, in the hope that we may see where justice is to be found in it and where injustice, how they differ, and which of the two will bring happiness to its possessor, no matter whether gods and men see that he has it or not.

Nonsense, said Glaucon; you promised to conduct the search yourself, because it would be a sin not to uphold justice by every means in your power.

That is true; I must do as you say, but you must all help.

We will.

I suspect, then, we may find what we are looking for in this way. I take it that our state, having been founded and built up on the right lines, is good in the complete sense of the word.

It must be.

Obviously, then, it is wise, brave, temperate, and just.

Obviously.

Then if we find some of these qualities in it, the remainder will be the one we have not found. It is as if we were looking somewhere for one of any four things: if we detected that one immediately, we should be satisfied; whereas if we recognized the other three first, that would be enough to indicate the thing we wanted; it could only be the remaining one. So here we have four qualities. Had we not better follow that method in looking for the one we want?

Surely.

To begin then: the first quality to come into view in our state seems to be its wisdom; and there appears to be something odd about this quality.[13]

What is there odd about it?

I think the state we have described really has wisdom; for it will be prudent in counsel, won't it?

Yes.

And prudence in counsel is clearly a form of knowledge; good counsel cannot be due to ignorance and stupidity.

Clearly.

But there are many various kinds of knowledge in our commonwealth. There is the knowledge possessed by the carpenters or the smiths, and the knowledge how to raise crops. Are we to call the state wise and prudent on the strength of these forms of skill?

No; they would only make it good at furniture-making or working in copper or agriculture.

Well then, is there any form of knowledge, possessed by some among the citizens of our new-founded commonwealth, which will enable it to take thought, not for some particular interest, but for the best possible conduct of the state as a whole in its internal and external relations?

Yes, there is.

What is it, and where does it reside?

It is precisely that art of guardianship which resides in those Rulers whom we just called Guardians in the full sense.

And what would you call the state on the strength of that knowledge?

Prudent and truly wise.

And do you think there will be more or fewer of these genuine Guardians in our state than there will be smiths?

Far fewer.

Fewer, in fact, than any of those other groups who are called after the kind of skill they possess?

Much fewer.

So, if a state is constituted on natural principles, the wisdom it possesses as a whole will be due to the knowledge residing in the smallest part, the one which takes the

lead and governs the rest. Such knowledge is the only kind that deserves the name of wisdom, and it appears to be ordained by nature that the class privileged to possess it should be the smallest of all.

Quite true.

Here then we have more or less made out one of our four qualities and its scat in the structure of the commonwealth.

To my satisfaction, at any rate.

Next there is courage. It is not hard to discern that quality or the part of the community in which it resides so as to entitle the whole to be called brave.

Why do you say so?

Because anyone who speaks of a state as either brave or cowardly can only be thinking of that part of it which takes the field and fight in its defence; the reason being, I imagine, that the character of the state is not determined by the bravery or cowardice of the other parts.

No.

Courage, then, is another quality which a community owes to a certain part of itself. And its being brave will mean that, in this part, it possesses the power of preserving, in all circumstances, a conviction about the sort of things that it is right to be afraid of— the conviction implanted by the education which the law-giver has established. Is not that what you mean by courage?

I do not quite understand. Will you say it again?

I am saying that courage means preserving something.

Yes, but what?

The conviction, inculcated by lawfully established education, about the sort of things which may rightly be feared. When I added "in all circumstances," I meant preserving it always and never abandoning it, whether under the influence of pain or of pleasure, of desire or of fear. If you like, I will give an illustration.

Please do.

You know how dyers who want wool to take a purple dye, first select the white wool from among all the other colours, next treat it very carefully to make it take the dye in its full brilliance, and only then dip it in the vat. Dyed in that way, wool gets a fast colour, which no washing, even with soap, will rob of its brilliance; whereas if they choose wool of any colour but white, or if

---

[13] Because the wisdom of the whole resides in the smallest part, as explained below.

they neglect to prepare it, you know what happens.

Yes, it looks washed-out and ridiculous.

That illustrates the result we were doing our best to achieve when we were choosing our fighting men and training their minds and bodies. Our only purpose was to contrive influences whereby they might take the colour of our institutions like a dye, so that, in virtue of having both the right temperament and the right education, their convictions about what ought to be feared and on all other subjects might be indelibly fixed, never to be washed out by pleasure and pain, desire and fear, solvents more terribly effective than all the soap and fuller's earth in the world. Such a power of constantly preserving, in accordance with our institutions, the right conviction about the things which ought, or ought not to be feared, is what I call courage. That is my position, unless you have some objection to make.

None at all, he replied; if the belief were such as might be found in a slave or an animal—correct, but not produced by education—you would hardly describe it as in accordance with our institutions, and you would give it some other name than courage.

Quite true.

Then I accept your account of courage.

You will do well to accept it, at any rate as applying to the courage of the ordinary citizen;[14] if you like we will go into it more fully some other time. At present we are in search of justice, rather than of courage; and for that purpose we have said enough.

I quite agree.

Two qualities, I went on, still remain to be made out in our state, temperance and the object of our whole inquiry, justice. Can we discover justice without troubling ourselves further about temperance?

I do not know, and I would rather not have justice come to light first, if that means that we should not go on to consider temperance. So if you want to please me, take temperance first.

Of course I have every wish to please you.

Do go on then.

I will. At first sight, temperance seems more like some sort of concord or harmony than the other qualities did.

How so?

Temperance surely means a kind of orderliness, a control of certain pleasures and appetites. People use the expression, "master of oneself," whatever that means, and various other phrases that point the same way.

Quite true.

Is not "master of oneself" an absurd expression? A man who was master of himself would presumably be also subject to himself, and the subject would be master; for all these terms apply to the same person.

No doubt.

I think, however, the phrase means that within the man himself, in his soul, there is a better part and a worse; and that he is his own master when the part which is better by nature has the worse under its control. It is certainly a term of praise; whereas it is considered a disgrace, when, through bad breeding or bad company, the better part is overwhelmed by the worse, like a small force outnumbered by a multitude. A man in that condition is called a slave to himself and intemperate.

Probably that is what is meant.

Then now look at our newly founded state and you will find one of these two conditions realized there. You will agree that it deserves to be called master of itself, if temperance and self-mastery exist where the better part rules the worse.

Yes, I can see that is true.

It is also true that the great mass of multifarious appetites and pleasures and pains will be found to occur chiefly in children and women and slaves, and, among free men so called, in the inferior multitude; whereas the simple and moderate desires which, with the aid of reason and right belief, are guided by reflection, you will find only in a few, and those with the best inborn dispositions and the best educated.

Yes, certainly.

Do you see that this state of things will exist in your commonwealth, where the desires of the inferior multitude will be controlled by the desires and wisdom of the superior few? Hence, if any society can be called master of itself and in control of pleasures and desires, it will be ours.

---

[14] As distinct from the perfect courage of the philosophic Ruler, based on immediate knowledge of values.

Quite so.

On all these grounds, then, we may describe it as temperate. Furthermore, in our state, if anywhere, the governors and the governed will share the same conviction on the question who ought to rule. Don't you think so?

I am quite sure of it.

Then, if that is their state of mind, in which of the two classes of citizens will temperance reside—in the governors or in the governed?

In both, I suppose.

So we were not wrong in divining a resemblance between temperance and some kind of harmony. Temperance is not like courage and wisdom, which made the state wise and brave by residing each in one particular part. Temperance works in a different way; it extends throughout the whole gamut of the state, producing a consonance of all its elements from the weakest to the strongest as measured by any standard you like to take—wisdom, bodily strength, numbers, or wealth. So we are entirely justified in identifying with temperance this unanimity or harmonious agreement between the naturally superior and inferior elements on the question which of the two should govern, whether in the state or in the individual.

I fully agree.

Good, said I. We have discovered in our commonwealth three out of our four qualities, to the best of our present judgment. What is the remaining one, required to make up its full complement of goodness? For clearly this will be justice.

Clearly.

Now is the moment, then, Glaucon, for us to keep the closest watch, like huntsmen standing round a covert, to make sure that justice does not slip through and vanish undetected. It must certainly be somewhere hereabouts; so keep your eyes open for a view of the quarry, and if you see it first, give me the alert.

I wish I could, he answered; but you will do better to give me a lead and not count on me for more than eyes to see what you show me.

Pray for luck, then, and follow me.

I will, if you will lead on.

The thicket looks rather impenetrable, said I; too dark for it to be easy to start up the game. However, we must push on.

Of course we must.

Here I gave the cry halloo. Glaucon, I exclaimed, I believe we are on the track and the quarry is not going to escape us altogether.

That is good news.

Really, I said, we have been extremely stupid. All this time the thing has been under our very noses from the start, and we never saw it. We have been as absurd as a person who hunts for something be has all the time got in his hand. Instead of looking at the thing, we have been staring into the distance. No doubt that is why it escaped us.

What do you mean?

I believe we have been talking about the thing all this while without ever understanding that we were giving some sort of account of it.

Do come to the point. I am all ears.

Listen, then, and judge whether I am right. You remember how, when we first began to establish our commonwealth and several times since, we have laid down, as a universal principle, that everyone ought to perform the one function in the community for which his nature best suited him. Well. I believe that that principle, or some form of it, is justice.

We certainly laid that down.

Yes, and surely we have often heard people say that justice means minding one's own business and not meddling with other men's concerns; and we have often said so ourselves.

We have.

Well, my friend, it may be that this minding of one's own business, when it takes a certain form, is actually the same thing as justice. Do you know what makes me think so?

No, tell me.

I think that this quality which makes it possible for the three we have already considered, wisdom, courage, and temperance, to take their place in the commonwealth, and so long as it remains present secures their continuance, must be the remaining one. And we said that, when three of the four were found, the one left over would be justice.

It must be so.

Well now, if we had to decide which of these qualities will contribute most to the excellence of our commonwealth, it would be hard to say whether it was the unanimity of rulers and subjects, or the soldier's fidelity to the established conviction about what is, or is not, to be feared, or the watchful intelligence of the Rulers; or whether its excellence were not above all due to the observance by everyone, child or woman, slave or freeman or artisan, ruler or ruled, of this principle that each one should do his own proper work without interfering with others.

It would be hard to decide, no doubt.

It seems, then, that this principle can at any rate claim to rival wisdom, temperance, and courage as conducing to the excellence of a state. And would you not say that the only possible competitor of these qualities must be justice?

Yes, undoubtedly.

Here is another thing which points to the same conclusion. The judging of lawsuits is a duty that you will lay upon your Rulers, isn't it?

Of course.

And the chief aim of their decisions will be that neither party shall have what belongs to another or be deprived of what is his own.

Yes.

Because that is just?

Yes.

So here again justice admittedly means that a man should possess and concern himself with what properly belongs to him.

True.

Again, do you agree with me that no great harm would be done to the community by a general interchange of most forms of work, the carpenter and the cobbler exchanging their positions and their tools and taking on each other's jobs, or even the same man undertaking both?

Yes, there would not be much harm in that.

But I think you will also agree that another kind of interchange would be disastrous. Suppose, for instance, someone whom nature designed to be an artisan or tradesman should be emboldened by some advantage, such as wealth or command of votes or bodily strength, to try to enter the order of fighting men; or some member of that order

should aspire, beyond his merits, to a seat in the council-chamber of the Guardians. Such interference and exchange of social positions and tools, or the attempt to combine all these forms of work in the same person, would be fatal to the commonwealth.

Most certainly.

Where there are three orders, then, any plurality of functions or shifting from one order to another is not merely utterly harmful to the community, but one might fairly call it the extreme of wrongdoing. And you will agree that to do the greatest of wrongs to one's own community is injustice.

Surely.

This, then, is injustice. And, conversely, let us repeat that when each order—tradesman, Auxiliary, Guardian—keeps to its own proper business in the commonwealth and does its own work, that is justice and what makes a just society.

I entirely agree,

THE THREE PARTS
OF THE SOUL

We must not be too positive yet, said I. If we find that this same quality when it exists in the individual can equally be identified with justice, then we can at once give our assent; there will be no more to be said; otherwise, we shall have to look further. For the moment, we had better finish the inquiry which we began with the idea that it would be easier to make out the nature of justice in the individual if we first tried to study it in something on a larger scale. That larger thing we took to be a state, and so we set about constructing the best one we could, being sure of finding justice in a state that was good. The discovery we made there must now be applied to the individual. If it is confirmed, all will be well; but if we find that justice in the individual is something different, we must go back to the state and test our new result. Perhaps if we brought the two cases into contact like flint and steel, we might strike out between them the spark of justice, and in its light confirm the conception in our own minds.

A good method. Let us follow it.

Now, I continued, if two things, one large, the other small, are called by the same name, they will be alike in that respect to which the common name applies. Accordingly, in so far as the quality of justice is concerned, there will be no difference between a just man and a just society.

No.

Well, but we decided that a society was just when each of the three types of human character it contained performed its own function; and again, it was temperate and brave and wise by virtue of certain other affections and states of mind of those same types.

True.

Accordingly, my friend, if we are to be justified in attributing those same virtues to the individual, we shall expect to find that the individual soul contains the same three elements and that they are affected in the same way as are the corresponding types in society.

That follows.

Here, then, we have stumbled upon another little problem: Does the soul contain these three elements or not?

Not such a very little one, I think. It may be a true saying, Socrates, that what is worth while is seldom easy.

Apparently; and let me tell you, Glaucon, it is my belief that we shall never reach the exact truth in this matter by following our present methods of discussion; the road leading to that goal is longer and more laborious. However, perhaps we can find an answer that will be up to the standard we have so far maintained in our speculations. Is not that enough? I should be satisfied for the moment.

Well, it will more than satisfy me, I replied.

Don't be disheartened, then, but go on.

Surely, I began, we must admit that the same elements and characters that appear in the state must exist in every one of us; where else could they have come from? It would be absurd to imagine that among peoples with a reputation for a high-spirited character, like the Thracians and Scythians and northerners generally, the states have not derived that character from their individual members; or that it is otherwise with the love of knowledge, which would be ascribed chiefly to our own part of the world, or with the love of money, which one would specially connect with Phoenicia and Egypt.

Certainly.

So far, then, we have a fact which is easily recognized. But here the difficulty begins. Are we using the same part of ourselves in all these three experiences, or a different part in each? Do we gain knowledge with one part, feel anger with another, and with yet a third desire the pleasures of food, sex, and so on? Or is the whole soul at work in every impulse and in all these forms of behaviour? The difficulty is to answer that question satisfactorily.

I quite agree.

Let us approach the problem whether these elements are distinct or identical in this way. It is clear that the same thing cannot act in two opposite ways or be in two opposite states at the same time, with respect to the same part of itself, and in relation to the same object. So if we find such contradictory actions or states among the elements concerned, we shall know that more than one must have been involved.

Very well.

Consider this proposition of mine, then. Can the same thing, at the same time and with respect to the same part of itself, be at rest and in motion?

Certainly not.

We had better state this principle in still more precise terms, to guard against misunderstanding later on. Suppose a man is standing still, but moving his head and arms. We should not allow anyone to say that the same man was both at rest and in motion at the same time, but only that part of him was at rest, part in motion. Isn't that so?

Yes.

An ingenious objector might refine still further and argue that a peg-top, spinning with its peg fixed at the same spot, or indeed any body that revolves in the same place, is both at rest and in motion as a whole. But we should not agree, because the parts in respect of which such a body is moving and at rest are not the same. It contains an axis and a circumference; and in respect of the axis it is at rest inasmuch as the axis is not inclined in any direction, while in respect of the circumference it revolves; and if, while it is spinning, the axis does lean out of the perpendicular in all directions, then it is in no way at rest.

That is true.

No objection of that sort, then, will disconcert us or make us believe that the same thing can ever act or be acted upon in two opposite ways, or be two opposite things, at the same time, in respect of the same part of itself, and in relation to the same object.

I can answer for myself at any rate.

Well, anyhow, as we do not want to spend time in reviewing all such objections to make sure that they are unsound, let us proceed on this assumption, with the understanding that, if we ever come to think otherwise, all the consequences based upon it will fall to the ground.

Yes, that is a good plan.

Now, would you class such things as assent and dissent, striving after something and refusing it, attraction and repulsion, as pairs of opposite actions or states of mind—no matter which?

Yes, they are opposites.

And would you not class all appetites such as hunger and thirst, and again willing and wishing, with the affirmative members of those pairs I have just mentioned? For instance, you would say that the soul of a man who desires something is striving after it, or trying to draw to itself the thing it wishes to possess, or again, in so far as it is willing to have its want satisfied, it is giving its assent to its own longing, as if to an inward question.

Yes.

And, on the other hand, disinclination, unwillingness, and dislike, we should class on the negative side with acts of rejection or repulsion.

Of course.

That being so, shall we say that appetites form one class, the most conspicuous being those we call thirst and hunger?

Yes.

Thirst being desire for drink; hunger, for food?

Yes.

Now, is thirst, just in so far as it is thirst, a desire in the soul for anything more than simply drink? Is it, for instance, thirst for hot drink or for cold, for much drink or for little, or in a word for drink of any particular kind? Is it not rather true that you will have a desire for cold drink only if you are feeling hot as well as thirsty, and for hot drink only if you are feeling cold; and if you want much drink or little, that will be because your thirst is a great thirst or a little one? But, just in itself, thirst or hunger is a desire for nothing more than its natural object, drink or food, pure and simple.

Yes, he agreed, each desire, just in itself, is simply for its own natural object. When the object is of such and such a particular kind, the desire will be correspondingly qualified.[15]

We must be careful here, or we might be troubled by the objection that no one desires mere food and drink, but always wholesome food and drink. We shall be told that what we desire is always something that is good; so if thirst is a desire, its object must be, like that of any other desire, something—drink or whatever it may be—that will be good for one.[16]

Yes, there might seem to be something in that objection.

But surely, wherever you have two correlative terms, if one is qualified, the other must always be qualified too; whereas if one is unqualified, so is the other.

I don't understand.

Well, "greater" is a relative term; and the greater is greater than the less; if it is much greater, then the less is much less; if it is greater at some moment, past or future, then the less is less at that same moment. The same principle applies to all such correlatives, like "more" and "fewer," "double" and "half"; and again to terms like "heavier"

---

[15] The object of the following subtle argument about relative terms is to distinguish thirst as a mere blind craving for drink from a more complex desire whose object includes the pleasure or health expected to result from drinking. We thus forestall the objection that all desires have "the good" (apparent or real) for their object and include an intellectual or rational element, so that the conflict of motives might be reduced to an intellectual debate, in the same "part" of the soul, on the comparative values of two incompatible ends.

[16] If this objection were admitted, it would follow that the desire would always be correspondingly qualified. It is necessary to insist that we do experience blind cravings which can be isolated from any judgment about the goodness of their object.

and "lighter," "quicker" and "slower," and to things like hot and cold.

Yes.

Or take the various branches of knowledge: is it not the same there? The object of knowledge pure and simple is the knowable—if that is the right word—without any qualification; whereas a particular kind of knowledge has an object of a particular kind. For example, as soon as men learnt how to build houses, their craft was distinguished from others under the name of architecture, because it had a unique character, which was itself due to the character of its object; and all other branches of craft and knowledge were distinguished in the same way.

True.

This, then, if you understand me now, is what I meant by saying that, where there are two correlatives, the one is qualified if, and only if, the other is so. I am not saying that the one must have the same quality as the other—that the science of health and disease is itself healthy and diseased, or the knowledge of good and evil is itself good and evil—but only that, as soon as you have a knowledge that is restricted to a particular kind of object, namely health and disease, the knowledge itself becomes a particular kind of knowledge. Hence we no longer call it merely knowledge, which would have for its object whatever can be known, but we add the qualification and call it medical science.

I understand now and I agree.

Now, to go back to thirst: is not that one of these relative terms? It is essentially thirst for something.

Yes, for drink.

And if the drink desired is of a certain kind, the thirst will be correspondingly qualified. But thirst which is just simply thirst is not for drink of any particular sort—much or little, good or bad—but for drink pure and simple.

Quite so.

We conclude, then, that the soul of a thirsty man, just in so far as he is thirsty, has no other wish than to drink. That is the object of its craving, and towards that it is impelled.

That is clear.

Now if there is ever something which at the same time pulls it the opposite way, that something must be an element in the soul other than the one which is thirsting and driving it like a beast to drink; in accordance with our principle that the same thing cannot behave in two opposite ways at the same time and towards the same object with the same part of itself. It is like an archer drawing the bow: it is not accurate to say that his hands are at the same time both pushing and pulling it. One hand does the pushing, the other the pulling.

Exactly.

Now, is it sometimes true that people are thirsty and yet unwilling to drink?

Yes, often.

What, then, can one say of them, if not that their soul contains something which urges them to drink and something which holds them back, and that this latter is a distinct thing and overpowers the other?

I agree.

And is it not true that the intervention of this inhibiting principle in such cases always has its origin in reflection; whereas the impulses driving and dragging the soul are engendered by external influences and abnormal conditions?[17]

Evidently.

We shall have good reason, then, to assert that they are two distinct principles. We may call that part of the soul whereby it reflects, rational; and the other, with which it feels hunger and thirst and is distracted by sexual passion and all the other desires, we will call irrational appetite, associated with pleasure in the replenishment of certain wants.

Yes, there is good ground for that view.

Let us take it, then, that we have now distinguished two elements in the soul. What of that passionate element which makes us feel angry and indignant? Is that a third, or identical in nature with one of those two?

It might perhaps be identified with appetite.

I am more inclined to put my faith in a story I once heard about Leontius, son of Aglaion. On his way up from the Piraeus

---

[17] Some of the most intense bodily desires are due to morbid conditions, e.g. thirst in fever, and even milder desires are caused by a departure from the normal state, which demands "replenishment."

outside the north wall, he noticed the bodies of some criminals lying on the ground, with the executioner standing by them. He wanted to go and look at them, but at the same time he was disgusted and tried to turn away. He struggled for some time and covered his eyes, but at last the desire was too much for him. Opening his eyes wide, he ran up to the bodies and cried, "There you are, curse you; feast yourselves on this lovely sight!"

Yes, I have heard that story too.

The point of it surely is that anger is sometimes in conflict with appetite, as if they were two distinct principles. Do we not often find a man whose desires would force him to go against his reason, reviling himself and indignant with this part of his nature which is trying to put constraint on him? It is like a struggle between two factions, in which indignation takes the side of reason. But I believe you have never observed, in yourself or anyone else, indignation make common cause with appetite in behaviour which reason decides to be wrong.

No, I am sure I have not.

Again, take a man who feels he is in the wrong. The more generous his nature, the less can he be indignant at any suffering, such as hunger and cold, inflicted by the man he has injured. He recognizes such treatment as just, and, as I say, his spirit refuses to be roused against it.

That is true.

But now contrast one who thinks it is he that is being wronged. His spirit boils with resentment and sides with the right as he conceives it. Persevering all the more for the hunger and cold and other pains he suffers, it triumphs and will not give in until its gallant struggle has ended in success or death; or until the restraining voice of reason, like a shepherd calling off his dog, makes it relent.

An apt comparison, he said; and in fact it fits the relation of our Auxiliaries to the Rulers: they were to be like watchdogs obeying the shepherds of the commonwealth.

Yes, you understand very well what I have in mind. But do you see how we have changed our view? A moment ago we were supposing this spirited element to be something of the nature of appetite; but now it appears that, when the soul is divided into

factions, it is far more ready to be up in arms on the side of reason.

Quite true.

Is it, then, distinct from the rational element or only a particular form of it, so that the soul will contain no more than two elements, reason and appetite? Or is the soul like the state, which had three orders to hold it together, traders, Auxiliaries, and counsellors? Does the spirited element make a third, the natural auxiliary of reason, when not corrupted by bad upbringing?

It must be a third.

Yes, I said, provided it can be shown to be distinct from reason, as we saw it was from appetite.

That is easily proved. You can see that much in children: they are full of passionate feelings from their birth; but some, I should say, never become rational, and most of them only late in life.

A very sound observation, said I, the truth of which may also be seen in animals. And besides, there is the witness of Homer in that line I quoted before: "He smote his breast and spoke, chiding his heart." The poet is plainly thinking of the two elements as distinct, when he makes the one which has chosen the better course after reflection rebuke the other for its unreasoning passion.

I entirely agree.

THE VIRTUES IN
THE INDIVIDUAL

And so, after a stormy passage, we have reached the land. We are fairly agreed that the same three elements exist alike in the state and in the individual soul.

That is so.

Does it not follow at once that state and individual will be wise or brave by virtue of the same element in each and in the same way? Both will possess in the same manner any quality that makes for excellence.

That must be true.

Then it applies to justice: we shall conclude that a man is just in the same way that a state was just. And we have surely not forgotten that justice in the state meant that each of the three orders in it was doing its own proper work. So we may henceforth bear in mind that each one of us likewise will be a just person, fulfilling his proper function, only if the several parts of our nature fulfil theirs.

Certainly.

And it will be the business of reason to rule with wisdom and forethought on behalf of the entire soul; while the spirited element ought to act as its subordinate and ally. The two will be brought into accord, as we said earlier, by that combination of mental and bodily training which will tune up one string of the instrument and relax the other, nourishing the reasoning part on the study of noble literature and allaying the other's wildness by harmony and rhythm. When both have been thus nurtured and trained to know their own true functions, they must be set in command over the appetites, which form the greater part of each man's soul and are by nature insatiably covetous. They must keep watch lest this part, by battening on the pleasures that are called bodily, should grow so great and powerful that it will no longer keep to its own work, but will try to enslave the others and usurp a dominion to which it has no right, thus turning the whole of life upside down. At the same time, those two together will be the best of guardians for the entire soul and for the body against all enemies from without: the one will take counsel, while the other will do battle, following its ruler's commands and by its own bravery giving effect to the ruler's designs.

Yes, that is all true.

And so we call an individual brave in virtue of this spirited part of his nature, when, in spite of pain or pleasure, it holds fast to the injunctions of reason about what he ought or ought not to be afraid of.

True.

And wise in virtue of that small part which rules and issues these injunctions, possessing as it does the knowledge of what is good for each of the three elements and for all of them in common.

Certainly.

And, again, temperate by reason of the unanimity and concord of all three, when there is no internal conflict between the ruling element and its two subjects, but all are agreed that reason should be ruler.

Yes, that is an exact account of temperance, whether in the state or in the individual.

Finally, a man will be just by observing the principle we have so often stated.

Necessarily.

Now is there any indistinctness in our vision of justice, that might make it seem somehow different from what we found it to be in the state?

I don't think so.

Because, if we have any lingering doubt, we might make sure by comparing it with some commonplace notions. Suppose, for instance, that a sum of money were entrusted to our state or to an individual of corresponding character and training, would anyone imagine that such a person would be specially likely to embezzle it?

No.

And would he not be incapable of sacrilege and theft, or of treachery to friend or country; never false to an oath or any other compact; the last to be guilty of adultery or of neglecting parents or the due service of the gods?

Yes.

And the reason for all this is that each part of his nature is exercising its proper function, of ruling or of being ruled.

Yes, exactly.

Are you satisfied, then, that justice is the power which produces states or individuals of whom that is true, or must we look further?

There is no need; I am quite satisfied.

And so our dream has come true—I mean the inkling we had that, by some happy chance, we had lighted upon a rudimentary form of justice from the very moment when we set about founding our commonwealth. Our principle that the born shoemaker or carpenter had better stick to his trade turns out to have been an adumbration of justice; and that is why it has helped us. But in reality justice, though evidently analogous to this principle, is not a matter of external behaviour, but of the inward self and of attending to all that is, in the fullest sense, a man's proper concern. The just man does not allow the several elements in his soul to usurp one another's functions; he is indeed one who sets his house in order, by self-mastery and discipline coming to be at peace with himself, and bringing into tune those three parts, like the terms in the proportion of a musical scale, the highest and lowest notes and the mean between them, with all the intermediate intervals. Only when he has linked these parts together in well-tempered harmony and has made himself one man instead of many, will he be ready to go about whatever he may have to do, whether it be making money and satisfying bodily wants, or business transactions, or the affairs of state. In all these fields when he speaks of just and honourable conduct, he will mean the behaviour that helps to produce and to preserve this habit of mind; and by wisdom he will mean the knowledge which presides over such conduct. Any action which tends to break down this habit will be for him unjust; and the notions governing it he will call ignorance and folly.

That is perfectly true, Socrates.

Good, said I. I believe we should not be thought altogether mistaken, if we claimed to have discovered the just man and the just state, and wherein their justice consists.

Indeed we should not.

Shall we make that claim, then?

Yes, we will.

So be it, said I. Next, I suppose, we have to consider injustice.

Evidently.

This must surely be a sort of civil strife among the three elements, whereby they usurp and encroach upon one another's functions and some one part of the soul rises up in rebellion against the whole, claiming a supremacy to which it has no right because its nature fits it only to be the servant of the ruling principle. Such turmoil and aberration we shall, I think, identify with injustice, intemperance, cowardice, ignorance, and in a word with all wickedness.

Exactly.

And now that we know the nature of justice and injustice, we can be equally clear about what is meant by acting justly and again by unjust action and wrongdoing.

How do you mean?

Plainly, they are exactly analogous to those wholesome and unwholesome activities which respectively produce a healthy or unhealthy condition in the body; in the same way just and unjust conduct produce a just or unjust character. Justice is produced in the soul, like health in the body, by establishing the elements concerned in their natural relations of control and subordination, whereas injustice is like disease and means that this natural order is inverted.

Quite so.

It appears, then, that virtue is as it were the health and comeliness and well-being of the soul, as wickedness is disease, deformity, and weakness.

True.

And also that virtue and wickedness are brought about by one's way of life, honourable or disgraceful.

That follows.

So now it only remains to consider which is the more profitable course: to do right and live honourably and be just, whether or not anyone knows what manner of man you are, or to do wrong and be unjust, provided that you can escape the chastisement which might make you a better man.

But really, Socrates, it seems to me ridiculous to ask that question now that the nature of justice and injustice has been brought to light. People think that all the luxury and wealth and power in the world cannot make life worth living when the bodily constitution is going to rack and ruin; and are we to believe that, when the very principle whereby we live is deranged and corrupted, life will be worth living so long as a man can do as he will, and wills to do anything rather than to free himself from vice and wrongdoing and to win justice and virtue?

Yes, I replied, it is a ridiculous question.

EQUALITY OF WOMEN

We must go back, then, to a subject which ought, perhaps, to have been treated earlier in its proper place; though, after all, it may be suitable that the women should have their turn on the stage when the men have quite finished their performance, especially since you are so insistent. In my judgment, then, the question under what conditions people born and educated as we have described should possess wives and children, and how they should treat them, can be rightly settled only by keeping to the course on which we started them at the outset. We undertook to put these men in the position of watch-dogs guarding a flock. Suppose we follow up the analogy and imagine them bred and reared in the same sort of way. We can then see if that plan will suit our purpose.

How will that be?

In this way. Which do we think right for watch-dogs: should the females guard the flock and hunt with the males and take a share in all they do, or should they be kept within doors as fit for no more than bearing and feeding their puppies, while all the hard work of looking after the flock is left to the males?

They are expected to take their full share, except that we treat them as not quite so strong.

Can you employ any creature for the same work as another, if you do not give them both the same upbringing and education?

No.

Then, if we are to set women to the same tasks as men, we must teach them the same things. They must have the same two branches of training for mind and body and also be taught the art of war, and they must receive the same treatment.

That seems to follow.

Possibly, if these proposals were carried out, they might be ridiculed as involving a good many breaches of custom.

They might indeed.

The most ridiculous—don't you think?—being the notion of women exercising naked along with the men in the wrestling-schools; some of them elderly women too, like the old men who still have a passion for exercise when they are wrinkled and not very agreeable to look at.

Yes, that would be thought laughable, according to our present notions.

Now we have started on this subject, we must not be frightened of the many witticisms that might be aimed at such a revolution, not only in the matter of bodily exercise but in the training of women's minds, and not least when it comes to their bearing arms and riding on horseback. Having begun upon these rules, we must not draw back from the harsher provisions. The wits may be asked to stop being witty and try to be serious; and we may remind them that it is not so long since the Greeks, like most foreign nations of the present day, thought it ridiculous and shameful for men to be seen naked. When gymnastic exercises were first introduced in Crete and later at Sparta, the humorists had their chance to make fun of them; but when experience had shown that nakedness is better uncovered than muffled up, the laughter died down and a practice which the reason approved ceased to look ridiculous to the eye. This shows how idle it is to think anything ludicrous but what is base. One who tries to raise a laugh at any spectacle save that of baseness and folly will also, in his serious moments, set before himself some other standard than goodness of what deserves to be held in honour.

Most assuredly.

The first thing to be settled, then, is whether these proposals are feasible; and it must be open to anyone, whether a humorist or serious-minded, to raise the question whether, in the case of mankind, the feminine nature is capable of taking part with the other sex in all occupations, or in none at all, or in some only; and in particular under which of these heads this business of military service falls. Well begun is half done, and would not this be the best way to begin?

Yes.

Shall we take the other side in this debate and argue against ourselves? We do not want the adversary's position to be taken by storm for lack of defenders.

I have no objection.

Let us state his case for him. "Socrates and Glaucon," he will say, "there is no need for others to dispute your position; you yourselves, at the very outset of founding your commonwealth, agreed that everyone should do the one work for which nature fits him." Yes, of course; I suppose we did. "And isn't there a very great difference in nature between man and woman?" Yes, surely. "Does not that natural difference imply a corresponding difference in the work to be given to each?" Yes. "But if so, surely you must be mistaken now and contradicting yourselves when you say that men and women, having such widely divergent natures, should do the same things?" What is your answer to that, my ingenious friend?

It is not easy to find one at the moment. I can only appeal to you to state the case on our own side, whatever it may be.

This, Glaucon, is one of many alarming objections which I foresaw some time ago. That is why I shrank from touching upon these laws concerning the possession of wives and the rearing of children.

It looks like anything but an easy problem.

True, I said; but whether a man tumbles into a swimming-pool or into mid-ocean, he has to swim all the time. So must we, and try if we can reach the shore, hoping for some Arion's dolphin or other miraculous deliverance to bring us safe to land.[18]

I suppose so.

Come then, let us see if we can find the way out. We did agree that different natures should have different occupations, and that the natures of man and woman are different; and yet we are now saying that these different natures are to have the same occupations. Is that the charge against us?

Exactly.

It is extraordinary, Glaucon, what an effect the practice of debating has upon people.

Why do you say that?

Because they often seem to fall unconsciously into mere disputes which they mistake for reasonable argument, through being unable to draw the distinctions proper to their subject; and so, instead of a philosophical exchange of ideas, they go off in chase of contradictions which are purely verbal.

I know that happens to many people; but does it apply to us at this moment?

Absolutely. At least I am afraid we are slipping unconsciously into a dispute about words. We have been strenuously insisting on the letter of our principle that different natures should not have the same occupations, as if we were scoring a point in a debate; but we have altogether neglected to consider what sort of sameness or difference we meant and in what respect these natures and occupations were to be defined as different or the same. Consequently, we might very well be asking one another whether there is not an opposition in nature between bald and long-haired men, and, when that was admitted, forbid one set to be shoemakers, if the other were following that trade.

That would be absurd.

Yes, but only because we never meant any and every sort of sameness or difference in nature, but the sort that was relevant to the occupations in question. We meant, for instance, that a man and a woman have the same nature if both have a talent for medicine; whereas two men have different natures if one is a born physician, the other a born carpenter.

Yes, of course.

If, then, we find that either the male sex or the female is specially qualified for any particular form of occupation, then that occupation, we shall say, ought to be assigned to one sex or the other. But if the only difference appears to be that the male begets and the female brings forth, we shall conclude that no difference between man and woman has yet been produced that is relevant to our purpose. We shall continue to think it proper for our Guardians and their wives to share in the same pursuits.

And quite rightly.

The next thing will be to ask our opponent to name any profession or occupation in civic life for the purposes of which woman's nature is different from man's.

That is a fair question.

He might reply, as you did just now, that it is not easy to find a satisfactory answer on the spur of the moment, but that there would be no difficulty after a little reflection.

Perhaps.

Suppose, then, we invite him to follow us and see if we can convince him that there is no occupation concerned with the management of social affairs that is peculiar to women. We will confront him with a question: When you speak of a man having a natural talent for something, do you mean that he finds it easy to learn, and after a little instruction can find out much more for himself; whereas a man who is not so gifted learns with difficulty and no amount of instruction and practice will make him even remember what he has been taught? Is the talented man one whose bodily powers are readily at the service of his mind, instead of being a hindrance? Are not these the marks by which you distinguish the presence of a natural gift for any pursuit?

Yes, precisely.

Now do you know of any human occupation in which the male sex is not superior to the female in all these respects? Need I waste time over exceptions like weaving and watching over saucepans and batches of

---

[18] The musician Arion, to escape the treachery of Corinthian sailors, leapt into the sea and was carried ashore at Taenarum by a dolphin, Herodotus, i. 24.

cakes, though women are supposed to be good at such things and get laughed at when a man does them better?

It is true, he replied, in almost everything one sex is easily beaten by the other. No doubt many women are better at many things than many men; but taking the sexes as a whole, it is as you say.

To conclude, then, there is no occupation concerned with the management of social affairs which belongs either to woman or to man, as such. Natural gifts are to be found here and there in both creatures alike; and every occupation is open to both, so far as their natures are concerned, though woman is for all purposes the weaker.

Certainly.

Is that a reason for making over all occupations to men only?

Of course not.

No, because one woman may have a natural gift for medicine or for music; another may not.

Surely.

Is it not also true that a woman may, or may not, be warlike or athletic?

I think so.

And again, one may love knowledge; another, hate it; one may be high-spirited; another, spiritless?

True again.

It follows that one woman will be fitted by nature to be a Guardian; another will not, because these were the qualities for which we selected our men Guardians. So for the purpose of keeping watch over the commonwealth, woman has the same nature as man, save in so far as she is weaker.

So it appears.

It follows that women of this type must be selected to share the life and duties of Guardians with men of the same type, since they are competent and of a like nature, and the same natures must be allowed the same pursuits.

Yes.

We come round, then, to our former position, that there is nothing contrary to nature in giving our Guardians' wives the same training for mind and body. The practice we proposed to establish was not impossible or visionary, since it was in accordance with nature. Rather, the contrary practice which now prevails turns out to be unnatural.

So it appears.

Well, we set out to inquire whether the plan we proposed was feasible and also the best. That it is feasible is now agreed; we must next settle whether it is the best.

Obviously.

Now, for the purpose of producing a woman fit to be a Guardian, we shall not have one education for men and another for women, precisely because the nature to be taken in hand is the same.

True.

What is your opinion on the question of one man being better than another? Do you think there is no such difference?

Certainly I do not.

And in this commonwealth of ours which will prove the better men—the Guardians who have received the education we described, or the shoemakers who have been trained to make shoes?

It is absurd to ask such a question.

Very well. So these Guardians will be the best of all the citizens?

By far.

And these women the best of all the women?

Yes.

Can anything be better for a commonwealth than to produce in it men and women of the best possible type?

No.

And that result will be brought about by such a system of mental and bodily training as we have described?

Surely.

We may conclude that the institution we proposed was not only practicable, but also the best for the commonwealth.

Yes.

The wives of our Guardians, then, must strip for exercise, since they will be clothed with virtue, and they must take their share in war and in the other social duties of guardianship. They are to have no other occupation; and in these duties the lighter part must fall to the women, because of the weakness of their sex. The man who laughs at naked women, exercising their bodies for the best of reasons, is like one that "gathers fruit unripe," for he does not know what it is that he is laughing at or what he is doing. There will never be a finer saying than the one which declares that whatever does good should be held in honour, and the only shame is in doing harm.

That is perfectly true.

ABOLITION OF THE FAMILY FOR THE GUARDIANS

So far, then, in regulating the position of women, we may claim to have come safely through with one hazardous proposal, that male and female Guardians shall have all occupations in common. The consistency of the argument is an assurance that the plan is a good one and also feasible. We are like swimmers who have breasted the first wave without being swallowed up.

Not such a small wave either.

You will not call it large when you see the next.

Let me have a look at the next one, then.

Here it is: a law which follows from that principle and all that has gone before, namely that, of these Guardians, no one man and one woman are to set up house together privately: wives are to be held in common by all; so too are the children, and no parent is to know his own child, nor any child his parent.

It will be much harder to convince people that that is either a feasible plan or a good one.

As to its being a good plan, I imagine no one would deny the immense advantage of wives and children being held in common, provided it can be done. I should expect dispute to arise chiefly over the question whether it is possible.

There may well be a good deal of dispute over both points.

You mean, I must meet attacks on two fronts. I was hoping to escape one by running away: if you agreed it was a good plan, then I should only have had to inquire whether it was feasible.

No, we have seen through that manœuvre. You will have to defend both positions.

Well, I must pay the penalty for my cowardice. But grant me one favour. Let me indulge my fancy, like one who entertains himself with idle day-dreams on a solitary walk. Before he has any notion how his desires can be realized, he will set aside that question, to save himself the trouble of reckoning what may or may not be possible. He will assume that his wish has come true, and amuse himself with settling all the details of what he means to do then. So a lazy mind encourages itself to be lazier than ever; and I am giving way to the same weakness myself. I want to put off till later that question, how the thing can be done. For the moment, with your leave, I shall assume it to be possible, and ask how the Rulers will work out the details in practice; and I shall argue that the plan, once carried into effect, would be the best thing in the world for our commonwealth and for its Guardians. That is what I shall now try to make out with your help, if you will allow me to postpone the other question.

Very good; I have no objection.

Well, if our Rulers are worthy of the name, and their Auxiliaries likewise, these latter will be ready to do what they are told, and the Rulers, in giving their commands, will themselves obey our laws and will be faithful to their spirit in any details we leave to their discretion.

No doubt.

It is for you, then, as their lawgiver, who have already selected the men, to select for association with them women who are so far as possible of the same natural capacity. Now since none of them will have any private home of his own, but they will share the same dwelling and eat at common tables, the two sexes will be together; and meeting without restriction for exercise and all through their upbringing, they will surely be drawn towards union with one another by a necessity of their nature—necessity is not too strong a word, I think?

Not too strong for the constraint of love, which for the mass of mankind is more persuasive and compelling than even the necessity of mathematical proof.

Exactly. But in the next place, Glaucon, anything like unregulated unions would be a profanation in a state whose citizens lead the good life. The Rulers will not allow such a thing.

No, it would not be right.

Clearly, then, we must have marriages, as sacred as we can make them; and this sanctity will attach to those which yield the best results.

Certainly.

How are we to get the best results? You must tell me, Glaucon, because I see you keep sporting dogs and a great many game birds at your house; and there is something about their mating and breeding that you must have noticed.

What is that?

In the first place, though they may all be of good stock, are there not some that turn out to be better than the rest?

There are.

And do you breed from all indiscriminately? Are you not careful to breed from the best so far as you can?

Yes.

And from those in their prime, rather than the very young or the very old?

Yes.

Otherwise, the stock of your birds or dogs would deteriorate very much, wouldn't it?

It would.

And the same is true of horses or of any animal?

It would be very strange if it were not.

Dear me, said I; we shall need consummate skill in our Rulers, if it is also true of the human race.

Well, it is true. But why must they be so skilful?

Because they will have to administer a large dose of that medicine we spoke of earlier. An ordinary doctor is thought good enough for a patient who will submit to be dieted and can do without medicine; but he must be much more of a man if drugs are required.

True, but how does that apply?

It applies to our Rulers: it seems they will have to give their subjects a considerable dose of imposition and deception for their good. We said, if you remember, that such expedients would be useful as a sort of medicine.

Yes, a very sound principle.

Well, it looks as if this sound principle will play no small part in this matter of marriage and child-bearing.

How so?

It follows from what we have just said that, if we are to keep our flock at the highest pitch of excellence, there should be as many unions of the best of both sexes, and as few of the inferior, as possible, and that only the offspring of the better unions

should be kept.[19] And again, no one but the Rulers must know how all this is being effected; otherwise our herd of Guardians may become rebellious.

Quite true.

We must, then, institute certain festivals at which we shall bring together the brides and bridegrooms. There will be sacrifices, and our poets will write songs befitting the occasion. The number of marriages we shall leave to the Rulers' discretion. They will aim at keeping the number of the citizens as constant as possible, having regard to losses caused by war, epidemics, and so on; and they must do their best to see that our state does not become either great or small.[20]

Very good.

I think they will have to invent some ingenious system of drawing lots, so that, at each pairing off, the inferior candidate may blame his luck rather than the Rulers.

Yes, certainly.

Moreover, young men who acquit themselves well in war and other duties, should

---

[19] That is, "kept as Guardians." The inferior children of Guardians were to be "thrust out among the craftsmen and farmers." A breeder of racehorses would keep the best foals, but not kill the rest.

[20] Plato seems to forget that these rules apply only to Guardians. If the much larger third class is to breed without restriction, a substantial rise in their numbers might entail suspension of all childbirth among Guardians, with a dysgenic effect. Plato, however, feared a decline, rather than a rise, in the birth-rate. (The state described in the Laws is always to have 5040 citizens, each holding one inalienable lot of land.) The "number of marriages" may include both the number of candidates admitted at each festival and the frequency of the festivals. But it is perhaps likely that the festivals are to be annual, so that women who had borne children since the last festival would be re-marriageable. If so, at each festival a fresh group will be called up, consisting of all who have reached the age of 25 for men or 20 for women since the previous festival. Some or all of these will be paired with one another or with members of older groups. The couples will cohabit during the festival, which might last (say) for a month. The marriages will then be dissolved and the partners remain celibate until the next festival at earliest. This follows from the statement that the resulting batch of children will all be born between 7 and 10 months after the festival.

be given, among other rewards and privileges, more liberal opportunities to sleep with a wife,[21] for the further purpose that, with good excuse, as many as possible of the children may be begotten of such fathers.

Yes.

As soon as children are born, they will be taken in charge by officers appointed for the purpose, who may be men or women or both, since offices are to be shared by both sexes. The children of the better parents they will carry to the crèche to be reared in the care of nurses living apart in a certain quarter of the city. Those of the inferior parents and any children of the rest that are born defective will be hidden away, in some appropriate manner that must be kept secret.[22]

They must be, if the breed of our Guardians is to be kept pure.

These officers will also superintend the nursing of the children. They will bring the mothers to the crèche when their breasts are full, while taking every precaution that no mother shall know her own child; and if the mothers have not enough milk, they will provide wetnurses. They will limit the time during which the mothers will suckle their children, and hand over all the hard work and sitting up at night to nurses and attendants.

That will make child-bearing an easy business for the Guardians' wives.

So it should be. To go on with our scheme: we said that children should be born from parents in the prime of life. Do you agree that this lasts about twenty years for a woman, and thirty for a man? A woman should bear children for the commonwealth from her twentieth to her fortieth year; a man should begin to beget them when he has passed "the racer's prime in swiftness," and continue till he is fifty-five.

Those are certainly the years in which both the bodily and the mental powers of man and woman are at their best.

If a man either above or below this age meddles with the begetting of children for the commonwealth, we shall hold it an offence against divine and human law. He will be begetting for his country a child conceived in darkness and dire incontinence, whose birth, if it escape detection, will not have been sanctioned by the sacrifices and prayers offered at each marriage festival, when priests and priestesses join with the whole community in praying that the children to be born may be even better and more useful citizens than their parents.

You are right.

The same law will apply to any man within the prescribed limits who touches a woman also of marriageable age when the Ruler has not paired them. We shall say that he is foisting on the commonwealth a bastard, unsanctioned by law or by religion.

Perfectly right.

As soon, however, as the men and the women have passed the age prescribed for producing children, we shall leave them free to form a connexion with whom they will, except that a man shall not take his daughter or daughter's daughter or mother or mother's mother, nor a woman her son or father or her son's son or father's father; and all this only after we have exhorted them to see that no child, if any be conceived, shall be brought to light, or, if they cannot prevent its birth, to dispose of it on the understanding that no such child can be reared.[23]

---

[21] Not to have several wives at once, but to be admitted at more frequent intervals to the periodic marriage festivals, not necessarily with a different wife each time.

[22] Infanticide of defective children was practiced at Sparta; but the vague expression used does not imply that all children of inferior Guardians are to be destroyed. Those not defective would be relegated to the third class. Promotion of children from that class was provided for above.

---

[23] The unofficial unions might be permanent. The only unions barred as incestuous are between parents and children, or grandparents and grandchildren (all such are included, since, if a woman cannot marry her father's father, a man cannot marry his son's daughter). It seems to follow that Plato did not regard the much more probable connexions of brothers and sisters as incestuous; and if so, he would see no reason against legal marriage of real brothers and sisters, who would not know they were so related. Such unions were regular in Egypt; and some modern authorities deny that they are dysgenic. Greek law allowed marriage between brother and half-sister by a different mother.

That too is reasonable. But how are they to distinguish fathers and daughters and those other relations you mentioned?

They will not, said I. But, reckoning from the day when he becomes a bridegroom, a man will call all children born in the tenth or the seventh month sons and daughters, and they will call him father. Their children he will call grandchildren, and they will call his group grandfathers and grandmothers; and all who are born within the period during which their mothers and fathers were having children will be called brothers and sisters. This will provide for those restrictions on unions that we mentioned; but the law will allow brothers and sisters to live together, if the lot so falls out and the Delphic oracle also approves.[24]

Very good.

This, then, Glaucon, is the manner in which the Guardians of your commonwealth are to hold their wives and children in common. Must we not next find arguments to establish that it is consistent with our other institutions and also by far the best plan?

Yes, surely.

We had better begin by asking what is the greatest good at which the lawgiver should aim in laying down the constitution of a state, and what is the worst evil. We can then consider whether our proposals are in keeping with that good and irreconcilable with the evil.

By all means.

Does not the worst evil for a state arise from anything that tends to rend it asunder and destroy its unity, while nothing does it more good than whatever tends to bind it together and make it one?

That is true.

And are not citizens bound together by sharing in the same pleasures and pains, all feeling glad or grieved on the same occasions of gain or loss; whereas the bond is broken when such feelings are no longer universal, but any event of public or personal concern fills some with joy and others with distress?

Certainly.

---

[24] This last speech deals with two distinct questions: (1) avoidance of incestuous union as above defined; (2) legal marriage of brothers and sisters.

And this disunion comes about when the words "mine" and "not mine," another's" and "not another's" are not applied to the same things throughout the community. The best ordered state will be the one in which the largest number of persons use these terms in the same sense, and which accordingly most nearly resembles a single person. When one of us hurts his finger, the whole extent of those bodily connexions which are gathered up in the soul and unified by its ruling element is made aware and it all shares as a whole in the pain of the suffering part; hence we say that the man has a pain in his finger. The same thing is true of the pain or pleasure felt when any other part of the person suffers or is relieved.

Yes; I agree that the best organized community comes nearest to that condition.

And so it will recognize as a part of itself the individual citizen to whom good or evil happens, and will share as a whole in his joy or sorrow.

It must, if the constitution is sound.

It is time now to go back to our own commonwealth and see whether these conclusions apply to it more than to any other type of state. In all alike there are rulers and common people, all of whom will call one another fellow citizens.

Yes.

But in other states the people have another name as well for their rulers, haven't they?

Yes; in most they call them masters; in democracies, simply the government.

And in ours?

The people will look upon their rulers as preservers and protectors.

And how will our rulers regard the people?

As those who maintain them and pay them wages.

And elsewhere?

As slaves.

And what do rulers elsewhere call one another?

Colleagues.

And ours?

Fellow Guardians.

And in other states may not a ruler regard one colleague as a friend in whom he has an interest, and another as a stranger with whom he has nothing in common?

Yes, that often happens.

But that could not be so with your Guardians? None of them could ever treat a fellow Guardian as a stranger.

Certainly not. He must regard everyone whom he meets as brother or sister, father or mother, son or daughter, grandchild or grandparent.

Very good; but here is a further point. Will you not require them, not merely to use these family terms, but to behave as a real family? Must they not show towards all whom they call "father" the customary reverence, care, and obedience due to a parent, if they look for any favour from gods or men, since to act otherwise is contrary to divine and human law? Should not all the citizens constantly reiterate in the hearing of the children from their earliest years such traditional maxims of conduct towards those whom they are taught to call father and their other kindred?

They should. It would be absurd that terms of kinship should be on their lips without any action to correspond.

In our community, then, above all others, when things go well or ill with any individual everyone will use that word "mine" in the same sense and say that all is going well or ill with him and his.

Quite true.

And, as we said, this way of speaking and thinking goes with fellow-feeling; so that our citizens, sharing as they do in a common interest which each will call his own, will have all their feelings of pleasure or pain in common.

Assuredly.

A result that will be due to our institutions, and in particular to our Guardians' holding their wives and children in common.

Very much so.

But you will remember how, when we compared a well-ordered community to the body which shares in the pleasures and pains of any member, we saw in this unity the greatest good that a state can enjoy. So the conclusion is that our commonwealth owes to this sharing of wives and children by its protectors its enjoyment of the greatest of all goods.

Yes, that follows.

Moreover, this agrees with our principle that they were not to have houses or lands or any property of their own, but to receive sustenance from the other citizens, as wages for their guardianship, and to consume it in common. Only so will they keep to their true character; and our present proposals will do still more to make them genuine Guardians. They will not rend the community asunder by each applying that word "mine" to different things and dragging off whatever he can get for himself into a private home, where he will have his separate family, forming a centre of exclusive joys and sorrows. Rather they will all, so far as may be, feel together and aim at the same ends, because they are convinced that all their interests are identical.

Quite so.

Again, if a man's person is his only private possession, lawsuits and prosecutions will all but vanish, and they will be free of those quarrels that arise from ownership of property and from having family ties. Nor would they be justified even in bringing actions for assault and outrage; for we shall pronounce it right and honourable for a man to defend himself against an assailant of his own age, and in that way they will be compelled to keep themselves fit.

That would be a sound law.

And it would also have the advantage that, if a man's anger can be satisfied in this way, a fit of passion is less likely to grow into a serious quarrel.

True.

But an older man will be given authority over all younger persons and power to correct them; whereas the younger will, naturally, not dare to strike the elder or do him any violence, except by command of a Ruler. He will not show him any sort of disrespect. Two guardian spirits, fear and reverence, will be enough to restrain him—reverence forbidding him to lay hands on a parent, and fear of all those others who as sons or brothers or fathers would come to the rescue.

Yes, that will be the result.

So our laws will secure that these men will live in complete peace with one another; and if they never quarrel among themselves, there is no fear of the rest of the community being divided either against them or against itself.

No.

There are other evils they will escape, so mean and petty that I hardly like to mention them: the poor man's flattery of the rich, and all the embarrassments and vexations of rearing a family and earning just enough to maintain a household; now borrowing and now refusing to repay, and by any and every means scraping together money to be handed over to wife and servants to spend. These sordid troubles are familiar and not worth describing.

Only too familiar.

Rid of all these cares, they will live a more enviable life than the Olympic victor, who is counted happy on the strength of far fewer blessings than our Guardians will enjoy. Their victory is the nobler, since by their success the whole commonwealth is preserved; and their reward of maintenance at the public cost is more complete, since their prize is to have every need of life supplied for themselves and for their children; their country honours them while they live, and when they die they receive a worthy burial.

Yes, they will be nobly rewarded.

Do you remember, then, how someone who shall be nameless reproached us for not making our Guardians happy: they were to possess nothing, though all the wealth of their fellow citizens was within their grasp? We replied, I believe, that we would consider that objection later, if it came in our way: for the moment we were bent on making our Guardians real guardians, and moulding our commonwealth with a view to the greatest happiness, not of one section of it, but of the whole.

Yes, I remember.

Well, it appears now that these protectors of our state will have a life better and more honourable than that of any Olympic victor; and we can hardly rank it on a level with the life of a shoemaker or other artisan or of a farmer.

I should think not.

However, it is right to repeat what I said at the time: if ever a Guardian tries to make himself happy in such a way that he will be a guardian no longer; if, not content with the moderation and security of this way of living which we think the best, he becomes possessed with some silly and childish notion of happiness, impelling him to make his power a means to appropriate all the citizens' wealth, then he will learn the wisdom of Hesiod's saying that the half is more than the whole.

My advice would certainly be that he should keep to his own way of living.

You do agree, then, that women are to take their full share with men in education, in the care of children, and in the guardianship of the other citizens; whether they stay at home or go out to war, they will be like watch-dogs which take their part either in guarding the fold or in hunting and share in every task so far as their strength allows. Such conduct will not be unwomanly, but all for the best and in accordance with the natural partnership of the sexes.

Yes, I agree.

THE PARADOX: PHILOSOPHERS MUST BE KINGS

But really, Socrates, Glaucon continued, if you are allowed to go on like this, I am afraid you will forget all about the question you thrust aside some time ago: whether a society so constituted can ever come into existence, and if so, how. No doubt, if it did exist, all manner of good things would come about. I can even add some that you have passed over. Men who acknowledged one another as fathers, sons, or brothers and always used those names among themselves would never desert one another; so they would fight with unequalled bravery. And if their womenfolk went out with them to war, either in the ranks or drawn up in the rear to intimidate the enemy and act as a reserve in case of need, I am sure all this would make them invincible. At home, too, I can see many advantages you have not mentioned. But, since I admit that our commonwealth would have all these merits and any number more, if once it came into existence, you need not describe it in further detail. All we have now to do is to convince ourselves that it can be brought into being and how.

This is a very sudden onslaught, said I; you have no mercy on my shilly-shallying. Perhaps you do not realize that, after I have barely escaped the first two waves, the third, which you are now bringing down upon me, is the most formidable of all. When you have seen what it is like and heard my reply, you will be ready to excuse the very natural fears which made me shrink from putting forward such a paradox for discussion.

The more you talk like that, he said, the less we shall be willing to let you off from telling us how this constitution can come into existence; so you had better waste no more time.

Well, said I, let me begin by reminding you that what brought us to this point was our inquiry into the nature of justice and injustice.

True; but what of that?

Merely this: suppose we do find out what justice is, are we going to demand that a man who is just shall have a character which exactly corresponds in every respect to the ideal of justice? Or shall we be satisfied if he comes as near to the ideal as possible and has in him a larger measure of that quality than the rest of the world?

That will satisfy me.

If so, when we set out to discover the essential nature of justice and injustice and what a perfectly just and a perfectly unjust man would be like, supposing them to exist, our purpose was to use them as ideal patterns: we were to observe the degree of happiness or unhappiness that each exhibited, and to draw the necessary inference that our own destiny would be like that of the one we most resembled. We did not set out to show that these ideals could exist in fact.

That is true.

Then suppose a painter had drawn an ideally beautiful figure complete to the last touch, would you think any the worse of him, if he could not show that a person as beautiful as that could exist?

No, I should not.

Well, we have been constructing in discourse the pattern of an ideal state. Is our theory any the worse, if we cannot prove it possible that a state so organized should be actually founded?

Surely not.

That, then, is the truth of the matter. But if, for your satisfaction, I am to do my best to show under what conditions our ideal would have the best chance of being realized, I must ask you once more to admit that the same principle applies here. Can theory ever be fully realized in practice? Is it not in the nature of things that action should come less close to truth than thought? People may not think so; but do you agree or not?

I do.

Then you must not insist upon my showing that this construction we have traced in thought could be reproduced in fact down to the last detail. You must admit that we shall have found a way to meet your demand for realization, if we can discover how a state might be constituted in the closest accordance with our description. Will not that content you? It would be enough for me.

And for me too.

Then our next attempt, it seems, must be to point out what defect in the working of existing states prevents them from being so organized, and what is the least change that would effect a transformation into this type of government—a single change if possible, or perhaps two; at any rate let us make the changes as few and insignificant as may be.

By all means.

Well, there is one change which, as I believe we can show, would bring about this revolution—not a small change, certainly, nor an easy one, but possible.

What is it?

I have now to confront what we called the third and greatest wave. But I must state my paradox, even though the wave should break in laughter over my head and drown me in ignominy. Now mark what I am going to say.

Go on.

Unless either philosophers become kings in their countries or those who are now called kings and rulers come to be sufficiently inspired with a genuine desire for wisdom; unless, that is to say, political power and philosophy meet together, while the many natures who now go their several ways in the one or the other direction are forcibly debarred from doing so, there can be no rest from troubles, my dear Glaucon, for states, nor yet, as I believe, for all mankind; nor can this commonwealth which we have imagined ever till then see the light of day and grow to its full stature. This it was that I have so long hung back from saying; I knew what a paradox it would be, because it is hard to see that there is no other way of happiness either for the state or for the individual.

Socrates, exclaimed Glaucon, after delivering yourself of such a pronouncement as that, you must expect a whole multitude of by no means contemptible assailants to fling off their coats, snatch up the handiest weapon, and make a rush at you, breathing fire and slaughter. If you cannot find arguments to beat them off and make your escape, you will learn what it means to be the target of scorn and derision.

Well, it was you who got me into this trouble.

Yes, and a good thing too. However, I will not leave you in the lurch. You shall have my friendly encouragement for what it is worth; and perhaps you may find me more complaisant than some would be in answering your questions. With such backing you must try to convince the unbelievers.

I will, now that I have such a powerful ally.

THE ALLEGORY
OF THE CAVE

Next, said I, here is a parable to illustrate the degrees in which our nature may be enlightened or unenlightened. Imagine the condition of men living in a sort of cavernous chamber underground, with an entrance open to the light and a long passage all down the cave.[25] Here they have been from childhood chained by the leg and also by the neck, so that they cannot move and can see only what is in front of them, because the chains will not let them turn their heads. At some distance higher up is the light of a fire burning behind them; and between the prisoners and the fire is a track[26] with a parapet built along it, like the screen at a puppet-show, which hides the performers while they show their puppets over the top.

I see, said he.

Now behind this parapet imagine persons carrying along various artificial objects, including figures of men and animals in wood or stone or other materials, which project above the parapet. Naturally, some of these persons will be talking, others silent.[27]

It is a strange picture, he said, and a strange sort of prisoners.

Like ourselves, I replied; for in the first place prisoners so confined would have seen nothing of themselves or of one another, except the shadows thrown by the fire-light on the wall of the Cave facing them, would they?

Not if all their lives they had been prevented from moving their heads.

And they would have seen as little of the objects carried past.

Of course.

Now, if they could talk to one another, would they not suppose that their words referred only to those passing shadows which they saw?[28]

Necessarily.

And suppose their prison had an echo from the wall facing them? When one of the people crossing behind them spoke, they could only suppose that the sound came from the shadow passing before their eyes.

No doubt.

In every way, then, such prisoners would recognize as reality nothing but the shadows of those artificial objects.

Inevitably.

Now consider what would happen if their release from the chains and the healing of their unwisdom should come about in this way. Suppose one of them set free and forced suddenly to stand up, turn his head, and walk with eyes lifted to the light; all these movements would be painful, and he would be too dazzled to make out the objects whose shadows he had been used to see. What do you think he would say, if

---

[25] The *length* of the "way in" (*eisodos*) to the chamber where the prisoners sit is an essential feature, explaining why no daylight reaches them.

[26] The track crosses the passage into the cave at right angles, and is *above* the parapet built along it.

[27] A modern Plato would compare his Cave to an underground cinema, where the audience

---

watch the play of shadows thrown by the film passing before a light at their backs. The film itself is only an image of "real" things and events in the world outside the cinema. For the film Plato has to substitute the clumsier apparatus of a procession of artificial objects carried on their heads by persons who are merely part of the machinery, providing for the movement of the objects and the sounds whose echo the prisoners hear. The parapet prevents these persons' shadows from being cast on the wall of the Cave.

[28] Adam's text and interpretation. The prisoners, having seen nothing but shadows, cannot think their words refer to the objects carried past behind their backs. For them shadows (images) are the only realities.

someone told him that what he had formerly seen was meaningless illusion, but now, being somewhat nearer to reality and turned towards more real objects, he was getting a truer view? Suppose further that he were shown the various objects being carried by and were made to say, in reply to questions, what each of them was. Would he not be perplexed and believe the objects now shown him to be not so real as what he formerly saw?

Yes, not nearly so real.

And if he were forced to look at the firelight itself, would not his eyes ache, so that he would try to escape and turn back to the things which he could see distinctly, convinced that they really were clearer than these other objects now being shown to him?

Yes.

And suppose someone were to drag him away forcibly up the steep and rugged ascent and not let him go until he had hauled him out into the sunlight, would he not suffer pain and vexation at such treatment, and, when he had come out into the light, find his eyes so full of its radiance that he could not see a single one of the things that he was now told were real?

Certainly he would not see them all at once.

He would need, then, to grow accustomed before he could see things in that upper world. At first it would be easiest to make out shadows, and then the images of men and things reflected in water, and later on the things themselves. After that, it would be easier to watch the heavenly bodies and the sky itself by night, looking at the light of the moon and stars rather than the Sun and the Sun's light in the day-time.

Yes, surely.

Last of all, he would be able to look at the Sun and contemplate its nature, not as it appears when reflected in water or any alien medium, but as it is in itself in its own domain.

No doubt.

And now he would begin to draw the conclusion that it is the Sun that produces the seasons and the course of the year and controls everything in the visible world, and moreover is in a way the cause of all that he and his companions used to see.

Clearly he would come at last to that conclusion.

Then if he called to mind his fellow prisoners and what passed for wisdom in his former dwelling-place, he would surely think himself happy in the change and be sorry for them. They may have had a practice of honouring and commending one another, with prizes for the man who had the keenest eye for the passing shadows and the best memory for the order in which they followed or accompanied one another, so that he could make a good guess as to which was going to come next.[29] Would our released prisoner be likely to covet those prizes or to envy the men exalted to honour and power in the Cave? Would he not feel like Homer's Achilles, that he would far sooner "be on earth as a hired servant in the house of a landless man" or endure anything rather than go back to his old beliefs and live in the old way?

Yes, he would prefer any fate to such a life.

Now imagine what would happen if he went down again to take his former seat in the Cave. Coming suddenly out of the sunlight, his eyes would be filled with darkness. He might be required once more to deliver his opinion on those shadows, in competition with the prisoners who had never been released, while his eyesight was still dim and unsteady; and it might take some time to become used to the darkness. They would laugh at him and say that he had gone up only to come back with his sight ruined; it was worth no one's while even to attempt the ascent. If they could lay hands on the man who was trying to set them free and lead them up, they would kill him.[30]

Yes, they would.

Every feature in this parable, my dear Glaucon, is meant to fit our earlier analysis. The prison dwelling corresponds to the region revealed to us through the sense of sight, and the firelight within it to the power of the Sun. The ascent to see the things in the upper world you may take as standing for the upward journey of the soul into the

---

[29] The empirical politician, with no philosophic insight, but only a "knack of remembering what usually happens" (*Gorg.* 501 a). He has *eikasia* = conjecture as to what is likely (*eikos*).

[30] An allusion to the fate of Socrates.

region of the intelligible; then you will be in possession of what I surmise, since that is what you wish to be told. Heaven knows whether it is true; but this, at any rate, is how it appears to me. In the world of knowledge, the last thing to be perceived and only with great difficulty is the essential Form of Goodness. Once it is perceived, the conclusion must follow that, for all things, this is the cause of whatever is right and good; in the visible world it gives birth to light and to the lord of light, while it is itself sovereign in the intelligible world and the parent of intelligence and truth. Without having had a vision of this Form no one can act with wisdom, either in his own life or in matters of state.

So far as I can understand, I share your belief.

Then you may also agree that it is no wonder if those who have reached this height are reluctant to manage the affairs of men. Their souls long to spend all their time in that upper world—naturally enough, if here once more our parable holds true. Nor, again, is it at all strange that one who comes from the contemplation of divine things to the miseries of human life should appear awkward and ridiculous when, with eyes still dazed and not yet accustomed to the darkness, he is compelled, in a law-court or elsewhere, to dispute about the shadows of justice or the images that cast those shadows, and to wrangle over the notions of what is right in the minds of men who have never beheld Justice itself.

It is not at all strange.

No; a sensible man will remember that the eyes may be confused in two ways—by a change from light to darkness or from darkness to light; and he will recognize that the same thing happens to the soul. When he sees it troubled and unable to discern anything clearly, instead of laughing thoughtlessly, he will ask whether, coming from a brighter existence, its unaccustomed vision is obscured by the darkness, in which case he will think its condition enviable and its life a happy one; or whether, emerging from the depths of ignorance, it is dazzled by excess of light. If so, he will rather feel sorry for it; or, if he were inclined to laugh, that would be less ridiculous than to laugh at the soul which has come down from the light.

That is a fair statement.

If this is true, then, we must conclude that education is not what it is said to be by some, who profess to put knowledge into a soul which does not possess it, as if they could put sight into blind eyes. On the contrary, our own account signifies that the soul of every man does possess the power of learning the truth and the organ to see it with; and that, just as one might have to turn the whole body round in order that the eye should see light instead of darkness, so the entire soul must be turned away from this changing world, until its eye can bear to contemplate reality and that supreme splendour which we have called the Good. Hence there may well be an art whose aim would be to effect this very thing, the conversion of the soul, in the readiest way; not to put the power of sight into the soul's eye, which already has it, but to ensure that, instead of looking in the wrong direction, it is turned the way it ought to be.

Yes, it may well be so.

It looks, then, as though wisdom were different from those ordinary virtues, as they are caned, which are not far removed from bodily qualities, in that they can be produced by habituation and exercise in a soul which has not possessed them from the first. Wisdom, it seems, is certainly the virtue of some diviner faculty, which never loses its power, though its use for good or harm depends on the direction towards which it is turned. You must have noticed in dishonest men with a reputation for sagacity the shrewd glance of a narrow intelligence piercing the objects to which it is directed. There is nothing wrong with their power of vision, but it has been forced into the service of evil, so that the keener its sight, the more harm it works.

Quite true.

And yet if the growth of a nature like this had been pruned from earliest childhood, cleared of those clinging overgrowths which come of gluttony and all luxurious pleasure and, like leaden weights charged with affinity to this mortal world, hang upon the soul, bending its vision downwards; if, freed from these, the soul were turned round towards true reality, then this same power in these very men would see the truth as keenly as the objects it is turned to now.

Yes, very likely.

Is it not also likely, or indeed certain after what has been said, that a state can never be properly governed either by the uneducated who know nothing of truth or by men who are allowed to spend all their days in the pursuit of culture? The ignorant have no single mark before their eyes at which they must aim in all the conduct of their own lives and of affairs of state; and the others will not engage in action if they can help it, dreaming that, while still alive, they have been translated to the Islands of the Blest.

Quite true.

It is for us, then, as founders of a commonwealth, to bring compulsion to bear on the noblest natures. They must be made to climb the ascent to the vision of Goodness, which we called the highest object of knowledge; and, when they have looked upon it long enough, they must not be allowed, as they now are, to remain on the heights, refusing to come down again to the prisoners or to take any part in their labours and rewards, however much or little these may be worth.

Shall we not be doing them an injustice, if we force on them a worse life than they might have?

You have forgotten again, my friend, that the law is not concerned to make any one class specially happy, but to ensure the welfare of the commonwealth as a whole. By persuasion or constraint it will unite the citizens in harmony, making them share whatever benefits each class can contribute to the common good; and its purpose in forming men of that spirit was not that each should be left to go his own way, but that they should be instrumental in binding the community into one.

True, I had forgotten.

You will see, then, Glaucon, that there will be no real injustice in compelling our philosophers to watch over and care for the other citizens. We can fairly tell them that their compeers in other states may quite reasonably refuse to collaborate: there they have sprung up, like a self-sown plant, in despite of their country's institutions; no one has fostered their growth, and they cannot be expected to show gratitude for a care they have never received. "But," we shall say, "it is not so with you. We have brought you into existence for your country's sake as well as for your own, to be like leaders and king-bees in a hive; you have been better and more thoroughly educated than those others and hence you are more capable of playing your part both as men of thought and as men of action. You must go down, then, each in his turn, to live with the rest and let your eyes grow accustomed to the darkness. You will then see a thousand times better than those who live there always; you will recognize every image for what it is and know what it represents, because you have seen justice, beauty, and goodness in their reality; and so you and we shall find life in our commonwealth no mere dream, as it is in most existing states, where men live fighting one another about shadows and quarrelling for power, as if that were a great prize; whereas in truth government can be at its best and free from dissension only where the destined rulers are least desirous of holding office."

Quite true.

Then will our pupils refuse to listen and to take their turns at sharing in the work of the community, though they may live together for most of their time in a purer air?

No; it is a fair demand, and they are fair-minded men. No doubt, unlike any ruler of the present day, they will think of holding power as an unavoidable necessity.

Yes, my friend; for the truth is that you can have a well-governed society only if you can discover for your future rulers a better way of life than being in office; then only will power be in the hands of men who are rich, not in gold, but in the wealth that brings happiness, a good and wise life. All goes wrong when, starved for lack of anything good in their own lives, men turn to public affairs hoping to snatch from thence the happiness they hunger for. They set about fighting for power, and this internecine conflict ruins them and their country. The life of true philosophy is the only one that looks down upon offices of state; and access to power must be confined to men who are not in love with it; otherwise rivals will start fighting. So whom else can you compel to undertake the guardianship of the commonwealth, if not those who, besides understanding best the principles of government, enjoy a nobler life than the politician's and look for rewards of a different kind?

There is indeed no other choice,

DEMOCRACY AND THE DEMOCRATIC MAN

Democracy, I suppose, should come next. A study of its rise and character should help us to recognize the democratic type of man and set him beside the others for judgment.

Certainly that course would fit in with our plan.

If the aim of life in an oligarchy is to become as rich as possible, that insatiable craving would bring about the transition to democracy. In this way: since the power of the ruling class is due to its wealth, they will not want to have laws restraining prodigal young men from ruining themselves by extravagance. They will hope to lend these spendthrifts money on their property and buy it up, so as to become richer and more influential than ever. We can see at once that a society cannot hold wealth in honour and at the same time establish a proper self-control in its citizens. One or the other must be sacrificed.

Yes, that is fairly obvious.

In an oligarchy, then, this neglect to curb riotous living sometimes reduces to poverty men of a not ungenerous nature. They settle down in idleness, some of them burdened with debt, some disfranchised, some both at once; and these drones are armed and can sting. Hating the men who have acquired their property and conspiring against them and the rest of society, they long for a revolution. Meanwhile the usurers, intent upon their own business, seem unaware of their existence; they are too busy planting their own stings into any fresh victim who offers them an opening to inject the poison of their money; and while they multiply their capital by usury, they are also multiplying the drones and the paupers. When the danger threatens to break out, they will do nothing to quench the flames, either in the way we mentioned, by forbidding a man to do what he likes with his own, or by the next best remedy, which would be a law enforcing a respect for right conduct. If it were enacted that, in general, voluntary contracts for a loan should be made at the lender's risk, there would be less of this shameless pursuit

of wealth and a scantier crop of those evils I have just described.

Quite true.

But, as things are, this is the plight to which the rulers of an oligarchy, for all these reasons, reduce their subjects. As for themselves, luxurious indolence of body and mind makes their young men too lazy and effeminate to resist pleasure or to endure pain; and the fathers, neglecting everything but money, have no higher ideals in life than the poor. Such being the condition of rulers and subjects, what will happen when they are thrown together, perhaps as fellow-travellers by sea or land to some festival or on a campaign, and can observe one another's demeanour in a moment of danger? The rich will have no chance to feel superior to the poor. On the contrary, the poor man, lean and sunburnt, may find himself posted in battle beside one who, thanks to his wealth and indoor life, is panting under his burden of fat and showing every mark of distress. "Such men," he will think, "are rich because we are cowards"; and when he and his friends meet in private, the word will go round: "These men are no good: they are at our mercy."

Yes, that is sure to happen.

This state, then, is in the same precarious condition as a person so unhealthy that the least shock from outside will upset the balance or even without that, internal disorder will break out. It falls sick and is at war with itself on the slightest occasion, as soon as one party or the other calls in allies from a neighbouring oligarchy or democracy; and sometimes civil war begins with no help from without.

Quite true.

And when the poor win, the result is a democracy. They kill some of the opposite party, banish others, and grant the rest an equal share in civil rights and government, officials being usually appointed by lot.

Yes, that is how a democracy comes to be established, whether by force of arms or because the other party is terrorized into giving way.

Now what is the character of this new régime? Obviously the way they govern themselves will throw light on the democratic type of man.

No doubt.

First of all, they are free. Liberty and free speech are rife everywhere; anyone is allowed to do what he likes.

Yes, so we are told.

That being so, every man will arrange his own manner of life to suit his pleasure. The result will be a greater variety of individuals than under any other constitution. So it may be the finest of all, with its variegated pattern of all sorts of characters. Many people may think it the best, just as women and children might admire a mixture of colours of every shade in the pattern of a dress. At any rate if we are in search of a constitution, here is a good place to look for one. A democracy is so free that it contains a sample of every kind; and perhaps anyone who intends to found a state, as we have been doing, ought first to visit this emporium of constitutions and choose the model he likes best.

He will find plenty to choose from.

Here, too, you are not obliged to be in authority, however competent you may be, or to submit to authority, if you do not like it; you need not fight when your fellow citizens are at war, nor remain at peace when they do, unless you want peace; and though you may have no legal right to hold office or sit on juries, you will do so all the same if the fancy takes you. A wonderfully pleasant life, surely, for the moment.

For the moment, no doubt.

There is a charm, too, in the forgiving spirit shown by some who have been sentenced by the courts. In a democracy you must have seen how men condemned to death or exile stay on and go about in public, and no one takes any more notice than he would of a spirit that walked invisible. There is so much tolerance and superiority to petty considerations; such a contempt for all those fine principles we laid down in founding our commonwealth, as when we said that only a very exceptional nature could turn out a good man, if he had not played as a child among things of beauty and given himself only to creditable pursuits. A democracy tramples all such notions under foot; with a magnificent indifference to the sort of life a man has led before he enters politics, it will promote to honour anyone who merely calls himself the people's friend.

Magnificent indeed.

These then, and such as these, are the features of a democracy, an agreeable form of anarchy with plenty of variety and an equality of a peculiar kind for equals and unequals alike.

All that is notoriously true.

Now consider the corresponding individual character. Or shall we take his origin first, as we did in the case of the constitution?

Yes.

I imagine him as the son of our miserly oligarch, brought up under his father's eye and in his father's ways. So he too will enforce a firm control over all such pleasures as lead to expense rather than profit—unnecessary pleasures, as they have been called. But, before going farther, shall we draw the distinction between necessary and unnecessary appetites, so as not to argue in the dark?[31]

Please do so.

There are appetites which cannot be got rid of, and there are all those which it does us good to fulfil. Our nature cannot help seeking to satisfy both these kinds; so they may fairly be described as necessary. On the other hand, "unnecessary" would be the right name for all appetites which can be got rid of by early training and which do us no good and in some cases do harm. Let us take an example of each kind, so as to form a general idea of them. The desire to eat enough plain food—just bread and meat—to keep in health and good condition may be called necessary. In the case of bread the necessity is twofold, since it not only does us good but is indispensable to life; whereas meat is only necessary in so far as it helps to keep us in good condition. Beyond these simple needs the desire for a whole variety of luxuries is unnecessary. Most people can get rid of it by early discipline and education; and it is as prejudicial to intelligence and self-control as it is to bodily health. Further, these unnecessary appetites might be called expensive, whereas the necessary ones are rather profitable, as helping a man

---

[31] A classification of appetites is needed because oligarchy, democracy, and despotism are based on the supremacy of three sorts of appetite: (1) the necessary, (2) the unnecessary and spendthrift, and (3) the lawless.

to do his work. The same distinctions could be drawn in the case of sexual appetite and all the rest.

Yes.

Now, when we were speaking just now of drones, we meant the sort of man who is under the sway of a host of unnecessary pleasures and appetites, in contrast with our miserly oligarch, over whom the necessary desires are in control. Accordingly, we can now go back to describe how the democratic type develops from the oligarchical. I imagine it usually happens in this way. When a young man, bred, as we were saying, in a stingy and uncultivated home, has once tasted the honey of the drones and keeps company with those dangerous and cunning creatures, who know how to purvey pleasures in all their multitudinous variety, then the oligarchical constitution of his soul begins to turn into a democracy. The corresponding revolution was effected in the state by one of the two factions calling in the help of partisans from outside. In the same way one of the conflicting sets of desires in the soul of this youth will be reinforced from without by a group of kindred passions; and if the resistance of the oligarchical faction in him is strengthened by remonstrances and reproaches coming from his father, perhaps, or his friends, the opposing parties will soon be battling within him. In some cases the democratic interest yields to the oligarchical: a sense of shame gains a footing in the young man's soul, and some appetites are crushed, others banished, until order is restored.

Yes, that happens sometimes.

But then again, perhaps, owing to the father's having no idea how to bring up his son, another brood of desires, akin to those which were banished, are secretly nursed up until they become numerous and strong. These draw the young man back into clandestine commerce with his old associates, and between them they breed a whole multitude. In the end, they seize the citadel of the young man's soul, finding it unguarded by the trusty sentinels which keep watch over the minds of men favoured by heaven. Knowledge, right principles, true thoughts, are not at their post; and the place lies open to the assault of false and presumptuous notions. So he turns again to those lotus-eaters and now throws in his lot with them openly.

If his family send reinforcements to the support of his thrifty instincts, the impostors who have seized the royal fortress shut the gates upon them, and will not even come to parley with the fatherly counsels of individual friends. In the internal conflict they gain the day; modesty and self-control, dishonoured and insulted as the weaknesses of an unmanly fool, are thrust out into exile; and the whole crew of unprofitable desires take a hand in banishing moderation and frugality, which, as they will have it, are nothing but churlish meanness. So they take possession of the soul which they have swept clean, as if purified for initiation into higher mysteries; and nothing remains but to marshal the great procession bringing home Insolence, Anarchy, Waste, and Impudence, those resplendent divinities crowned with garlands, whose praises they sing under flattering names: Insolence they call good breeding, Anarchy, freedom; Waste, magnificence; and Impudence, a manly spirit. Is not that a fair account of the revolution which gives free rein to unnecessary and harmful pleasures in a young man brought up in the satisfaction only of the necessary desires?

Yes, it is a vivid description.

In his life thenceforward he spends as much time and pains and money on his superfluous pleasures as on the necessary ones. If he is lucky enough not to be carried beyond all bounds, the tumult may begin to subside as he grows older. Then perhaps he may recall some of the banished virtues and cease to give himself up entirely to the passions which ousted them; and now he will set all his pleasures on a footing of equality, denying to none its equal rights and maintenance, and allowing each in turn, as it presents itself, to succeed, as if by the chance of the lot, to the government of his soul until it is satisfied. When he is told that some pleasures should be sought and valued as arising from desires of a higher order, others chastised and enslaved because the desires are base, he will shut the gates of the citadel against the messengers of truth, shaking his head and declaring that one appetite is as good as another and all must have their equal rights. So he spends his days indulging the pleasure of the moment, now intoxicated with wine and music, and then taking to a spare diet and drinking nothing but water; one day in hard training, the next doing nothing at all, the third apparently immersed in study. Every now and then he takes a part in politics, leaping to his feet to say or do whatever comes into his head. Or he will set out to rival someone he admires, a soldier it may be, or, if the fancy takes him, a man of business. His life is subject to no order or restraint, and he has no wish to change an existence which he calls pleasant, free, and happy.

That well describes the life of one whose motto is liberty and equality.

Yes, and his character contains the same fine variety of pattern that we found in the democratic state; it is as multifarious as that epitome of all types of constitution. Many a man, and many a woman too, will find in it something to envy. So we may see in him the counterpart of democracy, and call him the democratic man.

CHAPTER TWO

ARISTOTLE

Plato's strength and weakness lay in his gift to confront social reality with what *ought* to be. If that is utopian, every critic and reformer is a utopian. The *Republic* is not a work of abstract contemplation by an aloof philosopher addressed to no one in particular, but the impassioned plea of an Athenian old-family aristocrat. Opposing popular government, Plato recommended to his fellow citizens a constitution and way of life that in many respects, though not in all, resembled those of Sparta, a military and aristocratic state whose distinctive marks were discipline, unity, and complete subordination of the individual to the state. Deeply concerned about practical affairs as he was, Plato nevertheless often went beyond the analysis of what does happen, or is likely to happen, and let himself be carried off into the realm of the Ought. Looking into what may or ought to develop in the future, one is more likely to think in terms of the absolute and perfect, because the imagination of the future is pure idea, unmodified by that relentless relativist and compromiser—experience.

Plato found the corrective to his thinking in his own student, Aristotle (384–322 B.C.), not an Athenian, but a native of Stagira, a Greek colonial town on the Macedonia coast. Reared on the fringe of Greek civilization, Aristotle early acquired some of the worldly wisdom, detachment, and tolerance that were generally characteristic of colonial Greeks in constant touch with other peoples and cultures. Unlike Plato, Aristotle came from an upper-middle-class family, his father being a physician. At the age of seventeen, Aristotle went to Athens, the intellectual center of Greece, entered Plato's Academy, and studied under Plato for twenty years, until his master's death. During the subsequent twelve years, he traveled widely and spent several years at the Court of Philip of Macedon as tutor to his son, Alexander.

In 335 B.C. Aristotle returned to Athens and set up a school of his own, the Lyceum, whose teaching and research program included every branch of knowledge. In 323 B.C. Alexander suddenly died, and the national-democratic forces in Athens quickly rose against the Macedonian overlordship and its lieutenants and spokesmen in Greece. Aristotle, widely known for his intimate associations with the Macedonian monarchy and Alexander, was suspected of pro-Macedonian sentiments and indicted. However, Aristotle preferred exile to a court trial and possible sentence; he died the following year (322 B.C.) in Chalcis, a stronghold of Macedonian influence that gave him generous refuge during the last months of his life.

In the history of political philosophy no one has surpassed Aristotle in encyclopedic interest and accomplishment. From his father he inherited a flair for medical and biological subjects, and he may have practiced medicine for a time. This interest drew him into zoology, physics, and the natural sciences in general, and fostered in him the habit of observing and weighing data before expressing any general formulas and hypotheses. In philosophy proper, logic and metaphysics were his two main branches of study and writing; he also contributed to esthetics and rhetoric and wrote the first book on psychology; and his *Ethics* and *Politics* are the first systematic treatises in their respective fields. The *Politics* lacks the fire and poetic imagery of the *Republic,* but it is more systematic and analytical, and after twenty-three hundred years it is still an introductory textbook to the entire field of political science. It cannot easily be surpassed in clarity of thought, sobriety of expression, range of topics, and undogmatic openness of mind, for Aristotle prefers beings occasionally self-contradictory to being always right.

Aristotle opens the *Politics* with two important ideas: (1) that the state is a community, and (2) that it is the highest of all communities, "which embraces all the rest, aims at good in a greater degree than any other, and at the highest good." The first thesis came naturally to a Greek of the classical period: his *polis* was a city-state with a small area and population; lacking the impersonal anonymity of ancient empires or modern national states, it combined within itself the active citizenship of an early New England or modern Swiss community and the warmth and fellowship of a religious congregation, all deepened by a joint sharing in the arts and pleasures of life.

Aristotle may not have been the first to consider the state a community, but he was the first to define it clearly as such, and thus he laid the foundation for the *organic* conception of the state, one of the two major types into which all political theories of the state may roughly be divided. According to him, the state is a natural community, an organism with all the attributes of a living being. The other major type views the state as an instrument, a mechanism, a piece of machinery to be used for purposes and ends higher than itself. This type, called the *instrumentalist* view of the state, is actually older, having been propounded by the Sophists a century before Aristotle; however, it was rejected by Plato and revived only in modern times by Hobbes, Locke, and John Dewey.

Aristotle conceives of the state as "natural" in two ways. First, he briefly delineates the evolution of social institutions from the family through the village to the city-state; in this historical sense, the state is the natural and final stage in the growth of human relations. The state is also considered by Aristotle to be natural in a logical and philosophical sense: "The state is by nature clearly prior to the family and the individual, since the whole is of necessity prior to the part." Similarly, Aristotle says that "man is by nature a political animal," and that only gods or beasts can exist without the confines of the sheltering city.

But Aristotle maintains not only that the state is a community but that it is the *highest community* aiming at the highest good. The family is the first form of association, lowest in the chain of social evolution, and lowest on the rung of values, because it is established by nature "for the supply of men's everyday wants." The village is the second form of association, genetically more complex than the family, and aiming "at something more than the supply of daily needs," meeting at least some rudimentary and primitive cultural wants that the family cannot satisfy. The third and highest form of association is the city-state, highest in terms of social evolution and highest in terms of value and purpose: whereas family and village exist essentially for the preservation of life and the comforts of companionship, the "state exists for the sake of a good life, and not for the sake of life only," and "political society exists for the sake of noble actions, and not of mere companionship."

Unlike Plato, who conceives of reality in terms of unchanging and unchanging static essences and Ideas, Aristotle identifies the nature of a thing with the end toward which it is developing; at each unfinished stage, the thing is partly realizing its own nature and is fully itself when its end is wholly realized. Aristotle's biological, scientific, and historical interests enabled him to view the philosophical problem of reality from a more dynamic and relative standpoint than Plato's, and Aristotle's conception of the state therefore encompasses a wider range of forms of state, varying blends of idea and circumstance, of the perfect and the imperfect.

The state is the highest form of association, not only in terms of the social and institutional, or objective, values, but in terms of man's own nature. In the family, man reproduces himself; in the village, he satisfies elementary wants of human companionship; in the state alone, he realizes his entire self, and particularly the highest part of himself. Man thus represents a compound of qualities that are reflected in corresponding forms of association: his *material* appetites and biological urges, the lowest on the scale of values, are reflected in the family; his *social* sentiment, his desire for companionship and community, is expressed in the village; his *moral* nature, the quality that makes him most specifically human, is fulfilled in the state.

In modern thought, especially in the social sciences, a sharper distinction is drawn between the individual, social groups and associations, and, finally, the state. Aristotle sees all three as organically connected with one another. Man cannot be conceived as being apart from, or superior to, the state because, as was explained earlier, Aristotle considers that "the whole is of necessity prior to the part." Only a "beast or a god" is unable to live in society, or has no need for it. Man can realize himself, that which is most human in him, in society alone. Similarly, Aristotle recognizes no basic difference between social and political associations. To him, all associations are political, inasmuch as they aim at a common good through joint action; the state differs from other associations in that it aims at the highest good, the general advantage of all.

Since the seventeenth century the state has been sharply distinguished from all other organizations because it alone possesses sovereignty, or the highest authority in a politically organized community, and the legal monopoly of enforcing such authority in its territory. Aristotle knows not of the conceptual distinction, or contrast, between individual and society, nor can he visualize the later conflict between society (conceived as the sphere of unhindered and spontaneous activity) and the state (conceived as the sphere of regulated and compelled behavior). If Aristotle were to think at all of the state as sovereign, he would think of the *highest purpose* of the state rather than of its supreme authority over its citizens. His is a conception of *moral sovereignty* rather than of *legal sovereignty*. Nurtured in the tradition of the small city-state, Aristotle could still say that "the will to live together is friendship," and he would have abhorred the conception that the state is held together, not by personal bonds of fellowship and friendship, but by impersonal and anonymous rules of law, uniformly applying to vast territories and populations, as in modern states and empires.

In his organic view of the state Aristotle expresses more clearly what is implicit, and to some extent explicit, in Plato, but he is unwilling to go as far as his teacher. Unity became for Plato an ideal to which almost anything else was to be sacrificed, the happiness of the rulers as well as the ruled. By contrast, Aristotle warns against the dangers of excessive unity in the state; even if it could be attained, it ought to be rejected, "for it would be the destruction of the state." Moreover, Aristotle is doubtful whether such perfect unity is attainable, and he likens the guardian-rulers of the *Republic* to a "mere occupying garrison," with the result that Plato's ideally united state actually contains "two states in one, each hostile to the other."

Whereas Plato saw only a few basic differences of individuals, such as the differences between members of the three classes of the ideal state, Aristotle is aware of many more differences, and he expresses a truth that is as provocative today as ever, that "a state is not made up only of so many men, but of different kinds of men," and that "the nature of a state is to be a plurality." The danger of all organic theories of the state is that they tend to stress communal unity over individual differences and to subordinate the individual to the state. Plato's conception of the state carried the idea of unity, implicit in all organic theories, to the excess of self-destruction; Aristotle found the counterweight to such an extreme and perfectionist view in the elements of his thinking that pointed toward relativism and pluralism.

Aristotle's organic conception of the state has been used more eagerly and more frequently by conservatives and antidemocrats than by democratic political writers. Yet as time went on, the awareness grew that the state must be more than an instrument or piece of machinery and that the democratic state in particular should aim at becoming a community, not only of law, but of fellowship. Underlying the modern development of the welfare state is the notion that society must have no outcasts, that its inequalities must be reduced, and that the basic amenities of civilized life must be accessible to all.

The second basic doctrine of Aristotle, that the state is the highest community, is less likely to be accepted by democrats. Two objections can be raised: first, democrats are unwilling to concede that any institution per se is entitled to claim primary and exclusive loyalty. Man feels attached to various, and often conflicting, religious, social, economic, and political groups, and his conscience has to decide in each instance of conflict which loyalty comes first. In one instance he may put his church above his country; in another, his country above his economic interest, but there is no way of telling a priori that any institution is entitled to first allegiance under all circumstances. As a Greek, Aristotle would have felt little sympathy for such a conception of the state, which is implicit in all democratic political doctrines, because the small city-state with its intimate social life was church and state at the same time, and no sharp distinction was felt between socioeconomic and political institutions.

The second objection against the conception of the state as the highest community can be made by democrats on the ground, originally stated by the Sophists and later reemphasized by the Stoics, that man's loyalty is to mankind as a whole rather than to any particular fraction. This faith was given added force by the Judeo-Christian religious tradition, in which the oneness of God inspires the belief in the oneness of mankind.

By studying virtually all then-known constitutions and political systems, Aristotle laid the foundations of an important branch of political science: *comparative government and politics*. Of 158 such studies made by him, only one survives, the *Constitution of Athens,* discovered in 1890. The study of comparative political institutions is of interest to the political scientist as well as to the practicing statesman, who must know the varieties of political experience if he is to be able to remedy the defects of existing constitutions.

In considering the general problem of the various forms of government, Aristotle says, in an obvious reference to Plato, that "there are some who would have none but the most perfect." The knowledge of the best state may have some value as a norm and standard, but, on the other hand, "the best is often unattainable, and therefore the true legislator and statesman ought to be acquainted, not only with (1) that which is best in the abstract, but also with (2) that which is best relatively to circumstances." Where the attention to Plato, in the *Republic* at least, is centered on the desirable kind of state, Aristotle holds that we "should consider, not only what form of government is best, but also what is possible and what is easily attainable by all."

In classifying the forms of state, Aristotle distinguishes governments that are carried on "with a view to the common interest" from those that serve private interests, whether of one, of few, or of many. Of true governments, there are three: kingship, aristocracy, and constitutional government. Each form has its perversion, of which there are also three: tyranny, oligarchy, and democracy (the rule of the poor).

Of the three forms, Aristotle holds monarchy to be the most ideal kind of government. If a man "preeminent in virtue" can be found, who surpasses in virtue and political capacity "all the rest," he cannot be regarded as a part of the state, subject to the law like everybody else: "Such an one may truly be deemed a God among men." Since there is no law for men of preeminent virtue, monarchs "are themselves a law." Their superior virtue and political capacity give them the right to "practise compulsion and still live in harmony with their cities, if their own government is for the interest of the state."

Like Plato, Aristotle puts virtue of the rulers above consent of the ruled, although both would prefer to have the ruled submit voluntarily to their rulers, to avoid the necessity of compulsion. If a man of preeminent virtue be the monarch, Aristotle argues, "all should joyfully obey such a ruler, according to what seems to be the order of nature." Monarchy can be justified, however, by another consideration: that "a king is the resource of the better classes against the people," and that "the idea of a king is to be a protector of the rich against unjust treatment, of the people against insult and oppression."

Aristotle's deep sympathy for monarchy, as expressed in the *Politics* in so many passages, is to be understood in the light of his relations with the rising Macedonian monarchy. His father had been the royal physician at the Macedonian court, and Aristotle himself the tutor of Alexander. Both Philip and Alexander sought to conquer Greece intellectually as well as politically and militarily; just as in the struggle between Sparta and Athens, class loyalties often came before patriotism, and each city had its (antidemocratic) Spartan and (prodemocratic) Athenian party, so the Macedonian effort to annex Greece to its rule was accompanied by the growth of pro-Macedonian groups in the major Greek city-states. In Athens, the national and democratic movement was led by Demosthenes, to whom all monarchy, good or bad, was "un-Athenian"; the conservative classes, anxious above all to maintain their privileged social-economic position, received their intellectual support from Aristotle's school of philosophy and Plato's Academy, and they were therefore generally pro-Macedonian.

Aristocracy is nowhere described in the *Politics* systematically, perhaps because the problem of aristocracy and democracy (particularly in relation to Athenian self-government) was not of such practical importance as that of monarchy (particularly in relation to the Macedonian kingdom). Aristotle defines aristocracy as a "government formed of the best men absolutely," and not merely of men who are good relatively, that is, in relation to changing circumstances and constitutions. But Aristotle admits that, in addition to such a pure form of aristocracy, which is based on merit and virtue only, there is a type of aristocracy that also takes into account the elements of wealth. Generally, however, Aristotle speaks of monarchy and aristocracy as "the perfect state," the government of the best, both forms aiming at the general good; the main difference between the two consists in the fact that in monarchy virtue is centered in one "preeminent" man, whereas in aristocracy virtue is diffused among several men. The deteriorated form of aristocracy is oligarchy, in which government by the wealthy is carried on for their own benefit rather than for that of the whole state. Whereas merit and virtue are the distinctive qualities to be considered in selecting the rulers in an aristocracy, wealth is the basis of selection in an oligarchy.

The third of the true forms of state is constitutional government ("polity"). Aristotle defines it as the state that the citizens at large administer for the common interest. Constitutional government is a compromise between the two principles of freedom and wealth, the attempt to "unite the freedom of the poor and the wealth of the rich," without giving either principle exclusive predominance. Aristotle concedes that the doctrine

of the multitude being supreme rather than the few best, "though not free from difficulty, yet seems to contain an element of truth." When many ordinary persons meet together, their collective wisdom and experience may be superior to that of the few good,
"just as a feast to which many contribute is better than a dinner provided out of a single
purse." Aristotle suggests the general analogy of the user of a thing being a better judge
than its producer, and that, returning to culinary similes, "the guest will judge better of
a feast than the cook."

Thinking realistically of the stability of the state, Aristotle holds that the freedom of
the poor must be given some consideration, "for a state in which many poor men are excluded from office will necessarily be full of enemies." Aristotle never abandons the
ideal state (monarchy or aristocracy, that is, the rule of the best) as an "aspiration," but
he realizes that it assumes a standard of virtue "which is above ordinary persons"; in
practice, therefore, constitutional government, based on limited suffrage, turns out to
be "the best constitution for most states, and the best life for most men."

By relating forms of political organization to the social milieu that conditions them,
Aristotle anticipated some of the main doctrines of Montesquieu and, still more recently, the sociological approach to the study of politics. He saw the danger that would
arise if any principle singly and exclusively dominated the constitution, and he therefore advocated, for reasons of stability and practicability, *mixed constitutions,* such as
"polity" (constitutional government), based on the two principles of wealth and numbers. However, he realized that a mixed political system could exist in the long run only
if backed by a stable society without extremes of wealth and poverty.

Although many persons in the twentieth century find the cause of revolution in conspiracies of evil men, and its remedy in intimidation by investigatory committees or in
repression by antirevolutionary legislation, Aristotle states that "poverty is the parent
of revolution and crime," and that "when there is no middle class, and the poor greatly
exceed in number, troubles arise, and the state soon comes to an end." Because he realized that political stability depends on an equitable social and economic order, he was
opposed to selfish class rule by either an excessively wealthy plutocracy (called by him
"oligarchy") or by a propertyless proletariat (called by him "democracy"): "Thus it is
manifest that the best political community is formed by citizens of the middle class,
and that those states are likely to be well-administered, in which the middle class is
large, and stronger if possible than both the other classes, or at any rate than either
singly." The middle classes thus provided for Aristotle the balance and equilibrium
without which no constitution can endure.

The degenerate form of constitutional government (or "polity") is called by Aristotle
"democracy," and defined as a system in which "the poor rule." It is government by the
poor, and for the poor only, just as tyranny is government by one for his own benefit,
and oligarchy government by the wealthy few for their class benefit. But of the degenerate forms, government of the poor for the benefit of the poor ("democracy") is "the
most tolerable of the three." Aristotle names popular sovereignty and individual liberty
the two characteristic principles of democracy, and he condemns them, in language
similar to that of Plato, as incompatible with the stability of the existing moral and political order: "Men think that what is just is equal; and that equality is the supremacy of
the popular will; and that freedom means the doing what a man likes. In such democracies every one lives as he pleases."

Though Aristotle was more appreciative than Plato of the common sense and collective wisdom of the people, he was nevertheless afraid of government in which the democratic principle of popular sovereignty was allowed to operate without the modifying
influence of other principles, particularly wealth. In this fear of the sovereignty of the

majority, Aristotle is conservative rather than antidemocratic, and the godfather of all conservatives in history who have tried to harmonize respect for constitutional government with social and economic inequality.

Aristotle's conservative viewpoint is also clearly expressed in his conception of *citizenship*. He defines a citizen as follows: "he who has the power to take part in the deliberative or judicial administration of any state." Representative government was unknown to Aristotle because the Greek city-state was governed directly by its citizens, with but few representative elements. Aristotle could not have foreseen the modern concept of the citizen whose main (and often sole) political act is to vote (and frequently he neglects to do that) every few years in an election, and otherwise to leave the actual functions of government to professional legislators, judges, and civil servants. Within the small city-state, all slaves and the majority of the free were excluded from citizenship; to be a citizen meant to participate directly in the legislative and executive functions of government.

Aristotle's idea of citizenship is that of the economically independent gentleman who has enough experience, education, and leisure to devote himself to *active* citizenship, for "citizens must not lead the life of mechanics or tradesmen, for such life is ignoble, and inimical to virtue. Neither must they be husbandmen, since leisure is necessary both for the development of virtue and the performance of political duties." Stressing even more clearly the relation between property and virtue, Aristotle maintains that "the ruling class should be the owners of property, for they are citizens, and the citizens of a state should be in good circumstances; whereas mechanics or any other class which is not a producer of virtue have no share in the state."

Aristotle makes an important distinction between the "parts" of the state and its "necessary conditions." Only those who actively share, or have the means and leisure to share, in the government of the state are its component or integral parts. All the others are merely the "necessary condition" who provide the material environment within which the active citizens, freed from menial tasks, can function. Aristotle finds it "no more absurd" to exclude "the lower class" from citizenship than to exclude "slaves and freedmen," none of whom are resident aliens or foreigners; what the "lower class" has in common with slaves and freedmen is the fact that all its members are "necessary to the existence of the state" but not parts of the state. Aristotle even notes that in ancient times, the "artisan class *were* slaves or foreigners, and therefore the majority of them are so now." Although mechanics and laborers are not legally aliens, morally and politically they are, because "he who is excluded from the honors of the state is not better .than an alien."

In comparing the propertied citizens with the propertyless mechanics and laborers, Aristotle draws the analogy between ends and means, the latter existing for the sake of the former. Aristotle was unaware of the idea, expressed in religious terms by the Judeo-Christian teachings in antiquity, and in philosophical terms by Kant in modern times, that every man is, by virtue of being human, an end in himself, and must not be reduced to a means.

If free artisans and laborers are to be treated as means rather than ends, it is none too difficult for Aristotle to defend the institution of *slavery*. Whereas artisans and laborers are to be viewed as means in relation to the state only, slaves are means in every aspect of their existence; they belong "wholly" to their masters. Aristotle assumes that nature is universally ruled by the contrast of the superior and inferior: man is superior to the animals, the male to the female, the soul to the body, reason to passion. In all these divisions, it is just that the superior rule over the inferior, and such a rule is to the advantage of both. Among men, there are those "whose business is to use their body, and who can do nothing better," and they are by nature slaves. Just as it is fair to hunt against wild animals, so it is "against men who, though intended by nature to be governed, will not submit." Because the question of who is intended by nature to govern, or to be governed, is likely to be decided by the conquerors of a defeated nation rather than by an impartial, third-party court of appeal, Aristotle—in his doctrine of just wars of conquest and enslavement—anticipates Hegel's dictum that "world history is the world court."

Aristotle concedes to slaves the mental ability of apprehending the rational actions and orders of their masters but denies them the ability of acting rationally on their own initiative. The slave is a possession, a live tool; comparing slaves to tame animals, Aristotle notes the difference that the latter cannot even apprehend reason, whereas slaves do, but "the use made of slaves and of tame animals is not very different; for both with their bodies minister to the needs of life." Untouched by the monotheistic doctrine of the divinity and uniqueness of every human soul, Aristotle expresses the pagan view that "from the hour of their birth, some are marked out for subjection; others, for rule."

Aristotle was realistic enough to see that many were slaves by law rather than nature, particularly those who were reduced to slavery by conquest, a custom widely practiced in the wars of antiquity. Feeling strongly about the cultural unity (and superiority) of the Greeks, Aristotle was particularly disturbed by slavery in Greece, and said that "Hellenes do not like to call Hellenes slaves, but confine the term to barbarians." Just as Plato had urged that Greeks conduct war against one another with a higher set of standards than against "barbarians," Aristotle looked on the mastery-slavery relation as not befitting superior Greeks, because "some are slaves everywhere, others nowhere."

This difference, however, was not a fact to be observed, but a wish to be expressed, because Greeks did enslave one another, and some of those who were slaves were by nature (and often, by birth) free. Aristotle did not resolve the dilemma between his general theory of slavery, which was based on moral and rational superiority, and the slavery of his time, which was based on force, custom, and utility, and had little to do with moral superiority.

All in all, Aristotle's view of slavery was not too extreme for his time. By reminding the master that his rule over the slave must be based on moral excellence and that abuse of his authority was injurious to both, by allowing the possibility of friendship between them, by conceding to slaves the faculty of apprehending reason, Aristotle prepared the ground for more searching ideas. Yet his general acceptance of slavery shows how even a wise and great philosopher is captive of the institutions of his time, and of the prejudices that rationalize them.

Aristotle's views on *property* are developed in direct reference to Plato, but they are of more general bearing and constitute to this day the ablest defense of private property. In his polemic against Plato, Aristotle attributes to him the advocacy of a communist property scheme in the *Republic*. In fact, Plato proposed nothing of the sort: the workers, artisans, and farmers in the *Republic* live in a system of private ownership and management of property; as to the rulers, they own no means of production of any kind, and their only economic activity consists in consuming what they derive from the farming and working population as tribute befitting an austere yet noble style of living. Although Plato did not advocate economic communism, he nevertheless outlawed private property for the rulers as a possible menace to their sense of unity and their devotion to the state.

By contrast, Aristotle denies that private property is, in itself, a threat to moral perfection, and he defends his view on four grounds. First, he adduces the *incentive and progress* argument: when "every one has a distinct interest, men will not complain of one another, and they will make more progress, because every one will be attending to his own business." Thus, Aristotle links the idea of self-interest with that of social progress through greater individual effort and competence, whereas under a communist system, "those who labor much and get little will necessarily complain to those who labor little and receive or consume much." The collapse of Communist states in 1989 can in large part be traced to their nonrecognition of the profit motive in spurring individual initiative.

Aristotle's second argument in support of private property is the *pleasure* that the ownership of property gives, "for all, or almost all, men love money and other such objects in a measure." Aristotle sharply distinguishes such love of property from selfishness and miserliness, and considers it rather from the viewpoint of self-respect and material self-realization.

The third argument is that of *liberality.* Under common ownership, no one can afford to practice generosity and liberality because of the excessive equalization of property; it takes a system of private property, with at least some wealth and inequality, to "set an example of liberality or do any liberal action; for liberality consists in the use which is made of property."

Aristotle's fourth argument has a distinctly Burkean flavor: there must be something deeply and enduringly human in the idea of private property, if it has *existed* for such a *long time,* and "we should not disregard the experience of ages." As to communist practices, "in the multitude of years these things, if they were good, would certainly not have been unknown."

Aristotle is aware of the evils that befall men in a system of private property, but he says that they "are due to a very different cause—the wickedness of human nature." The cure for social imperfections is not equality of property but the moral improvement of man, and "the beginning of reform is not so much to equalize property as to train the nobler sort of natures not to desire more, and to prevent the lower from getting more; that is to say, they must be kept down, but not ill-treated." As a matter of public policy, the legislator ought to aim at equitable, rather than equal, distribution of property; what seems most important to Aristotle is *not who owns property but how property is used,* and that is an essentially moral question, not one of political economy.

Aristotle nevertheless realizes that excessive inequalities of wealth are dangerous to the balance and harmony of the state, and for this reason he praises with deep feeling the advantages of a society in which the middle classes are strongest. By contrast, where "some possess much, and the others nothing," constitutional government is impossible to maintain, and the state will be ruled by one of two extremes: either a plutocratic regime (oligarchy) for the exclusive benefit of the wealthy, or a proletarian regime (democracy) for the benefit of the urban poor, and "a tyranny may grow out of either extreme."

Unlike Plato, who searched for perfect justice, Aristotle understood that the basic issue is between the *rule of law* and the *rule of men.* Conceding that manmade law can never attain perfect justice, Aristotle nevertheless stresses that "the rule of the law is preferable to that of any individual," and that magistrates should regulate only matters on which the law is silent, because a general rule or principle cannot embrace all particulars. Whereas government based on law cannot be perfectly just, it is at least the lesser evil, when contrasted with the arbitrariness and passion inherent in government based on the rule of men.

The Aristotelian concept of the rule of law became one of the dominant political ideas to come forth from the Middle Ages—when interest in Aristotle revived—though during which political relations were still largely based on custom. In modern times the concept of the rule of law has become one of the pillars of the constitutional edifice of the United States and elsewhere. The constitutional state is perhaps the most important legacy Aristotle has bequeathed to posterity. In nondemocratic political systems still today, the strength or weakness of the rule of law is one of the clearest indications of the direction in which a particular state is moving. Historically, the rule of law has generally preceded democracy rather than been created by it. In ancient Greece, for example, the word "isonomia" (equality before the law) was coined before "demokratia" (rule of the people).

Aristotle's specific ideas, beliefs, and proposals are often conservative, even for his own time. But running through all his works, and implicit in his temper and personality, is a spirit that is wise and gentle, moderate, broad in outlook, open to new ideas, averse to dogmatism, conscious of the intricacy and complexity of human affairs, and imbued with sympathy that illuminates and enriches philosophical enquiry. Though explicitly conservative, Aristotle's thinking was suffused with qualities that characterize the liberal temper and the open mind.

ARISTOTLE

*Politics**

NATURE AND ORIGIN
OF THE STATE

Every state is a community of some kind, and every community is established with a view to some good; for mankind always act in order to obtain that which they think good. But, if all communities aim at some good, the state or political community, which is the highest of all, and which embraces all the rest, aims at good in a greater degree than any other, and at the highest good.

Some people think that the qualifications of a statesman, king, householder, and master are the same, and that they differ, not in kind, but only in the number of their subjects. For example, the ruler over a few is called a master; over more, the manager of a household; over a still larger number, a statesman or king, as if there were no difference between a great household and a small state. The distinction which is made between the king and the statesman is as follows: When the government is personal, the ruler is a king; when, according to the rules of the political science, the citizens rule and are ruled in turn, then he is called a statesman.

But all this is a mistake; for governments differ in kind, as will be evident to any one who considers the matter according to the method which has hitherto guided us. As in other departments of science, so in politics, the compound should always be resolved into the simple elements or least parts of the whole. We must therefore look at the

elements of which the state is composed, in order that we may see in what the different kinds of rule differ from one another, and whether any scientific result can be attained about each one of them.

He who thus considers things in their first growth and origin, whether a state or anything else, will obtain the clearest view of them. In the first place there must be a union of those who cannot exist without each other; namely, of male and female, that the race may continue (and this is a union which is formed, not of deliberate purpose, but because, in common with other animals and with plants, mankind have a natural desire to leave behind them an image of themselves), and of natural ruler and subject, that both may be preserved. For that which can foresee by the exercise of mind is by nature intended to be lord and master, and that which can with its body give effect to such foresight is a subject, and by nature a slave; hence master and slave have the same interest. Now nature has distinguished between the female and the slave. For she is not niggardly, like the smith who fashions the Delphian knife for many uses; she makes each thing for a single use, and every instrument is best made when intended for one and not for many uses. But among barbarians no distinction is made between women and slaves, because there is no natural ruler among them: they are a community of slaves, male and female.

Wherefore the poets say—

It is meet that Hellenes should rule over barbarians; as if they thought that the barbarian and the slave were by nature one.

---

*From Aristotle, *Politics* (trans. Benjamin Jowett, Oxford University Press). By permission.

Out of these two relationships between man and woman, master and slave, the first thing to arise is the family, and Hesiod is right when he says—

First house and wife and an ox for the plough,

for the ox is the poor man's slave. The family is the association established by nature for the supply of men's everyday wants, and the members of it are called by Charondas "companions of the cupboard," and by Epimenides the Cretan, "companions of the manger." But when several families are united, and the association aims at something more than the supply of daily needs, the first society to be formed is the village. And the most natural form of the village appears to be that of a colony from the family, composed of the children and grandchildren, who are said to be suckled "with the same milk." And this is the reason why Hellenic states were originally governed by kings; because the Hellenes were under royal rule before they came together, as the barbarians still are. Every family is ruled by the eldest, and therefore in the colonies of the family the kingly form of government prevailed because they were of the same blood. As Homer says:

Each one gives law to his children and to his wives.

For they lived dispersedly, as was the manner in ancient times. Wherefore men say that the Gods have a king, because they themselves either are or were in ancient times under the rule of a king. For they imagine, not only the forms of the Gods, but their ways of life to be like their own.

When several villages are united in a single complete community, large enough to be nearly or quite self-sufficing, the state comes into existence, originating in the bare needs of life, and continuing in existence for the sake of a good life. And therefore, if the earlier forms of society are natural, so is the state, for it is the end of them, and the nature of a thing is its end. For what each thing is when fully developed, we call its nature, whether we are speaking of a man, a horse, or a family. Besides, the final cause and end of a thing is the best, and to be self-sufficing is the end and the best.

Hence it is evident that the state is a creation of nature, and that man is by nature a political animal. And he who by nature and not by mere accident is without a state, is either a bad man or above humanity; he is like the

Tribeless, lawless, hearthless one,

whom Homer denounces—the natural outcast is forthwith a lover of war; he may be compared to an isolated piece at draughts.

Now, that man is more of a political animal than bees or any other gregarious animals is evident. Nature, as we often say, makes nothing in vain, and man is the only animal whom she has endowed with the gift of speech. And whereas mere voice is but an indication of pleasure or pain, and is therefore found in other animals (for their nature attains to the perception of pleasure and pain and the intimation of them to one another, and no further), the power of speech is intended to set forth the expedient and inexpedient, and therefore likewise the just and the unjust. And it is a characteristic of man that he alone has any sense of good and evil, of just and unjust, and the like, and the association of living beings who have this sense makes a family and a state.

Further, the state is by nature clearly prior to the family and to the individual, since the whole is of necessity prior to the part; for example, if the whole body be destroyed, there will be no foot or hand, except in an equivocal sense, as we might speak of a stone hand; for when destroyed the hand will be no better than that. But things are defined by their working and power; and we ought not to say that they are the same when they no longer have their proper quality, but only that they have the same name. The proof that the state is a creation of nature and prior to the individual is that the individual, when isolated, is not self-sufficing; and therefore he is like a part in relation to the whole. But he who is unable to live in society, or who has no need because he is sufficient for himself, must be either a beast or a god: he is no part of a state. A social instinct is implanted in all men by nature, and yet he who first founded the state was the greatest of benefactors.

For man, when perfected, is the best of animals, but, when separated from law and justice, he is the worst of all; since armed injustice is the more dangerous, and he is equipped at birth with arms, meant to be used by intelligence and virtue, which he may use for the worst ends. Wherefore, if he have not virtue, he is the most unholy and the most savage of animals, and the most full of lust and gluttony. But justice is the bond of men in states, for the administration of justice, which is the determination of what is just, is the principle of order in political society.

SLAVERY

But is there any one thus intended by nature to be a slave, and for whom such a condition is expedient and right, or rather is not all slavery a violation of nature?

There is no difficulty in answering this question, on grounds both of reason and of fact. For that some should rule and others be ruled is a thing not only necessary, but expedient; from the hour of their birth, some are marked out for subjection, others for rule.

And there are many kinds both of rulers and subjects (and that rule is the better which is exercised over better subjects—for example, to rule over men is better than to rule over wild beasts; for the work is better which is executed by better workmen, and where one man rules and another is ruled, they may be said to have a work); for in all things which form a composite whole and which are made up of parts, whether continuous or discrete, a distinction between the ruling and the subject element comes to light. Such a duality exists in living creatures, but not in them only; it originates in the constitution of the universe; even in things which have no life there is a ruling principle, as in a musical mode. But we are wandering from the subject. We will therefore restrict ourselves to the living creature, which, in the first place, consists of soul and body: and of these two, the one is by nature the ruler, and the other the subject. But then we must look for the intentions of nature in things which retain their nature, and not in things which are corrupted. And therefore we must study the man who is in the most perfect state both of body and

soul, for in him we shall see the true relation of the two; although in bad or corrupted natures the body will often appear to rule over the soul, because they are in an evil and unnatural condition. At all events we may firstly observe in living creatures both a despotical and a constitutional rule; for the soul rules the body with a despotical rule, whereas the intellect rules the appetites with a constitutional and royal rule. And it is clear that the rule of the soul over the body, and of the mind and the rational element over the passionate, is natural and expedient; whereas the equality of the two or the rule of the inferior is always hurtful. The same holds good of animals in relation to men; for tame animals have a better nature than wild, and all tame animals are better off when they are ruled by man; for then they are preserved. Again, the male is by nature superior, and the female inferior; and the one rules, and the other is ruled; this principle, of necessity, extends to all mankind. Where then there is such a difference as that between soul and body, or between men and animals (as in the case of those whose business is to use their body, and who can do nothing better), the lower sort are by nature slaves, and it is better for them as for all inferiors that they should be under the rule of a master. For he who can be, and therefore is, another's, and he who participates in rational principle enough to apprehend, but not to have, such a principle, is a slave by nature. Whereas the lower animals cannot even apprehend a principle, they obey their instincts. And indeed the use made of slaves and of tame animals is not very different; for both with their bodies minister to the needs of life. Nature would like to distinguish between the bodies of freemen and slaves, making the one strong for servile labour, the other upright, and although useless for such services, useful for political life in the arts both of war and peace. But the opposite often happens—that some have the souls and others have the bodies of freemen. And doubtless if men differed from one another in the mere forms of their bodies as much as the statues of the Gods do from men, all would acknowledge that the inferior class should be slaves of the superior. And if this is true of the body, how much more just that a similar distinction should exist in the soul? But the beauty of the body is seen, whereas the beauty of the soul is not seen. It is clear, then, that some men are by nature free, and others slaves, and that for these latter slavery is both expedient and right.

But that those who take the opposite view have in a certain way right on their side, may be easily seen. For the words slavery and slave are used in two senses. There is a slave or slavery by law as well as by nature. The law of which I speak is a sort of convention—the law by which whatever is taken in war is supposed to belong to the victors. But this right many jurists impeach, as they would an orator who brought forward an unconstitutional measure: they detest the notion that, because one man has the power of doing violence and is superior in brute strength, another shall be his slave and subject. Even among philosophers there is a difference of opinion. The origin of the dispute, and what makes the views invade each other's territory, is as follows: in some sense virtue, when furnished with means, has actually the greatest power of exercising force: and as superior power is only found where there is superior excellence of some kind, power seems to imply virtue, and the dispute to be simply one about justice (for it is due to one party identifying justice with goodwill, while the other identifies it with the mere rule of the stronger). If these views are thus set out separately, the other views have no force or plausibility against the view that the superior in virtue ought to rule, or be master. Others, clinging, as they think, simply to a principle of justice (for law and custom are a sort of justice), assume that slavery in accordance with the custom of war is justified by law, but at the same moment they deny this. For what if the cause of the war be unjust? And again, no one would ever say that he is a slave who is unworthy to be a slave. Were this the case, men of the highest rank would be slaves and the children of slaves if they or their parents chance to have been taken captive and sold. Wherefore Hellenes do not like to call Hellenes slaves, but confine the term to barbarians. Yet, in using this language, they really mean the natural slave of whom we spoke at first; for it must be admitted that some

are slaves everywhere, others nowhere. The same principle applies to nobility. Hellenes regard themselves as noble everywhere, and not only in their own country, but they deem the barbarians noble only when at home, thereby implying that there are two sorts of nobility and freedom, the one absolute, the other relative. The Helen of Theodectes says:

> Who would presume to call me servant who
> am on both sides sprung from the stem of
> the Gods?

What does this mean but that they distinguish freedom and slavery, noble and humble birth, by the two principles of good and evil? They think that as men and animals beget men and animals, so from good men a good man springs. But this is what nature, though she may intend it, cannot always accomplish.

We see then that there is some foundation for this difference of opinion, and that all are not either slaves by nature or freemen by nature, and also that there is in some cases a marked distinction between the two classes, rendering it expedient and right for the one to be slaves and the others to be masters: the one practising obedience, the others exercising the authority and lordship which nature intended them to have. The abuse of this authority is injurious to both; for the interests of part and whole, of body and soul, are the same, and the slave is a part of the master, a living but separated part of his bodily frame. Hence, where the relation of master and slave between them is natural they are friends and have a common interest, but where it rests merely on law and force the reverse is true.

CRITIQUE OF PLATO'S *REPUBLIC*

Our purpose is to consider what form of political community is best of all for those who are most able to realize their ideal of life. We must therefore examine not only this but other constitutions, both such as actually exist in well-governed states, and any theoretical forms which are held in esteem; that what is good and useful may be brought to light. And let no one suppose that in seeking for something beyond them we are anxious to make a sophistical display at any cost; we only undertake this inquiry because all the constitutions with which we are acquainted are faulty.

We will begin with the natural beginning of the subject. Three alternatives are conceivable: The members of a state must either have (1) all things or (2) nothing in common, or (3) some things in common and some not. That they should have nothing in common is clearly impossible, for the constitution is a community, and must at any rate have a common place—one city will be in one place, and the citizens are those who share in that one city. But should a well-ordered state have all things, as far as may be, in common, or some only and not others? For the citizens might conceivably have wives and children and property in common, as Socrates proposes in the *Republic* of Plato. Which is better, our present condition, or the proposed new order of society?

There are many difficulties in the community of women. And the principle on which Socrates rests the necessity of such an institution evidently is not established by his arguments. Further, as a means to the end which he ascribes to the state, the scheme, taken literally, is impracticable, and how we are to interpret it is nowhere precisely stated. I am speaking of the premiss from which the argument of Socrates proceeds, "that the greater the unity of the state the better." Is it not obvious that a state may at length attain such a degree of unity as to be no longer a state?—since the nature of a state is to be a plurality, and in tending to greater unity, from being a state, it becomes a family, and from being a family, an individual; for the family may be said to be more than the state, and the individual than the family. So that we ought not to attain this greatest unity even if we could, for it would be the destruction of the state. Again, a state is not made up only of so many men, but of different kinds of men; for similars do not constitute a state. It is not like a military alliance. The usefulness of the latter depends upon its quantity even where there is no difference in quality (for mutual protection is the end aimed at), just as a greater weight of anything is more useful than a less (in like manner, a state differs from a nation, when the nation has

not its population organized in villages, but lives an Arcadian sort of life); but the elements out of which a unity is to be formed differ in kind. Wherefore the principle of compensation, as I have already remarked in the *Ethics,* is the salvation of states. Even among freemen and equals this is a principle which must be maintained, for they cannot all rule together, but must change at the end of a year or some other period of time or in some order of succession. The result is that upon this plan they all govern; just as if shoemakers and carpenters were to exchange their occupations, and the same persons did not always continue shoemakers and carpenters. And since it is better that this should be so in politics as well, it is clear that while there should be continuance of the same persons in power where this is possible, yet where this is not possible by reason of the natural equality of the citizens, and at the same time it is just that all should share in the government (whether to govern be a good thing or a bad), an approximation to this is that equals should in turn retire from office and should, apart from official position, be treated alike. Thus the one party rule and the others are ruled in turn, as if they were no longer the same persons. In like manner when they hold office there is a variety in the offices held. Hence it is evident that a city is not by nature one in that sense which some persons affirm; and that what is said to be the greatest good of cities is in reality their destruction; but surely the good of things must be that which preserves them. Again, in another point of view, this extreme unification of the state is clearly not good; for a family is more self-sufficing than an individual, and a city than a family, and a city only comes into being when the community is large enough to be self-sufficing. If then self-sufficiency is to be desired, the lesser degree of unity is more desirable than the greater.

PROPERTY: EQUALITY OR INEQUALITY?

Next let us consider what should be our arrangements about property: should the citizens of the perfect state have their possessions in common or not? This question may be discussed separately from the enactments about women and children. Even supposing that the women and children belong to individuals, according to the custom which is at present universal, may there not be an advantage in having and using possessions in common? Three cases are possible: (1) the soil may be appropriated, but the produce may be thrown for consumption into the common stock; and this is the practice of some nations. Or (2), the soil may be common, and may be cultivated in common, but the produce divided among individuals for their private use; this is a form of common property which is said to exist among certain barbarians. Or (3), the soil and the produce may be alike common.

When the husbandmen are not the owners, the case will be different and easier to deal with; but when they till the ground for themselves the question of ownership will give a world of trouble. If they do not share equally in enjoyments and toils, those who labour much and get little will necessarily complain of those who labour little and receive or consume much. But indeed there is always a difficulty in men living together and having all human relations in common, but especially in their having common property. The partnerships of fellow-travelers are an example to the point; for they generally fall out over everyday matters and quarrel about any trifle which turns up. So with servants: we are most liable to take offense at those with whom we most frequently come into contact in daily life.

These are only some of the disadvantages which attend the community of property; the present arrangement, if improved as it might be by good customs and laws, would be far better, and would have the advantages of both systems. Property should be in a certain sense common, but, as a general rule, private; for, when every one has a distinct interest, men will not complain of one another, and they will make more progress, because every one will be attending to his own business. And yet by reason of goodness, and in respect of use, "Friends," as the proverb says, "will have all things common." Even now there are traces of such a principle, showing that it is not impracticable, but, in well-ordered states, exists already to a certain extent and may be carried further. For, although every man has his own property, some things he will place at the disposal of his friends, while of others

he shares the use with them. The Lacedaemonians, for example, use one another's slaves, and horses, and dogs, as if they were their own; and when they lack provisions on a journey, they appropriate what they find in the fields throughout the country. It is clearly better that property should be private, but the use of it common; and the special business of the legislator is to create in men this benevolent disposition. Again, how immeasurably greater is the pleasure, when a man feels a thing to be his own; for surely the love of self is a feeling implanted by nature and not given in vain, although selfishness is rightly censured; this, however, is not the mere love of self, but the love of self in excess, like the miser's love of money; for all, or almost all, men love money and other such objects in a measure. And further, there is the greatest pleasure in doing a kindness or service to friends or guests or companions, which can only be rendered when a man has private property. These advantages are lost by excessive unification of the state. The exhibition of two virtues, besides, is visibly annihilated in such a state: first, temperance towards women (for it is an honourable action to abstain from another's wife for temperance sake); secondly, liberality in the matter of property. No one, when men have all things in common, will any longer set an example of liberality or do any liberal action; for liberality consists in the use which is made of property.

Such legislation may have a specious appearance of benevolence; men readily listen to it, and are easily induced to believe that in some wonderful manner everybody will become everybody's friend, especially when some one is heard denouncing the evils now existing in states, suits about contracts, convictions for perjury, flatteries of rich men and the like, which are said to arise out of the possession of private property. These evils, however, are due to a very different cause—the wickedness of human nature. Indeed, we see that there is much more quarrelling among those who have all things in common, though there are not many of them when compared with the vast numbers who have private property.

Again, we ought to reckon, not only the evils from which the citizens will be saved, but also the advantages which they will lose.

The life which they are to lead appears to be quite impracticable. The error of Socrates must be attributed to the false notion of unity from which he starts. Unity there should be, both of the family and of the state, but in some respects only. For there is a point at which a state may attain such a degree of unity as to be no longer a state, or at which, without actually ceasing to exist, it will become an inferior state, like harmony passing into unison, or rhythm which has been reduced to a single foot. The state, as I was saying, is a plurality, which should be united and made into a community by education; and it is strange that the author of a system of education which he thinks will make the state virtuous should expect to improve his citizens by regulations of this sort, and not by philosophy or by customs and laws, like those which prevail at Sparta and Crete respecting common meals, whereby the legislator has made property common. Let us remember that we should not disregard the experience of ages; in the multitude of years these things, if they were good, would certainly not have been unknown; for almost everything has been found out, although sometimes they are not put together; in other cases men do not use the knowledge which they have. Great light would be thrown on this subject if we could see such a form of government in the actual process of construction; for the legislator could not form a state at all without distributing and dividing its constituents into associations for common meals, and into phratries and tribes. But all this legislation ends only in forbidding agriculture to the guardians, a prohibition which the Lacedaemonians try to enforce already.

But, indeed, Socrates has not said, nor is it easy to decide, what in such a community will be the general form of the state. The citizens who are not guardians are the majority, and about them nothing has been determined: are the husbandmen, too, to have their property in common? Or is each individual to have his own? and are the wives and children to be individual or common? If, like the guardians, they are to have all things in common, in what do they differ from them, or what will they gain by submitting to their government? Or, upon what principle would they submit, unless indeed the governing class adopt the ingenious policy of the Cretans, who give their slaves the same institutions as their own, but forbid them gymnastic exercises and the possession of arms. If, on the other hand, the inferior classes are to be like other cities in respect of marriage and property, what will be the form of the community? Must it not contain two states in one, each hostile to the other? He makes the guardians into a mere occupying garrison, while the husbandmen and artisans and the rest are the real citizens. But if so the suits and quarrels, and all the evils which Socrates affirms to exist in other states, will exist equally among them. He says indeed that, having so good an education, the citizens will not need many laws, for example laws about the city or about the markets; but then he confines his education to the guardians. Again, he makes the husbandmen owners of the property upon condition of their paying a tribute. But in that case they are likely to be much more unmanageable and conceited than the Helots, or Penestae, or slaves in general. And whether community of wives and property be necessary for the lower equally with the higher class or not, and the questions akin to this, what will be the education, form of government, laws of the lower class, Socrates has nowhere determined: neither is it easy to discover this, nor is their character of small importance if the common life of the guardians is to be maintained.

Again, if Socrates makes the women common, and retains private property, the men will see to the fields, but who will see to the house? And who will do so if the agricultural class have both their property and their wives in common? Once more: it is absurd to argue, from the analogy of the animals, that men and women should follow the same pursuits, for animals have not to manage a household. The government, too, as constituted by Socrates, contains elements of danger; for he makes the same persons always rule. And if this is often a cause of disturbance among the meaner sort, how much more among high-spirited warriors? But that the persons whom he makes rulers must be the same is evident; for the gold which the God mingles in the souls of men is not at one time given to one, at another time to another, but always to the same: as he says, "God mingles gold in some, and silver in others, from their very birth; but brass and iron in those who are meant to be artisans and husbandmen." Again, he deprives the guardians even of happiness, and says that the legislator ought to make the whole state happy. But the whole cannot be happy unless most, or all, or some of its parts enjoy happiness. In this respect happiness is not like the even principle in numbers, which may exist only in the whole, but in neither of the parts; not so happiness. And if the guardians are not happy, who are? Surely not the artisans, or the common people. The Republic of which Socrates discourses has all these difficulties, and others quite as great.

There is another point: Should not the amount of property be defined in some way which differs from this by being clearer? For Socrates says that a man should have so much property as will enable him to live temperately, which is only a way of saying "to live well"; this is too general a conception. Further, a man may live temperately and yet miserably. A better definition would be that a man must have so much property as will enable him to live not only temperately but liberally; if the two are parted, liberality will combine with luxury; temperance will be associated with toil. For liberality and temperance are the only eligible qualities which have to do with the use of property. A man cannot use property with mildness or courage, but temperately and liberally he may; and therefore the practice of these virtues is inseparable from property. There is an inconsistency, too, in equalizing the property and not regulating the number of the citizens; the population is to remain unlimited, and he thinks that it will be sufficiently equalized by a certain number of marriages being unfruitful, however many are born to others, because he finds this to be the case in existing states. But greater care will be required than now; for among ourselves, whatever may be the number of citizens, the property is always distributed among them, and therefore no one is in want; but, if the property were incapable of division as in the *Laws,* the supernumeraries, whether few or many, would get nothing. One would have thought that it was even more necessary to limit population than property; and that the limit should be fixed by calculating the chances of mortality in the children, and of sterility in married persons. The neglect of this subject,

which in existing states is so common, is a never-failing cause of poverty among the citizens; and poverty is the parent of revolution and crime. Pheidon the Corinthian, who was one of the most ancient legislators, thought that the families and the number of citizens ought to remain the same, although originally all the lots may have been of different sizes: but in the *Laws* the opposite principle is maintained. What in our opinion is the right arrangement will have to be explained hereafter.

Other constitutions have been proposed; some by private persons, others by philosophers and statesmen, which all come nearer to established or existing ones than either of Plato's. No one else has introduced such novelties as the community of women and children, or public tables for women: other legislators begin with what is necessary. In the opinion of some, the regulation of property is the chief point of all, that being the question upon which all revolutions turn. This danger was recognized by Phaleas of Chalcedon, who was the first to affirm that the citizens of a state ought to have equal possessions. He thought that in a new colony the equalization might be accomplished without difficulty, not so easily when a state was already established; and that then the shortest way of compassing the desired end would be for the rich to give and not to receive marriage portions, and for the poor not to give but to receive them.

Plato in the *Laws* was of opinion that, to a certain extent, accumulation should be allowed, forbidding, as I have already observed, any citizen to possess more than five times the minimum qualification. But those who make such laws should remember what they are apt to forget—that the legislator who fixes the amount of property should also fix the number of children; for, if the children are too many for the property, the law must be broken. And, besides the violation of the law, it is a bad thing that many from being rich should become poor; for men of ruined fortunes are sure to stir up revolutions. That the equilization of property exercises an influence on political society was clearly understood even by some of the old legislators. Laws were made by Solon and others prohibiting an individual from possessing as much land as he pleased;

and there are other laws in states which forbid the sale of property: among the Locrians, for example, there is a law that a man is not to sell his property unless he can prove unmistakably that some misfortune has befallen him. Again, there have been laws which enjoin the preservation of the original lots. Such a law existed in the island of Leucas, and the abrogation of it made the constitution too democratic, for the rulers no longer had the prescribed qualification. Again, where there is equality of property, the amount may be either too large or too small, and the possessor may be living either in luxury or penury. Clearly, then, the legislator ought not only to aim at the equalization of properties, but at moderation in their amount. Further, if he prescribe this moderate amount equally to all, he will be no nearer the mark; for it is not the possessions but the desires of mankind which require to be equalized, and this is impossible, unless a sufficient education is provided by the laws. But Phaleas will probably reply that this is precisely what he means; and that, in his opinion, there ought to be in states, not only equal property, but equal education. Still he should tell precisely what he means; and what, in his opinion, there ought to be in having one and the same for all, if it is of a sort that predisposes men to avarice, or ambition, or both. Moreover, civil troubles arise, not only out of the inequality of property, but out of the inequality of honour, though in opposite ways. For the common people quarrel about the inequality of property, the higher class about the equality of honour; as the poet says—

The bad and good alike in honour share.

There are crimes of which the motive is want; and for these Phaleas expects to find a cure in the equalization of property, which will take away from a man the temptation to be a highwayman, because he is hungry or cold. But want is not the sole incentive to crime; men also wish to enjoy themselves and not to be in a state of desire—they wish to cure some desire, going beyond the necessities of life, which preys upon them; nay, this is not the only reason—they may desire superfluities in order to enjoy pleasures unaccompanied with pain, and therefore they commit crimes.

Now what is the cure of these three disorders? Of the first, moderate possessions and occupation; of the second, habits of temperance; as to the third, if any desire pleasures which depend on themselves, they will find the satisfaction of their desires nowhere but in philosophy; for all other pleasures we are dependent on others. The fact is that the greatest crimes are caused by excess and not by necessity. Men do not become tyrants in order that they may not suffer cold; and hence great is the honour bestowed, not on him who kills a thief, but on him who kills a tyrant. Thus we see that the institutions of Phaleas avail only against petty crimes.

There is another objection to them. They are chiefly designed to promote the internal welfare of the state. But the legislator should consider also its relation to neighbouring nations, and to all who are outside of it. The government must be organized with a view to military strength; and of this he has said not a word. And so with respect to property: there should not only be enough to supply the internal wants of the state, but also to meet dangers coming from without. The property of the state should not be so large that more powerful neighbours may be tempted by it, while the owners are unable to repel the invaders; nor yet so small that the state is unable to maintain a war even against states of equal power, and of the same character. Phaleas has not laid down any rule; but we should bear in mind that abundance of wealth is an advantage. The best limit will probably be, that a more powerful neighbour must have no inducement to go to war with you by reason of the excess of your wealth, but only such as he would have had if you had possessed less. There is a story that Eubulus, when Autophradates was going to besiege Atarneus, told him to consider how long the operation would take, and then reckon up the cost which would be incurred in the time. "For," said he, "I am willing for a smaller sum than that to leave Atarneus at once." These words of Eubulus made an impression on Autophradates, and he desisted from the siege.

The equalization of property is one of the things that tend to prevent the citizens from quarrelling. Not that the gain in this direction is very great. For the nobles will be dissatisfied because they think themselves worthy of more than an equal share of honours; and this is often found to be a cause of sedition and revolution. And the avarice of mankind is insatiable; at one time two obols was pay enough; but now, when this sum has become customary, men always want more and more without end; for it is of the nature of desire not to be satisfied, and most men live only for the gratification of it. The beginning of reform is not so much to equalize property as to train the nobler sort of natures not to desire more, and to prevent the lower from getting more; that is to say, they must be kept down, but not ill-treated. Besides, the equalization proposed by Phaleas is imperfect; for he only equalizes land, whereas a man may be rich also in slaves, and cattle, and money, and in the abundance of what are called his movables. Now either all these things must be equalized, or some limit must be imposed on them, or they must all be let alone. It would appear that Phaleas is legislating for a small city only, if, as he supposes, all the artisans are to be public slaves and not to form a supplementary part of the body of citizens. But if there is a law that artisans are to be public slaves, it should only apply to those engaged on public works, as at Epidamnus, or at Athens on the plan which Diophantus once introduced.

From these observations any one may judge how far Phaleas was wrong or right in his ideas.

CITIZENSHIP

He who would inquire into the essence and attributes of various kinds of governments must first of all determine "What is a state?" At present this is a disputed question. Some say that the state has done a certain act; others, no, not the state, but the oligarchy or the tyrant. And the legislator or statesman is concerned entirely with the state; a constitution or government being an arrangement of the inhabitants of a state. But a state is composite, like any other whole made up of many parts;—these are the citizens, who compose it. It is evident, therefore, that we must begin by asking, "Who is the citizen," and what is the meaning of the term? For here again there may be a difference of opinion. He who is a citizen in a democracy will often not be a citizen in an oligarchy. Leaving out of consideration those who have been made citizens, or who

have obtained the name of citizen in any other accidental manner, we may say, first that a citizen is not a citizen because he lives in a certain place, for resident aliens and slaves share in the place; nor is he a citizen who has no legal right except that of suing and being sued; for this right may be enjoyed under the provisions of a treaty. Nay, resident aliens in many places do not possess even such rights completely, for they are obliged to have a patron, so that they do but imperfectly participate in citizenship, and we call them citizens only in a qualified sense, as we might apply the term to children who are too young to be on the register, or to old men who have been relieved from state duties. Of these we do not say quite simply that they are citizens, but add in the one case that they are not of age, and in the other, that they are past the age, or something of that sort; the precise expression is immaterial, for our meaning is clear. Similar difficulties to those which I have mentioned may be raised and answered about deprived citizens and about exiles. But the citizen whom we are seeking to define is a citizen in the strictest sense, against whom no such exception can be taken, and his special characteristic is that he shares in the administration of justice, and in offices. Now of offices some are discontinuous, and the same persons are not allowed to hold them twice, or can only hold them after a fixed interval; others have no limit of time—for example, the office of dicast or ecclesiast.[1] It may, indeed, be argued that these are not magistrates at all, and that their functions give them no share in the government. But surely it is ridiculous to say that those who have the supreme power do not govern. Let us not dwell further upon this, which is a purely verbal question; what we want is a common term including both dicast and ecclesiast. Let us, for the sake of distinction, call it "indefinite office," and we will assume that those who share in such office are citizens. This is the most comprehensive definition of a citizen, and best suits all those who are generally so called.

---

[1] "Dicast" = juryman and judge in one: "ecclesiast" = member of the ecclesia or assembly of the citizens.

But we must not forget that things of which the underlying principles differ in kind, one of them being first, another second, another third, have, when regarded in this relation, nothing, or hardly anything, worth mentioning in common. Now we see that governments differ in kind, and that some of them are prior and that others are posterior; those which are faulty or perverted are necessarily posterior to those which are perfect. (What we mean by perversion will be hereafter explained.) The citizen then of necessity differs under each form of government; and our definition is best adapted to the citizen of a democracy; but not necessarily to other states. For in some states the people are not acknowledged, nor have they any regular assembly, but only extraordinary ones; and suits are distributed by sections among the magistrates. At Lacedaemon, for instance, the Ephors determine suits about contracts, which they distribute among themselves, while the elders are judges of homicide, and other causes are decided by other magistrates. A similar principle prevails at Carthage; there certain magistrates decide all causes. We may, indeed, modify our definition of the citizen so as to include these states. In them it is the holder of a definite, not of an indefinite office, who legislates and judges, and to some or all such holders of definite offices is reserved the right of deliberating or judging about some things or about all things. The conception of the citizen now begins to clear up.

He who has the power to take part in the deliberative or judicial administration of any state is said by us to be a citizen of that state; and, speaking generally, a state is a body of citizens sufficing for the purposes of life.

There is a point nearly allied to the preceding: Whether the virtue of a good man and a good citizen is the same or not. But, before entering on this discussion, we must certainly first obtain some general notion of the virtue of the citizen. Like the sailor, the citizen is a member of a community. Now, sailors have different functions, for one of them is a rower, another a pilot, and a third a look-out man, a fourth is described by some similar term, and while the precise definition of each individual's virtue applies exclusively to him, there is, at the same time, a common definition applicable to them all. For they have all of them a common object, which is safety in navigation. Similarly, one citizen differs from another, but the salvation of the community is the common business of them all. This community is the constitution; the virtue of the citizen must therefore be relative to the constitution of which he is a member. If, then, there are many forms of government, it is evident that there is not one single virtue of the good citizen which is perfect virtue. But we say that the good man is he who has one single virtue which is perfect virtue. Hence it is evident that the good citizen need not of necessity possess the virtue which makes a good man.

The same question may also be approached by another road, from a consideration of the best constitution. If the state cannot be entirely composed of good men, and yet each citizen is expected to do his own business well, and must therefore have virtue, still, inasmuch as all the citizens cannot be alike, the virtue of the citizen and of the good man cannot coincide. All must have the virtue of the good citizen—thus, and thus only, can the state be perfect; but they will not have the virtue of a good man, unless we assume that in the good state all the citizens must be good.

Again, the state, as composed of unlikes, may be compared to the living being: as the first elements into which a living being is resolved are soul and body, as soul is made up of rational principle and appetite, the family of husband and wife, property of master and slave, so of all these, as well as other dissimilar elements, the state is composed; and, therefore, the virtue of all the citizens cannot possibly be the same, any more than the excellence of the leader of a chorus is the same as that of the performer who stands by his side. I have said enough to show why the two kinds of virtue cannot be absolutely and always the same.

But will there then be no case in which the virtue of the good citizen and the virtue of the good man coincide? To this we answer that the good *ruler* is a good and wise man, and that he who would be a statesman must be a wise man. And some persons say that even the education of the ruler should be of a special kind; for are not the children of kings instructed in riding and military exercises? As Euripides says:

No subtle arts for me, but what the state requires.

As though there were a special education needed by a ruler. If then the virtue of a good ruler is the same as that of a good man, and we assume further that the subject is a citizen as well as the ruler, the virtue of the good citizen and the virtue of the good man cannot be absolutely the same, although in some cases they may; for the virtue of a ruler differs from that of a citizen. It was the sense of this difference which made Jason say that "he felt hungry when he was not a tyrant," meaning that he could not endure to live in a private station. But, on the other hand, it may be argued that men are praised for knowing both how to rule and how to obey, and he is said to be a citizen of approved virtue who is able to do both. Now if we suppose the virtue of a good man to be that which rules, and the virtue of the citizen to include ruling and obeying, it cannot be said that they are equally worthy of praise. Since, then, it is sometimes thought that the ruler and the ruled must learn different things and not the same, but that the citizen must know and share in them both, the inference is obvious. There is, indeed, the rule of a master, which is concerned with menial offices—the master need not know how to perform these, but may employ others, in the execution of them: the other would be degrading; and by the other I mean the power actually to do menial duties, which vary much in character and are executed by various classes of slaves, such, for example, as handicraftsmen, who, as their name signifies, live by the labour of their hands:—under these the mechanic is included. Hence in ancient times, and among some nations, the working classes had no share in the government—a privilege which they only acquired under the extreme democracy. Certainly the good man and the statesman and the good citizen ought not to learn the crafts of inferiors except for their own occasional use; if they habitually practice them, there will cease to be a distinction between master and slave.

This is not the rule of which we are speaking; but there is a rule of another kind, which is exercised over freemen and equals by birth—a constitutional rule, which the ruler must learn by obeying, as he would learn the duties of a general of cavalry by being under the orders of a general of cavalry, or the duties of a general of infantry by being under the orders of a general of infantry, and by having had the command of a regiment and of a company. It has been well said that "he who has never learned to obey cannot be a good commander." The two are not the same, but the good citizen ought to be capable of both; he should know how to govern like a freeman, and how to obey like a freeman—these are the virtues of a citizen. And, although the temperance and justice of a ruler are distinct from those of a subject, the virtue of a good man will include both; for the virtue of the good man who is free and also a subject, e.g. his justice, will not be one but will comprise distinct kinds, the one qualifying him to rule, the other to obey, and differing as the temperance and courage of men and women differ. For a man would be thought a coward if he had no more courage than a courageous woman, and a woman would be thought loquacious if she imposed no more restraint on her conversation than the good man; and indeed their part in the management of the household is different, for the duty of the one is to acquire, and of the other to preserve. Practical wisdom only is characteristic of the ruler: it would seem that all other virtues must equally belong to ruler and subject. The virtue of the subject is certainly not wisdom, but only true opinion; he may be compared to the maker of the flute, while his master is like the flute-player or user of the flute.

From these considerations may be gathered the answer to the question, whether the virtue of the good man is the same as that of the good citizen, or different, and how far the same, and how far different.

There still remains one more question about the citizen: Is he only a true citizen who has a share of office, or is the mechanic to be included? If they who hold no office are to be deemed citizens, not every citizen can have this virtue of ruling and obeying; for this man is a citizen. And if none of the lower class are citizens, in which part of the state are they to be placed? For they are not resident aliens, and they are not foreigners. May we not reply, that as far as this objection goes there is no more absurdity in excluding them than in excluding slaves and freedmen from any of the above-mentioned classes? It must be admitted that we cannot consider all those to be citizens who are necessary to the existence of the state; for example, children are not citizens equally with grown-up men, who are citizens absolutely, but children, not being grown up, are only citizens on a certain assumption. Nay, in ancient times, and among some nations, the artisan class *were* slaves or foreigners, and therefore the majority of them are so now. The best form of state will not admit them to citizenship; but if they are admitted, then our definition of the virtue of a citizen will not apply to every citizen, not to every free man as such, but only to those who are freed from necessary services. The necessary people are either slaves who minister to the wants of individuals, or mechanics and labourers who are the servants of the community. These reflections carried a little further will explain their position; and indeed what has been said already is of itself, when understood, explanation enough.

Since there are many forms of government there must be many varieties of citizens, and especially of citizens who are subjects; so that under some governments the mechanic and the labourer will be citizens, but not in others, as, for example, in aristocracy or the so-called government of the best (if there be such an one), in which honours are given according to virtue and merit; for no man can practise virtue who is living the life of a mechanic or labourer. In oligarchies the qualification for office is high, and therefore no labourer can ever be a citizen; but a mechanic may, for an actual majority of them are rich. At Thebes there was a law that no man could hold office who had not retired from business for ten years. But in many states the law goes to the length of admitting aliens; for in some democracies a man is a citizen though his mother only be a citizen; and a similar principle is applied to illegitimate children; the law is relaxed when there is a dearth of population. But when the number of citizens increases, first the children of a male or a female slave are excluded; then those whose mothers only are citizens; and at last the right of citizenship is confined to those whose fathers and mothers are both citizens.

Hence, as is evident, there are different kinds of citizens; and he is a citizen in the highest sense who shares in the honours of the state. Compare Homer's words "like some dishonoured stranger"; he who is excluded from the honours of the state is no better than an alien. But when this exclusion is concealed, then the object is that the privileged class may deceive their fellow inhabitants.

As to the question whether the virtue of the good man is the same as that of the good citizen, the considerations already adduced prove that in some states the good man and the good citizen are the same, and in others different. When they are the same it is not every citizen who is a good man, but only the statesman and those who have or may have, alone or in conjunction with others, the conduct of public affairs.

As in other natural compounds the conditions of a composite whole are not necessarily organic parts of it, so in a state or in any other combination forming a unity not everything is a part, which is a necessary condition. The members of an association have necessarily some one thing the same and common to all, in which they share equally or unequally; for example, food or land or any other thing. But where there are two things of which one is a means and the other an end, they have nothing in common except that the one receives what the other produces. Such, for example, is the relation in which workmen and tools stand to their work; the house and the builder have nothing in common, but the art of the builder is for the sake of the house. And so states require property, but property, even though living beings are included in it, is no part of a state; for a state is not a community of living beings only, but a community of equals, aiming at the best life possible. Now, whereas happiness is the highest good, being a realization and perfect practice of virtue, which some can attain, while others have little or none of it, the various qualities of men are clearly the reason why there are various kinds of states and many forms of government; for different men seek after happiness in different ways and by different means, and so make for themselves different modes of life and forms of government. We must see also how many things are indispensable to the existence of a state, for what we call the parts of a state will be found among the indispensables. Let us then enumerate the functions of a state, and we shall easily elicit what we want:

First, there must be food; secondly, arts, for life requires many instruments; thirdly, there must be arms, for the members of a community have need of them, and in their own hands, too, in order to maintain authority both against disobedient subjects and against external assailants; fourthly, there must be a certain amount of revenue, both for internal needs, and for the purposes of war; fifthly, or rather first, there must be a care of religion, which is commonly called worship; sixthly, and most necessary of all, there must be a power of deciding what is for the public interest, and what is just in men's dealings with one another.

These are the services which every state may be said to need. For a state is not a mere aggregate of persons, but a union of them sufficing for the purposes of life; and if any of these things be wanting, it is as we maintain impossible that the community can be absolutely self-sufficing. A state then should be framed with a view to the fulfilment of these functions. There must be husbandmen to procure food, and artisans, and a warlike and a wealthy class, and priests, and judges to decide what is necessary and expedient.

Having determined these points, we have in the next place to consider whether all ought to share in every sort of occupation. Shall every man be at once husbandman, artisan, councillor, judge, or shall we suppose the several occupations just mentioned assigned to different persons? or, thirdly, shall some employments be assigned to individuals and others common to all? The same arrangement, however, does not occur in every constitution; as we were saying, all may be shared by all, or not all by all, but only by some; and hence arise the differences of constitutions, for in democracies all share in all, in oligarchies the opposite practice prevails. Now, since we are here speaking of the best form of government, i.e. that under which the state will be most happy (and happiness, as has been already said, cannot exist without virtue), it clearly follows that in the state which is best governed and possesses men who are just absolutely, and not merely relatively to the principle of the constitution, the citizens must not lead the life of mechanics or tradesmen, for such a life is ignoble, and inimical to virtue. Neither must they be husbandmen, since leisure is necessary both for the development of virtue and the performance of political duties.

Again, there is in a state a class of warriors, and another of councillors, who advise about the expedient and determine matters of law, and these seem in an especial manner parts of a state. Now, should these two classes be distinguished, or are both functions to be assigned to the same persons? Here again there is no difficulty in seeing that both functions will in one way belong to the same, in another, to different persons. To different persons in so far as these employments are suited to different primes of life, for the one requires wisdom and the other strength. But on the other hand, since it is an impossible thing that those who are able to use or to resist force should be willing to remain always in subjection, from this point of view the persons are the same; for those who carry arms can always determine the fate of the constitution. It remains therefore that both functions should be entrusted by the ideal constitution to the same persons, not, however, at the same time, but in the order prescribed by nature, who has given to young men strength and to older men wisdom. Such a distribution of duties will be expedient and also just, and is founded upon a principle of conformity to merit. Besides, the ruling class should be the owners of property, for they are citizens, and the citizens of a state should be in good circumstances; whereas mechanics or any other class which is not a producer of virtue have no share in the state. This follows from our first principle, for happiness cannot exist without virtue, and a city is not to be termed happy in regard to a portion of the citizens, but in regard to them all. And clearly property should be in their hands, since the husbandmen will of necessity be slaves or barbarian Perioeci.

Of the classes enumerated there remain only the priests, and the manner in which their office is to be regulated is obvious. No husbandman or mechanic should be appointed to it; for the Gods should receive honour from the citizens only. Now since the body of the citizens is divided into two classes, the warriors and the councillors, and it is beseeming that the worship of the Gods should be duly performed, and also a rest provided in their service for those who from age have given up active life, to the old men of these two classes should be assigned the duties of the priesthood.

We have shown what are the necessary conditions, and what the parts of a state: husbandmen, craftsmen, and labourers of all kinds are necessary to the existence of states, but the parts of the state are the warriors and councillors. And these are distinguished severally from one another, the distinction being in some cases permanent, in others not.

Since every political society is composed of rulers and subjects let us consider whether the relations of one to the other should interchange or be permanent. For the education of the citizens will necessarily vary with the answer given to this question. Now, if some men excelled others in the same degree in which gods and heroes are supposed to excel mankind in general (having in the first place a great advantage even in their bodies, and secondly in their minds), so that the superiority of the governors was undisputed and patent to their subjects, it would clearly be better that once for all the one class should rule and the others serve. But since this is unattainable, and kings have no marked superiority over their subjects, such as Scylax affirms to be found among the Indians, it is obviously necessary on many grounds that all the citizens alike should take their turn of governing and being governed. Equality consists in the same treatment of similar persons, and no government can stand which is not founded upon justice. For if the government be unjust every one in the country unites with the governed in the desire to have a revolution, and it is an impossibility that the members of the government can be so numerous as to be stronger than all their enemies put together. Yet that governors should excel their subjects is undeniable. How all this is to be effected, and in what way they will respectively share in the government, the legislator has to consider. The

subject has been already mentioned. Nature herself has provided the distinction when she made a difference between old and young within the same species, of whom she fitted the one to govern and the other to be governed. No one takes offence at being governed when he is young, nor does he think himself better than his governors, especially if he will enjoy the same privilege when he reaches the required age.

We conclude that from one point of view governors and governed are identical, and from another different. And therefore their education must be the same and also different. For he who would learn to command well must, as men say, first of all learn to obey. As I observed in the first part of this treatise, there is one rule which is for the sake of the rulers and another rule which is for the sake of the ruled; the former is a despotic, the latter a free government. Some commands differ not in the thing commanded, but in the intention with which they are imposed. Wherefore, many apparently menial offices are an honour to the free youth by whom they are performed; for actions do not differ as honourable or dishonourable in themselves so much as in the end and intention of them. But since we say that the virtue of the citizen and ruler is the same as that of the good man, and that the same person must first be a subject and then a ruler, the legislator has to see that they become good men, and by what means this may be accomplished, and what is the end of the perfect life.

Now the soul of man is divided into two parts, one of which has a rational principle in itself, and the other, not having a rational principle in itself, is able to obey such a principle. And we call a man in any way good because he has the virtues of these two parts. In which of them the end is more likely to be found is no matter of doubt to those who adopt our division; for in the world both of nature and of art the inferior always exists for the sake of the better or superior, and the better or superior is that which has a rational principle. This principle, too, in our ordinary way of speaking, is divided into two kinds, for there is a practical and a speculative principle. This part, then, must evidently be similarly divided. And there must be a corresponding division of actions; the actions of the naturally better part are to be preferred by those who have it in their power to attain to two out of the three or to all, for that is always to every one the most eligible which is the highest attainable by him. The whole of life is further divided into two parts, business and leisure, war and peace, and of actions some aim at what is necessary and useful, and some at what is honourable. And the preference given to one or the other class of actions must necessarily be like the preference given to one or other part of the soul and its actions over the other; there must be war for the sake of peace, business for the sake of leisure, things useful and necessary for the sake of things honourable. All these points the statesman should keep in view when he frames his laws; he should consider the parts of the soul and their functions, and above all the better and the end; he should also remember the diversities of human lives and actions. For men must be able to engage in business and go to war, but leisure and peace are better; they must do what is necessary and indeed what is useful, but what is honourable is better. On such principles children and persons of every age which requires education should be trained. Whereas even the Hellenes of the present day who are reputed to be best governed, and the legislators who gave them their constitutions, do not appear to have framed their governments with a regard to the best end, or to have given them laws and education with a view to all the virtues, but in a vulgar spirit have fallen back on those which promised to be more useful and profitable. Many modern writers have taken a similar view: they commend the Lacedaemonian constitution, and praise the legislator for making conquest and war his sole aim, a doctrine which may be refuted by argument and has long ago been refuted by facts. For most men desire empire in the hope of accumulating the goods of fortune; and on this ground Thibron and all those who have written about the Lacedaemonian constitution have praised their legislator, because the Lacedaemonians, by being trained to meet dangers, gained great power. But surely they are not a happy people now that their empire

has passed away, nor was their legislator right. How ridiculous is the result, if, while they are continuing in the observance of his laws and no one interferes with them, they have lost the better part of life! These writers further err about the sort of government which the legislator should approve, for the government of freemen is nobler and implies more virtue than despotic government. Neither is a city to be deemed happy or a legislator to be praised because he trains his citizens to conquer and obtain dominion over their neighbours, for there is great evil in this. On a similar principle any citizen who could, should obviously try to obtain the power in his own state—the crime which the Lacedaemonians accuse king Pausanias of attempting, although he had so great honour already. No such principle and no law having this object is either statesmanlike or useful or right. For the same things are best both for individuals and for states, and these are the things which the legislator ought to implant in the minds of his citizens. Neither should men study war with a view to the enslavement of those who do not deserve to be enslaved; but first of all they should provide against their own enslavement, and in the second place obtain empire for the good of the governed, and not for the sake of exercising a general despotism, and in the third place they should seek to be masters only over those who deserve to be slaves. Facts, as well as arguments, prove that the legislator should direct all his military and other measures to the provision of leisure and the establishment of peace. For most of these military states are safe only while they are at war, but fall when they have acquired their empire; like unused iron they lose their temper in time of peace. And for this the legislator is to blame, he never having taught them how to lead the life of peace.

POLITICAL SYSTEMS

Having determined these questions, we have next to consider whether there is only one form of government or many, and if many, what they are, and how many, and what are the differences between them.

A constitution is the arrangement of magistracies in a state, especially of the highest of all. The government is everywhere sovereign in the state, and the constitution is in fact the government. For example, in democracies the people are supreme, but in oligarchies, the few; and, therefore, we say that these two forms of government also are different: and so in other cases.

First, let us consider what is the purpose of a state, and how many forms of government there are by which human society is regulated. We have already said, in the first part of this treatise, when discussing household management and the rule of a master, that man is by nature a political animal. And therefore, men, even when they do not require one another's help, desire to live together; not but that they are also brought together by their common interests in proportion as they severally attain to any measure of well-being. This is certainly the chief end, both of individuals and of states. And also for the sake of mere life (in which there is possibly some noble element so long as the evils of existence do not greatly overbalance the good) mankind meet together and maintain the political community. And we all see that men cling to life even at the cost of enduring great misfortune, seeming to find in life a natural sweetness and happiness.

There is no difficulty in distinguishing the various kinds of authority; they have been often defined already in discussions outside the school. The rule of a master, although the slave by nature and the master by nature have in reality the same interests, is nevertheless exercised primarily with a view to the interest of the master, but accidentally considers the slave, since, if the slave perish, the rule of the master perishes with him. On the other hand, the government of a wife and children and of a household, which we have called household management, is exercised in the first instance for the good of the governed or for the common good of both parties, but essentially for the good of the governed, as we see to be the case in medicine, gymnastic, and the arts in general, which are only accidentally concerned with the good of the artists themselves. For there is no reason why the trainer may not sometimes practise gymnastics, and the helmsman is always one of the crew. The trainer or the helmsman considers the good of those committed to

his care. But, when he is one of the persons taken care of, he accidentally participates in the advantage, for the helmsman is also a sailor, and the trainer becomes one of those in training. And so in politics: when the state is framed upon the principle of equality and likeness, the citizens think that they ought to hold office by turns. Formerly, as is natural, every one would take his turn of service; and then again, somebody else would look after his interest, just as he, while in office, had looked after theirs. But nowadays, for the sake of the advantage which is to be gained from the public revenues and from office, men want to be always in office. One might imagine that the rulers, being sickly, were only kept in health while they continued in office; in that case we may be sure that they would be hunting after places. The conclusion is evident: that governments which have a regard to the common interest are constituted in accordance with strict principles of justice, and are therefore true forms; but those which regard only the interest of the rulers are all defective and perverted forms, for they are despotic, whereas a state is a community of freemen.

Having determined these points, we have next to consider how many forms of government there are, and what they are; and in the first place what are the true forms, for when they are determined the perversions of them will at once be apparent. The words constitution and government have the same meaning, and the government, which is the supreme authority in states, must be in the hands of one, or of a few, or of the many. The true forms of government, therefore, are those in which the one, or the few, or the many, govern with a view to the common interest; but governments which rule with a view to the private interest, whether of the one, or of the few, or of the many, are perversions. For the members of a state, if they are truly citizens, ought to participate in its advantages. Of forms of government in which one rules, we call that which regards the common interests, kingship or royalty; that in which more than one, but not many, rule, aristocracy; and it is so called, either because the rulers are the best men, or because they have at heart the best interests of the state and of the citizens. But when the citizens at large administer the state for the common interest, the government is called by the generic name—a constitution. And there is a reason for this use of language. One man or a few may excel in virtue; but as the number increases it becomes more difficult for them to attain perfection in every kind of virtue, though they may in military virtue, for this is found in the masses. Hence in a constitutional government the fighting-men have the supreme power, and those who possess arms are the citizens.

Of the above-mentioned forms, the perversions are as follows:—of royalty, tryanny; of aristocracy, oligarchy; of constitutional government, democracy. For tyranny is a kind of monarchy which has in view the interest of the monarch only; oligarchy has in view the interest of the wealthy; democracy, of the needy: none of them the common good of all.

DEMOCRACY AND OLIGARCHY

Let us begin by considering the common definitions of oligarchy and democracy, and what is justice oligarchical and democratical. For all men cling to justice of some kind, but their conceptions are imperfect and they do not express the whole idea. For example, justice is thought by them to be, and is, equality, not, however, for all, but only for equals. And inequality is thought to be, and is, justice; neither is this for all, but only for unequals. When the persons are omitted, then men judge erroneously. The reason is that they are passing judgment on themselves, and most people are bad judges in their own case. And whereas justice implies a relation to persons as well as to things, and a just distribution, as I have already said in the *Ethics,* implies the same ratio between the persons and between the things, they agree about the equality of the things, but dispute about the equality of the persons, chiefly for the reason which I have just given—because they are bad judges in their own affairs; and secondly, because both the parties to the argument are speaking of a limited and partial justice, but imagine themselves to be speaking of absolute justice. For the one party, if they are unequal in one respect, for example wealth, consider themselves to be unequal in all; and the other party, if they are equal in one

respect, for example free birth, consider themselves to be equal in all. But they leave out the capital point. For if men met and associated out of regard to wealth only, their share in the state would be proportioned to their property, and the oligarchical doctrine would then seem to carry the day. It would not be just that he who paid one mina should have the same share of a hundred minae, whether of the principal or of the profits, as he who paid the remaining ninety-nine. But a state exists for the sake of a good life, and not for the sake of life only: if life only were the object, slaves and brute animals might form a state, but they cannot, for they have no share in happiness or in a life of free choice. Nor does a state exist for the sake of alliance and security from injustice, nor yet for the sake of exchange and mutual intercourse; for then the Tyrrhenians and the Carthaginians, and all who have commercial treaties with one another, would be the citizens of one state. True, they have agreements about imports, and engagements that they will do no wrong to one another, and written articles of alliance. But there are no magistracies common to the contracting parties who will enforce their engagements; different states have each their own magistracies. Nor does one state take care that the citizens of the other are such as they ought to be, nor see that those who come under the terms of the treaty do no wrong or wickedness at all, but only that they do no injustice to one another. Whereas, those who care for good government take into consideration virtue and vice in states. Whence it may be further inferred that virtue must be the care of a state which is truly so called, and not merely enjoys the name: for without this end the community becomes a mere alliance which differs only in place from alliances of which the members live apart; and law is only a convention, "a surety to one another of justice," as the sophist Lycophron says, and has no real power to make the citizens good and just.

This is obvious; for suppose distinct places, such as Corinth and Megara, to be brought together so that their walls touched, still they would not be one city, not even if the citizens had the right to intermarry, which is one of the rights peculiarly characteristic of states. Again, if men dwelt at a distance from one another, but not so far off as to have no intercourse, and there were laws among them that they should not wrong each other in their exchanges, neither would this be a state. Let us suppose that one man is a carpenter, another a husbandman, another a shoemaker, and so on, and that their number is ten thousand: nevertheless, if they have nothing in common but exchange, alliance, and the like, that would not constitute a state. Why is this? Surely not because they are at a distance from one another: for even supposing that such a community were to meet in one place, but that each man had a house of his own, which was in a manner his state, and that they made alliance with one another, but only against evil-doers; still an accurate thinker would not deem this to be a state, if their intercourse with one another was of the same character after as before their union. It is clear then that a state is not a mere society, having a common place, established for the prevention of mutual crime and for the sake of exchange. These are conditions without which a state cannot exist; but all of them together do not constitute a state, which is a community of families and aggregations of families in well-being, for the sake of a perfect and self-suffcing life. Such a community can only be established among those who live in the same place and intermarry. Hence arise in cities family connexions, brotherhoods, common sacrifices, amusements which draw men together. But these are created by friendship, for the will to live together is friendship. The end of the state is the good life, and these are the means towards it. And the state is the union of families and villages in a perfect and self-suffcing life, by which we mean a happy and honourable life.

Our conclusion, then, is that political society exists for the sake of noble actions, and not of mere companionship. Hence they who contribute most to such a society have a greater share in it than those who have the same or a greater freedom or nobility of birth but are inferior to them in political virtue; or than those who exceed them in wealth but are surpassed by them in virtue.

From what has been said it will be clearly seen that all the partisans of different forms of government speak of a part of justice only.

There is also a doubt as to what is to be the supreme power in the state:—Is it the multitude? Or the wealthy? Or the good? Or the one best man? Or a tyrant? Any of these alternatives seems to involve disagreeable consequences. If the poor, for example, because they are more in number, divide among themselves the property of the rich—is not this unjust? No, by heaven (will be the reply), for the supreme authority justly willed it. But if this is not injustice, pray what is? Again, when in the first division all has been taken, and the majority divide anew the property of the minority, is it not evident, if this goes on, that they will ruin the state? Yet surely, virtue is not the ruin of those who possess her, nor is justice destructive of a state; and therefore this law of confiscation clearly cannot be just. If it were, all the acts of a tyrant must of necessity be just; for he only coerces other men by superior power, just as the multitude coerce the rich. But is it just then that the few and the wealthy should be the rulers? And what if they, in like manner, rob and plunder the people—is this just? If so, the other case will likewise be just. But there can be no doubt that all these things are wrong and unjust.

Then ought the good to rule and have supreme power? But in that case everybody else, being excluded from power, will be dishonoured. For the offices of a state are posts of honour; and if one set of men always hold them, the rest must be deprived of them. Then will it be well that the one best man should rule? Nay, that is still more oligarchical, for the number of those who are dishonoured is thereby increased. Some one may say that it is bad in any case for a man, subject as he is to all the accidents of human passion, to have the supreme power, rather than the law. But what if the law itself be democratical or oligarchical, how will that help us out of our difficulties? Not at all; the same consequences will follow.

Most of these questions may be reserved for another occasion. The principle that the multitude ought to be supreme rather than the few best is one that is maintained, and, though not free from difficulty, yet seems to contain an element of truth. For the many, of whom each individual is but an ordinary person, when they meet together may very likely be better than the few good, if regarded not individually but collectively, just as a feast to which many contribute is better than a dinner provided out of a single purse. For each individual among the many has a share of virtue and prudence, and when they meet together, they become in a manner one man, who has many feet, and hands, and senses; that is a figure of their mind and disposition. Hence the many are better judges than a single man of music and poetry; for some understand one part, and some another, and among them they understand the whole. There is a similar combination of qualities in good men, who differ from any individual of the many, as the beautiful are said to differ from those who are not beautiful, and works of art from realities, because in them the scattered elements are combined, although, if taken separately, the eye of one person or some other feature in another person would be fairer than in the picture. Whether this principle can apply to every democracy, and to all bodies of men, is not clear. Or rather, by heaven, in some cases it is impossible of application; for the argument would equally hold about brutes; and wherein, it will be asked, do some men differ from brutes? But there may be bodies of men about whom our statement is nevertheless true. And if so, the difficulty which has been already raised, and also another which is akin to it—viz. what power should be assigned to the mass of freemen and citizens, who are not rich and have no personal merit—are both solved. There is still a danger in allowing them to share the great offices of state, for their folly will lead them into error, and their dishonesty into crime. But there is a danger also in not letting them share, for a state in which many poor men are excluded from office will necessarily be full of enemies. The only way of escape is to assign to them some deliberative and judicial functions. For this reason Solon and certain other legislators give them the power of electing to offices, and of calling the magistrates to account, but they do not allow them to hold office singly. When they meet together their perceptions are quite good enough, and combined with the better class they are useful to the state (just as impure

food when mixed with what is pure sometimes makes the entire mass more wholesome than a small quantity of the pure would be), but each individual, left to himself, forms an imperfect judgment. On the other hand, the popular form of government involves certain difficulties. In the first place, it might be objected that he who can judge of the healing of a sick man would be one who could himself heal his disease, and make him whole—that is, in other words, the physician; and so in all professions and arts. As, then, the physician ought to be called to account by physicians, so ought men in general to be called to account by their peers. But physicians are of three kinds:—there is the ordinary practitioner, and there is the physician of the higher class, and thirdly the intelligent man who has studied the art: in all arts there is such a class; and we attribute the power of judging to them quite as much as to professors of the art. Secondly, does not the same principle apply to elections? For a right election can only be made by those who have knowledge; those who know geometry, for example, will choose a geometrician rightly, and those who know how to steer, a pilot; and, even if there be some occupations and arts in which private persons share in the ability to choose, they certainly cannot choose better than those who know. So that, according to this argument, neither the election of magistrates, nor the calling of them to account, should be entrusted to the many. Yet possibly these objections are to a great extent met by our old answer, that if the people are not utterly degraded, although individually they may be worse judges than those who have special knowledge—as a body they are as good or better. Moreover, there are some arts whose products are not judged of solely, or best, by the artists themselves, namely those arts whose products are recognized even by those who do not possess the art; for example, the knowledge of the house is not limited to the builder only; the user, or, in other words, the master, of the house will be even a better judge than the builder, just as the pilot will judge better of a rudder than the carpenter, and the guest will judge better of a feast than the cook.

This difficulty seems now to be sufficiently answered, but there is another akin to it. That inferior persons should have authority in greater matters than the good would appear to be a strange thing, yet the election and calling to account of the magistrates is the greatest of all. And these, as I was saying, are functions which in some states are assigned to the people, for the assembly is supreme in all such matters. Yet persons of any age, and having but a small property qualification, sit in the assembly and deliberate and judge, although for the great officers of state, such as treasurers and generals, a high qualification is required. This difficulty may be solved in the same manner as the preceding, and the present practice of democracies may be really defensible. For the power does not reside in the dicast, or senator, or ecclesiast, but in the court, and the senate, and the assembly, of which individual senators, or ecclesiasts, or dicasts, are only parts or members. And for this reason the many may claim to have a higher authority than the few; for the people, and the senate, and the courts consist of many persons, and their property collectively is greater than the property of one or of a few individuals holding great offices. But enough of this.

The discussion of the first question shows nothing so clearly as that laws, when good, should be supreme; and that the magistrate or magistrates should regulate those matters only on which the laws are unable to speak with precision owing to the difficulty of any general principle embracing all particulars. But what are good laws has not yet been clearly explained; the old difficulty remains. The goodness or badness, justice or injustice, of laws varies of necessity with the constitutions of states. This, however, is clear, that the laws must be adapted to the constitutions. But if so, true forms of government will of necessity have just laws, and perverted forms of government will have unjust laws.

MONARCHY

If, however, there be some one person, or more than one, although not enough to make up the full complement of a state, whose virtue is so preeminent that the virtues or the political capacity of all the rest admit of no comparison with his or theirs, he or they can be no longer regarded as part of a state;

for justice will not be done to the superior, if he is reckoned only as the equal of those who are so far inferior to him in virtue and in political capacity. Such an one may truly be deemed a God among men. Hence we see that legislation is necessarily concerned only with those who are equal in birth and in capacity; and that for men of preeminent virtue there is no law—they are themselves a law. Any one would be ridiculous who attempted to make laws for them: they would probably retort what, in the fable of Antisthenes, the lions said to the hares, when in the council of the beasts the latter began haranguing and claiming equality for all. And for this reason democratic states have instituted ostracism; equality is above all things their aim, and therefore they ostracized and banished from the city for a time those who seemed to predominate too much through their wealth, or the number of their friends, or through any other political influence. Mythology tells us that the Argonauts left Heracles behind for a similar reason; the ship Argo would not take him because she feared that he would have been too much for the rest of the crew. Wherefore those who denounce tryanny and blame the counsel which Periander gave to Thrasybulus cannot be held altogether just in their censure. The story is that Periander, when the herald was sent to ask counsel of him, said nothing, but only cut off the tallest ears of corn till he had brought the field to a level. The herald did not know the meaning of the action, but came and reported what he had seen to Thrasybulus, who understood that he was to cut off the principal men in the state; and this is a policy not only expedient for tyrants or in practice confined to them, but equally necessary in oligarchies and democracies. Ostracism is a measure of the same kind, which acts by disabling and banishing the most prominent citizens. Great powers do the same to whole cities and nations, as the Athenians did to the Samians, Chians, and Lesbians; no sooner had they obtained a firm grasp of the empire, than they humbled their allies contrary to treaty; and the Persian king has repeatedly crushed the Medes, Babylonians, and other nations, when their spirit has been stirred by the recollection of their former greatness.

The problem is a universal one, and equally concerns all forms of government, true as well as false; for, although perverted forms with a view to their own interests may adopt this policy, those which seek the common interest do so likewise. The same thing may be observed in the arts and sciences; for the painter will not allow the figure to have a foot which, however beautiful, is not in proportion, nor will the shipbuilder allow the stern or any other part of the vessel to be unduly large, any more than the chorus-master will allow any one who sings louder or better than all the rest to sing in the choir. Monarchs, too, may practise compulsion and still live in harmony with their cities, if their own government is for the interest of the state. Hence where there is an acknowledged superiority the argument in favor of ostracism is based upon a kind of political justice. It would certainly be better that the legislator should from the first so order his state as to have no need of such a remedy. But if the need arises, the next best thing is that he should endeavour to correct the evil by this or some similar measure. The principle, however, has not been fairly applied in states; for, instead of looking to the good of their own constitution, they have used ostracism for factious purposes. It is true that under perverted forms of government, and from their special point of view, such a measure is just and expedient, but it is also clear that it is not absolutely just. In the perfect state there would be great doubts about the use of it, not when applied to excess in strength, wealth, popularity, or the like, but when used against some one who is preeminent in virtue—what is to be done with him? Mankind will not say that such an one is to be expelled and exiled; on the other hand, he ought not to be a subject—that would be as if mankind should claim to rule over Zeus, dividing his offices among them. The only alternative is that all should joyfully obey such a ruler, according to what seems to be the order of nature, and that men like him should be kings in their state for life.

LIBERTY AND EQUALITY

The basis of a democratic state is liberty; which, according to the common opinion of men, can only be enjoyed in such a state;—this they affirm to be the great end of every democracy. One principle of liberty is for all to rule and be ruled in turn, and indeed democratic justice is the application of numerical not proportionate equality; whence it follows that the majority must be supreme, and that whatever the majority approve must be the end and the just. Every citizen, it is said, must have equality, and therefore in a democracy the poor have more power than the rich, because there are more of them, and the will of the majority is supreme. This, then, is one note of liberty which all democrats affirm to be the principle of their state. Another is that a man should live as he likes. This, they say, is the privilege of a freeman, since, on the other hand, not to live as a man likes is the mark of a slave. This is the second characteristic of democracy, whence has arisen the claim of men to be ruled by none, if possible, or, if this is impossible, to rule and be ruled in turns; and so it contributes to the freedom based upon equality.

Such being our foundation and such the principle from which we start, the characteristics of democracy are as follows:—the election of officers by all out of all; and that all should rule over each, and each in his turn over all; that the appointment to all offices, or to all but those which require experience and skill, should be made by lot; that no property qualification should be required for offices, or only a very low one; that a man should not hold the same office twice, or not often, or in the case of few except military offices: that the tenure of all offices, or of as many as possible, should be brief; that all men should sit in judgment, or that judges selected out of all should judge, in all matters, or in most and in the greatest and most important—such as the scrutiny of accounts, the constitution, and private contracts; that the assembly should be supreme over all causes, or at any rate over the most important, and the magistrates over none or only over a very few. Of all magistracies, a council is the most democratic when there is not the means of paying all the citizens, but when they are paid even this is robbed of its power; for the people then draw all cases to themselves, as I said in the previous discussion. The next characteristic of democracy is payment for services; assembly, law-courts, magistrates, everybody receives pay, when it is to be had; or when it is not to be had for all, then it is given to the law-courts and to the stated assemblies, to the council and to the magistrates, or at least to any of them who are compelled to have their meals together. And whereas oligarchy is characterized by birth, wealth, and education, the notes of democracy appear to be the opposite of these—low birth, poverty, mean employment. Another note is that no magistracy is perpetual, but if any such have survived some ancient change in the constitution it should be stripped of its power, and the holders should be elected by lot and no longer by vote. These are the points common to all democracies; but democracy and demos in their truest form are based upon the recognized principle of democratic justice, that all should count equally; for equality implies that the poor should have no more share in the government than the rich, and should not be the only rulers, but that all should rule equally according to their numbers. And in this way men think that they will secure equality and freedom in their state.

Next comes the question, how is this equality to be obtained? Are we to assign to a thousand poor men the property qualifications of five hundred rich men? and shall we give the thousand a power equal to that of the five hundred? or, if this is not to be the mode, ought we, still retaining the same ratio, to take equal numbers from each and give them the control of the elections and of the courts?—Which, according to the democratical notion, is the juster form of the constitution—this or one based on numbers only? Democrats say that justice is that to which the majority agree, oligarchs that to which the wealthier class; in their opinion the decision should be given according to the amount of property. In both principles there is some inequality and injustice. For if justice is the will of the few, any one person who has more wealth than all the rest of the rich put together, ought, upon the oligarchical principle, to have the sole power—but this would be tyranny; or if justice is the will of the majority, as I was before saying, they will unjustly confiscate the property of the wealthy minority. To find a principle of equality in which they both agree we must inquire into their respective ideas of justice.

Now they agree in saying that whatever is decided by the majority of the citizens is to be deemed law. Granted:—but not without some reserve; since there are two classes out of which a state is composed—the poor and the rich—that is to be deemed law, on which both or the greater part of both agree; and if they disagree, that which is approved by the greater number, and by those who have the higher qualification. For example, suppose that there are ten rich and twenty poor, and some measure is approved by six of the rich and is disapproved by fifteen of the poor, and the remaining four of the rich join with the party of the poor, and the remaining five of the poor with that of the rich; in such a case the will of those whose qualifications, when both sides are added up, are the greatest, should prevail. If they turn out to be equal, there is no greater difficulty than at present, when, if the assembly or the courts are divided, recourse is had to the lot, or to some similar expedient. But, although it may be difficult in theory to know what is just and equal, the practical difficulty of inducing those to forbear who can, if they like, encroach, is far greater, for the weaker are always asking for equality and justice, but the stronger care for none of these things.

THE RULE OF LAW

At this place in the discussion there impends the inquiry respecting the king who acts solely according to his own will; he has now to be considered. The so-called limited monarchy, or kingship according to law, as I have already remarked, is not a distinct form of government, for under all governments, as, for example, in a democracy or aristocracy, there may be a general holding office for life, and one person is often made supreme over the administration of a state. A magistracy of this kind exists at Epidamnus, and also at Opus, but in the latter city has a more limited power. Now, absolute monarchy, or the arbitrary rule of a sovereign over all the citizens, in a city which consists of equals, is thought by some to be quite contrary to nature; it is argued that those who are by nature equals must have the same natural right and worth, and that for unequals to have an equal share, or for equals to have an uneven share, in the offices of state, is as bad as for different bodily constitutions to have the same food and clothing. Wherefore it is thought to be just that among equals every one be ruled as well as rule, and therefore that all should have their turn. We thus arrive at law; for an order of succession implies law. And the rule of the law, it is argued, is preferable to that of any individual. On the same principle, even if it be better for certain individuals to govern, they should be made only guardians and ministers of the law. For magistrates there must be—this is admitted; but then men say that to give authority to any one man when all are equal is unjust. Nay, there may indeed be cases which the law seems unable to determine, but in such cases can a man? Nay, it will be replied, the law trains officers for this express purpose, and appoints them to determine matters which are left undecided by it, to the best of their judgment. Further, it permits them to make any amendment of the existing laws which experience suggests. Therefore he who bids the law rule may be deemed to bid God and Reason alone rule, but he who bids man rule adds an element of the beast; for desire is a wild beast, and passion perverts the minds of rulers, even when they are the best of men. The law is reason unaffected by desire. We are told that a patient should call in a physician; he will not get better if he is doctored out of a book. But the parallel of the arts is clearly not in point; for the physician does nothing contrary to rule from motives of friendship; he only cures a patient and takes a fee; whereas magistrates do many things from spite and partiality. And, indeed, if a man suspected the physician of being in league with his enemies to destroy him for a bribe, he would rather have recourse to the book. But certainly physicians, when they are sick, call in other physicians, and training-masters, when they are in training, other training-masters, as if they could not judge truly about their own case and might be influenced by their feelings. Hence it is evident that in seeking for justice men seek for the mean or neutral, for the law is the mean. Again, customary laws have more weight, and relate to more important matters, than written laws, and a man may be a safer ruler than the written law, but not safer than the customary law.

Again, it is by no means easy for one man to superintend many things; he will have to appoint a number of subordinates, and what difference does it make whether these subordinates always existed or were appointed by him because he needed them? If, as I said before, the good man has a right to rule because he is better, still two good men are better than one: this is the old saying—

two going together,

and the prayer of Agamemnon—

would that I had ten such counsellors!

And at this day there are magistrates, for example judges, who have authority to decide some matters which the law is unable to determine, since no one doubts that the law would command and decide in the best manner whatever it could. But some things can, and other things cannot, be comprehended under the law, and this is the origin of the vexed question whether the best law or the best man should rule. For matters of detail about which men deliberate cannot be included in legislation. Nor does any one deny that the decision of such matters must be left to man, but it is argued that there should be many judges, and not one only. For every ruler who has been trained by the law judges well; and it would surely seem strange that a person should see better with two eyes, or hear better with two ears, or act better with two hands or feet, than many with many; indeed, it is already the practice of kings to make to themselves many eyes and ears and hands and feet. For they make colleagues of those who are the friends of themselves and their governments. They must be friends of the monarch and of his government; if not his friends, they will not do what he wants; but friendship implies likeness and equality; and, therefore, if he thinks that his friends ought to rule, he must think that those who are equal to himself and like himself ought to rule equally with himself. These are the principal controversies relating to monarchy.

CONSTITUTIONAL GOVERNMENT

Polity or constitutional government may be described generally as a fusion of oligarchy and democracy; but the term is usually applied to those forms of government which incline towards democracy, and the term aristocracy to those which incline towards oligarchy, because birth and education are commonly the accompaniments of wealth. Moreover, the rich already possess the external advantages the want of which is a temptation to crime, and hence they are called noblemen and gentlemen. And inasmuch as aristocracy seeks to give predominance to the best of the citizens, people say also of oligarchies that they are composed of noblemen and gentlemen. Now it appears to be an impossible thing that the state which is governed not by the best citizens but by the worst should be well-governed, and equally impossible that the state which is ill-governed should be governed by the best. But we must remember that good laws, if they are not obeyed, do not constitute good government. Hence there are two parts of good government; one is the actual obedience of citizens to the laws, the other part is the goodness of the laws which they obey; they may obey bad laws as well as good. And there may be a further subdivision; they may obey either the best laws which are attainable to them, or the best absolutely.

The distribution of offices according to merit is a special characteristic of aristocracy, for the principle of an aristocracy is virtue, as wealth is of an oligarchy, and freedom of a democracy. In all of them there of course exists the right of the majority, and whatever seems good to the majority of those who share in the government has authority. Now in most states the form called polity exists, for the fusion goes no further than the attempt to unite the freedom of the poor and the wealth of the rich, who commonly take the place of the noble. But as there are three grounds on which men claim an equal share in the government, freedom, wealth, and virtue (for the fourth or good birth is the result of the two last, being only ancient wealth and virtue), it is clear that the admixture of the two elements, that is to say, of the rich and poor, is to be called a polity or constitutional government; and the union of the three is to be called aristocracy or the government of the best, and more than any other form of government, except the true and ideal, has a right to this name.

Thus far I have shown the existence of forms of states other than monarchy, democracy, and oligarchy, and what they are, and in what aristocracies differ from one another, and polities from aristocracies—that the two latter are not very unlike is obvious.

Next we have to consider how by the side of oligarchy and democracy the so-called polity or constitutional government springs up, and how it should be organized. The nature of it will be at once understood from a comparison of oligarchy and democracy; we must ascertain their different characteristics, and taking a portion from each, put the two together, like the parts of an indenture. Now there are three modes in which fusions of government may be affected. In the first mode we must combine the laws made by both governments, say concerning the administration of justice. In oligarchies they impose a fine on the rich if they do not serve as judges, and to the poor they give no pay; but in democracies they give pay to the poor and do not fine the rich. Now (1) the union of these two modes is a common or middle term between them, and is therefore characteristic of a constitutional government, for it is a combination of both. This is one mode of uniting the two elements. Or (2) a mean may be taken between the enactments of the two: thus democracies require no property qualification, or only a small one, from members of the assembly, oligarchies a high one; here neither of these is the common term, but a mean between them. (3) There is a third mode, in which something is borrowed from the oligarchical and something from the democratical principle. For example, the appointment of magistrates by lot is thought to be democratical, and the election of them oligarchical; democratical again when there is no property qualification, oligarchical when there is. In the aristocratical or constitutional state, one element will be taken from each—from oligarchy the principle of electing to offices, from democracy the disregard of qualification. Such are the various modes of combination.

There is a true union of oligarchy and democracy when the same state may be termed either a democracy or an oligarchy; those who use both names evidently feel that the fusion is complete. Such a fusion there is also in the mean; for both extremes appear in it. The Lacedaemonian constitution, for example, is often described as a democracy, because it has many democratical features. In the first place the youth receive a democratical education. For the sons of the poor are brought up with the sons of the rich, who are educated in such a manner as to make it possible for the sons of the poor to be educated like them. A similar equality prevails in the following period of life, and when the citizens are grown up to manhood the same rule is observed; there is no distinction between the rich and poor. In like manner they all have the same food at their public tables, and the rich wear only such clothing as any poor man can afford. Again, the people elect to one of the two greatest offices of state, and in the other they share; for they elect the Senators and share in the Ephoralty. By others the Spartan constitution is said to be an oligarchy, because it has many oligarchical elements. That all offices are filled by election and none by lot, is one of these oligarchical characteristics; that the power of inflicting death or banishment rests with a few persons is another; and there are others. In a well attempered polity there should appear to be both elements and yet neither; also the government should rely on itself, and not on foreign aid, and on itself not through the good will of a majority—they might be equally well-disposed when there is a vicious form of government—but through the general willingness of all classes in the state to maintain the constitution.

Enough of the manner in which a constitutional government, and in which the so-called aristocracies ought to be framed.

THE BEST STATE

In all arts and sciences which embrace the whole of any subject, and do not come into being in a fragmentary way, it is the province of a single art or science to consider all that appertains to a single subject. For example, the art of gymnastic considers not only the suitableness of different modes of training to different bodies (2) but what sort is absolutely the best (1); (for the absolutely best must suit that which is by nature best and best furnished with the means

of life), and also what common form of training is adapted to the great majority of men (4). And if a man does not desire the best habit of body, or the greatest skill in gymnastics, which might be attained by him, still the trainer or the teacher of gymnastic should be able to impart any lower degree of either (3). The same principle equally holds in medicine and ship-building, and the making of clothes, and in the arts generally.

Hence it is obvious that government too is the subject of a single science, which has to consider what government is best and of what sort it must be, to be most in accordance with our aspirations, if there were no external impediment, and also what kind of government is adapted to particular states. For the best is often unattainable, and therefore the true legislator and statesman ought to be acquainted, not only with (1) that which is best in the abstract, but also with (2) that which is best relatively to circumstances. We should be able further to say how a state may be constituted under any given conditions (3); both how it is originally formed and, when formed, how it may be longest preserved; the supposed state being so far from having the best constitution that it is unprovided even with the conditions necessary for the best; neither is it the best under the circumstances, but of an inferior type.

He ought, moreover, to know (4) the form of government which is best suited to states in general; for political writers, although they have excellent ideas, are often unpractical. We should consider, not only what form of government is best, but also what is possible and what is easily attainable by all. There are some who would have none but the most perfect; for this many natural advantages are required. Others, again, speak of a more attainable form, and, although they reject the constitution under which they are living, they extol some one in particular, for example the Lacedaemonian. Any change of government which has to be introduced should be one which men, starting from their existing constitutions, will be both willing and able to adopt, since there is quite as much trouble in the reformation of an old constitution as in the establishment of a new one, just as to unlearn is as hard as to learn. And therefore, in addition to the qualifications of the statesman already mentioned, he should be able to find remedies for the defects of existing constitutions, as has been said before. This he cannot do unless he knows how many forms of government there are. It is often supposed that there is only one kind of democracy and one of oligarchy. But this is a mistake; and, in order to avoid such mistakes, we must ascertain what differences there are in the constitutions of states, and in how many ways they are combined. The same political insight will enable a man to know which laws are the best, and which are suited to different constitutions; for the laws are, and ought to be, relative to the constitution, and not the constitution to the laws. A constitution is the organization of offices in a state, and determines what is to be the governing body, and what is the end of each community. But laws are not to be confounded with the principles of the constitution; they are the rules according to which the magistrates should administer the state, and proceed against offenders. So that we must know the varieties, and the number of varieties, of each form of government, if only with a view to making laws. For the same laws cannot be equally suited to all oligarchies or to all democracies, since there is certainly more than one form both of democracy and of oligarchy.

POLITICAL MODERATION
AND STABILITY:
THE MIDDLE CLASSES

We have now to inquire what is the best constitution for most states, and the best life for most men, neither assuming a standard of virtue which is above ordinary persons, nor an education which is exceptionally favoured by nature and circumstances, nor yet an ideal state which is an aspiration only, but having regard to the life in which the majority are able to share, and to the form of government which states in general can attain. As to those aristocracies, as they are called, of which we were just now speaking, they either lie beyond the possibilities of the greater number of states, or they approximate to the so-called constitutional government, and therefore need no separate discussion. And in fact the conclusion at which we arrive respecting all these forms

rests upon the same grounds. For if what was said in the *Ethics* is true, that the happy life is the life according to virtue lived without impediment, and that virtue is a mean, then the life which is in a mean, and in a mean attainable by every one, must be the best. And the same principles of virtue and vice are characteristic of cities and of constitutions; for the constitution is in a figure the life of the city.

Now in all states there are three elements: one class is very rich, another very poor, and a third in a mean. It is admitted that moderation and the mean are best, and therefore it will clearly be best to possess the gifts of fortune in moderation; for in that condition of life men are most ready to follow rational principle. But he who greatly excels in beauty, strength, birth, or wealth, or on the other hand who is very poor, or very weak, or very much disgraced, finds it difficult to follow rational principle. Of these two the one sort grow into violent and great criminals, the others into rogues and petty rascals. And two sorts of offences correspond to them, the one committed from violence, the other from roguery. Again, the middle class is least likely to shrink from rule, or to be overambitious for it; both of which are injuries to the state. Again, those who have too much of the goods of fortune, strength, wealth, friends, and the like, are neither willing nor able to submit to authority. The evil begins at home; for when they are boys, by reason of the luxury in which they are brought up, they never learn, even at school, the habit of obedience. On the other hand, the very poor, who are in the opposite extreme, are too degraded. So that the one class cannot obey, and can only rule despotically; the other knows not how to command and must be ruled like slaves. Thus arises a city, not of freemen, but of masters and slaves, the one despising, the other envying; and nothing can be more fatal to friendship and good fellowship in states than this: for good fellowship springs from friendship; when men are at enmity with one another, they would rather not even share the same path. But a city ought to be composed, as far as possible, of equals and similars; and these are generally the middle classes. Wherefore the city which is composed of middle-class citizens is necessarily best constituted in respect of the elements of which we say the fabric of the state naturally consists. And this is the class of citizens which is most secure in a state, for they do not, like the poor, covet their neighbours' goods; nor do others covet theirs, as the poor covet the goods of the rich; and as they neither plot against others, nor are themselves plotted against, they pass through life safely. Wisely then did Phocylides pray—"Many things are best in the mean; I desire to be of a middle condition in my city."

Thus it is manifest that the best political community is formed by citizens of the middle class, and that those states are likely to be well-administered, in which the middle class is large, and stronger if possible than both the other classes, or at any rate than either singly; for the addition of the middle class turns the scale, and prevents either of the extremes from being dominant. Great then is the good fortune of a state in which the citizens have a moderate and sufficient property; for where some possess much, and the others nothing, there may arise an extreme democracy, or a pure oligarchy; or a tyranny may grow out of either extreme— either out of the most rampant democracy, or out of an oligarchy; but it is not so likely to arise out of the middle constitutions and those akin to them. I will explain the reason of this hereafter, when I speak of the revolutions of states. The mean condition of states is clearly best, for no other is free from faction; and where the middle class is large, there are least likely to be factions and dissensions. For a similar reason large states are less liable to faction than small ones, because in them the middle class is large; whereas in small states it is easy to divide all the citizens into two classes who are either rich or poor, and to leave nothing in the middle. And democracies are safer and more permanent than oligarchies, because they have a middle class which is more numerous and has a greater share in the government; for when there is no middle class, and the poor greatly exceed in number, troubles arise, and the state soon comes to an end. A proof of the superiority of the middle class is that the best legislators have been of a middle condition; for example, Solon, as his own verses testify; and Lycurgus, for he was not a king; and Charondas, and almost all legislators.

These considerations will help us to understand why most governments are either democratical or oligarchical. The reason is that the middle class is seldom numerous in them, and whichever party, whether the rich or the common people, transgresses the mean and predominates, draws the constitution its own way, and thus arises either oligarchy or democracy. There is another reason—the poor and the rich quarrel with one another, and whichever side gets the better, instead of establishing a just or popular government, regards political supremacy as the prize of victory, and the one party sets up a democracy and the other an oligarchy. Further, both the parties which had the supremacy in Hellas looked only to the interest of their own form of government and established in states, the one, democracies, and the other, oligarchies; they thought of their own advantage, of the public not at all. For these reasons the middle form of government has rarely, if ever, existed, and among a very few only. One man alone of all who ever ruled in Hellas was induced to give this middle constitution to states. But it has now become a habit among the citizens of states, not even to care about equality; all men are seeking for dominion, or, if conquered, are willing to submit.

What then is the best form of government and what makes it the best, is evident; and of other constitutions, since we say that there are many kinds of democracy and many of oligarchy, it is not difficult to see which has the first and which the second or any other place in the order of excellence, now that we have determined which is the best. For that which is nearest to the best must of necessity be better, and that which is furthest from it worse, if we are judging absolutely and not relatively to given conditions: I say "relatively to given conditions," since a particular government may be preferable, but another form may be better for some people.

CAUSES OF REVOLUTION

In considering how dissensions and political revolutions arise, we must first of all ascertain the beginnings and causes of them which affect constitutions generally. They may be said to be three in number; and we have now to given an outline of each.

We want to know (1) what is the feeling? (2) what are the motives of those who make them? (3) whence arise political disturbances and quarrels? The universal and chief cause of this revolutionary feeling has been already mentioned; viz. the desire of equality, when men think that they are equal to others who have more than themselves; or, again, the desire of inequality and superiority, when conceiving themselves to be superior they think that they have not more but the same or less than their inferiors; pretensions which may and may not be just. Inferiors revolt in order that they may be equal, and equals that they may be superior. Such is the state of mind which creates revolutions. The motives for making them are the desire of gain and honour, or the fear of dishonour and loss; the authors of them want to divert punishment or dishonour from themselves or their friends. The causes and reasons of revolutions, whereby men are themselves affected in the way described, and about the things which I have mentioned, viewed in one way may be regarded as seven, and in another as more than seven. Two of them have been already noticed; but they act in a different manner, for men are excited against one another by the love of gain and honour—not, as in the case which I have just supposed, in order to obtain them for themselves, but at seeing others, justly or unjustly, engrossing them. Other causes are insolence, fear, excessive predominance, contempt, disproportionate increase in some part of the state; causes of another sort are election intrigues, carelessness, neglect about trifles, dissimilarity of elements.

HOW TO PREVENT REVOLUTION

We have next to consider what means there are of preserving constitutions in general, and in particular cases. In the first place it is evident that if we know the causes which destroy constitutions, we also know the causes which preserve them; for opposites produce opposites, and destruction is the opposite of preservation.

In all well-attempered governments there is nothing which should be more jealously maintained than the spirit of obedience to law, more especially in small matters; for transgression creeps in unperceived and at last ruins the state, just as the constant recurrence of small expenses in time eats up a fortune. The expense does not take place all at once, and therefore is not observed; the mind is deceived, as in the fallacy which says that "if each part is little, then the whole is little." And this is true in one way, but not in another, for the whole and the all are not little, although they are made up of littles.

In the first place, then, men should guard against the beginnings of change, and in the second place they should not rely upon the political devices of which I have already spoken invented only to deceive the people, for they are proved by experience to be useless. Further, we note that oligarchies as well as aristocracies may last not from any inherent stability in such forms of government, but because the rulers are on good terms both with the unenfranchised and with the governing classes, not maltreating any who are excluded from the government, but introducing into it the leading spirits among them. They should never wrong the ambitious in a matter of honour, or the common people in a matter of money; and they should treat one another and their fellow-citizens in a spirit of equality. The equality which the friends of democracy seek to establish for the multitude is not only just but likewise expedient among equals. Hence, if the governing class are numerous, many democratic institutions are useful; for example, the restriction of the tenure of offices to six months, that all those who are of equal rank may share in them. Indeed, equals or peers when they are numerous become a kind of democracy, and therefore demagogues are very likely to arise among them, as I have already remarked. The short tenure of office prevents oligarchies and aristocracies from falling into the hands of families, it is not easy for a person to do any great harm when his tenure of office is short, whereas long possession begets tyranny in oligarchies and democracies. For the aspirants to tyranny are either the principal men of the state, who in democracies are demagogues and in oligarchies members of ruling houses, or those who hold great offices, and have a long tenure of them.

Constitutions are preserved when their destroyers are at a distance, and sometimes also because they are near, for the fear of them makes the government keep in hand the constitution. Wherefore the ruler who has a care of the constitution should invent terrors, and bring distant dangers near, in order that the citizens may be on their guard, and, like sentinels in a night-watch, never relax their attention. He should endeavour too by help of the laws to control the contentions and quarrels of the notables, and to prevent those who have not hitherto taken part in them from catching the spirit of contention. No ordinary man can discern the beginning of evil, but only the true statesman.

As to the change produced in oligarchies and constitutional governments by the alteration of the qualification, when this arises, not out of any variation in the qualification but only out of the increase of money, it is well to compare the general valuation of property with that of past years, annually in those cities in which the census is taken annually, and in larger cities every third or fifth year. If the whole is many times greater or many times less than when the ratings recognized by the constitution were fixed, there should be power given by law to raise or lower the qualification as the amount is greater or less. Where this is not done a constitutional government passes into an oligarchy, and an oligarchy is narrowed to a rule of families; or in the opposite case constitutional government becomes democracy, and oligarchy either constitutional government or democracy.

It is a principle common to democracy, oligarchy, and every other form of government not to allow the disproportionate increase of any citizen, but to give moderate honour for a long time rather than great honour for a short time. For men are easily spoilt; not every one can bear prosperity. But if this rule is not observed, at any rate the honours which are given all at once should be taken away by degrees and not all at once. Especially should the laws provide against any one having too much power, whether derived from friends or money; if he has, he should be sent clean out of the country. And since innovations creep in through the private life of individuals also, there ought to be a magistracy which will have an eye to those whose life is not in harmony with the government, whether oligarchy or democracy or any other. And for

a like reason an increase of prosperity in any part of the state should be carefully watched. The proper remedy for this evil is always to give the management of affairs and offices of state to opposite elements; such opposites are the virtuous and the many, or the rich and the poor. Another way is to combine the poor and the rich in one body, or to increase the middle class: thus an end will be put to the revolutions which arise from inequality.

But above all every state should be so administered and so regulated by law that its magistrates cannot possibly make money. In oligarchies special precautions should be used against this evil. For the people do not take any great offence at being kept out of the government—indeed they are rather pleased than otherwise at having leisure for their private business—but what irritates them is to think that their rulers are stealing the public money; then they are doubly annoyed; for they lose both honour and profit. If office brought no profit, then and then only could democracy and aristocracy be combined; for both notables and people might have their wishes gratified. All would be able to hold office, which is the aim of democracy, and the notables would be magistrates, which is the aim of aristocracy. And this result may be accomplished when there is no possibility of making money out of the offices; for the poor will not want to have them when there is nothing to be gained from them—they would rather be attending to their own concerns; and the rich, who do not want money from the public treasury, will be able to take them; and so the poor will keep to their work and grow rich, and the notables will not he governed by the lower class. In order to avoid peculation of the public money, the transfer of the revenue should be made at a general assembly of the citizens, and duplicates of the accounts deposited with the different brotherhoods, companies, and tribes. And honours should be given by law to magistrates who have the reputation of being incorruptible. In democracies the rich should be spared; not only should their property not be divided, but their incomes also, which in some states are taken from them imperceptibly, should be protected. It is a good thing to prevent the wealthy citizens, even if they are willing, from undertaking expensive and useless public services, such as the giving of choruses, torch-races, and the like. In an oligarchy, on the other hand, great care should be taken of the poor, and lucrative offices should go to them; if any of the wealthy classes insult them, the offender should be punished more severely than if he had wronged one of his own class. Provision should be made that estates pass by inheritance and not by gift, and no person should have more than one inheritance; for in this way properties will be equalized, and more of the poor rise to competency. It is also expedient both in a democracy and in an oligarchy to assign to those who have less share in the government (i.e. to the rich in a democracy and to the poor in an oligarchy) an equality or preference in all but the principal offices of state. The latter should be entrusted chiefly or only to members of the governing class.

CHAPTER THREE

ST. AUGUSTINE

The destruction of Roman power in the fifth century was more than a political revolution. The Germanic conquerors from the North swept away an empire that seemed eternal and universal to its inhabitants, and wiped out a civilization and way of life that seemed imperishable. Yet the military helplessness of Rome was not so much the deeper cause of her fall as a symptom of her general decline and disintegration. Military defeat was the end, and not the beginning, of rot and decay.

Rome's decline can be said to have started in the growing betrayal of its pristine civic virtues and in her abandonment of republicanism in favor of despotic, monarchical imperialism. Amid immense material wealth there had been disturbing signs of failure of nerve and loss of faith; above all, unwillingness or inability to solve the social conflicts born of poverty, slavery, and serfdom had contributed to the weakening of the Roman empire and to its final conquest by barbarians emerging from a cultural nowhere—from the dark forests and endless plains beyond the confines of civilization.

The Gothic, Vandal, and Hun warriors could only destroy: they had no civilization of their own that they could substitute for, or mingle with, that of the Roman world. The recorded history of the west knows of no similar catastrophe, when a way of life was so thoroughly destroyed that men forgot what their ancestors had known for centuries, and had to start all over again groping toward a new existence.

It was a long and painful experience, and the process of gradual recovery from a near-mortal illness, the medieval period, fills the ten centuries between the fall of the Roman empire in the fifth century and the revival of ancient thought and learning in the fifteenth. Interest in this period had not been intense until recently, because it was assumed that nothing could henceforth have stopped the march of progress and scientific development, and that history was an unceasing process of liberty unfolding itself all over the world. This optimism, so typical of the eighteenth and nineteenth centuries, was rudely shaken in the twentieth century by World War II, which might have—had the allied nations been defeated—inaugurated a new dark age. The lesson of the fifth century is that an entire civilization can be razed from the earth, and humanity barbarized and decivilized.

When Rome was sacked by the Visigoths in A.D. 410, a popular explanation was that it was the fault of the Christians. Christianity had been officially tolerated in the Roman empire from A.D. 313, and eighty years later it became the official religion of state, paganism being proscribed and prohibited. Because the fall of Rome in A.D. 410 occurred so soon after the triumph of Christianity, many pagans and perhaps even some

Christians were inclined to see a connection between the rise of Christianity—so long considered officially a subversive movement—and the weakening of Roman power. From the traditional, pagan, upper-class Roman viewpoint, the Christian qualities of otherworldliness, meekness, pacifism, disregard for public affairs, and contempt for revered national deities had been persistently sapping the strength of Rome. Above all, the Christian refusal to recognize loyalty to Rome as the first loyalty, the dogged perseverance in putting a foreign religion above family, community, and state, must have appeared as a flagrant demonstration of "un-Roman" disloyalty.

Political-minded Romans of the old school were not deeply interested in religions as such, and as long as members of any creed were willing to make a formal gesture of obeisance to the ultimate authority of Rome and its personified imperial divinity, there was no cause for discord and conflict. Few empires and civilizations have, in fact, been as free from religious bigotry and persecution as Rome was, partly because of the moderation and political wisdom of its ruling classes and partly because religion was not taken seriously enough to turn men into tormentors and killers. The very polytheism of paganism ensured a basically tolerant attitude, as all pluralistic viewpoints tend to do. When Rome sought to extirpate Christianity by force in the second half of the third century, the charge was not against Christianity as a religion but against its alleged attempt to build up a state within the state, its boring from within every social class, and its gradual absorption of the Roman empire by infiltration and ideological appeals without overt acts of force.

Neither contempt nor ostracism, nor outright persecution, stopped the march of Christianity. In fact, in the fourth and fifth centuries, when Christianity became the religion of state, the roles were reversed, and paganism was put on the defensive and finally outlawed. The victory of Christianity appeared inevitable and providential to the Christian, because it was the only true religion; but to many pagans the effective extirpation of paganism by Christianity proved only that Christianity was more ruthless than its rival in the contest of persecution, and that the Roman emperors had made the mistake of treating the subversive Christians too leniently, wasting generosity on fanatics who would brook no compromise themselves if put in a position of authority.

When Rome was ravaged in 410, a wave of shock and horror swept through the world. For eight centuries Rome had proudly remained inviolate, growing from a small municipality into the center of a vast empire. The ease and speed with which this empire was broken up took everyone by surprise. The pagans, as we have said, ascribed the catastrophe to the betrayal of the old Roman deities under which Rome had risen to the position of the dominant world power, but Christians, too, were perplexed: it was hard to understand how Rome could be so shamed just after Christianity had become the religion of state, and many Christians began to wonder whether the official alliance of church and empire was such an advantage after all. If Rome was not strong enough to safeguard its own existence against heathen tribes, how could it be the source of worldly power that the church needed in spreading Christianity?

Some Christians who were particularly perturbed about what seemed the end of the world were recent converts; and yet, the strongest reaffirmation of Christian idealism was the work of a convert, St. Augustine (A.D. 354–430), a native and lifelong inhabitant of Roman North Africa. St. Augustine's parents were North Africans; his mother was a devout Christian, but his father never embraced the Christian faith. St. Augustine was baptized in Italy in A.D. 387, after many years of active and more than gay living, led in complete contradiction to Christian standards of morals and belief. But once he was baptized, he rose quickly in the hierarchy of the church; he was made Bishop of Hippo (the modern port of Buna, in Algeria) in 395, where he stayed until his death in 430.

St. Augustine was moved especially by the pagan attacks that attributed the fall of Rome to the victory of Christianity. He started the *City of God (De Civitate Dei)* in 413, and finished the voluminous work, consisting of twenty-two books, in 426. He set out to answer two main questions. The first concerns the pagan challenge to Christianity. Although from a purely theological viewpoint the issue of paganism is not so intense and controversial in the twentieth century as it was in the fifth, St. Augustine's critique is always vital and timely, if one substitutes for paganism the qualities with which he identified it: contempt for spiritual values, smugness, pride, and injustice.

The rebuttal of paganism, however, is only the more negative part of the *City of God.* Having demonstrated the hollowness and inconsistency of paganism, materialism, and worldly success, Augustine proceeds to his more constructive task: the vision of the heavenly city, as contrasted with the earthly city *(civitas terrena).* St. Augustine's use of the word *civitas,* however, should not be interpreted in a political sense; St. Augustine was not a constitutional lawyer or political theorist but a theologian. He was interested in God, Faith, and Salvation, and not so much in the organization of the state and its political-juridical relations to the church. His heavenly city, or City of God, is therefore not identical with the church, and the earthly city is not the state.

As a theologian and passionate Christian who took his faith seriously, St. Augustine was primarily concerned with *ways of life* and *not* with *organizations of life.* The great struggle in the universe is, then, not between church and state (as later writers mistakenly interpreted St. Augustine for sectarian purposes), but between two opposing ways of life: in the earthly city, the love of self, the lust of power predominate, whereas in the heavenly city the love of God, "even to the contempt of self," is the foundation of order. St. Augustine therefore divides the human race into two parts, "the one consisting of those who live according to man, the other of those who live according to God. And these we also mystically call the two cities, or the two communities of men, of which the one is predestined to reign eternally with God, and the other to suffer eternal punishment with the devil." St. Augustine himself thus emphasizes that the two communities of the heavenly and earthly cities can be called cities only in a mystical or allegorical sense.

Even more explicitly, St. Augustine often speaks of the heavenly city as the eternal kingdom of God that includes the angels preceding the creation of man and the saintly elect *(communio sanctorum);* by contrast, the earthly city is the "society of the impious" *(societas impiorum),* which includes fallen angels as well as human beings who "live after the flesh." Eternal reign with God is the destiny of the heavenly city, whereas eternal punishment with the devil is the doom awaiting the earthly city.

The basic conflict between Good and Evil rages not only in mankind as a whole but in every individual. Just as Plato had stated that the problem of the just society was that of the just individual "writ large," so St. Augustine notes that the struggle between Good and Evil in the world is closely related to, and a reflection of, the conflicts within the individual human being: "For in each individual there is first of all that which is reprobate, that from which we must begin, but in which we need not necessarily remain; afterwards is that which is well approved, to which we may by advancing attain, and in which, when we have reached it, we may abide." In fact, Plato had anticipated the idea of the complex structure of the individual human soul by viewing it as a composite of the three rivaling elements of appetite, courage, and reason, representing three types of men and three ways of living. Justice, or righteousness, is the central concept in Plato's *Republic:* an individual is just if the elements of his own soul are rightly ordered and arranged, and consequently he will also act justly in his relations with others by staying in his own station, by living the kind of life he was meant to live. St. Augustine transforms this secular conception of justice into a religious one: the essence of *justice* is the *relation between man and God,* from which right relations between man and man will inevitably follow.

If man is to become worthy of entry into the eternal kingdom of heaven, the City of God, there must be some agency on earth, St. Augustine realizes, that leads in the right direction. Although the central meaning of "heavenly city" is a way of life dedicated to the service of God, St. Augustine also uses this term "mystically," that is, symbolically, for the *church.* It is the part of the heavenly city that "sojourns on earth and lives by faith," and it "lives like a captive and stranger in the earthly city." In inspiring words that recall the Stoic message of universal unity and brotherhood, St. Augustine says that the heavenly city, "while it sojourns on earth, calls citizens out of all nations, and gathers together a society of pilgrims in all languages, not scrupling about diversities in the manners, laws, and institutions whereby earthly peace is secured and maintained," and that these diversities of men ought to be preserved, as long as men are united in God's service.

Yet St. Augustine nowhere clearly defines the church; in one place he calls it the Invisible Church of God's Elect (including some as yet to be converted), and in another, the Visible Church, made up of true believers and of those whose Christianity is little more than formal membership in the church. Because he failed to distinguish sharply the Invisible from the Visible Church, he claimed rights for the one that he would not have claimed for the other, particularly in relation to the state. As a result, his arguments were used later by adherents of papalist doctrines as well as by those who affirmed the sovereignty of mundane rulers over the church.

Just as the heavenly city symbolically represents, but is not identical with, the church, so the earthly city is symbolically reflected in the state. Strictly speaking, the *earthly city* is not identical with any empirical social or political organization but is the *community of the unrighteous,* including sinful members of the church and excluding righteous citizens of the state. Whereas the earthly city, as the incarnation of sin and lust, is the antithesis of any value whatsoever, the state, by contrast, has positive value, through it is not the absolute value inherent in the heavenly city.

The Greco-Roman background of St. Augustine comes out in his assumption that "the life of the wise man must be social," and that there is no man who "does not wish to have peace." The state, therefore, by providing social peace, "has its good in this world"; and St. Augustine recalls Greco-Roman ideas in saying that the state is, "in its own kind, better than all other human good. For it desires earthly peace for the sake of enjoying earthly goods."

At this point St. Augustine parts company with Plato and Cicero, who so strongly influenced him. The peace that the state provides is, according to St. Augustine, not an end in itself, but only a means, a condition that makes the service to God possible. The peace of the state is the temporary tranquillity that enables man to work for the heavenly city, which is "peace never-ending."

Peace is therefore conceived by St. Augustine in terms of justice (that is, the right relation of man and God); it is not merely the absence of social strife and conflict. Without justice there can be no peace, and this moral and religious conception is behind St. Augustine's famous statement: "Justice being taken away, then, what are kingdoms but great robberies?" St. Augustine goes on to say that, viewed from the standpoint of formal, effective authority, robberies (that is, bands of robbers) are but little kingdoms themselves; the difference, therefore, between a state and a band of robbers is qualitative and not quantitative.

St. Augustine thus Christianizes the classical approach to the theory of the state by imbuing the Platonic concept of justice and the Aristotelian notion of the good life with the ideals of Christianity, and his doctrine is firmly anchored in the Greco-Roman and Biblical conceptions of the state in terms of moral purpose rather than formal authority, the monopoly to use force, or sovereignty.

The strong influence of Greco-Roman conceptions and preconceptions on St. Augustine can also be seen in his attitude toward slavery. In essence, it is a Christianized version of Aristotle's rationalization of slavery. Man was created in God's image, to be master of irrational creatures, beasts, but not of fellow men. Slavery is therefore not the result of man's nature, as originally intended by God, but the "result of sin." It is both punishment and remedy for sin, as for Aristotle slavery is the just relation between those who possess virtue and those who do not.

St. Augustine specifically opposes the law of the Old Testament according to which all servitude was to be ended every seventh year, and states that bad slaves are made into good by the example of Christ, and that slaves should not refuse to serve wicked masters. St. Augustine appeals to the slaves to serve their masters "heartily and with good will, so that, if they cannot be freed by their masters, they may themselves make their slavery in some sort free, by serving not in crafty fear, but in faithful love, until all righteousness pass away, and all principality and every human power be brought to nothing, and God be in all." Like Aristotle, St. Augustine also appeals to the masters to act benevolently and responsibly; they "ought to feel their position of authority a greater burden than servants their service."

Yet St. Augustine never examined his theory in the light of empirical evidence: was it really true that slaves were worse sinners than the free? Although he occasionally notes that there are "many wicked masters who have religious men as their slaves," this observation leads him, not to a reexamination of his basic assumption that slavery is the punishment and remedy for sin, but to the more startling conclusion that even such slavery is legitimate because "it is a happier thing to be the slave of a man than of a lust." Weighed carefully, therefore, St. Augustine's theory of slavery, like that of the church in general, probably seemed more reasonable to masters than to slaves, although the institution of slavery was mitigated, in actual use, by the influence of Christianity.

St. Augustine, the greatest of the church Fathers, stood at the turning point of two worlds, that of antiquity and Christianity. The impact of Plato in particular, but also that of Aristotle, Cicero, and the Stoics, is clearly evident in his work, and he helped to transmit the ancient heritage to the new world that was being born. While the Roman empire was breaking up before his eyes, he sought to construe, as a Christian, the vision of a timeless empire in which peace and justice would reign: the City of God.

ST. AUGUSTINE

*The City of God**

JUSTICE—THE FOUNDATION OF THE STATE

Justice being taken away, then, what are kingdoms but great robberies? For what are robberies themselves, but little kingdoms? The band itself is made up of men; it is ruled by the authority of a prince, it is knit together by the pact of the confederacy; the booty is divided by the law agreed on. If, by the admittance of abandoned men, this evil increases to such a degree that it holds places, fixes abodes, takes possession of cities, and subdues peoples, it assumes the more plainly the name of a kingdom, because the reality is now manifestly conferred on it, not by the removal of covetousness, but by the addition of impunity. Indeed, that was an apt and true reply which was given to Alexander the Great by a pirate who had been seized. For when that king had asked the man what he meant by keeping hostile possession of the sea, he answered with bold pride, "What thou meanest by seizing the whole earth; but because I do it with a petty ship, I am called a robber, whilst thou who dost it with a great fleet art styled emperor."[1]

THE TRUE HAPPINESS OF THE RULER

For neither do we say that certain Christian emperors were therefore happy because

---

*From St. Augustine, *The City of God* (trans. Marcus Dods, in Vol. II of *A Select Library of the Nicene and Post-Nicene Fathers of the Christian Church,* ed. Philip Schaff, Buffalo, 1887).

[1] Cicero, *De Republica,* III.

they ruled a long time, or, dying a peaceful death, left their sons to succeed them in the empire, or subdued the enemies of the republic, or were able both to guard against and to suppress the attempt of hostile citizens rising against them. These and other gifts or comforts of this sorrowful life even certain worshippers of demons have merited to receive, who do not belong to the kingdom of God to which these belong; and this is to be traced to the mercy of God, who would not have those who believe in Him desire such things as the highest good. But we say that they are happy if they rule justly; if they are not lifted up amid the praises of those who pay them sublime honors, and the obsequiousness of those who salute them with an excessive humility, but remember that they are men; if they make their power the handmaid of His majesty by using it for the greatest possible extension of His worship; if they fear, love, worship God; if more than their own they love that kingdom in which they are not afraid to have partners; if they are slow to punish, ready to pardon; if they apply that punishment as necessary to government and defence of the republic, and not in order to gratify their own enmity; if they grant pardon, not that iniquity may go unpunished, but with the hope that the transgressor may amend his ways; if they compensate with the lenity of mercy and the liberality of benevolence for whatever severity they may be compelled to decree; if their luxury is as much restrained as it might have been unrestrained; if they prefer to govern depraved desires rather than any nation whatever; and if they do all these things, not through ardent desire of empty glory, but through love of eternal felicity, not neglecting to offer to the true God, who is their God, for their sins, the sacrifices of humility, contrition, and prayer. Such Christian emperors, we say, are happy in the present time by hope, and are destined to be so in the enjoyment of the reality itself, when that which we wait for shall have arrived.

THE EARTHLY AND THE HEAVENLY CITY

Accordingly, two cities have been formed by two loves: the earthly by the love of self, even to the contempt of God; the heavenly by the love of God, even to the contempt of self. The former, in a word, glories in itself, the latter in the Lord. For the one seeks glory from men; but the greatest glory of the other is God, the witness of conscience. The one lifts up its head in its own glory; the other says to its God, "Thou art my glory, and the lifter up of mine head."[2] In the one, the princes and the nations it subdues are ruled by the love of ruling; in the other, the princes and the subjects serve one another in love, the latter obeying, while the former take thought for all. The one delights in its own strength, represented in the persons of its rulers; the other says to its God, "I will love Thee, O Lord, my strength."[3] And therefore the wise men of the one city, living according to man, have sought for profit to their own bodies or souls, or both, and those who have known God "glorified Him not as God, neither were thankful, but became vain in their imaginations, and their foolish heart was darkened; professing themselves to be wise"—that is, glorying in their own wisdom, and being possessed by pride—"they became fools, and changed the glory of the incorruptible God into an image made like to corruptible man, and to birds, and four-footed beasts, and creeping things." For they were either leaders or followers of the people in adoring images, "and worshipped and served the creature more than the Creator, who is blessed for ever."[4] But in the other city there is no human wisdom, but only godliness, which offers due worship to the true God, and looks for its reward in the society of the saints, of holy angels as well as holy men, that God may be all in all.[5]

THE TWO TYPES OF MAN

Of the bliss of Paradise, of Paradise itself, and of the life of our first parents there, and of their sin and punishment, many have thought much, spoken much, written much. We ourselves, too, have spoken of these things in the foregoing books, and have written either what we read in the Holy Scriptures, or what we could reasonably deduce from them. And were we to enter into a more detailed investigation of these matters, an endless number of endless questions would arise, which would involve us in a larger work than the present occasion admits. We cannot be expected to find room for replying to every question that may be started by unoccupied and captious men, who are ever more ready to ask questions than capable of understanding the answer. Yet I trust we have already done justice to these great and difficult questions regarding the beginning of the world, or of the soul, or of the human race itself. This race we have distributed into two parts, the one consisting of those who live according to man, the other of those who live according to God. And these we also mystically call the two cities, or the two communities of men, of which the one is predestined to reign eternally with God, and the other to suffer eternal punishment with the devil. This, however, is their end, and of it we are to speak afterwards. At present, as we have said enough about their origin, whether among the angels, whose numbers we know not, or in the two first human beings, it seems suitable to attempt an account of their career, from the time when our two first parents began to propagate the race until all human generation shall cease. For this whole time or world-age, in which the dying give place and those who are born succeed, is the career of these two cities concerning which we treat.

Of these two first parents of the human race, then, Cain was the first-born, and he

---

[2] Ps. iii. 3.

[3] Ps. xviii. 1.

[4] Rom. i. 21–25.

---

[5] I Cor. xv. 28.

belonged to the city of men; after him was born Abel, who belonged to the city of God. For as in the individual the truth of the apostle's statement is discerned, "that is not first which is spiritual, but that which is natural, and afterward that which is spiritual,"[6] whence it comes to pass that each man, being derived from a condemned stock, is first of all born of Adam evil and carnal, and becomes good and spiritual only afterwards, when he is grafted into Christ by regeneration: so was it in the human race as a whole. When these two cities began to run their course by a series of deaths and births, the citizen of this world was the first-born, and after him the stranger in this world, the citizen of the city of God, pre-destinated by grace, elected by grace, by grace a stranger below, and by grace a citizen above. By grace—for so far as regards himself he is sprung from the same mass, all of which is condemned in its origin: but God, like a potter (for this comparison is introduced by the apostle judiciously, and not without thought), of the same lump made one vessel to honor, another to dishonor.[7] But first the vessel to dishonor was made, and after it another to honor. For in each individual, as I have already said, there is first of all that which is reprobate, that from which we must begin, but in which we need not necessarily remain; afterwards is that which is well-approved, to which we may by advancing attain, and in which, when we have reached it, we may abide. Not, indeed, that every wicked man shall be good, but that no one will be good who was not first of all wicked; but the sooner any one becomes a good man, the more speedily does he receive this title, and abolish the old name in the new. Accordingly, it is recorded of Cain that he built a city,[8] but Abel, being a sojourner, built none. For the city of the saints is above, although here below it begets citizens, in whom it sojourns till the time of its reign arrives, when it shall gather together all in the day of the resurrection; and then shall the promised kingdom be given to them, in which they shall reign with their Prince, the King of the ages, time without end.

CONFLICT AND PEACE IN THE EARTHLY CITY

But the earthly city, which shall not be everlasting (for it will no longer be a city when it has been committed to the extreme penalty), has its good in this world, and rejoices in it with such joy as such things can afford. But as this is not a good which can discharge its devotees of all distresses, this city is often divided against itself by litigations, wars, quarrels, and such victories as are either life-destroying or short-lived. For each part of it that arms against another part of it seeks to triumph over the nations though itself in bondage to vice. If, when it has conquered, it is inflated with pride, its victory is life-destroying; but if it turns its thoughts upon the common casualties of our mortal condition, and is rather anxious concerning the disasters that may befall it than elated with the successes already achieved, this victory, though of a higher kind, is still only short-lived; for it cannot abidingly rule over those whom it has victoriously subjugated. But the things which this city desires cannot justly be said to be evil, for it is itself, in its own kind, better than all other human good. For it desires earthly peace for the sake of enjoying earthly goods, and it makes war in order to attain to this peace; since, if it has conquered, and there remains no one to resist it, it enjoys a peace which it had not while there were opposing parties who contested for the enjoyment of those things which were too small to satisfy both. This peace is purchased by toilsome wars; it is obtained by what they style a glorious victory. Now, when victory remains with the party which had the juster cause, who hesitates to congratulate the victor, and style it a desirable peace? These things, then, are good things, and without doubt the gifts of God. But if they neglect the better things of the heavenly city, which are secured by eternal victory and peace never-ending, and so inordinately covet these present good things that they believe them to be the only desirable things, or love them better than those things which are believed to be better—if this be so, then it is necessary that misery follow and ever increase.

---

[6] I Cor. xv. 46.

[7] Rom. ix. 21.

[8] Gen. iv. 17.

THE LUST FOR POWER IN
THE EARTHLY CITY

Thus the founder of the earthly city was a fratricide. Overcome with envy, he slew his own brother, a citizen of the eternal city, and a sojourner on earth. So that we cannot be surprised that this first specimen, or, as the Greeks say, archetype of crime, should, long afterwards, find a corresponding crime at the foundation of that city which was destined to reign over so many nations, and be the head of this earthly city of which we speak. For that city also, as one of their poets has mentioned, "the first walls were stained with a brother's blood."[9] or, as Roman history records, Remus was slain by his brother Romulus. And thus there is no difference between the foundation of this city and of the earthly city, unless it be that Romulus and Remus were both citizens of the earthly city. Both desired to have the glory of founding the Roman republic, but both could not have as much glory as if one only claimed it; for he who wished to have the glory of ruling would certainly rule less if his power were shared by a living consort. In order, therefore, that the whole glory might be enjoyed by one, his consort was removed; and by this crime the empire was made larger indeed, but inferior, while otherwise it would have been less, but better. Now these brothers, Cain and Abel, were not both animated by the same earthly desires, nor did the murderer envy the other because he feared that, by both ruling, his own dominion would be curtailed—for Abel was not solicitous to rule in that city which his brother built—he was moved by that diabolical, envious hatred with which the evil regard the good, for no other reason than because they are good while themselves are evil. For the possession of goodness is by no means diminished by being shared with a partner either permanent or temporarily assumed; on the contrary, the possession of goodness is increased in proportion to the concord and charity of each of those who share it. In short, he who is unwilling to share this possession cannot have it; and he who is most willing to admit others to a share of it will have the greatest abundance to himself. The quarrel, then, between Romulus and Remus shows how the earthly city is divided against itself; that which fell out between Cain and Abel illustrated the hatred that subsists between the two cities, that of God and that of men. The wicked war with the wicked; the good also war with the wicked. But with the good, good men, or at least perfectly good men, cannot war; though, while only going on towards perfection, they war to this extent, that every good man resists others in those points in which he resists himself. And in each individual "the flesh lusteth against the spirit, and the spirit against the flesh."[10] This spiritual lusting, therefore, can be at war with the carnal lust of another man; or carnal lust may be at war with the spiritual desires of another, in some such way as good and wicked men are at war; or, still more certainly, the carnal lusts of two men, good but not yet perfect, contend together, just as the wicked contend with the wicked, until the health of those who are under the treatment of grace attains final victory.

LIMITATIONS OF
SOCIAL LIFE

We give a much more unlimited approval to their idea that the life of the wise man must be social. For how could the city of God either take a beginning or be developed, or attain its proper destiny, if the life of the saints were not a social life? But who can enumerate all the great grievances with which human society abounds in the misery of this mortal state? Who can weigh them? Hear how one of their comic writers makes one of his characters express the common feelings of all men in this matter: "I am married; this is one misery. Children are born to me; they are additional cares."[11] What shall I say of the miseries of love which Terence also recounts—"slights, suspicions, quarrels, war to-day, peace tomorrow?"[12] Is not human life full of such things? Do they not often occur even in

---

[9] Lucan, *Phar.* i. 95.

[10] Gal. v. 17.

[11] Terent. *Adelph.* v. 4.

[12] *Eunuch*, i. 1.

honorable friendships? On all hands we experience these slights, suspicions, quarrels, war, all of which are undoubted evils; while, on the other hand, peace is a doubtful good, because we do not know the heart of our friend, and though we did know it to-day, we should be as ignorant of what it might be to-morrow. Who ought to be, or who are more friendly than those who live in the same family? And yet who can rely even upon this friendship, seeing that secret treachery has often broken it up, and produced enmity as bitter as the amity was sweet, or seemed sweet by the most perfect dissimulation? It is on this account that the words of Cicero so move the heart of every one, and provoke a sigh: "There are no snares more dangerous than those which lurk under the guise of duty or the name of relationship. For the man who is your declared foe you can easily baffle by precaution; but this hidden, intestine, and domestic danger not merely exists, but overwhelms you before you can foresee and examine it."[13] Is It is also to this that allusion is made by the divine saying, "A man's foes are those of his own household"[14]—words which one cannot hear without pain; for though a man have sufficient fortitude to endure it with equanimity, and sufficient sagacity to baffle the malice of a pretended friend, yet if he himself is a good man, he cannot but be greatly pained at the discovery of the perfidy of wicked men, whether they have always been wicked and merely feigned goodness, or have fallen from a better to a malicious disposition. If, then, home, the natural refuge from the ills of life, is itself not safe, what shall we say of the city, which, as it is larger, is so much the more filled with lawsuits civil and criminal, and is never free from the fear, if sometimes from the actual outbreak, of disturbing and bloody insurrections and civil wars?

SHORTCOMINGS OF HUMAN JUSTICE

What shall I say of these judgments which men pronounce on men, and which are necessary in communities, whatever outward

peace they enjoy? Melancholy and lamentable judgments they are, since the judges are men who cannot discern the consciences of those at their bar, and are therefore frequently compelled to put innocent witnesses to the torture to ascertain the truth regarding the crimes of other men. What shall I say of torture applied to the accused himself? He is tortured to discover whether he is guilty, so that, though innocent, he suffers most undoubted punishment for crime that is still doubtful, not because it is proved that he committed it, but because it is not ascertained that he did not commit it. Thus the ignorance of the judge frequently involves an innocent person in suffering. And what is still more unendurable—a thing, indeed, to be bewailed, and, if that were possible, watered with fountains of tears—is this, that when the judge puts the accused to the question, that he may not unwittingly put an innocent man to death, the result of this lamentable ignorance is that this very person, whom he tortured that he might not condemn him if innocent, is condemned to death both tortured and innocent. For if he has chosen, in obedience to the philosophical instructions to the wise man, to quit this life rather than endure any longer such tortures, he declares that he has committed the crime which in fact he has not committed. And when he has been condemned and put to death, the judge is still in ignorance whether he has put to death an innocent or a guilty person, though he put the accused to the torture for the very purpose of saving himself from condemning the innocent; and consequently he has both tortured an innocent man to discover his innocence, and has put him to death without discovering it. If such darkness shrouds social life, will a wise judge take his seat on the bench or no? Beyond question he will. For human society, which he thinks it a wickedness to abandon, constrains him and compels him to this duty. And he thinks it no wickedness that innocent witnesses are tortured regarding the crimes of which other men are accused; or that the accused are put to the torture, so that they are often overcome with anguish, and, though innocent, make false confessions regarding themselves, and are punished; or that, though they be not condemned to die, they often die during, or in consequence of, the torture; or that sometimes the accusers,

---

[13] *In Verrem*, ii. I. 15.

[14] Matt. x. 36.

who perhaps have been prompted by a desire to benefit society by bringing criminals to justice, are themselves condemned through the ignorance of the judge, because they are unable to prove the truth of their accusations though they are true, and because the witnesses lie, and the accused endures the torture without being moved to confession. These numerous and important evils he does not consider sins; for the wise judge does these things, not with any intention of doing harm, but because his ignorance compels him, and because human society claims him as a judge. But though we therefore acquit the judge of malice, we must none the less condemn human life as miserable. And if he is compelled to torture and punish the innocent because his office and his ignorance constrain him, is he a happy as well as a guiltless man? Surely it were proof of more profound considerateness and finer feeling were he to recognize the misery of these necessities, and shrink from his own implication in that misery; and had he any piety about him, he would cry to God "From my necessities deliver Thou me."[15]

THE MISERY OF WAR

After the state or city comes the world, the third circle of human society—the first being the house, and the second the city. And the world, as it is larger, so it is fuller of dangers, as the greater sea is the more dangerous. And here, in the first place, man is separated from man by the difference of languages. For if two men, each ignorant of the other's language, meet, and are not compelled to pass, but, on the contrary, to remain in company, dumb animals, though of different species, would more easily hold intercourse than they, humans though they be. For their common nature is no help to friendliness when they are prevented by diversity of language from conveying their sentiments to one another; so that a man would more readily hold intercourse with his dog than with a foreigner. But the imperial city has endeavored to impose on subject nations not only her yoke, but her language, as a bond of peace, so that interpreters, far from being scarce, are numberless. This is true; but how

many great wars, how much slaughter and bloodshed, have provided this unity! And though these are past, the end of these miseries has not yet come. For though there have never been wanting, nor are yet wanting, hostile nations beyond the empire, against whom wars have been and are waged, yet, supposing there were no such nations, the very extent of the empire itself has produced wars of a more obnoxious description—social and civil wars—and with these the whole race has been agitated, either by the actual conflict or the fear of a renewed outbreak. If I attempted to give an adequate description of these manifold disasters, these stern and lasting necessities, though I am quite unequal to the task, what limit could I set? But, say they, the wise man will wage just wars. As if he would not all the rather lament the necessity of just wars, if he remembers that he is a man; for if they were not just he would not wage them, and would therefore be delivered from all wars. For it is the wrong-doing of the opposing party which compels the wise man to wage just wars; and this wrong-doing, even though it gave rise to no war, would still be matter of grief to man because it is man's wrong-doing. Let every one, then, who thinks with pain on all these great evils, so horrible, so ruthless, acknowledge that this is misery. And if any one either endures or thinks of them without mental pain, this is a more miserable plight still, for he thinks himself happy because he has lost human feeling.

THE OBJECTIVE OF WAR: PEACE

Whoever gives even moderate attention to human affairs and to our common nature, will recognize that if there is no man who does not wish to be joyful, neither is there any one who does not wish to have peace. For even they who make war desire nothing but victory—desire, that is to say, to attain to peace with glory. For what else is victory than the conquest of those who resist us? and when this is done there is peace. It is therefore with the desire for peace that wars are waged, even by those who take pleasure in exercising their warlike nature in command and battle. And hence it is obvious that peace is the end sought for by war. For

[15] Ps. xxv. 17.

every man seeks peace by waging war, but no man seeks war by making peace. For even they who intentionally interrupt the peace in which they are living have no hatred of peace, but only wish it changed into a peace that suits them better. They do not, therefore, wish to have no peace, but only one more to their mind. And in the case of sedition, when men have separated themselves from the community, they yet do not effect what they wish, unless they maintain some kind of peace with their fellow-conspirators. And therefore even robbers take care to maintain peace with their comrades, that they may with greater effect and greater safety invade the peace of other men. And if an individual happens to be of such unrivalled strength, and to be so jealous of partnership, that he trusts himself with no comrades, but makes his own plots, and commits depredations and murders on his own account, yet he maintains some shadow of peace with such persons as he is unable to kill, and from whom he wishes to conceal his deeds. In his own home, too, he makes it his aim to be at peace with his wife and children, and any other members of his household; for unquestionably their prompt obedience to his every look is a source of pleasure to him. And if this be not rendered, he is angry, he chides and punishes; and even by this storm he secures the calm peace of his own home, as occasion demands. For he sees that peace cannot be maintained unless all the members of the same domestic circle be subject to one head, such as he himself is in his own house. And therefore if a city or nation offered to submit itself to him, to serve him in the same style as he had made his household serve him, he would no longer lurk in brigand's hiding-places, but lift his head in open day as a king, though the same coveteousness and wickedness should remain in him. And thus all men desire to have peace with their own circle whom they wish to govern as suits themselves. For even those whom they make war against they wish to make their own, and impose on them the laws of their own peace.

But let us suppose a man such as poetry and mythology speak of—a man so unsociable and savage as to be called rather a semi-man than a man.[16] Although, then, his kingdom was the solitude of a dreary cave, and he himself was so singularly bad-hearted that he was named Κακός, which is the Greek word for *bad;* though he had no wife to soothe him with endearing talk, no children to play with, no sons to do his bidding, no friend to enliven him with intercourse, not even his father Vulcan (though in one respect he was happier than his father, not having begotten a monster like himself); although he gave to no man, but took as he wished whatever he could, from whomsoever he could, when he could; yet in that solitary den, the floor of which, as Virgil[17] says, was always reeking with recent slaughter, there was nothing else than peace sought, a peace in which no one should molest him, or disquiet him with any assault or alarm. With his own body he desired to be at peace, and he was satisfied only in proportion as he had this peace. For he ruled his members, and they obeyed him; and for the sake of pacifying his mortal nature, which rebelled when it needed anything, and of allaying the sedition of hunger which threatened to banish the soul from the body, he made forays, slew, and devoured, but used the ferocity and savageness he displayed in these actions only for the preservation of his own life's peace. So that, had he been willing to make with other men the same peace which he made with himself in his own cave, he would neither have been called bad, nor a monster, nor a semi-man. Or if the appearance of his body and his vomiting smoky fires frightened men from having any dealings with him, perhaps his fierce ways arose not from a desire to do mischief, but from the necessity of finding a living. But he may have had no existence, or, at least, he was not such as the poets fancifully describe him, for they had to exalt Hercules, and did so at the expense of Cacus. It is better, then, to believe that such a man or semi-man never existed, and that this, in common with many other fancies of the poets, is mere fiction. For the most savage animals (and he is said to have been almost a wild beast) encompass their own species with a ring of protecting peace. They cohabit, beget, produce, suckle, and bring up their young, though very many of them are not gregarious, but solitary—not

---

[16] He refers to the giant Cacus.

[17] *Aeneid,* viii. 195.

like sheep, deer, pigeons, starlings, bees, but such as lions, foxes, eagles, bats. For what tigress does not gently purr over her cubs, and lay aside her ferocity to fondle them? What kite, solitary as he is when circling over his prey, does not seek a mate, build a nest, hatch the eggs, bring up the young birds, and maintain with the mother of his family as peaceful a domestic alliance as he can? How much more powerfully do the laws of man's nature move him to hold fellowship and maintain peace with all men so far as in him lies, since even wicked men wage war to maintain the peace of their own circle, and wish that, if possible, all men belonged to them, that all men and things might serve but one head, and might, either through love or fear, yield themselves to peace with him! It is thus that pride in its perversity apes God. It abhors equality with other men under Him; but, instead of His rule, it seeks to impose a rule of its own upon its equals. It abhors, that is to say, the just peace of God, and loves its own unjust peace; but it cannot help loving peace of one kind or other. For there is no vice so clean contrary to nature that it obliterates even the faintest traces of nature.

He, then, who prefers what is right to what is wrong, and what is well-ordered to what is perverted, sees that the peace of unjust men is not worthy to be called peace in comparison with the peace of the just. And yet even what is perverted must of necessity be in harmony with, and in dependence on, and in some part of the order of things, for otherwise it would have no existence at all. Suppose a man hangs with his head downwards, this is certainly a perverted attitude of body and arrangement of its members; for that which nature requires to be above is beneath, and *vice versa*. This perversity disturbs the peace of the body, and is therefore painful. Nevertheless the spirit is at peace with its body, and labors for its preservation, and hence the suffering; but if it is banished from the body by its pains, then, so long as the bodily framework holds together, there is in the remains a kind of peace among the members, and hence the body remains suspended. And inasmuch as the earthly body tends towards the earth, and rests on the bond by which it is suspended, it tends thus to its natural peace, and the voice of its own weight demands a place for it to rest; and though now lifeless

and without feeling, it does not fall from the peace that is natural to its place in creation, whether it already has it, or is tending towards it. For if you apply embalming preparations to prevent the bodily frame from mouldering and dissolving, a kind of peace still unites part to part, and keeps the whole body in a suitable place on the earth—in other words, in a place that is at peace with the body. If, on the other hand, the body receive no such care, but be left to the natural course, it is disturbed by exhalations that do not harmonize with one another, and that offend our senses; for it is this which is perceived in putrefaction until it is assimilated to the elements of the world, and particle by particle enters into peace with them. Yet throughout this process the laws of the most high Creator and Governor are strictly observed, for it is by Him the peace of the universe is administered. For although minute animals are produced from the carcass of a larger animal, all these little atoms, by the law of the same Creator, serve the animals they belong to in peace. And although the flesh of dead animals be eaten by others, no matter where it be carried, nor what it be brought into contact with, nor what it be converted and changed into, it still is ruled by the same laws which pervade all things for the conservation of every mortal race, and which bring things that fit one another into harmony.

THE TRANQUILLITY OF ORDER IN THE UNIVERSE

The peace of the body then consists in the duly proportioned arrangement of its parts. The peace of the irrational soul is the harmonious repose of the appetites, and that of the rational soul the harmony of knowledge and action. The peace of body and soul is the well-ordered and harmonious life and health of the living creature. Peace between man and God is the well-ordered obedience of faith to eternal law. Peace between man and man is well-ordered concord. Domestic peace is the well-ordered concord between those of the family who rule and those who obey. Civil peace is a similar concord among the citizens. The peace of the celestial city is the perfectly ordered and harmonious enjoyment of God, and of one another in God. The peace of all things is the tranquillity of order. Order is the distribution which allots things equal and unequal, each to its own place. And hence, though the miserable, in so far as they are such, do certainly not enjoy peace, but are severed from that tranquillity of order in which there is no disturbance, nevertheless, inasmuch as they are deservedly and justly miserable, they are by their very misery connected with order. They are not, indeed, conjoined with the blessed, but they are disjoined from them by the law of order. And though they are disquieted, their circumstances are notwithstanding adjusted to them, and consequently they have some tranquillity of order, and therefore some peace. But they are wretched because, although not wholly miserable, they are not in that place where any mixture of misery is impossible. They would, however, be more wretched if they had not that peace which arises from being in harmony with the natural order of things. When they suffer, their peace is in so far disturbed; but their peace continues in so far as they do not suffer, and in so far as their nature continues to exist. As, then, there may be life without pain, while there cannot be pain without some kind of life, so there may be peace without war, but there cannot be war without some kind of peace, because war supposes the existence of some natures to wage it, and these natures cannot exist without peace of one kind or other.

And therefore there is a nature in which evil does not or even cannot exist; but there cannot be a nature in which there is no good. Hence not even the nature of the devil himself is evil, in so far as it is nature, but it was made evil by being perverted. Thus he did not abide in the truth,[18] but could not escape the judgment of the truth; he did not abide in the tranquillity of order, but did not therefore escape the power of the Ordainer. The good imparted by God to his nature did not screen him from the justice of God by which order was preserved in his punishment; neither did God punish the good which He had created, but the evil which the devil had committed. God did not take back all He had imparted to his nature, but something He took and something He left, that there might remain enough to be sensible of the loss of what was taken. And this very sensibility to pain is evidence of the good which has been taken away and the good which has been left. For, were nothing good left, there could be no pain on account of the good which had been lost. For he who sins is still worse if he rejoices in his loss of righteousness. But he who is in pain, if he derives no benefit from it, mourns at least the loss of health. And as righteousness and health are both good things, and as the loss of any good thing is matter of grief, not of joy—if, at least, there is no compensation, as spiritual righteousness may compensate for the loss of bodily health—certainly it is more suitable for a wicked man to grieve in punishment than to rejoice in his fault. As, then, the joy of a sinner who has abandoned what is good is evidence of a bad will, so his grief for the good he has lost when he is punished is evidence of a good nature. For he who laments the peace his nature has lost is stirred to do so by some relics of peace which make his nature friendly to itself. And it is very just that in the final punishment the wicked and godless should in anguish bewail the loss of the natural advantages they enjoyed, and should perceive that they were most justly taken from them by that God whose benign liberality they had despised. God, then, the most wise Creator and most just Ordainer of all natures, who placed the human race upon earth as its greatest ornament, imparted to men some good things adapted to this life, to wit, temporal peace, such as we can enjoy in this life from health and safety and human fellowship, and all things needful for the preservation and recovery of this peace, such as the objects which are accommodated to our outward senses, light, night, the air, and waters suitable for us, and everything the body requires to sustain, shelter, heal, or beautify it: and all under this most equitable condition, that every man who made a good use of these advantages suited to the peace of this mortal condition, should receive ampler and better blessings, namely, the peace of immortality, accompanied by glory and honor in an endless life made fit for the enjoyment of God and of one another in God; but that he who used the present blessings badly should both lose them and should not receive the others.

[18] John viii. 44.

RULERS AS SERVANTS
OF THE RULED

The whole use, then, of things temporal has a reference to this result of earthly peace in the earthly community, while in the city of God it is connected with eternal peace. And therefore, if we were irrational animals, we should desire nothing beyond the proper arrangement of the parts of the body and the satisfaction of the appetites—nothing, therefore, but bodily comfort and abundance of pleasures, that the peace of the body might contribute to the peace of the soul. For if bodily peace be wanting, a bar is put to the peace even of the irrational soul, since it cannot obtain the gratification of its appetites. And these two together help out the mutual peace of soul and body, the peace of harmonious life and health. For as animals, by shunning pain, show that they love bodily peace, and, by pursuing pleasure to gratify their appetites, show that they love peace of soul, so their shrinking from death is a sufficient indication of their intense love of that peace which binds soul and body in close alliance. But, as man has a rational soul, he subordinates all this which he has in common with the beasts to the peace of his rational soul, that his intellect may have free play and may regulate his actions, and that he may thus enjoy the well-ordered harmony of knowledge and action which constitutes, as we have said, the peace of the rational soul. And for this purpose he must desire to be neither molested by pain, nor disturbed by desire, nor extinguished by death, that he may arrive at some useful knowledge by which he may regulate his life and manners. But, owing to the liability of the human mind to fall into mistakes, this very pursuit of knowledge may be a snare to him unless he has a divine Master, whom he may obey without misgiving, and who may at the same time give him such help as to preserve his own freedom. And because, so long as he is in this mortal body, he is stranger to God, he walks by faith, not by sight; and he therefore refers all peace, bodily or spiritual or both, to that peace which mortal man has with the immortal God, so that he exhibits the well-ordered obedience of faith to eternal law. But as this divine Master inculcates two precepts—the love of God and the love of our neighbor—and as in these precepts a man finds three things he has to love—God, himself, and his neighbor—and that he who loves God loves himself thereby, it follows that he must endeavor to get his neighbor to love God, since he is ordered to love his neighbor as himself. He ought to make this endeavor in behalf of his wife, his children, his household, all within his reach, even as he would wish his neighbor to do the same for him if he needed it; and consequently he will be at peace, or in well-ordered concord, with all men, as far as in him lies. And this is the order of this concord, that a man, in the first place, injure no one, and, in the second, do good to every one he can reach. Primarily, therefore, his own household are his care, for the law of nature and of society gives him readier access to them and greater opportunity of serving them. And hence the apostle says, "Now, if any provide not for his own, and specially for those of his own house, he hath denied the faith, and is worse than an infidel."[19] This is the origin of domestic peace, or the well-ordered concord of those in the family who rule and those who obey. For they who care for the rest rule—the husband the wife, the parents the children, the masters the servants; and they who are cared for obey—the women their husbands, the children their parents, the servants their masters. But in the family of the just man who lives by faith and is as yet a pilgrim journeying on to the celestial city, even those who rule serve those whom they seem to command; for they rule not from a love of power, but from a sense of the duty they owe to others—not because they are proud of authority, but because they love mercy.

LIBERTY AND SLAVERY

This is prescribed by the order of nature: it is thus that God has created man. For "let them," He says, "have dominion over the fish of the sea, and over the fowl of the air, and over every creeping thing which creepeth on the earth."[20] He did not intend that His rational creature, who was made in His image, should have dominion over anything but the irrational creation—not man over

[19] I Tim. v. 8.

[20] Gen. i. 26.

man, but man over the beasts. And hence the righteous men in primitive times were made shepherds of cattle rather than kings of men, God intending thus to teach us what the relative position of the creatures is, and what the desert of sin; for it is with justice, we believe, that the condition of slavery is the result of sin. And this is why we do not find the word "slave" in any part of Scripture until righteous Noah branded the sin of his son with this name. It is a name, therefore, introduced by sin and not by nature. The origin of the Latin word for slave is supposed to be found in the circumstance that those who by the law of war were liable to be killed were sometimes preserved by their victors, and were hence called servants. And these circumstances could never have arisen save through sin. For even when we wage a just war, our adversaries must be sinning; and every victory, even though gained by wicked men, is a result of the first judgment of God, who humbles the vanquished either for the sake of removing or of punishing their sins. Witness that man of God, Daniel, who, when he was in captivity, confessed to God his own sins and the sins of his people, and declared with pious grief that these were the cause of the captivity.[21] The prime cause, then, of slavery is sin, which brings man under the dominion of his fellow—that which does not happen save by the judgment of God, with whom is no unrighteousness, and who knows how to award fit punishments to every variety of offence. But our Master in heaven says, "Every one who doeth sin is the servant of sin."[22] And thus there are many wicked masters who have religious men as their slaves, and who are yet themselves in bondage; "for of whom a man is overcome, of the same is he brought in bondage."[23] And beyond question it is a happier thing to be the slave of a man than of a lust; for even this very lust of ruling, to mention no others, lays waste men's hearts with the most ruthless dominion. Moreover, when men are subjected to one another in a peaceful order, the lowly position does as much good to the servant as the proud position does harm to the master. But

by nature, as God first created us, no one is the slave either of man or of sin. This servitude is, however, penal, and is appointed by that law which enjoins the preservation of the natural order and forbids its disturbance; for if nothing had been done in violation of that law, there would have been nothing to restrain by penal servitude. And therefore the apostle admonishes slaves to be subject to their masters, and to serve them heartily and with good-will, so that, if they cannot be freed by their masters, they may themselves make their slavery in some sort free, by serving not in crafty fear, but in faithful love, until all unrighteousness pass away, and all principality and every human power be brought to nothing, and God be all in all.

EQUITABLE RULE

And therefore, although our righteous fathers[24] had slaves, and administered their domestic affairs so as to distinguish between the condition of slaves and the heirship of sons in regard to the blessings of this life, yet in regard to the worship of God, in whom we hope for eternal blessings, they took an equally loving oversight of all the members of their household. And this is so much in accordance with the natural order, that the head of the household was called *paterfamilias;* and this name has been so generally accepted, that even those whose rule is unrighteous are glad to apply it to themselves. But those who are true fathers of their households desire and endeavor that all the members of their household, equally with their own children, should worship and win God, and should come to that heavenly home in which the duty of ruling men is no longer necessary, because the duty of caring for their everlasting happiness has also ceased; but, until they reach that home, masters ought to feel their position of authority a greater burden than servants their service. And if any member of the family interrupts the domestic peace by disobedience, he is corrected either by word or blow, or some kind of just and legitimate punishment, such as society permits, that he may himself be the better for it, and be readjusted to the

[21] Dan. ix.

[22] John viii. 34.

[23] II Pet. ii. 19.

[24] The patriarchs.

family harmony from which he had dislocated himself. For as it is not benevolent to give a man help at the expense of some greater benefit he might receive, so it is not innocent to spare a man at the risk of his falling into graver sin. To be innocent, we must not only do harm to no man, but also restrain him from sin or punish his sin, so that either the man himself who is punished may profit by his experience, or others be warned by his example. Since, then, the house ought to be the beginning or element of the city, and every beginning bears reference to some end of its own kind, and every element to the integrity of the whole of which it is an element, it follows plainly enough that domestic peace has a relation to civic peace—in other words, that the well-ordered concord of domestic obedience and domestic rule has a relation to the well-ordered concord of civic obedience and civic rule. And therefore it follows, further, that the father of the family ought to frame his domestic rule in accordance with the law of the city, so that the household may be in harmony with the civic order.

THE SUPRANATIONAL CHARACTER OF THE HEAVENLY CITY ON EARTH

But the families which do not live by faith seek their peace in the earthly advantages of this life; while the families which live by faith look for those eternal blessing which are promised, and use as pilgrims such advantages of time and of earth as do not fascinate and divert them from God, but rather aid them to endure with greater ease, and to keep down the number of those burdens of the corruptible body which weigh upon the soul. Thus the things necessary for this mortal life are used by both kinds of men and families alike, but each has its own peculiar and widely different aim in using them. The earthly city, which does not live by faith, seeks an earthly peace, and the end it proposes, in the well-ordered concord of civic obedience and rule, is the combination of men's wills to attain the things which are helpful to this life. The heavenly city, or rather the part of it which sojourns on earth and lives by faith, makes use of this peace only because it must, until this mortal condition which necessitates it shall pass away.

Consequently, so long as it lives like a captive and a stranger in the earthly city, though it has already received the promise of redemption, and the gift of the Spirit as the earnest of it, it makes no scruple to obey the laws of the earthly city, whereby the things necessary for the maintenance of this mortal life are administered; and thus, as this life is common to both cities, so there is a harmony between them in regard to what belongs to it. But, as the earthly city has had some philosophers whose doctrine is condemned by the divine teaching, and who, being deceived either by their own conjectures or by demons, supposed that many gods must be invited to take an interest in human affairs, and assigned to each a separate function and a separate department—to one the body, to another the soul; and in the body itself, to one the head, to another the neck, and each of the other members to one of the gods; and in like manner, in the soul, to one god the natural capacity was assigned, to another education, to another anger, to another lust; and so the various affairs of life were assigned—cattle to one, corn to another, wine to another, oil to another, the woods to another, money to another, navigation to another, wars and victories to another, marriages to another, births and fecundity to another, and other things to other gods: and as the celestial city, on the other hand, knew that one God only was to be worshipped, and that to Him alone was due that service which the Greeks call *latreia,* and which can be given only to a god, it has come to pass that the two cities could not have common laws of religion, and that the heavenly city has been compelled in this matter to dissent, and to become obnoxious to those who think differently, and to stand the brunt of their anger and hatred and persecutions, except in so far as the minds of their enemies have been alarmed by the multitude of the Christians, and quelled by the manifest protection of God accorded to them. This heavenly city, then, while it sojourns on earth, calls citizens out of all nations, and gathers together a society of pilgrims of all languages, not scrupling about diversities in the manners, laws, and institutions whereby earthly peace is secured and maintained, but recognizing that, however various these are, they all tend to one and the same end of earthly peace. It therefore is so far from rescinding and abolishing these diversities, that it even preserves and adopts them, so long only as no hindrance to the worship of the one supreme and true God is thus introduced. Even the heavenly city, therefore, while in its state of pilgrimage, avails itself of the peace of earth, and, so far as it can without injuring faith and godliness, desires and maintains a common agreement among men regarding the acquisition of the necessaries of life, and makes this earthly peace bear upon the peace of heaven; for this alone can be truly called and esteemed the peace of the reasonable creatures, consisting as it does in the perfectly ordered and harmonious enjoyment of God and of one another in God. When we shall have reached that peace, this mortal life shall give place to one that is eternal, and our body shall be no more this animal body which by its corruption weighs down the soul, but a spiritual body feeling no want, and in all its members subjected to the will. In its pilgrim state the heavenly city possesses this peace by faith; and by this faith it lives righteously when it refers to the attainment of that peace every good action towards God and man; for the life of the city is a social life.

CHAPTER FOUR

ST. THOMAS AQUINAS

One of the most paradoxical aspects of medieval life is the contradiction between the extreme pluralism of its institutions and the deep yearning for unity in its religious and philosophical ideas. The typical institution of the Middle Ages, the feudal system, represents the hallmark of diversity and decentralization that the western world has experienced. By contrast, medieval thinking on religious and secular matters took the *principle of unity* for granted: the oneness of God, of divine law and reason, permeated the whole universe, the heavens, nature, and society. Mankind was conceived as one community, subject to one eternal law and government. Diversities and pluralities were held to exist in the world of fact, but their reason for existence was related to a higher Whole possessing a unity to which they were subordinate.

The duality of man's body and soul was reflected in the two orders of the spiritual and mundane powers, church and empire, each claiming, in theory at least, universal jurisdiction. Both the papalist and imperialist parties were reluctant, in typical medieval fashion, to accept the dualism of church and empire as final. They agreed that there had to be a unifying principle within which the diversity of ecclesiastical and secular powers could be harmonized. The disagreement between papalists and imperialists arose over the nature of the unifying principle and the method of incorporating it into the solution of practical issues. Partisans of the church as well as of the empire also agreed on another major premise: that the *monarchical form of government in church and empire* was the necessary result of the unitary principle, which finds its highest embodiment in God's rule of the universe.

In the realm of thought, the medieval mind drew its nourishment and vitality from two sources: the religious inspiration of Christianity and the intellectual heritage of antiquity. The task of reconciling these two sources, Christian faith and pre-Christian philosophy, was relatively easy in the early medieval period: first, the classical heritage of thought was mainly kept alive in isolated islands of learning in churches and monasteries, and the *major ideological conflicts* in the *early Middle Ages* were *between church and heresy,* and not between theology and philosophy. Second, the relative quietude in this earlier period lay in the fact that, of the great classical philosophers, *Plato* was the *dominant influence,* whereas Aristotle, known only by a few writings on logic, played a minor part.

Plato's doctrine of vision as the ultimate form of knowing the Good, his concept of God, his tendency toward mysticism, his contempt of matter and idealization of spirit, his conception of Ideas as the essence of reality, his scheme of an ideal society in which the spiritual element would rule—all these Platonic strands could be easily woven into the texture of early Christian life and thought. As long as Christianity was still primarily faith and revelation, idea rather than institution, a fraternal community of love rather than an hierarchical organization endowed with the sword of law, Plato seemed to fit the mood and temper of Christian speculation. Of the two giants of the Christian tradition, St. Augustine and St. Thomas Aquinas, the first, St. Augustine, was thoroughly imbued with Platonic ideas; he was a Platonist not only on intellectual grounds, but also in personality, character, and style. And that he was clearly aware of his affinity is evidenced in *The City of God,* where he says that Plato was "justly preferred to all the other philosophers" of paganism, and that "it is evident that none come nearer to us than the Platonists."

But as the church became more and more a political organization struggling for world hegemony, possessing the best-trained bureaucracy of the Great Powers and utilizing diplomacy in peace and armies in war, its entire outlook changed. The original Augustinian conception of the Christian community as a community of the Elect and the conception of the direct participation of the Christian individual in divine grace and salvation were relegated to the background. When papal power reached its peak in the thirteenth century, the intellectual need of the institutionalized church was not so much mystic visions of a highly individual and personal kind but systematic and realistic elaboration of all thought in the light of collective traditions and newly emerging forces pointing to the future.

Particularly as humanistic studies spread in the eleventh and twelfth centuries in Bologna, Paris, Chartres, and Oxford, and classical knowledge became more easily accessible, the labors of publicists, philosophers, and theologians were increasingly devoted to the construction of a unified system of thought in which faith and reason, theology and philosophy, Christianity and pagan antiquity would be reconciled in harmony and lasting accord. The rising universities in Italy, France, England, and Germany—perhaps the most important single contribution of the Middle Ages to western civilization—provided an opportunity for general study and analysis. Originally intended for the training of the young in a single craft (medicine, law, theology), and therein resembling the medieval trade guilds, the universities soon followed the example set by the University of Paris, which was the first to include, early in the thirteenth century, the four faculties of theology, arts, law, and medicine. Henceforth the ideal of unity of knowledge remained the driving force of European universities; the application of the ideal changed with the outlook of the times.

Medieval scholasticism was the first great attempt, after the fall of the Roman empire, to unite in one body knowledge and revelation, philosophy and theology. The principle of unity was the *primacy of religion over philosophy,* of revelation over empirical verification, of faith over knowledge, of dogma over science. The scholastic philosophers did not invent the doctrine of the primacy of religion over philosophy but refined it in accordance with the needs of the time.

Tertullian (A.D. 160–220), one of the early church Fathers and like St. Augustine, a North African, had stated an extreme position by declaring that Christianity and philosophy were utterly irreconcilable, that heresies are the result of philosophy, and that there was the danger of a "mottled Christianity" of Platonic, Aristotelian, and Stoic elements. Sensing acutely that attempts to buttress religion by philosophy would eventually lead to the decline of faith, Tertullian sought to return to the primitive doctrine that religious belief should be based on simplicity of heart and not on subtlety of intellect.

St. Augustine was less extreme than Tertullian; he was not opposed to philosophy as such. According to St. Augustine, the possibility of reasoning originates in the act of faith. The road to truth begins with faith and revelation: "Seek not to understand that you may believe, but believe that you may understand." The Augustinian doctrine is thus an advance over the earlier church fathers because it is not hostile to understanding, provided that the basis and starting point of understanding are the acceptance of nonrational premises: faith and dogma. Yet in effect St. Augustine's method resulted in the enthronement of theology, and both his philosophy and his political thought are essentially theological speculation in content, expression, and symbolism.

From the fifth to the eighth century the main issue confronting western thought was not the struggle of one school against another but the very survival of traditional values and ideas in the aftermath of material and spiritual devastation on an unprecedented scale. Only in monasteries and churches was the connection between the tradition of civilization and the newly emerging medieval world always continued, and the link may have appeared at times to be tenuous indeed. But by the ninth century, physical recovery and consolidation had been attained to a considerable extent, and a more independent and typically medieval intellectual trend began to emerge: *scholasticism.* It was, in fact, as typical of the intellectual character of the Middle Ages as was feudalism of their social and economic system. From the ninth to the thirteenth century, scholasticism was the predominant pattern of thought.

The ecclesiastical domination of scholastic philosophy was assured in more than one way. Most philosophical writers and teachers were clerics, nurtured on church doctrine and subject to church discipline, and the one principle underlying their speculations was that reason should never contradict faith. Thus before the argument starts, the writer knows the answer. It is to be found in faith and belief, as stated by authoritative ecclesiastical sources.

In this respect, in scholastic philosophy the search for truth loses the dynamic and evolutionary quality of Greek philosophy, for among the exciting traits of Greek philosophy is that one never knows at the outset where the argument will lead, what the results of reasoning will be. Less influenced by experimental science than is modern thought, Greek philosophy, unhampered by ecclesiastical discipline, developed into greatness because it refused to take anything for granted. Whatever one may think of the conclusions arrived at by the various schools of Greek philosophy, one is always astounded anew by its exhilarating and bold spirit that challenges everything, that allows no argument to hide behind the protective cloak of authority, whatever its source may be.

The authoritative sources of the scholastic philosophers were the Bible, on which they relied heavily, the church fathers, and the relatively few known works of Greek and Roman antiquity. Aristotle, for example, was not adopted by the church until the thirteenth century; thereafter it became impious to attack him, although he had not been a Christian, and he was generally referred to as "the philosopher." Writers in ancient times relied far less on authority, and the literary technique of copious references and quotations in support of one's argument is largely an invention of these scholastic philosophers of the Middle Ages.

Another link between theology and philosophy in scholasticism was forged in the choice of issues. For example, the problem of free will was discussed in relation to the activities of God and the angels, from the spiritual nature of which deductions were made about analogous human problems. Revealed doctrine was the main source of chosen topics, and dogma was the method of regulation and control of philosophical writing. Finally, the influence of the Inquisition was also a limitation of untrammeled research and inquiry; the prospect of being burned alive probably tended to discourage unorthodox thinkers from going too far in the exploration of new ideas.

Scholastic philosophy reached its "golden age" in the thirteenth century, which was also the peak of papal power. The evolution of the church as an institution of universal aspirations demanded a universal, comprehensive, and systematic philosophy. The synthesis of theological doctrine, as elaborated and refined over a thousand years, provided one cornerstone of the new edifice. The rediscovery of Aristotle provided the other.

In the East the tradition of Aristotelian learning had never been abandoned; Constantinople in particular had long been a center of Greek scholarship. From Constantinople Greek studies spread to the Near East and were then carried by Arab and Jewish scholars to Spain. In the West, however, only a few of Aristotle's writings on logic were known before the middle of the twelfth century. From then on, and especially in the thirteenth century, the spread of Aristotelian studies was the outstanding intellectual event of the age. It began in Spain with translations of Arab and Hebrew versions of Aristotle into Latin. Toledo was one of the first centers of the Aristotelian revival, and it spread from there to Paris and Oxford, the two liveliest clearinghouses of new philosophical ideas in the thirteenth century. Gradually most of Aristotle's works were translated directly from Greek into Latin, and his metaphysics, physics, biology, psychology, politics, and ethics, in addition to his writings on logic already known, became the common property of the western world. At first the church was concerned about the spread of the new doctrines and sought to stem the tide of Aristotelianism by prohibition. But gradually the attitude of the church changed, and Aristotle moved from toleration into official acceptance.

The triumph of Aristotle in the thirteenth century was the work of many men, schools, and universities, but above all it was due to the influence of St. Thomas Aquinas (c. 1225–1274). He was born at the family castle at Roccasecca, halfway between Rome and Naples, of a landed family with an old military and political reputation. From an early age he was brought up by the Benedictines at the nearby monastery of Montecassino. At the age of barely eighteen, he joined the mendicant order of the Dominicans, against the vehement opposition of his family. He studied in Naples, Cologne, and Paris; in Paris he became well known, first as an outstanding student and then as a teacher of theology and philosophy.

Although St. Thomas Aquinas died before he was fifty, his literary output, about seventy works of all kinds and sizes, was truly encyclopedic. It marks the crowning achievement and summation of scholastic philosophy, his lasting accomplishment being the incorporation of Aristotelianism into Christian thought. With St. Augustine, St. Thomas Aquinas is one of the two leaders in the development of church doctrine. *Augustinianism* is the fusion of *Plato* and Christianity. *Thomism* is the synthesis of *Aristotle* and Christianity.

In the first few centuries of its existence, the strong mystical and idealistic tendency in Christianity found philosophical kinship and affinity in Plato; as St. Augustine himself said, Plato came near to Christian knowledge and revelation, and in a sense Christianity was Platonic from the beginning. By the thirteenth century, the nature of the Christian idea and church had changed considerably, and Platonism could no longer serve as the philosophical and metaphysical foundation of an institution in which the accent had changed from individual inspiration and illumination to institutional stability and sobriety. By accepting Thomism over Augustianism as its official doctrinal system, the church signified its preference of Aristotle to Plato. St. Augustine, the North African in whom the fires of faith burned with the intensity of his native sun, sought to reaffirm the spirit of the first Christians, for whom Christianity was faith and love, devoid of philosophy, argument, and law. The victory of Thomism over Augustinianism was the final commitment of the church to the long-term institutional, rational, legal viewpoint.

This victory is remarkable for two reasons. In the first place, it shows that the most decisive issue in the philosophical evolution of the church was in effect a repetition of the dialogue between Plato and Aristotle, adapted to the Christian world and its theology. Until the seventeenth century at least, it seemed that Plato and Aristotle had laid down for all time the two possible basic philosophical systems; with all its hostility to pre-Christian pagan philosophy, medieval scholasticism nevertheless was completely under the spell of Plato and Aristotle.

The second remarkable aspect of the victory of Thomism is the light it throws on the adaptability and high survival capacity of the church. As time went by, particularly from the eleventh century on, it became evident that theology was not enough, and that the challenge of budding humanism and secularism had to be met on its own ground. The adoption of Aristotle by the church, through St. Thomas, indicated its tremendous intellectual vitality and flexibility. In Aristotle the church found a systematic and encyclopedic body of thought, encompassing many disciplines and forming a coherent whole; it was moderate in temper and outlook, adaptable to changing circumstances, full of common sense, and therefore altogether human, supranational, and timeless. Though it lacked the spark and brilliance of Plato's philosophy, it was rich in solidity and endurance, characteristics that are prosaic but that wear well under all conditions. To be born, the church needed Plato. To last, it needed Aristotle.

Aristotle himself, as is true of any great disciple of any great teacher, never ceased to be a Platonist in a profound sense; the victory of Thomism over Augustinianism did not mean the elimination of the latter, or of Platonism, from the intellectual heritage of the church, but the relative stress of the Aristotelian over the Platonic system. Augustinian mysticism and emphasis on faith and individual illumination and grace, when politely relegated to a subordinate position in the official church theology, fled into the developing sects and creeds that sought to revive the original character of Christianity in the late Middle Ages. Their Augustinianism was later championed by the Protestant reformers, who were generally opposed to Thomism, in which they saw too much cold logic and too little personal inspiration. Martin Luther, himself an Augustinian monk, declared that he had not found any book that taught him as much of the meaning of God, Christ, man, and the world as he had learned from the Bible and St. Augustine, and that Aristotle is to theology what darkness is to light: "Only without Aristotle can we become theologians." Protestantism was thus a return to the beginnings of Christianity not only because of its stress on the earlier religious sources over the later, but because of its preference of St. Augustine to St. Thomas Aquinas, of Plato to Aristotle.

St. Thomas Aquinas' approach to the problem of faith and reason denoted as great a concession to rationalism in relation to the Augustinian solution, as the Augustinian solution had been an advance in relation to the antirationalism of Tertullian. St. Thomas conceived of faith and knowledge as divine in origin; therefore conflict between them could never be real, only apparent. He thought that the previous trouble had been due largely to the fact that theologians introduced theological criteria into philosophy, and philosophers attempted to philosophize in theology. However, once it is assumed that knowledge and faith are not opposing but supplementary modes of understanding God and the world, there is no need to reconcile conflict where there is no conflict.

Faith is not contrary to reason but *above reason,* and the results of faith are no less certain than those of reason; they are, in fact, more certain because faith is based on direct revelation of God and therefore closer to the source of all truth than is philosophy, which is based on human insight. If articles of faith could be rationally proved, they would become philosophy, and theology as a separate branch of thought would become unnecessary and disappear: the articles of faith, because of their very nature, however, cannot be intellectually proved; they have to be accepted by an act of *will*. Rational evidence can only support further rational propositions; it can never lead to the foundations of faith, which have to be accepted, not because they correspond to rational evidence, but because they are revealed by God as true. What man can therefore believe, he cannot know, and what he can know, he cannot believe.

If theological truth cannot be proved true by philosophy, neither can it be disproved. Conflict is thus impossible. Where it seems to arise, St. Thomas categorically states that faith is higher than knowledge in the hierarchy of truth, and that something must be wrong with philosophy if it seems to contradict revelation: philosophy is only relatively certain, whereas theology is absolutely certain, inasmuch as it is based on divine authority. St. Thomas thus conceives of faith and knowledge as autonomous in their respective spheres, yet does not separate them in tight compartments. Although faith does not interfere with the ordinary operations of reason, it keeps an overall watch over it, and gives it guidance and purpose.

No one in the history of the church has equaled St. Thomas Aquinas in blending the religious and rational motifs in one vast and rich pattern of thought in which there seems to be room, as in the work of Aristotle, for almost all forms of knowledge and insight. St. Thomas represents the high point of equilibrium that was compatible with the long-term interests of the church, and his position is an enormous concession to rationalism, compared with Tertullian's and St. Augustine's. After St. Thomas, and as early as the fourteenth century, the balance begins to move in the direction of rationalism; the fifteenth century, the cradle of the Renaissance, sees the rebirth of classical humanism, in which knowledge breaks with faith and claims supremacy over it.

The method of argument in St. Thomas' main treatise, the *Summa Theologica,* is characteristic of scholasticism. The entire work (three parts in twenty volumes) is arranged uniformly. Each major subject begins with a question and is subdivided into articles. Each article's heading is again a question, for example, "Whether the Angels Exist in Any Great Number?" The text of the article starts out with a series of "objections" presenting the incorrect doctrinal view (in this particular case, that the number of angels is not great). Immediately following the incorrect arguments presented in the objections, the correct doctrine is given, almost invariably in the form of a direct quotation from an authoritative source. Concerning the problem of the number of angels, St. Thomas quotes (Dan. 7:10): "Thousands of thousands ministered to Him, and ten thousand times a hundred thousand stood before Him." After thus establishing the large number of angels as incontrovertible, St. Thomas then adduces a number of reasons in support of the true doctrine stated in the quotation. Finally he replies specifically to each objection, demolishing them one by one.

A sense of complete certainty pervades the work. There is no slow and groping search toward the discovery of truth, and there are no questions (among the many thousand discussed) that must be kept open for further thought and inquiry. An element of dialectical reasoning in the method gives it its strength: the erroneous views are given a fair and full hearing. However, the end of the dialectical process, the truth, is not derived from the process of reasoning itself but from an authoritative source that reveals the true doctrine. After the true position is made known, reason then finds the supporting arguments. The medieval conception of *philosophy* as the *handmaiden of theology* is thus exemplified in the substance of scholasticism as well as in its method of argument.

St. Thomas Aquinas did not think of himself principally as a philosopher, and much less as a political philosopher, but as a theologian, a "catholic doctor" fervently devoted to Holy Doctrine. His political views may be best culled from two of his works, the short fragment, *On Kingship (De regno),* and *The Sum of Theology (Summa Theologica),* his chief work.

The pre-Thomistic medieval theory of the state, unfamiliar with Aristotle's *Politics* and *Ethics,* viewed the origin of political association, of government, as the result of sin and evil, of the distortion of man's natural and original impulses. St. Augustine had been a typical exponent of this Christian-Stoic conception of the state: God did not intend that man, "His rational creature, who was made in His image, should have dominion over anything but the irrational creation—not man over man, but man over the beasts." St. Thomas meets the Augustinian argument by interpreting the concept of "dominion" in two ways: if dominion refers to slavery, St. Thomas is willing to concede (with the Stoics and Roman lawyers) that there is no slavery in the state of nature. But if dominion refers to the "office of governing and directing free men," it is not incompatible with the state of innocence.

St. Thomas suggests two reasons for the necessity of government even in the state of innocence, before the occurrence of sin and evil: first, "Man is naturally a social being and so in the state of innocence he would have led a social life." Because there must be some organization of social life, government emerges as the specific organ of looking after the common good. Second, if one man surpasses others in knowledge and justice, it would be wrong to disregard such superiority for the benefit of all. St. Thomas thus bases the *need for government* on *man's social nature,* and the *organization of government* on the *superior wisdom and morality of the ruler for the benefit of the ruled.* In both views, his kinship to Aristotle is evident, and it constitutes a sharp break with the typical conceptions of state that had been prevalent until Aristotle's *Politics* became known again in the thirteenth century.

St. Thomas agrees with Aristotle that man's social impulse is the origin of the state, and the good life its purpose. But from here on, St. Thomas, the Christian theologian, goes beyond Aristotle. For the Greek, bound to this world, the good life of the community—though nowhere clearly defined—included practical and spiritual ends that could be attained by joint communal effort *here and now.* St. Thomas cannot be satisfied with the community as the ultimate point of reference and the creative source of spiritual values. His Christian, *other-worldy* concern leads him to the view that the Aristotelian doctrine of the good life is still one step short of the ultimate purpose of existence, because "through virtuous living man is further ordained to a higher end, which consists in the enjoyment of God." Whereas Aristotle, whose philosophy and ethics were humanistic and this-worldly, saw the end of man in values that exist within himself, St. Thomas sees, in addition to such man-centered values, an "extrinsic" good that does not exist in man himself and that is yet the supreme value, namely, "final beatitude which is looked for after death in the enjoyment of God."

Because society has the same end as the individual, the ultimate purpose of social life is not merely virtuous living, "but through virtuous living to attain to the possession of God." If man and society could attain this supreme end by human power, the king (as the supreme representative of human power) could guide them in the right direction. However, St. Thomas argues, the possession of God can be attained only by divine power, and human government is unable to guide men toward this end. The ministry of the kingdom of God is not in the hands of earthly kings, but of priests, and—above all—"the chief priest, the successor of St. Peter, the Vicar of Christ, the Roman Pontiff," to whom all kings are to be subject as to Christ himself.

St. Thomas always looks on the world in hierarchical terms, and his system of values is hierarchical, too. From the viewpoint of human and practical needs, the purposes of secular government are legitimate ends. But those ends are themselves means if viewed in relation to a still higher end, the highest of all: the possession of God. Applying the Aristotelian principle that "the one to whom it pertains to achieve the final end commands those who execute the things that are ordained to that end," St. Thomas arrives at the conclusion that *secular government* is *subject to the church* because the former is concerned with intermediate ends, whereas the latter is concerned with the ultimate end, the salvation of souls.

The question of toleration of heretics illustrates St. Thomas Aquinas' conception of the relation of state and church and also shows how seriously he took his religion. St. Thomas defines heretics as persons who profess the Christian faith "but corrupt its dogmas." The church treats heretics patiently, because it admonishes them twice before it takes drastic action. If the heretic remains stubborn, his crime is graver than other offenses; if forgers of money and other evildoers are put to death, "much more reason is there for heretics, as soon as they are convicted of heresy, to be not only excommunicated but even put to death." Excommunication separates the heretic from the church. In its mercy, the church, because it abhors the shedding of blood by its own organs, "delivers him to the secular tribunal to be exterminated thereby from the world by death." The church thus uses only spiritual weapons, whereas the state, as a temporal power, uses temporal weapons. Yet this separate of ecclesiastical and secular authorities is not final, because church and state cooperate in the highest task of all—the salvation of souls. The church possesses indirect power over secular authorities, employing them for its purposes whenever the defense of the faith so requires.

The death penalty in this world is mild compared with the punishment that awaits the sinner in hell. Of all crimes, the offenses against God are the most serious, and heresy ranks among them. The punishment for such crimes is eternal: first, the souls are punished by the real fire of hell; after the resurrection of the bodies, they, too, are burned in the fire of hell, but miraculously the bodies are never consumed by the fire. The degree of fire depends on the gravity of the sin committed, and heretics will be assigned to the hottest mansions in hell. Another miraculous provision prevents the dulling of the senses or loss of consciousness of the damned who are exposed to eternal hell-fire. The eternity of the penalty ensures that the degree of suffering is constant throughout and that there is no lessening of the pain through habit. The blessed in heaven will watch the sufferings of the damned in hell, in order that "the happiness of the saints may be more delightful to them"; they will rejoice not out of cruelty and hatred, but because they will recognize in these sufferings "the order of divine justice and their own deliverance which will fill them with joy."

St. Thomas was a man of kindness, charity, humility, moderation, and saintliness. His views on heresy, the treatment to be meted out to heretics in this world, and the eternal damnation awaiting them in the hottest chambers of hell are in stark contrast to St. Thomas the man; they reflect the nature of scholasticism at its peak. That dogmatic certainty is likely to lead to persecution of dissenters and eventually to death has been proved time and again in history, regardless of whether the dogmas are religious or political. Scholasticism must have been particularly certain of its premises and conclusions if a saintly and kindly man like St. Thomas Aquinas could hold such extreme views, however inextricably they were bound up with the theological and philosophical system he accepted as valid. Yet he could not go the whole way. He conceded that under certain circumstances heresy be tolerated: when heretics and unbelievers are numerous, the church may tolerate them in order to avoid disturbances of the peace.

As to the nature and form of political authority, St. Thomas Aquinas starts with the premise that government is related to the divine order. Therefore, because the commandments of God include the duty of obedience to superiors, "disobedience to the commands of a superior is a mortal sin." St. Thomas follows Aristotle in classifying the forms of government into good types, in which the interest of the governed is served, and bad types, in which the interest of the ruler or rulers prevails. But, whereas

Aristotle, with some hesitation and only under qualified circumstances, preferred monarchy as the best form of government, St. Thomas is much more unequivocal in his choice of *monarchy*.

Aristotle preferred monarchy because he believed that it was not likely that superior moral and intellectual qualities could be found in more than one man; his hesitation in committing himself absolutely can be attributed to his doubt that the right man can be found. St. Thomas, on the other hand, derives his preference for the monarchial form of government from his religious view of the world. He notices that "in the whole universe there is one God, Maker and Ruler of all things." In the multitude of bodily members, the heart rules all the others; among the bees, there is "one king bee," and generally "every natural government is government by one." The governing element represents, in a multiplicity of things, their purpose and guiding principle. In political society, the main practical task and purpose is the unity of peace. St. Thomas identifies unity with peace; he is therefore led to the conclusion that one ruler is most likely to maintain the peace that goes with complete unity, whereas a government made up of several persons might endanger social peace and stability through disagreement.

But St. Thomas seeks to delimit monarchy so that it will not degenerate into tyranny. First, he prefers elective to hereditary kingship: both papacy and empire were ruled by elective heads, as contrasted with the national dynasties in England and France that tended to become hereditary. Second, he suggests that the king's power "be so tempered that he cannot easily fall into tyranny." Without indicating in detail how this tempering is to be accomplished, St. Thomas in one passage stresses the important concept that "all should take some share in the government," and he also views sympathetically the idea of the *mixed constitution* in which monarchy is supplemented by aristocratic and popular elements of participation in government.

St. Thomas is aware that even a limited, or constitutional, monarchy, is no cure-all in itself and that it, too, may degenerate into tyranny. But he distinguishes minor tyranny from excessive tyranny. Regarding the first, he warns that hasty action against the tyrant may unleash unforeseen consequences worse than the evil to be remedied. He also says that *revolutionary resistance to minor tyranny*, if successful, is likely to lead to *even worse tyranny*, because the leader of the victorious revolution, "fearing to suffer from another what he did to his predecessor, oppresses the subjects with an even more grievous slavery." St. Thomas is perhaps the first writer on the problem of revolution who understands its inner dynamic, which cannot be halted at will once it is set in motion. He feared that revolution is nearly always a higher price than the evil it seeks to remedy; Edmund Burke was later to apply this Thomistic doctrine to the analysis and condemnation of the French Revolution.

Regarding *excessive tyranny* that becomes unbearable, St. Thomas does not endorse John of Salisbury's justification of *tyrannicide;* it is not up to private persons to decide that the king is a tyrant and then slay him. Such assumption of authority by subjects would be dangerous to the rulers as well as to the people, particularly because wicked men find the rule of a good king no less burdensome than that of a tyrant. If any action is to be taken against tyrants, it can be done only through public authority. Thus, if the people have the right to elect their king, they may lawfully depose him or restrict his power should he abuse it. But if the prince has been appointed by a higher sovereign, only that sovereign may depose him. In the event there is no human remedy, God alone can bring relief, for "it lies in his power to turn the cruel heart of the tyrant to mildness." St. Thomas relates the tyranny of the ruler to the sins of the ruled; tyrants rule by divine permission, as a punishment for the sins of the subjects. If God is to help them against the tyrant, the people must desist from sin.

The part of St. Thomas' political theory that is not primarily Aristotelian is his philosophy of law as developed in the *Summa Theologica*. The great contribution of the Middle Ages to the store of civilization is the conception of the *supremacy of law* based on the *custom of the community*. The origins of this conception are partly to be found in the Jewish-Christian doctrine of a divine law above the human law, and partly in the Stoic-Roman consciousness of the rational ordering of the world and its reflection in human society. The feudal system itself was largely a product of custom, and the relations between feudal lord and vassal were determined by custom, or law based on custom. The concept of sovereignty was not alien to the Middle Ages; but it was a sovereignty of the *law,* whereas in antiquity and in modern times the idea of sovereignty is attached to the *lawgiver*—a monarch or an aristocracy in the nondemocratic form of sovereignty, and the people in the democratic application of sovereignty. The medieval preference of communal custom to deliberate decision as the basis of the law was not mere philosophical predilection but the ideological reflection of a social reality in which status rather than contract was predominant, in which mobility was relatively low, and political authority greatly decentralized.

In his analysis of law, St. Thomas distinguishes four forms: eternal law, natural law, divine law, and human law. *Eternal law* is identical with the divine reason that governs the universe, and St. Thomas calls it eternal, because God's reason, God's rule of the world, "is not subject to time but is eternal."

As to *natural law,* St. Thomas says that all things, irrational animals and rational man, are subject to divine reason, to eternal law. But only man, as a rational creature, participates in divine providence and reason in a special way, for he provides for himself and for others, whereas all other creations of God, irrational animals and inanimate things, reflect divine reason only by receiving from it the inclinations to their proper acts and ends. Natural law is therefore man's active and transpersonal rationality, his "participation of the eternal law."

More specifically, St. Thomas divides natural law into three species: first, there is the good that man pursues in accordance with the nature he has in common with all substances, such as self-preservation. Next, there is the inclination he has toward certain forms of conduct that he shares with animals, such as "sexual intercourse, education of offspring and so forth." Third, there is the inclination in him that is specifically human, such as the desire to know God, live in society, and avoid offending those with whom one lives.

Divine law is related by St. Thomas to the fact that man's reason is neither the sole nor the most reliable guide to his apprehension of truth and justice. Divine law is communicated to man through revelation in the Old and New Testaments, and it is in no way contradictory to natural law apprehended by reason. St. Thomas' general doctrine that "grace does not abolish nature but perfects it" also applies to divine law, which is revealed by God as an act of grace.

The fourth, and lowest, form of law is *human law;* it is defined by St. Thomas as an "ordinance of reason for the common good, made by him who has care of the community, and promulgated." The need for human law arises out of two difficulties: first, the impossibility of perfectly apprehending, through the human mind, the dictates of divine reason; second, the difficulty of properly applying general principles of natural law to specific situations and circumstances.

There is little room for arbitrariness in St. Thomas' conception of human law, because it must meet several critical tests. First, for a command to have the nature of law, "it needs to be in accord with some rule of reason." Imperfect as the connection between a specific rule of law and first principles of reason may be, some link between the two must exist. The second major characteristic of law is, according to St. Thomas, that it be just and in harmony with the common good; otherwise it is "devoid of the nature of law." The third essential characteristic of the law is legitimacy: it must derive either from the people or from someone who has been entrusted by the people with the office of governing them. Though St. Thomas preferred monarchy to other forms of state, he sharply distinguished it from tyranny, which is illegitimate government. Finally, St. Thomas held that law, to be valid, must be duly promulgated. Unlike the precepts of reason and natural law, which can be grasped by logical deduction, human laws are not endowed with unerring finality; they apply to specific circumstances and therefore must be clearly and publicly promulgated. St. Thomas' insistence on publicity in the legal system is an important contribution to a principle that is one of the primary services the law renders to social life: security.

Forty-nine years after his death, St. Thomas Aquinas was canonized. It was officially held by the church that his doctrine could, not have come into existence without a miracle of God, and that his doctrine had done more to illuminate the church then the teachings of all other writers, teachers, and doctors together. From then on, the acceptance of Thomism as the official doctrine of the church has been steady. A large number of popes in the Middle Ages and in the modern period have declared Thomism to be the authoritative guide to doctrine and faith. Leo XIII issued the Encyclical *Aeterni Patris* on August 4, 1879, in which he ordered that the doctrines of St. Thomas, "the preeminent guardian and glory of the Catholic Church," be henceforth taught in its academies and schools. In later official pronouncements, Pope Leo XIII decreed that if other writers and theologians disagree with St. Thomas, the "former must be sacrificed to the latter."

The *Summa Theologica* was prescribed as the text of theology in Catholic universities and academies authorized to grant academic degrees and doctorates in philosophy, and all Catholic universities, colleges, and schools were put under the patronage of St. Thomas Aquinas. Pope Pius X declared in his pronouncement of June 29, 1914, that the "capital theses in the philosophy of St. Thomas are not to be placed in the category of opinions capable of being debated one way or another," and he warned all teachers of philosophy and theology that "if they deviated so much as a step, in metaphysics especially, from Aquinas, they exposed themselves to grave risk." The Code of Canon Law, promulgated on May 27, 1917, ordered teachers in Catholic schools to "deal in every particular with the studies of mental philosophy and theology and the education of pupils in such sciences according to the method, doctrine and principles of the Angelic Doctor and religiously to adhere thereto."

Since that time Thomism has been reaffirmed as the official doctrine of the Roman Catholic Church; in addition to conservative Catholic philosophers who are completely committed to the Thomistic line of thought, outstanding liberal Catholic thinkers like Jacques Maritain have also enthusiastically contributed to the renaissance of Thomism. This fact in itself demonstrates the vitality and flexibility of St. Thomas Aquinas' ideas.

How St. Thomas himself would react to the movement of setting him up as the authoritative source of doctrine is difficult to envision. He lived in a turbulent intellectual age that experimented with new sources and materials, and he refashioned the traditional approaches to basic philosophical problems. A profound believer, he nevertheless did not hesitate to reconstruct belief on new foundations. He might have felt that he was not a "Thomist" but a student and teacher seeking to reconcile faith and reason, and he might have doubted, in his modesty and humility, that his views commanded timeless authority.

ST. THOMAS AQUINAS

*On Kingship**

DEFINITION OF KINGSHIP

The first step in our undertaking must be to set forth what is to be understood by the term *king*.

In all things which are ordered towards an end, wherein this or that course may be adopted, some directive principle is needed through which the due end may be reached by the most direct route. A ship, for example, which moves in different directions according to the impulse of the changing winds, would never reach its destination were it not brought to port by the skill of the pilot. Now, man has an end to which his whole life and all his actions are ordered; for man is an intelligent agent, and it is clearly the part of an intelligent agent to act in view of an end. Men also adopt different methods in proceeding towards their proposed end, as the diversity of men's pursuits and actions clearly indicates. Consequently man needs some directive principle to guide him towards his end.

To be sure, the light of reason is placed by nature in every man, to guide him in his acts towards his end. Wherefore, if man were intended to live alone, as many animals do, he would require no other guide to his end. Each man would be a king unto himself, under God, the highest King, inasmuch as he would direct himself in his acts by the light of reason given him from on high. Yet it is natural for man, more than for any other animal, to be a social and political animal, to live in a group.

This is clearly a necessity of man's nature. For all other animals, nature has prepared food, hair as a covering, teeth, horns, claws as means of defence or at least speed in flight, while man alone was made without any natural provisions for these things. Instead of all these, man was endowed with reason, by the use of which he could procure all these things for himself by the work of his hands. Now, one man alone is not able to procure them all for himself, for one man could not sufficiently provide for life, unassisted. It is therefore natural that man should live in the society of many.

Moreover, all other animals are able to discern, by inborn skill, what is useful and what is injurious, even as the sheep naturally regards the wolf as his enemy. Some animals also recognize by natural skill certain medicinal herbs and other things necessary for their life. Man, on the contrary, has a natural knowledge of the things which are essential for his life only in a general fashion, inasmuch as he is able to attain knowledge of the particular things necessary for human life by reasoning from natural principles. But it is not possible for one man to arrive at a knowledge of all these things by his own individual reason. It is therefore necessary for man to live in a multitude so that each one may assist his fellows, and different men may be occupied in seeking, by their reason, to make different discoveries—one, for example, in medicine, one in this and another in that.

This point is further and most plainly evidenced by the fact that the use of speech is a prerogative proper to man. By this means, one man is able fully to express his conceptions

---

*From St. Thomas Aquinas, *On Kingship* (trans. Gerald B. Phelan, rev., with introduction and notes, by I. T. Eschmann; copyright, 1949, by The Pontifical Institute of Medieval Studies, Toronto). By permission.

to others. Other animals, it is true, express their feelings to one another in a general way, as a dog may express anger by barking and other animals give vent to other feelings in various fashions. But man communicates with his kind more completely than any other animal known to be gregarious, such as the crane, the ant or the bee.—With this in mind, Solomon says: "It is better that there be two than one; for they have the advantage of their company."

If, then, it is natural for man to live in the society of many, it is necessary that there exist among men some means by which the group may be governed. For where there are many men together and each one is looking after his own interest, the multitude would be broken up and scattered unless there were also an agency to take care of what appertains to the commonweal. In like manner, the body of a man or any other animal would disintegrate unless there were a general ruling force within the body which watches over the common good of all members.—With this in mind, Solomon says: "Where there is no governor, the people shall fall."

Indeed it is reasonable that this should happen, for what is proper and what is common are not identical. Things differ by what is proper to each: they are united by what they have in common. But diversity of effects is due to diversity of causes. Consequently, there must exist something which impels towards the common good of the many, over and above that which impels towards the particular good of each individual. Wherefore also in all things that are ordained towards one end, one thing is found to rule the rest. Thus in the corporeal universe, by the first body, i.e. the celestial body, the other bodies are regulated according to the order of Divine Providence; and all bodies are ruled by a rational creature. So, too, in the individual man, the soul rules the body; and among the parts of the soul, the irascible and the concupiscible parts are ruled by reason. Likewise, among the members of a body, one, such as the heart or the head, is the principal and moves all the others. Therefore in every multitude there must be some governing power.

Now it happens in certain things which are ordained towards an end that one may proceed in a right way and also in a wrong way. So, too, in the government of a multitude there is a distinction between right and wrong. A thing is rightly directed when it is led towards a befitting end; wrongly when it is led towards an unbefitting end. Now the end which befits a multitude of free men is different from that which befits a multitude of slaves, for the free man is one who exists for his own sake, while the slave, as such, exists for the sake of another. If, therefore, a multitude of free men is ordered by the ruler towards the common good of the multitude, that rulership will be right and just, as is suitable to free men. If, on the other hand, a rulership aims, not at the common good of the multitude, but at the private good of the ruler, it will be an unjust and perverted rulership. The Lord, therefore, threatens such rulers, saying by the mouth of Ezechiel: "Woe to the shepherds that feed themselves (seeking, that is, their own interest): should not the flocks be fed by the shepherd?" Shepherds indeed should seek the good of their flocks, and every ruler, the good of the multitude subject to him.

If an unjust government is carried on by one man alone, who seeks his own benefit from his rule and not the good of the multitude subject to him, such a ruler is called a *tyrant*—a word derived from *strength*—because he oppresses by might instead of ruling by justice. Thus among the ancients all powerful men were called tyrants. If an unjust government is carried on, not by one but by several, and if they be few, it is called an *oligarchy,* that is, the rule of a few. This occurs when a few, who differ from the tyrant only by the fact that they are more than one, oppress the people by means of their wealth. If, finally, the bad government is carried on by the multitude, it is called a *democracy, i.e.* control by the populace, which comes about when the plebeian people by force of numbers oppress the rich. In this way the whole people will be as one tyrant.

In like manner we must divide just governments. If the government is administered by many, it is given the name common to all forms of government, *viz. polity,* as for instance when a group of warriors exercise dominion over a city or province. If it is administered by a few men of virtue, this kind of government is called an *aristocracy, i.e.* noble governance, or governance by noble men, who for this reason are called the *Optimates.* And if a just government is in the hands of one man alone, he is properly called a *king.* Wherefore the Lord says by the mouth of Ezechiel: "My servant, David, shall be king over them and all of them shall have one shepherd."

From this it is clearly shown that the idea of king implies that he be one man who is chief and that he be a shepherd seeking the common good of the multitude and not his own.

Now since man must live in a group, because he is not sufficient unto himself to procure the necessities of life were he to remain solitary, it follows that a society will be the more perfect the more it is sufficient unto itself to procure the necessities of life. There is, to some extent, sufficiency for life in one *family of one household,* namely, insofar as pertains to the natural acts of nourishment and the begetting of offspring and other things of this kind. Self-sufficiency exists, furthermore, in one *street* with regard to those things which belong to the trade of one guild. In a *city,* which is the perfect community, it exists with regard to all the necessities of life. Still more self-sufficiency is found in a *province* because of the need of fighting together and of mutual help against enemies. Hence the man ruling a perfect community, *i.e.* a city or a province, is antonomastically called *the* king. The ruler of a household is called father, not king, although he bears a certain resemblance to the king, for which reason kings are sometimes called the fathers of their peoples.

It is plain, therefore, from what has been said, that a king is one who rules the people of one city or province, and rules them for the common good. Wherefore Solomon says: "The king ruleth over all the land subject to him."

RULE BY ONE OR BY MANY?

Having set forth these preliminary points we must now inquire what is better for a province or a city: whether to be ruled by one man or by many.

This question may be considered first from the viewpoint of the purpose of government. The aim of any ruler should be directed towards securing the welfare of that which he undertakes to rule. The duty of the pilot, for instance, is to preserve his ship amidst the perils of the sea and to bring it unharmed to the port of safety. Now the welfare and safety of a multitude formed into a society lies in the preservation of its unity, which is called peace. If this is removed, the benefit of social life is lost and, moreover, the multitude in its disagreement becomes a burden to itself. The chief concern of the ruler of a multitude, therefore, is to procure the unity of peace. It is not even legitimate for him to deliberate whether he shall establish peace in the multitude subject to him, just as a physician does not deliberate whether he shall heal the sick man encharged to him, for no one should deliberate about an end which he is obliged to seek, but only about the means to attain that end. Wherefore the Apostle, having commended the unity of the faithful people, says: "Be ye careful to keep the unity of the spirit in the bond of peace." Thus, the more efficacious a government is in keeping the unity of peace, the more useful it will be. For we call that more useful which leads more directly to the end. Now it is manifest that what is itself one can more efficaciously bring about unity than several—just as the most efficacious cause of heat is that which is by its nature hot. Therefore the rule of one man is more useful than the rule of many.

Furthermore, it is evident that several persons could by no means preserve the stability of the community if they totally disagreed. For union is necessary among them if they are to rule at all: several men, for instance, could not pull a ship in one direction unless joined together in some fashion. Now several are said to be united according as they come closer to being one. So one man rules better than several who come near being one.

Again, whatever is in accord with nature is best, for in all things nature does what is best. Now, every natural governance is governance by one. In the multitude of bodily members there is one which is the principal mover, namely, the heart; and among the powers of the soul one power presides as chief, namely, the reason. Among bees there is one king bee and in the whole universe there is One God, Maker and Ruler of all things. And there is a reason for this. Every multitude is derived from unity. Wherefore, if artificial things are an imitation of natural things and a work of art is better according as it attains a closer likeness to what is in nature, it follows that it is best for a human multitude to be ruled by one person.

This is also evident from experience. For provinces or cities which are not ruled by one person are torn with dissensions and tossed about without peace, so that the complaint seems to be fulfilled which the Lord uttered through the Prophet: "Many pastors have destroyed my vineyard." On the other hand, provinces and cities which are ruled under one king enjoy peace, flourish in justice, and delight in prosperity. Hence, the Lord by His prophets promises to His people as a great reward that He will give them one head and that "one Prince will be in the midst of them."

RESISTANCE TO TYRANTS

Therefore, since the rule of one man, which is the best, is to be preferred, and since it may happen that it be changed into a tyranny, which is the worst (all this is clear from what has been said), a scheme should be carefully worked out which would prevent the multitude ruled by a king from falling into the hands of a tyrant.

First, it is necessary that the man who is raised up to be king by those whom it concerns should be of such condition that it is improbable that he should become a tyrant. Wherefore Daniel, commending the providence of God with respect to the institution of the king says: "The Lord hath sought him a man according to his own heart, and the Lord hath appointed him to be prince over his people." Then, once the king is established, the government of the kingdom must be so arranged that opportunity to tyrannize is removed. At the same time his power should be so tempered that he cannot easily fall into tyranny. How these things may be done we must consider in what follows.

Finally, provision must be made for facing the situation should the king stray into tyranny.

Indeed, if there be not an excess of tyranny it is more expedient to tolerate the milder tyranny for a while than, by acting against the tyrant, to become involved in many perils more grievous than the tyranny itself. For it may happen that those who act against the tyrant are unable to prevail and

the tyrant then will rage the more. But should one be able to prevail against the tyrant, from this fact itself very grave dissensions among the people frequently ensue: the multitude may be broken up into factions either during their revolt against the tyrant, or in process of the organization of the government, after the tyrant has been overthrown. Moreover, it sometimes happens that while the multitude is driving out the tyrant by the help of some man, the latter, having received the power, thereupon seizes the tyranny. Then, fearing to suffer from another what he did to his predecessor, he oppresses his subjects with an even more grievous slavery. This is wont to happen in tyranny, namely, that the second becomes more grievous than the one preceding, inasmuch as, without abandoning the previous oppressions, he himself thinks up fresh ones from the malice of his heart. Whence in Syracuse, at a time when everyone desired the death of Dionysius, a certain old woman kept constantly praying that he might be unharmed and that he might survive her. When the tyrant learned this he asked why she did it. Then she said: "When I was a girl we had a harsh tyrant and I wished for his death; when he was killed, there succeeded him one who was a little harsher. I was very eager to see the end of his dominion also, and we began to have a third ruler still more harsh—that was you. So if you should be taken away, a worse would succeed in your place."

If the excess of tyranny is unbearable, some have been of the opinion that it would be an act of virtue for strong men to slay the tyrant and to expose themselves to the danger of death in order to set the multitude free. An example of this occurs even in the Old Testament, for a certain Aioth slew Eglon, King of Moab, who was oppressing the people of God under harsh slavery, thrusting a dagger into his thigh; and he was made a judge of the people.

But this opinion is not in accord with apostolic teaching. For Peter admonishes us to be reverently subject to our masters, not only to the good and gentle but also the froward: "For if one who suffers unjustly bear his trouble for conscience's sake, this is grace." Wherefore, when many emperors of the Romans tyrannically persecuted the faith of Christ, a great number both of the nobility and the common people were converted to the faith and were praised for patiently bearing death for Christ. They did not resist although they were armed, and this is plainly manifested in the case of the holy Theban legion. Aioth, then, must be considered rather as having slain a foe than assassinated a ruler, however tyrannical, of the people. Hence in the Old Testament we also read that they who killed Joas, the king of Juda, who had fallen away from the worship of God, were slain and their children spared according to the precept of the law.

Should private persons attempt on their own private presumption to kill the rulers, even though tyrants, this would be dangerous for the multitude as well as for their rulers. This is because the wicked usually expose themselves to dangers of this kind more than the good, for the rule of a king, no less than that of a tyrant, is burdensome to them since, according to the words of Solomon: "A wise king scattereth the wicked." Consequently, by presumption of this kind, danger to the people from the loss of a good king would be more probable than relief through the removal of a tyrant.

Furthermore, it seems that to proceed against the cruelty of tyrants is an action to be undertaken, not through the private presumption of a few, but rather by public authority.

If to provide itself with a king belongs to the right of a given multitude, it is not unjust that the king be deposed or have his power restricted by that same multitude if, becoming a tyrant, he abuses the royal power. It must not be thought that such a multitude is acting unfaithfully in deposing the tyrant, even though it had previously subjected itself to him in perpetuity, because he himself has deserved that the covenant with his subjects should not be kept, since, in ruling the multitude, he did not act faithfully as the office of a king demands. Thus did the Romans, who had accepted Tarquin the Proud as their king, cast him out from the kingship on account of his tyranny and the tyranny of his sons; and they set up in their place a lesser power, namely, the consular power. Similarly Domitian, who had succeeded those most moderate emperors, Vespasian, his father, and Titus, his brother, was slain by the Roman senate when he exercised tyranny, and all his wicked deeds were justly and profitably declared null and void by a decree of the senate. Thus it came about that Blessed John the Evangelist, the beloved disciple of God, who had been exiled to the island of Patmos by that very Domitian, was sent back to Ephesus by a decree of the senate.

If, on the other hand, it pertains to the right of a higher authority to provide a king for a certain multitude, a remedy against the wickedness of a tyrant is to be looked for from him. Thus when Archelaus, who had already begun to reign in Judaea in the place of Herod his father, was imitating his father's wickedness, a complaint against him having been laid before Caesar Augustus by the Jews, his power was at first diminished by depriving him of his title of king and by dividing one-half of his kingdom between his two brothers. Later, since he was not restrained from tyranny even by this means, Tiberius Caesar sent him into exile to Lugdunum, a city in Gaul.

Should no human aid whatsoever against a tyrant be forthcoming, recourse must be had to God, the King of all, Who is a helper in due time in tribulation. For it lies in His power to turn the cruel heart of the tyrant to mildness. According to Solomon: "The heart of the king is in the hand of the Lord, whithersoever He will He shall turn it." He it was who turned into mildness the cruelty of King Assuerus, who was preparing death for the Jews. He it was who so filled the cruel king Nabuchodonosor with piety that he became a proclaimer of the divine power. "Therefore," he said, "I, Nabuchodonosor do now praise and magnify and glorify the King of Heaven; because all His works are true and His ways judgments, and they that walk in pride He is able to abase." Those tyrants, however, whom he deems unworthy of conversion, he is able to put out of the way or to degrade, according to the words of the Wise Man: "God hath overturned the thrones of proud princes and hath set up the meek in their stead." He it was who, seeing the affliction of his people in Egypt and hearing their cry, hurled Pharaoh, a tyrant over God's people, with all his army into the sea. He it was who not only banished from his kingly throne the above-mentioned Nabuchodonosor because of his former pride, but also cast him from the fellowship of men and changed him into the likeness of a beast.

Indeed, his hand is not shortened that He cannot free His people from tyrants. For by Isaias He promised to give his people rest from their labours and lashings and harsh slavery in which they had formerly served; and by Ezechiel He says: "I will deliver my flock from their mouth," *i.e.* from the mouth of shepherds who feed themselves.

But to deserve to secure this benefit from God, the people must desist from sin, for it is by divine permission that wicked men receive power to rule as a punishment for sin, as the Lord says by the Prophet Osee: "I will give thee a king in my wrath" and it is said in *Job* that he "maketh a man that is a hypocrite to reign for the sins of the people." Sin must therefore be done away with in order that the scourge of tyrants may cease.

KINGS ARE SUBJECT TO PRIESTS

Just as the founding of a city or kingdom may suitably be learned from the way in which the world was created, so too the way to govern may be learned from the divine government of the world.

Before going into that, however, we should consider that to govern is to lead the thing governed in a suitable way towards its proper end. Thus a ship is said to be governed when, through the skill of the pilot, it is brought unharmed and by a direct route to harbour. Consequently, if a thing be directed to an end outside itself (as a ship to the harbour), it is the governor's duty, not only to preserve the thing unharmed, but further to guide it towards this end. If, on the contrary, there be a thing whose end is not outside itself, then the governor's endeavours will merely tend to preserve the thing undamaged in its proper perfection.

Nothing of this kind is to be found in reality, except God Himself, Who is the end of all. However, as concerns the thing which is directed to an end outside itself, care is exercised by different providers in different ways. One might have the task of preserving a thing in its being, another of bringing it to a further perfection. Such is clearly the case in the example of the ship; (the first meaning of the word *gubernator* [governor] is *pilot*). It is the carpenter's business to repair anything which might be broken, while the pilot bears the responsibility of bringing the ship to port. It is the same with man. The doctor sees to it that a man's life is preserved; the tradesman supplies the necessities of life; the teacher takes care that man may learn the truth; and the tutor sees that he lives according to reason.

Now if man were not ordained to another end outside himself, the above-mentioned cares would be sufficient for him. But as long as man's mortal life endures there is an extrinsic good for him, namely, final beatitude which is looked for after death in the enjoyment of God, for as the Apostle says: "As long as we are in the body we are far from the Lord." Consequently the Christian man, for whom that beatitude has been purchased by the blood of Christ, and who, in order to attain it, has received the earnest of the Holy Ghost, needs another and spiritual care to direct him to the harbour of eternal salvation, and this care is provided for the faithful by the ministers of the church of Christ.

Now the same judgment is to be formed about the end of society as a whole as about the end of one man. If, therefore, the ultimate end of man were some good that existed in himself, then the ultimate end of the multitude to be governed would likewise be for the multitude to acquire such good, and persevere in its possession. If such an ultimate end either of an individual man or a multitude were a corporeal one, namely, life and health of body, to govern would then be a physician's charge. If that ultimate end were an abundance of wealth, then knowledge of economics would have the last word in the community's government. If the good of the knowledge of truth were of such a kind that the multitude might attain to it, the king would have to be a teacher. It is, however, clear that the end of a multitude gathered together is to live virtuously. For men form a group for the purpose of *living well* together, a thing which the individual man living alone could not attain, and *good life* is virtuous life. Therefore, virtuous life is the end for which men gather together. The evidence for this lies in the fact that only those who render mutual assistance to one another in living well form a genuine part of an assembled multitude. If men assembled merely to live, then animals and slaves would form a part of the civil community. Or, if men assembled only to accrue wealth, then all those who traded together would belong to one city. Yet we see that only such are regarded as forming one multitude as are directed by the same laws and the same government to live well.

Yet through virtuous living man is further ordained to a higher end, which consists in the enjoyment of God, as we have said above. Consequently, since society must have the same end as the individual man, it is not the ultimate end of an assembled multitude to live virtuously, but through virtuous living to attain to the possession of God.

If this end could be attained by the power of human nature, then the duty of a king would have to include the direction of men to it. We are supposing, of course, that he is called king to whom the supreme power of governing in human affairs is entrusted. Now the higher the end to which a government is ordained, the loftier that government is. Indeed, we always find that the one to whom it pertains to achieve the final end commands those who execute the things that are ordained to that end. For example, the captain, whose business it is to regulate navigation, tells the shipbuilder what kind of ship he must construct to be suitable for navigation; and the ruler of a city, who makes use of arms, tells the blacksmith what kind of arms to make. But because a man does not attain his end, which is the possession of God, by human power but by divine—according to the words of the Apostle: "By the grace of God life everlasting"—, therefore the task of leading him to that last end does not pertain to human but to divine government.

Consequently, government of this kind pertains to that king who is not only a man, but also God, namely, our Lord Jesus Christ, Who by making men sons of God brought them to the glory of Heaven. This then is the government which has been delivered to Him and which "shall not be destroyed," on account of which He is called, in Holy Writ, not Priest only, but King. As Jeremias says: "The king shall reign and he shall be wise." Hence a royal priesthood is derived from Him, and what is more, all those who believe in Christ, insofar as they are His members, are called kings and priests.

Thus, in order that spiritual things might be distinguished from earthly things, the ministry of this kingdom has been entrusted not to earthly kings but to priests, and most of all to the chief priest, the successor of St. Peter, thě Vicar of Christ, the Roman Pontiff. To him all the kings of the Christian People are to be subject as to our Lord Jesus Christ Himself. For those to whom pertains the care of intermediate ends should be subject to him to whom pertains the care of the ultimate end, and be directed by his rule.

Because the priesthood of the gentiles and the whole worship of their gods existed merely for the acquisition of temporal goods (which were all ordained to the common good of the multitude, whose care devolved upon the king), the priests of the gentiles were very properly subject to the kings. Similarly, since in the old law earthly goods were promised to the religious people (not indeed by demons but by the true God), the priests of the old law, we read, were also subject to the kings. But in the new law there is a higher priesthood by which men are guided to heavenly goods. Consequently, in the law of Christ, kings must be subject to priests.

It was therefore also a marvellous disposition of Divine Providence that, in the city of Rome, which God had foreseen would be the principal seat of the Christian priesthood, the custom was gradually established that the rulers of the city should be subject to the priests, for as Valerius Maximus relates: "Our city has always considered that everything should yield precedence to religion, even those things in which it aimed to display the splendour of supreme majesty. We therefore unhesitatingly made the imperial dignity minister to religion, considering that the empire would thus hold control of human affairs if faithfully and constantly it were submissive to the divine power."

And because it was to come to pass that the religion of the Christian priesthood should especially thrive in France, God provided that among the Gauls too their tribal priests, called Druids, should lay down the law of all Gaul, as Julius Caesar relates in the book which he wrote about the Gallic war.

Summa Theologica*

WHETHER LAW IS SOMETHING PERTAINING TO REASON?

Objection 1   It seems that law is not something pertaining to reason. For the Apostle says (Rom, vii. 23): *I see another law in my members,* etc. But nothing pertaining to reason is in the members; since the reason does not make use of a bodily organ. Therefore law is not something pertaining to reason.

Obj. 2   Further, in the reason there is nothing else but power, habit, and act. But law is not the power itself of reason. In like manner, neither is it a habit of reason: because the habits of reason are the intellectual virtues of which we have spoken. Nor again is it an act of reason: because then law would cease, when the act of reason ceases, for instance, while we are asleep. Therefore law is nothing pertaining to reason.

Obj. 3   Further, the law moves those who are subject to it to act aright. But it belongs properly to the will to move to act, as is evident from what has been said. Therefore law pertains, not to the reason, but to the will; according to the words of the Jurist *(Lib. i. ff., De Const. Prin.): Whatsoever pleaseth the sovereign, has force of law.*

On the contrary, it belongs to the law to command and to forbid. But it belongs to reason to command. Therefore law is something pertaining to reason.

I answer that, law is a rule and measure of acts, whereby man is induced to act or is restrained from acting: for *lex* (law) is derived from *ligare* (to bind), because it binds one to act. Now the rule and measure of human acts is the reason, which is the first principle of human acts, as is evident from what has been stated above; since it belongs to the reason to direct to the end, which is the first principle in all matters of action, according to the Philosopher *(Phys. ii.).* Now that which is the principle in any genus, is the rule and measure of that genus: for instance, unity in the genus of numbers, and the first movement in the genus of movements. Consequently it follows that law is something pertaining to reason.

Reply Obj. 1   Since law is a kind of rule and measure, it may be in something in two ways. First, as in that which measures and rules: and since this is proper to reason, it follows that, in this way, law is in the reason alone.—Secondly, as in that which is measured and ruled. In this way, law is in all those things that are inclined to something by reason of some law: so that any inclination arising from a law, may be called a law, not essentially but by participation as it were. And thus the inclination of the members to concupiscence is called *the law of the members.*

Reply Obj. 2   Just as, in external action, we may consider the work and the work done, for instance the work of building and the house built; so in the acts of reason, we may consider the act itself of reason, *i.e.,* to understand and to reason, and something produced by this act. With regard to the speculative reason, this is first of all the definition; secondly, the proposition; thirdly, the syllogism or argument. And since also the practical reason makes use of a syllogism in respect of the work to be done, as stated above and as the Philosopher teaches *(Ethic.* vii.); hence we find in the practical reason something that holds the same position in regard to conclusions. Suchlike universal

*From St. Thomas Aquinas, *Summa Theologica* (trans. the Fathers of the English Dominican Province. Copyright by Benziger Bros., Inc., New York, 1947). By permission.

propositions of the practical intellect that are directed to actions have the nature of law. And these propositions are sometimes under our actual consideration, while sometimes they are retained in the reason by means of a habit.

Reply Obj. 3   Reason has its power of moving from the will: for it is due to the fact that one wills the end, that the reason issues its commands as regards things ordained to the end. But in order that the volition of what is commanded may have the nature of law, it needs to be in accord with some rule of reason. And in this sense is to be understood the saying that the will of the sovereign has the force of law; otherwise the sovereign's will would savour of lawlessness rather than of law.

WHETHER THE LAW IS ALWAYS DIRECTED TO THE COMMON GOOD?

Objection 1   It seems that the law is not always directed to the common good as to its end. For it belongs to law to command and to forbid. But commands are directed to certain individual goods. Therefore the end of the law is not always the common good.

Obj. 2   Further, the law directs man in his actions. But human actions are concerned with particular matters. Therefore the law is directed to some particular good.

Obj. 3   Further, Isidore says (*Etym.* ii.): *If the law is based on reason, whatever is based on reason will be a law.* But reason is the foundation not only of what is ordained to the common good, but also of that which is directed to private good. Therefore the law is not only directed to the good of all, but also to the private good of an individual.

On the contrary, Isidore says (*Etym.* v.) that *laws are enacted for no private profit, but for the common benefit of the citizens.*

I answer that the law belongs to that which is a principle of human acts, because it is their rule and measure. Now as reason is a principle of human acts, so in reason itself there is something which is the principle in respect of all the rest: wherefore to this principle chiefly and mainly law must

needs be referred.—Now the first principle in practical matters, which are the object of the practical reason, is the last end: and the last end of human life is bliss or happiness. Consequently the law must needs regard principally the relationship to happiness. Moreover, since every part is ordained to the whole, as imperfect to perfect; and since one man is a part of the perfect community, the law must needs regard properly the relationship to universal happiness. Wherefore the Philosopher, in the above definition of legal matters mentions both happiness and the body politic: for he says (*Ethic.* v.) that we call those legal matters *just, which are adapted to produce and preserve happiness and its parts for the body politic:* since the state is a perfect community, as he says in *Polit.* i.

Now in every genus, that which belongs to it chiefly is the principle of the others, and the others belong to that genus in subordination to that thing: thus fire, which is chief among hot things, is the cause of heat in mixed bodies, and these are said to be hot in so far as they have a share of fire. Consequently, since the law is chiefly ordained to the common good, any other precept in regard to some individual work, must needs be devoid of the nature of a law, save in so far as it regards the common good. Therefore every law is ordained to the common good.

Reply Obj. 1   A command denotes an application of a law to matters regulated by the law. Now the order to the common good, at which the law aims, is applicable to particular ends. And in this way commands are given even concerning particular matters.

Reply Obj. 2   Actions are indeed concerned with particular matters: but those particular matters are referable to the common good, not as to a common genus or species, but as to a common final cause, according as the common good is said to be the common end.

Reply Obj. 3   Just as nothing stands firm with regard to the speculative reason except that which is traced back to the first indemonstrable principles, so nothing stands firm with regard to the practical reason, unless it be directed to the last end which is the common good: and whatever stands to reason in this sense, has the nature of a law.

WHETHER THE REASON OF ANY MAN IS COMPETENT TO MAKE LAWS?

Objection 1   It seems that the reason of any man is competent to make laws. For the Apostle says: (Rom. ii. 14) that *when the Gentiles, who have not the law, do by nature those things that are of the law, . . . they are a law to themselves.* Now he says this of all in general. Therefore anyone can make a law for himself.

Obj. 2   Further, as the Philosopher says (*Ethic.* ii), *the intention of the lawgiver is to lead men to virtue.* But every man can lead another to virtue. Therefore the reason of any man is competent to make laws.

Obj. 3   Further, just as the sovereign of a state governs the state, so every father of a family governs his household. But the sovereign of a state can make laws for the state. Therefore every father of a family can make laws for his household.
  On the contrary, Isidore says (*Etym.* v.; and the passage is quoted in *Decretals, Dist.* ii): *A law is an ordinance of the people, whereby something is sanctioned by the Elders together with the Commonalty.*
  I answer that, a law, properly speaking, regards first and foremost the order to the common good. Now to order anything to the common good, belongs either to the whole people, or to someone who is the vice-gerent of the whole people. And therefore the making of a law belongs either to the whole people or to a public personage who has care of the whole people: since in all other matters the directing of anything to the end concerns him to whom the end belongs.

Reply Obj. 1   As stated above, a law is in a person not only as in one that rules, but also by participation as in one that is ruled. In the latter way each one is a law to himself, in so far as he shares the direction that he receives from one who rules him. Hence the same text goes on: *Who show the work of the law written in their hearts.*

Reply Obj. 2   A private person cannot lead another to virtue efficaciously: for he can only advise, and if his advice be not taken, it has no coercive power, such as the law

should have, in order to prove an efficacious inducement to virtue, as the Philosopher says (*Ethic.* x.). But this coercive power is vested in the whole people or in some public personage, to whom it belongs to inflict penalties. Wherefore the framing of laws belongs to him alone.

Reply Obj. 3   As one man is a part of the household, so a household is a part of the state: and the state is a perfect community, according to *Polit.* i. And therefore, as the good of one man is not the last end, but is ordained to the common good, so too the good of one household is ordained to the good of a single state, which is a perfect community. Consequently he that governs a family, can indeed make certain commands or ordinances, but not such as to have properly the force of law.

WHETHER PROMULGATION IS ESSENTIAL TO THE LAW?

Objection 1   It seems that promulgation is not essential to a law. For the natural law above all has the character of law. But the natural law needs no promulgation. Therefore it is not essential to a law that it be promulgated.

Obj. 2   Further, it belongs properly to a law to bind one to do or not to do something. But the obligation of fulfilling a law touches not only those in whose presence it is promulgated, but also others. Therefore promulgation is not essential to a law.

Obj. 3   Further, the binding force of a law extends even to the future, since *laws are binding in matters of the future,* as the jurists say *(Cod.* i., tit. *De lege et constit.).* But promulgation concerns those who are present. Therefore it is not essential to a law.
  On the contrary, it is laid down in the *Decretals (Append. Grat.)* that *laws are established when they are promulgated.*
  I answer that a law is imposed on others by way of a rule and measure. Now a rule or measure is imposed by being applied to those who are to be ruled and measured by it. Wherefore, in order that a law obtain the binding force which is proper to a law, it must needs be applied to the men who have to be ruled by it. Such application is made

by its being notified to them by promulgation. Wherefore promulgation is necessary for the law to obtain its force.

Thus from the four preceding articles, the definition of law may be gathered; and it is nothing else than an ordinance of reason for the common good, made by him who has care of the community, and promulgated.

Reply Obj. 1   The natural law is promulgated by the very fact that God instilled it into man's mind so as to be known by him naturally.

Reply Obj. 2   Those who are not present when a law is promulgated, are bound to observe the law, in so far as it is notified or can be notified to them by others, after it has been promulgated.

Reply Obj. 3   The promulgation that takes place now, extends to future time by reason of the durability of written characters, by which means it is continually promulgated. Hence Isidore says (*Etym.* ii) that *lex* (law) *is derived from legere* (to read) *because it is written.*

WHETHER THE NATURAL LAW IS THE SAME IN ALL MEN?

Objection 1   It seems that the natural law is not the same in all. For it is stated in the *Decretals (Dist.* i.) that *the natural law is that which is contained in the Law and the Gospel.* But this is not common to all men; because, as it is written (Rom. x. 16), *all do not obey the Gospel.* Therefore the natural law is not the same in all men.

Obj. 2   Further, *things which are according to the law are said to be just,* as stated in *Ethic.* v. But it is stated in the same book that nothing is so universally just as not to be subject to change in regard to some men. Therefore even the natural law is not the same in all men.

Obj. 3   Further, to the natural law belongs everything to which a man is inclined according to his nature. Now different men are naturally inclined to different things; some to the desire of pleasures, others to the desire of honours, and other men to other

things. Therefore there is not one natural law for all.

On the contrary, Isidore says (*Etym.* v.): *The natural law is common to all nations.*

I answer that to the natural law belong those things to which a man is inclined naturally: and among these it is proper to man to be inclined to act according to reason. Now the process of reason is from the common to the proper, as stated in *Phys.* i. The speculative reason, however, is differently situated in this matter, from the practical reason. For, since the speculative reason is busied chiefly with necessary things, which cannot be otherwise than they are, its proper conclusions, like the universal principles, contain the truth without fail. The practical reason, on the other hand, is busied with contingent matters, about which human actions are concerned: and consequently, although there is necessity in the general principles, the more we descend to matters of detail, the more frequently we encounter defects. Accordingly then in speculative matters truth is the same in all men, both as to principles and as to conclusions: although the truth is not known to all as regards the conclusions, but only as regards the principles which are called common notions. But in matters of action, truth or practical rectitude is not the same for all, as to matters of detail, but only as to the general principles: and where there is the same rectitude in matters of detail, it is not equally known to all.

It is therefore evident that, as regards the general principles whether of speculative or of practical reason, truth or rectitude is the same for all, and is equally known by all. As to the proper conclusions of the speculative reason, the truth is the same for all, but is not equally known to all: thus it is true for all that the three angles of a triangle are together equal to two right angles, although it is not known to all. But as to the proper conclusions of the practical reason, neither is the truth or rectitude the same for all, nor, where it is the same, is it equally known by all. Thus it is right and true for all to act according to reason: and from this principle it follows as a proper conclusion, that goods entrusted to another should be restored to their owner. Now this is true for the majority of cases: but it may happen in a particular case that it would be injurious, and therefore unreasonable, to restore goods held in trust; for instance if they are claimed for the purpose of fighting against one's country. And this principle will be found to fail the more, according as we descend further into detail, *e.g.,* if one were to say that goods held in trust should be restored with such and such a guarantee, or in such and such a way; because the greater the number of conditions added, the greater the number of ways in which the principle may fail, so that it be not right to restore or not to restore.

Consequently we must say that the natural law, as to general principles, is the same for all, both as to rectitude and as to knowledge. But as to certain matters of detail, which are conclusions, as it were, of those general principles, it is the same for all in the majority of cases, both as to rectitude and as to knowledge; and yet in some few cases it may fail, both as to rectitude, by reason of certain obstacles (just as natures subject to generation and corruption fail in some few cases on account of some obstacle), and as to knowledge, since in some the reason is perverted by passion, or evil habit, or an evil disposition of nature; thus formerly, theft, although it is expressly contrary to the natural law, was not considered wrong among the Germans, as Julius Caesar relates (*De Bello Gall,* vi.).

Reply Obj. 1 The meaning of the sentence quoted is not that whatever is contained in the Law and the Gospel belongs to the natural law, since they contain many things that are above nature; but that whatever belongs to the natural law is fully contained in them. Wherefore Gratian, after saying that *the natural law is what is contained in the Law and the Gospel,* adds at once, by way of example, *by which everyone is commanded to do to others as he would be done by.*

Reply Obj. 2 The saying of the Philosopher is to be understood of things that are naturally just, not as general principles, but as conclusions drawn from them, having rectitude in the majority of cases, but failing in a few.

Reply Obj. 3 As, in man, reason rules and commands the other powers, so all the natural inclinations belonging to the other powers must needs be directed according to reason. Wherefore it is universally right for all men, that all their inclinations should be directed according to reason.

WHETHER EVERY HUMAN LAW IS DERIVED FROM THE NATURAL LAW?

Objection 1 It seems that not every human law is derived from the natural law. For the Philosopher says (*Ethic.* v.) that *the legal just is that which originally was a matter of indifference.* But those things which arise from the natural law are not matters of indifference. Therefore the enactments of human laws are not all derived from the natural law.

Obj. 2 Further, positive law is contrasted with natural law, as stated by Isidore (*Etym.* v.) and the Philosopher (*Ethic.* v.). But those things which flow as conclusions from the general principles of the natural law belong to the natural law. Therefore that which is established by human law does not belong to the natural law.

Obj. 3 Further, the law of nature is the same for all; since the Philosopher says (*Ethic.* v.) that *the natural just is that which is equally valid everywhere.* If therefore human laws were derived from the natural law, it would follow that they too are the same for all: which is clearly false.

Obj. 4 Further, it is possible to give a reason for things which are derived from the natural law. But *it is not possible to give the reason for all the legal enactments of the lawgivers* (*Pandect. Justin.* Lib. I, Tit. III, Art. V, *De legibus,* etc.). Therefore not all human laws are derived from the natural law.

On the contrary, Tully says (*Rhetor.* ii.): *Things which emanated from nature and were approved by custom, were sanctioned by fear and reverence for the laws.*

I answer that, as Augustine says (*De Lib. Arb.* i.), *that which is not just seems to be no law at all:* wherefore the force of law depends on the extent of its justice. Now in human affairs a thing is said to be just, from being right, according to the rule of reason. But the first rule of reason is the law of nature, as is clear from what has been stated. Consequently every human law has just so much of the nature of law, as it is derived from the law of nature. But if in any point it deflects from the law of nature, it is no longer a law but a perversion of law.

But it must be noted that something may be derived from the natural law in two ways: first, as a conclusion from premises, secondly, by way of determination of certain generalities. The first way is like to that by which, in sciences, demonstrated conclusions are drawn from the principles: while the second mode is likened to that whereby, in the arts, general forms are particularized as to details: thus the craftsman needs to determine the general form of a house to some particular shape. Some things are therefore derived from the general principles of the natural law, by way of conclusions: e.g., that *one must not kill* may be derived as a conclusion from the principle that *one should do harm to no man:* while some are derived therefrom by way of determination; *e.g.,* the law of nature has it that the evil-doer should be punished: but that he be punished in this or that way, is a determination of the law of nature.

Accordingly both modes of derivation are found in the human law. But those things which are derived in the first way, are contained in human law not as emanating therefrom exclusively, but have some force from the natural law also. But those things which are derived in the second way, have no other force than that of human law.

Reply Obj. 1 The Philosopher is speaking of those enactments which are by way of determination or specification of the precepts of the natural law.

Reply Obj. 2 This argument avails for those things that are derived from the natural law, by way of conclusions.

Reply Obj. 3 The general principles of the natural law cannot be applied to all men in the same way on account of the great variety of human affairs: and hence arises the diversity of positive laws among various people.

Reply Obj. 4 These words of the Jurist are to be understood as referring to decisions of rulers in determining particular points of the natural law: on which determinations the judgment of expert and prudent men is based as on its principles; in so far, to wit, as they see at once what is the best thing to decide.

Hence the Philosopher says (*Ethic.* vi.) that in such matters, *we ought to pay as much attention to the undemonstrated sayings and opinions of persons who surpass us in experience, age and prudence, as to their demonstrations.*

WHETHER HUMAN LAW BINDS A MAN IN CONSCIENCE?

Objection 1 It seems that human law does not bind a man in conscience. For an inferior power has no jurisdiction in a court of higher power. But the power of man, which frames human law, is beneath the Divine power. Therefore human law cannot impose its precept in a Divine court, such as is the court of conscience.

Obj. 2 Further, the judgment of conscience depends chiefly on the commandments of God. But sometimes God's commandments are made void by human laws, according to Matth. xv. 6: *You have made void the commandment of God for your tradition.* Therefore human law does not bind a man in conscience.

Obj. 3 Further, human laws often bring loss of character and injury on man, according to Isa. x. 1 *et seq.: Woe to them that make wicked laws, and when they write, write injustice; to oppress the poor in judgment, and do violence to the cause of the humble of My people.* But it is lawful for anyone to avoid oppression and violence. Therefore human laws do not bind man in conscience.

On the contrary, it is written (I Pet. ii. 19.): *This is thanksworthy, if for conscience . . . a man endure sorrow, suffering wrongfully.*

I answer that, laws framed by man are either just or unjust. If they be just, they have the power of binding in conscience, from the eternal law whence they are derived, according to Prov. viii. 15: *By Me kings reign, and lawgivers decree just things.* Now laws are said to be just, both from the end, when, to wit, they are ordained to the common good,—and from their author, that is to say, when the law that is made does not exceed the power of the lawgiver,—and from their form, when, to wit, burdens are laid on the subjects, according to an equality of proportion and with a view to the common good. For, since one man is a part of the community, each man, in all that he is and has, belongs to the community; just as a part, in all that it is, belongs to the whole; wherefore nature inflicts a loss on the part, in order to save the whole: so that on this account, such laws as these, which impose proportionate burdens, are just and binding in conscience, and are legal laws.

On the other hand laws may be unjust in two ways: first, by being contrary to human good, through being opposed to the things mentioned above:—either in respect of the end, as when an authority imposes on his subjects burdensome laws, conducive, not to the common good, but rather to his own cupidity or vainglory;—or in respect of the author, as when a man makes a law that goes beyond the power committed to him;—or in respect of the form, as when burdens are imposed unequally on the community, although with a view to the common good. The like are acts of violence rather than laws; because, as Augustine says *(De Lib. A rb.i.), a law that is not just, seems to be no law at all.* Wherefore such laws do not bind in conscience, except perhaps in order to avoid scandal or disturbance, for which cause a man should even yield his right, according to Matth. v. 40, 41: *If a man . . . take away thy coat, let go thy cloak also unto him; and whosoever will force thee one mile, go with him two.*

Secondly, laws may be unjust through being opposed to the Divine good: such are the laws of tyrants inducing to idolatry, or to anything else contrary to the Divine law: and laws of this kind must nowise be observed, because, as stated in Acts v. 29, *we ought to obey God rather than men.*

Reply Obj. 1 As the Apostle says (Rom. xiii. 1, 2), all human power is from God . . . *therefore he that resisteth the power,* in matters that are within its scope, *resisteth the ordinance of God:* so that he becomes guilty according to his conscience.

Reply Obj. 2 This argument is true of laws that are contrary to the commandments of God, and which go beyond the scope of (human) power. Wherefore in such matters human law should not be obeyed.

Reply Obj. 3 This argument is true of a law that inflicts unjust hurt on its subjects. The power that man holds from God does not extend to this: wherefore neither in such matters is man bound to obey the law, provided he avoid giving scandal or inflicting a more grievous hurt.

WHETHER HUMAN LAW SHOULD ALWAYS BE CHANGED, WHENEVER SOMETHING BETTER OCCURS?

Objection 1 It seems that human law should be changed, whenever something better occurs. Because human laws are devised by human reason, like other arts. But in the other arts, the tenets of former times give place to others, if something better occurs. Therefore the same should apply to human laws.

Obj. 2 Further, by taking note of the past we can provide for the future. Now unless human laws had been changed when it was found possible to improve them, considerable inconvenience would have ensued; because the laws of old were crude in many points. Therefore it seems that laws should be changed, whenever anything better occurs to be enacted.

Obj. 3 Further, human laws are enacted about single acts of man. But we cannot acquire perfect knowledge in singular matters, except by experience, which *requires time,* as stated in *Ethic.* ii. Therefore it seems that as time goes on it is possible for something better to occur for legislation.

On the contrary, it is stated in the *Decretals (Dist.* xii.): *It is absurd, and a detestable shame, that we should suffer those traditions to be changed which we have received from the fathers of old.*

I answer that human law is rightly changed, in so far as such change is conducive to the common weal. But, to a certain extent, the mere change of law is of itself prejudicial to the common good: because custom avails much for the observance of laws, seeing that what is done contrary to general custom, even in slight matters, is looked upon as grave. Consequently, when a law is changed, the binding power of the law is diminished, in so far as custom is abolished. Wherefore human law should never be changed, unless, in some way or other, the common weal be compensated according to the extent of the harm done in this respect. Such compensation may arise either from some very great and very evident benefit conferred by the new enactment; or from the extreme urgency of the case, due to the fact that either the existing law is clearly unjust, or its observance extremely harmful.

Wherefore the Jurist says (*Pandect. Justin. i.*) *that in establishing new laws, there should be evidence of the benefit to be derived, before departing from a law which has long been considered just.*

Reply Obj. 1   Rules of art derive their force from reason alone: and therefore whenever something better occurs, the rule followed hitherto should be changed. But *laws derive very great force from custom,* as the Philosopher states (*Polit.* ii.): consequently they should not be quickly changed.

Reply Obj. 2   This argument proves that laws ought to be changed: not in view of any improvement, but for the sake of a great benefit or in a case of great urgency. This answer applies also to the Third Objection.

CHAPTER FIVE

MACHIAVELLI

Only in fifth-century Athens has the world seen the dazzling artistic brilliance and intellectual vitality that characterized the Renaissance. The rebirth and rediscovery of antiquity were both cause and effect: on the one hand, the Renaissance helped to revive the rational, this-worldly, secular, scientific spirit that had lain dormant through many centuries of medieval encasement; on the other hand, the Renaissance was itself the effect of man's growing restlessness as well as of changing social and technological conditions. In particular, printing destroyed the monopoly of knowledge that the clergy had enjoyed for a thousand years, and gunpowder destroyed the military monopoly of the nobility. Like travelers who return from their journey with their prejudices confirmed and strengthened, the men of the Renaissance, in traveling to the remote centuries of classical Greece and Rome, found what they looked for—an exciting world, the image of which had guided them on their voyage.

The most important discovery of the Renaissance—more significant than any single work of art or any one genius—was the *discovery of man*. In antiquity the sense of tribal kinship had not favored the growth of individualism, of isolation from the community. Stoicism and Christianity had been the first to contribute new and lasting elements to a conception of individuality: Stoicism, by stressing the idea of moral selfhood and responsibility, and Christianity, by insisting that man's innermost reality, his soul, was outside the sphere and jurisdiction of mundane authority, and that his salvation depended ultimately on his own decisions, his own works. But the social system of the Middle Ages, built on status and custom, discouraged the mobility and change that favor individualistic attitudes; it emphasized instead the class or group to which a person belonged. The Renaissance goes beyond the moral selfhood of Stoicism, the spiritual uniqueness of Christianity, the aesthetic individuality of the ancient Greeks, and views man in his totality, in his flesh and blood as well as in his mind and spirit—man in relation to himself, to society, to the world. Displacing God, *man* becomes the *center of the universe;* the values of this new solar system are inevitably different from those of the God-centered universe.

The Renaissance was the confluence of many streams and tributaries, yet the Italian share was predominant from beginning to end. Italy had never lost living contacts with its ancient past: The country was full of splendid cities founded in antiquity, it abounded in relics and monuments of past glories, and the language was still the language (with some minor changes) of Caesar and Cicero. The dead hand of uniformity had never lain as heavily on Italy as on other European countries in the Middle Ages, and the feudal system never permeated it as it did, for example, France, England, and Germany. Italy remained the only major area in which a vigorous communal life had weathered the storms of wars and invasions, and its city-states were for a long time islands of individualistic republicanism in a sea of European monarchical loyalties. The virtual destruction of the German empire as a world power by the papacy in the thirteenth century, and the later enslavement of the papacy to the French monarchy in the fourteenth century, gave the independent Italian city-states new opportunities for self-affirmation and increased self-confidence. Leadership in international trade, business, and finance made numerous Italian cities wealthy and prosperous, and provided the economic means for the literary, artistic, and scholarly activities of a new elite.

Among the centers of the Renaissance, Florence was always first, reaching its climax in Leonardo da Vinci (1452–1519), who most perfectly represented, and lived, the Renaissance ideal of *universal man,* creative in painting and the arts, inventive in science and engineering, and accomplished in philosophy and letters. In the study of politics, the New Learning finds its clearest expression in Niccolò Machiavelli (1469–1527).

At the age of twenty-nine Machiavelli entered the public service of his city, and there he remained for fourteen years. Although not employed on the highest levels of policy making, he was close enough to the inner circles of the administration to acquire first-hand knowledge of the mechanics of politics. Florence was at that time an independent republic, and Machiavelli was frequently sent on diplomatic missions to other Italian states and to great foreign powers like France and Germany. In 1512 he lost his job when the republican government, based on French support, was replaced by the absolutist regime of the Medici, who had been restored to power with papal help. Machiavelli was accused of serious crimes and tortured, but he was found innocent and banished to his small farm near Florence.

It was in such enforced leisure that he wrote *The Prince* (1513). The book was dedicated to Lorenzo di Medici, and Machiavelli fulsomely praised the dynasty that stood for the exact opposite of his erstwhile republican sentiments. He even hoped to have his political conversion rewarded by an opportunity to serve the new antirepublican regime, but in this expectation he failed. The further imposed idleness gave him enough time to work on his most elaborate political book, *The Discourses on the First Ten Books of Titus Livius* (1521). Taking Roman history as a starting point, *The Discourses* attempts to dissect the anatomy of the body politic, and on a much more philosophical and historical foundation than that of *The Prince. The Discourses* is interesting because Machiavelli affirms in it his republican sentiment; yet this personal preference does not alter his basic views on the process of politics, regardless of the form of its constitution, republican or despotic.

For all its breadth and elaborateness, and frequent depth and penetration, *The Discourses* is of interest primarily to students of political philosophy, whereas *The Prince,* pithy, shocking, persuasive, provocative, hard-hitting, is destined to remain one of the half-dozen political writings that have entered the general body of world literature. It is a reflection not only of man's political ambitions and passions but of man himself. If Machiavelli had painted, in medieval fashion, the devils who inhabit hell, his impact would have been much less intense on his contemporaries and on posterity. What Machiavelli did, however, was to portray something worse, real human beings; the shock of recognition has created around his work an aura of mixed horror and fascination, and it is hard to tell what is the stronger.

The most revolutionary aspect of *The Prince* is not so much what it says as what it ignores. Before Machiavelli, all political writing—from Plato and Aristotle through the Middle Ages to the Renaissance—had one central question: the *end of the state.* Political power was assumed to be a means only—a means in the service of higher ends, such as justice, the good life, freedom, or God. Machiavelli ignores the issue of the end of the state in extrapolitical (ethical, religious, cultural) terms. He assumes that *power* is *an end in itself,* and he confines his inquiries into the *means* that are best suited to *acquire, retain,* and *expand power.* Machiavelli thus separates power from morality, ethics, religion, and metaphysics, and sets up the *state* as an *autonomous system of values* independent of any other source.

If he follows the value system of the state, the statesman may violate other value systems, such as religion, ethics, or morality. Machiavelli thus develops the idea of the *reason of state,* under which many acts are permissive, even obligatory, that would be considered heinous crimes if judged in the court of religion or morality. Machiavelli does not assert that ethics and morality as such are inferior to the precepts of power, the reason of state; from a general, theoretical viewpoint, the canons of power and the tenets of morality are independent of each other. When it comes to practical collisions, it depends on who faces the alternatives. The moralist will recognize the supremacy of his moral code over competing systems of values. The ecclesiastic will not admit a rival to his religious code. Similarly, the statesman will be guided solely by the precepts of his code, whose end—the acquisition, retention, and expansion of power—is different from other codes, and whose means are therefore different, too.

In the actions of rulers "the end justifies the means. Let a prince therefore aim at conquering and maintaining the state, and the means will always be judged honourable and praised by every one." In *The Discourses,* Machiavelli defines the reason of state even more clearly: "For where the very safety of the country depends upon the resolution to be taken, no consideration of justice or injustice, humanity or cruelty, nor of glory or of shame, should be allowed to prevail. But putting all other considerations aside, the only question should be: What course will save the life and liberty of the country?"

Machiavelli never praises immorality for its own sake; his basic attitude is not one of nihilism: he neither assumes that there are no values in this world, nor wishes to create a world in which all values would be destroyed. Machiavelli is aware that civilization implies some sort of values. His *amorality* implies therefore, not the denial of moral values in all situations, but the affirmation that, in the specific situation of the statesman, the rules of power have priority over those of ethics and morality.

Machiavelli did not invent political murder, treachery, and fraud. But before his time such crimes were committed *de facto,* and no attempt was made to integrate them into a moral world of their own. The traditional reaction to political immorality had been either one of polite neglect, half-hearted excuse, or, at best, severe censure of individual violations of ethics and morality. The sanctity and inviolability of the moral code seemed, before Machiavelli, in no way impaired by the regrettable exceptions to the rule, regardless of how frequent they were. In Machiavelli, the traditional attitude of polite neglect and hypocritical, or sincere, regret is replaced by the positive affirmation that the reason of state is for the statesman the determining code of conduct, and that statecraft constitutes a value system of its own which is different from that of ethics and religion. What is evil from the viewpoint of morality and religion may therefore be good from the viewpoint of the reason of state, if it serves to acquire, retain, or expand power.

Good and *evil* are thus reduced from absolute to *relative* categories, and it depends on the basic assumption of a system of values whether a particular action is good or bad. If the basic assumption and objective of conduct is friendship, service, fellowship, justice, or God, the individual action will be judged good or bad to the extent that it agrees with, or deviates from, such assumptions and goals. If, as for the ruler, the basic assumption is power, the decision about whether a particular action is good or bad will depend on the extent to which it furthers the gain, retention, and growth of power. In this sense the use of poison may be called "good" if it does a good job in eliminating a political opponent, perhaps by acting slowly and imperceptibly so that the author of the crime cannot be easily detected. The attribution of "goodness" to poison in a specific case of political necessity does not imply a general justification for the use of poison. Assuming *power* as the *end of politics, goodness* thus *coincides with efficiency:* an efficient means of acquiring, consolidating, and expanding power is good; an inefficient means, bad.

Efficiency in politics is thus analogous to virtue in morals or religion, and inefficiency replaces the concept of sin. Machiavelli still uses the term "virtue" *(virtù),* but its meaning is different from, and even antithetical to, the Christian concept of virtue. As in so many other cases, Machiavelli—in typical Renaissance fashion—uses the term *virtù* in its original Roman meaning, and even adds some shades of meaning of his own. In classical, pre-Christian, Rome *virtus* (deriving from *vir,* man) meant "manliness," that is, military courage and intelligence combined with civic responsibility and personal integrity. In later Christian usage, "virtue" entirely lost its military connotation, and Christian virtue stood for humility and cheerful acceptance of suffering, and even female chastity, rather than for manly self-assertion. But even the classical Roman element of civic integrity in the concept of virtue was transformed by Christianity into religious and moral integrity, concerned above all with limitless faith in God and his commands rather than with the practice of political participation. Machiavelli goes back to the original pagan meaning of Roman virtue, but expands and adapts it to his thought and to the restless and violent world he lives in. Virtue for Machiavelli means *military valor,* and appropriately, therefore, the most comprehensive analysis of *virtù* is to be found in his *Art of War* (1521), although he frequently uses the concept in many of his other works, including *The Prince* and *The Discourses.*

Yet, as Machiavelli sees it, the quality of military valor is required in actual warfare as well as in extreme political crisis situations of acquiring, consolidating, and expanding of power, for in such conditions the boundary between conflict and peace, between chaos and stability is largely blurred. In such crisis situations, whether of actual warfare or of decisive political conflict, the concept of virtue implies the ability to understand reality and to adapt action to reality in a flexible and non-ideological, nondogmatic manner. This is the element of *prudence* in Machiavelli's concept of virtue, replacing the Roman quality of civic integrity and the Christian element of religious and moral loyalty in the pre-Renaissance and pre-Machiavellian meaning of virtue.

As in so many other areas of his thought, Machiavelli is more interested in means than in ends; in politics, for example, the end—the acquiring, consolidating, and expanding of power—is presumed to be naturally inherent in the ruler or would-be ruler, and need not be further argued. What captures Machiavelli's intellectual curiosity and literary imagination is the problem of technical skill of ruling, the ability of the leader to fight his way into political power by forcible or other means, coupled with the ability to "stay in business" and to expand his power. Consequently, when Machiavelli applies the term "virtue" *(virtù)* to the successful ruler, he means the ambitious, ruthless, crafty, successful ruler, and not the ruler who is a regular churchgoer, mindful of other men's wives, and generally a practicing moralist. In typical Renaissance style, Machiavelli even sees "grandeur" in elegant and magnificent crimes; this concept of an elegant or beautiful crime would have been unthinkable before a collapse of traditional standards of ethics.

Machiavelli's attitude to the Borgias is a revealing illustration of his more abstract concepts. Cardinal Rodrigo Borgia had four living children, three sons and one daughter, when he became pope in 1492 and assumed the name of Alexander VI. He appointed two of his sons as cardinals, and when he was away from Rome in 1501, he left his daughter, Lucrezia, in charge of the Vatican. Alexander VI had his personal hangman and poisoner. The latter, in particular, was constantly busy, and his victims included several cardinals. Alexander VI was one of the men whom Machiavelli most admired, and he writes of him as follows: "Alexander VI did nothing else but deceive men, he thought of nothing else, and found the occasion for it; no man was ever more able to give assurances, or affirmed things with stronger oaths, and no man observed them less; however, he always succeeded in his deceptions, as he well knew this aspect of things."

If Machiavelli admired Alexander VI, then he idolized his son, Caesar Borgia, Caesar assassinated his older brother and murdered the husband of his sister Lucrezia— hardly a typical family idyll of the Renaissance. The number of his other assassinations is legion, and his cruelty was matched only by his treachery and debauchery. Machiavelli knew Caesar Borgia personally and was fully aware of his criminal record. Yet it is generally believed that Caesar Borgia was Machiavelli's model in writing *The Prince;* certainly he is held up "as an example to be imitated by all who by fortune and with the arms of others have risen to power," and "one can find no better example than the actions of this man." Machiavelli had only one fault to find with Caesar Borgia: that he allowed, after the death of his father, Alexander VI, the election of Julian II as pope, because Julian was an enemy of the Borgias. What Machiavelli criticized in the career of his most admired hero was his one failure and not his life of crime.

Machiavelli's views on morals and religion illustrate his belief in the supremacy of power over other social values. He has no sense of religion as a deep personal experience, and the mystical element in religion—its supranatural and suprarational character—is alien to his outlook. Yet he has a positive attitude toward religion; albeit his *religion* becomes a *tool of influence and control* in the hands of the ruler over the ruled. Machiavelli sees in religion the poor man's reason, ethics, and morality put together, and "where religion exists it is easy to introduce armies and discipline." From his reading of history, however, Machiavelli is led to the generalization that "as the observance of divine institutions is the cause of the greatness of republics, so the disregard of them produces their ruin." The fear of the prince, Machiavelli adds, may temporarily supplant the fear of God, but the life of even an efficient ruler is short.

The role of religion as a mere instrument of political domination, cohesion, and unity becomes even clearer in Machiavelli's advice that the ruler support and spread religious doctrines and beliefs in miracles *that he knows to be false.* The main value of religion to the ruler lies in the fact that it helps him to keep the people "well conducted and united," and from this viewpoint of utility it makes no difference whether he spreads among them true or false religious ideas and beliefs.

Machiavelli's interest in Christianity is not philosophical or theological, but purely pragmatic and political. He is critical of Christianity because "it glorifies more the humble and contemplative men than the men of action," whereas the Roman pagan religion "deified only men who had achieved great glory, such as commanders of republics and chiefs of republics." Christianity idealizes, Machiavelli charges, "humility, lowliness, and a contempt for worldly objects," as contrasted with the pagan qualities of grandeur of soul, strength of body, and other qualities that "render men formidable." The only kind of strength that Christianity teaches is fortitude of soul in suffering; it does not teach the strength that goes into the achievement of great deeds.

Concerning the church, Machiavelli preferred two main charges. First, he states that the Italians have become "irreligious and bad" because of the "evil example of the court of Rome." The second and more serious accusation is that the church "has kept and still keeps our country divided." He goes on to say that the sole cause of Italian political disunity is the church. Having acquired jurisdiction over a considerable portion of Italy, "she has never had sufficient power or courage to enable her to make herself sole sovereign of all Italy." Though Machiavelli hated the papacy, he nevertheless would have been happy to see the papacy govern all Italy if her unity could not be attained by any other means. What Machiavelli primarily reproaches the papacy for is not its record of crime and iniquity but its political failure to rule the whole country.

The clue to Machiavelli is his *pessimism.* The pessimist sees mankind as essentially unchangeable, incapable of progressive improvability, and he denies that reason can cope with the hard and limiting facts of nature and history. By contrast, the optimist believes that man is improvable, that progress is possible, and that the chains of nature and history can be relaxed by the liberating and uplifting force of reason. Whereas the pessimist tends to look into the *past* and is primarily conscious of what *has* happened, the optimist looks into the *future* and wonders what *might* happen.

Machiavelli's pessimism is reflected in his conviction that moral considerations may be laudable in themselves (and in this he is less of a nihilist than the later nihilists and Machiavellians), but that the statesman cannot afford the luxury of practicing morality: "For how we live is so far removed from how we ought to live, that he who abandons what is done for what ought to be done, will rather learn to bring about his own ruin than his preservation." In the struggle between rulers, Machiavelli says, "There are two methods of fighting, the one by law, the other by force: the first method is that of men, the second of beasts; but as the first method is often insufficient, one must have recourse to the second. It is therefore necessary for a prince to know well how to use both the beast and the man."

Specifically, the *ruler must imitate the fox and the lion,* "for the lion cannot protect himself from the traps, and the fox cannot defend himself from wolves."

Should a ruler keep faith? This is Machiavelli's most famous question, and his answer to it is the best-known passage in *The Prince.* He admits that everybody knows how "laudable" it is for a ruler to keep faith. However, in the world of actual politics such laudable intentions may be irreconcilable with expediency and interest: "Therefore, a prudent ruler ought not to keep faith when by doing so it would be against his interest, and when the reasons which made him bind himself no longer exist. If men were all good, this precept would not be a good one; but as they are bad, and would not observe their faith with you, so you are not bound to keep faith with them."

Machiavelli thus takes a radically pessimistic view of human nature, and his psychological outlook is intimately related to his political philosophy. The theological conception of man's depravity, one of the central doctrines of the Reformation, must also have influenced Machiavelli and his contemporaries. Indeed, the political methods of the Renaissance were not known for their humanitarian mellowness. Death by poison and the silent dagger was a mere technical detail in the efficient execution of a political program, and there was little difference between kings and popes, princes and bishops. As a result, it was perhaps not unnatural for Machiavelli, as for many of his contemporaries, to take a dim view of human nature in general, and of human nature in the struggle for power in particular. Such skepticism easily developed into pessimism and outright cynicism.

Unlike later Machiavellians, Machiavelli himself was saved from extremism by prudence and moderation. In both *The Prince* and *The Discourses* there are numerous passages in which Machiavelli counsels rulers to be temperate, not to be uselessly cruel or arrogant, "for to incur hatred without any advantage is the greatest temerity and imprudence." The ruler should not use threats or insults, because neither diminishes the strength of the enemy but makes him only more cautious and disposed to hate. Machiavelli's rational skepticism, his horror of panaceas and cure-alls, his moderation and relativism, are apparent in his warning that no state should believe "that it can always follow a safe policy; rather let it think that all are doubtful. This is found in the nature of things, that one never tries to avoid one difficulty without running into another, but prudence consists in being able to know the nature of the difficulties, and taking the least harmful as good."

Machiavelli's sense of the complexity of human affairs, his realization that no policy can ever assure absolute safety, and his understanding that in practical politics the choice is often between a larger and a lesser evil rather than between evil and good—all these insights are intimately linked to the absence of ideological passion and fanaticism in his thought and feeling. What in some respects is the least satisfactory element in Machiavelli's thought—his scant concern for ends—is in other respects a source of strength which saves him from the excesses of ideological passion, in which hypocrisy easily mixes with cruelty. *Ideology* is essentially an *idea* (or ideas) *in the service of interest,* and to cover up this simple relation, ideologists rationalize, justify, obfuscate, and in extreme cases prevaricate and lie. Machiavelli's lack of commitment to ideological simplification and passionate abstraction is a built-in stabilizing and moderating force in his outlook. By contrast, this stabilizing element was lacking in some later self-styled Machiavellians who combined Machiavellian means with un-Machiavellian ends.

Machiavelli's fine *sense of the possible* makes his thought utilitarian, experimental, and relativistic. This basic quality—if not scientific in a strict sense—nevertheless partakes of one important aspect of science: empiricism, or the refusal to accept any solution as final.

Where Machiavelli is least scientific is where he thinks himself most scientific: in his belief that his analysis of power is based on solid facts of historical experience, that the record of man's behavior proves him a depraved and wily creature, and that a realistic theory of power must be based on such a pessimistic view of man. If Machiavelli's pessimism is the clue to his political philosophy, the weakness of his theory must be sought in his psychological conceptions. In detail a moderate, Machiavelli is an extremist when it comes to the whole. His doctrine of the badness of man is just as much an unscientific oversimplification as is the opposite extreme of the goodness of man. Man is somewhere between *angel and beast;* but Machiavelli says that the ruler is somewhere between *man and beast,* and that he "must know how to use both natures, and that the one without the other is not durable."

It would not be difficult to prove that human history has as much evidence of human goodness as of wickedness. It is a matter of ultimate—unprovable—personal philosophy of history whether one is more impressed by man's goodness than by his badness. But it is not sound philosophy of history, and still less is it sound science of politics, to reduce all history to one common denominator, be it goodness or badness.

Like other "realists" after him, Machiavelli identifies all too readily naked power politics with the whole of political reality, and he thus fails to grasp that ideas and ideals, if properly mobilized, can become potent facts, even decisive weapons, in the struggle for political survival. History is a vast graveyard filled with self-styled "realists" like Napoleon, Hitler, and Mussolini. They all underestimated the important imponderables in the equation of power and missed, in particular, the one component that in the end proved decisive: the will of man to be free, to put freedom above all other goods, even above life itself.

Machiavellian "realists" are usually realistic and rational in the choice of means with which they carry out their schemes of aggrandizement and expansion. But of what use is realism of means, if the ends themselves are utterly megalomaniac and unrealistic? Because Machiavelli was interested only in the means of acquiring, retaining, and expanding power, and not in the end of the state, he remained unaware of the *relations between means and ends*. Ends lead no existence apart from means but are continuously shaped by them. In the short run this inner connection may be concealed, but in the long run no great end can be accomplished by small means. The question, therefore, whether the political techniques and methods in *The Prince* are realistic even from the viewpoint of power cannot be separated from the still more basic issue of the end of power, inasmuch as the nature of the end determines the means most suited to it.

As one examines the references to rulers in *The Prince* more closely, one finds that Machiavelli was not interested in all forms of state, nor in all forms of power. What fascinated him above all was the *dynamics of illegitimate power;* he was little interested in states whose authority was legitimate, as in hereditary monarchies, but was primarily concerned with "new dominions both as to prince and state." He realized that "there is nothing more difficult to carry out, nor more doubtful of success, nor more dangerous to handle, than to initiate a new order of things." His primary concern with founders of new governments and states illuminates his attitude on the use of unethical means in politics. The "founders" of new states are, in effect, revolutionaries, and it is inevitable that in *reducing politics to war and revolution,* one arrives at an outlook in which the extraordinary becomes the ordinary, the abnormal the normal.

Because of his admiration for the outstanding man (and only outstanding men can successfully found "new dominions"), Machiavelli was little interested in the *institutional* framework of politics. He realized that in a period of institutional stability there is less need for the adventurer. In fact, as Machiavelli clearly sees, democrats hate war and revolution: The normal restraints and decencies are then imperiled by the necessity for sheer physical survival, and the habits of institutional stability are more easily subverted than in normal peacetime. The democratic theory of politics therefore tends to stress more the institutional framework of power than unique leader personalities, peace rather than war and revolution. Democrats have learned from long and painful experience that kindliness and decency flourish best in peaceful societies in which stable and just institutions make it difficult for lawless adventurers to thrive.

To the extent that democracies succeed in creating such societies, Machiavelli is wrong. To the extent that they fail, he is right. The ultimate commentary on *The Prince* is not in logic or morality, but in experience and history. Machiavelli laid bare the springs of human motivation with consummate and ruthless insight. It is hard to tell, in reading him, whether we shudder more when he tells the truth about human conduct, or more when he distorts the truth. He has, perhaps, rendered a service to humanity by pointing out the abysmal depth of demoralization and bestiality into which humans will sink for the sake of power. The twentieth century, in particular, has witnessed crimes of mass murder and genocide on a scale of which even Machiavelli, with all his interest in necessary, skillful, even elegant crimes, could never have dreamed. Our age is not one of facile optimism, and a balance will have to be struck between Machiavelli's pessimism about human nature and overconfident optimism, if an adequate approach to the theory and practice of politics is to be discovered.

MACHIAVELLI

*The Prince**

CONSTANT READINESS
FOR WAR

A prince should therefore have no other aim or thought, nor take up any other thing for his study, but war and its organisation and discipline, for that is the only art that is necessary to one who commands, and it is of such virtue that it not only maintains those who are born princes, but often enables men of private fortune to attain to that rank. And one sees, on the other hand, that when princes think more of luxury than of arms, they lose their state. The chief cause of the loss of states, is the contempt of this art, and the way to acquire them is to be well versed in the same.

Francesco Sforza, through being well armed, became, from private status, Duke of Milan; his sons, through wishing to avoid the fatigue and hardship of war, from dukes became private persons. For among other evils caused by being disarmed, it renders you contemptible; which is one of those disgraceful things which a prince must guard against, as will be explained later. Because there is no comparison whatever between an armed and a disarmed man, it is not reasonable to suppose that one who is armed will obey willingly one who is unarmed; or that any unarmed man will remain safe among armed servants. For one being disdainful and the other suspicious, it is not possible for them to act well together. And therefore a prince who is ignorant of military matters, besides the other misfortunes already

mentioned, cannot be esteemed by his soldiers, nor have confidence in them.

He ought, therefore, never to let his thoughts stray from the exercise of war; and in peace he ought to practise it more than in war, which he can do in two ways: by action and by study. As to action, he must, besides keeping his men well disciplined and exercised, engage continually in hunting, and thus accustom his body to hardships; and meanwhile learn the nature of the land, how steep the mountains are, how the valleys debouch, where the plains lie, and understand the nature of rivers and swamps. To all this he should devote great attention. This knowledge is useful in two ways. In the first place, one learns to know one's country, and can the better see how to defend it. Then by means of the knowledge and experience gained in one locality, one can easily understand any other that it may be necessary to observe; for the hills and valleys, plains and rivers of Tuscany, for instance, have a certain resemblance to those of other provinces, so that from a knowledge of the country in one province one can easily arrive at a knowledge of others. And that prince who is lacking in this skill is wanting in the first essentials of a leader; for it is this which teaches how to find the enemy, take up quarters, lead armies, plan battles and lay siege to towns with advantage.

Philopœmen, prince of the Achaei, among other praises bestowed on him by writers, is lauded because in times of peace he thought of nothing but the methods of warfare, and when he was in the country with his friends, he often stopped and asked them: If the enemy were on that hill and we found ourselves here with our army, which of us would have the advantage? How could we

* From Niccolò Machiavelli, *The Prince* (1513). Modern Library Edition. By permission of Random House, Inc.

safely approach him maintaining our order? If we wished to retire, what ought we to do? If they retired, how should we follow them? And he put before them as they went along all the contingencies that might happen to an army, heard their opinion, gave his own, fortifying it by argument; so that thanks to these constant reflections there could never happen any incident when actually leading his armies for which he was not prepared.

But as to exercise for the mind, the prince ought to read history and study the actions of eminent men, see how they acted in warfare, examine the causes of their victories and defeats in order to imitate the former and avoid the latter, and above all, do as some men have done in the past, who have imitated some one, who has been much praised and glorified, and have always kept his deeds and actions before them, as they say Alexander the Great imitated Achilles, Cæsar Alexander, and Scipio Cyrus. And whoever reads the life of Cyrus written by Xenophon, will perceive in the life of Scipio how gloriously he imitated the former, and how, in chastity, affability, humanity, and liberality Scipio conformed to those qualities of Cyrus as described by Xenophon.

A wise prince should follow similar methods and never remain idle in peaceful times, but industriously make good use of them, so that when fortune changes she may find him prepared to resist her blows, and to prevail in adversity.

WHY PRINCES ARE PRAISED OR BLAMED

It now remains to be seen what are the methods and rules for a prince as regards his subjects and friends. And as I know that many have written of this, I fear that my writing about it may be deemed presumptuous, differing as I do, especially in this matter, from the opinions of others. But my intention being to write something of use to those who understand, it appears to me more proper to go to the real truth of the matter than to its imagination; and many have imagined republics and principalities which have never been seen or known to exist in reality; for how we live is so far removed from how we ought to live, that he who abandons what is done for what ought

to be done, will rather learn to bring about his own ruin than his preservation. A man who wishes to make a profession of goodness in everything must necessarily come to grief among so many who are not good. Therefore it is necessary for a prince, who wishes to maintain himself, to learn how not to be good, and to use this knowledge and not use it, according to the necessity of the case.

Leaving on one side, then, those things which concern only an imaginary prince, and speaking of those that are real, I state that all men, and especially princes, who are placed at a greater height, are reputed for certain qualities which bring them either praise or blame. Thus one is considered liberal, another *misero* or miserly (using a Tuscan term, seeing that *avaro* with us still means one who is rapaciously acquisitive and *misero* one who makes grudging use of his own); one a free giver, another rapacious; one cruel, another merciful; one a breaker of his word, another trustworthy; one effeminate and pusillanimous, another fierce and high-spirited; one humane, another haughty; one lascivious, another chaste; one frank, another astute; one hard, another easy; one serious, another frivolous; one religious, another an unbeliever, and so on. I know that every one will admit that it would be highly praiseworthy in a prince to possess all the above-named qualities that are reputed good, but as they cannot all be possessed or observed, human conditions not permitting of it, it is necessary that he should be prudent enough to avoid scandal of those vices which would lose him the state, and guard himself if possible against those which will not lose it him, but if not able to, he can indulge them with less scruple. And yet he must not mind incurring the scandal of those vices, without which it would be difficult to save the state, for if one considers well, it will be found that some things which seem virtues would, if followed, lead to one's ruin, and some others which appear vices result in one's greater security and well-being.

LIBERALITY AND NIGGARDLINESS

Beginning now with the first qualities above named, say that it would be well to be considered liberal; nevertheless liberality such as the world understands it will injure you, because if used virtuously and in the proper way, it will not be known, and you will incur the disgrace of the contrary vice. But one who wishes to obtain the reputation of liberality among men, must not omit every kind of sumptuous display, and to such an extent that a prince of this character will consume by such means all his resources, and will be compelled, if he wishes to maintain his name for liberality, to impose heavy taxes on his people, become extortionate, and do everything possible to obtain money. This will make his subjects begin to hate him, and he will be little esteemed being poor, so that having by this liberality injured many and benefited but few, he will feel the first little disturbance and be endangered by every peril. If he recognises this and wishes to change his system, he incurs at once the charge of niggardliness.

A prince, therefore, not being able to exercise this virtue of liberality without risk if it be known, must not, if he be prudent, object to be called miserly. In course of time he will be thought more liberal, when it is seen that by his parsimony his revenue is sufficient, that he can defend himself against those who make war on him, and undertake enterprises without burdening his people, so that he is really liberal to all those from whom he does not take, who are infinite in number, and niggardly to all to whom he does not give, who are few. In our times we have seen nothing great done except by those who have been esteemed niggardly; the others have all been ruined. Pope Julius II, although he had made use of a reputation for liberality in order to attain the papacy, did not seek to retain it afterwards, so that he might be able to wage war. The present King of France has carried on so many wars without imposing an extraordinary tax, because his extra expenses were covered by the parsimony he had so long practised. The present King of Spain, if he had been thought liberal, would not have engaged in and been successful in so many enterprises.

For these reasons a prince must care little for the reputation of being a miser, if he wishes to avoid robbing his subjects, if he wishes to be able to defend himself, to avoid becoming poor and contemptible, and not to be forced to become rapacious; this

niggardliness is one of those vices which enable him to reign. If it is said that Cæsar attained the empire through liberality, and that many others have reached the highest positions through being liberal or being thought so, I would reply that you are either a prince already or else on the way to become one. In the first case, this liberality is harmful; in the second, it is certainly necessary to be considered liberal. Cæsar was one of those who wished to attain the mastery over Rome, but if after attaining it he had lived and had not moderated his expenses, he would have destroyed that empire. And should any one reply that there have been many princes, who have done great things with their armies, who have been thought extremely liberal, I would answer by saying that the prince may either spend his own wealth and that of his subjects or the wealth of others. In the first case he must be sparing, but for the rest he must not neglect to be very liberal. The liberality is very necessary to a prince who marches with his armies, and lives by plunder, sack and ransom, and is dealing with the wealth of others, for without it he would not be followed by his soldiers. And you may be very generous indeed with what is not the property of yourself or your subjects, as were Cyrus, Cæsar, and Alexander, for spending the wealth of others will not diminish your reputation, but increase it, only spending your own resources will injure you. There is nothing which destroys itself so much as liberality, for by using it you lose the power of using it, and become either poor and despicable, or, to escape poverty, rapacious and hated. And of all things that a prince must guard against, the most important are being despicable or hated, and liberality will lead you to one or other of these conditions. It is, therefore, wiser to have the name of a miser, which produces disgrace without hatred, than to incur of necessity the name of being rapacious, which produces both disgrace and hatred.

CRUELTY AND CLEMENCY: IS IT BETTER TO BE LOVED OR FEARED?

Proceeding to the other qualities before named, I say that every prince must desire to be considered merciful and not cruel. He must, however, take care not to misuse this mercifulness. Cesare Borgia was considered cruel, but his cruelty had brought order to the Romagna, united it, and reduced it to peace and fealty. If this is considered well, it will be seen that he was really much more merciful than the Florentine people, who, to avoid the name of cruelty, allowed Pistoia to be destroyed. A prince, therefore, must not mind incurring the charge of cruelty for the purpose of keeping his subjects united and faithful; for, with a very few examples, he will be more merciful than those who, from excess of tenderness, allow disorders to arise, from whence spring bloodshed and rapine; for these as a rule injure the whole community, while the executions carried out by the prince injure only individuals. And of all princes, it is impossible for a new prince to escape the reputation of cruelty, new states being always full of dangers. Wherefore Virgil through the mouth of Dido says:

Res dura, et regni novitas me talia cogunt Moliri, et late fines custode tueri.

Nevertheless, he must be cautious in believing and acting, and must not be afraid of his own shadow, and must proceed in a temperate manner with prudence and humanity, so that too much confidence does not render him incautious, and too much diffidence does not render him intolerant.

From this arises the question whether it is better to be loved more than feared, or feared more than loved. The reply is, that one ought to be both feared and loved, but as it is difficult for the two to go together, it is much safer to be feared than loved if one of the two has to be wanting. For it may be said of men in general that they are ungrateful, voluble, dissemblers, anxious to avoid danger, and covetous of gain; as long as you benefit them, they are entirely yours; they offer you their blood, their goods, their life, and their children, as I have before said, when the necessity is remote; but when it approaches, they revolt. And the prince who has relied solely on their words, without making other preparations, is ruined; for the friendship which is gained by, purchase and not through grandeur and nobility of spirit is bought but not secured, and in a pinch is not to be expended in your service. And men

have less scruple in offending one who makes himself loved than one who makes himself feared; for love is held by a chain of obligation which, men being selfish, is broken whenever it serves their purpose; but fear is maintained by a dread of punishment which never fails.

Still, a prince should make himself feared in such a way that if he does not gain love, he at any rate avoids hatred; for fear and the absence of hatred may well go together, and will be always attained by one who abstains from interfering with the property of his citizens and subjects or with their women. And when he is obliged to take the life of any one, let him do so when there is a proper justification and manifest reason for it; but above all he must abstain from taking the property of others, for men forget more easily the death of their father than the loss of their patrimony. Then also pretexts for seizing property are never wanting, and one who begins to live by rapine will always find some reason for taking the goods of others, whereas causes for taking life are rarer and more fleeting.

But when the prince is with his army and has a large number of soldiers under his control, then it is extremely necessary that he should not mind being thought cruel; for without this reputation he could not keep an army united or disposed to any duty. Among the noteworthy actions of Hannibal is numbered this, that although he had an enormous army, composed of men of all nations and fighting in foreign countries, there never arose any dissension either among them or against the prince, either in good fortune or in bad. This could not be due to anything but his inhuman cruelty, which together with his infinite other virtues, made him always venerated and terrible in the sight of his soldiers, and without it his other virtues would not have sufficed to produce that effect. Thoughtless writers admire on the one hand his actions, and on the other blame the principal cause of them.

And that it is true that his other virtues would not have sufficed may be seen from the case of Scipio (famous not only in regard to his own times, but all times of which memory remains), whose armies rebelled against him in Spain, which arose from nothing but his excessive kindness, which allowed more licence to the soldiers than was consonant with military discipline. He was reproached with this in the senate by Fabius Maximus, who called him a corrupter of the Roman militia. Locri having been destroyed by one of Scipio's officers was not revenged by him, nor was the insolence of that officer punished, simply by reason of his easy nature; so much so, that some one wishing to excuse him in the senate, said that there were many men who knew rather how not to err, than how to correct the errors of others. This disposition would in time have tarnished the fame and glory of Scipio had he persevered in it under the empire, but living under the rule of the senate this harmful quality was not only concealed but became a glory to him.

I conclude, therefore, with regard to being feared and loved, that men love at their own free will, but fear at the will of the prince, and that a wise prince must rely on what is in his power and not on what is in the power of others, and he must only contrive to avoid incurring hatred, as has been explained.

IN WHAT WAY PRINCES MUST KEEP FAITH

How laudable is it for a prince to keep good faith and live with integrity, and not with astuteness, every one knows. Still the experience of our times shows those princes to have done great things who have had little regard for good faith, and have been able by astuteness to confuse men's brains, and who have ultimately overcome those who have made loyalty their foundation.

You must know, then, that there are two methods of fighting, the one by law, the other by force: the first method is that of men, the second of beasts; but as the first method is often insufficient, one must have recourse to the second. It is therefore necessary for a prince to know well how to use both the beast and the man. This was covertly taught to rulers by ancient writers, who relate how Achilles and many others of those ancient princes were given to Chiron the centaur to be brought up and educated under his discipline. The parable of this semi-animal, semi-human teacher is meant to indicate that a prince must know how to use both natures, and that the one without the other is not durable.

A prince being thus obliged to know well how to act as a beast must imitate the fox and the lion, for the lion cannot protect himself from traps, and the fox cannot defend himself from wolves. One must therefore be a fox to recognise traps, and a lion to frighten wolves. Those that wish to be only lions do not understand this. Therefore, a prudent ruler ought not to keep faith when by so doing it would be against his interest, and when the reasons which made him bind himself no longer exist. If men were all good, this precept would not be a good one; but as they are bad, and would not observe their faith with you, so you are not bound to keep faith with them. Nor have legitimate grounds ever failed a prince who wished to show colourable excuse for the nonfulfilment of his promise. Of this one could furnish an infinite number of modern examples, and show how many times peace has been broken, and how many promises rendered worthless, by the faithlessness of princes, and those that have been best able to imitate the fox have succeeded best. But it is necessary to be able to disguise this character well, and to be a great feigner and dissembler; and men are so simple and so ready to obey present necessities, that one who deceives will always find those who allow themselves to be deceived.

I will only mention one modern instance. Alexander VI did nothing else but deceive men, he thought of nothing else, and found the occasion for it; no man was ever more able to give assurances, or affirmed things with stronger oaths, and no man observed them less; however, he always succeeded in his deceptions, as he well knew this aspect of things.

It is not, therefore, necessary for a prince to have all the above-named qualities, but it is very necessary to seem to have them. I would even be bold to say that to possess them and always to observe them is dangerous, but to appear to possess them is useful. Thus it is well to seem merciful, faithful, humane, sincere, religious, and also to be so; but you must have the mind so disposed that when it is needful to be otherwise you may be able to change to the opposite qualities. And it must be understood that a prince, and especially a new prince, cannot observe all those things which are considered good in men, being often obliged, in order to maintain the state, to act against faith, against charity, against humanity, and against religion. And, therefore, he must have a mind disposed to adapt itself according to the wind, and as the variations of fortune dictate, and, as I said before, not deviate from what is good, if possible, but be able to do evil if constrained.

A prince must take great care that nothing goes out of his mouth which is not full of the above-named five qualities, and, to see and hear him, he should seem to be all mercy, faith, integrity, humanity, and religion. And nothing is more necessary than to seem to have this last quality, for men in general judge more by the eyes than by the hands, for every one can see, but very few have to feel. Everybody sees what you appear to be, few feel what you are, and those few will not dare to oppose themselves to the many, who have the majesty of the state to defend them; and in the actions of men, and especially of princes, from which there is no appeal, the end justifies the means. Let a prince therefore aim at conquering and maintaining the state, and the means will always be judged honourable and praised by every one, for the vulgar is always taken by appearances and the issue of the event; and the world consists only of the vulgar, and the few who are not vulgar are isolated when the many have a rallying point in the prince. A certain prince of the present time, whom it is well not to name, never does anything but preach peace and good faith, but he is really a great enemy to both, and either of them, had he observed them, would have lost him state or reputation on many occasions.

PRINCES MUST AVOID BEING DESPISED OR HATED

But as I have now spoken of the most important of the qualities in question, I will now deal briefly and generally with the rest. The prince must, as already stated, avoid those things which will make him hated or despised; and whenever he succeeds in this, he will have done his part, and will find no danger in other vices. He will chiefly become hated, as I said, by being rapacious, and usurping the property and women of his subjects, which he must abstain from doing, and whenever one does not attack the property or honour of the generality of men, they will five contented; and one will only have to combat the ambition of a few, who can be easily held in check in many ways. He is rendered despicable by being thought changeable, frivolous, effeminate, timid, and irresolute; which a prince must guard against as a rock of danger, and so contrive that his actions show grandeur, spirit, gravity, and fortitude; and as to the government of his subjects, let his sentence be irrevocable, and let him adhere to his decisions so that no one may think of deceiving or cozening him.

The prince who creates such an opinion of himself gets a great reputation, and it is very difficult to conspire against one who has a great reputation, and he will not easily be attacked, so long as it is known that he is capable and reverenced by his subjects. For a prince must have two kinds of fear: one internal as regards his subjects, one external as regards foreign powers. From the latter he can defend himself with good arms and good friends, and he will always have good friends if he has good arms; and internal matters will always remain quiet, if they are not perturbed by conspiracy and there is no disturbance from without; and even if external powers sought to attack him, if he has ruled and lived as I have described, he will always if he stands firm, be able to sustain every shock, as I have shown that Nabis the Spartan did. But with regard to the subjects, if not acted on from outside, it is still to be feared lest they conspire in secret, from which the prince may guard himself well by avoiding hatred and contempt, and keeping the people satisfied with him, which it is necessary to accomplish, as has been related at length. And one of the most potent remedies that a prince has against conspiracies, is that of not being hated by the mass of the people; for whoever conspires always believes that he will satisfy the people by the death of their prince; but if he thought to offend them by doing this, he would fear to engage in such an undertaking, for the difficulties that conspirators have to meet are infinite. Experience shows that there have been very many conspiracies, but few have turned out well, for whoever conspires cannot act alone, and cannot find companions except among those who are discontented; and as soon as you have disclosed your intention to a malcontent, you give him the means of satisfying himself, for by revealing it he can hope to secure everything he wants; to such an extent that seeing a certain gain by doing this, and seeing on the other hand only a doubtful one and full of danger, he must either be a rare friend to you or else a very bitter enemy to the prince if he keeps faith with you. And to express the matter in a few words, I say, that on the side of the conspirator there is nothing but fear, jealousy, suspicion, and dread of punishment which frightens him; and on the side of the prince there is the majesty of government, the laws, the protection of friends and of the state which guard him. When to these things is added the goodwill of the people, it is impossible that any one should have the temerity to conspire. For whereas generally a conspirator has to fear before the execution of his plot, in this case, having the people for an enemy, he must also fear after his crime is accomplished, and thus he is not able to hope for any refuge.

Numberless instances might be given of this, but I will content myself with one which took place within the memory of our fathers. Messer Annibale Bentivogli, Prince of Bologna, ancestor of the present Messer Annibale, was killed by the Canneschi, who conspired against him. He left no relations but Messer Giovanni, who was then an infant, but after the murder the people rose up and killed all the Canneschi. This arose from the popular goodwill that the house of Bentivogli enjoyed at that time, which was so great that, as there was nobody left after the death of Annibale who could govern the state, the Bolognese hearing that there was one of the Bentivogli family in Florence, who had till then been thought the son of a blacksmith, came to fetch him and gave him the government of the city, and it was governed by him until Messer Giovanni was old enough to assume the government.

I conclude, therefore, that a prince need trouble little about conspiracies when the people are well disposed, but when they are hostile and hold him in hatred, then he must fear everything and everybody. Well-ordered states and wise princes have studied diligently not to drive the nobles to desperation, and to satisfy the populace and keep it contented, for this is one of the most important matters that a prince has to deal with.

Among the kingdoms that are well ordered and governed in our time is France, and there we find numberless good institutions on which depend the liberty and security of the king; of these the chief is the parliament and its authority, because he who established that kingdom, knowing the ambition and insolence of the great nobles, deemed it necessary to have a bit in their mouths to check them. And knowing on the other hand the hatred of the mass of the people against the great, based on fear, and wishing to secure them, he did not wish to make this the special care of the king, to relieve him of the dissatisfaction that he might incur among the nobles by favouring the people, and among the people by favouring the nobles, He therefore established a third judge that, without direct charge of the king, kept in check the great and favoured the lesser people. Nor could any better or more prudent measure have been adopted, nor better precaution for the safety of the king and the kingdom. From which another notable rule can be drawn, that princes should let the carrying out of unpopular duties devolve on others, and bestow favours themselves. I conclude again by saying that a prince must esteem his nobles, but not make himself hated by the populace.

THE USEFULNESS OF FORTRESSES

Some princes, in order to hold their possessions securely, have disarmed their citizens, some others have kept their subject lands divided into parts, others have fomented enmities against themselves, others have endeavoured to win over those whom they suspected at the commencement of their rule: some have constructed fortresses, others have cast them down and destroyed them. And although one cannot pronounce a definite judgment as to these things without going into the particulars of the state to which such a deliberation is to be applied, still I will speak in such a general way as the matter will permit.

A new prince has never been known to disarm his subjects, on the contrary, when he has found them disarmed he has always armed them, for by arming them these arms become your own, those that you suspected become faithful and those that were faithful remain so, and from being merely subjects become your partisans. And since all the subjects cannot be armed, when you give the privilege of arms to some, you can deal more safely with the others; and this different treatment that they recognise renders your men more obliged to you. The others will excuse you, judging that those have necessarily greater merit who have greater danger and heavier duties. But when you disarm them, you commence to offend them and show that you distrust them either through cowardice or lack of confidence, and both of these opinions generate hatred against you. And as you cannot remain unarmed, you are obliged to resort to a mercenary militia, of which we have already stated the value; and even if it were good it cannot be sufficient in number to defend you against powerful enemies and suspected subjects. Therefore, as I have said, a new prince in a new dominion always has his subjects armed. History is full of such examples.

But when a prince acquires a new state as an addition to his old one, then it is necessary to disarm that state, except those who in acquiring it have sided with you; and even these one must, when time and opportunity serve, render weak and effeminate, and arrange things so that all the arms of the new state are in the hands of your soldiers who live near you in your old state.

Our forefathers and those who were esteemed wise used to say that it was necessary to hold Pistoia by means of factions and Pisa with fortresses, and for this purpose they fomented differences in some of their subject towns in order to possess them more easily. In those days when there was a balance of power in Italy, this was doubtless well done, but does not seem to me to be a good precept for the present time, for I do not believe that the divisions thus created ever do any good; on the contrary it is certain that when the enemy approaches, the cities thus divided will be at once lost, for the weaker faction will always side with the enemy and the other will not be able to stand.

The Venetians, actuated, I believe, by the aforesaid motives, fomented the Guelf and Ghibelline factions in the cities subject to them, and although they never allowed them to come to bloodshed, they yet encouraged these differences among them, so that the citizens, being occupied in their own quarrels, might not act against them. This, however, did not avail them anything, as was seen when, after the defeat of Vailà, a part of those subjects immediately took courage and seized the whole state. Such methods, besides, argue weakness in a prince, for in a strong government such dissensions will never be permitted. They are profitable only in time of peace, as by such means it is easy to manage one's subjects, but when it comes to war, the fallacy of such a policy is at once shown.

Without doubt princes become great when they overcome difficulties and opposition, and therefore fortune, especially when it wants to render a new prince great, who has greater need of gaining a great reputation than a hereditary prince, raises up enemies and compels him to undertake wars against them, so that he may have cause to overcome them, and thus climb up higher by means of that ladder which his enemies have brought him. There are many who think therefore that a wise prince ought, when he has the chance, to foment astutely some enmity, so that by suppressing it he will augment his greatness.

Princes, and especially new ones, have found more faith and more usefulness in those men, whom at the beginning of their power they regarded with suspicion, than in those they at first confided in. Pandolfo Petrucci, Prince of Siena, governed his state more by those whom he suspected than by others. But of this we cannot speak at large, as it strays from the subject; I will merely say that these men who at the beginning of a new government were enemies, if they are of a kind to need support to maintain their position, can be very easily gained by the prince, and they are the more compelled to serve him faithfully as they know they must by their deeds cancel the bad opinion previously held of them, and thus the prince will always derive greater help from them than from those who, serving him with greater security, neglect his interests.

And as the matter requires it, I will not omit to remind a prince who has newly taken a state with the secret help of its inhabitants, that he must consider well the motives that have induced those who have favoured him to do so, and if it is not natural affection for him, but only because they were not contented with the state as it was, he will have great trouble and difficulty in maintaining their friendship, because it will be impossible for him to content them. And on well examining the cause of this in the examples drawn from ancient and modem times it will be seen that it is much easier to gain the friendship of those men who were contented with the previous condition and were therefore at first enemies, than that those who not being contented, became his friends and helped him to occupy it.

It has been the custom of princes in order to be able to hold their state securely, to erect fortresses, as a bridle and bit to those who have designs against them, and in order to have a secure refuge against a sudden assault. I approve this method, because it was anciently used. Nevertheless, Messer Niccolò Vitelli has been seen in our own time to destroy two fortresses in Città di Castello in order to keep that state. Guid'Ubaldo, Duke of Urbino, on returning to his dominions from which he had been driven by Cesare Borgia, razed to their foundations all the fortresses of that province, and considered that without them it would be more difficult for him to lose the state again. The Bentivogli, on returning to Bologna, took similar measures. Therefore fortresses may or may not be useful according to the times; if they do good in one way, they do harm in another. The question may be discussed thus: a prince who fears his own people more than foreigners ought to build fortresses, but he who has greater fear of foreigners than of his own people ought to do without them. The castle of Milan built by Francesco Sforza has given and will give more trouble to the house of Sforza than any other disorder in that state. Therefore the best fortress is to be found in the love of the people, for although you may have fortresses they will not save you if you are hated by the people. When once the people have taken arms against you, there will never be lacking foreigners to assist them. In our times we do not see that they have profited any ruler, except the Countess of Forli on the death of her consort Count Girolamo, for she was thus enabled to escape the popular rising and await help from Milan and recover the state; the circumstances being then such that no foreigner could assist the people. But afterwards they were of little use to her when Cesare Borgia attacked her and the people being hostile to her allied themselves with the foreigner. So that then and before it would have been safer for her not to have been hated by the people than to have had the fortresses. Having considered these things I would therefore praise the one who erects fortresses and the one who does not, and would blame any one who, trusting in them, recks little of being hated by his people.

HOW PRINCES GAIN REPUTATION

Nothing causes a prince to be so much esteemed as great enterprises and giving proof of prowess. We have in our own day Ferdinand, King of Aragon, the present King of Spain. He may almost be termed a new prince, because from a weak king he has become for fame and glory the first king in Christendom, and if you regard his actions you will find them all very great and some of them extraordinary. At the beginning of his reign he assailed Granada, and that enterprise was the foundation of his state. At first he did it at his leisure and with out fear of being interfered with; he kept the minds of the barons of Castile occupied in this enterprise, so that thinking only of that war they did not think of making innovations, and be thus acquired reputation and power over them without their being aware of it. He was able with the money of the Church and the people to maintain his armies, and by that long war to lay the foundations of his military power, which afterwards has made him famous. Besides this, to be able to undertake greater enterprises, and always under the pretext of religion, he had recourse to a pious cruelty, driving out the Moors from his kingdom and despoiling them. No more miserable or unusual example can be found. He also attacked Africa under the same pretext, undertook his Italian enterprise, and has lately attacked France; so that he has continually contrived great things, which have kept his subjects' minds uncertain and astonished, and occupied in watching their result. And these actions have arisen one out of the other, so that they have left no time for men to settle down and act against him.

It is also very profitable for a prince to give some outstanding example of his greatness in the internal administration, like those related of Messer Bernabò of Milan. When it happens that some one does something extraordinary, either good or evil, in civil life, he must find such means of rewarding or punishing him which will be much talked about. And above all a prince must endeavour in every action to obtain fame for being great and excellent.

A prince is further esteemed when he is a true friend or a true enemy, when, that is, he declares himself without reserve in favour of some one or against another. This policy is always more useful than remaining neutral. For if two neighbouring powers come to blows, they are either such that if one wins, you will have to fear the victor, or else not. In either of these two cases it will be better for you to declare yourself openly and make war, because in the first case if you do not declare yourself, you will fall a prey to the victor, to the pleasure and satisfaction of the one who has been defeated, and you will have no reason nor anything to defend you and nobody to receive you. For, whoever wins will not desire friends whom he suspects and who do not help him when in trouble, and whoever loses will not receive you as you did not take up arms to venture yourself in his cause.

Antiochus went to Greece, being sent by the Ætolians to expel the Romans. He sent orators to the Achaeians who were friends of the Romans to encourage them to remain neutral; on the other hand the Romans persuaded them to take up arms on their side. The matter was brought before the council of the Achaeians for deliberation, where the ambassador of Antiochus sought to persuade them to remain neutral, to which the Roman ambassador replied: "As to what is said that it is best and most useful for your state not to meddle in our war, nothing is further from the truth; for if you do not meddle in it you will become, without any favour or any reputation, the prize of the victor."

And it will always happen that the one who is not your friend will want you to remain neutral, and the one who is your friend will require you to declare yourself by taking arms. Irresolute princes, to avoid present dangers, usually follow the way of neutrality and are mostly ruined by it. But when the prince declares himself frankly in favour of one side, if the one to whom you adhere conquers, even if he is powerful and you remain at his discretion, he is under an obligation to you and friendship has been established, and men are never so dishonest as to oppress you with such a patent ingratitude. Moreover, victories are never so prosperous that the victor does not need to have some scruples, especially as to justice. But if your ally loses, you are sheltered by him, and so long as he can, he will assist you; you become the companion of a fortune which may rise again. In the second case, when those who fight are such that you have nothing to fear from the victor, it is still more prudent on your part to adhere to one; for you go to the ruin of one with the help of him who ought to save him if he were wise, and if he conquers he rests at your discretion, and it is impossible that he should not conquer with your help.

And here it should be noted that a prince ought never to make common cause with one more powerful than himself to injure another, unless necessity forces him to it, as before said; for if he wins you rest in his power, and princes must avoid as much as possible being under the will and pleasure of others. The Venetians united with France against the Duke of Milan, although they could have avoided that alliance, and from it resulted their own ruin. But when one cannot avoid it, as happened in the case of the Florentines when the Pope and Spain went with their armies to attack Lombardy, then the prince ought to join for the above reasons. Let no state believe that it can always follow a safe policy, rather let it think that all are doubtful. This is found in the nature of things, that one never tries to avoid one difficulty without running into another, but prudence consists in being able to know the nature of the difficulties, and taking the least harmful as good.

A prince must also show himself a lover of merit, give preferment to the able, and honour those who excel in every art. Moreover he must encourage his citizens to follow their callings quietly, whether in commerce, or agriculture, or any other trade that men follow, so that this one shall not refrain from improving his possessions through fear that they may be taken from him, and that one from starting a trade for fear of taxes; but he should offer rewards to whoever does these things, and to whoever seeks in any way to improve his city or state. Besides this, he ought, at convenient seasons of the year, to keep the people occupied with festivals and shows; and as every city is divided either into guilds or into classes, he ought to pay attention to all these groups, mingle with them from time to time, and give them an example of his humanity and munificence, always upholding, however, the majesty of his dignity, which must never be allowed to fail in anything whatever.

CHAPTER SIX

HOBBES

The modern age, conceived in the Renaissance and Reformation, was born in the crucible of civil and international war in the seventeenth century. A host of old and new issues—social, economic, constitutional—produced intense passions transformed by religion into irreconcilable hatreds. The Thirty Years' War (1618–1648) started with a Protestant revolt in Bohemia. The conflict soon broadened into a major conflagration, until most European states were finally involved; civil wars and revolutions sprang up in half a dozen countries, from Italy to England. Germany, the principal theater of military operations, was depopulated, impoverished, and ruined by the war. Neither Protestantism nor Catholicism won a conclusive victory, and men began to ask themselves whether moral and physical devastation could be justified by theological differences.

Until the age of discovery, that is, as long as the Mediterranean held the pivotal position in commerce and civilization, England lived on the rim of the world's center. But when geographical discovery and overseas expansion shifted the world's focal area from the Mediterranean basin—the "middle of the earth"—to the Atlantic shores of western Europe, England became the center of a new oceanic world largely of her own making, and her rising commercial and industrial wealth quickly put her in the front rank of European nations. Moreover, in the seventeenth century the foundations were laid for the future greatness of England in science, medicine, navigation, philosophy, economics, and politics. The nineteenth century is often called the "English century" because England then attained the peak of her visible power and world-wide influence. Yet the seventeenth is probably the most creative century in English history, and the success of the nineteenth century was built on the greatness of the seventeenth.

The turning point was marked by the Puritan Revolution and two civil wars (1642–1649), fought over fundamental issues that could not be resolved peaceably. First, there was the issue of *religious* liberty: the Church of England was criticized for being a state church, and its episcopal organization as well as its liturgy was rejected by many as being too close to Roman Catholicism. A sizable body of respectable Protestants favored presbyterianism as an alternative, and—on the theological left—the independent congregationalist sects began to press their demands. The slogan of King James I, "No Bishop, no King," made compromise with the Puritans difficult, and with the congregationalist sectarians impossible. The second main issue of the civil war was *constitutional:* who was sovereign, Parliament or the King? The third issue, cutting across religion and politics, was *social* and *economic:* to what extent should the merchants, financiers, lawyers, and tradesmen be included in the governing classes of the nation?

The class lines were by no means neatly drawn. The most prominent generals on the parliamentary side came from distinguished aristocratic or landowning families. Conversely, many urban elements, particularly in the North and West, supported the royalist side in the war. Yet on the whole the middle classes, tradesmen and yeoman farmers, supported the parliamentary party; and, though they were not agreed on the form of church government they wanted, they all abhorred the High Anglicanism and episcopalianism of the royalists, which seemed little different from Roman Catholicism—and Romanism meant Spain and France, the two national enemies of England. The parliamentary party was the more nationalistic; nationalism was of less import to those who upheld the doctrine of the divine right of kings.

The parliamentary party won because it commanded superior economic and financial resources, because the fleet was on its side, and because the New Model Army fought with invincible faith in its cause. King Charles I was publicly beheaded in London on January 30, 1649. The first middle-class revolution in history thus asserted itself successfully with decisive and unheard-of audacity. With the head of Charles I, the doctrine of the divine rights of kings rolled to the ground. His fate warned all rulers that political authority is closer to the earth and the people than to God and heaven.

The turbulent first half of the seventeenth century in England provides the background for the political philosophy of a lonely and complex figure, Thomas Hobbes (1588–1679). Hobbes' father was an impecunious vicar and something of a "character." Once, after a Saturday night of playing cards, he dozed in the pulpit and surprised the congregation by awakening with the cry of "Clubs is trumps." He got into a brawl with another parson and was forced to get away, abandoning his wife and three children. His brother, a well-to-do glover, who took charge of the deserted children, became particularly interested in young Thomas, who read and wrote at four, learned Greek and Latin at six, and went to Oxford at fifteen. Hobbes stayed at Oxford for five years but was not too happy about the course of studies, which seemed to him arid and old-fashioned.

On receiving his degree, Hobbes was recommended to Lord Cavendish (afterward the first Earl of Devonshire) for the post of companion and tutor of his eldest son, who was about the same age as Hobbes. The association with the Cavendish family lasted, with some interruptions, until Hobbes' death. Through his close connection with this family, one of the most aristocratic in England, he met men of affairs as well as outstanding scientists of the day, such as Bacon, Harvey, Descartes, and Galileo. Hobbes also traveled widely, and spent—in company with his Cavendish charges or on his own—about twenty years on the Continent, mostly in Paris; there he came in touch with the new philosophical and scientific developments of the time.

In 1640, when Parliament began to assert its authority, Hobbes fled to France, "the first of all that fled," as he later said of himself. He feared that his intimate associations with royalist circles might endanger his safety; in addition, his writings up to his flight to France had been clearly antiparliamentarian and antidemocratic. During his stay in Paris he instructed, from 1646 to 1648, Charles II, the son of the executed monarch, in mathematics. In 1651, Hobbes went back to England, because he "would not trust his safety with the French clergy," as he later explained. He declared his submission to the new republican regime and stayed in England until his death in 1679.

Hobbes' greatest work, the *Leviathan,* appeared in 1651, shortly before his return to England. The civil war provided some of the atmosphere of the book but little more. Hobbes' main views were formed long before the actual conflict broke out, although there had been no real peace in England since the ascension to the throne of James I in 1603. The *Leviathan* is not an apology for the Stuart monarchy, nor a grammar of despotic government, but the first general theory of politics in the English language.

Unlike most defenders of absolute government, who start out with the gospel of inequality, Hobbes argues that men are naturally equal in mind and body. As to strength of body, the weakest has enough strength to kill the strongest, either by slaying him secretly or by allying himself with others for the purpose. With regard to mental faculties, Hobbes finds an even greater natural equality. Prudence is a matter of time and experience that can be acquired by everybody. Most persons think that they have more wisdom than their fellow men, but this in itself, Hobbes remarks sardonically, is proof that men are equal rather than unequal.

This *basic equality of men* is a principal source of trouble and misery. Men have, in general, equal faculties; they also cherish like hopes and desires. If two men desire the same thing, which they cannot both obtain, they become enemies and seek to destroy each other. In the *state of nature,* therefore, men are in a *condition of war,* of "every man against every man," and Hobbes adds that the nature of the war consists, not in actual fighting, "but in the known disposition thereto." Force and fraud, the two cardinal virtues of war, flourish in this atmosphere of perpetual fear and strife, fed by three psychological causes: competition, diffidence, and glory. In such a condition, there is no place for industry, agriculture, navigation, trade; there are no arts or letters; no society; no amenities of civilized living, and, worst of all, there is "continual fear and danger of violent death; and the life of man, solitary, poor, nasty, brutish, and short."

Hobbes does not extensively discuss the question whether men have actually ever lived in such a state of nature. He notes that the "savage people in many places of America" have no government and live in the brutish manner described. Yet, even if the state of nature has never existed generally all over the world, one could envisage the kind of life men would lead if there were no government. His argument of the *state of nature* is, in other words, *philosophical* and *not historical*. On the basis of the anthropological data that we possess today but that were not accessible to Hobbes, we know that life is actually more regulated in the so-called primitive group than in the community of the more advanced stage. As a thoroughgoing individualist and rationalist, Hobbes was unaware that the family or clan, and not the individual, is the basic social unit in primitive society, and custom or social pressure, and not law, its mechanism of enforcing conformity.

Pessimistic as Hobbes may seem, he is not despondent about man's ability to overcome the predicament in which he finds himself in the state of nature. The *fear of death* is the passion that inclines men to peace: the attractions of power and glory give way to the desire for securing, as a minimum, life, and—if possible—the means of a commodious existence. Hobbes is a strong rationalist, but reason is for him not a *deus ex machina* that appears from nowhere to work miracles, but an integral part of man, his essential faculty that distinguishes him from animals. Once man realizes that his fear of death is primarily due to brutal competition, resulting in perpetual war of all against all, reason shows the way out: to accept the principle of not doing that to another "which thou thinkest unreasonable to be done by another to yourself."

However, on the basis of Hobbes' analysis of the nature of man, a contract among men not to do to one another what they would not wish to have done to themselves would not be sufficient. Though man has the capacity to learn prudence and moderation from his fear of death, his desire for power and glory may tempt him to break his pledge unless there is a restraining power strong enough to keep him to his promise, because "covenants, without the sword, are but words, and of no strength to secure a man at all." If men were peaceable enough, Hobbes notes, to observe covenants without a superior authority for their enforcement, there would be no need for government in the first place, because there would be peace without compulsion. To make the counsel of prudence, born of the fear of death, issue in effective peace, a sovereign authority—one man or an assembly of men—must be created to whom all power is transferred.

The *social contract* of Hobbes is made *between subjects and subjects, not between subjects and sovereign.* The sovereign is not a party to the contract, but its creation. In this conception of the social contract, the sovereign cannot commit any breach of covenant, because he is not a party to it. By participating in the creation of the sovereign, the subject is the author of all that the ruler does and must therefore not complain of any of the ruler's actions, because he would then be deliberately doing injury to himself. Hobbes concedes that the sovereign may commit iniquity but not "injustice or injury in the proper signification," because he cannot, by definition, act illegally: he determines what is just and unjust, and his action is law.

The question of the best form of state is not one of logic, according to Hobbes, but of convenience, that is, of the aptitude of the state to produce the security and peace of the people for which a government is instituted. However, on purely practical grounds Hobbes considers monarchy the best form of state because it suffers less from competition for office and power than do aristocracies and democracies; also, it is easier for one than for many to act resolutely and consistently.

Sovereign power is "incommunicable and inseparable," and Hobbes attacks any institution, town or private corporation, that may weaken the omnipotence of the state. He is vehemently opposed to division of powers or mixed government, and he goes so far as to say that there would have been no civil war in England if it had not been for the widespread opinion that sovereignty was divided between King, Lords, and Commons. There is particular danger in the liberty of the subject to challenge the wisdom of legality of the sovereign's actions, the "poisonous doctrine" that "every private man is judge of good and evil actions," and that "whatsoever a man does against his conscience is sin." Against such "seditious doctrines" Hobbes demands the unqualified obedience of the subject.

To keep the authority of the state strong, Hobbes advises the sovereign not to allow the growth of groups and institutions that intervene between state and individual. Hobbes is particularly anxious to prevent churches from interfering in any way with the activities of the state, and in his doctrine the church becomes, in effect, a department of the state. He reminds the clergy that it is not essential to the commonwealth, and that the safety of the church depends on the state rather than the state on the safety of the church.

Hobbes had no religion. He defines religion in general, together with true religion and superstition, as follows: *"Fear* of power invisible, feigned by the mind, or imagined from tales publicly allowed, *religion;* not allowed, *superstition.* And when the power imagined is truly such as we imagine, *true religion."* These definitions are included, not in a discussion of theology or metaphysics, but in a catalogue of human passions and their forms of expression. His approach to religion is by way of psychology and public policy, and not by way of theology or philosophy. His definitions of religion, superstition, and true religion are placed between "curiosity" and "panic terror," which placement suggests itself Hobbes' approach to religion.

From a strictly political viewpoint Hobbes saw in religions and churches the most serious danger of civil disobedience and disunity, and in the conflict of secular and divine commandments the most frequent pretext of sedition and civil war. He is skeptical about the origin of many commands that claim divine provenance, because it is difficult to know whether a command comes from God or from someone who abuses His name for private ends. But if there is a bona fide conflict between secular and divine laws, the subject should obey the civil sovereign, if compliance does not involve forfeiture of life eternal; if it does, the subject may prefer death of the body to eternal damnation of the soul.

Hobbes' advice to subjects to become martyrs for their consciences' sake, or obey the sovereign, is tantamount to establishing—for most people—the duty of unlimited obedience. Not feeling any deep sympathy for religion, Hobbes invites believers to prove their faith by their willingness to die for it. In his personal attitude, Hobbes preferred the "episcopacy" of the Anglican state church because it was the official church, and "the most commodious that a Christian King can use for the governing of Christ's flock." By contrast, Presbyterians and Puritans encroach on civil authority and encourage men to set themselves up as their own judges—a bad habit easily carried over into secular affairs.

Hobbes' heaviest assaults are directed against the Roman Catholic Church. Hobbes remembered—and the memory is maintained in England to this day by annual public ceremonies—the Catholic conspiracy of the Gunpowder Plot in 1605. The conspirators managed to introduce barrels of gunpowder into the cellars of Parliament just before it was to be opened by King James I, with the aim of blowing up King, Lords, and Commons in one big explosion. The plot failed, and the conspirators were executed, including the Provincial of the Jesuits in England. In 1610, while Hobbes was in Paris with young Cavendish on their first grand tour, King Henry IV of France, at first a Huguenot and later a convert to Catholicism, a conciliatory and temperate ruler, was stabbed to death by François Ravaillac, a Catholic fanatic. The murder made a lifelong impression on Hobbes, and he saw in the Roman Catholic Church the true exemplification of the kingdom of darkness: "For from the time that the Bishop of Rome had gotten to be acknowledged for bishop universal, by pretense of succession to St. Peter, their whole hierarchy, or kingdom of darkness, may be compared not unfitly to the *kingdom of fairies;* that is, to the old wives' *fables* in England concerning *ghosts* and *spirits,* and the feats they play in the night. And if a man consider the original of this ecclesiastical dominion, he will easily perceive that the Papacy is no other than the *ghost* of the deceased *Roman empire,* sitting crowned upon the grave thereof."

Called "father of atheists" even in the entourage of Charles II, Hobbes had to leave France in 1651 because he was afraid of the French clergy, not of politicians. After Charles II returned to England in 1660, Hobbes got into difficulties because of his alleged atheism, and the *Leviathan* could not be reprinted for several years, owing to the opposition of the bishops. In 1666 Hobbes—fearful of official proceedings against him—wrote an essay on heresy to prove why he could not be legally burned for his opinions. The first collected edition of his works in 1688 was published not in England, but in Holland.

In his treatment of the problem of *natural law* Hobbes reveals his novel doctrine. Since the Stoics, the conception has never died out in the West that civil (or positive) law is derived from, and inferior to, a higher law, a "law behind the law"—the law of nature. In the Bible, too, the law of kings and princes is held to be subordinate to the law of God. This Stoic-Jewish-Christian tradition has had a civilizing effect on the western world because it has always reminded rulers that above their edicts and commands there is a higher law, founded on natural reason or divine revelation. Hobbes rejects this approach to the problem of the validity of law on the ground that it places validity beyond the formal source of the legal sovereign. According to Hobbes, there can be no unjust law—the cardinal issue of legal philosophy—because laws are the "rules of just and unjust." As to the relations between civil law and natural law, Hobbes maintains that they "contain each other." In fact, the law of nature is not law at all, but only "qualities that dispose men to peace and obedience."

Hobbes lists equity, justice, gratitude, and "other moral virtues" as the laws of nature. These qualities are not true laws, because, before the state is established, there is no authority to decide finally which idea of the law is binding. In practice, therefore, the law of nature is nothing but a set of general principles of the civil law; the main formal difference lies in the fact that the civil law is written, whereas the natural law is unwritten. Thus Hobbes sought to sweep away the doctrine of natural law from the theory of the state. With penetrating insight he foresaw the revolutionary implications of natural law ideas as they became manifest only a century later in the American and French revolutions. Locke, too, admitted the revolutionary possibilities of the doctrine of natural law, but, unlike Hobbes, he was not overly frightened by the prospect.

Hobbes' hostility to natural law, whether based on reason or religious faith, is not only linked to his conception of sovereignty and government, but is closely related to his total rejection of values and universally valid ethical ideas. According to Hobbes, "good" and "evil" are not ethical qualities of an object or action, but merely expressions of an individual's feelings about them: "But whatsoever is the object of any man's appetite or desire, that is it which he for his part calls *good:* and the object of his hate and aversion, *evil;* and of his contempt, *vile* and *inconsiderable.* For these words of good, evil, and contemptible are ever used with relation to the person that uses them: there being nothing simply and absolutely so; nor any common rule of good and evil, to be taken from the nature of the objects themselves." This *emotive theory of value,* as the modern philosophical school of logical positivism calls it, thus denies to statements of value any objective validity or even meaning, since such statements—in the eyes of both Hobbes and the logical positivists—merely tell us something about the feelings of a person with respect to some actions, but say nothing meaningful or valid about the actions themselves.

This general rejection by Hobbes of any concept of universal values can also be seen in his treatment of the problem of the *forms of government* Aristotle divided all forms of government into two broad groups, and the basic criterion of his distinction was entirely ethical: whether a government operates in the interests of the people (monarchy, aristocracy, constitutional government) or of the rulers (tyranny, oligarchy, dictatorship of the poor). Hobbes rejects this ethical distinction completely, and holds that governments can only differ as to their numerical composition, that is, government by one (monarchy), by a few (aristocracy), or by the people (democracy). Terms like "tyranny," "oligarchy," and "anarchy" are not, according to Hobbes, names for ethically deficient forms of government, but simply indicate that a particular person "mislikes" a monarchical, aristocratic, or democratic form of government. Hobbes rejects here again, as in his analysis of natural law and the more general problem of values, the possibility of rational argument and valid ethical conclusions: if he comes out in favor of monarchy against aristocracy and democracy, his preference is not based on any moral position, but solely on his assertion that monarchy is more "convenient," in the sense that it is likely to be more effective than its rivals, and will result in more peace and security for the people.

On the whole, the practical effect of Hobbes has been to strengthen the *doctrine of the absolute state.* Yet the complex character of his ideas has puzzled his political friends and opponents. Conservatives who believe in legitimate monarchy criticize Hobbes first for being little interested in the divine right of monarchs and in monarchy as a moral institution. Hobbes was solely concerned with the pragmatic question of *effective* government, and legitimacy did not interest him at all. Thus, when he returned to England in 1651, he sent his submission to the Council of State. Though he was a lifelong supporter of the royalist cause, he was willing to submit to Cromwell's regime, because at the time it was the effective government that maintained law and order in England. In 1656, Hobbes boasted of the influence of the *Leviathan* on "the minds of a thousand gentlemen to a conscientious obedience to the present government [of Cromwell], which otherwise would have wavered in that point." After King Charles II returned to England in 1660, and the monarchy was restored, Hobbes explained that the "gentlemen" had appeased Cromwell in order to protect their property and influence for serving the king better later on. This may be realism, but it cannot appeal to a conservative who bases loyalty on moral sentiment.

Moreover, monarchists could never be satisfied with Hobbes' preference for monarchy as the best form of government. No theory of monarchy can be construed without some element of mysticism to make its authority acceptable. Hobbes' preference was entirely devoid of mysticism; his approach was utilitarian and pragmatic. The Hobbesian monarch cannot hide his ineffectiveness behind the cloak of divine or traditional authority. He must "deliver the goods," if he is to retain his regal office. Religious conservatives have charged Hobbes with atheism because he treats the church as he treats other associations, that is, subordinates it to the state, as he subordinates theology to philosophy. For a long time, atheism and agnosticism were branded as Hobbism.

Hobbes' main opponents have been the adherents of parliamentary government and limited powers; because this doctrine has become the dominant tradition in the English-speaking countries, there has been no Hobbesian school in British and American political thought. By contrast, Hobbes has markedly influenced various countries with traditions of absolute, despotic government.

Yet to call Hobbes a spiritual father of modern totalitarianism is more untenable than would appear from a cursory glance at several key phrases in the *Leviathan*. First, government is set up, according to Hobbes, by a covenant that transfers all power and authority to the sovereign. This *contractual foundation of government* is anathema to modern totalitarians who attacked the contractual theory of the state because contract implies mutuality of some sort, and, still more important because there can be no contract without consent. Democracy is government by consent.

Second, Hobbes assigns to the state a prosaic business: to maintain *order and security for the benefit of the citizens.* By contrast, the aim of the modern totalitarian state was anti-individualistic and antihedonistic: the goal of public policy was dictated, not by the longing of citizens for happiness, but by a collective purpose, such as the glory of the master race in Nazi Germany, the revival of the Roman empire in Fascist Italy, and the triumph of the proletariat in Soviet Russia. Race, Empire, and Class are modern totalitarian substitutes for Hobbes' bourgeois ideals of Thrift, Industry, and "Commodious Living."

Third, the Hobbesian state is *authoritarian,* not totalitarian. Above all, Hobbes pleads for equality before the law, so that the "rich and mighty" have no legal advantage over "poor and obscure persons." Hobbes' authoritarianism thus lacks one of the most characteristic features of the modern totalitarian state: inequality before the law, and the resulting sense of personal insecurity. Authority in the Hobbesian state is concentrated in the political sphere, and in it alone. The sovereign will normally permit his subjects "the liberty to buy and sell and otherwise to contract with one another, to choose their own abode, their own diet, their own trade of life, and institute their children as they themselves see fit; and the like." The Hobbesian belief in economic *laissez faire* is the exact opposite of rigid economic planning. Similarly, the Hobbesian freedom of bringing up one's children is antithetical to the regimenting and drilling of children in modern totalitarian regimes.

Fourth, Hobbes holds that the sovereign may be one man or an assembly of men, whereas modern totalitarianism—in fact, if not always in theory—was addicted to the leadership principle. Hobbes preferred monarchy for practical reasons, but he was free from the mysticism that has endowed totalitarian leaders with alleged charismatic and prophetic gifts. The Hobbesian sovereign is a *supreme administrator and lawgiver* but not a top spellbinder, propagandist, or showman.

Fifth, Hobbes recognizes that war is one of the two main forces (the other being the danger of internal disorder) that drive men to set up a state. But whenever he speaks of war, it is *defensive war,* and there is no glorification of war, let alone of aggressive war, in the *Leviathan.* By contrast, totalitarian fascists looked on war as something highly *desirable,* and on imperialist war as the highest form of national life; communists—while rejecting, in theory, war between nations—accepted the inevitability of war between classes, and the liquidation of the bourgeoisie by violent means.

Sixth, the totalitarian state insisted on outer as well as inner conformity; in fact, it considered ideas more dangerous than actions. By contrast, the Hobbesian sovereign desires merely—for purposes of maintaining the peace—*outer conformity* of the subjects to the law. The subject is bound to obey the law, but "not bound to believe it," and human governors can take no notice of his "belief and interior cogitations." What Hobbes is concerned about is social peace, not Truth, whereas totalitarians of all times are willing to destroy man for the sake of preserving Truth, if a choice has to be made.

Seventh, and finally, the Hobbesian state does not completely swallow the individual: "A man cannot lay down the right of resisting them that assault him by force to take away his life." Since the purpose of civil society is the preservation and protection of man's life, Hobbes recognizes the inalienable *right of the individual to resist* when his life is at stake, because "man by nature chooses the lesser evil, which is danger of death in resisting, rather than the greater, which is certain and present death in not resisting." For a long time this cautionary qualification seemed unimportant, because the sanctity of human life, as a principle at least, was universally accepted. But when, in World War II, millions of people were murdered in gas chambers and concentration camps in pursuance of deliberate state policy, the Hobbesian stress on the inalienability of human life as the irreducible minimum of the state's purpose acquired new meaning.

The fact that Hobbes was not—intellectually or emotionally—of the totalitarian cast should not create the impression that he was a democrat in disguise. He was not. The Hobbesian state finds its realization in neither the modern democratic state nor the totalitarian dictatorship of the fascist or communist brand. In modern times, political Hobbism is to be found in countries that possess social and economic conditions similar to those of seventeenth-century England—some nations in Latin America and Asia. Dictatorships in Latin America in the nineteenth and twentieth centuries closely approximated the Hobbesian state: society was still in a precapitalist or, at best, early capitalist stage. Economic *laissez faire* was mingled, in such countries, with strong political authority, usually in the form of an open or concealed dictatorship. But the dictatorship was authoritarian, not totalitarian. In cultural, religious, educational, social, and economic affairs it was often very lenient. Compared with an advanced democracy, the Hobbesian state may appear dismal enough. Compared with twentieth-century totalitarianism, it is a vision of refined political civilization.

The Hobbesian theory of politics rests largely on a hypothesis—the solitary, combative, competitive character of man—that is only a half-truth. It is difficult to see how the brutes who lead a life of nasty savagery in the Hobbesian state of nature should suddenly display the prudent reasoning and cooperative effort that go into the making of the social contract creating the sovereign. A group that knows the institution of the contract is well beyond the state of nature, and it would perhaps be truer to say that contract is the product of society rather than society the product of contract. Yet these difficulties rest, not on varying sets of historical facts, but on different interpretations of human nature. If one rejects Hobbes' psychological assumptions as too pessimistic and mechanistic, one will be unable to accept, to that extent, the political ideas derived from them.

The truth of Hobbes' psychological tenets will ultimately be tested by the facts of social life rather than by philosophical arguments. In the area of domestic political organization, the state of nature with its horrors and barbarisms has disappeared. In the area of international relations, Hobbes noted in 1651, independent sovereign states live in the state of nature, "are in continual jealousies, and in the state and posture of gladiators; having their weapons pointing, and their eyes fixed, on one another; that is, their forts, garrisons, and guns upon the frontiers of their kingdoms, and continual spies upon their neighbors; which is a posture of war. But because they uphold thereby the industry of their subjects, there does not follow from it that misery which accompanies the liberty of particular men." As long as the sovereign states of the world continue to exist in the state of nature, a condition of brutish savagery, the Hobbesian view of man will continue to be true of the behavior of states toward one another.

Hobbes' observation that the fear of death is an important motive in creating a social order is profound. In the forty-five years after World War II, relative peace between the Soviet Union and the United States was maintained as the result of this fear, which took on new meaning in the atomic age. If humanity cannot find its purpose in the pursuit of more positive goals, then perhaps its best chance of survival may be in the more modest Hobbesian motive.

HOBBES

*Leviathan**

THE STATE OF NATURE

Nature has made men so equal in the faculties of the body and mind, as that though there be found one man sometimes manifestly stronger in body, or of quicker mind than another, yet when all is reckoned together, the difference between man and man is not so considerable, as that one man can thereupon claim to himself any benefit to which another man may not pretend as well as he. For as to the strength of body, the weakest has strength enough to kill the strongest, either by secret machinations, or by confederacy with others that are in the same danger with himself.

And as to the faculties of the mind, setting aside the arts grounded upon words, and especially that skill of proceeding upon general and infallible rules, called science, which very few have, and but in few things, as being not a native faculty, born with us, nor attained, as prudence, while we look after somewhat else, I find yet a greater equality among men than that of strength. For prudence is but experience, which equal time equally bestows on all men in those things they equally apply themselves unto. That which may perhaps make such equality incredible is but a vain conceit of one's own wisdom, which almost all men think they have in a greater degree than the vulgar; that is, than all men but themselves, and a few others, whom by fame, or for concurring with themselves, they approve. For such is the nature of men, that howsoever they may acknowledge many others to be more witty, or more eloquent, or more learned, yet they will hardly believe there be many so wise as themselves; for they see their own wit at hand, and other men's at a distance. But this proves rather that men are in that point equal, than unequal. For there is not ordinarily a greater sign of the equal distribution of anything than that every man is contented with his share.

From this equality or ability arises equality of hope in the attaining of our ends. And therefore if any two men desire the same thing, which nevertheless they cannot both enjoy, they become enemies; and in the way to their end, which is principally their own conservation, and sometimes their delectation only, endeavour to destroy or subdue one another. And from hence it comes to pass that where an invader has no more to fear than another man's single power, if one plant, sow, build, or possess a convenient seat, others may probably be expected to come prepared with forces united, to dispossess and deprive him, not only of the fruit of his labour, but also of his life or liberty. And the invader again is in the like danger of another.

And from this diffidence of one another, there is no way for any man to secure himself, so reasonable, as anticipation; that is, by force, or wiles, to master the persons of all men he can, so long till he see no other power great enough to endanger him; and this is no more than his own conservation requires, and is generally allowed. Also because there be some that, taking pleasure in contemplating their own power in the acts of conquest, which they pursue farther than their security requires, if others, that otherwise would be glad to be at case within modest bounds, should not by invasion increase

---

*From Thomas Hobbes, *Leviathan* (1651). Spelling and punctuation have been modernized for this selection.

their power, they would not be able, long time, by standing only on their defence, to subsist. And by consequence, such augmentation of dominion over men being necessary to a man's conservation, it ought to be allowed him.

Again, men have no pleasure, but on the contrary a great deal of grief, in keeping company where there is no power able to over-awe them all. For every man looks that his companion should value him at the same rate he sets upon himself; and upon all signs of contempt, or undervaluing, naturally endeavours, as far as he dares (which, among them that have no common power to keep them in quiet, is far enough to make them destroy each other), to extort a greater value from his contemners, by damage; and from others, by the example.

So that in the nature of man, we find three principal causes of quarrel. First, competition; secondly, diffidence; thirdly, glory.

The first makes men invade for gain; the second, for safety; and the third, for reputation. The first use violence, to make themselves masters of other men's persons, wives, children, and cattle; the second, to defend them; the third, for trifles, as a word, a smile, a different opinion, and any other sign of undervalue, either direct in their persons, or by reflection in their kindred, their friends, their nation, their profession, or other name.

Hereby it is manifest that, during the time men live without a common power to keep them all in awe, they are in that condition which is called war; and such a war as is of every man against every man. For *war* consists not in battle only, or the act of fighting, but in a tract of time, wherein the will to contend by battle is sufficiently known; and therefore the notion of *time* is to be considered in the nature of war, as it is in the nature of weather. For as the nature of foul weather lies not in a shower or two or rain, but in an inclination thereto of many days together, so the nature of war consists not in actual fighting, but in the known disposition thereto, during all the time there is no assurance to the contrary. All other time is *peace*.

Whatsoever therefore is consequent to a time of war, where every man is enemy to every man, the same is consequent to the time wherein men live without other security

than what their own strength, and their own invention, shall furnish them withal. In such condition, there is no place for industry, because the fruit thereof is uncertain; and consequently no culture of the earth; no navigation nor use of the commodities that may be imported by sea; no commodious building; no instruments of moving, and removing, such things as require much force; no knowledge of the face of the earth; no account of time; no arts; no letters; no society and, which is the worst of all, continual fear, and danger of violent death; and the life of man, solitary, poor, nasty, brutish, and short.

It may seem strange to some man that has not well weighted these things that nature should thus dissociate, and render men apt to invade and destroy one another; and he may therefore, not trusting to this inference, made from the passions, desire perhaps to have the same confirmed by experience. Let him therefore consider with himself: when taking a journey, he arms himself, and seeks to go well accompanied; when going to sleep, he locks his doors; when even in his house he locks his chests; and this when he knows there be laws, and public officers, armed, to revenge all injuries shall be done him; what opinion he has of his fellow-subjects, when he rides armed; of his fellow citizens, when he locks his doors; and of his children and servants, when he locks his chests. Does he not there as much accuse mankind by his actions as I do by my words? But neither of us accuse man's nature in it. The desire, and other passions of man, are in themselves no sin. No more are the actions that proceed from those passions, till they know a law that forbids them, which till laws be made they cannot know, nor can any law be made till they have agreed upon the person that shall make it.

It may peradventure be thought there was never such a time, nor condition of war, as this; and I believe it was never generally so over all the world; but there are many places where they live so now. For the savage people in many places of America, except the government of small families, the concord whereof depends on natural lust, have no government at all, and live at this day in that brutish manner, as I said before. Howsoever, it may be perceived what manner of life there would be, where there were no common power to fear, by the manner of life which men that have formerly lived under a peaceful government used to degenerate into in civil war.

But though there had never been any time wherein particular men were in a condition of war one against another, yet in all times kings and persons of sovereign authority, because of their independency, are in continual jealousies and in the state and posture of gladiators, having their weapons pointing and their eyes fixed on one another; that is, their forts, garrisons and guns upon the frontiers of their kingdoms, and continual spies upon their neighbours, which is a posture of war. But because they uphold thereby the industry of their subjects, there does not follow from it that misery which accompanies the liberty of particular men.

To this war of every man against every man this also is consequent: that nothing can be unjust. The notions of right and wrong, justice and injustice, have there no place. Where there is no common power, there is no law: where no law, no injustice. Force and fraud are in war the two cardinal virtues. Justice and injustice are none of the faculties neither of the body nor mind. If they were, they might be in a man that were alone in the world, as well as his senses and passions. They are qualities that relate to men in society, not in solitude. It is consequent also to the same condition that there be no propriety, no dominion, no *mine* and *thine* distinct, but only that to be every man's that he can get, and for so long as he can keep it. And thus much for the ill condition which man by mere nature is actually placed in, though with a possibility to come out of it, consisting partly in the passions, partly in his reason.

The passions that incline men to peace are fear of death, desire of such things as are necessary to commodious living, and a hope by their industry to obtain them. And reason suggests convenient articles of peace, upon which men may be drawn to agreement. These articles are they which otherwise are called the laws of nature.

THE SOCIAL CONTRACT

The *right of nature,* which writers commonly call *jus naturale,* is the liberty each man has to use his own power, as he will himself, for the preservation of his own nature, that is to say, of his own life, and consequently of doing anything which in his own judgment and reason he shall conceive to be the aptest means thereunto.

By *liberty* is understood, according to the proper signification of the word, the absence of external impediments, which impediments may oft take away part of a man's power to do what he would, but cannot hinder him from using the power left him, according as his judgment and reason shall dictate to him.

A law of nature, *lex naturalis,* is a precept or general rule, found out by reason, by which a man is forbidden to do that which is destructive of his life or takes away the means of preserving the same, and to omit that by which he thinks it may be best preserved. For though they that speak of this subject use to confound *jus* and *lex, right* and *law,* yet they ought to be distinguished, because right consists in liberty to do or to forbear, whereas law determines and binds to one of them, so that law and right differ as much as obligation and liberty, which in one and the same matter are inconsistent.

And because the condition of man, as has been declared in the precedent chapter, is a condition of war of every one against every one, in which case every one is governed by his own reason, and there is nothing he can make use of that may not be a help unto him in preserving his life against his enemies; it follows that in such a condition every man has a right to every thing, even to one another's body. And therefore, as long as this natural right of every man to every thing endures, there can be no security to any man, how strong or wise soever he be, of living out the time which nature ordinarily allows men to live. And consequently it is a precept, or general rule of reason, *that every man ought to endeavour peace as far as he has hope of obtaining it, and when he cannot obtain it, that he may seek, and use, all helps and advantages of war.* The first branch of which rule contains the first, and fundamental, law of nature: which is, *to seek peace and follow it.* The second, the sum of the right of nature: which is, *by all means we can to defend ourselves.*

From this fundamental law of nature, by which men are commanded to endeavour peace, is derived this second law: *that a man be willing, when others are so too, as far-forth as for peace and defence of himself he shall think it necessary, to lay down this right to all things, and be contented with so much liberty against other men as he would allow other men against himself.* For as long as every man holds this right of doing any thing he likes, so long are all men in the condition of war. But if other men will not lay down their right as well as he, then there is no reason for any one to divest himself of his, for that were to expose himself to prey, which no man is bound to, rather than to dispose himself to peace. This is that law of the Gospel: *whatsoever you require that others should do to you, that do ye to them.* And that law of all men: *quod tibi fieri non vis, alteri ne feceris.*

To *lay down* a man's *right* to any thing is to *divest* himself of the *liberty* of hindering another of the benefit of his own right to the same. For he that renounces or passes away his right, gives not to any other man a right which he had not before, because there is nothing to which every man had not right by nature, but only stands out of his way that he may enjoy his own original right without hindrance from him, not without hindrance from another. So that the effect which redounds to one man by another man's defect of right, is but so much diminution of impediments to the use of his own right original. Right is laid aside either by simply renouncing it or by transferring it to another. By *simply* renouncing: when he cares not to whom the benefit thereof redounds. By transferring: when he intends the benefit thereof to some certain person or persons. And when a man has in either manner abandoned or granted away his right, then he is said to be obliged, or bound, not to hinder those to whom such right is granted or abandoned from the benefit of it, and that he *ought,* and it is his duty, not to make void that voluntary act of his own, and that such hindrance is injustice and injury, as being *sine jure,* the right being before being renounced or transferred. So that *injury,* or *injustice,* in the controversies of the world is somewhat like to that which in the disputations of scholars is called *absurdity.* For as it is there called an absurdity to contradict what one maintained in the beginning, so in the world it is called injustice and injury

voluntarily to undo that which from the beginning he had voluntarily done. The way by which a man either simply renounces or transfers his right, is a declaration, or signification, by some voluntary and sufficient sign, or signs, that he does so renounce or transfer, or has so renounced or transferred the same to him that accepts it. And these signs are either words only, or actions only, or—as it happens most often—both words and actions. And the same are the bonds by which men are bound and obliged: bonds that have their strength, not from their own nature, for nothing is more easily broken than a man's word, but from fear of some evil consequence upon the rupture.

Whensoever a man transfers his right or renounces it, it is either in consideration of some right reciprocally transferred to himself, or for some other good he hopes for thereby. For it is a voluntary act: and of the voluntary acts of every man the object is some *good to himself.* And therefore there be some rights which no man can be understood by any words, or other signs, to have abandoned or transferred. As first a man cannot lay down the right of resisting them that assault him by force to take away his life, because he cannot be understood to aim thereby at any good to himself. The same may be said of wounds, and chains, and imprisonment: both because there is no benefit consequent to such patience, as there is to the patience of suffering another to be wounded or imprisoned, as also because a man cannot tell, when he sees men proceed against him by violence, whether they intend his death or not. And lastly, the motive and end for which this renouncing and transferring of right is introduced, is nothing else but the security of a man's person in his life and in the means of so preserving life as not to be weary of it. And therefore if a man by words, or other signs, seems to despoil himself of the end for which those signs were intended, he is not to be understood as if he meant it or that it was his will, but that he was ignorant of how such words and actions were to be interpreted. The mutual transferring of right is that which men call *contract.*

A covenant not to defend myself from force, by force, is always void. For, as I have showed before, no man can transfer, or lay down, his right to save himself from death, wounds, and imprisonment, the avoiding whereof is the only end of laying down any right; and therefore the promise of not resisting force in no covenant transfers any right nor is obliging. For though a man may covenant thus, *unless I do so or so, kill me,* he cannot covenant thus, *unless I do so or so, I will not resist you when you come to kill me.* For man by nature chooses the lesser evil, which is danger of death in resisting, rather than the greater, which is certain and present death in not resisting. And this is granted to be true by all men, in that they lead criminals to execution and prison with armed men, notwithstanding that such criminals have consented to the law by which they are condemned.

A covenant to accuse oneself, without assurance of pardon, is likewise invalid. For in the condition of nature, where every man is judge, there is no place for accusation, and in the civil state the accusation is followed with punishment which, being force, a man is not obliged not to resist. The same is also true of the accusation of those, by whose condemnation a man falls into misery, as of a father, wife, or benefactor. For the testimony of such an accuser, if it be not willingly given, is presumed to be corrupted by nature, and therefore not to be received: and where a man's testimony is not to be credited, he is not bound to give it. Also accusations upon torture are not to be reputed as testimonies. For torture is to be used but as means of conjecture and light in the further examination and search of truth; and what is in that case confessed, tends to the ease of him that is tortured, not to the informing of the torturers, and therefore ought not to have the credit of a sufficient testimony: for whether he deliver himself by true or false accusation, he does it by the right of preserving his own life.

THE COMMONWEALTH

The final cause, end, or design of men who naturally love liberty and dominion over others, in the introduction of that restraint upon themselves in which we see them live in commonwealths, is the foresight of their own preservation and of a more contented life thereby; that is to say, of getting themselves out from that miserable condition of war which is necessarily consequent, as has been shown, to the natural passions of men, when there is no visible power to keep them in awe, and tie them by fear of punishment to the performance of their covenants and observation of the laws of nature.

For the laws of nature, as *justice, equity, modesty, mercy,* and, in sum, *doing to others, as we would be done to,* of themselves, without the terror of some power to cause them to be observed, are contrary to our natural passions that carry us to partiality, pride, revenge, and the like. And covenants, without the sword, are but words, and of no strength to secure a man at all. Therefore notwithstanding the laws of nature (which everyone has then kept, when he has the will to keep them, when he can do it safely), if there be no power erected, or not great enough for our security, every man will, and may, lawfully rely on his own strength and art for caution against all other men. And in all places where men have lived by small families, to rob and spoil one another has been a trade, and so far from being reputed against the law of nature, that the greater spoils they gained, the greater was their honour; and men observed no other laws therein, but the laws of honour, that is, to abstain from cruelty, leaving to men their lives and instruments of husbandry.

The only way to erect such a common power, as may be able to defend them from the invasion of foreigners and the injuries of one another, and thereby to secure them in such sort as that by their own industry and by the fruits of the earth they may nourish themselves and live contentedly, is to confer all their power and strength upon one man, or upon one assembly of men, that may reduce all their wills, by plurality of voices, unto one will: which is as much as to say, to appoint one man, or assembly of men, to bear their persons, and every one to own and acknowledge himself to be author of whatsoever he that so bears their person shall act, or cause to be acted, in those things which concern the common peace and safety, and therein to submit their wills, every one to his will, and their judgments to his judgment. This is more than consent, or concord; it is a real unity of them all, in one and the same person, made by covenant of every man with every man, in such manner as if every man should say to every man, *I authorize and give up my right of governing myself, to this man, or to this assembly of men, on this condition, that thou give up thy right to him, and authorize all his actions in like manner.* This done, the multitude so united in one person is called a Commonwealth, in Latin, *civitas.* This is the generation of that great *Leviathan,* or rather, to speak more reverently, of that *mortal god* to which we owe, under the *immortal God,* our peace and defence. For by this authority, given him by every particular man in the commonwealth, he has the use of so much power and strength conferred on him that by terror thereof he is enabled to form the wills of them all, to peace at home, and mutual aid against their enemies abroad. And in him consists the essence of the commonwealth; which, to define it, is *one person, of whose acts a great multitude, by mutual covenants one with another, have made themselves every one the author, to the end he may use the strength and means of them all, as he shall think expedient, for their peace and common defence.*

And he that carries this person is called Sovereign, and said to have *sovereign power;* and every one besides, his subject.

The attaining to this sovereign power is by two ways. One, by natural force, as when a man makes his children to submit themselves and their children to his government, as being able to destroy them if they refuse, or by war subdues his enemies to his will, giving them their lives on that condition. The other is when men agree among themselves to submit to some man, or assembly of men, voluntarily, on confidence to be protected by him against all others. This latter may be called a political commonwealth, or commonwealth by *institution;* and the former, a commonwealth by *acquistion.*

RIGHTS OF THE SOVEREIGN

A *commonwealth* is said to be *instituted* when a *multitude* of men do agree and *covenant, every one with every one,* that to whatsoever *man,* or *assembly of men,* shall be given by the major part the *right* to *present* the person of them all, that is to say, to be their *representative,* every one—as well he that *voted for it,* as he that *voted against it,* shall *authorize* all the actions and judg-

ments of that man, or assembly of men, in the same manner as if they were his own, to the end, to live peaceably amongst themselves, and be protected against other men.

From this institution of a commonwealth are derived all the *rights* and *faculties* of him, or them, on whom the sovereign power is conferred by the consent of the people assembled.

First, because they covenant, it is to be understood, they are not obliged by former covenant to any thing repugnant hereunto. And consequently they that have already instituted a commonwealth, being thereby bound by covenant to own the actions and judgments of one, cannot lawfully make a new covenant, among themselves, to be obedient to any other, in any thing whatsoever, without his permission. And therefore, they that are subjects to a monarch cannot without his leave cast off monarchy, and return to the confusion of a disunited multitude, nor transfer their person from him that bears it to another man, or other assembly of men: for they are bound, every man to every man, to own and be reputed author of all that he that already is their sovereign, shall do and judge fit to be done; so that any one man dissenting, all the rest should break their covenant made to that man, which is injustice, and they have also every man given the sovereignty to him that bears their person, and therefore if they depose him, they take from him that which is his own, and so again it is injustice. Besides, if he that attempts to depose his sovereign be killed, or punished by him for such attempt, he is author of his own punishment, as being by the institution author of all his sovereign shall do; and because it is injustice for a man to do any thing for which he may be punished by his own authority, he is also, upon that title, unjust. And whereas some men have pretended for their disobedience to their sovereign a new covenant made, not with men, but with God, this also is unjust, for there is no covenant with God but by mediation of somebody that represents God's person, which none does but God's lieutenant, who has the sovereignty under God. But this pretence of covenant with God is so evident a lie, even in the pretenders' own consciences, that it is not only an act of an unjust, but also of a vile and unmanly disposition.

Secondly, because the right of bearing the person of them all is given to him they make sovereign, by covenant only of one to another, and not of him to any of them, there can happen no breach of covenant on the part of the sovereign, and consequently none of his subjects, by any pretence of forfeiture, can be freed from his subjection. That he which is made sovereign makes no covenant with his subjects beforehand, is manifest, because either he must make it with the whole multitude, as one party to the covenant, or he must make a several covenant with every man. With the whole, as one party, it is impossible, because as yet they are not one person; and if he make so many covenants as there be men, those covenants after he has the sovereignty are void, because what act soever can be pretended by any one of them for breach thereof, is the act both of himself and of all the rest, because done in the person and by the right of every one of them in particular. Besides, if any one, or more of them, pretend a breach of the covenant made by the sovereign at his institution, and others, or one other of his subjects, or himself alone, pretend there was no such breach, there is in this case no judge to decide the controversy. It returns therefore to the sword again, and every man recovers the right of protecting himself by his own strength, contrary to the design they had in the institution. It is therefore in vain to grant sovereignty by way of precedent covenant. The opinion that any monarch receives his power by covenant, that is to say, on condition, proceeds from want of understanding this easy truth: that covenants, being but words and breath, have no force to oblige, contain, constrain, or protect any man, but what it has from the public sword, that is, from the united hands of that man, or assembly of men, that has the sovereignty, and whose actions are avouched by them all and performed by the strength of them all, in him united. But when an assembly of men is made sovereign, then no man imagines any such covenant to have passed in the institution, for no man is so dull as to say for example, the people of Rome made a covenant with the Romans to hold the sovereignty on such or such conditions which, not performed, the Romans might lawfully depose the Roman people. That men see not the reason to be alike in a monarchy and in a popular government, proceeds from the ambition of some that are kinder to the government of an assembly, whereof they may hope to participate, than of monarchy, which they despair to enjoy.

Thirdly, because the major part has by consenting voices declared a sovereign, he that dissented must now consent with the rest, that is, be contented to avow all the actions he shall do, or else justly be destroyed by the rest. For if he voluntarily entered into the congregation of them that were assembled, he sufficiently declared thereby his will, and therefore tacitly covenanted, to stand to what the major part should ordain; and therefore if he refuse to stand thereto, or make protestation against any of their decrees, he does contrary to his covenant, and therefore unjustly. And whether he be of the congregation or not, and whether his consent be asked or not, he must either submit to their decrees, or be left in the condition of war he was in before; wherein he might without injustice be destroyed by any man whatsoever.

Fourthly, because every subject is by this institution author of all the actions and judgments of the sovereign instituted, it follows that whatsoever he does, it can be no injury to any of his subjects, nor ought he to be by any of them accused of injustice. For he that does anything by authority from another, does therein no injury to him by whose authority he acts, but by this institution of a commonwealth every particular man is author of all the sovereign does, and consequently he that complains of injury from his sovereign, complains of that whereof he himself is author, and therefore ought not to accuse any man but himself; no, nor himself of injury, because to do injury to one's self is impossible. It is true that they that have sovereign power may commit iniquity, but not injustice, or injury, in the proper signification.

Fifthly, and consequently to that which was said last, no man that has sovereign power can justly be put to death, or otherwise in any manner by his subjects punished. For seeing every subject is author of the actions of his sovereign, he punishes another for the actions committed by himself.

And because the end of this institution is the peace and defence of them all, and whosoever has right to the end has right to the means, it belongs of right to whatsoever man or assembly that has the sovereignty, to be judge both of the means of peace and defence and also of the hindrances and disturbances of the same, and to do whatsoever he shall think necessary to be done, both beforehand for the preserving of peace and security, by prevention of discord at home and hostility from abroad, and, when peace and security are lost, for the recovery of the same. And therefore:

Sixthly, it is annexed to the sovereignty to be judge of what opinions and doctrines are averse, and what conducing to peace, and consequently on what occasions, how far, and what men are to be trusted withal, in speaking to multitudes of people, and who shall examine the doctrines of all books before they be published. For the actions of men proceed from their opinions, and in the well-governing of opinions consists the well-governing of men's actions, in order to their peace and concord. And though in matter of doctrine nothing ought to be regarded but the truth, yet this is not repugnant to regulating the same by peace. For doctrine repugnant to peace can no more be true than peace and concord can be against the law of nature. It is true that in a commonwealth where by the negligence or unskilfulness of governors and teachers false doctrines are by time generally received, the contrary truths may be generally offensive. Yet the most sudden and rough bustling in of a new truth that can be, does never break the peace, but only sometimes awake the war. For those men that are so remissly governed that they dare take up arms to defend or introduce an opinion, are still in war, and their condition not peace, but only a cessation of arms for fear of one another; and they live, as it were, in the precincts of battle continually. It belongs therefore to him that has the sovereign power to be judge, or constitute all judges of opinions and doctrines as a thing necessary to peace, thereby to prevent discord and civil war.

Seventhly, is annexed to the sovereignty the whole power of prescribing the rules whereby every man may know what goods he may enjoy, and what actions he may do, without being molested by any of his fellow-subjects; and this is it men call *propriety*. For before constitution of sovereign power,

as has already been shown, all men had right to all things, which necessarily causes war: and therefore this propriety, being necessary to peace and depending on sovereign power, is the act of that power, in order to the public peace. These rules of propriety, or *meum* and *tuum*, and of *good, evil, lawful* and *unlawful* in the actions of subjects, are the civil laws, that is to say, the laws of each commonwealth in particular, though the name of civil law be now restrained to the ancient civil laws of the city of Rome which being the head of a great part of the world, her laws at that time were in these parts the civil law.

Eighthly, is annexed to the sovereignty the right of judicature, that is to say, of hearing and deciding all controversies which may arise concerning law, either civil or natural, or concerning fact. For without the decision of controversies, there is no protection of one subject against the injuries of another; the laws concerning *meum* and *tuum* are in vain; and to every man remains, from the natural and necessary appetite of his own conservation, the right of protecting himself by his private strength, which is the condition of war and contrary to the end for which every commonwealth is instituted.

These are the rights which make the essence of sovereignty, and which are the marks whereby a man may discern in what man, or assembly of men, the sovereign power is placed and resides. For these are incommunicable and inseparable. The power to coin money, to dispose of the estate and persons of infant heirs, to have preemption in markets, and all other statute prerogatives may be transferred by the sovereign, and yet the power to protect his subjects be retained. But if he transfer the *militia*, he retains the judicature in vain, for want of execution of the laws; or if he grant away the power of raising money, the *militia* is in vain; or if he give away the government of doctrines, men will be frightened into rebellion with the fear of spirits. And so if we consider any one of the said rights, we shall presently see that the holding of all the rest will produce no effect in the conservation of peace and justice, the end for which all commonwealths are instituted. And this division is it, whereof it is said, *a kingdom divided in itself cannot stand:* for unless this division precede, division into opposite armies can never happen. If there had not first been an opinion received of the greatest part of England that these powers were divided between the King and the Lords and the House of Commons, the people had never been divided and fallen into this civil war; first between those that disagreed in politics; and after between the dissenters about the liberty of religion; which have so instructed men in this point of sovereign right that there be few now in England that do not see that these rights are inseparable, and will be so generally acknowledged at the next return of peace, and so continue till their miseries are forgotten, and no longer, except the vulgar be better taught than they have hitherto been.

But a man may here object that the condition of subjects is very miserable, as being obnoxious to the lusts and other irregular passions of him or them that have so unlimited a power in their hands. And commonly they that live under a monarch, think it the fault of monarchy; and they that live under the government of democracy or other sovereign assembly, attribute all the inconvenience to that form of commonwealth; whereas the power in all forms, if they be perfect enough to protect them, is the same: not considering that the state of man can never be without some incommodity or other, and that the greatest that in any form of government can possibly happen to the people in general is scarce sensible in respect of the miseries and horrible calamities that accompany a civil war or that dissolute condition of masterless men, without subjection to laws and a coercive power to tie their hands from rapine and revenge: nor considering that the greatest pressure of sovereign governors proceeds not from any delight or profit they can expect in the damage or weakening of their subjects, in whose vigour consists their own strength and glory, but in the restiveness of themselves that, unwillingly contributing to their own defence, make it necessary for their governors to draw from them what they can in time of peace, that they may have means on any emergent occasion, or sudden need, to resist, or take advantage on their enemies.

For all men are by nature provided of notable multiplying glasses, that is their passions and self-love, through which every little payment appears a great grievance, but are destitute of those prospective glasses, namely moral and civil science, to see afar off the miseries that hang over them, and cannot without such payments be avoided.

LIBERTY OF THE SUBJECT

But as men, for the attaining of peace and conservation of themselves thereby, have made an artificial man, which we call a commonwealth, so also have they made artificial chains, called *civil laws,* which they themselves, by mutual covenants, have fastened at one end to the lips of that man, or assembly, to whom they have given the sovereign power, and at the other end to their own ears. These bonds, in their own nature but weak, may nevertheless be made to hold by the danger, though not by the difficulty, of breaking them.

In relation to these bonds only it is that I am to speak now of the *liberty* of *subjects.* For seeing there is no commonwealth in the world, wherein there be rules enough set down for the regulating of all the actions and words of men, as being a thing impossible, it follows necessarily that in all kinds of actions by the laws praetermitted, men have the liberty of doing what their own reasons shall suggest, for the most profitable to themselves. For if we take liberty in the proper sense for corporal liberty, that is to say, freedom from chains and prison, it were very absurd for men to clamour, as they do, for the liberty they so manifestly enjoy. Again, if we take liberty for an exemption from laws, it is no less absurd for men to demand, as they do, that liberty by which all other men may be masters of their lives. And yet, as absurd as it is, this is it they demand, not knowing that the laws are of no power to protect them without a sword in the hands of a man, or men, to cause those laws to be put in execution. The liberty of a subject lies therefore only in those things which, in regulating their actions, the sovereign has praetermitted: such as is the liberty to buy, and sell, and otherwise contract with one another; to choose their own abode, their own diet, their own trade of life, and institute their children as they themselves think fit; and the like.

Nevertheless we are not to understand that by such liberty the sovereign power of life and death is either abolished or limited. For it has been already shown that nothing the sovereign representative can do to a subject, on what pretence soever, can properly be called injustice or injury, because every subject is author of every act the sovereign does, so that he never wants right to any thing, otherwise than as he is himself the subject of God, and bound thereby to observe the laws of nature. And therefore it may, and does often, happen in commonwealths that a subject may be put to death by the command of the sovereign power, and yet neither do the other wrong: as when Jephtha caused his daughter to be sacrificed, in which—and the like cases—he that so dies, had liberty to do the action for which he is nevertheless without injury put to death. And the same holds also in a sovereign prince that puts to death an innocent subject. For though the action be against the law of nature as being contrary to equity, as was the killing of Uriah by David, yet it was not an injury to Uriah, but to God. Not to Uriah, because the right to do what he pleased was given him by Uriah himself: and yet to God, because David was God's subject and prohibited all iniquity by the law of nature, which distinction David himself, when he repented the fact, evidently confirmed saying, *To thee only have I sinned.* In the same manner, the people of Athens, when they banished the most potent of their commonwealth for ten years, thought they committed no injustice; and yet they never questioned what crime he had done, but what hurt he would do: nay, they commanded the banishment of they knew not whom; and every citizen bringing his oystershell into the market place, written with the name of him he desired should be banished, without actually accusing him, sometimes banished an Aristides for his reputation of justice, and sometimes a scurrilous jester, as Hyperbolus, to make a jest of it. And yet a man cannot say the sovereign people of Athens wanted right to banish them, or an Athenian the liberty to jest, or to be just.

The liberty whereof there is so frequent and honourable mention in the histories and philosophy of the ancient Greeks and Romans, and in the writings and discourse of those that from them have received all their learning in the politics, is not the liberty of particular men, but the liberty of the commonwealth: which is the same with that which every man then should have if there were no civil laws, nor commonwealth at all. And the effects of it also be the same. For as among masterless men there is perpetual war of every man against his neighbour; no inheritance to transmit to the son, nor to expect from the father; no propriety of goods or lands; no security; but a full and absolute liberty in every particular man: so in states and commonwealths not dependent on one another, every commonwealth, not every man, has an absolute liberty to do what it shall judge, that is to say, what that man, or assembly that represents it, shall judge most conducing to their benefit. But withal, they live in the condition of a perpetual war and upon the confines of battle, with their frontiers armed and cannons planted against their neighbours round about. The Athenians and Romans were free, that is, free commonwealths: not that any particular men had the liberty to resist their own representative, but that their representative had the liberty to resist or invade other people. There is written on the turrets of the city of Lucca in great characters at this day the word "Libertas"; yet no man can thence infer that a particular man has more liberty or immunity from the service of the commonwealth there than in Constantinople. Whether a commonwealth be monarchical, or popular, the freedom is still the same.

But it is an easy thing for men to be deceived by the specious name of liberty, and for want of judgment to distinguish, mistake that for their private inheritance and birthright which is the right of the public only. And when the same error is confirmed by the authority of men in reputation for their writings on this subject, it is no wonder if it produce sedition and change of government. In these western parts of the world, we are made to receive our opinions concerning the institution and rights of commonwealths from Aristotle, Cicero, and other men, Greeks and Romans, that, living under popular states, derived those rights, not from the principles of nature, but transcribed them into their books out of the practice of their own commonwealths which were popular; as the grammarians describe the rules of language out of the practice of the time, or the rules of poetry out of the poems of Homer and Virgil. And because the Athenians were taught, to keep them from desire of changing their government, that they were freemen, and all that lived under monarchy were slaves, therefore Aristotle puts it down in his *Politics* (*lib.* 6, *cap.* ii): "In democracy, liberty is to be supposed: for it is commonly held that no man is free in any other government." And as Aristotle, so Cicero and other writers have grounded their civil doctrine on the opinions of the Romans, who were taught to hate monarchy, at first, by them that, having deposed their sovereign, shared among them the sovereignty of Rome, and afterwards by their successors. And by reading of these Greek and Latin authors, men from their childhood have gotten a habit, under a false show of liberty, of favouring tumults and of licentious controlling the actions of their sovereigns, and again of controlling those controllers; with the effusion of so much blood, as I think I may truly say, there was never any thing so dearly bought as these western parts have bought the learning of the Greek and Latin tongues.

To come now to the particulars of the true liberty of a subject; that is to say, what are the things which, though commanded by the sovereign, be may nevertheless, without injustice, refuse to do; we are to consider what rights we pass away when we make a commonwealth, or, which is all one, what liberty we deny ourselves by owning all the actions, without exception, of the man, or assembly, we make our sovereign. For in the act of our *submission* consists both our *obligation* and our *liberty*, which must therefore be inferred by arguments taken from thence, there being no obligation on any man which arises not from some act of his own, for all men equally are by nature free. And because such arguments must either be drawn from the express words, *I authorize all his actions,* or from the intention of him that submits himself to his power, which intention is to be understood by the end for which he so submits, the obligation and liberty of the subject is to be derived either from those words or others equivalent, or else from the end of the institution of sovereignty, namely, the

peace of the subjects within themselves, and their defence against a common enemy.

First therefore, seeing sovereignty by institution is by covenant of every one to every one, and sovereignty by acquisition, by covenants of the vanquished to the victor, or the child to the parent, it is manifest that every subject has liberty in all those things, the right whereof cannot by covenant be transferred. I have shown before that covenants not to defend a man's own body are void. Therefore, if the sovereign command a man, though justly condemned, to kill, wound, or maim himself, or not to resist those that assault him, or to abstain from the use of food, air, medicine, or any other thing without which he cannot live, yet has that man the liberty to disobey.

If a man be interrogated by the sovereign, or his authority, concerning a crime done by himself, he is not bound, without assurance of pardon, to confess it, because no man can be obliged by covenant to accuse himself.

Again, the consent of a subject to sovereign power is contained in these words, *I authorize, or take upon me, all his actions,* in which there is no restriction at all of his former natural liberty: for by allowing him to *kill* me, I am not bound to kill myself when he commands me. It is one thing to say, *kill me, or my fellow, if you please;* another thing to say, *I will kill myself, or my fellow.* It follows therefore that no man is bound by the words themselves either to kill himself, or any other man, and consequently, that the obligation a man may sometimes have, upon the command of the sovereign to execute any dangerous or dishonourable office, depends not on the words of our submission, but on the intention, which is to be understood by the end thereof. When therefore our refusal to obey frustrates the end for which the sovereignty was ordained, then there is no liberty to refuse: otherwise there is.

The obligation of subjects to the sovereign is understood to last as long, and no longer, than the power lasts by which he is able to protect them. For the right men have by nature to protect themselves when none else can protect them, can by no covenant be relinquished. The sovereignty is the soul of the commonwealth which, once departed from the body, the members do no more receive their motion from it. The end of obedience is protection which, wheresoever a man sees it either in his own or in another's sword, nature applies his obedience to it, and his endeavour to maintain it. And though sovereignty, in the intention of them that make it, be immortal, yet is it in its own nature, not only subject to violent death by foreign war, but also through the ignorance and passions of men, it has in it—from the very institution—many seeds of a natural mortality by intestine discord.

CIVIL LAW AND NATURAL LAW

By civil laws I understand the laws that men are therefore bound to observe because they are members, not of this or that commonwealth in particular, but of a commonwealth. For the knowledge of particular laws belongs to them that profess the study of the laws of their several countries; but the knowledge of civil law in general, to any man. The ancient law of Rome was called their *civil law,* from the word *civitas,* which signifies a commonwealth: and those countries which, having been under the Roman empire and governed by that law, retain still such part thereof as they think fit, call that part the civil law, to distinguish it from the rest of their own civil laws. But that is not it I intend to speak of here; my design being not to show what is law here and there, but what is law, as Plato, Aristotle, Cicero and divers others have done, without taking upon them the profession of the study of the law.

And first it is manifest that law in general is not counsel, but command; nor a command of any man to any man, but only of him whose command is addressed to one formerly obliged to obey him. And as for civil law, it adds only the name of the, person commanding, which is *persona civitatis,* the person of the commonwealth.

Which considered, I define civil law in this manner. Civil law *is to every subject those rules which the commonwealth has commanded him, by word, writing, or other sufficient sign of the will, to make use of, for the distinction of right and wrong; that is to say, of what is contrary, and what is not contrary to the rule.*

In which definition, there is nothing that is not at first sight evident. For every man sees that some laws are addressed to all the subjects in general, some to particular provinces; some to particular vocations; and some to particular men; and are therefore laws to every of those to whom the command is directed, and to none else. As also, that laws are the rules of just and unjust; nothing being reputed unjust that is not contrary to some law. Likewise, that none can make laws but the commonwealth, because our subjection is to the commonwealth only, and that commands are to be signified by sufficient signs, because a man knows not otherwise how to obey them. And therefore, whatsoever can from this definition by necessary consequence be deduced, ought to be acknowledged for truth. Now I deduce from it this that follows.

The legislator in all commonwealths is only the sovereign, be he one man, as in a monarchy, or one assembly of men, as in a democracy or aristocracy. For the legislator is he that makes the law. And the commonwealth only prescribes and commands the observation of those rules which we call law: therefore the commonwealth is the legislator. But the commonwealth is no person, nor has capacity to do any thing, but by the representative, that is, the sovereign; and therefore the sovereign is the sole legislator. For the same reason, none can abrogate a law made, but the sovereign; because a law is not abrogated, but by another law that forbids it to be put in execution.

The sovereign of a commonwealth, be it an assembly, or one man, is not subject to the civil laws. For having power to make and repeal laws, he may, when he pleases, free himself from that subjection by repealing those laws that trouble him, and making of new; and consequently he was free before. For he is free that can be free when he will: nor is it possible for any person to be bound to himself, because he that can bind can release; and therefore he that is bound to himself only, is not bound.

When long use obtains the authority of a law, it is not the length of time that makes the authority, but the will of the sovereign signified by his silence, for silence is sometimes an argument of consent; and it is no longer law than the sovereign shall be silent therein. And therefore if the sovereign shall have a question of right grounded, not upon his present will, but upon the laws formerly made, the length of time shall bring no prejudice to his right, but the question shall be judged by equity. For many unjust actions and unjust sentences go uncontrolled a longer time than any man can remember. And our lawyers account no customs law, but such as are reasonable, and that evil customs are to be abolished. But the judgment of what is reasonable, and of what is to be abolished, belongs to him that makes the law, which is the sovereign assembly, or monarch.

The law of nature and the civil law contain each other, and are of equal extent. For the laws of nature, which consist in equity, justice, gratitude and other moral virtues on these depending in the condition of mere nature, as I have said before, are not properly laws, but qualities that dispose men to peace and obedience. When a commonwealth is once settled, then are they actually laws, and not before, as being then the commands of the commonwealth, and therefore also civil laws: for it is the sovereign power that obliges men to obey them. For in the differences of private men to declare what is equity, what is justice, and what is moral virtue, and to make them binding, there is need of the ordinances of sovereign power, and punishments to be ordained for such as shall break them, which ordinances are therefore part of the civil law. The law of nature therefore is a part of the civil law in all commonwealths of the world. Reciprocally also, the civil law is a part of the dictates of nature. For justice, that is to say, performance of covenant, and giving to every man his own, is a dictate of the law of nature. But every subject in a commonwealth has covenanted to obey the civil law, either one with another, as when they assemble to make a common representative, or with the representative itself one by one, when subdued by the sword they promise obedience that they may receive life; and therefore obedience to the civil law is part also of the law of nature. Civil and natural law are not different kinds, but different parts of law, whereof one part, being written, is called civil, the other, unwritten, natural. But the right of nature, that is, the

natural liberty of man, may by the civil law be abridged and restrained: nay, the end of making laws is no other but such restraint, without the which there cannot possibly be any peace. And law was brought into the world for nothing else but to limit the natural liberty of particular men in such manner, as they might not hurt, but assist one another and join together against a common enemy.

That law can never be against reason, our lawyers are agreed; and that not the letter, that is, every construction of it, but that which is according to the intention of the legislator, is the law. And it is true: but the doubt is of whose reason it is that shall be received for law. It is not meant of any private reason; for then there would be as much contradiction in the laws, as there is in the Schools, nor yet, as Sir Edward Coke makes it, *an artificial perfection of reason, gotten by long study, observation, and experience,* as his was. For it is possible long study may increase and confirm erroneous sentences: and when men build on false grounds, the more they build, the greater is the ruin: and of those that study and observe with equal time and diligence, the reasons and resolutions are, and must remain, discordant: and therefore it is not that *juris prudentia,* or wisdom of subordinate judges, but the reason of this our artificial man the commonwealth, and his command, that makes law: and the commonwealth being in their representative but one person, there cannot easily arise any contradiction in the laws; and when there does, the same reason is able, by interpretation, or alteration, to take it away. In all courts of justice, the sovereign, which is the person of the commonwealth, is he that judges: the subordinate judge ought to have regard to the reason which moved his sovereign to make such law, that his sentence may be according thereunto; which then is his sovereign's sentence; otherwise it is his own, and an unjust one.

The interpretation of the laws of nature, in a commonwealth, depends not on the books of moral philosophy. The authority of writers, without the authority of the commonwealth, makes not their opinions law, be they never so true. That which I have written in this treatise concerning the moral virtues, and of their necessity for the procuring and maintaining peace, though it be evident truth, is not therefore presently law; but because in all commonwealths in the world it is part of the civil law. For though it be naturally reasonable, yet it is by the sovereign power that it is law: otherwise it were a great error to call the laws of nature unwritten laws; whereof we see so many volumes published, and in them so many contradictions of one another, and of themselves.

The interpretation of the law of nature is the sentence of the judge constituted by the sovereign authority, to hear and determine such controversies, as depend thereon, and consists in the application of the law to the present case. For in the act of judicature, the judge does no more but consider whether the demand of the party be consonant to natural reason and equity, and the sentence he gives is therefore the interpretation of the law of nature; which interpretation is authentic, not because it is his private sentence, but because he gives it by authority of the sovereign, whereby it becomes the sovereign's sentence; which is law for that time, to the parties pleading.

SUBVERSIVE POLITICAL DOCTRINES

Though nothing can be immortal which mortals make, yet, if men had the use of reason they pretend to, their commonwealths might be secured at least from perishing by internal diseases. For by the nature of their institution they are designed to live as long as mankind, or as the laws of nature, or as justice itself which gives them life. Therefore when they come to be dissolved, not by external violence, but intestine disorder, the fault is not in men as they are the *matter,* but as they are the *makers* and orderers of them. For men, as they become at least weary of irregular jostling and hewing one another, and desire with all their hearts to conform themselves into one firm and lasting edifice, so for want both of the art of making fit laws to square their actions by, and also of humility and patience to suffer the rude and cumbersome points of their present greatness to be taken off,

they cannot without the help of a very able architect be compiled into any other than a crazy building, such as hardly lasting out their own time, must assuredly fall upon the heads of their posterity.

Among the *infirmities* therefore of a commonwealth, I will reckon in the first place those that arise from an imperfect institution, and resemble the diseases of a natural body which proceed from a defectuous procreation.

Of which this is one, *that a man, to obtain a kingdom, is sometimes content with less power than to the peace and defence of the commonwealth is necessarily required.* From whence it comes to pass that when the exercise of the power laid by is for the public safety to be resumed, it has the resemblance of an unjust act, which disposes great numbers of men, when occasion is presented, to rebel, in the same manner as the bodies of children, gotten by diseased parents, are subject either to untimely death or, to purge the ill quality derived from their vicious conception, by breaking out into biles and scabs. And when kings deny themselves some such necessary power, it is not always, though sometimes, out of ignorance of what is necessary to the office they undertake, but many times out of a hope to recover the same again at their pleasure. Wherein they reason not well, because such as will hold them to their promises shall be maintained against them by foreign commonwealths, who in order to the good of their own subjects let slip few occasions to *weaken* the estate of their neighbours. So was Thomas Becket, archbishop of Canterbury, supported against Henry the Second by the Pope, the subjection of ecclesiastics to the commonwealth having been dispensed with by William the Conqueror at his reception, when he took an oath not to infringe the liberty of the church. And so were the barons, whose power was by William Rufus, to have their help in transferring the succession from his elder brother to himself, increased to a degree inconsistent with the sovereign power, maintained in their rebellion against King John, by the French.

Nor does this happen in monarchy only. For whereas the style of the ancient Roman commonwealth was *The Senate and People of Rome,* neither senate nor people pretended to the whole power, which first caused the seditions of Tiberius Gracchus, Caius Gracchus, Lucius Saturninus, and others, and afterwards the wars between the senate and the people, under Marius and Sulla; and again under Pompey and Caesar, to the extinction of their democracy, and the setting up of monarchy.

The people of Athens bound themselves but from one only action, which was that no man on pain of death should propound the renewing of the war for the island of Salamis; and yet thereby, if Solon had not caused to be given out he was mad, and afterwards in gesture and habit of a madman, and in verse, propounded it to the people that flocked about him, they had had an enemy perpetually in readiness, even at the gates of their city; such damage, or shifts, are all commonwealths forced to that have their power never so little limited.

In the second place, *diseases* of a commonwealth that proceed from the poison of seditious doctrines, whereof one is *that every private man is judge of good and evil actions.* This is true in the condition of mere nature, where there are no civil laws, and also under civil government in such cases as are not determined by the law. But otherwise, it is manifest that the measure of good and evil actions is the civil law, and the judge the legislator who is always representative of the commonwealth. From this false doctrine, men are disposed to debate with themselves and dispute the commands of the commonwealth, and afterwards to obey or disobey them, as in their private judgments they shall think fit; whereby the commonwealth is distracted and *weakened.*

Another doctrine repugnant to civil society is that *whatsoever a man does against his conscience is sin,* and it depends on the presumption of making himself judge of good and evil. For a man's conscience and his judgment is the same thing, and as the judgment, so also the conscience may be erroneous. Therefore, though he that is subject to no civil law sins in all he does against his conscience, because he has no other rule to follow but his own reason, yet it is not so with him that lives in a commonwealth, because the law is the public conscience, by which he has already undertaken to be guided. Otherwise in such diversity as there

is of private consciences, which are but private opinions, the commonwealth must needs be distracted, and no man dare to obey the sovereign power further than it shall seem good in his own eyes.

It has been also commonly taught *that faith and sanctity are not to be attained by study and reason, but by supernatural inspiration or infusion.* Which granted, I see not why any man should render a reason of his faith; or why every Christian should not be also a prophet; or why any man should take the law of his country, rather than his own inspiration, for the rule of his action. And thus we fall again in the fault of taking upon us to judge of good and evil, or to make judges of it such private men as pretend to be supernaturally inspired, to the dissolution of all civil government. Faith comes by hearing, and hearing by those accidents which guide us into the presence of them that speak to us; which accidents are all contrived by God Almighty, and yet are not supernatural, but only, for the great number of them that concur to every effect, unobservable. Faith and sanctity are indeed not very frequent; but yet they are not miracles, but brought to pass by education, discipline, correction, and other natural ways by which God works them in his elect, at such times as he thinks fit. And these three opinions, pernicious to peace and government, have in this part of the world proceeded chiefly from the tongues and pens of unlearned divines who, joining the words of Holy Scripture together otherwise than is agreeable to reason, do what they can to make men think that sanctity and natural reason cannot stand together.

A fourth opinion, repugnant to the nature of commonwealth, is this, *that he that has the sovereign power is subject to the civil laws.* It is true that sovereigns are all subject to the laws of nature, because such laws be divine and cannot by any man or commonwealth be abrogated. But to those laws which the sovereign himself, that is, which the commonwealth makes, he is not subject. For to be subject to laws is to be subject to the commonwealth, that is, to the sovereign representative, that is to himself; which is not subjection, but freedom from the laws. Which error, because it sets the laws above the sovereign, sets also a judge above him, and a power to punish him; which is to make a new sovereign; and again for the same reason a third, to punish the second; and so continually without end, to the confusion and dissolution of the commonwealth.

A fifth doctrine, that tends to the dissolution of the commonwealth, is *that every private man has an absolute propriety in his goods, such as excludes the right of the sovereign.* Every man has indeed a propriety that excludes the right of every other subject; and he has it only from the sovereign power, without the protection whereof every other man should have equal right to the same. But if the right of the sovereign also be excluded, he cannot perform the office they have put him into, which is to defend them both from foreign enemies and from the injuries of one another; and consequently there is no longer a commonwealth.

And if the propriety of subjects exclude not the right of the sovereign representative to their goods, much less to their offices of judicature, or execution, in which they represent the sovereign himself.

There is a sixth doctrine, plainly and directly against the essence of a commonwealth; and it is this, *that the sovereign power may be divided.* For what is it to divide the power of a commonwealth, but to dissolve it; for powers divided mutually destroy each other. And for these doctrines men are chiefly beholding to some of those that, making profession of the laws, endeavour to make them depend upon their own learning and not upon the legislative power.

CHAPTER SEVEN

LOCKE

Revolutionary Puritanism ruled England until 1660 but was unable to establish itself permanently. Cromwell died in 1658, and in less than two years Charles II was restored to the throne. After civil war and dictatorship the return to monarchy seemed the best prospect of peace. In bringing Charles II back to a throne, no clear delimitation between royal and parliamentary authority was made. It was hoped that a practical equilibrium could be obtained without formal constitutional charters, if the king would avoid the arbitrary government of his executed father, and if Parliament would be satisfied with less than absolute supremacy, such as it had exercised in the years 1642–1649, the period of civil war. Yet Charles II lacked the wisdom, or even desire, to contribute his share to the growth of a balanced constitution. His reign lasted from 1660–1685, during which years he increasingly antagonized his subjects on the two key issues of religion and Parliament. A crypto-Catholic, he sought to strengthen the influence of Catholics and fatally returned to the ways of his father by ruling without summoning Parliament for several years.

Charles II was succeeded by his brother, James II, who was an open Catholic and more authoritarian than Charles. James II sought to convert England to Catholicism by prerogative and force, and he methodically subverted the authority of Parliament either by exempting individuals from the law or by suspending laws altogether. He appointed and dismissed judges arbitrarily and built up a standing army to buttress his autocracy. By identifying despotism with Roman Catholicism he outraged not only his subjects' religion and liberty but their very patriotism.

France and Spain were England's chief opponents in the struggle for hegemony, and James II sealed his position as a traitor to the nation when it became known that he, like Charles II and many politicians, was secretly receiving money from Louis XIV of France. In 1688, Whig and Tory leaders invited Prince William of Orange to come to England and deliver it from Romanism and absolutism. William arrived in England in November, and there was great jubilation and almost no resistance. James II saw himself abandoned by Parliament, church, and army, and on December 22, 1688, stealthily sailed for France, never to return. Royal absolutism in England was dead.

Prince William summoned a "Convention Parliament" that met in January of 1689. The first business was to fill the vacant throne. James II was declared to have subverted the Constitution of the Kingdom by breaking the "original contract" between King and people and to have violated the fundamental laws "by the advice of Jesuits and other wicked persons," and to have, by his flight and misdeeds, abdicated the throne. Parliament then invited Prince William and his wife Mary to become King and Queen of

England. But the Crown was not given to them without condition. The "Declaration of Right" (passed later in the year as the Bill of Rights) was the instrument that conferred the Crown on William and Mary.

The Bill of Rights begins with a recital of the iniquities and illegalities of James II. The first of the twelve charges accuses him of having assumed and exercised the power to dispense with and suspend laws, and to execute laws, without consent of Parliament. This was the crux of the "Glorious" or "Bloodless" Revolution of 1688: who is to be supreme, king or Parliament? The clear and unmistakable words of the Bill of Rights settled the question once and for all. By denying the king the right to levy money without grant of Parliament, and by prohibiting the raising or keeping of a standing army in time of peace without the consent of Parliament, the Bill of Rights deprived the king of the fiscal and military means of governing without the active consent of Parliament.

Another important condition was attached by Parliament to the British monarchy: no person who professes the Roman Catholic religion or is married to a Roman Catholic may inherit or hold the throne. The work of the Glorious Revolution went further. Judges were made irremovable during good behavior; they could no longer be removed by the arbitrary will of the king, as James II had removed judges who interpreted the law contrary to his wishes. To make the change of the times even more marked, judges were henceforth to be removable only on the address of both Houses of Parliament. The abolition of censorship made for free expression of thought in religious and political matters, and toleration was legally granted to Protestant dissenters; thus the road was opened for the general principle of separating religious faith from political loyalty.

The Glorious Revolution established the first constitutional monarchy in a major European country, and its general character remained unchanged until the reform of parliamentary representation in 1832. The bloodless revolution of 1832, transferring political power from the gentry to the middle class, would have been impossible without the Bloodless Revolution of 1688. At that time the liberal foundations of British government were judiciously laid, and the British system of today is the direct descendant of the Revolution of 1688. The peaceful revolution of 1945, by which the British working class became one of the principal political elements in the state through the election of a Labour Party majority in Parliament, is the twentieth-century version of the Reform Act of 1832, and both go back to 1688–1689. *Revolution by consent* sounds like a contradiction in itself, yet the examples of 1688, 1832, and 1945 prove that it is possible to effect fundamental political and social change without bloodshed.

The spirit of this rational liberalism is best reflected in the work of John Locke (1632–1704), specifically, in his *Two Treatises of Government* (1690). Locke was born of a middle-class Puritan family; his father had fought in the civil war on the side of the Parliamentary party. He went to Oxford in 1652, and stayed on after graduation as a senior student and tutor. His connection with the university lasted until 1684, when he was deprived of his appointment for political reasons. His interests were at first concentrated on philosophy, then on science, and he became a fellow of the Royal Society, England's first scientific society, shortly after its incorporation. Locke also studied and, on many occasions, practiced medicine. In 1667, he met Thomas Sydenham, the leading English medical figure in both clinical work and research. The two men became life-long close friends, and Locke worked with Sydenham both in his clinical practice and in his research. Sydenham believed that medical experience was the only "true teacher" and there is no doubt that Sydenham's medical views, then strongly rejected by the more conservative "establishment" of the medical profession, influenced and reinforced Locke's general sympathies toward experience as the source of knowledge.

Locke's knowledge of medicine led to a chance meeting with Lord Ashley in 1666. Lord Ashley was the leader of the Whig party and one of the central figures in public life. Locke, who saved the statesman's life by a skillful operation, became attached to his career and household for the next fifteen years. He assisted him in political and commercial affairs, and helped him draw up the *Fundamental Constitutions of Carolina* (1669), of which colony Lord Ashley was one of the founders and chief owners. The Carolina constitution guaranteed religious toleration but accepted Negro slavery as a form of rightful property. In 1672 Lord Ashley was raised to the peerage as Earl of Shaftesbury, and shortly thereafter he was appointed Lord High Chancellor of England. Locke followed Shaftesbury into the government and retained his position until 1675, when Shaftesbury fell in disgrace.

Locke then went to France, where he spent four years, mostly in Montpellier and Paris. On his return to England in 1679 he found political unrest growing. Shaftesbury became the principal leader of the opposition against the court, and he was finally forced to flee to Holland, where he died in 1683. Later in the same year Locke himself, fearful for his safety in England, fled to Holland, where he stayed until early in 1689. He left Holland on the same boat that carried Princess Mary of Orange to England.

Locke's exile in Holland was not free from harassment and uncertainty; yet he always looked back on it with nostalgia. He was captivated by the spirit of freedom and manliness he saw in Holland, and he envied the country that had become the center of political and religious refugees from all Europe, including the British Isles. Locke's liberalism was formed in its fundamentals before he set foot on Dutch soil, but his experience there showed him that liberalism in religion and politics could work, and it reinforced his determination to help rid England of the illiberal government of Charles II, and—later—the despotic obscurantism of James II. The first of Locke's four *Letters Concerning Toleration* was composed and first published in Holland, and an abstract of Locke's chief philosophical work, the *Essay Concerning Human Understanding,* the foundation of modern empiricism, was also first published there.

On his arrival in England the new government offered Locke an ambassadorship in Vienna or Berlin, but, as he preferred to remain in England, he accepted instead an appointment as Commissioner of Appeals, which enabled him to stay away from London much of the time, his health having begun to fail him. In 1696 he was made Commissioner of Trade and Plantations, the forerunner of the later Board of Trade and Colonial Office. Whereas Hobbes had little or no practical acquaintance with government, Locke had wide administrative and political experience both before and after his exile. Hobbes had spent his years of exile in absolutist France, Locke in liberal Holland.

Locke's *Two Treatises of Government* is often dismissed as a mere apology for the victorious Whigs in the Revolution of 1688–1689. Such dismissal is clearly not borne out by the facts relating to the history and publication of the book. The *Two Treatises* was begun in 1679 and substantially finished in 1681. Its purpose was to provide the intellectual armory for the planned revolutionary overthrow of Charles II by the Earl of Shaftesbury and his Whig friends. After Locke returned to England in February, 1689, he revised the *Two Treatises* to take into account the fact that the revolution had already occurred. Although the first edition of the *Two Treatises* carries the year 1690 as the date of publication, the book was actually on sale in October of 1689, since publishers then—as now—had the habit of putting a later date on publications than the actual date on which they appeared. In the Preface to the *Two Treatises* Locke implies that the text presented to the public is only part of a larger work, written at an earlier date.

Yet Locke seems to lend some weight to the idea of looking at the *Two Treatises* as an apology for the victorious Whigs in the Revolution of 1688–1689, for in the Preface to the *Two Treatises,* obviously written after his return in 1689, he expresses the hope that the pages of the *Two Treatises* as published "are sufficient to establish the throne of our great restorer, our present King William," and "to justify to the world the people of

England whose love of their just and natural rights, with their resolution to preserve them, saved the nation when it was on the very brink of slavery and ruin." Locke nowhere says or implies that he wrote the *Two Treatises* for the purpose of justifying the Revolution of 1688–1689. He was confident that the book which he composed in 1679–1681 and in which he, in principle, both attacked despotism and justified its overthrow by revolution would also hold good in 1689, although the specific circumstances of English politics had changed in the meantime. The specific issue was no longer a revolution to be carried out by the Liberal political leaders, but a Liberal revolution which had actually taken place.

Every piece of significant political writing is a fragment of the autobiography of its age; yet it becomes great only if, in addition to its vital connection with the period from which it springs, it possesses a universal appeal because of its general human interest. A political treatise that is wholly submerged in the issues of its own age can never rise above the level of a partisan pamphlet. On the other hand, a political work that is isolated from its own age is bound to be and and abstract. The *Two Treatises* could not have been written by someone without the practical experience and interest of Locke; yet without Locke's philosophical rationalism, luminous common sense, and liberality of spirit it could never have become the Bible of modern liberalism.

Like Hobbes, Locke starts out with the concept of the *state of nature*. Yet from this starting point on, Locke travels a different road and arrives at a different destination. Unlike Hobbes, whose state of nature is little different from the jungle in which force and fraud reign supreme, Locke takes an optimistic view. In Hobbes' state of nature there is no natural law, only natural right, each individual doing as he sees fit for his preservation and enhancement of power. By contrast, Locke's conception of man in the state of nature is not noticeably different from man in organized society. Locke cannot conceive of human beings living together without some sort of law and order, and in the state of nature it is the *law of nature* that rules: "The state of nature has a law of nature to govern it, which obliges every one; and reason, which is that law, teaches all mankind who will but consult it, that, being all equal and independent, no one ought to harm another in his life, health, liberty, or possessions."

The law of nature, through the instrument of reason, defines what is right and wrong; if a violation of the law occurs, the execution of the penalty is, in the state of nature, "put into every man's hands, whereby every one has a right to punish the transgressors of that law to such a degree, as may hinder its violation." Locke penetratingly notes that without some agency of enforcement there can be no law, and that in the law of nature the injured party is authorized to be judge in his own case and to execute the judgment against the culprit.

In actuality, the legal situation that Locke describes as the state of nature still exists (as it did in Locke's time) in two areas. First, within the so-called primitive community there is a body of law that is generally known to its members. In the event of transgression, the injured party (or his family) pursues the malefactor, punishes him, or takes reparation from him. The kin of the murdered victim, who slays the assassin, does not commit murder in the eyes of the primitive community, but reestablishes thereby the sanctity of the law: he is the authorized agent of the law to defend it against the assassin, because as yet there are no third-party judges and specialized law-enforcement agencies. Second, the state of nature still exists between so-called advanced nations. To be sure, there is a body of law, international law, that is binding and recognized as such; yet, when a violation of international law occurs and there is no international judicature and enforcement agency, the injured state is authorized to punish the transgressor. Such penalties or reprisals are not considered contrary to international law but are viewed as acts in behalf of its defense and reestablishment.

The law of the state of nature is thus deficient in three important points. First, it is not sufficiently clear. If all men were guided by pure reason, they would all see the same law. But men are biased by their interests and mistake their interest for general rules of law. Second, there is no third-party judge who has no personal stake in disputes. Men who judge their own conflicts are apt to be carried away by passion and revenge. Third, in the state of nature the injured party is not always strong enough to execute the just sentence of the law: "Thus mankind, notwithstanding all the privileges of the state of nature, but being in an ill condition while they remain in it, are quickly driven into society." The purpose of the social contract is to establish organized law and order so that the uncertainties of the state of nature will be replaced by the predictability of known laws and impartial institutions.

Within a group, men quickly form society, because the advantages of the state of nature seem to them to be outweighed by its disadvantages. After society is set up by contract, government is established, not by a contract, but by a *fiduciary trust*. The legislature is "the supreme power" to which all other powers, particularly the executive, "must be subordinate." Yet the legislature is only relatively supreme among organs of government. Above the legislature there is still something higher: the people. Locke conceives of the institution of the legislature as a "fiduciary power." Ordinarily there are three parties to a trust: the trustor, who creates the trust; the trustee, who is charged with the administration of the trust; and the beneficiary, in whose interest the trust is created. According to Locke's view of government, there are only two parties to the trust: the people, who are both trustor and beneficiary, and the legislature, who is trustee.

The principal characteristic of a trust is the fact that the trustee assumes primarily obligations rather than rights. The purpose of the trust is determined by the interest of the beneficiary and not by the will of the trustee. The trustee is little more than a servant of both trustor and beneficiary, and he may be recalled by the trustor in the event of neglect of duty. Because the legislature is no more than a trustee, "there remains still in the people a supreme power to remove or alter the legislative when they find the legislative act contrary to the trust reposed in them; for all power given with trust for the attaining an end, being limited by that end, whenever that end is manifestly neglected or opposed, the trust must necessarily be forfeited, and the power devolve to the hands of those that gave it, who may place it anew where they shall think best for their safety and security."

Locke thus goes further than the makers of the Glorious Revolution who accused James II of having violated the "original contract between King and people." The contractual conception of kingship was a tremendous attack on the theory of kingship by divine right, according to which the king—and the king only—received his right to govern from God. In the doctrine of contract, people and king were put on the same plane as equals. Locke completes this progression by his conception of government as trust: only the people as trustor (and beneficiary) have rights; the government as trustee has only duties, which are defined by the interests of the trustor and beneficiary, and not by those of the trustee. In the theory of divine right, only the ruler has rights; in the theory of contract, both people and government have rights; in Locke's conception of *government as trust, only the people have rights*.

When Hobbes described the establishment of society and government, he carefully confined the act of covenant to the subjects; they set up the sovereign, transferring to him all power. There was no contract between subjects and sovereign, only between subjects and subjects, because Hobbes was anxious to avoid a conception of government that had duties, under a contract, toward the governed. Similarly, Locke confines the act of covenant to the setting up of society but not of government; yet his aim is exactly the opposite of Hobbes'. Locke's government is not a party to any contract with the people, because he does not wish to give the state any rights against the people. Locke's state never becomes the Hobbesian sovereign but always remains an instrument of the purposes that society sets for it. As a strong believer in natural law, Locke assigned to government the task of *finding the law* rather than of making it in the Hobbesian manner. *Law precedes the state* in Locke, but follows it in Hobbes.

Among the rights which precede government Locke stresses that of *property*. The principal purpose of government, the reason why men give up the state of nature for civil society, is "for the mutual preservation of their lives, liberties, and estates, which I call by the general name, property." This broad Lockean concept of property exceeds man's purely economic needs and interests and encompasses almost the whole orbit of his "life, liberty, and pursuit of happiness." When Locke speaks of property, he thinks of a wider range of action and opportunity that is implied in ordinary language. By linking property with life and liberty, Locke undoubtedly showed how important it seemed to him. Yet by the same token, the link of property with life and liberty also shows that Locke thought of property as liberating its owner rather than as enslaving others. To Locke, property meant, not the exercise of power over others, but the protection against power of others—particularly the power of government or of custom or privilege.

Locke's theory of property starts with the inquiry of how private property can be justified at all. Because every man has a property in his own person, the "labor of his body and the work of his hands we may say are properly his." *Labor creates property:* the human effort that is "mixed" with natural resources is the determining criterion which alone justifies private property. Thus Locke avoids justifying property on the ground that "the law" protects it, and instead goes back to the law behind the law, the law of nature, according to which man's property in his own body also extends to its labor.

But labor does more than create property. It also *determines the value of property.* "It is labor indeed," Locke says, "that puts the difference of value on everything." In fact, he stresses the proportion of labor in value highly enough to say that "of the products of the earth useful to the life of man nine-tenths are the effects of labor."

The Lockean theory of property was later used in defense of capitalism; but in the hands of pre-Marxian socialists it became a powerful weapon of attacking capitalism. When Locke defended property on the ground of individual effort and initiative, he protected the productive capacities of a new system of commercial and industrial capitalism against the restrictive traditions of a repressive state. By making labor the title to property and the source of value, Locke translated the rise of a new class to power into terms of a new political economy. Although himself a mercantilist, Locke's economic philosophy helped to liberate the ingenious and industrious entrepreneur from paralyzing force and custom. The socialists used—a century and a half after Locke—his labor theory of property to demand communal control or ownership of the basic means of production; they did not thereby prove that they were more progressive than Locke, but that economic facts had changed since 1690, resulting in the concentration of property and control in industry and finance.

Locke did not work out a consistently clear theory as to *how much property* a person may fairly claim for himself. In general, he acknowledges that the right to property is limited: "As much as anyone can make use of to any advantage of life before it spoils, so much he may by his labor fix a property in; whatever is beyond this, is more than his share, and belongs to others. Nothing was made by God for man to spoil or destroy." This relative equality of property, based on man's limited capacity to consume, would have lasted forever, "had not the invention of money, and by tacit agreement of men to put a value on it, introduced (by consent) larger possessions and a right to them."

The criterion which Locke here applies is that of waste. Before money was invented, man had no moral right to hoard the products of the earth and allow them to rot and spoil. His ability to use perishable goods determined the amount of property he could rightfully own. In a later phase, man would exchange perishable fruit (like plums) for durable ones (like nuts). By disposing of the plums he had done his duty toward society, for he had prevented them from wasting in his possession. From durable nuts to even more durable gold, or "a sparkling pebble or diamond," was only a small and logical step. And if he kept on hoarding these durable goods (like gold and diamonds and money) "all his life, he invaded not the right of others."

Thus Locke arrives at defining money "as some lasting thing that men might keep without spoiling, and that, by mutual consent, men would take in exchange for the truly useful but perishable supports of life." In his doctrine of property Locke makes no serious attempt to reconcile the teaching of natural law, which postulates a reasonable equality of property, with the inequality of property that stems, by consent among men, from the use of money.

Property precedes government and is the "great and chief end" for which men unite into political society. It follows that the state "cannot take from any man any part of his property without his own consent." Even if a commonwealth is based on freely elected representative institutions, it cannot "dispose of the estates of the subjects arbitrarily." The Fourteenth Amendment to the Constitution of the United States embodies this Lockean idea, that no State shall "deprive any person of life, liberty, or property, without due process of law."

Locke felt—understandably enough in the light of Stuart despotism—a profound distrust of executive power; he had more confidence in the legislature, as representing the will of the people or at least the majority of the electorate. The executive power "is visibly subordinate and accountable" to the legislature, "and may be at pleasure changed and displaced." The legislature is supreme, but not absolutely; it is supreme only in relation to other organs of government, and the limitations of the legislature are the end of government, that is, the protection of life, liberty, and property of men.

Specifically, Locke lists four major limitations on the powers of the legislature: first, the law must apply equally to all, rich and poor, favorite at court and countryman at plough; second, the law must not be arbitrary and oppressive, but must be designed for the good of the people; third, the legislature must not raise taxes without the consent of the people or their representatives; fourth, the legislature must not transfer its law-making power to anybody else. In this fourth limitation Locke expresses his opposition to government by administrative decree instead of by legislative assembly. Executive power always harbors the peril of uncertainty and arbitrariness, whereas government by legislature means certainty and the Rule of Law.

This part of Locke's political philosophy has retained more vitality in the United States than in England. There the development of cabinet government since the eighteenth century has controverted some of Locke's misgivings about the inherent evil of a strong and effective executive. Despite Locke's fears, England has not become a despotism, although her legislature has been overshadowed by the executive (itself, however, a committee of the legislature). In the United States, on the other hand, the Lockean sanctification of the legislature as contrasted with the devil theory of the executive has not lost its vote-getting magic.

Hobbes was so strongly impressed with the need for compulsion to maintain social cohesion that he could not envisage society without government. The dissolution of government meant for him the end of all order and restraint, the cessation of civilized living, and the return to the barbarous state of nature. Locke enunciates one of the principal doctrines of classical liberalism by drawing a *sharp distinction between state and society*. Of the two, society is by far the more important and enduring. The dissolution of government does not entail that of society, whereas if society "is dissolved, it is certain that the government of that society cannot remain." Locke mentions that the destruction of society usually occurs by external force, by conquerors' swords that "mangle society to pieces." But when government is dissolved from within, Locke does not anticipate chaos—as did Hobbes—but trusts that society will set up a new government to serve its ends and purposes. In general, government dissolves from within if it violates the trust given to it by the people, who then set up a new government.

Absolute monarchy is, according to Locke, *no form of civil government* at all, and, in fact, worse than the state of nature. In the latter, everybody is judge in his own case, whereas in absolute monarchy there is only one person who has that liberty: the king. In civil society, government approaches dissolution whenever the legislators "endeavor to take away and destroy the property of the people, or to reduce them to slavery under arbitrary power." Similarly, government may be destroyed from within by the chief executive if he overrides the laws of the legislature by his own arbitrary will, hinders the legislative assembly from meeting or acting freely, prevents free elections, or delivers the people into the subjection of a foreign power: "In these, and the like cases, when the government is dissolved, the people are at liberty to provide for themselves by erecting a new legislature differing from the other by the change of persons, or form, or both, as they shall find it most for their safety and good."

Before Locke, theories of disobedience usually contained an element of apology when it came to justifying resistance to authority. Locke reversed the position by declaring the arbitrary ruler an outcast and rebel against the law, whereas the people defined the law by revolting against such despots: "In all states and conditions the true remedy of force without authority is to oppose force to it," and the ruler who uses force without authority should be treated like an aggressor in war. Locke qualifies his theory of resistance in two ways; first, force is to be used by the people only against unjust and unlawful force; second, the right of disobedience may not be exercised by one man or a small group of citizens who feel themselves oppressed, but only by the majority of the people when they have suffered from mischief and oppression.

Locke's insistence that there is a higher law above the law of the state has led to the conception, so deeply ingrained in the traditions of democratic nations, that obedience to the law is a high, but not the highest, civic virtue. Opponents of democratic government have charged that making political rule dependent on consent of the ruled "lays a ferment for frequent rebellion," as Locke puts it. Locke does not deny the charge, but asserts that his hypothesis invites *anarchy and rebellion* no more than any other. First, when the people are made miserable, they will rebel under any form of government, let the governors be "sacred and divine, descended or authorized from heaven, give them out for whom or what you please, the same will happen." Second, Locke emphasizes that men do not revolt "upon every little mismanagement in public affairs" (or "for light and transient causes," as the Declaration of Independence puts it). Third, and here Locke moves from the defensive to the offensive, government by consent coupled with the right of the people to rebel is "the best fence against rebellion." The more the channels of free communication and consent are maintained in a society, the less the need for revolution.

What was an argument in 1690 has since become a matter of experience. The most effective reply to the charge that democracy contains within itself the seeds of anarchy and rebellion is to be found in the political history of the last three centuries. The British and American systems of government, based on the Lockean recognition of the right to rebel, have proved themselves the strongest and most enduring political societies the world has seen, and the same could be said of smaller countries like Holland, Switzerland, and the Scandinavian nations. By contrast, where the right to revolution has been rejected in the name of order and stability, the political results have been *coups d'état,* blood purges, plots and counterplots, conspiracies, and violent swings from one extreme to another—the political record, specifically, of militaristic dictatorships and totalitarian regimes.

By committing themselves to Locke's theories of government, the British supplied the case for the American Revolution and the later peaceful attainment of independence by other colonies, culminating in the virtually complete liquidation of the British Empire in the two decades following World War II. The text of the Declaration is pure Locke, and the main elements of the American constitutional system—limited government, inalienable individual rights, inviolability of property—are all directly traceable to Locke. Writing in the expanding commercial society of his own, his ideas fitted even more the needs of a dynamic pioneering society on the American continent.

Above all, Locke's defense of the right to rebel seemed to the makers of the American Revolution eminently reasonable. Thomas Jefferson, in many respects a Lockean rationalist and lover of freedom and toleration, expressed the American version of Locke's theory of rebellion in the classical phrase that the "tree of liberty must be refreshed from time to time with the blood of patriots and tyrants." Whatever the social or economic system that may exist at a particular time, the right to rebel remains the great, perhaps the greatest, tradition of British and American politics. Rebelliousness too, can, paradoxically, grow into tradition: the tradition of the dignity of man and of his unbreakable spirit.

LOCKE

Two Treatises of Government *

THE STATE OF NATURE

To understand political power aright, and derive it from its original, we must consider, what state all men are naturally in, and that is, a state of perfect freedom to order their actions, and dispose of their possessions and persons, as they think fit, within the bounds of the law of nature, without asking leave, or depending upon the will of any other man.

A state also of equality, wherein all the power and jurisdiction is reciprocal, no one having more than another; there being nothing more evident, than that creatures of the same species and rank, promiscuously born to all the same advantages of nature, and the use of the same faculties, should also be equal one amongst another without subordination or subjection, unless the lord and master of them all should, by any manifest declaration of his will, set one above another, and confer on him, by an evident and clear appointment, an undoubted right to dominion and sovereignty.

This equality of men by nature, the judicious Hooker looks upon as so evident in itself, and beyond all question, that he makes it the foundation of that obligation to mutual love amongst men, on which he builds the duties they owe one another, and from whence he derives the great maxims of justice and charity. His words are:

The like natural inducement hath brought men to know that it is no less their duty, to love others than themselves; for seeing

those things which are equal, must needs all have one measure; if I cannot but wish to receive good, even as much at every man's hands, as any man can wish unto his own soul, how should I look to have any part of my desire herein satisfied, unless myself be careful to satisfy the like desire, which is undoubtedly in other men. We all being of one and the same nature; to have any thing offered them repugnant to this desire, must needs in all respects grieve them as much as me; so that if I do harm, I must look to suffer, there being no reason that others should shew greater measure of love to me, than they have by me shewed unto them; my desire therefore to be loved of my equals in nature, as much as possible may be, imposeth upon me a natural duty of bearing to themward fully the like affection; from which relation of equality between ourselves and them that are as ourselves, what several rules and canons natural reason hath drawn, for direction of life, no man is ignorant.

—*Eccl. Pol.,* lib.i.

But though this be a state of liberty, yet it is not a state of licence: though man in that state have an uncontrollable liberty to dispose of his person or possessions, yet he has not liberty to destroy himself, or so much as any creature in his possession, but where some nobler use than its bare preservation calls for it. The state of nature has a law of nature to govern it, which obliges every one, and reason, which is that law, teaches all mankind, who will but consult it, that being all equal and independent, no one ought to harm another in his life, health, liberty, or possessions: for men being all the workmanship of one omnipotent, and infinitely wise

---

*From John Locke, *Two Treatises of Government* (1690).

maker; all the servants of one sovereign master, sent into the world by his order, and about his business; they are his property, whose workmanship they are, made to last during his, not one another's pleasure: and being furnished with like faculties, sharing all in one community of nature, there cannot be supposed any such subordination among us, that may authorize us to destroy one another, as if we were made for one another's uses, as the inferior ranks of creatures are for ours. Every one, as he is bound to preserve himself, and not to quit his station wilfully, so by the like reason, when his own preservation comes not in competition, ought he as much as he can to preserve the rest of mankind, and not unless it be to do justice on an offender, take away, or impair the life, or what tends to the preservation of the life, the liberty, health, limb or goods of another.

And that all men may be restrained from invading others rights, and from doing hurt to one another, and the law of nature be observed, which willeth the peace and preservation of all mankind, the execution of the law of nature is, in that state, put into every man's hands, whereby every one has a right to punish the transgressors of that law to such a degree, as may hinder its violation. For the law of nature would, as all other laws that concern men in this world, be in vain, if there were nobody that in the state of nature had a power to execute that law, and thereby preserve the innocent and restrain offenders. And if any one in the state of nature may punish another for any evil he has done, every one may do so: for in that state of perfect equality where naturally there is no superiority or jurisdiction of one over another, what any may do in prosecution of that law, every one must needs have a right to do.

And thus, in the state of nature, one man comes by a power over another; but yet no absolute or arbitrary power, to use a criminal, when he has got him in his hands, according to the passionate heats, or boundless extravagancy of his own will; but only to retribute to him, so far as calm reason and conscience dictates, what is proportionate to his transgression, which is so much as may serve for reparation and restraint: for these two are the only reasons why one man may lawfully do harm to another, which is that we call punishment. In transgressing the law of nature, the offender declares himself to live by another rule than that of reason and common equity, which is that measure God has set to the actions of men for their mutual security, and so he becomes dangerous to mankind, the tie, which is to secure them from injury and violence, being slighted and broken by him, which being a trespass against the whole species, and the peace and safety of it, provided for by the law of nature, every man upon this score, by the right he hath to preserve mankind in general, may restrain, or where it is necessary, destroy things noxious to them, and so may bring such evil on any one, who hath transgressed that law, as may make him repent the doing of it, and thereby deter him, and, by his example others, from doing the like mischief. And in this case, and upon this ground, every man hath a right to punish the offender, and be executioner of the law of nature.

I doubt not but this will seem a very strange doctrine to some men; but before they condemn it, I desire them to resolve me, by what right any prince or state can put to death, or punish an alien, for any crime he commits in their country. 'Tis certain their laws, by virtue of any sanction they receive from the promulgated will of the legislative, reach not a stranger: they speak not to him, nor, if they did, is he bound to hearken to them. The legislative authority, by which they are in force over the subjects of that commonwealth, hath no power over him. Those who have the supreme power of making laws in England, France or Holland, are to an Indian, but like the rest of the world, men without authority: and therefore, if by the law of nature every man hath not a power to punish offences against it, as he soberly judges the case to require, I see not how the magistrates of any community can punish an alien of another country; since, in reference to him, they can have no more power than what every man naturally may have over another.

Besides the crime which consists in violating the law, and varying from the right rule of reason, whereby a man so far becomes degenerate, and declares himself to quit the principles of human nature and to be a noxious creature, there is commonly injury done, and some person or other, some other man receives damage by his transgression; in which case he who hath received any damage, has, besides the right of punishment common to him with other men, a particular right to seek reparation from him that has done it: and any other person, who finds it just, may also join with him that is injured, and assist him in recovering from the offender so much as may make satisfaction for the harm he has suffered.

From these two distinct rights, the one of punishing the crime for restraint, and preventing the like offence, which right of punishing is in everybody; the other of taking reparation, which belongs only to the injured party, comes it to pass that the magistrate, who by being magistrate hath the common right of punishing put into his hands, can often, where the public good demands not the execution of the law, remit the punishment of criminal offences by his own authority, but yet cannot remit the satisfaction due to any private man for the damage he has received. That, he who has suffered the damage has a right to demand in his own name, and he alone can remit: the damnified person has this power of appropriating to himself the goods or service of the offender, by right of self-preservation, as every man has a power to punish the crime, to prevent its being committed again, by the right he has of preserving all mankind, and doing all reasonable things he can in order to that end: and thus it is, that every man, in the state of nature, has a power to kill a murderer, both to deter others from doing the like injury, which no reparation can compensate, by the example of the punishment that attends it from every body, and also to secure men from the attempts of a criminal, who having renounced reason, the common rule and measure God hath given to mankind, hath, by the unjust violence and slaughter he hath committed upon one, declared war against all mankind, and therefore may be destroyed as a lion or a tiger, one of those wild savage beasts, with whom men can have no society nor security: and upon this is grounded that great law of nature, *Whoso sheddeth man's blood, by man shall his blood be shed.* And Cain was so fully convinced, that every one had a right to destroy such a criminal, that after the murder of his brother, he cries out,

Every one that findeth me shall slay me; so plain was it writ in the hearts of all mankind.

By the same reason may a man in the state of nature punish the lesser breaches of that law. It will perhaps be demanded, with death? I answer, each transgression may be punished to that degree, and with so much severity, as will suffice to make it an ill bargain to the offender, give him cause to repent, and terrify others from doing the like. Every offence, that can be committed in the state of nature, may in the state of nature be also punished equally, and as far forth as it may, in a commonwealth: for though it would be besides my present purpose, to enter here into the particulars of the law of nature, or its measures of punishment; yet, it is certain there is such a law, and that too as intelligible and plain to a rational creature, and a studier of that law, as the positive laws of commonwealths: nay, possibly plainer; as much as reason is easier to be understood, than the fancies and intricate contrivances of men, following contrary and hidden interests put into words; for so truly are a great part of the municipal laws of countries, which are only so far right, as they are founded on the law of nature, by which they are to be regulated and interpreted.

To this strange doctrine, *viz.,* that in the state of nature every one has the executive power of the law of nature, I doubt not but it will be objected, that it is unreasonable for men to be judges in their own cases, that self-love will make men partial to themselves and their friends: and on the other side, ill-nature, passion and revenge will carry them too far in punishing others; and hence nothing but confusion and disorder will follow; and that therefore God hath certainly appointed government to restrain the partiality and violence of men. I easily grant that civil government is the proper remedy for the inconveniences of the state of nature, which must certainly be great where men may be judges in their own case, since 'tis easy to be imagined, that he who was so unjust as to do his brother an injury, will scarce be so just as to condemn himself for it; but I shall desire those who make this objection, to remember, that absolute monarchs are but men; and if government is to be the remedy of those evils, which necessarily follow from men's being judges in their own cases, and the state of nature is therefore not to be endured, I desire to know what kind of government that is, and bow much better it is than the state of nature, where one man commanding a multitude, has the liberty to be judge in his own case, and may do to all his subjects whatever he pleases, without the least question or control of those who execute his pleasure? and in whatsoever he doth, whether led by reason, mistake or passion, must be submitted to? which men in the state of nature are not bound to do one to another. And if he that judges, judges amiss in his own, or any other case, he is answerable for it to the rest of mankind.

'Tis often asked as a mighty objection, where are, or ever were there any men in such a state of nature? To which it may suffice as an answer at present, that since all princes and rulers of *independent* governments all through the world, are in a state of nature, 'tis plain the world never was, nor never will be, without numbers of men in that state. I have named all governors of *independent* communities, whether they are, or are not, in league with others: for 'tis not every compact that puts an end to the state of nature between men, but only this one of agreeing together mutually to enter into one community, and make one body politic; other promises, and compacts, men may make one with another, and yet still be in the state of nature. The promises and bargains for truck, etc., between the two men in the desert island, mentioned by Garcilasso de la Vega, in his history of Peru; or between a Swiss and an Indian, in the woods of America, are binding to them, though they are perfectly in a state of nature, in reference to one another: for truth and keeping of faith belongs to men as men, and not as members of society.

To those that say, there were never any men in the state of nature, I will not only oppose the authority of the judicious Hooker, *Eccl. Pol.* lib. i. *sect.* 10, where he says,

the laws which have been hitherto mentioned, *i.e.,* the laws of nature, do bind men absolutely, even as they are men, although they have never any settled fellowship, never any solemn agreement amongst

themselves what to do, or not to do: but forasmuch as we are not by ourselves sufficient to furnish ourselves with competent store of things, needful for such a life as our nature doth desire, a life fit for the dignity of man; therefore to supply those defects and imperfections which are in us, as living singly and solely by ourselves, we are naturally induced to seek communion and fellowship with others: this was the cause of men uniting themselves at first in politic societies.

But I moreover affirm, that all men are naturally in that state, and remain so, till by their own consents they make themselves members of some politic society; and I doubt not in the sequel of this discourse, to make it very clear.

THE STATE OF WAR

The state of war is a state of enmity and destruction; and therefore declaring by word or action, not a passionate and hasty, but sedate, settled design upon another man's life, puts him in a state of war with him against whom he has declared such an intention, and so has exposed his life to the other's power to be taken away by him, or any one that joins with him in his defence, and espouses his quarrel, it being reasonable and just I should have a right to destroy that which threatens me with destruction; for by the fundamental law of nature, man being to be preserved, as much as possible, when all cannot be preserved, the safety of the innocent is to be preferred; and one may destroy a man who makes war upon him, or has discovered an enmity to his being, for the same reason that he may kill a wolf or a lion, because such men are not under the ties of the common law of reason, have no other rule but that of force and violence, and so may be treated as beasts of prey, those dangerous and noxious creatures that will be sure to destroy him whenever he falls into their power.

And hence it is that he who attempts to get another man into his absolute power does thereby put himself into a state of war with him; it being to be understood as a declaration of a design upon his life. For I have reason to conclude that he who would get me into his power without my consent would use me as he pleased when he had got me there, and destroy me too when he had a fancy to it, for nobody can desire to have me in his absolute power unless it be to compel me by force to that which is against the right of my freedom—*i.e.,* make me a slave. To be free from such force is the only security of my preservation, and reason bids me look on him as an enemy to my preservation who would take away that freedom which is the fence to it; so that he who makes an attempt to enslave me thereby puts himself into a state of war with me. He that in the state of nature would take away the freedom that belongs to any one in that state must necessarily be supposed to have a design to take away everything else, that freedom being the foundation of all the rest; as he that in the state of society would take away the freedom belonging to those of that society or commonwealth must be supposed to design to take away from them everything else, and so be looked on as in a state of war.

This makes it lawful for a man to kill a thief who has not in the least hurt him, nor declared any design upon his life, any farther than by the use of force, so to get him in his power as to take away his money, or what he pleases, from him; because using force, where he has no right to get me into his power, let his pretence be what it will, I have no reason to suppose that he who would take away my liberty would not, when he had me in his power, take away everything else. And therefore it is lawful for me to treat him as one who has put himself into a state of war with me—*i.e.,* kill him if I can; for to that hazard does he justly expose himself whoever introduces a state of war, and is aggressor in it.

And here we have the plain difference between the state of nature and the state of war, which however some men have confounded, are as far distant as a state of peace, goodwill, mutual assistance, and preservation; and a state of enmity, malice, violence and mutual destruction are one from another. Men living together according to reason without a common superior on earth, with authority to judge between them, are properly in the state of nature. But force, or a declared design of force upon the person of another, where there is no common superior on earth to appeal to for

relief, is the state of war; and 'tis the want of such an appeal gives a man the right of war even against an aggressor, though he be in society and a fellow-subject. Thus, a thief whom I cannot harm, but by appeal to the law, for having stolen all that I am worth, I may kill when he sets on me to rob me but of my horse or coat, because the law, which was made for my preservation, where it cannot interpose to secure my life from present force, which if lost is capable of no reparation, permits me my own defence and the right of war, a liberty to kill the aggressor, because the aggressor allows not time to appeal to our common judge, nor the decision of the law, for remedy in a case where the mischief may be irreparable. Want of a common judge with authority puts all men in a state of nature; force without right upon a man's person makes a state of war both where there is, and is not, a common judge.

But when the actual force is over, the state of war ceases between those that are in society and are equally on both sides subjected to the fair determination of the law; because then there lies open the remedy of appeal for the past injury, and to prevent future harm; but where no such appeal is, as in the state of nature, for want of positive laws, and judges with authority to appeal to, the state of war, once begun, continues with a right to the innocent party to destroy the other whenever he can, until the aggressor offers peace, and desires reconciliation on such terms as may repair any wrongs he has already done, and secure the innocent for the future; nay, where an appeal to the law and constituted judges lies open, but the remedy is denied by a manifest perverting of justice, and a barefaced wresting of the laws to protect or indemnify the violence or injuries of some men or party of men, there it is hard to imagine any thing but a state of war: for wherever violence is used, and injury done, though by hands appointed to administer justice, it is still violence and injury, however coloured with the name, pretences, or forms of law, the end whereof being to protect and redress the innocent, by an unbiased application of it, to all who are under it; wherever that is not *bona fide* done, war is made upon the sufferers, who having no appeal on earth to right them, they are left to the only remedy in such cases, an appeal to heaven.

To avoid this state of war (wherein there is no appeal but to heaven, and wherein every the least difference is apt to end, where there is no authority to decide between the contenders) is one great reason of men's putting themselves into society, and quitting the state of nature. For where there is an authority, a power on earth from which relief can be had by appeal, there the continuance of the state of war is excluded, and the controversy is decided by that power.

SLAVERY

The natural liberty of man is to be free from any superior power on earth, and not to be under the will or legislative authority of man, but to have only the law of nature for his rule. The liberty of man in society is to be under no other legislative power but that established by consent in the commonwealth, nor under the dominion of any will, or restraint of any law, but what the legislative shall enact according to the trust put in it. Freedom, then, is not what Sir Robert Filmer tells us, *O.A. 55. A liberty for every one to do what he lists, to live as he pleases, and not to be tied by any laws,* but freedom of men under government is to have a standing rule to live by, common to every one of that society, and made by the legislative power erected in it. A liberty to follow my own will in all things where the rule prescribes not, not to be subject to the inconstant, uncertain, unknown, arbitrary will of another man, as freedom of nature is to be under no other restraint but the law of nature.

This freedom from absolute, arbitrary power is so necessary to, and closely joined with, a man's preservation, that he cannot part with it but by what forfeits his preservation and life together. For a man, not having the power of his own life, cannot, by compact or his own consent, enslave himself to any one, nor put himself under the absolute, arbitrary power of another to take away his life when he pleases. Nobody can give more power than he has himself, and he that cannot take away his own life cannot give another power over it. Indeed, having by his fault forfeited his own life by some act that deserves death, he to whom he has forfeited it may, when he has him in his power, delay to take it, and make use of him to his own service; and he does him no injury by it. For, whenever he finds the hardship of his slavery outweigh the value of his life, 'tis in his power, by resisting the will of his master, to draw on himself the death he desires.

PROPERTY

God, who hath given the world to men in common, hath also given them reason to make use of it to the best advantage of life and convenience. The earth and all that is therein is given to men for the support and comfort of their being. And though all the fruits it naturally produces, and beasts it feeds, belong to mankind in common, as they are produced by the spontaneous hand of nature, and no body has originally a private dominion exclusive of the rest of mankind in any of them, as they are thus in their natural state, yet being given for the use of men, there must of necessity be a means to appropriate them some way or other before they can be of any use, or at all beneficial, to any particular man. The fruit or venison which nourishes the wild Indian, who knows no enclosure, and is still a tenant in common, must be his, and so his—*i.e.,* a part of him, that another can no longer have any right to it before it can do him any good for the support of his life.

Though the earth and all inferior creatures be common to all men, yet every man has a *property* in his own *person.* This nobody has any right to but himself. The *labour* of his body and the *work* of his hands, we may say, are properly his. Whatsoever, then, he removes out of the state that nature hath provided and left it in, he hath mixed his labour with it, and joined to it something that is his own, and thereby makes it his property. It being by him removed from the common state nature placed it in, it hath by this labour something annexed to it that excludes the common right of other men. For this labour being the unquestionable property of the labourer, no man but he can have a right to what that is once joined to, at least where there is enough, and as good left in common for others.

He that is nourished by the acorns he picked up under an oak, or the apples he gathered from the trees in the wood, has certainly appropriated them to himself.

Nobody can deny but the nourishment is his. I ask, then, when did they begin to be his? when he digested? or when he ate? or when he boiled? or when he brought them home? or when he picked them up? And 'tis plain, if the first gathering made them not his, nothing else could. That labour put a distinction between them and common. That added something to them more than Nature, the common mother of all, had done, and so they became his private right. And will any one say he had no right to those acorns or apples he thus appropriated because he had not the consent of all mankind to make them his? Was it a robbery thus to assume to himself what belonged to all in common? If such a consent as that was necessary, man had starved, notwithstanding the plenty God had given him. We see in commons, which remain so by compact, that 'tis the taking any part of what is common, and removing it out of the state Nature leaves it in, which begins the property, without which the common is of no use. And the taking of this or that part does not depend on the express consent of all the commoners. Thus, the grass my horse has bit, the turfs my servant has cut, and the ore I have digged in any place, where I have a right to them in common with others, become my property without the assignation or consent of any body. The labour that was mine, removing them out of that common state they were in, hath fixed my property in them.

It will perhaps be objected to this, that if gathering the acorns or other fruits of the earth, etc., makes a right to them, then any one may engross as much as he will. To which I answer, Not so. The same law of nature that does by this means give us property, does also bound that property too. *God has given us all things richly,* I *Tim.* vi. 12. Is the voice of reason confirmed by inspiration? But how far has he given it us, *to enjoy?* As much as any one can make use of to any advantage of life before it spoils, so much he may by his labour fix a property in. Whatever is beyond this is more than his share, and belongs to others. Nothing was made by God for man to spoil or destroy. And thus considering the plenty of natural provisions there was a long time in the world, and the few spenders, and to how small a part of that provision the industry of one man could extend itself and engross it to the prejudice of others, especially keeping within the bonds set by reason of what might serve for his use, there could be then little room for quarrels or contentions about property so established.

But the chief matter of property being now not the fruits of the earth and the beasts that subsist on it, but the earth itself, as that which takes in and carries with it all the rest, I think it is plain that property in that too is acquired as the former. As much land as a man tills, plants, improves, cultivates, and can use the product of, so much is his property. He by his labour does, as it were, enclose it from the common. Nor will it invalidate his right to say, Every body else has an equal title to it, and therefore he cannot appropriate, he cannot enclose, without the consent of all his fellow commoners, all mankind. God, when he gave the world in common to all mankind, commanded man also to labour, and the penury of his condition required it of him. God and his reason commanded him to subdue the earth—*i.e.,* improve it for the benefit of life and therein lay out something upon it that was his own, his labour. He that, in obedience to this command of God, subdued, tilled, and sowed any part of it, thereby annexed to it something that was his property, which another had no title to, nor could without injury take from him.

Nor was this appropriation of any parcel of land, by improving it, any prejudice to any other man, since there was still enough and as good left, and more than the yet unprovided could use. So that, in effect, there was never the less left for others because of his enclosure for himself. For he that leaves as much as another can make use of does as good as take nothing at all. No body could think himself injured by the drinking of another man, though he took a good draught, who had a whole river of the same water left him to quench his thirst. And the case of land and water, where there is enough of both, is perfectly the same.

God gave the world to men in common, but since he gave it them for their benefit and the greatest conveniences of life they were capable to draw from it, it cannot be supposed he meant it should always remain common and uncultivated. He gave it to the use of the industrious and rational (and labour was to be his title to it); not to the fancy or covetousness of the quarrelsome and contentious. He that had as good left for his improvement as was already taken up needed not complain, ought not to meddle with what was already improved by another's labour; if he did 'tis plain he desired the benefit of another's pains, which he had no right to, and not the ground which God had given him, in common with others, to labour on, and whereof there was as good left as that already possessed, and more than he knew what to do with, or his industry could reach to.

Nor is it so strange as perhaps before consideration, it may appear, that the property of labour should be able to overbalance the community of land, for 'tis labour indeed that puts the difference of value on every thing; and let any one consider what the difference is between an acre of land planted with tobacco or sugar, sown with wheat or barley, and an acre of the same land lying in common without any husbandry upon it, and he will find that the improvement of labour makes the far greater part of the value. I think it will be but a very modest computation to say, that of the products of the earth useful to the life of man, nine-tenths are the effects of labour: nay, if we will rightly estimate things as they come to our use, and cast up the several expenses about them, what in them is purely owing to nature and what to labour, we shall find that in most of them ninety-nine hundredths are wholly to be put on the account of labour.

There cannot be a clearer demonstration of any thing than several nations of the Americans are of this, who are rich in land and poor in all the comforts of life; whom nature, having furnished as liberally as any other people with the materials of plenty, *i.e.,* a fruitful soil, apt to produce in abundance what might serve for food, raiment, and delight; yet, for want of improving it by labour, have not one hundredth part of the conveniences we enjoy. And a king of a large and fruitful territory there feeds, lodges, and is clad worse than a day labourer in England.

From all which it is evident, that though the things of nature are given in common, man (by being master of himself, and proprietor of his own person, and the actions or labour of it) had still in himself the great foundation of property; and that which made up the great part of what he applied to the support or comfort of his being, when invention and arts had improved the conveniences of life, was perfectly his own, and did not belong in common to others.

Thus labour, in the beginning, gave a right of property, wherever any one was pleased to employ it, upon what was common, which remained a long while, the far greater part, and is yet more than mankind makes use of. Men at first, for the most part, contented themselves with what unassisted nature offered to their necessities, and though afterwards, in some parts of the world, where the increase of people and stock, with the use of money, had made land scarce, and so of some value, the several communities settled the bounds of their distinct territories, and, by laws, within themselves, regulated the properties of the private men of their society, and so, by compact and agreement, settled the property which labour and industry began; and the leagues that have been made between several states and kingdoms, either expressly or tacitly disowning all claim and right to the land in the other's possession, have, by common consent, given up their pretences to their natural common right, which originally they had to those countries; and so have, by positive agreement, settled a property amongst themselves, in distinct parts of the world; yet there are still great tracts of ground to be found, which the inhabitants thereof, not having joined with the rest of mankind in the consent of the use of their common money, lie waste, and are more than the people who dwell on it, do, or can make use of, and so still lie in common; though this can scarce happen amongst that part of mankind that have consented to the use of money.

The greatest part of things really useful to the life of man, and such as the necessity of subsisting made the first commoners of the world look after, as it doth the Americans now, are generally things of short duration, such as, if they are not consumed by use, will decay and perish of themselves. Gold, silver, and diamonds are things that fancy or agreement hath put the value on, more than real use and the necessary support of life. Now of those good things which nature hath provided in common, every one had a right (as hath been said) to as much as he could use, and had a property in all that he could effect with his labour; all that his industry could extend to, to alter from the state nature had put it in, was his. He that gathered a hundred bushels of acorns or apples had thereby a property in them, they were his goods as soon as gathered. He was only to look that he used them before they spoiled, else he took more than his share, and robbed others. And, indeed, it was a foolish thing, as well as dishonest, to hoard up more than he could make use of. If he gave away a part to any body else, so that it perished not uselessly in his possession, these he also made use of. And if he also bartered away plums that would have rotted in a week, for nuts that would last good for his eating a whole year, he did no injury; he wasted not the common stock; destroyed no part of the portion of goods that belonged to others, so long as nothing perished uselessly in his hands. Again, if he would give his nuts for a piece of metal, pleased with its colour, or exchange his sheep for shells, or wool for a sparkling pebble or a diamond, and keep those by him all his life, he invaded not the right of others; he might heap up as much of these durable things as he pleased; the exceeding of the bounds of his just property not lying in the largeness of his possession, but the perishing of anything uselessly in it.

And thus came in the use of money, some lasting thing that men might keep without spoiling, and that, by mutual consent, men would take in exchange for the truly useful but perishable supports of life.

And as different degrees of industry were apt to give men possessions in different proportions, so this invention of money gave them the opportunity to continue and enlarge them. For supposing an island, separate from all possible commerce with the rest of the world, wherein there were but a hundred families, but there were sheep, horses, and cows, with other useful animals, wholesome fruits, and land enough for corn for a hundred thousand times as many, but nothing in the island, either because of its commonness or perishableness, fit to supply the place of money. What reason could any one have there to enlarge his possessions beyond the use of his family, and a plentiful supply to its consumption, either in what their own industry produced,

or they could barter for like perishable, useful commodities with others? Where there is not something both lasting and scarce, and so valuable to be hoarded up, there men will not be apt to enlarge their possessions of land, were it never so rich, never so free for them to take. For I ask, what would a man value ten thousand or an hundred thousand acres of excellent land, ready cultivated and well stocked, too, with cattle, in the middle of the inland parts of America, where he had no hopes of commerce with other parts of the world, to draw money to him by the sale of the product? It would not be worth the enclosing, and we should see him give up again to the wild common of nature whatever was more than would supply the conveniences of life, to be had there for him and his family.

Thus, in the beginning, all the world was America, and more so than that is now; for no such thing as money was any where known. Find out something that hath the use and value of money amongst his neighbours, you shall see the same man will begin presently to enlarge his possessions.

But since gold and silver, being little useful to the life of man, in proportion to food, raiment, and carriage, has its value only from the consent of men, whereof labour yet makes in great part the measure, it is plain that the consent of men have agreed to a disproportionate and unequal possession of the earth, I mean out of the bounds of society and compact; for in governments the laws regulate it, they having, by consent, found out and agreed in a way how a man may rightfully, and without injury, possess more than he himself can make use of by receiving gold and silver, which may continue long in a man's possession without decaying for the overplus, and agreeing those metals should have a value.

POLITICAL SOCIETY

Man being born, as has been proved, with a title to perfect freedom and an uncontrolled enjoyment of all the rights and privileges of the law of nature, equally with any other man, or number of men in the world, hath by nature a power not only to preserve his property, that is, his life, liberty, and estate, against the injuries and attempts of other men, but to judge of and punish the breaches of that law in others, as he is persuaded the offence deserves, even with death itself, in crimes where the heinousness of the fact, in his opinion, requires it. But because no political society can be, nor subsist, without having in itself the power to preserve the property, and in order thereunto punish the offences of all those of that society: there, and there only, is political society, where every one of the members hath quitted this natural power, resigned it up into the hands of the community in all cases that exclude him not from appealing for protection to the law established by it. And thus all private judgement of every particular member being excluded, the community comes to be umpire, by settled standing rules; indifferent, and the same to all parties: And by men having authority from the community for the execution of those rules, decides all the differences that may happen between any members of that society concerning any matter of right, and punishes those offences which any member hath committed against the society with such penalties as the law has established; whereby it is easy to discern who are, and who are not, in political society together. Those who are united into one body, and have a common established law and judicature to appeal to, with authority to decide controversies between them and punish offenders, are in civil society one with, another; but those who have no such common appeal, I mean on earth, are still in the state of nature, each being, where there is no other, judge for himself and executioner; which is, as I have before showed it, the perfect state of nature.

And thus the commonwealth comes by a power to set down what punishment shall belong to the several transgressions they think worthy of it, committed amongst the members of that society (which is the power of making laws) as well as it has the power to punish any injury done unto any of its members by anyone that is not of it (which is the power of war and peace); and all this for the preservation of the property of all the members of that society, as far as is possible. But though every man entered into society has quitted his power to punish offences against the law of nature in prosecution of his own private judgement, yet with the judgement of offences which he has given up to the legislative in all cases where

he can appeal to the magistrate, he has given up a right to the commonwealth to employ his force for the execution of the judgements of the commonwealth whenever he shall be called to it, which, indeed, are his own judgements, they being made by himself or his representative. And herein we have the original of the legislative and executive power of civil society, which is to judge by standing laws how far offences are to be punished when committed within the commonwealth; and also by occasional judgements founded on the present circumstances of the fact, how far injuries from without are to be vindicated, and in both these to employ all the force of all the members when there shall be need.

Wherever therefore any number of men are so united into one society as to quit every one his executive power of the law of nature, and to resign it to the public, there and there only is a political or civil society. And this is done wherever any number of men, in the state of nature, enter into society to make one people, one body politic under one supreme government: or else when anyone joins himself to and incorporates with any government already made. For hereby he authorizes the society, or which is all one, the legislative thereof, to make laws for him as the public good of the society shall require, to the execution whereof his own assistance (as to his own decrees) is due. And this puts men out of a state of nature into that of a commonwealth, by setting up a judge on earth with authority to determine all the controversies and redress the injuries that may happen to any member of the commonwealth; which judge is the legislative or magistrates appointed by it. And wherever there are any number of men, however associated, that have no such decisive power to appeal to, there they are still in the state of nature.

And hence it is evident that absolute monarchy, which by some men is counted for the only government in the world, is indeed inconsistent with civil society, and so can be no form of civil government at all. For the end of civil society being to avoid and remedy those inconveniences of the state of nature which necessarily follow from every man's being judge in his own case, by setting up a known authority, to which everyone of that society may appeal upon any injury received, or controversy that may arise, and which everyone of the society ought to obey, wherever any persons are who have not such an authority to appeal to, for the decision of any difference between them there, those persons are still in the state of nature. And so is every absolute prince in respect of those who are under his *dominion*.

For he being supposed to have all, both legislative and executive, power in himself alone, there is no judge to be found, no appeal lies open to anyone, who may fairly and indifferently, and with authority decide, and from whence relief and redress may by expected of any injury or inconveniency that may be suffered from him, or by his order. So that such a man, however entitled, Czar, or Grand Signior, or how you please, is as much in the state of nature, with all under his dominion, as he is with the rest of mankind. For wherever any two men are, who have no standing rule and common judge to appeal to on earth, for the determination of controversies of right betwixt them, there they are still in the state of nature, and under all the inconveniences of it, with only this woeful difference to the subject, or rather slave of an absolute prince. That whereas, in the ordinary state of nature, he has a liberty to judge of his right, and according to the best of his power, to maintain it; but whenever his property is invaded by the will and order of his monarch, he has not only no appeal, as those in society ought to have, but, as if he were degraded from the common state of rational creatures, is denied a liberty to judge of, or defend his right, and so is exposed to all the misery and inconveniences that a man can fear from one, who being in the unrestrained state of nature, is yet corrupted with flattery and armed with power.

THE END OF GOVERNMENT

If man in the state of nature be so free as has been said; if he be absolute lord of his own person and possessions; equal to the greatest and subject to no body, why will he part with his freedom? Why will he give up this empire, and subject himself to the dominion and control of any other power? To which 'tis obvious to answer, that though in the state of nature he hath such a right, yet the enjoyment of it is very uncertain and constantly exposed to the invasion of others; for all being kings as much as he, every man his equal, and the greater part no strict observers of equity and justice, the enjoyment of the property he has in this state is very unsafe, very unsecure. This makes him willing to quit this condition which, however free, is full of fears and continual dangers; and 'tis not without reason that he seeks out and is willing to join in society with others who are already united, or have a mind to unite for the mutual preservation of their lives, liberties, and estates, which I call by the general name, property.

The great and chief end therefore, of men's uniting into commonwealths, and putting themselves under government, is the preservation of their property; to which in the state of nature there are many things wanting.

First, There wants an established, settled, known law, received and allowed by common consent to be the standard of right and wrong, and the common measure to decide all controversies between them. For though the law of nature be plain and intelligible to all rational creatures, yet men, being biased by their interest, as well as ignorant for want of study of it, are not apt to allow of it as a law binding to them in the application of it to their particular cases.

Secondly, In the state of nature there wants a known and indifferent judge, with authority to determine all differences according to the established law. For everyone in that state being both judge and executioner of the law of nature, men being partial to themselves, passion and revenge is very apt to carry them too far, and with too much heat in their own cases, as well as negligence and unconcernedness, make them too remiss in other men's.

Thirdly, In the state of nature there often wants power to back and support the sentence when right, and to give it due execution. They who by any injustice offended, will seldom fail where they are able by force to make good their injustice. Such resistance many times makes the punishment dangerous, and frequently destructive to those who attempt it.

Thus mankind, notwithstanding all the privileges of the state of nature, being but in an ill condition while they remain in it, are quickly driven into society. Hence it comes to pass, that we seldom find any number of men live any time together in this state. The inconveniences that they are therein exposed to by the irregular and uncertain exercise of the power every man has of punishing the transgressions of others, make them take sanctuary under the established laws of government, and therein seek the preservation of their property. 'Tis this makes them so willingly give up every one his single power of punishing to be exercised by such alone as shall be appointed to it amongst them, and by such rules as the community, or those authorized by them to that purpose, shall agree on. And in this we have the original right and rise of both the legislative and executive power as well as of the governments and societies themselves.

THE LIMITS
OF GOVERNMENT

The great end of men's entering into society being the enjoyment of their properties in peace and safety, and the great instrument and means of that being the laws established in that society, the first and fundamental positive law of all commonwealths is the establishing of the legislative power; as the first and fundamental natural law, which is to govern even the legislative itself, is the preservation of the society, and (as far as will consist with the public good) of every person in it. This legislative is not only the supreme power of the commonwealth, but sacred and unalterable in the hands where the community have once placed it; nor can any edict of anybody else, in what form soever conceived, or by what power soever backed, have the force and obligation of a law which has not its sanction from that legislative which the public has chosen and appointed; for without this the law could not have that which is absolutely necessary to its being a law, the consent of the society, over whom nobody can have a power to make laws but by their own consent and by authority received from them; and therefore all the obedience, which by the most solemn ties anyone can be obliged to pay, ultimately terminates in this supreme power, and is directed by those laws which it enacts. Nor can any oaths to any foreign power whatsoever, or any domestic subordinate power, discharge any member of the society from his obedience to the legislative, acting pursuant to their trust, nor oblige him to any obedience contrary to the laws so enacted or farther than they do allow, it being ridiculous to imagine one can be tied ultimately to obey any power in the society which is not the supreme.

Though the legislative, whether placed in one or more, whether it be always in being or only by intervals, though it be the supreme power in every commonwealth, yet.

First, It is not, nor can possibly be, absolutely arbitrary over the lives and fortunes of the people. For it being but the joint power of every member of the society given up to that person or assembly which is legislator, it can be no more than those persons had in a state of nature before they entered into society, and gave it up to the community. For nobody can transfer to another more power than he has in himself, and nobody has an absolute arbitrary power over himself, or over any other, to destroy his own life, or take away the life or property of another. A man, as has been proved, cannot subject himself to the arbitrary power of another; and having, in the state of nature, no arbitrary power over the life, liberty, or possession of another, but only so much as the law of nature gave him for the preservation of himself and the rest of mankind, this is all he doth, or can give up to the commonwealth, and by it to the legislative power, so that the legislative can have no more than this. Their power in the utmost bounds of it is limited to the public good of the society. It is a power that hath no other end but preservation, and therefore can never have a right to destroy, enslave, or designedly to impoverish the subjects; the obligations of the law of nature cease not in society, but only in many cases are drawn closer, and have, by human laws, known penalties annexed to them to enforce their observation. Thus the law of nature stands as an eternal rule to all men, legislators as well as others.

The rules that they make for other men's actions must, as well as their own and other men's actions, be conformable to the law of nature, *i.e.,* to the will of God, of which that is a declaration, and the fundamental law of nature being the preservation of mankind, no human sanction can be good or valid against it.

Secondly, The legislative or supreme authority cannot assume to itself a power to rule by extemporary arbitrary decrees, but is bound to dispense justice and decide the rights of the subject by promulgated standing laws, and known authorized judges. For the law of nature being unwritten, and so nowhere to be found but in the minds of men, they who, through passion or interest, shall miscite or misapply it, cannot so easily be convinced of their mistake where there is no established judge; and so it serves not as it ought, to determine the rights and fence the properties of those that live under it, especially where everyone is judge, interpreter, and executioner of it too, and that in his own case; and he that has right on his side, having ordinarily but his own single strength, hath not force enough to defend himself from injuries or to punish delinquents. To avoid these inconveniencies which disorder men's properties in the state of nature, men unite into societies that they may have the united strength of the whole society to secure and defend their properties, and may have standing rules to bound it by which everyone may know what is his. To this end it is that men give up all their natural power to the society they enter into, and the community put the legislative power into such hands as they think fit, with this trust, that they shall be governed by declared laws, or else their peace, quiet, and property will still be at the same uncertainty as it was in the state of nature.

Absolute arbitrary power, or governing without settled standing laws, can neither of them consist with the ends of society and government, which men would not quit the freedom of the state of nature for, and tie themselves up under, were it not to preserve their lives, liberties, and fortunes, and by stated rules of right and property to secure their peace and quiet. It cannot be supposed that they should intend, had they a power so to do, to give to any one or more an absolute arbitrary power over their persons and estates, and put a force into the magistrate's hand to execute his unlimited will arbitrarily upon them; this were to put themselves into a worse condition than the state of nature, wherein they had a liberty to defend their right against the injuries of others, and were upon equal terms of force to maintain it, whether invaded by a single man or many in combination. Whereas by supposing they have given up themselves to the absolute arbitrary power and will of a legislator, they have disarmed themselves, and armed him to make a prey of them when he pleases; he being in a much worse condition that is exposed to the arbitrary power of one man who has the command of a hundred thousand than he that is exposed to the arbitrary power of a hundred thousand single men, nobody being secure, that his will who has such a command is better than that of other men, though his force be a hundred thousand times stronger. And, therefore, whatever form the commonwealth is under, the ruling power ought to govern by declared and received laws, and not by extemporary dictates and undetermined resolutions, for then mankind will be in a far worse condition than in the state of nature if they shall have armed one or a few men with the joint power of a multitude, to force them to obey at pleasure the exorbitant and unlimited decrees of their sudden thoughts, or unrestrained, and till that moment, unknown wills, without having any measures set down which may guide and justify their actions. For all the power the government has, being only for the good of the society, as it ought not to be arbitrary and at pleasure, so it ought to be exercised by established and promulgated laws, that both the people may know their duty, and be safe and secure within the limits of the law, and the rulers, too, kept within their due bounds, and not to be tempted by the power they have in their hands to employ it to purposes, and by such measures as they would not have known, and own not willingly.

Thirdly, The supreme power cannot take from any man any part of his property without his own consent. For the preservation of property being the end of government, and that for which men enter into society, it necessarily supposes and requires that the people should have property, without which they must be supposed to lose that by entering into society which was the end for which they entered into it; too gross an absurdity for any man to own. Men therefore in society having property, they have such a right to the goods, which by the law of the community are theirs, that nobody hath a right to their substance, or any part of it, from them without their own consent; without this they have no property at all. For I have truly no property in that which another can by right take from me when he pleases against my consent. Hence it is a mistake to think that the supreme or legislative power of any commonwealth can do what it will, and dispose of the estates of the subject arbitrarily, or take any part of them at pleasure. This is not much to be feared in governments where the legislative consists wholly or in part in assemblies which are variable, whose members upon the dissolution of the assembly are subjects under the common laws of their country, equally with the rest. But in governments where the legislative is in one lasting assembly, always in being, or in one man as in absolute monarchies, there is danger still, that they will think themselves to have a distinct interest from the rest of the community, and so will be apt to increase their own riches and power by taking what they think fit from the people. For a man's property is not at all secure, though there be good and equitable laws to set the bounds of it between him and his fellow-subjects, if he who commands those subjects have power to take from any private man what part he pleases of his property, and use and dispose of it as he thinks good.

But government, into whatsoever hands it is put, being as I have before showed, entrusted with this condition, and for this end, that men might have and secure their properties, the prince or senate, however it may have power to make laws for the regulating of property between the subjects one amongst another, yet can never have a power to take to themselves the whole, or any part of the subjects' property, without their own consent; for this would be in effect to leave them no property at all. And to let us see that even absolute power, where it is necessary, is not arbitrary by being absolute, but is still limited by that reason, and confined to those

ends which required it in some cases to be absolute, we need look no farther than the common practice of martial discipline. For the preservation of the army, and in it of the whole commonwealth, requires an absolute obedience to the command of every superior officer, and it is justly death to disobey or dispute the most dangerous or unreasonable of them; but yet we see that neither the sergeant that could command a soldier to march up to the mouth of a cannon, or stand in a breach where he is almost sure to perish, can command that soldier to give him one penny of his money; nor the general that can condemn him to death for deserting his post, or not obeying the most desperate orders, cannot yet with all his absolute power of life and death dispose of one farthing of that soldier's estate, or seize one jot of his goods; whom yet be can command anything, and hang for the least disobedience. Because such a blind obedience is necessary to that end for which the commander has his power, *viz.* the preservation of the rest, but the disposing of his goods has nothing to do with it.

'Tis true, governments cannot be supported without great charge, and 'tis fit everyone who enjoys his share of the protection should pay out of his estate his proportion for the maintenance of it. But still it must be with his own consent, *i.e.*, the consent of the majority, giving it either by themselves or their representatives chosen by them; for if anyone shall claim a power to lay and levy taxes on the people by his own authority, and without such consent of the people, he thereby invades the fundamental law of property, and subverts the end of government. For what property have I in that which another may by right take when he pleases himself?

Fourthly, The legislative cannot transfer the power of making laws to any other hands, for it being but a delegated power from the people, they who have it cannot pass it over to others. The people alone can appoint the form of the commonwealth, which is by constituting the legislative, and appointing in whose hands that shall be. And when the people have said, We will submit, and be governed by laws made by such men, and in such forms, nobody else can say other men shall make laws for them; nor can they be bound by any laws but such as are enacted by those whom they have chosen and authorized to make laws for them. The power of the legislative being derived from the people by a positive voluntary grant and institution, can be no other than what that positive grant conveyed, which being only to make laws, and not to make legislators, the legislative can have no power to transfer their authority of making laws, and place it in other hands.

These are the bounds which the trust that is put in them by the society and the law of God and nature have set to the legislative power of every commonwealth, in all forms of government.

First, They are to govern by promulgated established laws, not to be varied in particular cases, but to have one rule for rich and poor, for the favourite at Court, and the countryman at plough.

Secondly, These laws also ought to be designed for no other end ultimately but the good of the people.

Thirdly, They must not raise taxes on the property of the people without the consent of the people given by themselves or their deputies. And this properly concerns only such governments where the legislative is always in being, or at least where the people have not reserved any part of the legislative to deputies, to be from time to time chosen by themselves.

Fourthly, The legislative neither must nor can transfer the power of making laws to anybody else, or place it anywhere but where the people have.

THE RIGHT TO REBEL

The reason why men enter into society is the preservation of their property; and the end why they choose and authorize a legislative is that there may be laws made, and rules set, as guards and fences to the properties of all the members of the society, to limit the power and moderate the dominion of every part and member of the society. For since it can never be supposed to be the will of the society that the legislative should have a power to destroy that which every one designs to secure by entering into society, and

for which the people submitted themselves to legislators of their own making: whenever the legislators endeavour to take away and destroy the property of the people, or to reduce them to slavery under arbitrary power, they put themselves into a state of war with the people, who are thereupon absolved from any farther obedience, and are left to the common refuge which God hath provided for all men against force and violence. Whensoever therefore the legislative shall transgress this fundamental rule of society, and either by ambition, fear, folly, or corruption, endeavour to grasp themselves, or put into the hands of any other, an absolute power over the lives, liberties, and estates of the people, by this breach of trust they forfeit the power the people had put into their hands for quite contrary ends, and it devolves to the people; who have a right to resume their original liberty, and by the establishment of a new legislative (such as they shall think fit), provide for their own safety and security, which is the end for which they are in society. What I have said here concerning the legislative in general holds true also concerning the supreme executor, who having a double trust put in him, both to have a part in the legislative and the supreme execution of the law, acts against both, when he goes about to set up his own arbitrary will as the law of the society. He acts also contrary to his trust when he employs the force, treasure, and offices of the society to corrupt the representatives and gain them to his purposes, when he openly pre-engages the electors, and prescribes, to their choice, such whom he has, by solicitations, threats, promises, or otherwise, won to his designs, and employs them to bring in such who have promised beforehand what to vote and what to enact. Thus to regulate candidates and electors, and new model the ways of election, what is it but to cut up the government by the roots, and poison the very fountain of public security? For the people having reserved to themselves the choice of their representatives as the fence to their properties, could do it for no other end but that they might always be freely chosen, and so chosen, freely act and advise as the necessity of the commonwealth and the public good should, upon examination and mature debate, be judged to require. This, those who give their votes before they hear the debate, and have weighed the reasons on all sides, are not capable of doing. To prepare such an assembly as this, and endeavour to set up the declared abettors of his own will, for the true representatives of the people, and the law-makers of the society, is certainly as great a breach of trust, and as perfect a declaration of a design to subvert the government, as is possible to be met with. To which, if one shall add rewards and punishments visibly employed to the same end, and all the arts of perverted law made use of to take off and destroy all that stand in the way of such a design, and will not comply and consent to betray the liberties of their country, 'twill be past doubt what is doing. What power they ought to have in the society who thus employ it contrary to the trust went along with it in its first institution, is easy to determine; and one cannot but see that he who has once attempted any such thing as this cannot any longer be trusted.

To this, perhaps, it will be said, that the people being ignorant and always discontented, to lay the foundation of government in the unsteady opinion and uncertain humour of the people, is to expose it to certain ruin; and no government will be able long to subsist if the people may set up a new legislative whenever they take offence at the old one. To this I answer, quite the contrary. People are not so easily got out of their old forms as some are apt to suggest. They are hardly to be prevailed with to amend the acknowledged faults in the frame they have been accustomed to. And if there be any original defects, or adventitious ones introduced by time or corruption, 'tis not an easy thing to get them changed, even when all the world sees there is an opportunity for it. This slowness and aversion in the people to quit their old constitutions has in the many revolutions [that] have been seen in this kingdom, in this and former ages, still kept us to, or after some interval of fruitless attempts, still brought us back again to our old legislative king, lords and commons; and whatever provocations have made the crown be taken from some of our princes' heads, they never carried the people so far as to place it in another line.

But 'twill be said, this hypothesis lays a ferment for frequent rebellion. To which I answer:

First, No more than any other hypothesis. For when the people are made miserable, and find themselves exposed to the ill usage of arbitrary power; cry up their governors as much as you will for sons of *Jupiter,* let them be sacred and divine, descended or authorized from Heaven; give them out for whom or what you please, the same will happen. The people generally ill treated, and contrary to right, will be ready upon any occasion to ease themselves of a burden that sits heavy upon them. They will wish and seek for the opportunity, which in the change, weakness, and accidents of human affairs, seldom delays long to offer itself. He must have lived but a little while in the world, who has not seen examples of this in his time; and he must have read very little who cannot produce examples of it in all sorts of governments in the world.

Secondly, I answer, such revolutions happen not upon every little mismanagement in public affairs. Great mistakes in the ruling part, many wrong and inconvenient laws, and all the slips of human frailty will be borne by the people without mutiny or murmur. But if a long train of abuses, prevarications, and artifices, all tending the same way, make the design visible to the people, and they cannot but feel what they lie under, and see whither they are going, 'tis not to be wondered that they should then rouse themselves, and endeavour to put the rule into such hands which may secure to them the ends for which government was at first erected, and without which, ancient names and specious forms are so far from being better, that they are much worse than the state of nature or pure anarchy; the inconveniencies being all as great and as near, but the remedy farther off and more difficult.

Thirdly, I answer, That this power in the people of providing for their safety anew by a new legislative when their legislators have acted contrary to their trust by invading their property, is the best fence against rebellion, and the probablest means to hinder it. For rebellion being an opposition, not to persons, but authority, which is founded only in the constitutions and laws of the government; those, whoever they be, who by force break through, and by force justify their violation of them, are truly and properly rebels. For when men, by entering into society and civil government, have excluded force, and introduced laws for the preservation of property, peace, and unity amongst themselves; those who set up force again in opposition to the laws, do *rebellare*—that is, bring back again the state of war, and are properly rebels, which they who are in power, by the pretence they have to authority, the temptation of force they have in their hands, and the flattery of those about them being likeliest to do, the properest way to prevent the evil is to shew them the danger and injustice of it who are under the greatest temptation to run into it.

In both the forementioned cases, when either the legislative is changed, or the legislators act contrary to the end for which they were constituted, those who are guilty are guilty of rebellion. For if any one by force takes away the established legislative of any society, and the laws by them made, pursuant to their trust, he thereby takes away the umpirage which every one had consented to for a peaceable decision of all their controversies, and a bar to the state of war amongst them. They who remove or change the legislative take away this decisive power, which no body can have but by the appointment and consent of the people; and so destroying the authority which the people did, and no body else can set up, and introducing a power which the people hath not authorized, actually introduce a state of war, which is that of force without authority; and thus by removing the legislative established by the society, in whose decisions the people acquiesced and united as to that of their own will, they untie the knot, and expose the people anew to the state of war. And if those, who by force take away the legislative, are rebels, the legislators themselves, as has been shown, can be no less esteemed so, when they who were set up for the protection and preservation of the people, their liberties and properties shall by force invade and endeavour to take them away; and so they putting themselves into a state of war with those who made them the protectors and guardians of their peace, are properly, and with the greatest aggravation, *rebellantes,* rebels.

But if they who say it lays a foundation for rebellion mean that it may occasion civil wars or intestine broils to tell the people

they are absolved from obedience when illegal attempts are made upon their liberties or properties, and may oppose the unlawful violence of those who were their magistrates when they invade their properties, contrary to the trust put in them; and that, therefore, this doctrine is not to be allowed, being so destructive to the peace of the world; they may as well say, upon the same ground, that honest men may not oppose robbers or pirates, because this may occasion disorder or bloodshed. If any mischief come in such cases, it is not to be charged upon him who defends his own right, but on him that invades his neighbour's. If the innocent honest man must quietly quit all he has for peace sake to him who will lay violent hands upon it, I desire it may be considered what a kind of peace there will be in the world which consists only in violence and rapine, and which is to be maintained only for the benefit of robbers and oppressors. Who would not think it an admirable peace betwixt the mighty and the mean, when the lamb, without resistance, yielded his throat to be torn by the imperious wolf? *Polyphemus's* den gives us a perfect pattern of such a peace. Such a government wherein *Ulysses* and his companions had nothing to do but quietly to suffer themselves to be devoured. And no doubt, *Ulysses,* who was a prudent man, preached up passive obedience, and exhorted them to a quiet submission by representing to them of what concernment peace was to mankind, and by showing the inconveniences might happen if they should offer to resist *Polyphemus,* who had now the power over them.

The end of government is the good of mankind; and which is best for mankind, that the people should be always exposed to the boundless will of tyranny, or that the rulers should be sometimes liable to be opposed when they grow exorbitant in the use of their power, and employ it for the destruction, and not the preservation, of the properties of their people?

Nor let any one say that mischief can arise from hence as often as it shall please a busy head or turbulent spirit to desire the alteration of the government. 'Tis true such men may stir whenever they please, but it will be only to their own just ruin and perdition. For till the mischief be grown general, and the ill designs of the rulers become visible, or their attempts sensible to the greater part, the people, who are more disposed to suffer than right themselves by resistance, are not apt to stir. The examples of particular injustice or oppression of here and there an unfortunate man moves them not. But if they universally have a persuasion grounded upon manifest evidence that designs are carrying on against their liberties, and the general course and tendency of things cannot but give them strong suspicions of the evil intention of their governors, who is to be blamed for it? Who can help it if they, who might avoid it, bring themselves into this suspicion? Are the people to be blamed if they have the sense of rational creatures, and can think of things no otherwise than as they find and feel them? And is it not rather their fault who put things in such a posture that they would not have them thought as they are? I grant that the pride, ambition, and turbulency of private men have sometimes caused great disorders in commonwealths, and factions have been fatal to states and kingdoms. But whether the mischief has oftener begun in the people's wantonness, and a desire to cast off the lawful authority of their rulers, or in the rulers' insolence and endeavours to get and exercise an arbitrary power over their people, whether oppression or disobedience gave the first rise to the disorder, I leave it to impartial history to determine. This I am sure, whoever, either ruler or subject, by force goes about to invade the rights of either prince 'or people, and lays the foundation for overturning the constitution and frame of any just government, he is guilty of the greatest crime I think a man is capable of, being to answer for all those mischiefs of blood, rapine, and desolation, which the breaking to pieces of governments bring on a country; and he who does it is justly to be esteemed the common enemy and pest of mankind, and is to be treated accordingly.

That subjects or foreigners attempting by force on the properties of any people may be resisted with force is agreed on all hands; but that magistrates doing the same thing may be resisted, has of late been denied; as if those who had the greatest privileges and advantages by the law had thereby a power to break those laws by which alone they were set in a better place than their brethren; whereas their offence is thereby

the greater, both as being ungrateful for the greater share they have by the law, and breaking also that trust which is put into their hands by their brethren.

Whosoever uses force without right, as every one does in society who does it without law, puts himself into a state of war with those against whom he so uses it, and in that state all former ties are cancelled, all other rights cease, and every one has a right to defend himself, and to resist the aggressor.

Here 'tis like the common question will be made, Who shall be judge whether the prince or legislative act contrary to their trust? This, perhaps, ill-affected and factious men may spread amongst the people, when the prince only makes use of his due prerogative. To this I reply, The people shall be judge; for who shall be judge whether his trustee or deputy acts well and according to the trust reposed in him, but he who deputes him and must, by having deputed him, have still a power to discard him when he fails in his trust? If this be reasonable in particular cases of private men, why should it be otherwise in that of the greatest moment, where the welfare of millions is concerned and also where the evil, if not prevented, is greater, and the redress very difficult, dear, and dangerous?

But, farther, this question, (Who shall be judge?) cannot mean that there is no judge at all. For where there is no judicature on earth to decide controversies amongst men, God in Heaven is judge. He alone, 'tis true, is judge of the right. But every man is judge for himself, as in all other cases so in this, whether another hath put himself into a state of war with him, and whether he should appeal to the supreme Judge, as *Jephtha* did.

If a controversy arise betwixt a prince and some of the people in a matter where the law is silent or doubtful, and the thing be of great consequence, I should think the proper umpire, in such a case, should be the body of the people. For in such cases where the prince hath a trust reposed in him, and is dispensed from the common, ordinary rules of the law; there, if any men find themselves aggrieved, and think the prince acts contrary to, or beyond that trust, who so proper to judge as the body of the people (who at first lodged that trust in him) how far they meant it should extend? But if the prince, or whoever they be in the administration, decline that way of determination, the appeal then lies nowhere but to Heaven. Force between either persons, who have no known superior on earth, or which permits no appeal to a judge on earth, being properly a state of war, wherein the appeal lies only to Heaven; and in that state the injured party must judge for himself when he will think fit to make use of that appeal and put himself upon it.

To conclude, The power that every individual gave the society when he entered into it, can never revert to the individuals again, as long as the society lasts, but will always remain in the community; because without this there can be no community, no commonwealth, which is contrary to the original agreement; so also when the society hath placed the legislative in any assembly of men, to continue in them and their successors, with direction and authority for providing such successors, the legislative can never revert to the people whilst that government lasts; because, having provided a legislative with power to continue for ever, they have given up their political power to the legislative, and cannot resume it. But if they have set limits to the duration of their legislative, and made this supreme power in any person or assembly only temporary; or else when, by the miscarriages of those in authority, it is forfeited; upon the forfeiture of their rulers or at the determination of the time set, it reverts to the society, and the people have a right to act as supreme, and continue the legislative in themselves or place it in a new form, or new hands, as they think good.

CHAPTER EIGHT

ROUSSEAU

The French Revolution is the dominating event of the eighteenth century, and its impetus is far from being spent even today. Its intellectual preparation ran through three generations, and all significant issues were subjected to critical inquiry and examination. The impact of the debate was intensified by its being carried on in human rather than in national terms, and the universal recognition of France's intellectual leadership in the Age of Reason was a source of her ultimate political leadership, because progressive and democratic forces throughout the world identified themselves with the cause of French freedom.

If the Age of Reason ended, politically, in the Age of Revolution, the fault was not that of philosophers and publicists but of the traditional forces that, by stubbornly resisting mild reform, made radical revolution inevitable. Voltaire and Montesquieu were liberal conservatives of the upper classes, and their purpose was to prevent revolution rather than to promote it; and social revolution was furthest from their thoughts. The England they adored was dominated by a wealthy and vigorous aristocracy. The suffrage was confined to a small number of persons, and Parliament represented primarily the interests of the landowning classes. The political recognition of the English middle classes came in 1832, a century after Voltaire and Montesquieu had visited England, and the acceptance of popular democracy occurred even later.

The whole eighteenth century in France was a race between time and disaster. During the first half of the century, criticism of existing institutions was directed more openly against the church than against the state, although once the principle of ecclesiastical authority was undermined, the issue of political authority was bound to be raised. The social centers of the era were the elegant Parisian *salons,* in which the sparkling wit of the *philosophes* mingled with the charm of beautiful women and the skeptical nonchalance of leisurely aristocrats. The people were still inarticulate; Voltaire spoke of them as *la canaille,* and not a few of the early leaders of the Enlightenment felt the same sentiment toward the masses, whom they met only as untutored servants, workers, or peasants.

Voltaire was little interested in forms of government; a benevolent despot, enlightened enough to protect intellectual liberty and personal property, would have suited his taste best, because he was more interested in the monarch's enlightenment than in his autocratic government. He would rather, he said, "obey a fine lion, much stronger than himself, than two hundred rats of his own species." Though completely unaware of the existence of the social question as a chief driving force of revolution, Voltaire nevertheless opened the way for change by his ruthless and ridiculing attacks on intellectual obscurantism and inequality before the law.

In the second half of the eighteenth century, political criticism and philosophical expression became more daring and outspoken. The monument to that era is the *Encyclopédie* (1751–1772), edited by Diderot and containing contributions from the leading men of the time, d'Alembert, Holbach, Helvétius, Turgot, Haller, Morellet, Quesnay, and, at the beginning, also from Voltaire and Montesquieu. The *Encyclopédie* was originally designed to be mainly a translation of Chambers' *Cyclopaedia,* published in London in 1727, but Diderot desired to produce a work of more original and ambitious scope. The *Encyclopédie* was the first large-scale synthesis of all knowledge, and it represented—more than any other encyclopedia before or after—a whole temper and philosophical outlook.

The *encyclopédistes* belonged to varied schools of thought in science, philosophy, theology, and the arts, yet a collective intellectual denominator soon emerged: naturalism and empiricism in philosophy, deism or agnosticism in theology, utilitarianism in social institutions, constitutionalism in government, and support for industry and commerce in economics. The faith of the *encyclopédistes* was humanitarian, rationalist, and scientific: they believed that nature and society are governed, not by an incomprehensible and arbitrary fate or divine providence, but by an intelligible rational order, and that man's increase of knowledge is the best guide to his happiness and progress.

Despite its novel ideas and emphases, the rational outlook of the Enlightenment was traditional—and the tradition that had sprung from Greece was even older than the rivaling dogmas of church and religion. The historical achievement of the Enlightenment consisted not so much in having discovered the possibilities of reason but in having converted such a large part of the ruling classes of the time to its tenets. There was room for feeling and emotion in this age of rationalism, but they were subordinated to the primacy of reason and stylized in form and expression. The first to attack, not this or that idea or philosophy, but the very foundations of traditional civilization, had to be someone who was not a part of it: Jean Jacques Rousseau (1712–1778).

Before Rousseau appeared on the literary scene in Europe, critics of the existing order had slowly been widening their orbit of interest to include the people in their plans of reform. But "the people" meant primarily the discriminated Third Estate of prosperous and respectable merchants, lawyers, and intellectuals. Rousseau is the first modern writer on politics who was *of* the people: the submerged, inarticulate masses of the *petite bourgeoisie,* the poor artisans and workingmen, the small peasants, the restless and rootless, the *déclassés,* for whom there was no room, and no hope, in the existing order of things.

Rousseau was born of a poor family in Geneva, his French ancestors having migrated there as religious refugees in the sixteenth century. Rousseau's mother died a few days after his birth, and his father, an impecunious watchmaker and more enthusiastic dancing master, was unable to raise Jean Jacques in any coherent fashion. From the age of twelve Rousseau was apprenticed to various masters, but he failed to establish himself in any art or trade. At sixteen he ran away from Geneva, and for the remainder of his life could claim no permanent abode anywhere.

Voltaire and Montesquieu had traveled through Europe in grand style; Rousseau saw much of the Continent through the eyes of a penniless, and at times hunted, vagabond, who did not always know where his next meal would come from and where he would sleep. Poverty made him commit minor thefts and larcenies, change his religion for temporary material advantage, and accept charity from people he detested. He was valet to an Italian aristocrat, secretary to a French diplomat, and a music teacher (with but few pupils); he often survived by dint of his own ingenuity and the charity of others, particularly women, who played a large part in his life from his early youth. He never ceased to attract women and to be attracted by them.

In 1744 Rousseau went to Paris, having visited it first in 1742. He tried his hand at various schemes, the theater, opera, music, poetry, without making much of a success at anything. Yet his personality opened for him the doors of the best *salons* in Paris, where he met leading Encyclopédists as well as influential women, with several of whom he maintained close ties of friendship. But he never became, nor did he wish to become, a part of the fashionable set of Paris. He had love affairs with society women, but of all his associations with women the one that lasted longest was with Thérèse Levasseur, a servant girl who worked in Rousseau's small hotel in Paris. As he said later in his *Confessions:* "At first I sought to give myself amusement, but I saw I had gone further and had given myself a companion."

Though enjoying, out of vanity, the company of the rich and powerful, he resented being admitted to the exalted society as a matter of personal privilege, and he never shed his plebeian, Puritanical background of a low middle-class family in Geneva. His complex feelings of pleasure and resentment regarding his social standing made it difficult for him to establish lasting human relations, except with Thérèse Levasseur, with whom he lived from his early days in Paris to the end of his life.

In 1749 the Academy of Dijon announced a prize for the best essay on the question: "Has the progress of sciences and arts contributed to corrupt or purify morality?" In his *Confessions* Rousseau later describes his immediate reaction: "Instantly I saw another universe, and I become another man." He set to work feverishly on the essay and submitted it to the Academy. In 1750 the Academy rewarded it the first prize, and it was published in 1751 under the title *A Discourse on the Moral Effects of the Arts and Sciences.*

Rousseau's thesis was the exact opposite of what was conventionally thought at that time, and he was bold enough to *extol natural man* at the expense of so-called civilized man, for "our minds have been corrupted in proportion as the arts and sciences have improved." The much vaunted politeness, the glory of civilized refinement, is for Rousseau but a "uniform and perfidious veil" under which he sees "jealousy, suspicion, fear, coolness, reserve, hate, and fraud."

In surveying history in support of his cult of natural simplicity, Rousseau is full of enthusiasm for Sparta, a "republic of demi-gods rather than of men," famous for the happy ignorance of its inhabitants, "eternal proof of the vanity of science." By contrast, he denigrates Athens, the center of vice, doomed to perish because of its elegance, luxury, wealth, art, and science: "From Athens we derive those astonishing performances which will serve as models to every corrupt age."

Rousseau sees a direct causal relation between luxury, constantly expanding needs, and the rise of art and science, after which true courage flags and the virtues disappear. Roman history, Rousseau holds, supports this view: as long as Rome was poor and simple, she was able to command respect and conquer an empire; after having developed luxury and engulfed the riches of the universe, Rome "fell a prey to peoples who knew not even what riches were." Rousseau inveighs against orators and philosophers as guides to superficiality and perversion. Philosophers consecrate themselves to the destruction of "all that men hold sacred," and Rousseau calls them "charlatans" who sow confusion among men and undermine their simple ideas of patriotism and religion.

Anticipating his own later views on education in *Emile* (1762), Rousseau writes in his first *Discourse* that traditional education is too vocational and too highly specialized, that children remain ignorant of their own language while being taught other languages not spoken anywhere, and that the moral virtues are neglected: "But magnanimity, equity, temperance, humanity and courage will be words of which they know not the meaning." Finally, Rousseau makes the charge that is as timely today as in 1749. "We have physicists, geometricians, chemists, astronomers, poets, musicians, and painters in plenty; but we have no longer a citizen among us."

In 1753 Rousseau competed again in a contest of the Academy of Dijon; the subject was "What is the origin of inequality among men, and is it authorized by natural law?" His first *Discourse* had brought him immediate fame and sensational success. In writing his *Discourse on the Origin of Inequality* (1755), Rousseau felt he no longer needed to shock and captivate his audience by paradoxes and one-sided arguments, and he composed a much more systematic essay, one of the most influential in the history of democratic and socialist thought. He did not win this time, but the second *Discourse* is more important than the first, particularly in relation to the development of Rousseau's political ideas.

Rousseau distinguishes two kinds of inequality. The first is *natural* and consists in differences of age, health, bodily strength, and the qualities of mind and soul. The second is moral or *political inequality,* which owes its existence to social institutions and consists in privileges of wealth, honor, and power. Rousseau finds that natural inequalities are not substantial, that the problem of inequality arises with the formation of society. Nature destined man to live a healthy, simple life and to satisfy his essential needs ("food, a female, and sleep"). By contrast, man in society, or civilized man, has developed varied and unhealthful habits of eating and sleeping, and his mental and physical exhaustion is the result of the pains, anxieties, and torments of civilized living. *Civilization* is thus a *hopeless race to discover remedies for the evils it produces.* The man of nature knows less medicine than civilized man, but the latter brings upon himself more diseases than medicine can cure. Reflection is contrary to nature, and a thinking man, Rousseau says, is "a depraved animal."

This motif ran through the first *Discourse on the Arts and Sciences,* and Rousseau now announces the idea—so contrary to the commonplaces of his time—that human understanding is not the sole domain of reason but is "greatly indebted to passions." In the state of nature, man was guided by two sentiments: self-interest and pity, and having no moral obligations with others, he could not be "good or bad, virtuous or vicious." Rousseau specifically rejects Hobbes' view of the state of nature in which man, not knowing goodness, must therefore be wicked, and he asserts that man's sense of compassion is the original sentiment from which all later virtues flow. Reason and thinking come afterward and isolate man from his fellows, whereas compassion unites him with others. Uncivilized man is always "foolishly ready to obey the first promptings of humanity. It is the populace that flocks together at riots and street-brawls, while the wise man prudently makes off. It is the mob and the market-women who part the combatants, and hinder gentle-folks from cutting one another's throats."

Turning to the origin of inequality in society, Rousseau starts out with a passage that has a distinctly socialist and revolutionary flavor: "The first man who, having enclosed a piece of ground, bethought himself of saying *This is mine,* and found people simple enough to believe him, was the real founder of civil society." The natural voice of compassion was stilled by the usurpations of the rich and the robberies of the poor, and the newborn society thus led to a "horrible state of war." The rich then devised a plan by which they would better enjoy their power and possession without the threat of constant war.

The first step was easy, to obtain agreement among the rich themselves to set up a system of law and government for the maintenance of peace. The second step, "the profoundest plan that ever entered the mind of man," was to employ the forces of the poor for the creation of government, under which all would be protected and their possessions safeguarded: "Such was, or may well have been, the origin of society and law, which bound new fetters on the poor, and gave new powers to the rich; which irretrievably destroyed natural liberty, eternally fixed the law of property and inequality, converted clever usurpation into unalterable right, and, for the advantage of a few ambitious individuals, subjected all mankind to perpetual labor, slavery and wretchedness."

In the long run, however, Rousseau foresees that from extreme inequality of fortunes and conditions spring divisions and dissensions that undermine the fabric of society and government. Despotism arises out of these disorders, but despotism is the "last term of inequality." Popular insurrection deposes the despot, or even puts him to death: "As he was maintained by force alone, it is force alone that overthrows him." This was strong language for the middle of the eighteenth century, when revolution was not thought of as yet and when free expression was curbed by both church and state.

The concluding words of the *Discourse on the Origin of Inequality* made it plain that Rousseau was not referring to hypothetical states of nature or society but to the injustices of contemporary France, "since it is plainly contrary to the laws of nature, however defined, that children should command old men, fools wise men, and that the privileged few should gorge themselves with superfluities, while the starving multitude are in want of the bare necessities of life."

At the time of uttering this ringing challenge, Rousseau did not earn enough to rent a house, much less own one, or to provide enough of the bare necessities for himself and the woman who shared his existence. During most of his life Rousseau lived in houses and cottages that his friends gave him rent-free, and Thérèse Levasseur received more gifts (often rather unashamedly soliciting them from friends) than proud and sensitive Jean Jacques would have cared to know. While he was not of the "starving multitude," he was close enough to its worries, its tragedies, and petty cares, to know how poverty could deprave and degrade men and women who were originally good.

In 1755 Rousseau published the *Discourse on Political Economy* in Diderot's *Encyclopédie*. Rousseau's regular assignments for the *Encyclopédie* covered music, and the *Discourse on Political Economy* is less remarkable for its economic observations than for the fact that it is his first constructive approach to a theory of the state, whereas the first two *Discourses* had been mainly critical. The *Discourse on Political Economy* is important in the development of Rousseau's political ideas, inasmuch as it contains the first statement of the concept of the General Will, his most original contribution to political philosophy. Thus, when Rousseau published his most famous work, *The Social Contract,* in 1762, its chief ideas were not the result of a sudden inspiration; they had matured in him over the years and had been partially expressed in his three *Discourses.*

The main concern of *The Social Contract* is the central issue of all political speculation: *political obligation.* "The problem," Rousseau says, "is to find a form of association which will defend and protect with the whole common force the person and goods of each associate, and in which each, while uniting himself with all, may still obey himself alone, and remain as free as before." In the very beginning of the book, Rousseau puts the same question in a more dramatic form: "Man is born free; and everywhere he is in chains."

Like his predecessors, Rousseau uses the conceptions of the state of nature and the social contract that puts an end to it. Rousseau's conception of man's life in the state of nature is not quite so gloomy as that of Hobbes, nor as optimistic as that of Locke. Each man pursues his self-interest in the state of nature until he discovers that his power to preserve himself individually against the threats and hindrances of others is not strong enough. The purpose of the social contract is thus to combine security, which comes from collective association, with liberty, which the individual had before the making of the contract. But the social contract consists in "the total alienation of each associate, together with all his rights, to the whole community."

The total surrender of the individual to the sovereign community is completely contrary to Locke and recalls Hobbes' view of the social contract, in which the individual also surrenders himself completely to the sovereign. But whereas Hobbes' subject is completely submissive to his sovereign, Rousseau reflects this kind of social peace without liberty: "Tranquillity is also found in dungeons; but is that enough to make them desirable places to live in?" To renounce liberty, Rousseau says, is to renounce being a man, for there can be no obligation that is not, to some extent at least, mutual. In Rousseau's social contract man does not surrender completely to a sovereign ruler, but each man gives himself to all, and therefore gives himself to nobody in particular: "As there is no associate over whom he does not acquire the same right as he yields others over himself, he gains an equivalent for everything he loses, and an increase of force for the preservation of what he has."

Rousseau shows in *The Social Contract* a much greater appreciation of civil society, as compared with the state of nature, than he showed in his earlier writings. In the state of nature, Rousseau now says, man is guided by instinct only, whereas in society he is inspired by justice and morality. Man loses through the social contract his *natural liberty* and an unlimited right to everything he can lay his hands on, but he gains *civil liberty* and property rights in all he possesses. The liberty of the state of nature is no true liberty, because it is merely enslavement to uncontrolled appetites. By contrast, *moral liberty,* which man acquires solely in the civil state, makes him master of himself, because "obedience to a law which we prescribe to ourselves is liberty."

These three forms of liberty progress from the lower to the higher. Natural liberty is devoid of any reflective or rational elements, and its boundary—constantly shifting—is simply the strength of the individual to assert himself. Civil liberty has a firmer and more rational foundation—the laws and rules of the political community which determine what each member may and may not do in relation to other members. However, if the rules and laws of a political community are created by all its members, then civil liberty rises to the level of moral liberty, for in obeying laws we ourselves have made, we remain free. Whereas civil liberty creates individual rights and freedoms in relation to others, moral liberty is the only type of freedom in which the individual is free in relation to himself.

Once men have created society, the alternative is no longer between liberty limited by no rules (or by one's strength only, as in the state of nature) and liberty limited by rules, for the very concept of civil society requires laws. In civil society, the alternative is between obeying laws in the making of which the citizens have not participated, and obeying laws in which we ourselves have participated in making. In the first case, we obey the will of others, which makes us morally unfree. In the second case, we obey the will of ourselves, which condition alone can make us free. If there has to be law—and where there is society, there must be law—self-imposed law is thus the closest approximation to freedom that man can attain in civil society. Rousseau was fully aware of the paradox that law by its very nature limits freedom and that there can be no freedom without law. "By what inconceivable art," he asks, "has a means been found of making men free by making them subject?" and he answers that "these wonders are the work of law. It is to law alone that men owe justice and liberty."

Rousseau's conception of sovereignty differs from both Hobbes' and Locke's. In Hobbes' the people set up a sovereign and transfer all power to him. In Locke's social contract the people set up a limited government for limited purposes, but Locke shuns the conception of sovereignty—popular or monarchical—as a symbol of political absolutism. Rousseau's sovereign is the people, constituted as a political community through the social contract.

Unlike nearly all other major political thinkers, Rousseau considers the *sovereignty of the people inalienable and indivisible.* The people cannot give away, or transfer, to any person or body their ultimate right of self-government, of deciding their own destiny. Whereas Hobbes identified the sovereign with the ruler who exercises sovereignty, Rousseau draws a sharp distinction between sovereignty, which always and wholly resides in the people, and government, which is but a temporary agent (as in Locke's conception) of the sovereign people. Whereas, in Locke, the people transfer the exercise of their supreme authority, legislative, executive, and judicial, to organs of government, Rousseau's concept of inalienable and indivisible sovereignty does not permit the people to transfer their legislative function, the supreme authority in the state. As to the executive and judicial functions, Rousseau realizes that they have to be exercised by special organs of government, but they are completely subordinated to the sovereign people, and there is no hint or suggestion of separation, or balance, of powers.

Rousseau's system of government is unmitigated popular sovereignty, unmodified by competing or balancing powers; this aspect of Rousseau has always strongly appealed to adherents of radical and uncompromising democracy. Rousseau thought that the people of England were mistaken in thinking themselves free; they were actually free only once every few years when electing Members of Parliament. Sovereignty lies in the General Will of the people, and will cannot be represented.

In the *Discourse on Political Economy* Rousseau had already dealt with the problem of the General Will, the key conception in his political philosophy. He sees the body politic "possessed of a will; and this General Will, which tends always to the preservation and welfare of the whole and of every part, and is the source of the laws, constitutes for all the members of the state, in their relation to one another and to it, the rule of what is just or unjust." By introducing the concept of the *General Will,* Rousseau fundamentally alters the mechanistic concept of the state as an instrument (shared by both Hobbes and Locke) and revives the *organic* theory of the state, which goes back to Plato and Aristotle.

Rousseau is keenly aware of the life of groups, which is more than a charter or articles of incorporation. The state is not the only group with a General Will; particular societies and associations, too, have a General Will in relation to their members, though in relation to the state their will is particular, because the General Will of the state is the most comprehensive of all, embracing all members of the community.

Rousseau himself admits, before his critics and commentators made the discovery, that the distinction between the General Will and particular wills is "always very difficult to make." The General Will is not an empirical fact so much as a *moral fact,* and "it is needful only to act justly, to be certain of following the General Will." By establishing the reign of virtue, all particular wills will be brought in conformity with the General Will. The General Will, therefore, is not something that can be legislated against the people from the outside, but is a moral attitude in the heart of the citizens, and "nothing can take the place of morality in the maintenance of government."

The character of the General Will is determined by two elements: first, it *aims at the general good,* and, second, it *must come from all* and *apply to all.* The first refers to the object of the will; the second, to its origin. The Will of All must therefore not be confused with the General Will: "The latter considers only the common interest, while the former takes private interest into account, and is no more than a sum of particular wills." The generality of the will is not so much a matter of numbers as of intrinsic quality and goodness. The people always will be good, but they do not always understand it, particularly when factions make it difficult for the independent citizen to pursue the common good. Nor can the General Will be represented, because representative assemblies tend to develop particular interests of their own, forgetting those of the community. Obviously referring to the direct democracies of Swiss city-republics, Rousseau glowingly describes how "bands of peasants are seen regulating affairs of state under an oak, and always acting wisely," and he prefers the methods of these "happiest people in the world" to the ingenious methods of party government through representation, as practiced in other nations.

Rousseau recognizes that in direct popular government unanimity is, in practice, impossible, and that the vote of the majority binds the minority. The question of how the minority can be free and yet be bound to obey the majority is rejected by Rousseau as wrongly put: when a citizen objects to a proposed law in the popular assembly and finds himself in a minority, he does not thereby lose his freedom, for his minority vote merely proves that he did not recognize the General Will, rather than that the majority, as such, has a right to rule over him. Rousseau cautiously adds that this conception of freedom of the individual "presupposes, indeed, that all the qualities of the General Will still reside in the majority: when they cease to do so, whatever side a man may take, liberty is no longer possible."

Obeying the General Will is thus the expression of the moral freedom of the individual, and if he refuses to obey, he may be compelled to do so: "This means nothing less than that he will be forced to be free." Here Rousseau revives his basic distinction between the apparent liberty of man in the state of nature, which actually is enslavement to selfish appetites, and his moral liberty in civil society, which consists in obeying laws, general in scope and origin, which he, as a member of the body politic, has helped to make.

Yet it takes more than one brief phrase to interpret a thinker as an authoritarian, particularly a thinker who felt drawn to the lowly, the weak, the oppressed, and who proclaimed liberty, justice, and equality as the ends of law and government. Perhaps this famous phrase—that man can be forced to be free—is an extreme case of Rousseau's love of colorful images and verbal fireworks, as exemplified, for example, by the opening words of the *social contract,* "Man is born free; and everywhere he is in chains," which also cannot be accepted literally and which yet try to say something important.

The phrase "forcing man to be free" is obviously self-contradictory, if one looks at the ordinary meaning of these words. It may be safely presumed that Rousseau was fully aware of this contradiction if one interprets the words force and freedom according to everyday usage in which force and freedom are contradictory. The contradiction becomes, however, less obvious and simple if we recall that Rousseau distinguishes civil liberty from moral liberty, and that moral liberty can be attained only through the General Will creating laws which come from all, apply to all, and aim at the general good. When a civil society is in the process of being set up by the social contract, individuals may stay out of the rights and obligations thereby created by either leaving the civil society, that is, by emigrating, or by remaining "as foreigners among citizens." Once the state is set up, "residence constitutes consent; to dwell in its territory to submit to its sovereignty." In the light of many modern totalitarian practices of preventing people from leaving their country for another, Rousseau adds the interesting comment that residence should be construed as consent to the political institutions of a state only if it is free and voluntary, as is the case in a "free state," for in states which are not free, "lack of a refuge, necessity, or violence may detain a man in a country against his will; and then his residing there no longer by itself implies his consent to the contract or to its violation."

However, the citizen of the free state cannot give his consent selectively to one law but not to another: "The citizen gives his consent to all the laws, including those which are passed in spite of his opposition, and even those which punish him when he dares to break any of them." The concept of the General Will involves the participation of every citizen in the making of laws; by taking part in the process on a free and equal basis with all other citizens, he obliges himself in advance to obey the law even if he has voted against it, since "the vote of the majority always binds the rest." However, Rousseau is no adherent of majoritarian tyranny and caprice, for the obligation of the citizen to obey the law he has opposed or voted against before its being enacted presupposes that "all the qualities of the General Will still reside in the majority," including its quality of aiming at the common good. But if the General Will, as expressed by the majority, meets both its empirical requirement—that it come from all and that it apply to all—and its moral or rational requirement—that it aim at the common good, then liberty—in Rousseau's (and, later, Kant's) sense of *moral liberty*—means no more, *but also no less,* than obeying the laws one has participated in creating. What Rousseau thus tries to convey in the provocative and attention-catching phrase of forcing man to be free if he disobeys the General Will is the notion that one cannot have it both ways, that the very concept of civil society implies the abandonment of natural liberty, in which one's freedom is limited only by his strength. All civilization implies rational self-restraint, and political civilization, too, implies the rational understanding on the part of the citizen in the free state that in the notion of liberty as subjection to self-imposed law the importance of the word "subjection" is equal to that of "self-imposed." In the first draft of *The Social Contract* Rousseau plainly states that the General Will is more than pure will, that, in fact, it is "in each individual a pure act of understanding, which reasons while the passions are silent on what a man may demand of his neighbor and on what his neighbor has a right to demand of him."

Like most democratic theorists of the state, Rousseau was anxious to base political obligation on consent and thus save the idea of individual liberty in the realm of government. Yet he saw beyond the mechanical constructions of liberal political theory, which assumed that the public good would somehow be the final product of all individual private wills and interests. He attributes to the people inalienable sovereignty, but a moral obligation is attached to this precious possession: each citizen must will the general good, because popular sovereignty means the General Will, and self-government is therefore not mere submission to the common good, but its active cultivation: "There can be no patriotism without liberty, no liberty without virtue, no virtue without citizens; create citizens, and you have everything you need; without them, you will have nothing but debased slaves, from the rulers of the state downward."

Some defenders of totalitarian states have sought to claim Rousseau as an intellectual progenitor of unlimited collectivism and oppressive anti-individualism. True, the organic element in Rousseau's doctrine may be abused, and has been abused, for antidemocratic purposes. Yet the master conception of *The Social Contract*—is a community of free men living in a small state in which democracy can be practiced directly by the people, a community of men who see in freedom not only an invitation to personal enjoyment and advantage but also shared responsibility for the welfare of the whole.

Before Rousseau, the classical doctrine of Plato and Aristotle emphasized good government at the expense of self-government. The aim was the good life, not government of the people by the people. The more modern idea of Locke and the liberal school was concerned principally with self-government; it relegated the problem of good government into the background, or it was assumed that good government would naturally result from a combination of public *laissez faire* and private pursuit of individual advantage. Rousseau is the first modern writer to attempt, not always successfully, to synthesize *good government with self-government* in the key concept of the General Will: the realization of what is best for the community is not enough; it must also be *willed* by the community.

This synthesis explains why Rousseau has been claimed by adherents of the organic theory of the state as well as by followers of liberal democracy, though their conclusions may be antagonistic to each other. The more one is addicted to an extreme view of either the organic or the liberal theory in politics, the easier it is to appropriate only one part of Rousseau. The more one seeks to preserve what is best in the organic theory of the state and to fuse it with liberal democracy, the more one runs into philosophical difficulties that, in the end, resemble those of Rousseau.

Rousseau also saw more clearly than the conventional liberal doctrinaries that the end of government is not confined to the protection of individual liberty but also includes *equality,* because "liberty cannot exist without it." Rousseau reverses in *The Social Contract* the hostility to property that he showed in the first two *Discourses;* here he accepts property as an essential institution of society. But in *The Social Contract* he does not abandon the ideal of economic equality, though the concept of equality should not be taken in a literal sense. No citizen "shall ever be wealthy even to buy another, and none poor enough to be forced to sell himself." Rousseau realizes that in practice it is difficult to maintain the ideal of equitable distribution of property, but it "is precisely because the force of circumstances tends continually to destroy equality that the force of legislation should always tend to its maintenance."

Whereas Locke failed to see property as a relation of domination of man over man, Rousseau clearly recognized *property* as a form of *private domination* that had to be kept under control by the General Will, the public interest of the community. Rousseau's theory of equitable distribution of property was, however, hardly socialist in the modern sense of the term, because he was not thinking of an industrial society, in which the problem of socialized property chiefly arises, but of communities of small peasants and craftsmen (as in Switzerland), in which individual economic independence and an approximation to the ideal of equal property are feasible. Yet indirectly, this part of Rousseau—the stress on equality—has aided the development of socialist sentiment by sharpening the awareness that political liberty and crass economic inequality are ultimately incompatible if democracy is to survive and expand.

Since the eighteenth century the record of free government everywhere has proved that there can be no reliance on contrivances and institutions alone in the eternal struggle for liberty, and that its survival depends, in the last analysis, on those moral qualities that Rousseau calls the General Will, justice, virtue. The General Will, like individual virtue, cannot be defined in detail; it is an impulse that animates and guides civic action. It receives its ultimate valid definition in the lives of free men rather than in philosophical distinctions.

Rousseau was first vindicated historically by the success of the American Revolution, and the opening words of the Constitution of the United States, "We the people . . . ," were of the spirit of Jean Jacques Rousseau. In the French Revolution, only a few years later, the French nation discovered its communal solidarity in a new birth of individual freedom and popular government. Since then, the message of Rousseau has been carried to all corners of the world, and its vitality and persistent timeliness continue to inspire free men and free women everywhere.

ROUSSEAU

The Social Contract *

MAN IS BORN FREE

Man is born free; and everywhere he is in chains. One thinks himself the master of others, and still remains a greater slave than they. How did this change come about? I do not know. What can make it legitimate? That question I think I can answer.

If I took into account only force, and the effects derived from it, I should say: "As long as a people is compelled to obey, and obeys, it does well; as soon as it can shake off the yoke, and shakes it off, it does still better; for, regaining its liberty by the same right as took it away, either it is justified in resuming it, or there was no justification for those who took it away." But the social order is a sacred right which is the basis of all other rights. Nevertheless, this right does not come from nature, and must therefore be founded on conventions. Before coming to that, I have to prove what I have just asserted.

THE RIGHT OF
THE STRONGEST

The strongest is never strong enough to be always the master, unless he transforms strength into right, and obedience into duty. Hence the right of the strongest, which, though to all seeming meant ironically, is really laid down as a fundamental principle. But are we never to have an explanation of this phrase? Force is a physical power, and I fail to see what moral effect it can have.

*From Jean Jacques Rousseau, *The Social Contract and Discourses* (1762, trans. G.D.H. Cole, Everyman's Library Edition, 1947). By permission of E.P. Dutton & Co., and J.M. Dent & Sons, Ltd.

To yield to force is an act of necessity, not of will—at the most, an act of prudence. In what sense can it be a duty?

Suppose for a moment that this so-called "right" exists. I maintain that the sole result is a mass of inexplicable nonsense. For, if force creates right, the effect changes with the cause: every force that is greater than the first succeeds to its right. As soon as it is possible to disobey with impunity, disobedience is legitimate; and, the strongest being always in the right, the only thing that matters is to act so as to become the strongest. But what kind of right is that which perishes when force fails? If we must obey perforce, there is no need to obey because we ought; and if we are not forced to obey, we are under no obligation to do so. Clearly, the word "right" adds nothing to force: in this connection, it means absolutely nothing.

Obey the powers that be. If this means yield to force, it is a good precept, but superfluous: I can answer for its never being violated. All power comes from God, I admit; but so does all sickness: does that mean that we are forbidden to call in the doctor? A brigand surprises me at the edge of a wood: must I not merely surrender my purse on compulsion; but, even if I could withhold it, am I in conscience bound to give it up? For certainly the pistol he holds is also a power.

Let us then admit that force does not create right, and that we are obliged to obey only legitimate powers. In that case, my original question recurs.

SLAVERY

Since no man has a natural authority over his fellow, and force creates no right, we must conclude that conventions form the basis of all legitimate authority among men.

If an individual, says Grotius, can alienate his liberty and make himself the slave of a master, why could not a whole people do the same and make itself subject to a king? There are in this passage plenty of ambiguous words which would need explaining; but let us confine ourselves to the word *alienate*. To alienate is to give or to sell. Now, a man who becomes the slave of another does not give himself; he sells himself, at the least for his subsistence: but for what does a people sell itself? A king is so far from furnishing his subjects with their subsistence that he gets his own only from them; and, according to Rabelais, kings do not live on nothing. Do subjects then give their persons on condition that the king takes their goods also? I fail to see what they have left to preserve.

It will be said that the despot assures his subjects civil tranquillity. Granted; but what do they gain, if the wars his ambition brings down upon them, his insatiable avidity, and the vexatious conduct of his ministers press harder on them than their own dissensions would have done? What do they gain, if the very tranquillity they enjoy is one of their miseries? Tranquillity is found also in dungeons; but is that enough to make them desirable places to live in? The Greeks imprisoned in the cave of the Cyclops lived there very tranquilly, while they were awaiting their turn to be devoured.

To say that a man gives himself gratuitously, is to say what is absurd and inconceivable; such an act is null and illegitimate, from the mere fact that he who does it is out of his mind. To say the same of a whole people is to suppose a people of madmen; and madness creates no right.

Even if each man could alienate himself, he could not alienate his children: they are born men and free; their liberty belongs to them, and no one but they has the right to dispose of it. Before they come to years of discretion, the father can, in their name, lay down conditions for their preservation and well-being, but he cannot give them irrevocably and without conditions: such a gift is contrary to the ends of nature, and exceeds the rights of paternity. It would therefore be necessary, in order to legitimize an arbitrary

government, that in every generation the people should be in a position to accept or reject it; but, were this so, the government would be no longer arbitrary.

To renounce liberty is to renounce being a man, to surrender the rights of humanity and even its duties. For him who renounces everything no indemnity is possible. Such a renunciation is incompatible with man's nature; to remove all liberty from his will is to remove all morality from his acts. Finally, it is an empty and contradictory convention that sets up, on the one side, absolute authority, and, on the other, unlimited obedience. Is it not clear that we can be under no obligation to a person from whom we have the right to exact everything? Does not this condition alone, in the absence of equivalence or exchange, in itself involve the nullity of the act? For what right can my slave have against me, when all that he has belongs to me, and, his right being mine, this right of mine against myself is a phrase devoid of meaning?

Grotius and the rest find in war another origin for the so-called right of slavery. The victor having, as they hold, the right of killing the vanquished, the latter can buy back his life at the price of his liberty; and this convention is the more legitimate because it is to the advantage of both parties.

But it is clear that this supposed right to kill the conquered is by no means deducible from the state of war. Men, from the mere fact that, while they are living in their primitive independence, they have no mutual relations stable enough to constitute either the state of peace or the state of war, cannot be naturally enemies. War is constituted by a relation between things, and not between persons; and, as the state of war cannot arise out of simple personal relations, but only out of real relations, private war, or war of man with man, can exist neither in the state of nature, where there is no constant property, nor in the social state, where everything is under the authority of the laws.

Individual combats, duels, and encounters, are acts which cannot constitute a state; while the private wars, authorized by the Establishments of Louis IX, King of France, and suspended by the Peace of God, are abuses of feudalism, in itself an absurd system if ever there was one, and contrary to the principles of natural right and to all good polity.

War then is a relation, not between man and man, but between State and State, and individuals are enemies only accidentally, not as men, nor even as citizens,[1] but as soldiers; not as members of their country, but as its defenders. Finally, each State can have for enemies only other States, and not men; for between things disparate in nature there can be no real relation.

Furthermore, this principle is in conformity with the established rules of all times and the constant practice of all civilized peoples. Declarations of war are intimations less to powers than to their subjects. The foreigner, whether king, individual, or people, who robs, kills, or detains the subjects, without declaring war on the prince, is not an enemy, but a brigand. Even in real war, a just prince, while laying hands, in the enemy's country, on all that belongs to the public, respects the lives and goods of individuals: he respects rights on which his own are founded. The object of the war being the destruction of the hostile State, the other side has a right to kill its defenders, while they are bearing arms; but as soon as they lay them down and surrender, they cease to be enemies or instruments of the enemy, and become once more merely men, whose life no one has any right to take. Sometimes it is possible to kill the State without killing a single one of its members; and war gives no right which is not necessary to the gaining of its object. These principles are not those of Grotius: they are not based on the authority of poets, but derived from the nature of reality and based on reason.

The right of conquest has no foundation other than the right of the strongest. If war does not give the conqueror the right to massacre the conquered peoples, the right to enslave them cannot be based upon a right which does not exist. No one has a right to kill an enemy except when he cannot make him a slave, and the right to enslave him cannot therefore be derived from the right to kill him. It is accordingly an unfair exchange to make him buy at the price of his liberty his life, over which the victor holds no right. Is it not clear that there is a vicious circle in founding the right of life and death on the right of slavery, and the right of slavery on the right of life and death?

Even if we assume this terrible right to kill everybody, I maintain that a slave made in war, or a conquered people, is under no obligation to a master, except to obey him as far as he is compelled to do so. By taking an equivalent for his life, the victor has not done him a favour; instead of killing him without profit, he has killed him usefully. So far then is he from acquiring over him any authority in addition to that of force, that the state of war continues to subsist between them: their mutual relation is the effect of it, and the usage of the right of war does not imply a treaty of peace. A convention has indeed been made; but this convention, so far from destroying the state of war, presupposes its continuance.

So, from whatever aspect we regard the question, the right of slavery is null and void, not only as being illegitimate, but also because it is absurd and meaningless. The words *slave* and *right* contradict each other, and are mutually exclusive. It will always be equally foolish for a man to say to a man or to a people: "I make with you a convention wholly at your expense and wholly to my advantage; I shall keep it as long as I like, and you will keep it as long as I like."

---

[1] The Romans, who understood and respected the right of war more than any other nation on earth, carried their scruples on this head so far that a citizen was not allowed to serve as a volunteer without engaging himself expressly against the enemy, and against such and such an enemy by name. A legion in which the younger Cato was seeing his first service under Popilius having been reconstructed, the elder Cato wrote to Popilius that, if he wished his son to continue serving under him, he must administer to him a new military oath, because, the first having been annulled, he was no longer able to bear arms against the enemy. The same Cato wrote to his son telling him to take great care not to go into battle before taking this new oath. I know that the siege of Clusium and other isolated events can be quoted against me; but I am citing laws and customs. The Romans are the people that least often transgressed its laws; and no other people has had such good ones.

THE FIRST CONVENTION
OF SOCIETY

Even if I granted all that I have been refuting, the friends of despotism would be no better off. There will always be a great difference between subduing a multitude and ruling a society. Even if scattered individuals were successively enslaved by one man, however numerous they might be, I still see no more than a master and his slaves, and certainly not a people and its ruler; I see what may be termed an aggregation, but not an association; there is as yet neither public good nor body politic. The man in question, even if he has enslaved half the world, is still only an individual; his interest, apart from that of others, is still a purely private interest. If this same man comes to die, his empire, after him, remains scattered and without unity, as an oak falls and dissolves into a heap of ashes when the fire has consumed it.

A people, says Grotius, can give itself to a king. Then, according to Grotius, a people is a people before it gives itself. The gift is itself a civil act, and implies public deliberation. It would be better, before examining the act by which a people gives itself to a king, to examine that by which it has become a people; for this act, being necessarily prior to the other, is the true foundation of society.

Indeed, if there were no prior convention, where, unless the election were unanimous, would be the obligation on the minority to submit to the choice of the majority? How have a hundred men who wish for a master the right to vote on behalf of ten who do not? The law of majority voting is itself something established by convention, and presupposes unanimity, on one occasion at least.

THE SOCIAL COMPACT

I suppose men to have reached the point at which the obstacles in the way of their preservation in the state of nature show their power of resistance to be greater than the resources at the disposal of each individual for his maintenance in that state, The primitive condition can then subsist no longer; and the human race would perish unless it changed its manner of existence.

But, as men cannot engender new forces, but only unite and direct existing ones, they have no other means of preserving themselves than the formation, by aggregation, of a sum of forces great enough to overcome the resistance. These they have to bring into play by means of a single motive power, and cause to act in concert.

This sum of forces can arise only where several persons come together: but, as the force and liberty of each man are the chief instruments of his self-preservation, how can he pledge them without harming his own interests, and neglecting the care he owes to himself? This difficulty, in its bearing on my present subject, may be stated in the following terms:

"The problem is to find a form of association which will defend and protect with the whole common force the person and goods of each associate, and in which each, while uniting himself with all, may still obey himself alone, and remain as free as before." This is the fundamental problem of which the *Social Contract* provides the solution.

The clauses of this contract are so determined by the nature of the act that the slightest modification would make them vain and ineffective; so that, although they have perhaps never been formally set forth, they are everywhere the same and everywhere tacitly admitted and recognized, until, on the violation of the social compact, each regains his original rights and resumes his natural liberty, while losing the conventional liberty in favour of which he renounced it.

These clauses, properly understood, may be reduced to one—the total alienation of each associate, together with all his rights, to the whole community; for, in the first place, as each gives himself absolutely, the conditions are the same for all; and, this being so, no one has any interest in making them burdensome to others.

Moreover, the alienation being without reserve, the union is as perfect as it can be, and no associate has anything more to demand: for, if the individuals retained certain rights, as there would be no common superior to decide between them and the public, each, being on one point his own judge, would ask to be so on all; the state of nature would thus continue, and the association would necessarily become inoperative or tyrannical.

Finally, each man, in giving himself to all, gives himself to nobody; and as there is no associate over which he does not acquire the same right as he yields others over himself, he gains an equivalent for everything he loses, and an increase of force for the preservation of what he has.

If then we discard from the social compact what is not of its essence, we shall find that it reduces itself to the following terms:

"Each of us puts his person and all his power in common under the supreme direction of the general will, and, in our corporate capacity, we receive each member as an indivisible part of the whole."

At once, in place of the individual personality of each contracting party, this act of association creates a moral and collective body, composed of as many members as the assembly contains voters, and receiving from this act its unity, its common identity, its life, and its will. This public person, so formed by the union of all other persons, formerly took the name of city,[2] and now takes that of *Republic* or *body politic;* it is called by its members *State* when passive, *Sovereign* when active, and *Power* when

_____

[2] The real meaning of this word has been almost wholly lost in modern times; most people mistake a town for a city, and a townsman for a citizen. They do not know that houses make a town, but citizens a city. The same mistake long ago cost the Carthaginians dear. I have never read of the title of citizens being given to the subjects of any prince, not even the ancient Macedonians or the English of to-day, though they are nearer liberty than any one else. The French alone everywhere familiarly adopt the name of citizens, because, as can be seen from their dictionaries, they have no idea of its meaning, otherwise they would be guilty in usurping it, of the crime of *lèse-majesté:* among them, the name expresses a virtue, and not a right. When Bodin spoke of our citizens and townsmen, he fell into a bad blunder in taking the one class for the other. M. d'Alembert has avoided the error, and, in his article on Geneva, has clearly distinguished the four orders of men (or even five, counting mere foreigners) who dwell in our town, of which two only compose the Republic. No other French writer, to my knowledge, has understood the real meaning of the word citizen.

compared with others like itself. Those who are associated in it take collectively the name of *people,* and severally are called *citizens,* as sharing in the sovereign power, and *subjects,* as being under the laws of the State. But these terms are often confused and taken one for another: it is enough to know how to distinguish them when they are being used with precision.

THE SOVEREIGN

This formula shows us that the act of association comprises a mutual undertaking between the public and the individuals, and that each individual, in making a contract, as we may say, with himself, is bound in a double capacity; as a member of the Sovereign he is bound to the individuals, and as a member of the State to the Sovereign. But the maxim of civil right, that no one is bound by undertakings made to himself, does not apply in this case; for there is a great difference between incurring an obligation to yourself and incurring one to a whole of which you form a part.

Attention must further be called to the fact that public deliberation, while competent to bind all the subjects to the Sovereign, because of the two different capacities in which each of them may be regarded, cannot, for the opposite reason, bind the Sovereign to itself; and that it is consequently against the nature of the body politic for the Sovereign to impose on itself a law which it cannot infringe. Being able to regard itself in only one capacity, it is in the position of an individual who makes a contract with himself; and this makes it clear that there neither is nor can be any kind of fundamental law binding on the body of the people— not even the social contract itself. This does not mean that the body politic cannot enter into undertakings with others, provided the contract is not infringed by them; for in relation to what is external to it, it becomes a simple being, an individual.

But the body politic or the Sovereign, drawing its being wholly from the sanctity of the contract, can never bind itself, even to an outsider, to do anything derogatory to the original act, for instance, to alienate any part of itself, or to submit to another Sovereign. Violation of the act by which it exists would be self-annihilation; and that which is itself nothing can create nothing.

As soon as this multitude is so united in one body, it is impossible to offend against one of the members without attacking the body, and still more to offend against the body without the members resenting it. Duty and interest therefore equally oblige the two contracting parties to give each other help; and the same men should seek to combine, in their double capacity, all the advantages dependent upon that capacity.

Again, the Sovereign, being formed wholly of the individuals who compose it, neither has nor can have any interest contrary to theirs; and consequently the sovereign power need give no guarantee to its subjects, because it is impossible for the body to wish to hurt all its members. We shall also see later on that it cannot hurt any in particular. The Sovereign, merely by virtue of what it is, is always what it should be.

This, however, is not the case with the relation of the subjects to the Sovereign, which, despite the common interest, would have no security that they would fulfil their undertakings, unless it found means to assure itself of their fidelity.

In fact, each individual, as a man, may have a particular will contrary or dissimilar to the general will which he has as a citizen. His particular interest may speak to him quite differently from the common interest: his absolute and naturally independent existence may make him look upon what he owes to the common cause as a gratuitous contribution, the loss of which will do less harm to others than the payment of it is burdensome to himself; and, regarding the moral person which constitutes the State as a *persona ficta,* because not a man, he may wish to enjoy the rights of citizenship without being ready to fulfil the duties of a subject. The continuance of such an injustice could not but prove the undoing of the body politic.

In order then that the social compact may not be an empty formula, it tacitly includes the undertaking, which alone can give force to the rest, that whoever refuses to obey the general will shall be compelled to do so by the whole body. This means nothing less than that he will be forced to be free; for this is the condition which, by giving each citizen to his country, secures him against all personal dependence. In this lies the key to the working of the political machine; this alone legitimizes civil undertakings, which, without it, would be absurd, tyrannical, and liable to the most frightful abuses.

THE CIVIL STATE

The passage from the state of nature to the civil state produces a very remarkable change in man, by substituting justice for instinct in his conduct, and giving his actions the morality they had formerly lacked. Then only, when the voice of duty takes the place of physical impulses and right of appetite, does man, who so far had considered only himself, find that he is forced to act on different principles, and to consult his reason before listening to his inclinations. Although, in this state, he deprives himself of some advantages which he got from nature, he gains in return others so great, his faculties are so stimulated and developed, his ideas so extended, his feelings so ennobled, and his whole soul so uplifted, that, did not the abuses of this new condition often degrade him below that which he left, he would be bound to bless continually the happy moment which took him from it for ever, and, instead of a stupid and unimaginative animal, made him an intelligent being and a man.

Let us draw up the whole account in terms easily commensurable. What man loses by the social contract is his natural liberty and an unlimited right to everything he tries to get and succeeds in getting; what he gains is civil liberty and the proprietorship of all he possesses. If we are to avoid mistakes in weighing one against the other, we must clearly distinguish natural liberty, which is bounded only by the strength of the individual, from civil liberty, which is limited by the general will; and possession, which is merely the effect of force or the right of the first occupier, from property, which can be founded only on a positive title.

We might, over and above all this, add, to what man acquires in the civil state, moral liberty, which alone makes him truly master of himself; for the mere impulse of appetite is slavery, while obedience to a law which we prescribe to ourselves is liberty. But I have already said too much on this head, and the philosophical meaning of the word liberty does not now concern us.

THE INALIENABILITY
OF SOVEREIGNTY

The first and most important deduction from the principles we have so far laid down is that the general will alone can direct the State according to the object for which it was instituted, i.e. the common good: for if the clashing of particular interests made the establishment of societies necessary, the agreement of these very interests made it possible. The common element in these different interests is what forms the social tie; and, were there no point of agreement between them all, no society could exist. It is solely on the basis of this common interest that every society should be governed.

I hold then that Sovereignty, being nothing less than the exercise of the general will, can never be alienated, and that the Sovereign, who is no less than a collective being, cannot be represented except by himself: the power indeed may be transmitted, but not the will.

In reality, if it is not impossible for a particular will to agree on some point with the general will, it is at least impossible for the agreement to be lasting and constant; for the particular will tends, by its very nature, to partiality, while the general will tends to equality. It is even more impossible to have any guarantee of this agreement; for even if it should always exist, it would be the effect not of art, but of chance. The Sovereign may indeed say: "I now will actually what this man wills, or at least what he says he wills"; but it cannot say: "What he wills to-morrow, I too shall will" because it is absurd for the will to bind itself for the future, nor is it incumbent on any will to consent to anything that is not for the good of the being who wills. If then the people promises simply to obey, by that very act it dissolves itself and loses what makes it a people; the moment a master exists, there is no longer a Sovereign, and from that moment the body politic has ceased to exist.

This does not mean that the commands of the rulers cannot pass for general wills, so long as the Sovereign, being free to oppose them, offers no opposition. In such a case, universal silence is taken to imply the consent of the people. This will be explained later on.

THE INDIVISIBILITY
OF SOVEREIGNTY

Sovereignty, for the same reason as makes it inalienable, is indivisible; for will either is, or is not, general;[3] it is the will either of the body of the people, or only of a part of it. In the first case, the will, when declared, is an act of Sovereignty and constitutes law: in the second, it is merely a particular will, or act of magistracy—at the most a decree.

But our political theorists, unable to divide Sovereignty in principle, divide it according to its object: into force and will; into legislative power and executive power; into rights of taxation, justice, and war; into internal administration and power of foreign treaty. Sometimes they confuse all these sections, and sometimes they distinguish them; they turn the Sovereign into a fantastic being composed of several connected pieces: it is as if they were making man of several bodies, one with eyes, one with arms, another with feet, and each with nothing besides. We are told that the jugglers of Japan dismember a child before the eyes of the spectators; then they throw all the members into the air one after another, and the child falls down alive and whole. The conjuring tricks of our political theorists are very like that; they first dismember the body politic by an illusion worthy of a fair, and then join it together again we know not how.

This error is due to a lack of exact notions concerning the Sovereign authority, and to taking for parts of it what are only emanations from it. Thus, for example, the acts of declaring war and making peace have been regarded as acts of Sovereignty; but this is not the case, as these acts do not constitute law, but merely the application of a law, a particular act which decides how the law applies, as we shall see clearly when the idea attached to the word "law" has been defined.

---

[3] To be general, a will need not always be unanimous; but every vote must be counted: any exclusion is a breach of generality.

If we examined the other divisions in the same manner, we should find, that, whenever Sovereignty seems to be divided, there is an illusion: the rights which are taken as being part of Sovereignty are really all subordinate, and always imply supreme wills of which they only sanction the execution.

It would be impossible to estimate the obscurity this lack of exactness has thrown over the decisions of writers who have dealt with political right, when they have used the principles laid down by them to pass judgment on the respective rights of kings and peoples. Every one can see, in Chapters III and IV of the first book of Grotius, how the learned man and his translator, Barbeyrac, entangle and tie themselves up in their own sophistries, for fear of saying too little or too much of what they think, and so offending the interests they have to conciliate. Grotius, a refugee in France, ill content with his own country, and desirous of paying his court to Louis XIII, to whom his book is dedicated, spares no pains to rob the peoples of all their rights and invest kings with them by every conceivable artifice. This would also have been much to the taste of Barbeyrac, who dedicated his translation to George I of England. But unfortunately the expulsion of James II, which he called his "abdication," compelled him to use all reserve, to shuffle and to tergiversate, in order to avoid making William out a usurper. If these two writers had adopted the true principles, all difficulties would have been removed, and they would have been always consistent; but it would have been a sad truth for them to tell, and would have paid court for them to no one save the people. Moreover, truth is no road to fortune, and the people dispenses neither ambassadorships, nor professorships, nor pensions.

INFALLIBILITY OF
THE GENERAL WILL

It follows from what has gone before that the general will is always right and tends to the public advantage; but it does not follow that the deliberations of the people are always equally correct. Our will is always for our own good, but we do not always see what that is; the people is never corrupted, but it is often deceived, and on such occasions only does it seem to will what is bad.

There is often a great deal of difference between the will of all and the general will; the latter considers only the common interest, while the former takes private interest into account, and is no more than a sum of particular wills: but take away from these same wills the pluses and minuses that cancel one another,[4] and the general will remains as the sum of the differences.

If, when the people, being furnished with adequate information, held its deliberations, the citizens had no communication one with another, the grand total of the small differences would always give the general will, and the decision would always be good. But when factions arise, and partial associations are formed at the expense of the great association, the will of each of these associations becomes general in relation to its members, while it remains particular in relation to the State: it may then be said that there are no longer as many votes as there are men, but only as many as there are associations. The differences become less numerous and give a less general result. Lastly, when one of these associations is so great as to prevail over all the rest, the result is no longer a sum of small differences, but a single difference; in this case there is no longer a general will, and the opinion which prevails is purely particular.

It is therefore essential, if the general will is to be able to express itself, that there should be no partial society within the State, and that each citizen should think only his own thoughts[5] which was indeed

---

[4] "Every interest," says the Marquis d'Argenson, "has different principles. The agreement of two particular interests is formed by opposition to a third." He might have added that the agreement of all interests is formed by opposition to that of each. If there were no different interests, the common interest would be barely felt, as it would encounter no obstacle; all would go on of its own accord, and politics would cease to be an art.

[5] "In fact," says Machiavelli, "there are some divisions that are harmful to a Republic and some that are advantageous. Those which stir up sects and parties are harmful; those attended by neither are advantageous. Since, then, the founder of a Republic cannot help enmities arising, he ought at least to prevent them from growing into sects" (*History of Florence,* Book VII).

the sublime and unique system established by the great Lycurgus. But if there are partial societies, it is best to have as many as possible and to prevent them from being unequal, as was done by Solon, Numa, and Servius. These precautions are the only ones than can guarantee that the general will shall be always enlightened, and that the people shall in no way deceive itself.

LIMITS OF THE SOVEREIGN POWER

If the State is a moral person whose life is in the union of its members, and if the most important of its cares is the care for its own preservation, it must have a universal and compelling force, in order to move and dispose each part as may be most advantageous to the whole. As nature gives each man absolute power over all his members, the social compact gives the body politic absolute power over all its members also; and it is this power which, under the direction of the general will, bears, as I have said, the name of Sovereignty.

But, besides the public person, we have to consider the private persons composing it, whose life and liberty are naturally independent of it. We are bound then to distinguish clearly between the respective rights of the citizens and the Sovereign,[6] and between the duties the former have to fulfil as subjects, and the natural rights they should enjoy as men.

Each man alienates, I admit, by the social compact, only such part of his powers, goods, and liberty as it is important for the community to control; but it must also be granted that the Sovereign is sole judge of what is important.

Every service a citizen can render the State he ought to render as soon as the Sovereign demands it; but the Sovereign, for its part, cannot impose upon its subjects any fetters that are useless to the community, nor can it even wish to do so; for no more by the law of reason than by the law of nature can anything occur without a cause.

The undertakings which bind us to the social body are obligatory only because they are mutual; and their nature is such that in fulfilling them we cannot work for others without working for ourselves. Why is it that the general will is always in the right, and that all continually will the happiness of each one, unless it is because there is not a man who does not think of "each" as meaning him, and consider himself in voting for all? This proves that equality of rights and the idea of justice which such equality creates originate in the preference each man gives to himself, and accordingly in the very nature of man. It proves that the general will, to be really such, must be general in its object as well as its essence; that it must both come from all and apply to all; and that it loses its natural rectitude when it is directed to some particular and determinate object, because in such a case we are judging of something foreign to us, and have no true principle of equity to guide us.

Indeed, as soon as a question of particular fact or right arises on a point not previously regulated by a general convention, the matter becomes contentious. It is a case in which the individuals concerned are one party, and the public the other, but in which I can see neither the law that ought to be followed nor the judge who ought to give the decision. In such a case, it would be absurd to propose to refer the question to an express decision of the general will, which can be only the conclusion reached by one of the parties and in consequence will be, for the other party, merely an external and particular will, inclined on this occasion to injustice and subject to error. Thus, just as a particular will cannot stand for the general will, the general will, in turn, changes its nature, when its object is particular, and, as general, cannot pronounce on a man or a fact. When, for instance, the people of Athens nominated or displaced its rulers, decreed honours to one, and imposed penalties on another, and, by a multitude of particular decrees, exercised all the functions of government indiscriminately, it had in such cases no longer a general will in the strict sense; it was acting no longer as Sovereign, but as magistrate. This will seem contrary to current views; but I must be given time to expound my own.

---

[6] Attentive readers, do not, I pray, be in a hurry to charge me with contradicting myself. The terminology made it unavoidable, considering the poverty of the language; but wait and see.

It should be seen from the foregoing that what makes the will general is less the number of votes than the common interest uniting them; for, under this system, each necessarily submits to the conditions he imposes on others: and this admirable agreement between interest and justice gives to the common deliberations an equitable character which at once vanishes when any particular question is discussed, in the absence of a common interest to unite and identify the ruling of the judge with that of the party.

From whatever side we approach our principle, we reach the same conclusion, that the social compact sets up among the citizens an equality of such a kind, that they all bind themselves to observe the same conditions and should therefore all enjoy the same rights. Thus, from the very nature of the compact, every act of Sovereignty, i.e. every authentic act of the general will, binds or favours all the citizens equally; so that the Sovereign recognizes only the body of the nation, and draws no distinctions between those of whom it is made up. What, then, strictly speaking, is an act of Sovereignty? It is not a convention between a superior and an inferior, but a conviction between the body and each of its members. It is legitimate, because based on the social contract, and equitable, because common to all; useful, because it can have no other object than the common good, and stable, because guaranteed by the public force and the supreme power. So long as the subjects have to submit only to conventions of this sort, they obey no one but their own will; and to ask how far the respective rights of the Sovereign and the citizens extend, is to ask up to what point the latter can enter into undertakings with themselves, each with all, and all with each.

We can see from this that the sovereign power, absolute, sacred, and inviolable as it is, does not and cannot exceed the limits of general conventions, and that every man may dispose at will of such goods and liberty as these conventions leave him; so that the Sovereign never has a right to lay more charges on one subject than on another, because, in that case, the question becomes particular, and ceases to be within its competency.

When these distinctions have once been admitted, it is seen to be so untrue that there is, in the social contract, any real renunciation on the part of the individuals, that the position in which they find themselves as a result of the contract is really preferable to that in which they were before. Instead of a renunciation, they have made an advantageous exchange: instead of an uncertain and precarious way of living they have got one that is better and more secure; instead of natural independence they have got liberty, instead of the power to harm others security for themselves, and instead of their strength, which others might overcome, a right which social union makes invincible. Their very life, which they have devoted to the State, is by it constantly protected; and when they risk it in the State's defence, what more are they doing than giving back what they have received from it? What are they doing that they would not do more often and with greater danger in the state of nature, in which they would inevitably have to fight battles at the peril of their lives in defence of that which is the means of their preservation? All have indeed to fight when their country needs them; but then no one has ever to fight for himself. Do we not gain something by running, on behalf of what gives us our security, only some of the risks we should have to run for ourselves, as soon as we lost it?

LAW

By the social compact we have given the body politic existence and life; we have now by legislation to give it movement and will. For the original act by which the body is formed and united still in no respect determines what it ought to do for its preservation.

What is well and in conformity with order is so by the nature of things and independently of human conventions. All justice comes from God, who is its sole source; but if we knew how to receive so high an inspiration, we should need neither government nor laws. Doubtless, there is a universal justice emanating from reason alone; but this justice, to be admitted among us, must be mutual. Humanly speaking, in default of natural sanctions, the laws of justice are ineffective among men: they merely make for the good of the wicked and the undoing of the just, when the just man observes them towards everybody and nobody observes them towards him. Conventions and laws are therefore needed to join rights to duties and refer justice to its object. In the state of nature, where everything is common, I owe nothing to him whom I have promised nothing; I recognize as belonging to others only what is of no use to me. In the state of society all rights are fixed by law, and the case becomes different.

But what, after all, is a law? As long as we remain satisfied with attaching purely metaphysical ideas to the word, we shall go on arguing without arriving at an understanding; and when we have defined a law of nature, we shall be no nearer the definition of a law of the State,

I have already said that there can be no general will directed to a particular object. Such an object must be either within or outside the State. If outside, a will which is alien to it cannot be, in relation to it, general; if within, it is part of the State, and in that case there arises a relation between whole and part which makes them two separate beings, of which the part is one, and the whole minus the part the other. But the whole minus a part cannot be the whole; and while this relation persists, there can be no whole, but only two unequal parts; and it follows that the will of one is no longer in any respect general in relation to the other.

But when the whole people decrees for the whole people, it is considering only itself; and if a relation is then formed, it is between two aspects of the entire object, without there being any division of the whole. In that case the matter about which the decree is made is, like the decreeing will, general. This act is what I call a law.

When I say that the object of laws is always general, I mean that law considers subjects *en masse* and actions in the abstract, and never a particular person or action. Thus the law may indeed decree that there shall be privileges, but cannot confer them on anybody by name. It may set up several classes of citizens, and even lay down the qualifications for membership of these classes, but it cannot nominate such and such persons as belonging to them; it may establish a monarchical government and hereditary succession, but it cannot choose a king, or nominate a royal family. In a word,

no function which has a particular object belongs to the legislative power.

On this view, we at once see that it can no longer be asked whose business it is to make laws, since they are acts of the general will; nor whether the prince is above the law, since he is a member of the State; nor whether the law can be unjust, since no one is unjust to himself; nor how we can be both free and subject to the laws, since they are but registers of our wills.

We see further that, as the law unites universality of will with universality of object, what a man, whoever he be, commands of his own motion cannot be a law; and even what the Sovereign commands with regard to a particular matter is no nearer being a law, but is a decree, an act, not of sovereignty, but of magistracy.

I therefore give the name "Republic" to every State that is governed by laws, no matter what the form of its administration may be: for only in such a case does the public interest govern, and the *res publica* rank as a *reality*. Every legitimate government is republican;[7] what government is I will explain later on.

Laws are, properly speaking, only the conditions of civil association. The people, being subject to the laws, ought to be their author: the conditions of the society ought to be regulated solely by those who come together to form it. But how are they to regulate them? Is it to be by common agreement, by a sudden inspiration? Has the body politic an organ to declare its will? Who can give it the foresight to formulate and announce its acts in advance? Or how is it to announce them in the hour of need? How can a blind multitude, which often does not know what it wills, because it rarely knows what is good for it, carry out for itself so great and difficult an enterprise as a system of legislation? Of itself the people wills always the good, but of itself it by no means always sees it. The general will is always in the right, but the judgment which guides it

---

[7] I understand by this word, not merely an aristocracy or a democracy, but generally any government directed by the general will, which is the law. To be legitimate, the government must be, not one with the Sovereign, but its minister. In such a case even a monarchy is a Republic.

is not always enlightened. It must be got to see objects as they are, and sometimes as they ought to appear to it; it must be shown the good road it is in search of, secured from the seductive influences of individual wills, taught to see times and spaces as a series, and made to weigh the attractions of present and sensible advantages against the danger of distant and hidden evils. The individuals see the good they reject; the public wills the good it does not see. All stand equally in need of guidance. The former must be compelled to bring their wills into conformity with their reason; the latter must be taught to know what it wills. If that is done, public enlightenment leads to the union of understanding and will in the social body: the parts are made to work exactly together, and the whole is raised to its highest power. This makes a legislator necessary.

THE LEGISLATOR

In order to discover the rules of society best suited to nations, a superior intelligence beholding all the passions of men without experiencing any of them would be needed. This intelligence would have to be wholly unrelated to our nature, while knowing it through and through; its happiness would have to be independent of us, and yet ready to occupy itself with ours; and lastly, it would have, in the march of time, to look forward to a distant glory, and, working in one century, to be able to enjoy in the next.[8] It would take gods to give men laws.

What Caligula argued from the facts, Plato, in the dialogue called the *Politicus,* argued in defining the civil or kingly man, on the basis of right. But if great princes are rare, how much more so are great legislators! The former have only to follow the pattern which the latter have to lay down. The legislator is the engineer who invents the machine, the prince merely the mechanic who sets it up and makes it go. "At the birth of societies," says Montesquieu, "the rulers

of Republics establish institutions, and afterwards the institutions mould the rulers."[9]

He who dares to undertake the making of a people's institutions ought to feel himself capable, so to speak, of changing human nature, of transforming each individual, who is by himself a complete and solitary whole, into part of a greater whole from which he in a manner receives his life and being; of altering man's constitution for the purpose of strengthening it; and of substituting a partial and moral existence for the physical and independent existence nature has conferred on us all. He must, in a word, take away from man his own resources and give him instead new ones alien to him, and incapable of being made use of without the help of other men. The more completely these natural resources are annihilated, the greater and more lasting are those which he acquires, and the more stable and perfect the new institutions; so that if each citizen is nothing and can do nothing without the rest, and the resources acquired by the whole are equal or superior to the aggregate of the resources of all the individuals, it may be said that legislation is at the highest possible point of perfection.

The legislator occupies in every respect an extraordinary position in the State. If he should do so by reason of his genius, he does so no less by reason of his office, which is neither magistracy, nor Sovereignty. This office, which sets up the Republic, nowhere enters into its constitution; it is an individual and superior function, which has nothing in common with human empire; for if he who holds command over men ought not to have command over the laws, he who has command over the laws ought not any more to have it over men; or else his laws would be the ministers of his passions and would often merely serve to perpetuate his injustices: his private aims would inevitably mar the sanctity of his work.

When Lycurgus gave laws to his country, he began by resigning the throne. It was the custom of most Greek towns to entrust the establishment of their laws to foreigners. The Republics of modern Italy in many cases followed this examples; Geneva did

---

[8] A people becomes famous only when its legislation begins to decline. We do not know for how many centuries the system of Lycurgus made the Spartans happy before the rest of Greece took any notice of it.

---

[9] Montesquieu, *The Greatness and Decadence of the Romans,* chap. i.

the same and profited by it.[10] Rome, when it was most prosperous, suffered a revival of all the crimes of tyranny, and was brought to the verge of destruction, because it put the legislative authority and the sovereign power into the same hands.

Nevertheless, the decemvirs themselves never claimed the right to pass any law merely on their own authority. "Nothing we propose to you," they said to the people, "can pass into law without your consent. Romans, be yourselves the authors of the laws which are to make you happy."

He, therefore, who draws up the laws has, or should have, no right of legislation, and the people cannot, even if it wishes, deprive itself of this incommunicable right, because, according to the fundamental compact, only the general will can bind the individuals, and there can be no assurance that a particular will is in conformity with the general will, until it has been put to the free vote of the people. This I have said already; but it is worth while to repeat it.

Thus in the task of legislation we find together two things which appear to be incompatible: an enterprise too difficult for human powers, and, for its execution, an authority that is no authority.

There is a further difficulty that deserves attention. Wise men, if they try to speak their language to the common herd instead of its own, cannot possibly make themselves understood. There are a thousand kinds of ideas which it is impossible to translate into popular language. Conceptions that are too general and objects that are too remote are equally out of its range: each individual, having no taste for any other plan of government than that which suits his particular interest, finds it difficult to realize the advantages he might hope to draw from the continual privations good laws impose. For a young people to be able to relish sound principles of political theory and follow the fundamental rules of statecraft, the effect

would have to become the cause; the social spirit, which should be created by these institutions, would have to preside over their very foundation; and men would have to be before law what they should become by means of law. The legislator therefore, being unable to appeal to either force or reason, must have recourse to an authority of a different order, capable of constraining without violence and persuading without convincing.

This is what has, in all ages, compelled the fathers of nations to have recourse to divine intervention and credit the gods with their own wisdom, in order that the peoples, submitting to the laws of the State as to those of nature, and recognizing the same power in the formation of the city as in that of man, might obey freely, and bear with docility the yoke of the public happiness.

This sublime reason, far above the range of the common herd, is that whose decisions the legislator puts into the mouth of the immortals, in order to constrain by divine authority those whom human prudence could not move.[11] But it is not anybody who can make the gods speak, or get himself believed when he proclaims himself their interpreter. The great soul of the legislator is the only miracle that can prove his mission. Any man may grave tablets of stone, or buy an oracle, or feign secret intercourse with some divinity, or train a bird to whisper in his ear, or find other vulgar ways of imposing on the people. He whose knowledge goes no further may perhaps gather round him a band of fools; but he will never found an empire, and his extravagances will quickly perish with him. Idle tricks form a passing tie; only wisdom can make it lasting. The Judaic law, which still subsists, and that of the child of Ishmael, which, for ten centuries, has ruled half the world, still proclaim the great men who laid them down; and, while the pride of philosophy or the blind spirit of faction sees in them no more

---

[10] Those who know Calvin only as a theologian much underestimate the extent of his genius. The codification of our wise edicts, in which he played a large part, does him no less honour than his *Institutes*. Whatever revolution time may bring in our religion, so long as the spirit of patriotism and liberty still lives among us, the memory of this great man will be for ever blessed.

[11] "In truth," says Machiavelli, "there has never been, in any country, an extraordinary legislator who has not had recourse to God; for otherwise his laws would not have been accepted: there are, in fact, many useful truths of which a wise man may have knowledge without their having in themselves such clear reasons for their being so as to be able to convince others" (*Discourses on Livy,* Bk. V, chap. xi).

than lucky impostures, the true political theorist admires, in the institutions they set up, the great and powerful genius which presides over things made to endure.

We should not, with Warburton, conclude from this that politics and religion have among us a common object, but that, in the first periods of nations, the one is used as an instrument for the other.

THE PEOPLE

As nature has set bounds to the stature of a well-made man, and, outside those limits, makes nothing but giants or dwarfs, similarly, for the constitution of a State to be at its best, it is possible to fix limits that will make it neither too large for good government, nor too small for self-maintenance. In every body politic there is a maximum strength which it cannot exceed and which it only loses by increasing in size. Every extension of the social tie means its relaxation; and, generally speaking, a small State is stronger in proportion than a great one.

A thousand arguments could be advanced in favour of this principle. First, long distances make administration more difficult, just as a weight becomes heavier at the end of a longer lever. Administration therefore becomes more and more burdensome as the distance grows greater; for, in the first place, each city has its own, which is paid for by the people: each district its own, still paid for by the people: then comes each province, and then the great governments, satrapies, and viceroyalties, always costing more the higher you go, and always at the expense of the unfortunate people. Last of all comes the supreme administration, which eclipses all the rest. All these overcharges are a continual drain upon the subjects; so far from being better governed by all these different orders, they are worse governed than if there were only a single authority over them. In the meantime, there scarce remain resources enough to meet emergencies; and, when recourse must be had to these, the State is always on the eve of destruction.

This is not all; not only has the government less vigour and promptitude for securing the observance of the laws, preventing nuisances, correcting abuses, and guarding against seditious undertakings begun in distant places; the people has less affection for its rulers, whom it never sees, for its country, which, to its eyes, seems like the world, and for its fellow citizens, most of whom are unknown to it. The same laws cannot suit so many diverse provinces with different customs, situated in the most various climates, and incapable of enduring a uniform government. Different laws lead only to trouble and confusion among peoples which, living under the same rulers and in constant communication one with another, intermingle and intermarry, and, coming under the sway of new customs, never know if they can call their very patrimony their own. Talent is buried, virtue unknown, and vice unpunished, among such a multitude of men who do not know one another, gathered together in one place at the seat of the central administration. The leaders, overwhelmed with business, see nothing for themselves; the State is governed by clerks. Finally, the measures which have to be taken to maintain the general authority, which all these distant officials wish to escape or to impose upon, absorb all the energy of the public, so that there is none left for the happiness of the people. There is hardly enough to defend it when need arises, and thus a body which is too big for its constitution gives way and falls crushed under its own weight.

Again, the State must assure itself a safe foundation, if it is to have stability, and to be able to resist the shocks it cannot help experiencing, as well as the efforts it will be forced to make for its maintenance; for all peoples have a kind of centrifugal force that makes them continually act one against another, and tend to aggrandize themselves at their neighbours' expense, like the vortices of Descartes. Thus the weak run the risk of being soon swallowed up; and it is almost impossible for any one to preserve itself except by putting itself in a state of equilibrium with all, so that the pressure is on all sides practically equal.

It may therefore be seen that there are reasons for expansion and reasons for contraction; and it is no small part of the statesman's skill to hit between them the mean that is most favourable to the preservation of the State. It may be said that the reason for expansion, being merely external and relative, ought to be subordinate to the reasons for contraction, which are internal and absolute. A strong and healthy constitution is the first thing to look for; and it is better to count on the vigour which comes of good government than on the resources a great territory furnishes.

It may be added that there have been known States so constituted that the necessity of making conquests entered into their very constitution, and that, in order to maintain themselves, they were forced to expand ceaselessly. It may be that they congratulated themselves greatly on this fortunate necessity, which none the less indicated to them, along with the limits of their greatness, the inevitable moment of their fall.

GOVERNMENT IN GENERAL

I warn the reader that this chapter requires careful reading, and that I am unable to make myself clear to those who refuse to be attentive.

Every free action is produced by the concurrence of two causes; one moral, i.e. the will which determines the act; the other physical, i.e. the power which executes it. When I walk towards an object, it is necessary first that I should will to go there, and, in the second place, that my feet should carry me. If a paralytic wills to run and an active man wills not to, they will both stay where they are. The body politic has the same motive powers; here too force and will are distinguished, will under the name of legislative power and force under that of executive power. Without their concurrence, nothing is, or should be, done.

We have seen that the legislative power belongs to the people, and can belong to it alone. It may, on the other hand, readily be seen, from the principles laid down above, that the executive power cannot belong to the generality as legislature or Sovereign, because it consists wholly of particular acts which fall outside the competency of the law, and consequently of the Sovereign, whose acts must always be laws.

The public force therefore needs an agent of its own to bind it together and set it to work under the direction of the general will, to serve as a means of communication between the State and the Sovereign, and to do for the collective person more or less what the union of soul and body does for man.

Here we have what is, in the State, the basis of government, often wrongly confused with the Sovereign, whose minister it is.

What then is government? An intermediate body set up between the subjects and the Sovereign, to secure their mutual correspondence, charged with the execution of the laws and the maintenance of liberty, both civil and political.

The members of this body are called magistrates or *kings,* that is to say *governors,* and the whole body bears the name *prince.*[12] Thus those who hold that the act, by which a people puts itself under a prince, is not a contract, are certainly right. It is simply and solely a commission, an employment, in which the rulers, mere officials of the Sovereign, exercise in their own name the power of which it makes them depositaries. This power it can limit, modify, or recover at pleasure; for the alienation of such a right is incompatible with the nature of the social body, and contrary to the end of association.

I call then *government,* or supreme administration, the legitimate exercise of the executive power, and prince or magistrate the man or the body entrusted with that administration.

In government reside the intermediate forces whose relations make up that of the whole to the whole, or of the Sovereign to the State. This last relation may be represented as that between the extreme terms of the continuous proportion, which has government as its mean proportional. The government gets from the Sovereign the orders it gives the people, and, for the State to be properly balanced, there must, when everything is reckoned in, be equality between the product or power of the government taken in itself, and the product or power of the citizens, who are on the one hand sovereign and on the other subject.

Furthermore, none of these three terms can be altered without the equality being instantly destroyed. If the Sovereign desires to govern, or the magistrate to give laws, or if the subjects refuse to obey, disorder takes the place of regularity, force and will no longer act together, and the State is dissolved

---

[12] Thus at Venice the College, even in the absence of the Doge, is called "Most Serene Prince."

and falls into despotism or anarchy. Lastly, as there is only one mean proportional between each relation, there is also only one good government possible for a State. But, as countless events may change the relations of a people, not only may different governments be good for different peoples, but also for the same people at different times.

In attempting to give some idea of the various relations that may hold between these two extreme terms, I shall take as an example the number of a people, which is the most easily expressible.

Suppose the State is composed of ten thousand citizens. The Sovereign can only be considered collectively and as a body; but each member, as being a subject, is regarded as an individual: thus the Sovereign is to the subject as ten thousand to one, i.e. each member of the State has as his share only a ten-thousandth part of the sovereign authority, although he is wholly under its control. If the people numbers a hundred thousand, the condition of the subject undergoes no change, and each equally is under the whole authority of the laws, while his vote, being reduced to one hundred thousandth part, has ten times less influence in drawing them up. The subject therefore remaining always a unit, the relation between him and the Sovereign increases with the number of citizens. From this it follows that, the larger the State, the less the liberty.

When I say the relation increases, I mean that it grows more unequal. Thus the greater it is in the geometrical sense, the less relation there is in the ordinary sense of the word. In the former sense, the relation, considered according to quantity, is expressed by the quotient; in the latter, considered according to identity, it is reckoned by similarity.

Now, the less relation the particular wills have to the general will, that is, morals and manners to laws, the more should the repressive force be increased The government, then, to be good, should be proportionately stronger as the people is more numerous.

On the other hand, as the growth of the State gives the depositaries of the public authority more temptations and chances of abusing their power, the greater the force with which the government ought to be endowed for keeping the people in hand, the greater too should be the force at the disposal of the Sovereign for keeping the government in hand. I am speaking, not of absolute force, but of the relative force of the different parts of the state.

It follows from this double relation that the continuous proportion between the Sovereign, the prince, and the people, is by no means an arbitrary idea, but a necessary consequence of the nature of the body politic. It follows further that, one of the extreme terms, viz. the people, as subject, being fixed and represented by unity, whenever the duplicate ratio increases or diminishes, the simple ratio does the same, and is changed accordingly. From this we see that there is not a single unique and absolute form of government, but as many governments differing in nature as there are States differing in size.

If, ridiculing this system, any one were to say that, in order to find the mean proportional and give form to the body of the government, it is only necessary, according to me, to find the square root of the number of the people, I should answer that I am here taking this number only as an instance; that the relations of which I am speaking are not measured by the number of men alone, but generally by the amount of action, which is a combination of a multitude of causes; and that, further, if, to save words, I borrow for a moment the terms of geometry, I am none the less well aware that moral quantities do not allow of geometrical accuracy.

The government is on a small scale what the body politic which includes it is on a great one. It is a moral person endowed with certain faculties, active like the Sovereign and passive like the State, and capable of being resolved into other similar relations. This accordingly gives rise to a new proportion, within which there is yet another, according to the arrangement of the magistracies, till an indivisible middle term is reached, i.e. a single ruler or supreme magistrate, who may be represented, in the midst of this progression, as the unity between the fractional and the ordinal series.

Without encumbering ourselves with this multiplication of terms, let us rest content with regarding government as a new body within the State, distinct from the people and the Sovereign, and intermediate between them.

There is between these two bodies this essential difference, that the State exists by itself, and the government only through the Sovereign. Thus the dominant will of the prince is, or should be, nothing but the general will or the law; his force is only the public force concentrated in his hands, and, as soon as he tries to base any absolute and independent act on his own authority, the tie that binds the whole together begins to be loosened. If finally the prince should come to have a particular will more active than the will of the Sovereign, and should employ the public force in his hands in obedience to this particular will, there would be, so to speak, two Sovereigns, one rightful and the other actual, the social union would evaporate instantly, and the body politic would be dissolved.

However, in order that the government may have a true existence and a real life distinguishing it from the body of the State, and in order that all its members may be able to act in concert and fulfil the end for which it was set up, it must have a particular personality, a sensibility common to its members, and a force and will of its own making for its preservation. This particular existence implies assemblies, councils, power of deliberation and decision, rights, titles, and privileges belonging exclusively to the prince and making the office of magistrate more honourable in proportion as it is more troublesome. The difficulties lie in the manner of so ordering this subordinate whole within the whole, that it in no way alters the general constitution by affirmation of its own, and always distinguishes the particular force it possesses, which is destined to aid in its preservation, from the public force, which is destined to the preservation of the State; and, in a word, is always ready to sacrifice the government to the people, and never to sacrifice the people to the government.

Furthermore, although the artificial body of the government is the work of another artificial body, and has, we may say, only a borrowed and subordinate life, this does not prevent it from being able to act with more or less vigour or promptitude, or from being, so to speak, in more or less robust health. Finally, without departing directly from the end for which it was instituted, it may deviate more or less from it, according to the manner of its constitution.

From all these differences arise the various relations which the government ought to bear to the body of the State, according to the accidental and particular relations by which the State itself is modified, for often the government that is best in itself will become the most pernicious, if the relations in which it stands have altered according to the defects of the body politic to which it belongs.

DEMOCRACY

He who makes the law knows better than any one else how it should be executed and interpreted. It seems then impossible to have a better constitution than that in which the executive and legislative powers are united; but this very fact renders the government in certain respects inadequate, because things which should be distinguished are confounded, and the prince and the Sovereign, being the same person, form, so to speak, no more than a government without government.

It is not good for him who makes the laws to execute them, or for the body of the people to turn its attention away from a general standpoint and devote it to particular objects. Nothing is more dangerous than the influence of private interests in public affairs, and the abuse of the laws by the government is a less evil than the corruption of the legislator, which is the inevitable sequel to a particular standpoint. In such a case, the State being altered in substance, all reformation becomes impossible. A people that would never misuse governmental powers would never misuse independence; a people that would always govern well would not need to be governed.

If we take the term in the strict sense, there never has been a real democracy, and there never will be. It is against the natural order for the many to govern and the few to be governed. It is unimaginable that the people should remain continually assembled to devote their time to public affairs, and it is clear that they cannot set up commissions for that purpose without the form of administration being changed.

In fact, I can confidently lay down as a principle that, when the functions of government are shared by several tribunals, the less numerous sooner or later acquire the greatest authority, if only because they are in position to expedite affairs, and power thus naturally comes into their hands.

Besides, how many conditions that are difficult to unite does such a government presuppose! First, a very small State, where the people can readily be got together and where each citizen can with ease know all the rest; secondly, great simplicity of manners, to prevent business from multiplying and raising thorny problems; next, a large measure of equality in rank and fortune, without which equality of rights and authority cannot long subsist; lastly, little or no luxury—for luxury either comes of riches or makes them necessary; it corrupts at once rich and poor, the rich by possession and the poor by covetousness; it sells the country to softness and vanity, and takes away from the State all its citizens, to make them slaves one to another, and one and all to public opinion.

This is why a famous writer has made virtue the fundamental principle of Republics; for all these conditions could not exist without virtue. But, for want of the necessary distinctions, that great thinker was often inexact, and sometimes obscure, and did not see that, the sovereign authority being everywhere the same, the same principle should be found in every well-constituted State, in a greater or less degree, it is true, according to the form of the government.

It may be added that there is no government so subject to civil wars and intestine agitations as democratic or popular government, because there is none which has so strong and continual a tendency to change to another form, or which demands more vigilance and courage for its maintenance as it is. Under such a constitution above all, the citizen should arm himself with strength and constancy, and say, every day of his life, what a virtuous Count Palatine said in the Diet of Poland: "Malo periculosam libertatem quam quieturn servitium."

Were there a people of gods, their government would be democratic. So perfect a government is not for men.

DEPUTIES OR REPRESENTATIVES

As soon as public service ceases to be the chief business of the citizens, and they would rather serve with their money than with their persons, the State is not far from its fall. When it is necessary to march out to war, they pay troops and stay at home: when it is necessary to meet in council, they name deputies and stay at home. By reason of idleness and money, they end by having soldiers to enslave their country and representatives to sell it.

It is through the hustle of commerce and the arts, through the greedy self-interest of profit, and through softness and love of amenities that personal services are replaced by money payments. Men surrender a part of their profits in order to have time to increase them at leisure. Make gifts of money, and you will not be long without chains. The word "finance" is a slavish word, unknown in the city-state. In a country that is truly free, the citizens do everything with their own arms and nothing by means of money; so far from paying to be exempted from their duties, they would even pay for the privilege of fulfilling them themselves. I am far from taking the common view: I hold enforced labour to be less opposed to liberty than taxes.

The better the constitution of a State is, the more do public affairs encroach on private in the minds of the citizens. Private affairs are even of much less importance, because the aggregate of the common happiness furnishes a greater proportion of that of each individual, so that there is less for him to seek in particular cares. In a well-ordered city every man flies to the assemblies: under a bad government no one cares to stir a step to get to them, because no one is interested in what happens there, because it is foreseen that the general will not prevail, and lastly because domestic cares are all-absorbing. Good laws lead to the making of better ones; bad ones bring about worse. As soon as any man says of the affairs of the State *What does it matter to me?* the State may be given up for lost.

The lukewarmness of patriotism, the activity of private interest, the vastness of States, conquest, and the abuse of government suggested the method of having deputies or representatives of the people in the national assemblies. These are what, in some countries, men have presumed to call the Third Estate. Thus the individual interest of two orders is put first and second;

the public interest occupies only the third place.

Sovereignty, for the same reason as makes it inalienable, cannot be represented; it lies essentially in the general will, and will does not admit of representation: it is either the same, or other; there is no intermediate possibility. The deputies of the people, therefore, are not and cannot be its representatives: they are merely its stewards, and can carry through no definitive acts. Every law the people has not ratified in person is null and void—is, in fact, not a law. The people of England regards itself as free; but it is grossly mistaken; it is free only during the election of members of parliament. As soon as they are elected, slavery overtakes it, and it is nothing. The use it makes of the short moments of liberty it enjoys shows indeed that it deserves to lose them.

The idea of representation is modern; it comes to us from feudal government, from that iniquitous and absurd system which degrades humanity and dishonours the name of man. In ancient republics and even in monarchies, the people never had representatives; the word itself was unknown. It is very singular that in Rome, where the tribunes were so sacrosanct, it was never even imagined that they could usurp the functions of the people, and that in the midst of so great a multitude they never attempted to pass on their own authority a single *plebiscitum*. We can, however, form an idea of the difficulties caused sometimes by the people being so numerous, from what happened in the time of the Gracchi, when some of the citizens had to cast their votes from the roofs of buildings.

Where right and liberty are everything, disadvantages count for nothing. Among this wise people everything was given its just value, its lictors were allowed to do what its tribunes would never have dared to attempt; for it had no fear that its lictors would try to represent it.

To explain, however, in what way the tribunes did sometimes represent it, it is enough to conceive how the government represents the Sovereign. Law being purely the declaration of the general will, it is clear that, in the exercise of the legislative power, the people cannot be represented; but in that of the executive power, which is only the force that is applied to give the law effect, it both can and should be represented. We thus see that if we looked closely into the matter we should find that very few nations have any laws. However that may be, it is certain that the tribunes, possessing no executive power, could never represent the Roman people by right of the powers entrusted to them, but only by usurping those of the senate.

In Greece, all that the people had to do, it did for itself; it was constantly assembled in the public square. The Greeks lived in a mild climate; they had no natural greed; slaves did their work for them; their great concern was with liberty. Lacking the same advantages, how can you preserve the same rights? Your severer climates add to your needs;[13] for half the year your public squares are uninhabitable; the flatness of your languages unfits them for being heard in the open air; you sacrifice more for profit than for liberty, and fear slavery less than poverty.

What then? Is liberty maintained only by the help of slavery? It may be so. Extremes meet. Everything that is not in the course of nature has its disadvantages, civil society most of all. There are some unhappy circumstances in which we can only keep our liberty at others' expense, and where the citizen can be perfectly free only when the slave is most a slave. Such was the case with Sparta. As for you, modern peoples, you have no slaves, but you are slaves yourselves; you pay for their liberty with your own. It is in vain that you boast of this preference; I find in it more cowardice than humanity.

I do not mean by all this that it is necessary to have slaves, or that the right of slavery is legitimate: I am merely giving the reason why modern peoples, believing themselves to be free, have representatives, while ancient peoples had none. In any case, the moment a people allows itself to be represented, it is no longer free: it no longer exists.

All things considered, I do not see that it is possible henceforth for the Sovereign to

---

[13] To adopt in cold countries the luxury and effeminacy of the East is to desire to submit to its chains; it is indeed to bow to them far more inevitably in our case than in theirs.

preserve among us the exercise of its rights, unless the city is very small. But if it is very small, it will be conquered? No. I will show later on how the external strength of a great people may be combined with the convenient polity and good order of a small State.

VOTING

It may be seen that the way in which general business is managed may give a clear enough indication of the actual state of morals and the health of the body politic. The more concert reigns in the assemblies, that is, the nearer opinion approaches unanimity, the greater is the dominance of the general will. On the other hand, long debates, dissensions, and tumult proclaim the ascendancy of particular interests and the decline of the State.

This seems less clear when two or more orders enter into the constitution, as patricians and plebeians did at Rome; for quarrels between these two orders often disturbed the comitia, even in the best days of the Republic. But the exception is rather apparent than real; for then, through the defect that is inherent in the body politic, there were, so to speak, two States in one, and what is not true of the two together is true of either separately. Indeed, even in the most stormy times, the *plebiscita* of the people, when the senate did not interfere with them, always went through quietly and by large majorities. The citizens having but one interest, the people had but a single will.

At the other extremity of the circle, unanimity recurs; this is the case when the citizens, having fallen into servitude, have lost both liberty and will. Fear and flattery then change votes into acclamation; deliberation ceases, and only worship or malediction is left. Such was the vile manner in which the senate expressed its views under the emperors. It did so sometimes with absurd precautions. Tacitus observes that, under Otho, the senators, while they heaped curses on Vitellius, contrived at the same time to make a deafening noise, in order that, should he ever become their master, he might not know what each of them had said.

On these various considerations depend the rules by which the methods of counting votes and comparing opinions should be regulated, according as the general will is more or less easy to discover, and the State more or less in its decline.

There is but one law which, from its nature, needs unanimous consent. This is the social compact; for civil association is the most voluntary of all acts. Every man being born free and his own master, no one, under any pretext whatsoever, can make any man subject without his consent. To decide that the son of a slave is born a slave is to decide that he is not born a man.

If then there are opponents when the social compact is made, their opposition does not invalidate the contract, but merely prevents them from being included in it. They are foreigners among citizens. When the State is instituted, residence constitutes consent; to dwell within its territory is to submit to the Sovereign.[14]

Apart from this primitive contract, the vote of the majority always binds all the rest. This follows from the contract itself. But it is asked how a man can be both free and forced to conform to wills that are not his own. How are the opponents at once free and subject to laws they have not agreed to?

I retort that the question is wrongly put. The citizen gives his consent to all the laws, including those which are passed in spite of his opposition, and even those which punish him when he dares to break any of them. The constant will of all the members of the State is the general will; by virtue of it they are citizens and free.[15] When in the popular assembly a law is proposed, what the people is asked is not exactly whether it approves or rejects the proposal, but whether it is in conformity with the general will, which is their will. Each man, in giving his vote,

---

[14] This should of course be understood as applying to a free State; for elsewhere family, goods, lack of a refuge, necessity, or violence may detain a man in a country against his will; and then his dwelling there no longer by itself implies his consent to the contract or to its violation.

[15] At Genoa, the word "Liberty" may be read over the front of the prisons and on the chains of the galley-slaves. This application of the device is good and just. It is indeed only malefactors of all estates who prevent the citizen from being free. In the country in which all such men were in the galleys, the most perfect liberty would be enjoyed.

states his opinion on that point; and the general will is found by counting votes. When therefore the opinion that is contrary to my own prevails, this proves neither more nor less than that I was mistaken, and that what I thought to be the general will was not so. If my particular opinion had carried the day I should have achieved the opposite of what was my will; and it is in that case that I should not have been free.

This presupposes, indeed, that all the qualities of the general will still reside in the majority: when they cease to do so, whatever side a man may take, liberty is no longer possible.

In my earlier demonstration of how particular wills are substituted for the general will in public deliberation, I have adequately pointed out the practicable methods of avoiding this abuse; and I shall have more to say of them later on. I have also given the principles for determining the proportional number of votes for declaring that will. A difference of one vote destroys equality; a single opponent destroys unanimity; but between equality and unanimity, there are several grades of unequal division, at each of which this proportion may be fixed in accordance with the condition and the needs of the body politic.

There are two general rules that may serve to regulate this relation. First, the more grave and important the questions discussed, the nearer should the opinion that is to prevail approach unanimity. Secondly, the more the matter in hand calls for speed, the smaller the prescribed difference in the numbers of votes may be allowed to become: where an instant decision has to be reached, a majority of one vote should be enough. The first of these two rules seems more in harmony with the laws, and the second with practical affairs. In any case, it is the combination of them that gives the best proportions for determining the majority necessary.

CHAPTER NINE

MILL

Alexis de Tocqueville's *Democracy in America* (1835–1840), translated into English almost immediately after publication, aroused considerable attention on both sides of the Atlantic. One of the most enthusiastic English reviewers of the work was John Stuart Mill (1806–1873), who compared Tocqueville to Montesquieu and thought that nothing equally profound had yet been written on the subject of democracy. Tocqueville seemed to Mill to have "changed the face of political philosophy" by posing new questions that went to the core of democracy as a system of government and way of life.

Mill was impressed by the fact that the tendencies which Tocqueville had noted in America—the drive toward equality of conditions with its new problems and pressures—were also gradually permeating England. He shared Tocqueville's concern about the possibility of the tyranny of the majority in democracy, and he added that "it is not from the separate interests, real or imaginary, that minorities are in danger; but from its antipathies of religion, political party, or race." The more perfectly each knows himself the equal of any other individual, "the more helpless he feels against the aggregate mass; and the more incredible it appears to him that the opinions of all the world can possibly be erroneous."

In his *Autobiography,* too, Mill avows how much he owes to Tocqueville from whom he learned the specific virtues and defects of democracy. In turn, Tocqueville wrote to Mill that of all reviewers of *Democracy in America* he was the one who best understood the meaning of the work; the two met during Tocqueville's second visit to England in 1835, and their friendly association lasted until Tocqueville's death in 1859.

Mill's *Autobiography* (1873), one of the most fascinating autobiographies of a political philosopher, is remarkable for several reasons. It provides a lifelike, and occasionally intimate, account of the Benthamite circle, Mill's father, James, being the leading disciple of the master. The *Autobiography* also spans an important era of nineteenth-century intellectual history. Mill's interest was not confined to England, and he was particularly conversant with developments in France and the United States. Above all, the *Autobiography* is noteworthy for its account of the intellectual development of Mill himself.

For the generation of Bentham as for that of James Mill, democracy still was an objective to aim at, a goal to work for. John Stuart Mill, who belongs to the third generation of Utilitarianism, lived in a world in which middle-class reform had attained a high degree of realization and—gradually shedding the magic of the envisioned future—had begun to reveal its own shortcomings and imperfections. The heyday of middle-class democracy heralded the first dawn of the next phase of social and political development, pointing toward socialism and the welfare state.

Mill typifies in his own life history the evolution of nineteenth-century liberalism. Born and reared as an orthodox and uncontaminated Benthamite, he ended as a "qualified socialist." From a personal viewpoint, moreover, the *Autobiography* is a remarkable record of human endurance. James Mill had definite ideas on how to educate John Stuart from the moment he was born. At the age of three, John began to learn Greek, and Latin at the much later age of seven. By this time he already had acquired a solid knowledge of Greek literature and philosophy, including Plato, Herodotus, and Xenophon. He also learned arithmetic and ancient and modern history. When he came to the American war, Mill recalls, he took the side of England, but he quickly was set right by his father who, like all Philosophical Radicals, regarded the United States as the advance guard of democracy and the model of future developments in England.

From his eighth year on, Mill went thoroughly through Latin literature and broadened his knowledge of Greek literature by reading Thucydides, Homer, Euripides, Sophocles, and Polybius. At the same time, he delved into algebra, geometry, the differential calculus, and other portions of high mathematics. He also read books on experimental science and, at the age of twelve, began a course of study in logic from Aristotle to Hobbes. At thirteen, Mill's primary study was political economy, particularly Smith and David Ricardo, the latter being a close friend of Mill's father. At fourteen Mill went to France for a year, spending part of his time with the family of General Sir Samuel Bentham, Jeremy's brother. Mill fell in love with France, later returned there for prolonged visits, and died in Avignon in 1873.

At the age of seventeen, Mill joined the staff of the East India Company as a clerk, became head of his department in 1856, and retired two years later. Most of his immense literary output was accomplished while he held a full-time and absorbing job. In 1865 Mill was asked by a body of voters in Westminster to stand for Parliament. He was convinced that no numerous or influential body of any constituency would wish to be represented by a person of his opinions. He also held the fixed conviction that a candidate should neither incur election expenses nor canvass his constituency. He nevertheless won with a small majority over his Conservative opponent, but he stayed in the House of Commons for only three years. In the election of 1868 he was defeated, but he confesses in his *Autobiography* that he was less surprised by his defeat than by his having been elected the first time.

In his teens Mill wrote and published essays on various political and philosophical topics and contributed to the *Westminster Review,* the official organ of Philosophical Radicalism from its foundation in 1824. In 1834 he published the *System of Logic,* his principal work on philosophy. In 1848 he brought out his *Political Economy,* next to Adam Smith's *Wealth of Nations* the most authoritative work in its field for several generations, and long the most popular textbook in economics in England and the United States.

Yet Mill's claim to enduring fame derives from *On Liberty* (1859); he predicted that of all his writings *On Liberty* was likely to survive longest, and his prediction has come true. Mill says in the *Autobiography* that he wrote *On Liberty* at a time when there may have seemed comparatively little need for it. But he foresaw that illiberal forces in modern society would gain in weight, and he hoped that men then would turn to the teachings of *On Liberty.* Though Mill modestly disclaimed originality other than that which "every thoughtful mind gives to its own mode of conceiving and expressing truths which are common property," *On Liberty* long has been held to be, together with Milton's *Areopagitica,* the finest and most moving essay on liberty in English, perhaps in any language. As time goes on, *On Liberty* grows in stature and meaning because its predictions have come to life more realistically, and more tragically, than seemed possible in the middle of the nineteenth century, when belief in the progress of liberty was well-nigh universal.

Mill explodes the illusion that the evolution of government from tyranny to popular self-rule necessarily solves the problem of liberty. Like Tocqueville, he sees that *society* may practice a social tyranny more formidable than many kinds of political oppression, because social tyranny leaves fewer means of escape, "penetrating much more deeply into the details of life, and enslaving the soul itself." Protection against political tyranny therefore is not enough; there also must be protection against the tyranny of prevailing opinion and feeling. Unless *absolute freedom* of opinion and sentiment—scientific, moral, and theological—is guaranteed, a society is not completely free. Mill makes the point, seldom made in the optimistic nineteenth century, that the natural disposition of man is to impose his views, as ruler or fellow citizen, on others, and that want of power is often the cause of toleration of dissent.

The issue of liberty is one not only of power but of right and obligation, and it makes little difference how numerous the dissentient minority is: "If all mankind minus one, were of one opinion, and only one person were of the contrary opinion, mankind would be no more justified in silencing that one person, than he, if he had the power, would be justified in silencing mankind." Silencing an unorthodox opinion is not only wrong but harmful, because it robs mankind of an opportunity to become acquainted with ideas that may possibly be true, or partly true: "All silencing of discussion is an assumption of infallibility."

Mill recognizes that each individual can grasp no more than some aspects of truth, and that the imperfection of truth is due to the partial knowledge that man is able to attain in his limited experience of the world. Not only is society no infallible judge of truth, but even "ages are no more infallible than individuals." History is full of opinions held by one age to be the ultimate truth and considered by subsequent ages to be false and absurd.

Just as liberty is not complete unless it is absolute, so discussion must be completely unhampered, and free discussion must not be ruled out when "pushed to an extreme," because the arguments for a case are not good unless they are good for an extreme case. Mill is aware of the favorite argument that some opinions must be protected from public discussion and attack because of their usefulness to society, and he retorts that the "usefulness of an opinion is itself a matter of opinion."

Mill does not believe in the "pleasant falsehood" that truth inevitably triumphs over persecution; history "teems with instances of truth put down by persecution." He cites numerous examples of successful persecution in religion in support of his view that "persecution has always succeeded, save where the heretics were too strong a party to be effectually persecuted." The greatest harm of persecution is not done to those who are heretics but to those who are not, because the mental development of the latter is stifled by the fear of heresy. In an atmosphere of cowed conformity and slavish submission there may be a few exceptional great individual thinkers, but not an intellectually active people: "No one can be a great thinker who does not recognize, that as a thinker it is his first duty to follow his intellect to whatever conclusions it may lead."

Mill particularly warns against the blind acceptance of dead formulas as truth, without the challenge of discussion. For its own vitality and survival, truth needs to be "fully, frequently, and fearlessly" discussed, and Mill adds the not unimportant point that the opposing opinion be presented by someone who really believes in it. Only in the constant process of being challenged and assailed can truth grow and establish itself:

"Both teachers and learners go to sleep at their post, as soon as there is no enemy in the field."

In summary, says Mill, the necessity of freedom of opinion, and freedom of expression, may be based upon three grounds. First, any opinion we silence may be true, and in silencing it we assume our own *infallibility*. Second, though the *silenced opinion* be on the whole erroneous, it may be *partly true*, and because the prevailing opinion on any subject is rarely the *complete truth*, "it is only by the collision of adverse opinions that the remainder of the truth has any chance of being supplied." Third, even if the prevailing opinion be the *complete truth*, it will inevitably become dogma, prejudice, and formula unless it is exposed to the *challenge of free discussion*.

In his *Autobiography*, Mill says that his father felt himself more indebted for his mental culture to Plato than to any other writer. He shares his father's high esteem for Plato, not because of any sympathy with Plato's specific political or social views, but because of his admiration for the Socratic method, "unsurpassed" in correcting errors and clearing up confusions through relentless exposure of generalities, the "perpetual testing of all general statements by particular instances." Long before instrumentalism made its formal contribution to philosophy, Mill was an instrumentalist in his approach to the problem of truth. He recognized that truth never is finished, certain, and timeless, but that it always is unfinished, tentative, and temporary, subject to new data and experiences; that the quest for truth is an endless road; and that the free debate between opposite viewpoints is more likely to result in an approximation of truth than is the one-sided assertion of dogma and creed which are beyond dispute. In this concept of truth as a dynamic process of colliding opposites, Mill sacrifices the certainty that is devoid of mental freedom to the uncertainty that is the pride of intellectual liberty.

In championing liberty, Mill has a broad goal in mind: the "Greek ideal of self-development." It is the privilege of every human being to use and interpret experience in his own way, and the act of choosing between alternatives brings man's moral faculties into play. A person who acts according to custom and tradition makes no choice, and he who lets others choose his plan of life for him has no need of any faculty other than ape-like imitation. Different persons should be permitted to lead different lives; and the plea for *variety* in *On Liberty* is as strong as that for *freedom*. The very progress of industrial civilization creates a uniformity of conditions that makes it difficult for persons to remain individuals, because "they now read the same things, listen to the same things, go to the same places, have their hopes and fears directed to the same objects, have the same rights and liberties, and the same means of asserting them." Moreover, Mill feels that "genius" is an absolutely indispensable ingredient in social progress: "there are but few persons, in comparison with the whole of mankind, whose experiments, if adopted by others, would be likely to be any improvement on established practice," and "genius can only breathe freely in an atmosphere of freedom." Liberty, therefore, is essential not just to individual advancement but to societal progression.

Mill reminds those who are willing to repress individual liberty for the sake of a strong state that the worth of a state is no more than the worth of the individuals composing it. The concluding words of *On Liberty* contain a message that always is timely: "A state which dwarfs its men, in order that they may be more docile instruments in its hands even for beneficial purposes—will find that with small men no great thing can really be accomplished; and that the perfection of machinery to which it has sacrificed everything, will in the end avail it nothing, for want of the vital power which, in order that the machine might work smoothly, it has preferred to banish."

Mill understood that the issue of liberty is closely related to the larger question of social power and organization. Bred as an orthodox economist, his faith in *laissez faire* was originally stronger than that of Bentham himself; but as time went on, Mill gradually abandoned what was reactionary in the economic philosophy of *laissez faire*. Although in the first edition of his *Political Economy* (1848) his general view of socialism was that it was neither desirable nor practicable, in subsequent editions he revised his attitude. As a utilitarian and pragmatist, Mill was unwilling to commit himself to any economic perspective without qualifications. He felt that the decision between capitalism and socialism ultimately would be based upon one chief consideration "which of the two systems is consistent with the greatest amount of human liberty and spontaneity." It would be rash to predict that socialism would be unable to realize a great part of its aspirations, and the best way to find out, Mill thought, was to give socialists an opportunity of trial.

With regard to individual property, Mill held that the aim of an enlightened social policy should be not to destroy it, but to improve it, and to enable every member of the community to own property. The ultimate form of ownership of the means of production would not be, Mill says in the *Political Economy,* that of capitalist chiefs, with the workers deprived of any voice in the management, but the "association of the laborers themselves on terms of equality, collectively owning the capital with which they carry on their operations, and working under managers elected and removable by themselves."

In 1869 Mill began a book on socialism but did not finish it. *Chapters on Socialism,* published in 1879 by his stepdaughter, contains further important additions to Mill's previously held ideas. Avoiding an extreme position, Mill asserts on the one hand, that the present system is "not hurrying us into a state of general indigence and slavery from which only socialism can save us." Though the evils and injustices of capitalism are great, they are not increasing but generally decreasing. On the other hand, Mill foresees that individual property is only of provisional existence, though it still has a long term before it, and that the nature of property would change in the course of time. Property denotes in every state of society the largest power of exclusive control over things, "and sometimes, unfortunately, over persons," but these powers vary greatly in accordance with the conceptions of right and justice held in different countries and times. In his *Autobiography,* Mill sums up most succinctly the problem of socialism as he saw it: how to "unite the greatest individual liberty of action with a common ownership in the raw material of the globe, and an equal participation of all in the benefits of combined labor."

In his analysis of socialist ideas and proposals, Mill does not mention Marx and Engels—probably because he was not familiar with their writings—and relies most heavily upon Robert Owen, Charles Fourier, Saint-Simon, and Louis Blanc. Mill foresaw that socialism would run into a dead end if it gave up its liberal heritage and embraced the philosophy of the all-powerful state. He therefore was solely interested in French and British socialists, who stressed the cooperative, individualist, and fraternal elements in socialism as a new way of life. He ignored the doctrines of revolution and dictatorship. He was an idealist, not scientific, socialist.

Mill felt that socialism was more than a legal problem of transferring productive property from private to public ownership and also more than a purely economic problem of organizing the economy on the foundations of new principles of the common good rather than entrepreneurial profits. He thought that socialism would demand a higher moral and intellectual level of the people than did capitalism. He therefore emphasized that socialist experiments along cooperative lines should be tried first among "elite groups" of workers before such experiments of a broader scope would be justified. In particular, he opposed wholesale transfer of private property to public ownership, because he seriously doubted whether in a collectivized economy "there would be any asylum left for individuality of character; whether public opinion would not be a tyrannical yoke; whether the absolute dependence of each on all, and surveillance of each by all, would not grind all down into a tame uniformity of thoughts, feelings, and actions."

Mill was aware that many democratic socialists of his time felt unconcerned about possible deleterious political effects of large-scale public ownership and operation of the economy by the state as long as the government would be elected by democratic procedures and as long as a free press would continue. Mill did not share this optimistic expectation, and argued that, under a fully collectivized economy, "not all the freedom of the press and popular constitution would make this or any other country free otherwise than in name." The abandonment of large-scale nationalization as a goal by socialist parties vindicates Mill's conviction that an economically all-powerful state cannot be politically liberal in relation to the individual. Mill favored cooperation within working places and competition between them.

Mill's other most enduring work, in addition to *On Liberty,* is *Utilitarianism* (1861), originally published in three parts in *Fraser's Magazine.* Mill mostly wrote *Utilitarianism* in 1854, slightly before *On Liberty,* though it was not published until after *On Liberty.* The subject of *Utilitarianism* is the *summum bonum,* or ultimate good. Following Bentham, Mill holds this to be happiness.

Mill's theory of utilitarianism generally is held to differ from Bentham's in Mill's introduction of quality of pleasures and pains. Mill states: "It is quite compatible with the principle of utility to recognize the fact, that some *kinds* of pleasure are more desirable and more valuable than others. It would be absurd that while, in estimating all other things, quality is considered as well as quantity, the estimation of pleasures should be supposed to depend on quantity alone."

Historically, the great objection to utilitarianism stems from its emphasis on pleasure and pain. Carlyle called utilitarianism "pig philosophy." Does the exaltation of pleasures and pains necessarily reduce humanity to swine? Mill responds this way: "When thus attacked, the Epicureans have always answered, that it is not they, but their accusers, who represent human nature in a degrading light; since the accusation supposes human beings to be capable of no pleasures except those of which swine are capable."

Mill holds in *Utilitarianism* that the highest form of pleasure is sympathetic affection. For individuals who are "tolerably fortunate in their outward lot" who do not find happiness, the "cause generally is . . . caring for nobody but themselves." Public and private affections provide much of life's joy. Mill believes in a "powerful natural sentiment" that can form the basis for utilitarian morality: "This firm foundation is . . . the social feelings of mankind; the desire to be in unity with our fellow creatures . . . "

Mill's most amazing claim for utilitarianism is contained in these lines: "In the golden rule of Jesus of Nazareth, we read the complete spirit of the ethics of utility. To do as you would be done by, and to love your neighbour as yourself, constitute the ideal perfection of utilitarian morality." How is Mill able to say this, as he believes pleasure and freedom from pain are the only desirable ends? How can the golden rule not only be reconcilable with the principle of utility but its "complete spirit"?

Mill's answer is found in his conception of pleasure and pain. He believes that pleasures and pains have both quality and quantity. He further believes that the highest quality pleasure—the most intense pleasure—is sympathetic affection, loving one's neighbors. Individuals experience their greatest, highest pleasure, according to Mill, when they help others to be happy. In this way, to love one's neighbor as oneself is not merely reconcilable with, but constitutes the "ideal perfection" of, utilitarian ethics.

Mill does not believe the happiest person necessarily is the one who is happiest for the greatest period of time. Indeed, he holds that one of two pleasures can have a "superiority in quality" so great compared to quantity as in comparison to render the latter of "small account." The quality of pleasures differs so markedly that an individual who experiences high quality pleasures even for a short period of time can be happier over-all—can have a higher quotient of happiness—than an individual who experiences lower quality pleasures for a longer period of time.

Mill holds in *Utilitarianism* that the "utilitarian morality does recognize in human beings the power of sacrificing their own greatest good for the good of others." How is this possible? If one genuinely loves one's neighbor as oneself, there is no greater pleasure than loving others. Humans become happiest through the happiness of others.

It is unnecessary to postulate as Aristotle does in *Nichomachean Ethics* that the greatest happiness comes about through a single act of self-sacrifice. Aristotle writes "it is true of the good man . . . that he does many acts for the sake of his friends and country, and if necessary dies for them . . . since he would prefer a short period of intense pleasure to a long one of mild enjoyment, a twelve-month of noble life to many years of humdrum existence, and one great and noble action to many trivial ones." Rather, it is the spirit that enables self-sacrifice that is enjoined by utilitarian ethics. It is this spirit that is such great happiness, regardless of whether or how it is called upon to act or not.

The sublime quality of happiness that one receives in being able to make the ultimate sacrifice allows one to transcend the earthly and touch the ethereal. If one genuinely loves others, there is no greater happiness than sacrificing oneself for another. The only correction that should be made in Mill's statement for it really to be compatible with Christian ethics is that "the utilitarian morality does recognize in human beings the power of *realizing* their own greatest good in the good of others."

Mill is a great optimist. He writes in *Utilitarianism* that "no one whose opinion deserves a moment's consideration can doubt that most of the great positive evils of the world are in themselves removable, and will, if human affairs continue to improve, be in the end reduced within narrow limits. Poverty, in any sense implying suffering, may be completely extinguished by the wisdom of society. . . . Even that most intractable of enemies, disease, may be indefinitely reduced in dimensions. . . . And every advance in that direction relieves us from some, not only of the chances which cut short our own lives, but, what concerns us still more, which deprive us of those in whom our happiness is wrapt up. . . . All the grand sources, in short, of human suffering are in a great degree, many of them almost entirely, conquerable by human care and effort."

Like other democrats and liberals, Mill's thought on the subject of political and economic liberty suffers from tensions and dilemmas that are not so much a result of personal inconsistencies as of deeper tensions between democracy and liberalism. In dealing with both political and economic liberty, Mill always tries to reconcile his emotional attachment for the negative conception of liberty (liberalism) with his intellectual acceptance of the positive conception of liberty (democracy). Despite the evolution of his thought through several phases of diverse emphases, his ultimate and decisive commitment was to the more difficult ideal of liberalism than the more appealing ideal of democracy. This is true of his concern with both political and economic liberty.

An area of great interest to Mill was women's rights. His interest in this area was furthered by his wife, the former Harriet Taylor. While it seems almost inconceivable in 2001, in 1900, women almost everywhere were denied the suffrage. In the fifth chapter of *Utilitarianism,* on justice, Mill prophetically writes that "the entire history of social improvement has been a series of transitions by which one custom or institution after another . . . has passed into the rank of a universally stigmatized injustice and tyranny. So it has been with the distinctions of slaves and freemen, nobles and serfs, patricians and plebeians; and so it will be, and in part already is, with the aristocracies of color, race, and sex."

Mill turned to the topic of women's rights in *The Subjection of Women* (1869). He here takes the position, exceedingly controversial for his time, that "the principle which regulates the existing social relations between the two sexes—the legal subordination of one sex to the other—is wrong in itself, and . . . ought to be replaced by a principle of perfect equality." He particularly is concerned with legal equality in marriage: "The moral regeneration of mankind will only really commence when the most fundamental of social relations is placed under the rule of equal justice."

Mill attempted to advance legal equality between the sexes while a member of Parliament. During debate on the Reform Bill of 1867, extending the right to vote, he moved that "man" should be replaced by "person," the first time the question of women's right to vote was heard in Parliament and a half-century before similar legislation passed. On this, as many other issues, he deeply felt and was ahead of his time.

Mill was the greatest philosophical liberal of the nineteenth century; William Gladstone, who called Mill the "saint of rationalism," was the greatest political liberal (and Liberal). Mill's thought forms a bridge between the classical liberals of the nineteenth century and democratic socialists and democratic interventionist welfare state capitalists of the twentieth—from Bentham to Fabianism and Keynesians.

On Liberty remains, moreover, the best libertarian statement. In putting forward in *On Liberty* his "one very simple principle . . . that the sole end for which mankind are warranted, individually or collectively, in interfering with the liberty of action of any of their number is self-protection," Mill exactly states libertarianism. As he continues, "the only purpose for which power can be rightfully exercised over any member of a civilised community, against his will, is to prevent harm to others." Unfortunately, Mill conflated the libertarian standard for coercive involvement in others' lives of doing no harm to others with the far more general standard merely of an individual not engaging in activity that "concerns" others, and he thus was not a consistent libertarian.

Mill was the first intellectual of major stature to adopt a sympathetic attitude toward socialism, without being dogmatic. He sought the greatest happiness for all. He prefaced *On Liberty* with this passage from Wilhem von Humboldt: "The grand, leading principle, towards which every argument unfolded in these pages directly converges, is the absolute and essential importance of human development in its richest diversity."

MILL

*On Liberty**

LIBERTY AND AUTHORITY

The subject of this Essay is not the so-called Liberty of the Will, so unfortunately opposed to the misnamed doctrine of Philosophical Necessity; but Civil, or Social Liberty: the nature and limits of the power which can be legitimately exercised by society over the individual. A question seldom stated, and hardly ever discussed, in general terms, but which profoundly influences the practical controversies of the age by its latent presence, and is likely soon to make itself recognized as the vital question of the future. It is so far from being new, that, in a certain sense, it has divided mankind, almost from the remotest ages; but in the stage of progress into which the more civilized portions of the species have now entered, it presents itself under new conditions, and requires a different and more fundamental treatment.

The struggle between Liberty and Authority is the most conspicuous feature in the portions of history with which we are earliest familiar, particularly in that of Greece, Rome, and England. But in old times this contest was between subjects, or some classes of subjects, and the Government. By liberty, was meant protection against the tyranny of the political rulers. The rulers were conceived (except in some of the popular governments of Greece) as in a necessarily antagonistic position to the people whom they ruled. They consisted of a governing One, or a governing tribe or caste, who derived their authority from inheritance or conquest, who, at all events,

did not hold it at the pleasure of the governed, and whose supremacy men did not venture, perhaps did not desire, to contest, whatever precautions might be taken against its oppressive exercise. Their power was regarded as necessary, but also as highly dangerous; as a weapon which they would attempt to use against their subjects, no less than against external enemies. To prevent the weaker members of the community from being preyed upon by innumerable vultures, it was needful that there should be an animal of prey stronger than the rest, commissioned to keep them down. But as the king of the vultures would be no less bent upon preying on the flock than any of the minor harpies, it was indispensable to be in a perpetual attitude of defense against his beak and claws. The aim, therefore, of patriots was to set limits to the power which the ruler should be suffered to exercise over the community; and this limitation was what they meant by liberty. It was attempted in two ways. First, by obtaining a recognition of certain immunities, called political liberties or rights, (which it was to be regarded as a breach of duty in the ruler to infringe, and which, if he did infringe, specific resistance, or general rebellion, was held to be justifiable). A second, and generally a later expedient, was the establishment of constitutional checks, (by which the consent of the community, or of a body of some sort, supposed to represent its interests, was made a necessary condition to some of the more important acts of the governing power). To the first of these modes of limitation, the ruling power, in most European countries, was compelled, more or less, to submit. It was not so with the second; and, to attain this, or when already in some

---

*From John Stuart Mill, *On Liberty* (1859).

degree possessed, to attain it more completely, became everywhere the principal object of the lovers of liberty. And so long as mankind were content to combat one enemy by another, and to be ruled by a master, on condition of being guaranteed more or less efficaciously against his tyranny, they did not carry their aspirations beyond this point.

A time, however, came, in the progress of human affairs, when men ceased to think it a necessity of nature that their governors should be an independent power, opposed in interest to themselves. It appeared to them much better that the various magistrates of the State should be their tenants or delegates, revocable at their pleasure. In that way alone, it seemed, could they have complete security that the powers of government would never be abused to their disadvantage. By degrees this new demand for elective and temporary rulers became the prominent object of the exertions of the popular party, wherever any such party existed; and superseded, to a considerable extent, the previous efforts to limit the power of rulers. As the struggle proceeded for making the ruling power emanate from the periodical choice of the ruled, some persons began to think that too much importance had been attached to the limitation of the power itself. *That* (it might seem) was a resource against rulers whose interests were habitually opposed to those of the people. What was now wanted was, that the rulers should be identified with the people; that their interest and will should be the interest and will of the nation. The nation did not need to be protected against its own will. There was no fear of tyrannizing over itself. Let the rulers be effectually responsible to it, promptly removable by it, and it could afford to trust them with power of which it could itself dictate the use to be made. Their power was but the nation's own power, concentrated, and in a form convenient for exercise. This mode of thought, or rather perhaps of feeling, was common among the last generation of European liberalism, in the Continental section of which it still apparently predominates. Those who admit any limit to what a government may do, except in the case of such governments as they think ought not to exist, stand out as brilliant exceptions among the political thinkers of the Continent. A similar tone of sentiment might by this time have been prevalent in our own country, if the circumstances which for a time encouraged it, had continued unaltered.

But, in political and philosophical theories, as well as in persons, success discloses faults and infirmities which failure might have concealed from observation. The notion, that the people have no need to limit their power over themselves, might seem axiomatic, when popular government was a thing only dreamed about, or read of as having existed at some distant period of the past. Neither was that notion necessarily disturbed by such temporary aberrations as those of the French Revolution, the worst of which were the work of an usurping few, and which, in any case, belonged, not to the permanent working of popular institutions, but to a sudden and convulsive outbreak against monarchical and aristocratic despotism. In time, however, a democratic republic came to occupy a large portion of the earth's surface, and made itself felt as one of the most powerful members of the community of nations; and elective and responsible government became subject to the observations and criticisms which wait upon a great existing fact. It was now perceived that such phrases as "self-government," and "the power of the people over themselves," do not express the true state of the case. The "people" who exercise the power are not always the same people with those over whom it is exercised; and the "self-government" spoken of is not the government of each by himself, but of each by all the rest. The will of the people, moreover, practically means the will of the most numerous or the most active *part* of the people: the majority, or those who succeed in making themselves accepted as the majority; the people, consequently, *may* desire to oppress a part of their number; and precautions are as much needed against this as against any other abuse of power. The limitation, therefore, of the power of government over individuals loses none of its importance when the holders of power are regularly accountable to the community, that is, to the strongest party therein. This view of things, recommending itself equally to the intelligence of thinkers and to the inclination of those important classes in

European society to whose real or supposed interests democracy is adverse, has had no difficulty in establishing itself; and in political speculations "the tyranny of the majority" is now generally included among the evils against which society requires to be on its guard.

Like other tyrannies, the tyranny of the majority was at first, and is still vulgarly, held in dread, chiefly as operating through the acts of the public authorities. But reflecting persons perceived that when society is itself the tyrant—society collectively, over the separate individuals who compose it—its means of tyrannizing are not restricted to the acts which it may do by the hands of its political functionaries. Society can and does execute its own mandates: and if it issues wrong mandates instead of right, or any mandates at all in things with which it ought not to meddle, it practices a social tyranny more formidable than many kinds of political oppression, since, though not usually upheld by such extreme penalties, it leaves fewer means of escape, penetrating much more deeply into the details of life, and enslaving the soul itself. Protection, therefore, against the tyranny of the magistrate is not enough: there needs protection also against the tyranny of the prevailing opinion and feeling; against the tendency of society to impose, by other means than civil penalties, its own ideas and practices as rules of conduct on those who dissent from them; to fetter the development, and, if possible, prevent the formation, of any individuality not in harmony with its ways, and compel all characters to fashion themselves upon the model of its own. There is a limit to the legitimate interference of collective opinion with individual independence: and to find that limit, and maintain it against encroachment, is as indispensable to a good condition of human affairs, as protection against political despotism.

But though this proposition is not likely to be contested in general terms, the practical question, where to place the limit—how to make the fitting adjustment between individual independence and social control—is a subject on which nearly everything remains to be done.

The object of this Essay is to assert one very simple principle, as entitled to govern absolutely the dealings of society with the individual in the way of compulsion and control, whether the means used be physical force in the form of legal penalties, or the moral coercion of public opinion. That principle is, that the sole end for which mankind are warranted, individually or collectively, in interfering with the liberty of action of any of their number, is self-protection. That the only purpose for which power can be rightfully exercised over any member of a civilized community, against his will, is to prevent harm to others. His own good, either physical or moral, is not a sufficient warrant. He cannot rightfully be compelled to do or forbear because it will be better for him to do so, because it will make him happier, because, in the opinions of others, to do so would be wise, or even right. These are good reasons for remonstrating with him, or reasoning with him, or persuading him, or entreating him, but not for compelling him, or visiting him with any evil in case he do otherwise. To justify that, the conduct from which it is desired to deter him, must be calculated to produce evil to some one else. The only part of the conduct of any one, for which he is amenable to society, is that which concerns others. In the part which merely concerns himself, his independence is, of right, absolute. Over himself, over his own body and mind, the individual is sovereign.

It is, perhaps, hardly necessary to say that this doctrine is meant to apply only to human beings in the maturity of their faculties. We are not speaking of children, or of young persons below the age which the law may fix as that of manhood or womanhood. Those who are still in a state to require being taken care of by others, must be protected against their own actions as well as against external injury. For the same reason, we may leave out of consideration those backward states of society in which the race itself may be considered as in its nonage. The early difficulties in the way of spontaneous progress are so great, that there is seldom any choice of means for overcoming them; and a ruler full of the spirit of improvement is warranted in the use of any expedients that will attain an end, perhaps otherwise unattainable. Despotism is a legitimate mode of government in dealing with barbarians, provided the end be their improvement, and the means justified by actually effecting that end. Liberty, as a principle, has no application to any state of things anterior to the time when mankind have become capable of being improved by free and equal discussion. Until then, there is nothing for them but implicit obedience to an Akbar or a Charlemagne, if they are so fortunate as to find one. But as soon as mankind have attained the capacity of being guided to their own improvement by conviction or persuasion (a period long since reached in all nations with whom we need here concern ourselves), compulsion, either in the direct form or in that of pains and penalties for non-compliance, is no longer admissible as a means to their own good, and justifiable only for the security of others.

It is proper to state that I forego any advantage which could be derived to my argument from the idea of abstract right, as a thing independent of utility. I regard utility as the ultimate appeal on all ethical questions; but it must be utility in the largest sense, grounded on the permanent interests of man as a progressive being. Those interests, I contend, authorize the subjection of individual spontaneity to external control, only in respect to those actions of each, which concern the interest of other people. If any one does an act hurtful to others, there is a prima facie case for punishing him, by law, or, where legal penalties are not safely applicable, by general disapprobation. There are also many positive acts for the benefit of others, which he may rightfully be compelled to perform; such as, to give evidence in a court of justice; to bear his fair share in the common defense, or in any other joint work necessary to the interest of the society of which he enjoys the protection; and to perform certain acts of individual beneficence, such as saving a fellow creature's life, or interposing to protect the defenseless against ill-usage, things which whenever it is obviously a man's duty to do, he may rightfully be made responsible to society for not doing. A person may cause evil to others not only by his actions but by his inaction, and in either case he is justly accountable to them for the injury. The latter case, it is true, requires a much more cautious exercise of compulsion than the former. To make any one answerable for

doing evil to others, is the rule; to make him answerable for not preventing evil, is, comparatively speaking, the exception. Yet there are many cases clear enough and grave enough to justify that exception. In all things which regard the external relations of the individual, he is *de jure* amenable to those whose interests are concerned, and if need be, to society as their protector. There are often good reasons for not holding him to the responsibility; but these reasons must arise from the special expediencies of the case: either because it is a kind of case in which he is on the whole likely to act better, when left to his own discretion, than when controlled in any way in which society have it in their power to control him; or because the attempt to exercise control would produce other evils, greater than those which it would prevent. When such reasons as these preclude the enforcement of responsibility, the conscience of the agent himself should step into the vacant judgment-seat, and protect those interests of others which have no external protection; judging himself all the more rigidly, because the case does not admit of his being made accountable to the judgment of his fellow creatures.

But there is a sphere of action in which society, as distinguished from the individual, has, if any, only an indirect interest: comprehending all that portion of a person's life and conduct which affects only himself, or if it also affects others, only with their free, voluntary, and undeceived consent and participation. When I say only himself, I mean directly, and in the first instance: for whatever affects himself, may affect others through himself; and the objection which may be grounded on this contingency will receive consideration in the sequel. This, then, is the appropriate region of human liberty. It comprises, first, the inward domain of consciousness; demanding liberty of conscience, in the most comprehensive sense; liberty of thought and feeling; absolute freedom of opinion and sentiment on all subjects, practical or speculative, scientific, moral, or theological. The liberty of expressing and publishing opinions may seem to fall under a different principle, since it belongs to that part of the conduct of an individual which concerns other people; but, being almost of as much importance as the liberty of thought itself, and resting in great part on the same reasons, is practically in-separable from it. Secondly, the principle requires liberty of tastes and pursuits; of framing the plan of our life to suit our own character; of doing as we like, subject to such consequences as may follow: without impediment from our fellow creatures, so long as what we do does not harm them, even though they should think our conduct foolish, perverse, or wrong. Thirdly, from this liberty of each individual, follows the liberty, within the same limits, of combina-tion among individuals; freedom to unite, for any purpose not involving harm to oth-ers: the persons combining being supposed to be of full age, and not forced or deceived.

No society in which these liberties are not, on the whole, respected, is free, what-ever may be its form of government; and none is completely free in which they do not exist absolute and unqualified. The only freedom which deserves the name, is that of pursuing our own good in our own way, so long as we do not attempt to deprive others of theirs, or impede their efforts to obtain it. Each is the proper guardian of his own health, whether bodily, or mental and spiri-tual. Mankind are greater gainers by suffer-ing each other to live as seems good to themselves, than by compelling each to live as seems good to the rest.

LIBERTY OF THOUGHT AND DISCUSSION

The time, it is to be hoped, is gone by, when any defense would be necessary of the "lib-erty of the press" as one of the securities against corrupt or tyrannical government. No argument, we may suppose, can now be needed, against permitting a legislature or an executive, not identified in interest with the people, to prescribe opinions to them, and determine what doctrines or what argu-ments they shall be allowed to hear. This aspect of the question, besides, has been so often and so triumphantly enforced by pre-ceding writers, that it needs not be specially insisted on in this place. Though the law of England, on the subject of the press, is as servile to this day as it was in the time of the Tudors, there is little danger of its being actually put in force against political discussion, except during some temporary panic, when fear of insurrection drives

ministers and judges from their propriety;[1] and, speaking generally, it is not, in con-stitutional countries, to be apprehended, that the government, whether completely re-sponsible to the people or not, will often at-tempt to control the expression of opinion, except when in doing so it makes itself the organ of the general intolerance of the pub-lic. Let us suppose, therefore, that the gov-ernment is entirely at one with the people, and never thinks of exerting any power of coercion unless in agreement with what it conceives to be their voice. But I deny the

---

[1] These words had scarcely been written, when, as if to give them an emphatic contradic-tion, occurred the Government Press Prosecu-tions of 1858. That ill-judged interference with the liberty of public discussion has not, however, induced me to alter a single word in the text, nor has it at all weakened my conviction that, mo-ments of panic excepted, the era of pains and penalties for political discussion has, in our own country, passed away. For, in the first place, the prosecutions were not persisted in; and, in the second, they were never, properly speaking, po-litical prosecutions. The offense charged was not that of criticizing institutions, or the acts or per-sons of rulers, but of circulating what was deemed an immoral doctrine, the lawfulness of Tyrannicide.

If the arguments of the present chapter are of any validity, there ought to exist the fullest lib-erty of professing and discussing, as a matter of ethical conviction, any doctrine, however im-moral it may be considered. It would, therefore, be irrelevant and out of place to examine here, whether the doctrine of Tyrannicide deserves that title. I shall content myself with saying that the subject has been at all times one of the open questions of morals; that the act of a private cit-izen in striking down a criminal, who, by raising himself above the law, has placed himself be-yond the reach of legal punishment or control, has been accounted by whole nations, and by some of the best and wisest of men, not a crime, but an act of exalted virtue; and that, right or wrong, it is not of the nature of assassination, but of civil war. As such, I hold that the instigation to it, in a specific case, may be a proper subject of punishment, but only if an overt act has fol-lowed, and at least a probable connection can be established between the act and the instigation. Even then, it is not a foreign government, but the very government assailed, which alone, in the exercise of self-defense, can legitimately punish attacks directed against its own existence.

right of the people to exercise such coercion, either by themselves or by their government. The power itself is illegitimate. The best government has no more title to it than the worst. It is as noxious, or more noxious, when exerted in accordance with public opinion, than when in opposition to it. If all mankind minus one, were of one opinion, and only one person were of the contrary opinion, mankind would be no more justified in silencing that one person, than he, if he had the power, would be justified in silencing mankind. Were an opinion a personal possession of no value except to the owner; if to be obstructed in the enjoyment of it were simply a private injury, it would make some difference whether the injury was inflicted only on a few persons or on many. But the peculiar evil of silencing the expression of an opinion is, that it is robbing the human race; posterity as well as the existing generation; those who dissent from the opinion, still more than those who hold it. If the opinion is right, they are deprived of the opportunity of exchanging error for truth: if wrong, they lose, what is almost as great a benefit, the clearer perception and livelier impression of truth, produced by its collision with error.

It is necessary to consider separately these two hypotheses, each of which has a distinct branch of the argument corresponding to it. We can never be sure that the opinion we are endeavoring to stifle is a false opinion; and if we were sure, stifling it would be an evil still.

First: the opinion which it is attempted to suppress by authority may possibly be true. Those who desire to suppress it, of course deny its truth; but they are not infallible. They have no authority to decide the question for all mankind, and exclude every other person from the means of judging. To refuse a hearing to an opinion, because they are sure that it is false, is to assume that *their* certainty is the same thing as *absolute* certainty. All silencing of discussion is an assumption of infallibility. Its condemnation may be allowed to rest on this common argument, not the worse for being common.

Unfortunately for the good sense of mankind, the fact of their fallibility is far from carrying the weight in their practical judgment, which is always allowed to it in theory; for while every one well knows himself to be fallible, few think it necessary to take any precautions against their own fallibility, or admit the supposition that any opinion, of which they feel very certain, may be one of the examples of the error to which they acknowledge themselves to be liable. Absolute princes, or others who are accustomed to unlimited deference, usually feel this complete confidence in their own opinions on nearly all subjects. People more happily situated, who sometimes hear their opinions disputed, and are not wholly unused to be set right when they are wrong, place the same unbounded reliance only on such of their opinions as are shared by all who surround them, or to whom they habitually defer: for in proportion to a man's want of confidence in his own solitary judgment, does he usually repose, with implicit trust, on the infallibility of "the world" in general. And the world, to each individual, means the part of it with which he comes in contact; his party, his sect, his church, his class of society: the man may be called, by comparison, almost liberal and large-minded to whom it means anything so comprehensive as his own country or his own age. Nor is his faith in this collective authority at all shaken by his being aware that other ages, countries, sects, churches, classes, and parties have thought, and even now think, the exact reverse. He devolves upon his own world the responsibility of being in the right against the dissentient worlds of other people; and it never troubles him that mere accident has decided which of these numerous worlds is the object of his reliance, and that the same causes which make him a Churchman in London, would have made him a Buddhist or a Confucian in Pekin. Yet it is as evident in itself, as any amount of argument can make it, that ages are no more infallible than individuals; every age having held many opinions which subsequent ages have deemed not only false but absurd; and it is as certain that many opinions, now general, will be rejected by future ages, as it is that many, once general, are rejected by the present.

The objection likely to be made to this argument would probably take some such form as the following. There is no greater assumption of infallibility in forbidding the propagation of error, than in any other thing which is done by public authority on its own judgment and responsibility. Judgment is given to men that they may use it. Because it may be used erroneously, are men to be told that they ought not to use it at all? To prohibit what they think pernicious, is not claiming exemption from error, but fulfilling the duty incumbent on them, although fallible, of acting on their conscientious conviction. If we were never to act on our opinions, because those opinions may be wrong, we should leave all our interests uncared for, and all our duties unperformed. An objection which applies to all conduct, can be no valid objection to any conduct in particular. It is the duty of governments, and of individuals, to form the truest opinions they can; to form them carefully, and never impose them upon others unless they are quite sure of being right. But when they are sure (such reasoners may say), it is not conscientiousness but cowardice to shrink from acting on their opinions, and allow doctrines which they honestly think dangerous to the welfare of mankind, either in this life or in another, to be scattered abroad without restraint, because other people, in less enlightened times, have persecuted opinions now believed to be true. Let us take care, it may be said, not to make the same mistake: but governments and nations have made mistakes in other things, which are not denied to be fit subjects for the exercise of authority: they have laid on bad taxes, made unjust wars. Ought we therefore to lay on no taxes, and, under whatever provocation, make no wars? Men, and governments, must act to the best of their ability. There is no such thing as absolute certainty, but there is assurance sufficient for the purposes of human life. We may, and must, assume our opinion to be true for the guidance of our own conduct: and it is assuming no more when we forbid bad men to pervert society by the propagation of opinions which we regard as false and pernicious.

I answer, that it is assuming very much more. There is the greatest difference between presuming an opinion to be true, because, with every opportunity for contesting it, it has not been refuted, and assuming its truth for the purpose of not permitting its refutation. Complete liberty of contradicting and disproving our opinion, is the very condition which justifies us in assuming its truth for purposes of action; and on no other

terms can a being with human faculties have any rational assurance of being right.

When we consider either the history of opinion, or the ordinary conduct of human life, to what is it to be ascribed that the one and the other are no worse than they are? Not certainly to the inherent force of the human understanding; for, on any matter not self-evident, there are ninety-nine persons totally incapable of judging of it, for one who is capable; and the capacity of the hundredth person is only comparative; for the majority of the eminent men of every past generation held many opinions now known to be erroneous, and did or approved numerous things which no one will now justify. Why is it, then, that there is on the whole a preponderance among mankind of rational opinions and rational conduct? If there really is this preponderance—which there must be unless human affairs are, and have always been, in an almost desperate state—it is owing to a quality of the human mind, the source of everything respectable in man either as an intellectual or as a moral being, namely, that his errors are corrigible. He is capable of rectifying his mistakes, by discussion and experience. Not by experience alone. There must be discussion, to show how experience is to be interpreted. Wrong opinions and practices gradually yield to fact and argument: but facts and arguments, to produce any effect on the mind, must be brought before it. Very few facts are able to tell their own story, without comments to bring out their meaning. The whole strength and value, then, of human judgment, depending on the one property, that it can be set right when it is wrong, reliance can be placed on it only when the means of setting it right are kept constantly at hand. In the case of any person whose judgment is really deserving of confidence, how has it become so? Because he has kept his mind open to criticism of his opinions and conduct. Because it has been his practice to listen to all that could be said against him; to profit by as much of it as was just, and expound to himself, and upon occasion to others, the fallacy of what was fallacious. Because he has felt, that the only way in which a human being can make some approach to knowing the whole of a subject, is by hearing what can be said about it by persons of every variety of opinion, and studying all modes in which it can be looked at by every character of mind. No wise man ever acquired his wisdom in any mode but this; nor is it in the nature of human intellect to become wise in any other manner. The steady habit of correcting and completing his own opinion by collating it with those of others, so far from causing doubt and hesitation in carrying it into practice, is the only stable foundation for a just reliance on it: for, being cognizant of all that can, at least obviously, be said against him, and having taken up his position against all gain-sayers—knowing that he has sought for objections and difficulties, instead of avoiding them, and has shut out no light which can be thrown upon the subject from any quarter—he has a right to think his judgment better than that of any person, or any multitude, who have not gone through a similar process.

It is not too much to require that what the wisest of mankind, those who are best entitled to trust their own judgment, find necessary to warrant their relying on it, should be submitted to by that miscellaneous collection of a few wise and many foolish individuals, called the public. The most intolerant of churches, the Roman Catholic Church, even at the canonization of a saint, admits, and listens patiently to, a "devil's advocate." The holiest of men, it appears, cannot be admitted to posthumous honors, until all that the devil could say against him is known and weighed. If even the Newtonian philosophy were not permitted to be questioned, mankind could not feel as complete assurance of its truth as they now do. The beliefs which we have most warrant for, have no safeguard to rest on, but a standing invitation to the whole world to prove them unfounded. If the challenge is not accepted, or is accepted and the attempt fails, we are far enough from certainty still; but we have done the best that the existing state of human reason admits of; we have neglected nothing that could give the truth a chance of reaching us: if the lists are kept open, we may hope that if there be a better truth, it will be found when the human mind is capable of receiving it; and in the meantime we may rely on having attained such approach to truth, as is possible in our own day. This is the amount of certainty attainable by a fallible being, and this the sole way of attaining it.

Strange it is, that men should admit the validity of the arguments for free discussion, but object to their being "pushed to an extreme"; not seeing that unless the reasons are good for an extreme case, they are not good for any case. Strange that they should imagine that they are not assuming infallibility, when they acknowledge that there should be free discussion on all subjects which can possibly be *doubtful*, but think that some particular principle or doctrine should be forbidden to be questioned because it is so *certain*, that is, because *they are certain* that it is certain. To call any proposition certain, while there is any one who would deny its certainty if permitted, but who is not permitted, is to assume that we ourselves, and those who agree with us, are the judges of certainty, and judges without hearing the other side.

In the present age—which has been described as "destitute of faith, but terrified at scepticism"—in which people feel sure, not so much that their opinions are true, as that they should not know what to do without them—the claims of an opinion to be protected from public attack are rested not so much on its truth, as on its importance to society. There are, it is alleged, certain beliefs, so useful, not to say indispensable to well-being, that it is as much the duty of governments to uphold those beliefs, as to protect any other of the interests of society. In a case of such necessity, and so directly in the line of their duty, something less than infallibility may, it is maintained, warrant, and even bind, governments, to act on their own opinion, confirmed by the general opinion of mankind. It is also often argued, and still oftener thought, that none but bad men would desire to weaken these salutary beliefs; and there can be nothing wrong, it is thought, in restraining bad men, and prohibiting what only such men would wish to practice. This mode of thinking makes the justification of restraints on discussion not a question of the truth of doctrines, but of their usefulness; and flatters itself by that means to escape the responsibility of claiming to be an infallible judge of opinions. But those who thus satisfy themselves, do not perceive that the assumption of infallibility is merely shifted from one point to another. The usefulness of an opinion is itself matter of opinion: as disputable, as open to discussion, and requiring discussion as much, as the opinion itself. There is the same need of an infallible judge of opinions to decide an opinion to be noxious, as to decide it to be false, unless the opinion condemned has full opportunity of defending itself. And it will not do to say that the heretic may be allowed to maintain the utility or harmlessness of his opinion, though forbidden to maintain its truth. The truth of an opinion is part of its utility. If we would know whether or not it is desirable that a proposition should be believed, is it possible to exclude the consideration of whether or not it is true? In the opinion, not of bad men, but of the best men, no belief which is contrary to truth can be really useful: and can you prevent such men from urging that plea, when they are charged with culpability for denying some doctrine which they are told is useful, but which they believe to be false? Those who are on the side of received opinions, never fail to take all possible advantage of this plea; you do not find *them* handling the question of utility as if it could be completely abstracted from that of truth: on the contrary, it is, above all, because their doctrine is the "truth," that the knowledge or the belief of it is held to be so indispensable. There can be no fair discussion of the question of usefulness, when an argument so vital may be employed on one side, but not on the other. And in point of fact, when law or public feeling do not permit the truth of an opinion to be disputed, they are just as little tolerant of a denial of its usefulness. The utmost they allow is an extenuation of its absolute necessity, or of the positive guilt of rejecting it.

In order more fully to illustrate the mischief of denying a hearing to opinions because we, in our own judgment, have condemned them, it will be desirable to fix down the discussion to a concrete case; and I choose, by preference, the cases which are least favorable to me—in which the argument against freedom of opinion, both on the score of truth and on that of utility, is considered the strongest. Let the opinions impugned be the belief in a God and in a future state, or any of the commonly received doctrines of morality. To fight the battle on such ground, gives a great advantage to an unfair antagonist; since he will be sure to say (and many who have no desire to be unfair will say it internally), Are these the doctrines which you do not deem sufficiently certain to be taken under the protection of law? Is

the belief in a God one of the opinions, to feel sure of which, you hold to be assuming infallibility? But I must be permitted to observe, that it is not the feeling sure of a doctrine (be it what it may) which I call an assumption of infallibility. It is the undertaking to decide that question *for others,* without allowing them to hear what can be said on the contrary side. And I denounce and reprobate this pretension not the less, if put forth on the side of my most solemn convictions. However positive any one's persuasion may be, not only of the falsity but of the pernicious consequences—not only of the pernicious consequences, but (to adopt expressions which I altogether condemn) the immorality and impiety of an opinion; yet if, in pursuance of that private judgment, though backed by the public judgment of his country or his contemporaries, he prevents the opinion from being heard in its defense, he assumes infallibility. And so far from the assumption being less objectionable or less dangerous because the opinion is called immoral or impious, this is the case of all others in which it is most fatal. These are exactly the occasions on which the men of one generation commit those dreadful mistakes, which excite the astonishment and horror of posterity. It is among such that we find the instances memorable in history, when the arm of the law has been employed to root out the best men and the noblest doctrines; with deplorable success as to the men, though some of the doctrines have survived to be (as if in mockery) invoked, in defense of similar conduct towards those who dissent from *them,* or from their received interpretation.

Mankind can hardly be too often reminded, that there was once a man named Socrates, between whom and the legal authorities and public opinion of his time, there took place a memorable collision. Born in an age and country abounding in individual greatness, this man has been handed down to us by those who best knew both him and the age, as the most virtuous man in it; while *we* know him as the head and prototype of all subsequent teachers of virtue, the source equally of the lofty inspiration of Plato and the judicious utilitarianism of Aristotle, *i maestri di color che sanno,* the two headsprings of ethical as of all other philosophy. This acknowledged master of all the eminent thinkers who have since lived—whose fame, still growing after more than two thousand years, all but outweighs the whole remainder of the names which make his native city illustrious—was put to death by his countrymen, after a judicial conviction, for impiety and immorality. Impiety, in denying the gods recognized by the State; indeed his accuser asserted (see the *Apologia*) that he believed in no gods at all. Immorality, in being, by his doctrines and instructions, a "corruptor of youth." Of these charges the tribunal, there is every ground for believing, honestly found him guilty, and condemned the man who probably of all then born had deserved best of mankind, to be put to death as a criminal.

To pass from this to the only other instance of judicial iniquity, the mention of which, after the condemnation of Socrates, would not be an anti-climax: the event which took place on Calvary rather more than eighteen hundred years ago. The man who left on the memory of those who witnessed his life and conversation, such an impression of his moral grandeur, that eighteen subsequent centuries have done homage to him as the Almighty in person, was ignominiously put to death, as what? As a blasphemer. Men did not merely mistake their benefactor; they mistook him for the exact contrary of what he was, and treated him as that prodigy of impiety, which they themselves are now held to be, for their treatment of him. The feelings with which mankind now regard these lamentable transactions, especially the later of the two, render them extremely unjust in their judgment of the unhappy actors. These were, to all appearance, not bad men—not worse than men commonly are, but rather the contrary: men who possessed in a full, or somewhat more than a full measure, the religious, moral, and patriotic feelings of their time and people: the very kind of men who, in all times, our own included, have every chance of passing through life blameless and respected. The high-priest who rent his garments when the words were pronounced, which, according to all the ideas of his country, constituted the blackest guilt, was in all probability quite as sincere in his horror and indignation, as the generality of respectable and pious men now are in the religious and moral sentiments they profess;

and most of those who now shudder at his conduct, if they had lived in his time, and been born Jews, would have acted precisely as he did. Orthodox Christians who are tempted to think that those who stoned to death the first martyrs must have been worse men than they themselves are, ought to remember that one of those persecutors was Saint Paul.

Let us add one more example, the most striking of all, if the impressiveness of an error is measured by the wisdom and virtue of him who falls into it. If ever any one, possessed of power, had grounds for thinking himself the best and most enlightened among his contemporaries, it was the Emperor Marcus Aurelius. Absolute monarch of the whole civilized world, he preserved through life not only the most unblemished justice, but what was less to be expected from his Stoical breeding, the tenderest heart. The few failings which are attributed to him, were all on the side of indulgence: while his writings, the highest ethical product of the ancient mind, differ scarcely perceptibly, if they differ at all, from the most characteristic teachings of Christ. This man, a better Christian in all but the dogmatic sense of the word, than almost any of the ostensibly Christian sovereigns who have since reigned, persecuted Christianity. Placed at the summit of all the previous attainments of humanity, with an open, unfettered intellect, and a character which led him of himself to embody in his moral writings the Christian ideal, he yet failed to see that Christianity was to be a good and not an evil to the world, with his duties to which he was so deeply penetrated. Existing society he knew to be in a deplorable state. But such as it was, he saw, or thought he saw, that it was held together, and prevented from being worse, by belief and reverence of the received divinities. As a ruler of mankind, he deemed it his duty not to suffer society to fall in pieces; and saw not how, if its existing ties were removed, any others could be formed which could again knit it together. The new religion openly aimed at dissolving these ties: unless, therefore, it was his duty to adopt that religion, it seemed to be his duty to put it down. Inasmuch then as the theology of Christianity did not appear to him true or of divine origin; inasmuch as this strange history of a crucified God was not credible to him, and a system which purported to rest entirely upon a foundation to him so wholly unbelievable, could not be foreseen by him to be that renovating agency which, after all abatements, it has in fact proved to be; the gentlest and most amiable of philosophers and rulers, under a solemn sense of duty, authorized the persecution of Christianity. To my mind this is one of the most tragical facts in all history. It is a bitter thought, how different a thing the Christianity of the world might have been, if the Christian faith had been adopted as the religion of the empire under the auspices of Marcus Aurelius instead of those of Constantine. But it would be equally unjust to him and false to truth, to deny, that no one plea which can be urged for punishing anti-Christian teaching, was wanting to Marcus Aurelius for punishing, as he did, the propagation of Christianity. No Christian more firmly believes that Atheism is false, and tends to the dissolution of society, than Marcus Aurelius believed the same things of Christianity; he who, of all men then living, might have been thought the most capable of appreciating it. Unless any one who approves of punishment for the promulgation of opinions, flatters himself that he is a wiser and better man than Marcus Aurelius—more deeply versed in the wisdom of his time, more elevated in his intellect above it—more earnest in his search for truth, or more singleminded in his devotion to it when found;—let him abstain from that assumption of the joint infallibility of himself and the multitude, which the great Antoninus made with so unfortunate a result.

Aware of the impossibility of defending the use of punishment for restraining irreligious opinions, by any argument which will not justify Marcus Antoninus, the enemies of religious freedom, when hard pressed, occasionally accept this consequence, and say, with Dr. Johnson, that the persecutors of Christianity were in the right; that persecution is an ordeal through which truth ought to pass, and always passes successfully, legal penalties being, in the end, powerless against truth, though sometimes beneficially effective against mischievous errors. This is a form of the argument for religious intolerance, sufficiently remarkable not to be passed without notice.

A theory which maintains that truth may justifiably be persecuted because persecution cannot possibly do it any harm, cannot be charged with being intentionally hostile to the reception of new truths; but we cannot commend the generosity of its dealing with the persons to whom mankind are indebted for them. To discover to the world something which deeply concerns it, and of which it was previously ignorant; to prove to it that it had been mistaken on some vital point of temporal or spiritual interest, is as important a service as a human being can render to his fellow creatures, and in certain cases, as in those of the early Christians and of the Reformers, those who think with Dr. Johnson believe it to have been the most precious gift which could be bestowed on mankind. That the authors of such splendid benefits should be requited by martyrdom; that their reward should be to be dealt with as the vilest of criminals, is not, upon this theory, a deplorable error and misfortune, for which humanity should mourn in sackcloth and ashes, but the normal and justifiable state of things. The propounder of a new truth, according to this doctrine, should stand, as stood, in the legislation of the Locrians, the proposer of a new law, with a halter round his neck, to be instantly tightened if the public assembly did not, on hearing his reasons, then and there adopt his proposition. People who defend this mode of treating benefactors, cannot be supposed to set much value on the benefit; and I believe this view of the subject is mostly confined to the sort of persons who think that new truths may have been desirable once, but that we have had enough of them now.

But, indeed, the dictum that truth always triumphs over persecution, is one of those pleasant falsehoods which men repeat after one another till they pass into commonplaces, but which all experience refutes. History teems with instances of truth put down by persecution. If not suppressed for ever, it may be thrown back for centuries. To speak only of religious opinions: the Reformation broke out at least twenty times before Luther, and was put down. Arnold of Brescia was put down. Fra Dolcino was put down. Savonarola was put down. The Albigeois were put down. The Vaudois were put down. The Lollards were put down. The Hussites were put down. Even after the era of Luther, wherever persecution was persisted in, it was successful. In Spain, Italy, Flanders, the Austrian empire, Protestantism was rooted out; and, most likely, would have been so in England, had Queen Mary lived, or Queen Elizabeth died. Persecution has always succeeded, save where the heretics were too strong a party to be effectually persecuted. No reasonable person can doubt that Christianity might have been extirpated in the Roman Empire. It spread, and became predominant, because the persecutions were only occasional, lasting but a short time, and separated by long intervals of almost undisturbed propagandism. It is a piece of idle sentimentality that truth, merely as truth, has any inherent power denied to error, of prevailing against the dungeon and the stake. Men are not more zealous for truth than they often are for error, and a sufficient application of legal or even of social penalties will generally succeed in stopping the propagation of either. The real advantage which truth has, consists in this, that when an opinion is true, it may be extinguished once, twice, or many times, but in the course of ages there will generally be found persons to rediscover it, until some one of its reappearances falls on a time when from favorable circumstances it escapes persecution until it has made such head as to withstand all subsequent attempts to suppress it.

What is boasted of at the present time as the revival of religion, is always, in narrow and uncultivated minds, at least as much the revival of bigotry; and where there is the strong permanent leaven of intolerance in the feelings of a people, which at all times abides in the middle classes of this country, it needs but little to provoke them into actively persecuting those whom they have never ceased to think proper objects of persecution. For it is this—it is the opinions men entertain, and the feelings they cherish, respecting those who disown the beliefs they deem important, which makes this country not a place of mental freedom. For a long time past, the chief mischief of the legal penalties is that they strengthen the social stigma. It is that stigma which is really effective, and so effective is it, that the profession of opinions which are under the ban of society is much less common in England, than is, in many other countries, the avowal of those which incur risk of judicial punishment. In respect to all persons but those whose pecuniary circumstances make them independent of the goodwill of other people, opinion, on this subject, is as efficacious as law; men might as well be imprisoned, as excluded from the means of earning their bread. Those whose bread is already secured, and who desire no favors from men in power, or from bodies of men, or from the public, have nothing to fear from the open avowal of any opinions, but to be ill-thought of and ill-spoken of, and this it ought not to require a very heroic mold to enable them to bear. There is no room for any appeal *ad misericordiam* in behalf of such persons. But though we do not now inflict so much evil on those who think differently from us, as it was formerly our custom to do, it may be that we do ourselves as much evil as ever by our treatment of them. Socrates was put to death, but the Socratic philosophy rose like the sun in heaven, and spread its illumination over the whole intellectual firmament. Christians were cast to the lions, but the Christian church grew up a stately and spreading tree, overtopping the older and less vigorous growths, and stifling them by its shade. Our merely social intolerance kills no one, roots out no opinions, but induces men to disguise them, or to abstain from any active effort for their diffusion. With us, heretical opinions do not perceptibly gain, or even lose, ground in each decade or generation; they never blaze out far and wide, but continue to smolder in the narrow circles of thinking and studious persons among whom they originate, without ever lighting up the general affairs of mankind with either a true or a deceptive light. And thus is kept up a state of things very satisfactory to some minds, because, without the unpleasant process of fining or imprisoning anybody, it maintains all prevailing opinions outwardly undisturbed, while it does not absolutely interdict the exercise of reason by dissentients afflicted with the malady of thought. A convenient plan for having peace in the intellectual world, and keeping all things going on therein very much as they do already. But the price paid for this sort of intellectual pacification, is the sacrifice of the entire moral courage of the human mind. A state of things in which a large portion of the most active and inquiring intellects find it advisable to keep the general principles and grounds of their convictions within their own breasts, and attempt, in what they address to the public, to fit as much as they can of their own conclusions to premises which they have internally renounced, cannot send forth the open, fearless characters, and logical, consistent intellects who once adorned the thinking world. The sort of men who can be looked for under it, are either mere conformers to commonplace, or time-servers for truth, whose arguments on all great subjects are meant for their hearers, and are not those which have convinced themselves. Those who avoid this alternative, do so by narrowing their thoughts and interest to things which can be spoken of without venturing within the region of principles, that is, to small practical matters, which would come right of themselves, if but the minds of mankind were strengthened and enlarged, and which will never be made effectually right until then: while that which would strengthen and enlarge men's minds, free and daring speculation on the highest subjects, is abandoned.

Those in whose eyes this reticence on the part of heretics is no evil, should consider in the first place, that in consequence of it there is never any fair and thorough discussion of heretical opinions; and that such of them as could not stand such a discussion, though they may be prevented from spreading, do not disappear. But it is not the minds of heretics that are deteriorated most, by the ban placed on all inquiry which does not end in the orthodox conclusions. The greatest harm done is to those who are not heretics, and whose whole mental development is cramped, and their reason cowed, by the fear of heresy. Who can compute what the world loses in the multitude of promising intellects combined with timid characters, who dare not follow out any bold, vigorous, independent train of thought, lest it should land them in something which would admit of being considered irreligious or immoral? Among them we may occasionally see some man of deep conscientiousness, and subtle and refined understanding, who spends a life in sophisticating with an intellect which he cannot silence, and exhausts the resources of ingenuity in attempting to reconcile the promptings of his conscience and reason with orthodoxy, which yet he does not, perhaps, to the end succeed in doing. No one can be a great thinker who does not recognize, that as a thinker it is his first duty to follow his intellect to whatever conclusions it may lead. Truth gains more even by the errors of one who, with due study and preparation, thinks for himself, than by the true opinions of those who only hold them because they do not suffer themselves to think. Not that it is solely, or chiefly, to form great thinkers, that freedom of thinking is required. On the contrary, it is as much and even more indispensable, to enable average human beings to attain the mental stature which they are capable of. There have been, and may again be, great individual thinkers, in a general atmosphere of mental slavery. But there never has been, nor ever will be, in that atmosphere, an intellectually active people. When any people has made a temporary approach to such a character, it has been because the dread of heterodox speculation was for a time suspended. Where there is a tacit convention that principles are not to be disputed; where the discussion of the greatest questions which can occupy humanity is considered to be closed, we cannot hope to find that generally high scale of mental activity which has made some periods, of history so remarkable. Never when controversy avoided the subjects which are large and important enough to kindle enthusiasm, was the mind of a people stirred up from its foundations, and the impulse given which raised even persons of the most ordinary intellect to something of the dignity of thinking beings. Of such we have had an example in the condition of Europe during the times immediately following the Reformation; another, though limited to the Continent and to a more cultivated class, in the speculative movement of the latter half of the eighteenth century; and a third, of still briefer duration, in the intellectual fermentation of Germany during the Goethian and Fichtean period. These periods differed widely in the particular opinions which they developed; but were alike in this, that during all three the yoke of authority was broken. In each, an old mental despotism had been thrown off, and no new one had yet taken its place. The impulse given at these three periods has made Europe what it now is. Every single improvement which has taken place either in the human mind or in institutions, may be traced distinctly to one or other of them. Appearances have for some time indicated that all three impulses are wellnigh spent; and we can expect no fresh start, until we again assert our mental freedom.

Let us now pass to the second division of the argument, and dismissing the supposition that any of the received opinions may be false, let us assume them to be true, and examine into the worth of the manner in which they are likely to be held, when their truth is not freely and openly canvassed. However unwillingly a person who has a strong opinion may admit the possibility that his opinion may be false, he ought to be moved by the consideration that however true it may be, if it is not fully, frequently, and fearlessly discussed, it will be held as a dead dogma, not a living truth.

There is a class of persons (happily not quite so numerous as formerly) who think it enough if a person assents undoubtingly to what they think true, though he has no knowledge whatever of the grounds of the opinion, and could not make a tenable defense of it against the most superficial objections. Such persons, if they can once get their creed taught from authority, naturally think that no good, and some harm, comes of its being allowed to be questioned. Where their influence prevails, they make it nearly impossible for the received opinion to be rejected wisely and considerately, though it may still be rejected rashly and ignorantly; for to shut out discussion entirely is seldom possible and, when it once gets in, beliefs not grounded on conviction are apt to give way before the slightest semblance of an argument. Waiving, however, this possibility—assuming that the true opinion abides in the mind, but abides as a prejudice, a belief independent of, and proof against, argument—this is not the way in which truth ought to be held by a rational being. This is not knowing the truth. Truth, thus held, is but one superstition the more accidentally clinging to the words which enunciate a truth.

If the intellect and judgment of mankind ought to be cultivated, a thing which Protestants at least do not deny, on what can these faculties be more appropriately exercised by any one, than on the things which concern him so much that it is considered necessary for him to hold opinions on them? If the cultivation of the understanding consists in one thing more than in another, it is surely in learning the grounds of one's own opinions. Whatever people believe, on subjects on which it is of the first importance to believe rightly, they ought to be able to defend against at least the common objections. But, some one may say, "Let them be *taught* the grounds of their opinions. It does not follow that opinions must be merely parroted because they are never heard controverted. Persons who learn geometry do not simply commit the theorems to memory, but understand and learn likewise the demonstrations; and it would be absurd to say that they remain ignorant of the grounds of geometrical truths, because they never hear any one deny, and attempt to disprove them." Undoubtedly: and such teaching suffices on a subject like mathematics, where there is nothing at all to be said on the wrong side of the question. The peculiarity of the evidence of mathematical truths is, that all the argument is on one side. There are no objections, and no answers to objections. But on every subject on which difference of opinion is possible, the truth depends on a balance to be struck between two sets of conflicting reasons. Even in natural philosophy, there is always some other explanation possible of the same facts; some geocentric theory instead of heliocentric, some phlogiston instead of oxygen; and it has to be shown why that other theory cannot be the true one: and until this is shown, and until we know how it is shown, we do not understand the grounds of our opinion. But when we turn to subjects infinitely more complicated, to morals, religion, politics, social relations, and the business of life, three-fourths of the arguments for every disputed opinion consist in dispelling the appearances which favor some opinion different from it. The greatest orator, save one, of antiquity, has left it on record that he always studied his adversary's case with as great, if not with still greater, intensity than even his own. What Cicero practiced as the means of forensic success, requires to be imitated by all who study any subject in order to arrive at the truth. He who knows only his own side of the case, knows little of that. His reasons may be good, and no one may have been able to refute them. But if he is equally unable to refute the reasons on the opposite side; if he does not so much as know what they are, he has no ground for preferring either opinion. The rational position for him would be suspension of judgment, and unless he contents himself with that, he is either led by authority, or adopts, like the generality of the world, the side to which he feels most inclination. Nor is it enough that he should hear the arguments of adversaries from his own teachers, presented as they state them, and accompanied by what they offer as refutations. That is not the way to do justice to the arguments, or bring them into real contact with his own mind. He must be able to hear them from persons who actually believe them; who defend them in earnest, and do their very utmost for them. He must know them in their most plausible and persuasive form; he must feel the whole force of the difficulty which the true view of the subject has to encounter and dispose of; else he will never really possess himself of the portion of truth which meets and removes that difficulty. Ninety-nine in a hundred of what are called educated men are in this condition; even of those who can argue fluently for their opinions. Their conclusion may be true, but it might be false for anything they know: they have never thrown themselves into the mental position of those who think differently from them, and considered what such persons may have to say; and consequently they do not, in any proper sense of the word, know the doctrine which they themselves profess. They do not know those parts of it which explain and justify the remainder; the considerations which show that a fact which seemingly conflicts with another is reconcilable with it, or that, of two apparently strong reasons, one and not the other ought to be preferred. All that part of the truth which turns the scale, and decides the judgment of a completely informed mind, they are strangers to; nor is it ever really known, but to those who have attended equally and impartially to both sides, and endeavored to see the reasons of both in the strongest light. So essential is this discipline to a real understanding of moral and human subjects, that if opponents of all important truths do not exist, it is indispensable to imagine them, and supply them with the strongest

arguments which the most skillful devil's advocate can conjure up.

To abate the force of these considerations, an enemy of free discussion may be supposed to say, that there is no necessity for mankind in general to know and understand all that can be said against or for their opinions by philosophers and theologians. That it is not needful for common men to be able to expose all the misstatements or fallacies of an ingenious opponent. That it is enough if there is always somebody capable of answering them, so that nothing likely to mislead uninstructed persons remains unrefuted. That simple minds, having been taught the obvious grounds of the truths inculcated on them, may trust to authority for the rest, and being aware that they have neither knowledge nor talent to resolve every difficulty which can be raised, may repose in the assurance that all those which have been raised have been or can be answered, by those who are specially trained to the task.

Conceding to this view of the subject the utmost that can be claimed for it by those most easily satisfied with the amount of understanding of truth which ought to accompany the belief of it; even so, the argument for free discussion is no way weakened. For even this doctrine acknowledges that mankind ought to have a rational assurance that all objections have been satisfactorily answered; and how are they to be answered if that which requires to be answered is not spoken? or how can the answer be known to be satisfactory, if the objectors have no opportunity of showing that it is unsatisfactory? If not the public, at least the philosophers and theologians who are to resolve the difficulties, must make themselves familiar with those difficulties in their most puzzling form; and this cannot be accomplished unless they are freely stated, and placed in the most advantageous light which they admit of. The Catholic Church has its own way of dealing with this embarrassing problem. It makes a broad separation between those who can be permitted to receive its doctrines on conviction, and those who must accept them on trust. Neither, indeed, are allowed any choice as to what they will accept; but the clergy, such at least can be fully confided in, may admissibly and meritoriously make themselves acquainted with the arguments of opponents, in order to answer them, and may, therefore, read heretical books; the laity, not unless by special permission, hard to be obtained. This discipline recognizes a knowledge of the enemy's case as beneficial to the teachers, but finds means, consistent with this, of denying it to the rest of the world: thus giving to the *élite* more mental culture, though not more mental freedom, than it allows to the mass. By this device it succeeds in obtaining the kind of mental superiority which its purposes require; for though culture without freedom never made a large and liberal mind, it can make a clever *nisi prius* advocate of a cause. But in countries professing Protestantism, this resource is denied; since Protestants hold, at least in theory, that the responsibility for the choice of a religion must be borne by each for himself, and cannot be thrown off upon teachers. Besides, in the present state of the world, it is practically impossible that writings which are read by the instructed can be kept from the uninstructed. If the teachers of mankind are to be cognizant of all that they ought to know, everything must be free to be written and published without restraint.

If, however, the mischievous operation of the absence of free discussion, when the received opinions are true, were confined to leaving men ignorant of the grounds of those opinions, it might be thought that this, if an intellectual, is no moral evil, and does not affect the worth of the opinions, regarded in their influence on the character. The fact, however, is, that not only the grounds of the opinion are forgotten in the absence of discussion, but too often the meaning of the opinion itself. The words which convey it, cease to suggest ideas, or suggest only a small portion of those they were originally employed to communicate. Instead of a vivid conception and a living belief, there remain only a few phrases retained by rote; or, if any part, the shell and husk only of the meaning is retained, the finer essence being lost. The great chapter in human history which this fact occupies and fills, cannot be too earnestly studied and meditated on.

It is illustrated in the experience of almost all ethical doctrines and religious creeds. They are all full of meaning and vitality to those who originate them, and to the direct disciples of the originators. Their meaning continues to be felt in undiminished strength, and is perhaps brought out into even fuller consciousness, so long as the struggle lasts to give the doctrine or creed an ascendancy over other creeds. At last it either prevails, and becomes the general opinion, or its progress stops; it keeps possession of the ground it has gained, but ceases to spread further. When either of these results has become apparent, controversy on the subject flags, and gradually dies away. The doctrine has taken its place, if not as a received opinion, as one of the admitted sects or divisions of opinion: those who hold it have generally inherited, not adopted it; and conversion from one of these doctrines to another, being now an exceptional fact, occupies little place in the thoughts of their professors. Instead of being, as at first, constantly on the alert either to defend themselves against the world, or to bring the world over to them, they have subsided into acquiescence, and neither listen, when they can help it, to arguments against their creed, nor trouble dissentients (if there be such) with arguments in its favor. From this time may usually be dated the decline in the living power of the doctrine. We often hear the teachers of all creeds lamenting the difficulty of keeping up in the minds of believers a lively apprehension of the truth which they nominally recognize, so that it may penetrate the feelings, and acquire a real mastery over the conduct. No such difficulty is complained of while the creed is still fighting for its existence: even the weaker combatants then know and feel what they are fighting for, and the difference between it and other doctrines; and in that period of every creed's existence, not a few persons may be found, who have realized its fundamental principles in all the forms of thought, have weighed and considered them in all their important bearings, and have experienced the full effect on the character, which belief in that creed ought to produce in a mind thoroughly imbued with it. But when it has come to be an hereditary creed, and to be received passively, not actively—when the mind is no longer compelled, in the same degree as at first, to exercise its vital powers on the questions which its belief presents to it, there is a progressive tendency to forget all of the belief except the formularies, or to give it a dull and torpid assent, as if accepting it on trust dispensed with the necessity of realizing it in consciousness, or testing it by personal experience; until it almost ceases to connect itself at all with the inner life of the human being. Then are seen the cases, so frequent in this age of the world as almost to form the majority, in which the creed remains as it were outside the mind, encrusting and petrifying it against all other influences addressed to the higher parts of our nature; manifesting its power by not suffering any fresh and living conviction to get in, but itself doing nothing for the mind or heart, except standing sentinel over them to keep them vacant.

To what an extent doctrines intrinsically fitted to make the deepest impression upon the mind may remain in it as dead beliefs, without being ever realized in the imagination, the feelings, or the understanding, is exemplified by the manner in which the majority of believers hold the doctrines of Christianity. By Christianity I here mean what is accounted such by all churches and sects—the maxims and precepts contained in the New Testament. These are considered sacred, and accepted as laws, by all professing Christians. Yet it is scarcely too much to say that not one Christian in a thousand guides or tests his individual conduct by reference to those laws. The standard to which he does refer it, is the custom of his nation, his class, or his religious profession. He has thus, on the one hand, a collection of ethical maxims, which he believes to have been vouchsafed to him by infallible wisdom as rules for his government; and on the other, a set of everyday judgments and practices, which go a certain length with some of those maxims, not so great a length with others, stand in direct opposition to some, and are, on the whole, a compromise between the Christian creed and the interests and suggestions of worldly life. To the first of these standards he gives his homage; to the other his real allegiance. All Christians believe that the blessed are the poor and humble, and those who are ill-used by the world; that it is easier for a camel to pass through the eye of a needle than for a rich man to enter the kingdom of heaven; that they should judge not, lest they be judged; that they should swear not at all; that they should love their neighbor as themselves;

that if one take their cloak, they should give him their coat also; that they should take no thought for the morrow; that if they would be perfect, they should sell all that they have and give it to the poor. They are not insincere when they say that they believe these things. They do believe them, as people believe what they have always heard lauded and never discussed. But in the sense of that living belief which regulates conduct, they believe these doctrines just up to the point to which it is usual to act upon them. The doctrines in their integrity are serviceable to pelt adversaries with; and it is understood that they are to be put forward (when possible) as the reasons for whatever people do that they think laudable. But any one who reminded them that the maxims require an infinity of things which they never even think of doing, would gain nothing but to be classed among those very unpopular characters who affect to be better than other people. The doctrines have no hold on ordinary believers—are not a power in their minds. They have an habitual respect for the sound of them, but no feeling which spreads from the words to the things signified, and forces the mind to take *them* in, and make them conform to the formula. Whenever conduct is concerned, they look round for Mr. A and B to direct them how far to go in obeying Christ.

Now we may be well assured that the case was not thus, but far otherwise, with the early Christians. Had it been thus, Christianity never would have expanded from an obscure sect of the despised Hebrews into the religion of the Roman empire. When their enemies said, "See how these Christians love one another" (a remark not likely to be made by anybody now), they assuredly had a much livelier feeling of the meaning of their creed than they have ever had since. And to this cause, probably, it is chiefly owing that Christianity now makes so little progress in extending its domain, and after eighteen centuries, is still nearly confined to Europeans and the descendants of Europeans. Even with the strictly religious, who are much in earnest about their doctrines, and attach a greater amount of meaning to many of them than people in general, it commonly happens that the part which is thus comparatively active in their minds is that which was made by Calvin, or Knox, or some such person much nearer in character to themselves. The sayings of Christ co-exist passively in their minds, producing hardly any effect beyond what is caused by mere listening to words so amiable and bland. There are many reasons, doubtless, why doctrines which are the badge of a sect retain more of their vitality than those common to all recognized sects, and why more pains are taken by teachers to keep their meaning alive; but one reason certainly is, that the peculiar doctrines are more questioned, and have to be oftener defended against open gainsayers. Both teachers and learners go to sleep at their post, as soon as there is no enemy in the field.

The same thing holds true, generally speaking, of all traditional doctrines—those of prudence and knowledge of life, as well as morals or religion. All languages and literatures are full of general observations on life, both as to what it is, and how to conduct oneself in it; observations which everybody knows, which everybody repeats, or hears with acquiescence, which are received as truisms, yet of which most people first truly learn the meaning, when experience, generally of a painful kind, has made it a reality to them. How often, when smarting under some unforeseen misfortune or disappointment, does a person call to mind some proverb or common saying, familiar to him all his life, the meaning of which, if he had ever before felt it as he does now, would have saved him from the calamity. There are indeed reasons for this, other than the absence of discussion: there are many truths of which the full meaning *cannot* be realized, until personal experience has brought it home. But much more of the meaning even of these would have been understood, and what was understood would have been far more deeply impressed on the mind, if the man had been accustomed to hear it argued *pro* and *con* by people who did understand it. The fatal tendency of mankind to leave off thinking about a thing when it is no longer doubtful, is the cause of half their errors. A contemporary author has well spoken of "the deep slumber of a described opinion."

But what! (it may be asked) Is the absence of unanimity an indispensable condition of true knowledge? Is it necessary that some part of mankind should persist in error, to enable any to realize the truth? Does a belief cease to be real and vital as soon as it is generally received—and is a proposition never thoroughly understood and felt unless some doubt of it remains? As soon as mankind have unanimously accepted a truth, does the truth perish within them? The highest aim and best result of improved intelligence, it has hitherto been thought, is to unite mankind more and more in the acknowledgment of all important truths: and does the intelligence only last as long as it has not achieved its object? Do the fruits of conquest perish by the very completeness of the victory?

I affirm no such thing. As mankind improve, the number of doctrines which are no longer disputed or doubted will be constantly on the increase: and the well-being of mankind may almost be measured by the number and gravity of the truths which have reached the point of being uncontested. The cessation, on one question after another, of serious controversy, is one of the necessary incidents of the consolidation of opinion; a consolidation as salutary in the case of true opinions, as it is dangerous and noxious when the opinions are erroneous. But though this gradual narrowing of the bounds of diversity of opinion is necessary in both senses of the term, being at once inevitable and indispensable, we are not therefore obliged to conclude that all its consequences must be beneficial. The loss of so important an aid to the intelligent and living apprehension of a truth, as is afforded by the necessity of explaining it to, or defending it against, opponents, though not sufficient to outweigh, is no trifling drawback from the benefit of its universal recognition. Where this advantage can no longer be had, I confess I should like to see the teachers of mankind endeavoring to provide a substitute for it; some contrivance for making the difficulties of the question as present to the learner's consciousness, as if they were pressed upon him by a dissentient champion, eager for his conversion.

But instead of seeking contrivances for this purpose, they have lost those they formerly had. The Socratic dialectics, so magnificently exemplified in the dialogues of Plato, were a contrivance of this description. They were essentially a negative discussion of the great questions of philosophy and life, directed with consummate skill to the purpose of convincing any one who had merely adopted the commonplaces of received opinion, that he did not understand the subject—that he as yet attached no definite meaning to the doctrines he professed; in order that, becoming aware of his ignorance, he might be put in the way to attain a stable belief, resting on a clear apprehension both of the meaning of doctrines and of their evidence. The school disputations of the Middle Ages had a somewhat similar object. They were intended to make sure that the pupil understood his own opinion, and (by necessary correlation) the opinion opposed to it, and could enforce the grounds of the one and confute those of the other. These last-mentioned contests had indeed the incurable defect, that the premises appealed to were taken from authority, not from reason; and, as a discipline to the mind, they were in every respect inferior to the powerful dialectics which formed the intellects of the "Socratici viri": but the modern mind owes far more to both than it is generally willing to admit, and the present modes of education contain nothing which in the smallest degree supplies the place either of the one or of the other. A person who derives all his instruction from teachers or books, even if he escape the besetting temptation of contenting himself with cram, is under no compulsion to hear both sides; accordingly it is far from a frequent accomplishment, even among thinkers, to know both sides; and the weakest part of what everybody says in defense of his opinion, is what he intends as a reply to antagonists. It is the fashion of the present time to disparage negative logic—that which points out weaknesses in theory or errors in practice, without establishing positive truths. Such negative criticism would indeed be poor enough as an ultimate result; but as a means to attaining any positive knowledge or conviction worthy the name, it cannot be valued too highly; and until people are again systematically trained to it, there will be few great thinkers, and a low general average of intellect, in any but the mathematical and physical departments of speculation. On any other subject no one's opinions deserve the name of knowledge, except so far as he has either had forced upon him by others, or gone through of himself, the same mental

process which would have been required of him in carrying on an active controversy with opponents. That, therefore, which when absent, it is so indispensable, but so difficult, to create, how worse than absurd it is to forego, when spontaneously offering itself! If there are any persons who contest a received opinion, or who will do so if law or opinion will let them, let us thank them for it, open our minds to listen to them, and rejoice that there is some one to do for us what we otherwise ought, if we have any regard for either the certainty or the vitality of our convictions, to do with much greater labor for ourselves.

It still remains to speak of one of the principal causes which make diversity of opinion advantageous, and will continue to do so until mankind shall have entered a stage of intellectual advancement which at present seems at an incalculable distance. We have hitherto considered only two possibilities: that the received opinion may be false, and some other opinion, consequently, true; or that, the received opinion being true, a conflict with the opposite error is essential to a clear apprehension and deep feeling of its truth. But there is a commoner case than either of these; when the conflicting doctrines, instead of being one true and the other false, share the truth between them; and the nonconforming opinion is needed to supply the remainder of the truth, of which the received doctrine embodies only a part. Popular opinions, on subjects not palpable to sense, are often true, but seldom or never the whole truth. They are a part of the truth; sometimes a greater, sometimes a smaller part, but exaggerated, distorted, and disjoined from the truths by which they ought to be accompanied and limited. Heretical opinions, on the other hand, are generally some of these suppressed and neglected truths, bursting the bonds which kept them down, and either seeking reconciliation with the truth contained in the common opinion, or fronting it as enemies, and setting themselves up, with similar exclusiveness, as the whole truth. The latter case is hitherto the most frequent, as, in the human mind, one-sidedness has always been the rule, and many-sidedness the exception. Hence, even in revolutions of opinion, one part of the truth usually sets while another rises. Even progress, which ought to superadd, for the most part only substitutes, one partial and incomplete truth for another; improvement consisting chiefly in this, that the new fragment of truth is more wanted, more adapted to the needs of the time, than that which it displaces. Such being the partial character of prevailing opinions, even when resting on a true foundation, every opinion which embodies somewhat of the portion of truth which the common opinion omits, ought to be considered precious, with whatever amount of error and confusion that truth may be blended. No sober judge of human affairs will feel bound to be indignant because those who force on our notice truths which we should otherwise have overlooked, overlook some of those which we see. Rather, he will think that so long as popular truth is one-sided, it is more desirable than otherwise that unpopular truth should have one-sided asserters too; such being usually the most energetic, and the most likely to compel reluctant attention to the fragment of wisdom which they proclaim as if it were the whole.

Thus, in the eighteenth century, when nearly all the instructed, and all those of the uninstructed who were led by them, were lost in admiration of what is called civilization, and of the marvels of modern science, literature, and philosophy, and while greatly overrating the amount of unlikeness between the men of modern and those of ancient times, indulged the belief that the whole of the difference was in their own favor; with what a salutary shock did the paradoxes of Rousseau explode like bombshells in the midst, dislocating the compact mass of one-sided opinion, and forcing its elements to recombine in a better form and with additional ingredients. Not that the current opinions were on the whole farther from the truth than Rousseau's were; on the contrary, they were nearer to it; they contained more of positive truth, and very much less of error. Nevertheless there lay in Rousseau's doctrine, and has floated down the stream of opinion along with it, a considerable amount of exactly those truths which the popular opinion wanted; and these are the deposit which was left behind when the flood subsided. The superior worth of simplicity of life, the enervating and demoralizing effect of the trammels and hypocrisies of artificial society, are ideas which have never been

entirely absent from cultivated minds since Rousseau wrote; and they will in time produce their due effect, though at present needing to be asserted as much as ever, and to be asserted by deeds, for words, on this subject, have nearly exhausted their power.

In politics, again, it is almost a commonplace, that a party of order or stability, and a party of progress or reform, are both necessary elements of a healthy state of political life; until the one or the other shall have so enlarged its mental grasp as to be a party equally of order and of progress, knowing and distinguishing what is fit to be preserved from what ought to be swept away. Each of these modes of thinking derives its utility from the deficiencies of the other; but it is in a great measure the opposition of the other that keeps each within the limits of reason and sanity. Unless opinions favorable to democracy and to aristocracy, to property and to equality, to co-operation and to competition, to luxury and to abstinence, to sociality and individuality, to liberty and discipline, and all the other standing antagonisms of practical life, are expressed with equal freedom, and enforced and defended with equal talent and energy, there is no chance of both elements obtaining their due; one scale is sure to go up, and the other down. Truth, in the great practical concerns of life, is so much a question of the reconciling and combining of opposites, that very few have minds sufficiently capacious and impartial to make the adjustment with an approach to correctness, and it has to be made by the rough process of a struggle between combatants fighting under hostile banners. On any of the great open questions just enumerated, if either of the two opinions has a better claim than the other, not merely to be tolerated, but to be encouraged and countenanced, it is the one which happens at the particular time and place to be in a minority. That is the opinion which, for the time being, represents the neglected interests, the side of human well-being which is in danger of obtaining less than its share. I am aware that there is not, in this country, any tolerance of differences of opinion on most of these topics. They are adduced to show, by admitted and multiplied examples, the universality of the fact, that only through diversity of opinion is there, in the existing state of human intellect, a chance of fair play to all sides of the truth. When there are persons to be found, who form an exception to the apparent unanimity of the world on any subject, even if the world is in the right, it is always probable that dissentients have something worth hearing to say for themselves, and that truth would lose something by their silence.

It may be objected, "But *some* received principles, especially on the highest and most vital subjects, are more than half-truths. The Christian morality, for instance, is the whole truth on that subject, and if any one teaches a morality which varies from it, he is wholly in error." As this is of all cases the most important in practice, none can be fitter to test the general maxim. But before pronouncing what Christian morality is or is not, it would be desirable to decide what is meant by Christian morality. If it means the morality of the New Testament, I wonder that any one who derives his knowledge of this from the book itself, can suppose that it was announced, or intended, as a complete doctrine of morals. The Gospel always refers to a pre-existing morality, and confines its precepts to the particulars in which that morality was to be corrected, or superseded by a wider and higher; expressing itself, moreover, in terms most general, often impossible to be interpreted literally, and possessing rather the impressiveness of poetry or eloquence than the precision of legislation. To extract from it a body of ethical doctrine, has never been possible without eking it out from the Old Testament, that is, from a system elaborate indeed, but in many respects barbarous, and intended only for a barbarous people. St. Paul, a declared enemy to this Judaical mode of interpreting the doctrine and filling up the scheme of his Master, equally assumes a pre-existing morality, namely that of the Greeks and Romans; and his advice to Christians is in a great measure a system of accommodation to that; even to the extent of giving an apparent sanction to slavery. What is called Christian, but should rather be termed theological, morality, was not the work of Christ or the Apostles, but is of much later origin, having been gradually built up by the Catholic Church of the first five centuries, and though not implicitly adopted by moderns and Protestants, has been much less modified by them than

might have been expected. For the most part, indeed, they have contented themselves with cutting off the additions which had been made to it in the Middle Ages, each sect supplying the place by fresh additions, adopted to its own character and tendencies. That mankind owe a great debt to this morality, and to its early teachers, I should be the last person to deny; but I do not scruple to say of it, that it is, in many important points, incomplete and one-sided, and that unless ideas and feelings, not sanctioned by it, had contributed to the formation of European life and character, human affairs would have been in a worse condition than they now are. Christian morality (so called) has all the characters of a reaction; it is, in great part, a protest against Paganism. Its ideal is negative rather than positive; passive rather than active; innocence rather than Nobleness; Abstinence from Evil, rather than energetic Pursuit of Good: in its precepts (as has been well said) "thou shalt not" predominates unduly over "thou shalt." In its horror of sensuality, it made an idol of asceticism, which has been gradually compromised away into one of legality. It holds out the hope of heaven and the threat of hell, as the appointed and appropriate motives to a virtuous life: in this falling far below the best of the ancients, and doing what lies in it to give to human morality an essentially selfish character, by disconnecting each man's feelings of duty from the interests of his fellow-creatures, except so far as a self-interested inducement is offered to him for consulting them. It is essentially a doctrine of passive obedience; it inculcates submission to all authorities, found established; who indeed are not to be actively obeyed when they command what religion forbids, but who are not to be resisted, far less rebelled against, for any amount of wrong to ourselves. And while, in the morality of the best Pagan nations, duty to the State holds even a disproportionate place, infringing on the just liberty of the individual; in purely Christian ethics, that grand department of duty is scarcely noticed or acknowledged. It is in the Koran, not the New Testament, that we read the maxim—"A ruler who appoints any man to an office, when there is in his dominions another man better qualified for it, sins against God and against the State." What little recognition the idea of obligation to the public attains in modern morality, is derived from Greek and Roman sources, not from Christian; as, even in the morality of private life, whatever exists of magnanimity, high-mindedness, personal dignity, even the sense of honor, is derived from the purely human, not the religious part of our education, and never could have grown out of a standard of ethics in which the only worth, professedly recognized, is that of obedience.

I am as far as any one from pretending that these defects are necessarily inherent in the Christian ethics, in every manner in which it can be conceived, or that the many requisites of a complete moral doctrine which it does not contain, do not admit of being reconciled with it. Far less would I insinuate this of the doctrines and precepts of Christ himself. I believe that the sayings of Christ are all, that I can see any evidence of their having been intended to be; that they are irreconcilable with nothing which a comprehensive morality requires; that everything which is excellent in ethics may be brought within them, with no greater violence to their language than has been done to it by all who have attempted to deduce from them any practical system of conduct whatever. But it is quite consistent with this, to believe that they contain, and were meant to contain, only a part of the truth; that many essential elements of the highest morality are among the things which are not provided for, nor intended to be provided for, in the recorded deliverances of the Founder of Christianity, and which have been entirely thrown aside in the system of ethics erected on the basis of those deliverances by the Christian Church. And this being so, I think it a great error to persist in attempting to find in the Christian doctrine that complete rule for our guidance, which its author intended it to sanction and enforce, but only partially to provide. I believe, too, that this narrow theory is becoming a grave practical evil, detracting greatly from the value of the moral training and instruction, which so many well-meaning persons are now at length exerting themselves to promote. I much fear that by attempting to form the mind and feelings on an exclusively religious type, and discarding those secular standards (as for want of a better

name they may be called) which heretofore co-existed with and supplemented the Christian ethics, receiving some of its spirit, and infusing into it some of theirs, there will result, and is even now resulting, a low, abject, servile type of character, which, submit itself as it may to what it deems the Supreme Will, is incapable of rising to or sympathizing in the conception of Supreme Goodness. I believe that other ethics than any which can be evolved from exclusively Christian sources, must exist side by side with Christian ethics to produce the moral regeneration of mankind; and that the Christian system is no exception to the rule, that in an imperfect state of the human mind, the interests of truth require a diversity of opinions. It is not necessary that in ceasing to ignore the moral truths not contained in Christianity, men should ignore any of those which it does contain. Such prejudice, or oversight, when it occurs, is altogether an evil; but it is one from which we cannot hope to be always exempt, and must be regarded as the price paid for an inestimable good. The exclusive pretension made by a part of the truth to be the whole, must and ought to be protested against; and if a reactionary impulse should make the protestors unjust in their turn, this one-sidedness, like the other, may be lamented, but must be tolerated. If Christians would teach infidels to be just to Christianity, they should themselves be just to infidelity. It can do truth no service to blink the fact, known to all who have the most ordinary acquaintance with literary history, that a large portion of the noblest and most valuable moral teaching has been the work, not only of men who did not know, but of men who knew and rejected, the Christian faith.

I do not pretend that the most unlimited use of the freedom of enunciating all possible opinions would put an end to the evils of religious or philosophical sectarianism. Every truth which men of narrow capacity are in earnest about, is sure to be asserted, inculcated, and in many ways even acted on, as if no other truth existed in the world, or at all events none that could limit or qualify the first. I acknowledge that the tendency of all opinions to become sectarian is not cured by the freest discussion, but is often heightened and exacerbated thereby; the truth which ought to have been, but was not, seen, being rejected all the more violently because proclaimed by persons regarded as opponents. But it is not on the impassioned partisan, it is on the calmer and more disinterested bystander, that this collision of opinions works its salutary effect. Not the violent conflict between parts of the truth, but the quiet suppression of half of it, is the formidable evil; there is always hope when people are forced to listen to both sides; it is when they attend only to one that errors harden into prejudices, and truth itself ceases to have the effect of truth, by being exaggerated into falsehood. And since there are few mental attributes more rare than that judicial faculty which can sit in intelligent judgment between two sides of a question, of which only one is represented by an advocate before it, truth has no chance but in proportion as every side of it, every opinion which embodies any fraction of the truth, not only finds advocates, but is so advocated as to be listened to.

We have now recognized the necessity to the mental well-being of mankind (on which all their other well-being depends) of freedom of opinion, and freedom of the expression of opinion, on four distinct grounds; which we will now briefly recapitulate.

First, if any opinion is compelled to silence, that opinion may, for aught we can certainly know, be true. To deny this is to assume our own infallibility.

Secondly, though the silenced opinion be an error, it may, and very commonly does, contain a portion of truth; and since the general or prevailing opinion on any subject is rarely or never the whole truth, it is only by the collision of adverse opinions that the remainder of the truth has any chance of being supplied.

Thirdly, even if the received opinion be not only true, but the whole truth; unless it is suffered to be, and actually is, vigorously and earnestly contested, it will, by most of those who receive it, be held in the manner of a prejudice, with little comprehension or feeling of its rational grounds. And not only this, but, fourthly, the meaning of the doctrine itself will be in danger of being lost, or enfeebled, and deprived of its vital effect on the character and conduct: the dogma becoming a mere formal profession, inefficacious for good, but cumbering the ground,

and preventing the growth of any real and heartfelt conviction, from reason or personal experience.

INDIVIDUALITY AS ONE OF THE ELEMENTS OF WELL-BEING

Such being the reasons which make it imperative that human beings should be free to form opinions, and to express their opinions without reserve; and such the baneful consequences to the intellectual, and through that to the moral nature of man, unless this liberty is either conceded, or asserted in spite of prohibition; let us next examine whether the same reasons do not require that men should be free to act upon their opinions—to carry these out in their lives, without hindrance, either physical or moral, from their fellow men, so long as it is at their own risk and peril. This last proviso is of course indispensable. No one pretends that actions should be as free as opinions. On the contrary, even opinions lose their immunity, when the circumstances in which they are expressed are such as to constitute their expression a positive instigation to some mischievous act. An opinion that corn-dealers are starvers of the poor, or that private property is robbery, ought to be unmolested when simply circulated through the press, but may justly incur punishment when delivered orally to an excited mob assembled before the house of a corn-dealer, or when handed about among the same mob in the form of a placard. Acts, of whatever kind, which, without justifiable cause, do harm to others, may be, and in the more important cases absolutely require to be, controlled by the unfavorable sentiments, and, when needful, by the active interference of mankind. The liberty of the individual must be thus far limited; he must not make himself a nuisance to other people. But if he refrains from molesting others in what concerns them, and merely acts according to his own inclination and judgment in things which concern himself, the same reasons which show that opinion should be free, prove also that he should be allowed, without molestation, to carry his opinions into practice at his own cost. That mankind are not infallible; that their truths, for the most part, are only half-truths; that unity of opinion, unless resulting from the fullest and freest comparison of opposite opinions, is not desirable, and diversity not an evil, but a good, until mankind are much more capable than at present of recognizing all sides of the truth, are principles applicable to men's modes of action, not less than to their opinions. As it is useful that mankind are imperfect there should be different opinions, so it is that there should be experiments of living; that free scope should be given to varieties of character, short of injury to others; and that the worth of different modes of life should be proved practically, when any one thinks fit to try them. It is desirable, in short, that in things which do not primarily concern others, individuality should assert itself. Where (not the person's own character) but the traditions or customs of other people are the rule of conduct, there is wanting one of the principal ingredients of human happiness, and quite the chief ingredient of individual and social progress.

In maintaining the principle, the greatest difficulty to be encountered does not lie in the appreciation of means towards an acknowledged end, but in the indifference of persons in general to the end itself. If it were felt that the free development of individuality is one of the leading essentials of well-being; that it is not only a co-ordinate element with all that is designated by the terms civilization, instruction, education, culture, but is itself a necessary part and condition of all those things; there would be no danger that liberty should be undervalued, and the adjustment of the boundaries between it and social control would present no extraordinary difficulty. But the evil is, that individual spontaneity is hardly recognized by the common modes of thinking, as having any intrinsic worth, or deserving any regard on its own account. The majority, being satisfied with the ways of mankind as they now are (for it is they who make them what they are), cannot comprehend why those ways should not be good enough for everybody; and what is more, spontaneity forms no part of the ideal of the majority of moral and social reformers, but is rather looked on with jealousy, as a troublesome and perhaps rebellious obstruction to the general acceptance of what these reformers, in their own judgment, think would be best for mankind. Few persons, out of Germany, even comprehend the meaning of the doctrine which Wilhelm von Humboldt, so eminent both as a savant and as a politician, made the text of a treatise—that "the end of man, or that which is prescribed by the eternal or immutable dictates of reason, and not suggested by vague and transient desires, is the highest and most harmonious development of his powers to a complete and consistent whole"; that, therefore, the object "towards which every human being must ceaselessly direct his efforts, and on which especially those who design to influence their fellow men must ever keep their eyes, is the individuality of power and development"; that for this there are two requisites, "freedom, and variety of situations"; and that from the union of these arise "individual vigor and manifold diversity," which combine themselves in "originality."

Little, however, as people are accustomed to a doctrine like that of von Humboldt, and surprising as it may be to them to find so high a value attached to individuality, the question, one must nevertheless think, can only be one of degree. No one's idea of excellence in conduct is that people should do absolutely nothing but copy one another. No one would assert that people ought not to put into their mode of life, and into the conduct of their concerns, any impress whatever of their own judgment, or of their own individual character. On the other hand, it would be absurd to pretend that people ought to live as if nothing whatever had been known in the world before they came into it; as if experience had as yet done nothing towards showing that one mode of existence, or of conduct, is preferable to another. Nobody denies that people should be so taught and trained in youth, as to know and benefit by the ascertained results of human experience. But it is the privilege and proper condition of a human being, arrived at the maturity of his faculties, to use and interpret experience in his own way. It is for him to find out what part of recorded experience is properly applicable to his own circumstances and character. The traditions and customs of other people are, to a certain extent, evidence of what their experience has taught *them;* presumptive evidence, and as such, have a claim to his deference: but, in the first place, their experience may be too narrow; or they may not have interpreted it rightly. Secondly, their interpretation of experience may be correct, but unsuitable to him. Customs are made for customary circumstances, and customary characters; and his circumstances or his character may be uncustomary. Thirdly, though the customs be both good as customs, and suitable to him, yet to conform to custom, merely *as* custom, does not educate or develop in him any of the qualities which are the distinctive endowment of a human being. The human facilities of perception, judgment, discriminative feeling, mental activity, and even moral preference, are exercised only in making a choice. He who does anything because it is the custom, makes no choice. He gains no practice either in discerning or in desiring what is best. The mental and moral, like the muscular powers, are improved only by being used. The faculties are called into no exercise by doing a thing merely because others do it, no more than by believing a thing only because others believe it. If the grounds of an opinion are not conclusive to the person's own reason, his reason cannot be strengthened, but is likely to be weakened, by his adopting it: and if the inducements to an act are not such as are consentaneous to his own feelings and character (where affection, or the rights of others, are not concerned) it is so much done towards rendering his feelings and character inert and torpid, instead of active and energetic.

He who lets the world, or his own portion of it, choose his plan of life for him, has no need of any other faculty than the ape-like one of imitation. He who chooses his plan for himself, employs all his faculties. He must use observation to see, reasoning and judgment to foresee, activity to gather materials for decision, discrimination to decide, and when he has decided, firmness and self-control to hold to his deliberate decision. And these qualities he requires and exercises exactly in proportion as the part of his conduct which he determines according to his own judgment and feelings is a large one. It is possible that he might be guided in some good path, and kept out of harm's way, without any of these things. But what will be his comparative worth as a human being? It really is of importance, not only what men do, but also what manner of men they are that do it. Among the works of man, which human life is rightly employed in perfecting and beautifying, the first in importance surely is man himself. Supposing it were possible to get houses built, corn grown, battles fought, causes tried, and even churches erected and prayers said, by machinery—by automatons in human form—it would be a considerable loss to exchange for these automatons even the men and women who at present inhabit the more civilized parts of the world, and who assuredly are but starved specimens of what nature can and will produce. Human nature is not a machine to be built after a model, and set to do exactly the work prescribed for it, but a tree, which requires to grow and develop itself on all sides, according to the tendency of the inward forces which make it a living thing.

It will probably be conceded that it is desirable people should exercise their understandings, and that an intelligent following of custom, or even occasionally an intelligent deviation from custom, is better than a blind and simply mechanical adhesion to it. To a certain extent it is admitted, that our understanding should be our own: but there is not the same willingness to admit that our desires and impulses should be our own likewise; or that to possess impulses of our own, and of any strength, is anything but a peril and a snare. Yet desires and impulses are as much a part of a perfect human being, as beliefs and restraints: and strong impulses are only perilous when not properly balanced; when one set of aims and inclinations is developed into strength, while others, which ought to co-exist with them, remain weak and inactive. It is not because men's desires are strong that they act ill; it is because their consciences are weak. There is no natural connection between strong impulses and a weak conscience. The natural connection is the other way. To say that one person's desires and feelings are stronger and more various than those of another, is merely to say that he has more of the raw material of human nature, and is therefore capable, perhaps of more evil, but certainly or more good. Strong impulses are but another name for energy. Energy may be turned to bad uses; but more good may always be made of an energetic nature, than of an indolent and impassive one. Those who have most natural feeling, are always those whose cultivated feelings may be made the strongest. The same strong susceptibilities which make the personal impulses vivid and powerful, are also the source from whence are generated the most passionate love of virtue, and the sternest self-control. It is through the cultivation of these, that society both does its duty and protects its interests: not by rejecting the stuff of which heroes are made, because it knows not how to make them. A person whose desires and impulses are his own—are the expression of his own nature, as it has been developed and modified by his own culture—is said to have a character. One whose desires and impulses are not his own, has no character, no more than a steam-engine has a character. If, in addition to being his own, his impulses are strong, and are under the government of a strong will, he has an energetic character. Whoever thinks that individuality of desires and impulses should not be encouraged to unfold itself, must maintain that society has no need of strong natures—is not the better for containing many persons who have much character—and that a high general average of energy is not desirable.

In some early states of society, these forces might be, and were, too much ahead of the power which society then possessed of disciplining and controlling them. There has been a time when the element of spontaneity and individuality was in excess, and the social principle had a hard struggle with it. The difficulty then was, to induce men of strong bodies or minds to pay obedience to any rules which required them to control their impulses. To overcome this difficulty, law and discipline, like the Popes struggling against the Emperors, asserted a power over the whole man, claiming to control all his life in order to control his character—which society had not found any other sufficient means of binding. But society has now fairly got the better of individuality; and the danger which threatens human nature is not the excess, but the deficiency, of personal impulses and preferences. Things are vastly changed, since the passions of those who were strong by station or by personal endowment were in a state of habitual rebellion against laws and ordinances, and required to be rigorously chained up to enable the persons within their reach to enjoy any particle of security. In our times, from the highest class of society down to the lowest, every one lives as under the eye of a hostile and dreaded censorship. Not only in what concerns others, but in what concerns only themselves, the individual or the family do not ask themselves—what do I prefer? or, what would suit my character and disposition? or, what would allow the best and highest in me to have fair play, and enable it to grow and thrive? They ask themselves, what is suitable to my position? what is usually done by persons of my station and pecuniary circumstances? or (worse still) what is usually done by persons of a station and circumstances superior to mine? I do not mean that they choose what is customary, in preference to what suits their own inclination. It does not occur to them to have any inclination, except for what is customary. Thus the mind itself is bowed to the yoke: even in what people do for pleasure, conformity is the first thing thought of; they like in crowds; they exercise choice only among things commonly done: peculiarity of taste, eccentricity of conduct, are shunned equally with crimes: until by dint of not following their own nature, they have no nature to follow: their human capacities are withered and starved: they become incapable of any strong wishes or native pleasures, and are generally without either opinions or feelings of home growth, or properly their own. Now is this, or is it not, the desirable condition of human nature?

It is so, on the Calvinistic theory. According to that, the one great offense of man is self-will. All the good of which humanity is capable, is comprised in obedience. You have no choice; thus you must do, and no otherwise: "whatever is not a duty, is a sin." Human nature being radically corrupt, there is no redemption for any one until human nature is killed within him. To one holding this theory of life, crushing out any of the human faculties, capacities, and susceptibilities, is no evil: man needs no capacity, but that of surrendering himself to the will of God: and if he uses any of his faculties for any other purpose but to do that supposed will more effectually, he is better without them. This is the theory of Calvinism; and it is held, in a mitigated form, by many who do not consider themselves Calvinists; the mitigation consisting in giving a less ascetic interpretation to the alleged will of God; asserting it to be his will that mankind should gratify some of their inclinations; of course not in the manner they themselves prefer, but in the way of obedience, that is, in a way prescribed to them by authority; and, therefore, by the necessary conditions of the case, the same for all.

In some such insidious form there is at present a strong tendency to this narrow theory of life, and to the pinched and hidebound type of human character which it patronizes. Many persons, no doubt, sincerely think that human beings thus cramped and dwarfed, are as their Maker designed them to be; just as many have thought that trees are a much finer thing when clipped into pollards, or cut out into figures of animals, than as nature made them. But if it be any part of religion to believe that man was made by a good Being, it is more consistent with that faith to believe, that this Being gave all human faculties that they might be cultivated and unfolded, not rooted out and consumed, and that he takes delight in every nearer approach made by his creatures to the ideal conception embodied in them, every increase in any of their capabilities of comprehension, of action, or of enjoyment. There is a different type of human excellence from the Calvinistic; a conception of humanity as having its nature bestowed on it for other purposes than merely to be abnegated. "Pagan self-assertion" is one of the elements of human worth, as well as "Christian self-denial." There is a Greek ideal of self-development, which the Platonic and Christian ideal of self-government blends with, but does not supersede. It may be better to be a John Knox than an Alcibiades, but it is better to be a Pericles than either; nor would a Pericles, if we had one in these days, be without anything good which belonged to John Knox.

It is not by wearing down into uniformity all that is individual in themselves, but by cultivating it and calling it forth, within the limits imposed by the rights and interests of others, that human beings become a noble and beautiful object of contemplation; and as the works partake the character of those who do them, by the same process human life also becomes rich, diversified, and animating, furnishing more abundant aliment to high thoughts and elevating feelings, and strengthening the tie which binds every individual to the race, by making the race

infinitely better worth belonging to. In proportion to the development of his individuality, each person becomes more valuable to himself, and is therefore capable of being more valuable to others. There is a greater fullness of life about his own existence, and when there is more life in the units there is more in the mass which is composed of them. As much compression as is necessary to prevent the stronger specimens of human nature from encroaching on the rights of others, cannot be dispensed with; but for this there is ample compensation even in the point of view of human development. The means of development which the individual loses by being prevented from gratifying his inclinations to the injury of others, are chiefly obtained at the expense of the development of other people. And even to himself there is a full equivalent in the better development of the social part of his nature, rendered possible by the restraint put upon the selfish part. To be held to rigid rules of justice for the sake of others, develops the feelings and capacities which have the good of others for their object. But to be restrained in things not affecting their good, by their mere displeasure, develops nothing valuable, except such force of character as may unfold itself in resisting the restraint. If acquiesced in, it dulls and blunts the whole nature. To give any fair plan to the nature of each, it is essential that different persons should be allowed to lead different lives. In proportion as this latitude has been exercised in any age, has that age been noteworthy to posterity. Even despotism does not produce its worst effects, so long as individuality exists under it; and whatever crushes individuality is despotism, by whatever name it may be called, and whether it professes to be enforcing the will of God or the injunctions of men.

Having said that Individuality is the same thing with development, and that it is only the cultivation of individuality which produces, or can produce, well-developed human beings, I might here close the argument: for what more or better can be said of any condition of human affairs, than that it begins human beings themselves nearer to the best thing they can be? or what worse can be said of any obstruction to good, than that it prevents this? Doubtless, however, these considerations will not suffice to convince those who most need convincing; and it is necessary further to show, that these developed human beings are of some use to the undeveloped—to point out to those who do not desire liberty, and would not avail themselves of it, that they may be in some intelligible manner rewarded for allowing other people to make use of it without hindrance.

In the first place, then, I would suggest that they might possibly learn something from them. It will not be denied by anybody, that originality is a valuable element in human affairs. There is always need of persons not only to discover new truths, and point out when what were once truths are true no longer, but also to commence new practices, and set the example of more enlightened conduct, and better taste and sense in human life. This cannot well be gainsaid by anybody who does not believe that the world has already attained perfection in all its ways and practices. It is true that this benefit is not capable of being rendered by everybody alike: there are but few persons, in comparison with the whole of mankind, whose experiments, if adopted by others, would be likely to be any improvement on established practice. But these few are the salt of the earth; without them, human life would become a stagnant pool. Not only is it they who introduce good things which did not before exist; it is they who keep the life in those which already existed. If there were nothing new to be done, would human intellect cease to be necessary? Would it be a reason why those who do the old things should forget why they are done, and do them like cattle, not like human beings? There is only too great a tendency in the best beliefs and practices to degenerate into the mechanical; and unless there were a succession of persons whose ever-recurring originality prevents the grounds of those beliefs and practices from becoming merely traditional, such dead matter would not resist the smallest shock from anything really alive, and there would be no reason why civilization should not die out, as in the Byzantine Empire. Persons of genius, it is true, are, and are always likely to be, a small minority; but in order to have them, it is necessary to preserve the soil in which they grow. Genius can only breathe freely in an *atmosphere* of freedom. Persons of genius are, *ex vi termini, more* individual than any other people—less capable, consequently, of fitting themselves, without hurtful compression, into any of the small number of molds which society provides in order to save its members the trouble of forming their own character. If from timidity they consent to be forced into one of these molds, and to let all that part of themselves which cannot expand under the pressure remain unexpanded, society will be little the better for their genius. If they are of a strong character, and break their fetters, they become a mark for the society which has not succeeded in reducing them to commonplace, to point at with solemn warning as "wild," "erratic," and the like; much as if one should complain of the Niagara river for not flowing smoothly between its banks like a Dutch canal.

I insist thus emphatically on the importance of genius, and the necessity of allowing it to unfold itself freely both in thought and in practice, being well aware that no one will deny the position in theory, but knowing also that almost every one, in reality, is totally indifferent to it. People think genius a fine thing if it enables a man to write an exciting poem, or paint a picture. But in its true sense, that of originality in thought and action, though no one says that it is not a thing to be admired, nearly all, at heart, think that they can do very well without it. Unhappily this is too natural to be wondered at. Originality is the one thing which unoriginal minds cannot feel the use of. They cannot see what it is to do for them: how should they? If they could see what it would do for them, it would not be originality. The first service which originality has to render them, is that of opening their eyes: which being once fully done, they would have a chance of being themselves original. Meanwhile, recollecting that nothing was ever yet done which some one was not the first to do, and that all good things which exist are the fruits of originality, let them be modest enough to believe that there is something still left for it to accomplish, and assure themselves that they are more in need of originality, the less they are conscious of the want.

In sober truth, whatever homage may be professed, or even paid, to real or supposed mental superiority, the general tendency of things throughout the world is to render mediocrity the ascendant power among mankind. In ancient history, in the Middle Ages, and in a diminishing degree through the long transition from feudality to the present time, the individual was a power in himself; and if he had either great talents or a high social position, he was a considerable power. At present individuals are lost in the crowd. In politics it is almost a triviality to say that public opinion now rules the world. The only power deserving the name is that of masses, and of governments while they make themselves the organ of the tendencies and instincts of masses. This is as true in the moral and social relations of private life as in public transactions. Those whose opinions go by the name of public opinion, are not always the same sort of public: in America they are the whole white population; in England, chiefly the middle class. But they are always a mass, that is to say, collective mediocrity. And what is a still greater novelty, the mass do not now take their opinions from dignitaries in Church or State, from ostensible leaders, or from books. Their thinking is done for them by men much like themselves, addressing them or speaking in their name, on the spur of the moment, through the newspapers. I am not complaining of all this. I do not assert that anything better is compatible, as a general rule, with the present low state of the human mind. But that does not hinder the government of mediocrity from being mediocre government. No government by a democracy or numerous aristocracy, either in its political acts or in the opinions, qualifies, and tone of mind which it fosters, ever did or could rise above mediocrity, except in so far as the sovereign Many have let themselves be guided (which in their best times they always have done) by the counsels and influence of a more highly gifted and instructed One or Few. The initiation of all wise or noble things, comes and must come from individuals; generally at first from some one individual. The honor and glory of the average man is that he is capable of following that initiative; that he can respond internally to wise and noble things, and be led to them with his eyes open. I am not countenancing the sort of "hero-worship" which

applauds the strong man of genius for forcibly seizing on the government of the world and making it do his bidding in spite of itself. All he can claim is, freedom to point out the way. The power of compelling others into it, is not only inconsistent with the freedom and development of all the rest, but corrupting to the strong man himself. It does seem, however, that when the opinions of masses of merely average men are everywhere become or becoming the dominant power, the counterpoise and corrective to that tendency would be, the more and more pronounced individuality of those who stand on the higher eminences of thought. It is in these circumstances most especially, that exceptional individuals, instead of being deterred, should be encouraged in acting differently from the mass. In other times there was no advantage in their doing so, unless they acted not only differently, but better. In this age, the mere example of nonconformity, the mere refusal to bend the knee to custom, is itself a service. Precisely because the tyranny of opinion is such as to make eccentricity a reproach, it is desirable, in order to break through that tyranny, that people should be eccentric. Eccentricity has always abounded when and where strength of character has abounded; and the amount of eccentricity in a society has generally been proportional to the amount of genius, mental vigor, and moral courage which it contained. That so few now dare to be eccentric, marks the chief danger of the time.

The worth of a State, in the long run, is the worth of the individuals composing it; and a State which postpones the interests of *their* mental expansion and elevation, to a little more of administrative skill, or of that semblance of it which practice gives, in the details of business; a State which dwarfs its men, in order that they may be more docile instruments in its hands even for beneficial purposes—will find that with small men no great thing can really be accomplished; and that the perfection of machinery to which it has sacrificed everything, will in the end avail it nothing, for want of the vital power which, in order that the machine might work more smoothly, it has preferred to banish.

*Utilitarianism**

The creed which accepts as the foundation of morals "utility" or the "greatest happiness principle" holds that actions are right in proportion as they tend to promote happiness; wrong as they tend to produce the reverse of happiness. By happiness is intended pleasure and the absence of pain; by unhappiness, pain and the privation of pleasure. To give a clear view of the moral standard set up by the theory, much more requires to be said; in particular, what things it includes in the ideas of pain and pleasure, and to what extent this is left an open question. But these supplementary explanations do not affect the theory of life on which this theory of morality is grounded—namely, that pleasure and freedom from pain are the only things desirable as ends; and that all desirable things (which are as numerous in the utilitarian as in any other scheme) are desirable either for pleasure inherent in themselves or as means to the promotion of pleasure and the prevention of pain.

Now such a theory of life excites in many minds, and among them in some of the most estimable in feeling and purpose, inveterate dislike. To suppose that life has (as they express it) no higher end than pleasure—no better and nobler object of desire and pursuit—they designate as utterly mean and groveling, as a doctrine worthy only of swine, to whom the following of Epicurus were, at a very early period, contemptuously likened; and modern holders of the doctrine are occasionally made the subject of equally polite comparisons by its German, French, and English assailants.

When thus attacked, the Epicureans have always answered that it is not they, but their accusers, who represent human nature in a degrading light, since the accusation supposes human beings to be capable of no pleasures except those of which swine are capable. The comparison of the Epicurean life to that of beasts is felt as degrading, precisely because a beast's pleasures do not satisfy a human being's conceptions of happiness. Human beings have faculties more elevated than the animal appetites and, when once made conscious of them, do not regard anything as happiness which does not include their gratification. I do not, indeed, consider the Epicureans to have been by any means faultless in drawing out their scheme of consequences from the utilitarian principle. To do this in any sufficient manner, many Stoic, as well as Christian, elements require to be included. But there is no known Epicurean theory of life which does not assign to the pleasures of the intellect, of the feelings and imagination, and of the moral sentiments a much higher value as pleasures than to those of mere sensation. It must be admitted, however, that utilitarian writers in general have placed the superiority of mental over bodily pleasure chiefly in the greater permanency, safety, uncostliness, etc., of the former—that is, in their circumstantial advantages rather than in their intrinsic nature. And on all these points utilitarians have fully proved their case; but they might have taken the other and, as it may be called, higher ground with entire consistency. It is quite compatible with the principle of utility to recognize the fact that some kinds of pleasure are more desirable and more valuable than others. It would be absurd that, while in estimating all other things quality is considered as well as quantity, the estimation of pleasure should be supposed to depend on quantity alone. . . .

Now it is an unquestionable fact that those who are equally acquainted with and equally capable of appreciating and enjoying both do give a most marked preference to the manner of existence which employs

---

* From John Stuart Mill, *Utilitarianism* (1861).

their higher faculties. Few human creatures would consent to be changed into any of the lower animals for a promise of the fullest allowance of a beast's pleasures; no intelligent human being would consent to be a fool, no instructed person would be an ignoramus, no person of feeling and conscience would be selfish and base, even though they should be persuaded that the fool, the dunce, or the rascal is better satisfied with his lot than they are with theirs. They would not resign what they possess more than he for the most complete satisfaction of all the desires which they have in common with him. If they ever fancy they would, it is only in cases of unhappiness so extreme that to escape from it they would exchange their lot for almost any other, however undesirable in their own eyes. A being of higher faculties requires more to make him happy, is capable probably of more acute suffering, and certainly accessible to it at more points, than one of an inferior type; but in spite of these liabilities, he can never really wish to sink into what he feels to be a lower grade of existence. We may give what explanation we please of this unwillingness; we may attribute it to pride, a name which is given indiscriminately to some of the most and to some of the least estimable feelings of which mankind are capable; we may refer it to the love of liberty and personal independence, an appeal to which was with the Stoics one of the most effective means for the inculcation of it; to the love of power or to the love of excitement, both of which do really enter into and contribute to it; but its most appropriate appellation is a sense of dignity, which all human beings possess in one form or other, and in some, though by no means in exact, proportion to their higher faculties, and which is so essential a part of the happiness of those in whom it is strong that nothing which conflicts with it could be otherwise than momentarily an object of desire to them. Whoever supposes that this preference takes place at a sacrifice of happiness—that the superior being, in anything like equal circumstances, is not happier than the inferior—confounds the two very different ideas of happiness and content. . . .

It may be objected that many who are capable of the higher pleasures occasionally, under the influence of temptation, postpone them to the lower. But this is quite compatible with a full appreciation of the intrinsic superiority of the higher. Men often, from infirmity of character, make their election for the nearer good, though they know it to be the less valuable; and this no less when the choice is between two bodily pleasures than when it is between bodily and mental. They pursue sensual indulgences to the injury of health, though perfectly aware that health is the greater good. It may be further objected that many who begin with youthful enthusiasm for everything noble, as they advance in years, sink into indolence and selfishness. But I do not believe that those who undergo this very common change voluntarily choose the lower description of pleasures in preference to the higher. I believe that, before they devote themselves exclusively to the one, they have already become incapable of the other. Capacity for the nobler feelings is in most natures a very tender plant, easily killed, not only by hostile influences, but by mere want of sustenance; and in the majority of young persons it speedily dies away if the occupations to which their position in life has devoted them, and the society into which it has thrown them, are not favorable to keeping that higher capacity in exercise. Men lose their high aspirations as they lose their intellectual tastes, because they have not time or opportunity for indulging them; and they addict themselves to inferior pleasures, not because they deliberately prefer them, but because they are either the only ones to which they have access or the only ones which they are any longer capable of enjoying. . . .

I must again repeat what the assailants of utilitarianism seldom have the justice to acknowledge, that the happiness which forms the utilitarian standard of what is right in conduct is not the agent's own happiness but that of all concerned. As between his own happiness and that of others, utilitarianism requires him to be as strictly impartial as a disinterested and benevolent spectator. In the golden rule of Jesus of Nazareth, we read the complete spirit of the ethics of utility. "To do as you would be done by," and "to love your neighbor as yourself," constitute the ideal perfection of utilitarian morality. As the means of making the nearest approach to this ideal, utility would enjoin, first, that laws and social arrangements should place the happiness or (as, speaking practically, it may be called) the interest of every individual as nearly as possible in harmony with the interest of the whole; and secondly, that education and opinion, which have so vast a power over human character, should so use that power as to establish in the mind of every individual an indissoluble association between his own happiness and the good of the whole, especially between his own happiness and the practice of such modes of conduct, negative and positive, as regard for the universal happiness prescribes: so that not only he may be unable to conceive the possibility of happiness to himself, consistently with conduct opposed to the general good, but also that a direct impulse to promote the general good may be in every individual one of the habitual motives of action, and the sentiments connected therewith may fill a large and prominent place in every human being's sentient existence.

The Subjection of Women*

The object of this essay is to explain as clearly as I am able, the grounds of an opinion which I have held from the very earliest period when I had formed any opinions at all on social or political matters, and which, instead of being weakened or modified, has been constantly growing stronger by the progress of reflection and the experience of life: That the principle which regulates the existing social relations between the two sexes—the legal subordination of one sex to the other—is wrong in itself, and now one of the chief hindrances to human improvement; and that it ought to be replaced by a principle of perfect equality, admitting no power or privilege on the one side, nor disability on the other.

The generality of a practice is in some cases a strong presumption that it is, or at all events once was, conducive to laudable ends. This is the case, when the practice was first adopted, or afterwards kept up, as a means to such ends, and was grounded on experience of the mode in which they could be most effectually attained. If the authority of men over women, when first established, had been the result of a conscientious comparison between different modes of constituting the government of society; if, after trying various other modes of social organization—the government of women over men, equality between the two, and such mixed and divided modes of government as might be invented—it had been decided, on the testimony of experience, that the mode in which women are wholly under the rule of men, having no share at all in public concerns, and each in private being under the legal obligation of obedience to the man

with whom she has associated her destiny, was the arrangement most conducive to the happiness and well being of both; its general adoption might then be fairly thought to be some evidence that, at the time when it was adopted, it was the best: though even then the considerations which recommended it may, like so many other primeval social facts of the greatest importance, have subsequently, in the course of ages, ceased to exist. But the state of the case is in every respect the reverse of this. In the first place, the opinion in favor of the present system, which entirely subordinates the weaker sex to the stronger, rests upon theory only; for there never has been trial made of any other: so that experience, in the sense in which it is vulgarly opposed to theory, cannot be pretended to have pronounced any verdict. And in the second place, the adoption of this system of inequality never was the result of deliberation, or forethought, or any social ideas, or any notion whatever of what conduced to the benefit of humanity or the good order of society. It arose simply from the fact that from the very earliest twilight of human society, every woman (owing to the value attached to her by men, combined with her inferiority in muscular strength) was found in a state of bondage to some man. Laws and systems of polity always begin by recognizing the relations they find already existing between individuals. They convert what was a mere physical fact into a legal right, give it the sanction of society, and principally aim at the substitution of public and organized means of asserting and protecting these rights, instead of the irregular and lawless conflict of physical strength. Those who had already been compelled to obedience became in this manner legally bound to it. Slavery, from being a mere affair of force between the master and the slave, became regularized and a matter of

---

*From John Stuart Mill, *The Subjection of Women* (1869).

compact among the masters, who, binding themselves to one another for common protection, guaranteed by their collective strength the private possessions of each, including his slaves. In early times, the great majority of the male sex were slaves, as well as the whole of the female. And many ages elapsed, some of them ages of high cultivation, before any thinker was bold enough to question the rightfulness, and the absolute social necessity, either of the one slavery or of the other. By degrees such thinkers did arise: and (the general progress of society assisting) the slavery of the male sex has, in all the countries of Christian Europe at least (though, in one of them, only within the last few years) been at length abolished, and that of the female sex has been gradually changed into a milder form of dependence. But this dependence, as it exists at present, is not an original institution, taking a fresh start from considerations of justice and social expediency—it is the primitive state of slavery lasting on, through successive mitigations and modifications occasioned by the same causes which have softened the general manners, and brought all human relations more under the control of justice and the influence of humanity. It has not lost the taint of its brutal origin. No presumption in its favor, therefore, can be drawn from the fact of its existence. The only such presumption which it could be supposed to have, must be grounded on its having lasted till now, when so many other things which came down from the same odious source have been done away with. And this, indeed, is what makes it strange to ordinary ears, to hear it asserted that the inequality of rights between men and women has no other source than the law of the strongest.

That this statement should have the effect of a paradox, is in some respects creditable to the progress of civilization, and the improvement of the moral sentiments of mankind. We now live—that is to say, one or two of the most advanced nations of the world now live—in a state in which the law of the strongest seems to be entirely abandoned as the regulating principle of the world's affairs: nobody professes it, and, as regards most of the relations between human beings, nobody is permitted to practice it. When any one succeeds in doing so, it is under cover of some pretext which gives him the semblance of having some general social interest on his side. This being the ostensible state of things, people flatter themselves that the rule of mere force is ended; that the law of the strongest cannot be the reason of existence of anything which has remained in full operation down to the present time. However any of our present institutions may have begun, it can only, they think, have been preserved to this period of advanced civilization by a well-grounded feeling of its adaptation to human nature, and conduciveness to the general good. They do not understand the great vitality and durability of institutions which place right on the side of might; how intensely they are clung to; how the good as well as the bad propensities and sentiments of those who have power in their hands, become identified with retaining it; how slowly these bad institutions give way, one at a time, the weakest first, beginning with those which are least interwoven with the daily habits of life; and how very rarely those who have obtained legal power because they first had physical, have ever lost their hold of it until the physical power had passed over to the other side. Such shifting of the physical force not having taken place in the case of women; this fact, combined with all the peculiar and characteristic features of the particular case, made it certain from the first that this branch of the system of right founded on might, though softened in its most atrocious features at an earlier period than several of the others, would be the very last to disappear. It was inevitable that this one case of a social relation grounded on force, would survive through generations of institutions grounded on equal justice, an almost solitary exception to the general character of their laws and customs; but which, so long as it does not proclaim its own origin, and as discussion has not brought out its true character, is not felt to jar with modern civilization, any more than domestic slavery among the Greeks jarred with their notion of themselves as a free people.

All causes, social and natural, combine to make it unlikely that women should be collectively rebellious to the power of men. They are so far in a position different from all other subject classes, that their masters require something more from them than actual service. Men do not want solely the obedience of women, they want their sentiments. All men, except the most brutish, desire to have, in the woman most nearly connected with them, not a forced slave but a willing one, not a slave merely, but a favorite. They have therefore put everything in practice to enslave their minds. The masters of all other slaves rely, for maintaining obedience, on fear; either fear of themselves, or religious fears. The masters of women wanted more than simple obedience, and they turned the whole force of education to effect their purpose. All women are brought up from the very earliest years in the belief that their ideal of character is the very opposite to that of men; not self-will, and government by self-control, but submission, and yielding to the control of others. All the moralities tell them that it is the duty of women, and all the current sentimentalities that it is their nature, to live for others; to make complete abnegation of themselves, and to have no life but in their affections. And by their affections are meant the only ones they are allowed to have—those to the men with whom they are connected, or to the children who constitute an additional and indefeasible tie between them and a man. When we put together three things—first, the natural attraction between opposite sexes; secondly, the wife's entire dependence on the husband, every privilege or pleasure she has being either his gift, or depending entirely on his will; and lastly, that the principal object of human pursuit, consideration, and all objects of social ambition, can in general be sought or obtained by her only through him, it would be a miracle if the object of being attractive to men had not become the polar star of feminine education and formation of character. And, this great means of influence over the minds of women having been acquired, an instinct of selfishness made men avail themselves of it to the utmost as a means of holding women in subjection, by representing to them meekness, submissiveness, and resignation of all individual will into the hands of a man, as an essential part of sexual attractiveness. Can it be doubted that any of the other yokes which mankind have succeeded in breaking, would have subsisted till now if the same means had existed, and had been as sedulously used, to

bow down their minds to it? If it had been made the object of the life of every young plebeian to find personal favor in the eyes of some patrician, of every young serf with some seigneur; if domestication with him, and a share of his personal affections, had been held out as the prize which they all should look out for, the most gifted and aspiring being able to reckon on the most desirable prizes; and if, when this prize had been obtained, they had been shut out by a wall of brass from all interests not centering in him, all feelings and desires but those which he shared or inculcated; would not serfs and seigneurs, plebeians and patricians, have been as broadly distinguished at this day as men and women are? and would not all but a thinker here and there, have believed the distinction to be a fundamental and unalterable fact in human nature?

I am far from pretending that wives are in general no better treated than slaves; but no slave is a slave to the same lengths, and in so full a sense of the word, as a wife is. Hardly any slave, except one immediately attached to the master's person, is a slave at all hours and all minutes; in general he has, like a soldier, his fixed task, and when it is done, or when he is off duty, he disposes, within certain limits, of his own time, and has a family life into which the master rarely intrudes. "Uncle Tom" under his first master had his own life in his "cabin," almost as much as any man whose work takes him away from home, is able to have in his own family. But it cannot be so with the wife. Above all, a female slave has (in Christian countries) an admitted right, and is considered under a moral obligation, to refuse to her master the last familiarity. Not so the wife: however brutal a tyrant she may unfortunately be chained to—though she may know that he hates her, though it may be his daily pleasure to torture her, and though she may feel it impossible not to loathe him—he can claim from her and enforce the lowest degradation of a human being, that of being made the instrument of an animal function contrary to her inclinations. While she is held in this worst description of slavery as to her own person, what is her position in regard to the children in whom she and her master have a joint interest? They are by law *his* children. He alone has any legal rights over them. Not one act can she do towards or in relation to them, except by delegation from him. Even after he is dead she is not their legal guardian, unless he by will has made her so. He could even send them away from her, and deprive her of the means of seeing or corresponding with them, until this power was in some degree restricted by Serjeant Talfourd's Act. This is her legal state. And from this state she has no means of withdrawing herself. If she leaves her husband, she can take nothing with her, neither her children nor anything which is rightfully her own. If he chooses, he can compel her to return, by law, or by physical force; or he may content himself with seizing for his own use anything which she may earn, or which may be given to her by her relations. It is only legal separation by a decree of a court of justice, which entitles her to live apart, without being forced back into the custody of an exasperated jailer—or which empowers her to apply any earnings to her own use, without fear that a man whom perhaps she has not seen for twenty years will pounce upon her some day and carry all off. This legal separation, until lately, the courts of justice would only give at an expense which made it inaccessible to any one out of the higher ranks. Even now it is only given in cases of desertion, or of the extreme of cruelty; and yet complaints are made every day that it is granted too easily. Surely, if a woman is denied any lot in life but that of being the personal body-servant of a despot, and is dependent for everything upon the chance of finding one who may be disposed to make a favorite of her instead of merely a drudge, it is a very cruel aggravation of her fate that she should be allowed to try this chance only once. The natural sequel and corollary from this state of things would be, that since her all in life depends upon obtaining a good master, she should be allowed to change again and again until she finds one. I am not saying that she ought to be allowed this privilege. That is a totally different consideration. The question of divorce, in the sense involving liberty of remarriage, is one into which it is foreign to my purpose to enter. All I now say is, that to those to whom nothing but servitude is allowed, the free choice of servitude is the only, though a most insufficient, alleviation. Its refusal completes the assimilation of the wife to the slave—and the slave under not the mildest form of slavery: for in some slave codes the slave could, under certain circumstances of ill usage, legally compel the master to sell him. But no amount of ill usage, without adultery superadded, will in England free a wife from her tormentor.

When we consider how vast is the number of men, in any great country, who are little higher than brutes, and that this never prevents them from being able, through the law of marriage, to obtain a victim, the breadth and depth of human misery caused in this shape alone by the abuse of the institution swells to something appalling. Yet these are only the extreme cases. They are the lowest abysses, but there is a sad succession of depth after depth before reaching them. In domestic as in political tyranny, the case of absolute monsters chiefly illustrates the institution by showing that there is scarcely any horror which may not occur under it if the despot pleases, and thus setting in a strong light what must be the terrible frequency of things only a little less atrocious.

The equality of married persons before the law, is not only the sole mode in which that particular relation can be made consistent with justice to both sides, and conducive to the happiness of both, but it is the only means of rendering the daily life of mankind, in any high sense, a school of moral cultivation. Though the truth may not be felt or generally acknowledged for generations to come, the only school of genuine moral sentiment is society between equals. The moral education of mankind has hitherto emanated chiefly from the law of force, and is adapted almost solely to the relations which force creates. In the less advanced states of society, people hardly recognize any relation with their equals. To be an equal is to be an enemy. Society, from its highest place to its lowest, is one long chain, or rather ladder, where every individual is either above or below his nearest neighbor, and wherever he does not command he must obey. Existing moralities, accordingly, are mainly fitted to a relation of command and obedience. Yet command and obedience are but unfortunate necessities of human life: society in equality is its normal state. Already in modern life, and more and more as it progressively improves, command and obedience become exceptional facts in life, equal association its general rule. The morality of the first ages rested on the obligation to submit to power; that of the ages next following, on the right of the weak to the forbearance and protection of the strong. How much longer is one form of society and life to content itself with the morality made for another? We have had the morality of submission, and the morality of chivalry and generosity; the time is now come for the morality of justice. Whenever, in former ages, any approach has been made to society in equality, Justice has asserted its claims as the foundation of virtue. It was thus in the free republics of antiquity. But even in the best of these, the equals were limited to the free male citizens; slaves, women, and the unenfranchised residents were under the law of force. The joint influence of Roman civilization and of Christianity obliterated these distinctions, and in theory (if only partially in practice) declared the claims of the human being, as such, to be paramount to those of sex, class, or social position. The barriers which had begun to be levelled were raised again by the northern conquests; and the whole of modern history consists of the slow process by which they have since been wearing away. We are entering into an order of things in which justice will again be the primary virtue; grounded as before on equal, but now also on sympathetic association; having its root no longer in the instinct of equals for self-protection, but in a cultivated sympathy between them; and no one being now left out, but an equal measure being extended to all. It is no novelty that mankind do not distinctly foresee their own changes, and that their sentiments are adapted to past, not to coming ages. To see the futurity of the species has always been the privilege of the intellectual élite, or of those who have learnt from them; to have the feelings of that futurity has been the distinction, and usually the martyrdom, of a still rarer élite. Institutions, books, education, society, all go on training human beings for the old, long after the new has come; much more when it is only coming. But the true virtue of human beings is fitness to live together as equals; claiming nothing for themselves but what they as freely concede to every one else; regarding

command of any kind as an exceptional necessity, and in all cases a temporary one; and preferring, whenever possible, the society of those with whom leading and following can be alternate and reciprocal. To these virtues, nothing in life as at present constituted gives cultivation by exercise. The family is a school of despotism, in which the virtues of despotism, but also its vices, are largely nourished. Citizenship, in free countries, is partly a school of society in equality; but citizenship fills only a small place in modern life, and does not come near the daily habits or inmost sentiments. The family, justly constituted, would be the real school of the virtues of freedom. It is sure to be a sufficient one of everything else. It will always be a school of obedience for the children, of command for the parents. What is needed is, that it should be a school of sympathy in equality, of living together in love, without power on one side or obedience on the other. This it ought to be between the parents. It would then be an exercise of those virtues which each requires to fit them for all other association, and a model to the children of the feelings and conduct which their temporary training by means of obedience is designed to render habitual, and therefore natural, to them. The moral training of mankind will never be adapted to the conditions of the life for which all other human progress is a preparation, until they practice in the family the same moral rule which is adapted to the normal constitution of human society.

The moral regeneration of mankind will only really commence, when the most fundamental of the social relations is placed under the rule of equal justice, and when human beings learn to cultivate their strongest sympathy with an equal in rights and in cultivation.

Thus far, the benefits which it has appeared that the world would gain by ceasing to make sex a disqualification for privileges and a badge of subjection, are social rather than individual; consisting in an increase of the general fund of thinking and acting power, and an improvement in the general conditions of the association of men with women. But it would be a grievous understatement of the case to omit the most direct benefit of all, the unspeakable gain in private happiness to the liberated half of the species; the difference to them between a life of subjection to the will of others, and a life of rational freedom. After the primary necessities of food and raiment, freedom is the first and strongest want of human nature. While mankind are lawless, their desire is for lawless freedom. When they have learnt to understand the meaning of duty and the value of reason, they incline more and more to be guided and restrained by these in the exercise of their freedom; but they do not therefore desire freedom less; they do not become disposed to accept the will of other people as the representative and interpreter of those guiding principles. On the contrary, the communities in which the reason has been most cultivated, and in which the idea of social duty has been most powerful, are those which have most strongly asserted the freedom of action of the individual—the liberty of each to govern his conduct by his own feelings of duty, and by such laws and social restraints as his own conscience can subscribe to.

He who would rightly appreciate the worth of personal independence as an element of happiness, should consider the value he himself puts upon it as an ingredient of his own.

Every restraint on the freedom of conduct of any of their human fellow creatures, (otherwise than by making them responsible for any evil actually caused by it), dries up *pro tanto* the principal fountain of human happiness, and leaves the species less rich, to an inappreciable degree, in all that makes life valuable to the individual human being.

CHAPTER TEN

MARX

In the nineteenth century, democracy seemed the goal toward which the whole world was inevitably moving. In some countries it was more cheerfully welcomed and more faithfully practiced than in others, but even politically backward states like Russia and Germany had to pay homage to political virtue by gradually broadening, in form, though not always in substance, the range of self-government. In the twentieth century, political hypocrisy, like other expressions of nineteenth-century politeness and formality, became no longer obligatory, and attacks upon democracy were carried out in the open, without the protective facade of apparent concessions to the principle of democracy. During the two decades between World Wars I and II, fascism (merged with the imperial ambitions of Germany, Japan, and Italy), was the main challenge to the democratic way of life for a time, it was so successful that it was openly hailed even in democratic states as "the wave of the future" by its sympathizers, or by those who felt that democracy was done for in a vain attempt to stem the tide of fascism.

World War II destroyed the military ambitions of the fascist Axis. The strains and stresses of war revealed the hollowness of fascism's claim to have inaugurated a new way of life that combined scientific and industrial efficiency with youthful and dynamic heroism. Yet World War II was hardly over when communism emerged as the new threat to democracy. At the end of World War I, when Russia was the only communist state in the world, and when its industrial and military power seemed to be low, communism was interpreted as a specifically Russian phenomenon without much practical applicability elsewhere. But the defeat of Nazi Germany by Russian armies in World War II revealed the extent to which the strength of Communist Russia had been underrated. When the war was over, Russia was the dominant military power in eastern Europe, and it quickly communized Poland, Rumania, Bulgaria, Hungary, Czechoslovakia, and East Germany.

Though the Russian armies were the principal instrument in spreading communism, the force of communist ideology was of vital significance. Whereas fascism did not possess a single creative or constructive idea that went beyond crass national egotism and lust for power, communism—unhampered, in particular, by the deadly burden of fascist racism—addressed itself to the world as the true heir of the libertarian, egalitarian democratic tradition. Also, whereas fascism proudly proclaimed its "pagan" character in relation to the democratic way of life, which it rejected *in toto,* communism is more "heretical" in terms of the democratic tradition: it accepts the democratic ideals of liberty, equality, and fraternity, and its charge against democracy is not, as was the charge of fascism, that democracy is too faithful to its ideals, but that it has, in fact, betrayed them. Just as in religion paganism generally has been less ruinous than heresy, because the former rejects the perceived truth in its entirety, whereas the latter mingles the true with the false, so communism, in the long run, proved more dangerous than fascism, precisely because communism contains important elements of the democratic tradition, distorted as they may be in practice.

In Europe, communism represented itself with considerable success, even in the eyes of many conservatives, as the authentic fighter against social and economic injustice. In Asia, communism was hunger become articulate, longing for faith and action. Whereas the western democracies taught Asia the right to be happy, without giving it the means to achieve happiness, communism promised the masses of landless, destitute, and forgotten Asians a new life of equality and abundance.

The greatest single influence in the development of revolutionary communism was Karl Marx (1818–1883). He was born in the Rhineland, which more than any other part of Germany had been strongly permeated with democratic ideas by the French Revolution. Marx attended the University of Berlin for several years, where he studied jurisprudence, philosophy, and history. But he quickly became engaged in political activities and in 1842 joined the staff of the *Rheinische Zeitung,* a democratic newspaper in Cologne. In the following year the paper was suppressed by the Prussian Government, and Marx went to Paris, then the European headquarters of radical movements.

In Paris, Marx met Proudhon, the leading French socialist thinker, Bakunin, the Russian anarchist, and Friedrich Engels (1820–1895), a Rhinelander like Marx, and soon to become his lifelong companion and close collaborator. Engels was the son of a German textile manufacturer with business interests in Germany and England, and he was sent by his father to Manchester in 1842. His *Condition of the Working Class in England* (1844) was a remarkably penetrating study of squalor, drabness, and poverty in the midst of luxurious wealth, and Engels was the first to draw Marx's attention to England as a laboratory in which industrial capitalism could be most accurately observed.

In 1845 Marx was expelled from France through the intervention of the Prussian Government, and he went to Brussels, another center of political refugees from all over Europe. There Marx composed, with the aid of Engels, the *Communist Manifesto* (1848), the most influential of all his writings, a pamphlet that has made history, inspired devotion and hatred, and divided mankind as profoundly as any other political document. Marx participated in the revolutions of 1848 in France and Germany, and early in 1849 he again was expelled by the Prussian Government, forbidden to return to his native land.

He went to London in the late summer of 1849, soon followed by Engels. Marx had planned to stay in England for only a few weeks, but he stayed there until his death in 1883. He spent most of his time in the British Museum, digging up obscure sources throwing light on the history and working of industrial capitalism. The first volume of *Das Kapital,* his monumental analysis of the capitalist system, was published in 1867; the second and third volumes appeared posthumously in 1885–1895, edited by Engels.

Marx's writings show little penetration of English *political* ideas and ways of thought, and his lack of insight into the forces and motivations of English politics would have been little better or worse had he stayed in Germany all his life. By contrast, his writings demonstrate a profound knowledge of the English *economic* system, based on detailed and painstaking research. Marx was one of the first social scientists to use neglected government reports and statistical materials as a basic tool of research in the study of social and economic problems. Yet it never occurred to him that the self-analysis of English capitalism, to which he owed the documentary sources of his grand indictment, might eventually evolve into peaceful self-improvement and change.

Marx's analysis of the capitalist system has influenced the making of history even more than the writing of history. Regardless of what one accepts or rejects of Marx's social, economic, political, and philosophical ideas, it is impossible to bypass him. He said of himself that he was not a "Marxist," and those who insist on all or nothing in relation to his ideas, betray Marx in his own painful and long search for a philosophy that he did not receive ready-made from any master but gathered, and added to his own life experience, from diverse sources: German philosophy, French revolutionary politics, and English economics.

In German philosophy, it was above all Hegel who greatly influenced Marx. Although Marx very early criticized Hegel, he never abandoned the basic categories of Hegel's thought. Like Hegel, Marx felt that history had meaning, and that it moved in a set pattern toward a known goal. In a rationalized version of the religious conception of history, in which history derives meaning from God and moves toward the kingdom of God, Hegel replaced God with the concept of Spirit or Reason, and history was seen by Hegel as the progressive unfolding of Reason. Marx held that history had both a meaning and a goal, and the historical process was dominated by the struggles between social classes; each phase of the struggle, as in Hegel, represented a higher phase of human evolution than the preceding one. The goal of history was predetermined for Marx: the classless society, leading to full human freedom.

This philosophy of history has, in Hegel, a conscious religious connotation, and in Marx, too, there is a quasi-religious element. As in religion, Hegel and Marx both view history as a perpetual struggle between lower and higher forces; however, the outcome of the struggle is predetermined. In religion, God triumphs when mankind finally turns toward him and abandons the false idols of lust and greed. In Hegel, the outcome is certain: the final victory of Reason and Spirit over enslavement to caprice and passion. In Marx, the outcome is the abolition of capitalism, and the destruction of all forms of injustice and exploitation in a new society based on freedom and fraternal cooperation. Many who embrace Marxism come from the ranks of persons who have lost faith in traditional forms of supernatural religion, but who still need the psychic support often derived from religious beliefs. Marxists find comfort in the feeling that man is not alone in this world, that there is meaning in the cosmos and in human history, and that mankind is inexorably moving toward a noble goal, compared with which one's temporary and individual sufferings and frustrations are not too important.

Thus, while Marx was personally a convinced atheist and insisted that his thought was guided by strictly scientific criteria, the historical influence of Marxism was not so much in the realm of scientific analysis as in its popular appeal as a *new religion* of the dispossessed and oppressed. The devout follower of the Marxian faith has an unshakable conviction that he knows what the meaning of history is, the goal toward which it is moving, that he has joined the forces that in the end must win, and that opposing the coming of communism is not only wrong but also futile, since "the march of history" cannot be stopped by any "reactionary" individual or group. In underdeveloped countries in particular, in which literacy is low, the spread of Marxism was overwhelmingly a quasi-religious phenomenon rather than a sign of expanding science.

French *revolutionary politics* was another important source for Marx's intellectual development. With his instinct of genius, Marx realized that, if revolution was the principal method of destroying a capitalist society, France and her revolutionary experience served as the best laboratory. France was among the most advanced major western nations because its revolutions were most clearly based on social antagonisms. Marx fully understood that the English Puritan revolution in the 1640s was a war between the middle class and the existing order based on landed property, but this social aspect of the

Puritan revolution was too commingled with religious and political issues to serve as a pure, or almost pure, case of a social revolution. Moreover, the Puritan revolution was finally brought to a conclusion by the moderate settlement of the Glorious (and bloodless) Revolution of 1688, a conclusion which had little appeal for Marx. Similarly, the American Revolution was not the perfect case of a class war that Marx looked for. In Marx's mind, the American Revolution was a class war between the rising bourgeoisie and the aristocratic order in the American colonies. Yet the political issue of independence befuddled the class issue, and once the revolutionary struggle was won, the United States seemed to show few symptoms of intense conflict between its social classes.

In France, Marx felt, the historical development was different. The French Revolution of 1789 was by common agreement a purely social revolution of the peasants and urban middle classes against the aristocratic order. However, whereas revolutionary activity came to an end in England in 1688 and in the United States in the 1780s, the French Revolution of 1789 was merely the beginning of a series of revolutionary upheavals the end of which was not in sight. France experienced major revolutionary upheavals in 1830 and 1848, experiences which both England and the United States were spared. Finally, France was the scene of the short-lived proletarian dictatorship of the Paris Commune in 1871, the first of its kind in modern history. For Marx, both England and the United States had become too conservative after their successful revolutions; on the European continent, there was no other major nation in which social revolution was as much an integral part of the national experience as was France. As to Germany, Marx considered it intellectually and politically provincial, held back by feudal anachronisms and national disunity; Italy was economically backward and politically disunited, and until these two issues were resolved, there was little chance for a social revolution. Russia seemed to Marx more Asian than European, and although he sensed that Russia was a sleeping giant, he nevertheless shared the prejudices of many Germans that Russia, and Slavdom in general, was not culturally, socially, and economically in the same league with the more advanced nations of the West.

Finally, Marx perceptively saw that industrial capitalism and economic science could best be studied in England. Since Marx viewed economic forces as the main driving force in history, and since he felt that industrial civilization was irresistibly spreading throughout the whole world, he was convinced that England was the country to live in if one wanted to study industrial capitalism firsthand, and that English (and Scottish) economic analysis was the most advanced of any country. While Marx had no doubt that English economic doctrines were no more than a rationalization and justification of the capitalist system, they nevertheless supplied him with the basic concepts and tools of economic analysis which could also be used in demonstrating that capitalism was both wasteful and exploitative.

Above all, Marx shares with English classical economics basic presuppositions and tacit assumptions which are as important as his explicit rejection of specific doctrines of its leading representatives. For example, Marx looks upon *work* as man's most creative and noblest form of personal self-fulfillment. His quarrel with English classical economic theory and capitalist practice is not that they, too, take such a high view of work, but that under capitalism work becomes a mechanism of exploitation, degrading the worker to a soulless robot, enslaved to the "fetishism of commodities."

In Marx's thought, the classless communist society of the future was by no means to abolish the duty to work. The first stage of communism, Marx argued, would be guided by the principle of "from each according to his ability, to each according to his work." In the second, and higher, phase of communism, the principle of "from each according to his ability, to each according to his needs" would prevail. Most students of Marx concentrate on the difference of awards for work in the second as compared with the first stage of communism, but they often overlook that even in the second stage man is still expected to contribute to the best of his ability, that is, to perform socially useful work. Even in the second stage of communism, when the new man of communist society has become cooperative and has lost the competitive and acquisitive vices of capitalism and when production creates abundance, work is still, Marx says, "the primary necessity of life."

This Marxian worship of work is strictly adhered to by communists today. Communist states, for example, have not provided monetary relief for the unemployed, since an unemployed person is expected to work in any job he can find, regardless of pay, skill, or location. Interestingly, in noncommunist countries the religion of work has been greatly weakened in recent years, and liberal thinkers have attacked the idea of work as the main channel of personal self-fulfillment. In communist countries the duty to work is still an article of faith that must not be challenged. Though they rarely quote from the Bible, on this particular issue communists like to cite the Biblical injunction that "he who does not work, neither shall he eat"—although in communist literature this is often called a "socialist principle."

Marx's conception of *property* is closely related to that held by classical English liberal thinkers from Locke on. Locke and later English economists assumed that private property was a *relation of man to things,* and not a power relation between men—provided government does not meddle in the economy, thus injecting an element of compulsion into the property relation. Marx retains the basic concept of English classical economics of property as a relation of man to things, but according to Marx such property without power can exist only under public ownership, whereas private property is by definition a power relation. Marx thought that he completely rejected classical economic thought on property, since he reversed the roles of public and private property as viewed by the classical economists. Yet he still shares with them the belief—or illusion—that *any* form of productive property (private in the case of the classical economists, public in the case of Marx) can be interpreted as being a purely technical relationship between man and things, or as the "administration of things," as Marx referred to public ownership in a communist society.

The three major sources of Marx's intellectual development—German philosophy, French revolutionary politics, English political economy—nourished his thought from his youth to his old age. Early in his life, however, Marx was influenced by another powerful movement that was particularly strong in Germany: *romanticism.* From a purely literary viewpoint, romanticism was a movement of protest against the classical literary traditions of reason, order, measure, and form, as represented above all by the great age of French cultural predominance in the eighteenth century. In its social outlook, romanticism was a protest against the rising industrialization. The romantics felt that industrial civilization was destroying the natural and organic bonds of life that characterized preindustrial Europe, and that, as a result, man in an industrial society was becoming estranged or "alienated" from his fellow men, from nature, and—most important of all—from himself. The romantics had no positive program to cope with the evils of industrialism. Some romantics felt that the only solution was to abandon industrialism altogether and to return to the agrarian life of the preindustrial age—a highly impractical program quickly overtaken by events, since masses of propertyless farm workers kept on streaming into the cities. Other romantics withdrew from the ugly world of industrialism into a philosophy of extreme individualism—a solution which was purely literary rather than social, and which could only be adopted by a few individuals, but which provided no answer to problems affecting society as a whole.

In his *Economic and Philosophical Manuscripts,* written by Marx in 1844, at the age of twenty-six, Marx reflects the romantics' concern about alienation, but under a different perspective. Whereas the romantics saw the evil in industrialism as a new way of life, Marx perceived alienation as the result of *capitalist* industrialism. Under capitalism, Marx said in his *Economic and Philosophical Manuscripts,* man is alienated from his work, the objects he produces, his employers, other workers, nature, and from himself. Under capitalism, Marx argues, the worker does not work in order to fulfill himself as a person, for his work "is not voluntary but imposed, *forced* labor." His work does not satisfy his own needs, but is merely a means to satisfy the needs of others, the capitalist employers who use the worker as an instrument of profit making. The worker thus "sinks to the level of a commodity," producing palaces for the rich, but hovels for the poor. The worker is also alienated from the capitalist employer, who appropriates the products of labor and enjoys pleasures and privileges denied to the worker. Being alienated from the product of his labor, the worker is also alienated from other men. Marx vehemently attacks the role of money in the new capitalist economy. Money is the "highest good, and so its possessor is good." Money is the "visible deity" of capitalist industrialism, transforming all natural human relations into monetary relations. Since in a capitalist society everything can be bought with money, Marx affirms the need for a society in which man is related to his fellow men as an individual human being, in which love cannot be bought, but can "only be exchanged for love."

Marx showed in his *Economic and Philosophical Manuscripts* that man's predicament had economic, as well as ethical and psychological facets. However, in a crucial change of outlook Marx quickly abandoned the ethical element in his conception of communism, and in *The German Ideology,* written jointly with Frederick Engels in 1846, the Left Hegelians were subjected to a strong attack for talking of "human nature, of Man in general" rather than of man as a member of a particular class. The individualistic leanings of the *Manuscripts* were replaced by the concept of class, to which Marx adhered for the rest of his life, and the ideal of love and fellowship was replaced by that of class struggle and hatred. In the *Communist Manifesto* he specifically ridicules and attacks philosophical socialists who talk about the "alienation of humanity" or about the "philosophical foundation of socialism." Marx also attacks ethically oriented socialists as "utopians," because they reject revolutionary action and "wish to attain their ends by peaceful means, and endeavor, by small experiments, necessarily doomed to failure, and by the force of example, to pave the way for the new social gospel."

Since Marx himself had expressed, in the *Economic and Philosophical Manuscripts* of 1844, ideas which were akin to those of the philosophical and ethical socialists, he decided not to publish what he later considered a juvenile aberration. In fact, the *Manuscripts* were not published during his lifetime, and even after his death Engels, his literary executor, refrained from publishing them. In 1932, the *Manuscripts* were finally published for the first time in German, followed by translation into English nearly three decades later. Since then, the *Manuscripts*—with their fashionable doctrine of "human alienation"—have been used in communist and noncommunist countries for diverse purposes. In communist countries, particularly in Eastern Europe, the *Manuscripts* served as a weapon used by *liberal* elements who sought to discredit totalitarian attitudes and ideas of orthodox communism. While more liberally minded thinkers in Eastern Europe could not propagate liberalism by name, they could advocate some of its substance under the protective shield of the "Young Marx." In noncommunist countries, by contrast, the *Manuscripts* have served the opposite goal of making *Marxism* respectable, since Marx has been presented as a humanist socialist and liberal individualist primarily concerned with man's need for self-fulfillment through love and free cooperation. Whatever the merits of these two *political* efforts in communist and non-communist countries—to make liberalism respectable in the former and Marxism in the latter—from the purely analytical and historical viewpoint the middle-aged and mature Marx cannot be turned into a liberal humanist, since from *The German Ideology* on, he saw in the liberal, humanist brand of socialism the most dangerous enemy of communism. This attitude of Marx was later faithfully emulated by communists, who consistently considered democratic socialists of the British Labor party type as more dangerous and damaging to the cause of communism than the openly conservative parties of a capitalist society.

As Marx became involved in practical political activities in his early life, he criticized the philosophical socialists, and philosophers in general, for analyzing society rather than actively trying to change it. Marx believed as he expressed it in one of his early writings (*Theses on Feuerbach,* 1845), "in practice man must prove the truth"; thus the easier method of discovering truth through revelation and authority, whether based on Marx or any other god or prophet, is excluded. The *Theses on Feuerbach* were written by Marx when he was only twenty-seven, and his conception of the task of philosophy is clearly indicated by his charge that "the philosophers have only *interpreted* the world, the point however is to *change* it." This activist approach to philosophy is distinctly un-Hegelian, and Marx's life was dedicated to the anti-Hegelian proposition that the actual was far from rational, and that the rational would finally be imposed upon actuality, not by a mystical world spirit, but by the new social class that was the heir of bourgeois science and rationalism: the proletariat.

Marx's philosophy of history and politics has to be gathered from many incidental remarks and comments in his writings and letters, as he never wrote a systematic statement on the basic assumptions of his thought. In the preface to his *Critique of Political Economy* (1859), Marx briefly states his general philosophy of history, based on the thesis that "the anatomy of civil society is to be found in political economy." Pre-Marxian social analysis had emphasized law and politics as the determining factors in society and social change. Marx reverses the scale of importance and considers the "productive forces" of society as the basis, whereas legal relations and forms of government are the "superstructure." Marx puts it in this fashion: "The mode of production of the material means of existence conditions the whole process of social, political, and intellectual life."

One of Marx's most famous sayings is that *men's social existence determines their consciousness,* and not, as had been generally accepted before Marx, that the "consciousness of men determines their existence." What Marx stresses here is that men's ideas are not accidental and haphazard, or freely left to their choice. Thus the legal, political, and religious ideas of a pastoral civilization will fundamentally differ from those of an agricultural, feudal society, and both will have little in common with the social, political, religious, and intellectual outlook of modern capitalist society.

Turning to the question of what causes historical change, Marx renounces the study of monarchs and their relations with court ladies and fellow dynasts, and he is equally dissatisfied with the study of history as a long list of battles and wars. Instead, Marx attempts to find the deeper causes of historical change in forces that go beyond the power of individual rulers and victorious war leaders: "At a certain stage of their development the material productive forces of society come into contradiction with the existing productive relationships, or, what is but a legal expression for these, with the property relationships within which they have moved before. From forms of development of the productive forces these relationships are transformed into their fetters.

Then an epoch of social revolution opens. With the change in the economic foundation the whole vast superstructure is more or less rapidly transformed." Thus, when new *productive forces* developed within the *productive relationships* of the feudal system, social revolution was, according to Marx, inevitable, because the productive relationships of the feudal system (property relations, market controls, internal customs and tariffs, monetary instability) did not permit the utilization of the newly developing productive forces of industrial capitalism. What has doomed all historically known economic systems is the fact, according to Marx, that when new productive forces develop, the existing productive relationships stand in the way of their proper utilization. Each system thus becomes eventually wasteful in terms of the potentialities that have developed in its womb but that are not permitted to be born and to grow.

The capitalist system, too, shows the same tendency, according to Marx, and is due to undergo the same fate when the *productive forces* (the capacity to produce) have *outstripped* the *productive relationships* (law of property, production for private profit). The capitalist system as a system of social, economic, and legal relations thus eventually stands in the way of the scientific resources and technological know-how that are not permitted to be fully utilized. Only the public ownership of the means of production will, according to Marx, bring into existence a new system of productive relationships (production for common use rather than private profit) that will match the tremendous forces of production actually or potentially existent and known to man.

In the *Communist Manifesto,* Marx and Engels explain how social change through revolution actually occurs. When the forces of production begin to outstrip the methods of production (or productive relationships), the owners of the means of production do not step aside and thus accelerate the inevitable course of history. Bound by the limitations of their ideology (which, in turn, reflects the existing modes of production), they sincerely believe that the existing system is economically the most efficient, socially the most equitable, and generally in harmony with the laws of nature and the will of whatever god they venerate. It is not a question of the greed of the individual feudal landowner (who obstructs the birth of the more productive capitalist system) or of the selfishness of the individual capitalist (who impedes the nationalization of the means of production). The owners of the means of production will utilize all the instruments of the legal, political, and ideological superstructure to block the growth of the forces that represent the potentially more progressive economic system. For this reason Marx and Engels state early in the *Communist Manifesto* that the "history of all hitherto existing society is the history of class struggles." In the nineteenth century, the bourgeoisie liked to think of itself as conservative, law-abiding, and antirevolutionary—once it had won its class struggle. Yet Marx and Engels remind the bourgeoisie that, historically, it "has played a most revolutionary part."

The end of capitalism will be brought about, according to the *Communist Manifesto,* not by "subversive" conspiracies of professional agitators and revolutionaries, but by the same inexorable laws of social change that destroyed previous systems. Just as feudalism, for example, prepared its own grave by developing these forces—the urban bourgeoisie—which eventually destroyed it, capitalism does the same thing: "The essential condition for the existence and for the sway of the bourgeois class is the formation and augmentation of capital; the condition for capital is wage-labor. Wage-labor rests exclusively on competition between the laborers. The advance of industry, whose involuntary promoter is the bourgeoisie, replaces the isolation of the laborers, due to competition, by their revolutionary combinations, due to association. The development of modern industry, therefore, cuts from under its feet the very foundation on which the

bourgeoisie produces and appropriates products. What the bourgeoisie therefore produces, above all, are its own grave-diggers. Its fall and the victory of the proletariat are
equally inevitable."

As Marx and Engels look at history, they can find no instance where a major social
and economic system has freely abdicated to its successor. Therefore the communists
"openly declare that their ends can be attained only by the forcible overthrow of all existing social conditions." This is one of the crucial tenets of Marxist revolutionary
communism, and the one that most clearly opposed it irreconcilably to democracy, be it
capitalist or socialist democracy.

Marx had no clear-cut theory as to how the political transformation from capitalist to
proletarian rule could come about. Though in the *Communist Manifesto* he believed in
the need for revolution, he was less dogmatic later. Speaking in 1872 at a public meeting in Amsterdam following the Congress of the International, Marx declared that the
means of attaining power for the working class are not everywhere the same: "We know
that we must take into consideration the institutions, the habits and customs of different
regions, and we do not deny that there are countries like America, England, and—if I
knew your institutions better I would perhaps add Holland—where the workers can attain their objective by peaceful means. But such is not the case in all other countries."

Marx never fully pursued the implications of this distinction, and the generally accepted doctrine of communist Marxism is the impossibility of fundamental social and
economic change except by class war, violence, and revolution. If Marx had accorded
the political factor its due weight, if he had studied the implications of the Reform Act
of 1832—a bloodless revolution in which the governing class peacefully ceded its position to the new middle class—he might have foreseen that socialism, too, might be accomplished without violence in countries whose democratic tradition was strong
enough to absorb far-reaching social and economic changes without civil war.

A full recognition of the cultural and political factors in the equation of social
change would have amounted to a virtual abandonment, however, of the central position of Marx: that history is the history of class wars, and that ruling classes defend
their position to the last, not because of selfish greed, but because their ideological
framework, the superstructure of the economic system, compels them to identify their
privileged position with that of the whole community. Conversely, the proletariat attacks the capitalist system, and finally overthrows it, according to Marx, not because
of some abstract ideals of justice, but because the inevitable evolution of capitalism
puts the proletariat in a position of misery and exploitation, while men, knowledge,
and resources lie idle.

In Hegel, *war between nations* is the vehicle of historical decision and progress, and
the World Spirit assigns to different nations special missions at particular times. In
Marx, social change and progress are attained by *war between classes,* and in each historical epoch one particular class is assigned the mission of representing the idea of
progress. For Hegel, world history culminates in the Germanic peoples, which embody
the finest flowering of freedom and spirit. For Marx, history culminates in the proletariat, which embodies the highest social principles of progress and rational ordering of
society. Just as Hegel assumed that the process of the fulfillment of spirit and freedom
was consummated in Prussianized Germany, Marx assumed that the process of history,
the record of class wars, would be consummated in the final victory of the proletariat,
after which the dynamics of class war would be followed by the *statics of the classless
society.*

No one before Marx saw as clearly as he did the *intimate relationship between private
property and power.* In particular, Marx demonstrated that the link between power and

property was heightened to its extreme in the capitalist system, inasmuch as its scientific, technological, and managerial forces made possible an accumulation of economic power in the hands of the few, such as would have been impossible before the Industrial Revolution. Yet, realistic as Marx was in his appraisal of *private* property as a system of private government and power of man over man, he was utopian in assuming that property lost the character of power merely by being collectivized. The Marx-Engels doctrine of the "withering away of the state" in the classless society is based on the hypothesis that property in a socialist or communist society ceases to be a system of power when owned by the whole community. Whereas private ownership of the means of production under capitalism, Marx and Engels argue, entails the domination of man over man, public ownership of the means of production under socialism or communism will lead to the "administration of things," so that the state (in its historical meaning as a system of force) would wither away by itself, as there would no longer be any need for it.

The *administration of things* is a matter of technical *knowledge* and not of political *will*. Government as an agency of settling disputes between men by force would be replaced in the classless society by administration as a scientific method of using resources in the best way in accordance with verifiable procedures of science and technology. Locke was the first modern writer to define property as a relationship of man to things, inasmuch as he saw the origin of property in the admixture of human effort to natural resources. Marx's concept of *publicly owned property as a relationship between man and things* closely follows Locke's concept of private property.

The ideal of classical liberalism and that of Marx-Engels have a common utopian element: both assume that human nature can be so improved and perfected by the right kind of institutional changes that government as a mechanism of force becomes superfluous. In the classical doctrine of liberal democracy, the equitable distribution of private property seemed to point to such a state of harmony; in the doctrine of Marx-Engels, the transformation of individual work into collective work in the capitalist factory pointed to the practical conclusion that collective ownership of the means of production would assure a basic equality of men that would make government in the traditional sense unnecessary. Both classical democracy and Marxism suffer from an excessive optimism with regard to the perfectibility of man, and both wrongly assume that any system of society can be devised that can achieve perfect harmony of interests. Nevertheless, the liberal doctrine of "the less government, the better" and the Marxian doctrine of the "withering away of the state" can be valuable as permanent reminders that the state exists for man, and not man for the state. Whereas a society without force and government is humanly unattainable, the ideal at least of a civilized community should be that of the lowest possible amount of force and compulsion in human relations.

The main difference between the theory of classical democracy and that of Marx-Engels is that the former envisaged a free, harmoniously ordered society as the result of peaceful, gradual growth, whereas Marx-Engels saw in revolution, civil war, and the dictatorship of the proletariat the preparatory stages of peace and harmony. Experience has shown since Marx-Engels that revolution and dictatorship are less likely to induce the state to wither away, or even decrease the use of force and violence, than the slower and more difficult methods of peaceful persuasion and consent. The failure to see the fatal relationship between means and ends is one of the most striking philosophical and practical weaknesses of Marxism, and the one that fundamentally separates it from liberal democracy.

There were two major countries in the nineteenth century in which the ideas of Marx and Engels became important ideological and political forces: Germany and Russia.

Despite the facade of the legislative Reichstag, Germany was in fact a political autocracy that did not permit the development of genuine representative government. Philosophically, Marxism may be Hegelianism put upside down (as Marx claimed), but Hegel upside down is still Hegel, and the fixed determinism and closed system of Marxism appealed to much that was deeply rooted in the German philosophical tradition. Just as Hegel had asserted that the *state* was an *objective reality,* and its laws, like those of nature, beyond the whim and caprice of the individual, Marx now claimed that the *laws of society* followed an inexorable course, possessing the same *scientific validity* that Hegel had claimed for the laws of the state. By contrast, the liberal philosophical tradition of the West has always rejected the Hegel-Marx conception that human reason can only *understand* the laws of the state or society, and has affirmed the possibility of rational control and creative change of social and political institutions. The experience of free government forms the psychological foundation of the western conceptions of state and society, just as the experience of autocratic government in Germany provides the psychological background for the determinism of Hegel and Marx.

MARX AND ENGELS

The Communist Manifesto *

A spectre is haunting Europe—the spectre of Communism. All the powers of old Europe have entered into a holy alliance to exorcise this spectre: Pope and Czar, Metternich and Guizot, French Radicals and German police-spies.

Where is the party in opposition that has not been decried as communistic by its opponents in power? Where the Opposition that has not hurled back the branding reproach of Communism, against the more advanced opposition parties, as well as against its reactionary adversaries?

Two things result from this fact:

I. Communism is already acknowledged by all European powers to be itself a power.

II. It is high time that Communists should openly, in the face of the whole world, publish their views, their aims, their tendencies, and meet this nursery tale of the spectre of Communism with a manifesto of the party itself.

To this end, Communists of various nationalities have assembled in London, and sketched the following manifesto, to be published in the English, French, German, Italian, Flemish and Danish languages.

BOURGEOIS AND PROLETARIANS

The history of all hitherto existing society is the history of class struggles.

Freeman and slave, patrician and plebeian, lord and serf, guild-master and journeyman, in a word, oppressor and oppressed, stood in constant opposition to one another, carried on an uninterrupted, now hidden, now open fight, a fight that each time ended, either in a revolutionary reconstitution of society at large, or in the common ruin of the contending classes.

In the earlier epochs of history, we find almost everywhere a complicated arrangement of society into various orders, a manifold gradation of social rank. In ancient Rome we have patricians, knights, plebeians, slaves; in the Middle Ages, feudal lords, vassals, guildmasters, journeymen, apprentices, serfs; in almost all of these classes, again, subordinate gradations.

The modern bourgeois society that has sprouted from the ruins of feudal society, has not done away with class antagonisms. It has but established new classes, new conditions of oppression, new forms of struggle in place of the old ones.

Our epoch, the epoch of the bourgeoisie, possesses, however, this distinctive feature: It has simplified the class antagonisms. Society as a whole is more and more splitting up into two great hostile camps, into two great classes directly facing each other—bourgeoisie and proletariat.

From the serfs of the Middle Ages sprang the chartered burghers of the earliest towns. From these burgesses the first elements of the bourgeoisie were developed.

The discovery of America, the rounding of the Cape, opened up fresh ground for the rising bourgeoisie. The East-Indian and Chinese markets, the colonisation of America, trade with the colonies, the increase in the means of exchange and in commodities generally, gave to commerce, to navigation, to industry, an impulse never before

---

* (1848; English trans. of 1888, ed. Friedrich Engels.)

known, and thereby, to the revolutionary element in the tottering feudal society at rapid development.

The feudal system of industry, in which industrial production was monopolised by closed guilds, now no longer sufficed for the growing wants of the new markets. The manufacturing system took its place. The guild-masters were pushed aside by the manufacturing middle class; division of labour between the different corporate guilds vanished in the face of division of labour in each single workshop.

Meantime the markets kept ever growing, the demand ever rising. Even manufacture no longer sufficed. Thereupon, steam and machinery revolutionised industrial production. The place of manufacture was taken by the giant, modern industry, the place of the industrial middle class, by industrial millionaires—the leaders of whole industrial armies, the modern bourgeoisie.

Modern industry has established the world market, for which the discovery of America paved the way. This market has given an immense development to commerce, to navigation, to communication by land. This development has, in its turn, reacted on the extension of industry; and in proportion as industry, commerce, navigation, railways extended, in the same proportion the bourgeoisie developed, increased its capital, and pushed into the background every class handed down from the Middle Ages.

We see, therefore, how the modern bourgeoisie is itself the product of a long course of development, of a series of revolutions in the modes of production and of exchange.

Each step in the development of the bourgeoisie was accompanied by a corresponding political advance of that class. An oppressed class under the sway of the feudal nobility, it became an armed and self-governing association in the mediæval commune; here independent urban republic (as in Italy and Germany), there taxable "third estate" of the monarchy (as in France); afterwards, in the period of manufacture proper, serving either the semi-feudal or the absolute monarchy as a counterpoise against the nobility, and, in fact, cornerstone of the great monarchies in general—the bourgeoisie has at last, since the establishment of modern industry and of the world market, conquered for itself, in the modern

representative state, exclusive political sway. The executive of the modern state is but a committee for managing the common affairs of the whole bourgeosie.

The bourgeoisie has played a most revolutionary rôle in history.

The bourgeoisie, wherever it has got the upper hand, has put an end to all feudal, patriarchal, idyllic relations. It has pitilessly torn asunder the motley feudal ties that bound man to his "natural superiors," and has left no other bond between man and man than naked self-interest, than callous "cash payment." It has drowned the most heavenly ecstasies of religious fervour, of chivalrous enthusiasm, of philistine sentimentalism, in the icy water of egotistical calculation. It has resolved personal worth into exchange value, and in place of the numberless indefeasible chartered freedoms, has set up that single, unconscionable freedom—Free Trade. In one word, for exploitation, veiled by religious and political illusions, it has substituted naked, shameless, direct, brutal exploitation.

The bourgeoisie has stripped of its halo every occupation hitherto honoured and looked up to with reverent awe. It has converted the physician, the lawyer, the priest, the poet, the man of science, into its paid wage-labourers.

The bourgeoisie has torn away from the family its sentimental veil, and has reduced the family relation to a mere money relation.

The bourgeoisie has disclosed how it came to pass that the brutal display of vigour in the Middle Ages, which reactionaries so much admire, found its fitting complement in the most slothful indolence. It has been the first to show what man's activity can bring about. It has accomplished wonders far surpassing Egyptian pyramids, Roman aqueducts, and Gothic cathedrals; it has conducted expeditions that put in the shade all former migrations of nations and crusades.

The bourgeoisie cannot exist without constantly revolutionising the instruments of production, and thereby the relations of production, and with them the whole relations of society. Conservation of the old modes of production in unaltered form, was, on the contrary, the first condition of existence for all earlier industrial classes. Constant revolutionising of production, uninterrupted disturbance of all social conditions, ever-lasting uncertainty and agitation distinguish the bourgeois epoch from all earlier ones. All fixed, fast-frozen relations, with their train of ancient and venerable prejudices and opinions, are swept away, all new-formed ones become antiquated before they can ossify. All that is solid melts into air, all that is holy is profaned, and man is at last compelled to face with sober senses his real conditions of life and his relations with his kind.

The need of a constantly expanding market for its products chases the bourgeoisie over the whole surface of the globe. It must nestle everywhere, settle everywhere, establish connections everywhere.

The bourgeoisie has through its exploitation of the world market given a cosmopolitan character to production and consumption in every country. To the great chagrin of reactionaries, it has drawn from under the feet of industry the national ground on which it stood. All old-established national industries have been destroyed or are daily being destroyed. They are dislodged by new industries, whose introduction becomes a life and death question for all civilised nations, by industries that no longer work up indigenous raw material, but raw material drawn from the remotest zones; industries whose products are consumed, not only at home, but in every quarter of the globe. In place of the old wants, satisfied by the production of the country, we find new wants, requiring for their satisfaction the products of distant lands and climes. In place of the old local and national seclusion and self-sufficiency, we have intercourse in every direction, universal interdependence of nations. And as in material, so also in intellectual production. The intellectual creations of individual nations become common property. National one-sidedness and narrow-mindedness become more and more impossible, and from the numerous national and local literatures there arises a world literature.

The bourgeoisie, by the rapid improvement of all instruments of production, by the immensely facilitated means of communication, draws all nations, even the most barbarian, into civilisation. The cheap prices of its commodities are the heavy artillery with which it batters down all Chinese walls, with which it forces the barbarians' intensely obstinate hatred of foreigners to capitulate. It compels all nations, on pain of extinction, to adopt the bourgeois mode of production; it compels them to introduce what it calls civilisation into their midst, *i.e.,* to become bourgeois themselves. In a word, it creates a world after its own image.

The bourgeoisie has subjected the country to the rule of the towns. It has created enormous cities, has greatly increased the urban population as compared with the rural, and has thus rescued a considerable part of the population from the idiocy of rural life. Just as it has made the country dependent on the towns, so it has made barbarian and semi-barbarian countries dependent on the civilised ones, nations of peasants on nations of bourgeois, the East on the West.

The bourgeoisie keeps more and more doing away with the scattered state of the population, of the means of production, and of property. It has agglomerated population, centralised means of production, and has concentrated property in a few hands. The necessary consequence of this was political centralisation. Independent, or but loosely connected provinces, with separate interests, laws, governments and systems of taxation, became lumped together into one nation, with one government, one code of laws, one national class interest, one frontier and one customs tariff.

The bourgeoisie, during its rule of scarce one hundred years, has created more massive and more colossal productive forces than have all preceding generations together. Subjection of nature's forces to man, machinery, application of chemistry to industry and agriculture, steam-navigation, railways, electric telegraphs, clearing of whole continents for cultivation, canalisation of rivers, whole populations conjured out of the ground—what earlier century had even a presentiment that such productive forces slumbered in the lap of social labour?

We see then that the means of production and of exchange, which served as the foundation for the growth of the bourgeoisie, were generated in feudal society. At a certain stage in the development of these means of production and of exchange, the conditions under which feudal society produced and exchanged, the feudal organisation of agriculture and manufacturing industry, in a word, the feudal relations of property became no longer compatible with the already developed productive forces; they became so many fetters. They had to be burst asunder; they were burst asunder.

Into their place stepped free competition, accompanied by a social and political constitution adapted to it, and by the economic and political sway of the bourgeois class.

A similar movement is going on before our own eyes. Modern bourgeois society with its relations of production, of exchange and of property, a society that has conjured up such gigantic means of production and of exchange, is like the sorcerer who is no longer able to control the powers of the nether world whom he has called up by his spells. For many a decade past the history of industry and commerce is but the history of the revolt of modern productive forces against modern conditions of production, against the property relations that are the conditions for the existence of the bourgeoisie and of its rule. It is enough to mention the commercial crises that by their periodical return put the existence of the entire bourgeois society on trial, each time more threateningly. In these crises a great part not only of the existing products, but also of the previously created productive forces, are periodically destroyed. In these crises there breaks out an epidemic that, in all earlier epochs, would have seemed an absurdity—the epidemic of over-production. Society suddenly finds itself put back into a state of momentary barbarism; it appears as if a famine, a universal war of devastation had cut off the supply of every means of subsistence; industry and commerce seem to be destroyed. And why? Because there is too much civilization, too much means of subsistence, too much industry, too much commerce. The productive forces at the disposal of society no longer tend to further the development of the conditions of bourgeois property; on the contrary, they have become too powerful for these conditions, by which they are fettered, and no sooner do they overcome these fetters than they bring disorder into the whole of bourgeois society, endanger the existence of bourgeois property. The conditions of bourgeois society are too narrow to comprise the wealth created by them. And how does the bourgeoisie get over these crises? On the one

hand by enforced destruction of a mass of productive forces; on the other, by the conquest of new markets, and by the more thorough exploitation of the old ones. That is to say, by paving the way for more extensive and more destructive crises, and by diminishing the means whereby crises are prevented.

The weapons with which the bourgeoisie felled feudalism to the ground are now turned against the bourgeoisie itself.

But not only has the bourgeoisie forged the weapons that bring death to itself; it has also called into existence the men who are to wield those weapons—the modern working class—the proletarians.

In proportion as the bourgeoisie, i.e., capital, is developed, in the same proportion is the proletariat, the modern working class, developed—a class of labourers, who live only so long as they find work, and who find work only so long as their labour increases capital. These labourers, who must sell themselves piecemeal, are a commodity, like every other article of commerce, and are consequently exposed to all the vicissitudes of competition, to all the fluctuations of the market.

Owing to the extensive use of machinery and to division of labour, the work of the proletarians has lost all individual character, and, consequently, all charm for the workman. He becomes an appendage of the machine, and it is only the most simple, most monotonous, and most easily acquired knack, that is required of him. Hence, the cost of production of a workman is restricted, almost entirely, to the means of subsistence that he requires for his maintenance, and for the propagation of his race. But the price of a commodity, and therefore also of labour, is equal to its cost of production. In proportion, therefore, as the repulsiveness of the work increases, the wage decreases. Nay more, in proportion as the use of machinery and division of labour increases, in the same proportion the burden of toil also increases, whether by prolongation of the working hours, by increase of the work exacted in a given time, or by increased speed of the machinery, etc.

Modern industry has converted the little workshop of the patriarchal master into the great factory of the industrial capitalist. Masses of labourers, crowded into the factory, are organised like soldiers. As privates of the industrial army they are placed under the command of a perfect hierarchy of officers and sergeants. Not only are they slaves of the bourgeois class, and of the bourgeois state; they are daily and hourly enslaved by the machine, by the overseer, and, above all, by the individual bourgeois manufacturer himself. The more openly this despotism proclaims gain to be its end and aim, the more petty, the more hateful and the more embittering it is.

The less the skill and exertion of strength implied in manual labour, in other words, the more modern industry develops, the more is the labour of men superseded by that of women. Differences of age and sex have no longer any distinctive social validity for the working class. All are instruments of labour, more or less expensive to use, according to their age and sex.

No sooner has the labourer received his wages in cash, for the moment escaping exploitation by the manufacturer, than he is set upon by the other portions of the bourgeoisie, the landlord, the shopkeeper, the pawnbroker, etc.

The lower strata of the middle class—the small tradespeople, shopkeepers, and retired tradesman generally, the handicraftsmen and peasants—all these sink gradually into the proletariat, partly because their diminutive capital does not suffice for the scale on which modern industry is carried on, and is swamped in the competition with the large capitalists, partly because their specialised skill is rendered worthless by new methods of production. Thus the proletariat is recruited from all classes of the population.

The proletariat goes through various stages of development. With its birth begins its struggle with the bourgeoisie. At first the contest is carried on by individual labourers, then by the work people of a factory, then by the operatives of one trade, in one locality, against the individual bourgeois who directly exploits them. They direct their attacks not against the bourgeois conditions of production, but against the instruments of production themselves; they destroy imported wares that compete with their labour, they smash machinery to pieces, they set factories ablaze, they seek to restore by force the vanished status of the workman of the Middle Ages.

At this stage the labourers still form an incoherent mass scattered over the whole country, and broken up by their mutual competition. If anywhere they unite to form more compact bodies, this is not yet the consequence of their own active union, but of the union of the bourgeoisie, which class, in order to attain its own political ends, is compelled to set the whole proletariat in motion, and is moreover still able to do so for a time. At this stage, therefore, the proletarians do not fight their enemies, but the enemies of their enemies, the remnants of absolute monarchy, the landowners, the non-industrial bourgeois, the petty bourgeoisie. Thus the whole historical movement is concentrated in the hands of the bourgeoisie; every victory so obtained is a victory for the bourgeoisie.

But with the development of industry the proletariat not only increases in number; it becomes concentrated in greater masses, its strength grows, and it feels that strength more. The various interests and conditions of life within the ranks of the proletariat are more and more equalised, in proportion as machinery obliterates all distinctions of labour and nearly everywhere reduces wages to the same low level. The growing competition among the bourgeois, and the resulting commercial crises, makes the wages of the workers ever more fluctuating. The unceasing improvement of machinery, ever more rapidly developing, makes their livelihood more and more precarious; the collisions between individual workmen and individual bourgeois take more and more the character of collisions between two classes. Thereupon the workers begin to form combinations (trade unions) against the bourgeoisie; they club together in order to keep up the rate of wages; they found permanent associations in order to make provision beforehand for these occasional revolts. Here and there the contest breaks out into riots.

Now and then the workers are victorious, but only for a time. The real fruit of their battles lies, not in the immediate result, but in the ever expanding union of the workers. This union is furthered by the improved means of communication which are created by modern industry, and which place the workers of different localities in contact with one another. It was just this contact that was needed to centralise the numerous local struggles, all of the same character, into one national struggle between classes. But every class struggle is a political struggle. And that union, to attain which the burghers of the Middle Ages, with their miserable highways, required centuries, the modern proletarians, thanks to railways, achieve in a few years.

This organisation of the proletarians into a class, and consequently into a political party, is continually being upset again by the competition between the workers themselves. But it ever rises up again, stronger, firmer, mightier. It compels legislative recognition of particular interests of the workers, by taking advantage of the divisions among the bourgeoisie itself. Thus the ten-hour bill in England was carried.

Altogether, collisions between the classes of the old society further the course of development of the proletariat in many ways. The bourgeoisie finds itself involved in a constant battle. At first with the aristocracy; later on, with those portions of the bourgeoisie itself whose interests have become antagonistic to the progress of industry; at all times with the bourgeoisie of foreign countries. In all these battles it sees itself compelled to appeal to the proletariat, to ask for its help, and thus, to drag it into the political arena. The bourgeoisie itself, therefore, supplies the proletariat with its own elements of political and general education, in other words, it furnishes the proletariat with weapons for fighting the bourgeoisie.

Further, as we have already seen, entire sections of the ruling classes are, by the advance of industry, precipitated into the proletariat, or are at least threatened in their conditions of existence. These also supply the proletariat with fresh elements of enlightenment and progress.

Finally, in times when the class struggle nears the decisive hour, the process of dissolution going on within the ruling class, in fact within the whole range of old society, assumes such a violent, glaring character, that a small section of the ruling class cuts itself adrift, and joins the revolutionary class, the class that holds the future in its hands. Just as, therefore, at an earlier period, a section of the nobility went over to the bourgeoisie, so now a portion of the bourgeoisie goes over to the proletariat, and in particular, a portion of the bourgeois ideologists, who have raised themselves to the level of comprehending theoretically the historical movement as a whole.

Of all the classes that stand face to face with the bourgeoisie today, the proletariat alone is a really revolutionary class. The other classes decay and finally disappear in the face of modern industry: the proletariat is its special and essential product.

The lower middle class, the small manufacturer, the shopkeeper, the artisan, the peasant, all these fight against the bourgeoisie, to save from extinction their existence as fractions of the middle class. They are therefore not revolutionary but conservative. Nay more, they are reactionary, for they try to roll back the wheel of history. If by chance they are revolutionary, they are so only in view of their impending transfer into the proletariat; they thus defend not their present, but their future interests; they desert their own standpoint to adopt that of the proletariat.

The "dangerous class," the social scum *(Lumpenproletariat),* that passively rotting mass thrown off by the lowest layers of old society, may, here and there, be swept into the movement by a proletarian revolution; its conditions of life, however, prepare it far more for the part of a bribed tool of reactionary intrigue.

The social conditions of the old society no longer exist for the proletariat. The proletarian is without property; his relation to his wife and children has no longer anything in common with bourgeois family relations; modern industrial labour, modern subjection to capital, the same in England as in France, in America as in Germany, has stripped him of every trace of national character. Law, morality, religion, are to him so many bourgeois prejudices, behind which lurk in ambush just as many bourgeois interests.

All the preceding classes that got the upper hand, sought to fortify their already acquired status by subjecting society at large to their conditions of appropriation. The proletarians cannot become masters of the productive forces of society, except by abolishing their own previous mode of appropriation, and thereby also every other previous mode of appropriation. They have nothing of their own to secure and to fortify; their mission is to destroy all previous securities for, and insurances of, individual property.

All previous historical movements were movements of minorities, or in the interest of minorities. The proletarian movement is the self-conscious, independent movement of the immense majority, in the interest of the immense majority. The proletariat, the lowest stratum of our present society, cannot stir, cannot raise itself up, without the whole super-incumbent strata of official society being sprung into the air.

Though not in substance, yet in form, the struggle of the proletariat with the bourgeoisie is at first a national struggle. The proletariat of each country must, of course, first of all settle matters with its own bourgeoisie.

In depicting the most general phases of the development of the proletariat, we traced the more or less veiled civil war, raging within existing society, up to the point where that war breaks out into open revolution, and where the violent overthrow of the bourgeoisie lays the foundation for the sway of the proletariat.

Hitherto, every form of society has been based, as we have already seen, on the antagonism of oppressing and oppressed classes. But in order to oppress a class, certain conditions must be assured to it under which it can, at least, continue its slavish existence. The serf, in the period of serfdom, raised himself to membership in the commune, just as the petty bourgeois, under the yoke of feudal absolutism, managed to develop into a bourgeois. The modern labourer, on the contrary, instead of rising with the progress of industry, sinks deeper and deeper below the conditions of existence of his own class. He becomes a pauper, and pauperism develops more rapidly than population and wealth. And here it becomes evident, that the bourgeoisie is unfit any longer to be the ruling class in society, and to impose its conditions of existence upon society as an over-riding law. It is unfit to rule because it is incompetent to assure an existence to its slave within his slavery, because it cannot help letting him sink into such a state, that it has to feed him, instead of being fed by him. Society can no longer live under this bourgeoisie, in other words, its existence is no longer compatible with society.

The essential condition for the existence and sway of the bourgeois class, is the formation and augmentation of capital; the condition for capital is wage-labour. Wage-labour rests exclusively on competition between the labourers. The advance of industry, whose involuntary promoter is the bourgeoisie, replaces the isolation of the labourers, due to competition, by their revolutionary combination, due to association. The development of modern industry, therefore, cuts from under its feet the very foundation on which the bourgeoisie produces and appropriates products. What the bourgeoisie therefore produces, above all, are its own grave-diggers. Its fall and the victory of the proletariat are equally inevitable.

PROLETARIANS AND COMMUNISTS

In what relation do the Communists stand to the proletarians as a whole?

The Communists do not form a separate party opposed to other working class parties.

They have no interests separate and apart from those of the proletariat as a whole.

They do not set up any sectarian principles of their own, by which to shape and mould the proletarian movement.

The Communists are distinguished from the other working class parties by this only: 1. In the national struggles of the proletarians of the different countries, they point out and bring to the front the common interests of the entire proletariat, independently of all nationality. 2. In the various stages of development which the struggle of the working class against the bourgeoisie has to pass through, they always and everywhere represent the interests of the movement as a whole.

The Communists, therefore, are on the one hand, practically, the most advanced and resolute section of the working class parties of every country, that section which pushes forward all others; on the other hand, theoretically, they have over the great mass of the proletariat the advantage of clearly understanding the line of march, the conditions, and the ultimate general results of the proletarian movement.

The immediate aim of the Communists is the same as that of all the other proletarian parties: Formation of the proletariat into a class, overthrow of bourgeois supremacy, conquest of political power by the proletariat.

The theoretical conclusions of the Communists are in no way based on ideas or principles that have been invented, or discovered, by this or that would-be universal reformer.

They merely express, in general terms, actual relations springing from an existing class struggle, from a historical movement going on under our very eyes. The abolition of existing property relations is not at all a distinctive feature of Communism.

All property relations in the past have continually been subject to historical change consequent upon the change in historical conditions.

The French Revolution, for example, abolished feudal property in favour of bourgeois property.

The distinguishing feature of Communism is not the abolition of property generally, but the abolition of bourgeois property. But modern bourgeois private property is the final and most complete expression of the system of producing and appropriating products that is based on class antagonisms, on the exploitation of the many by the few.

In this sense, the theory of the Communists may be summed up in the single sentence: Abolition of private property.

We Communists have been reproached with the desire of abolishing the right of personally acquiring property as the fruit of a man's own labour, which property is alleged to be the groundwork of all personal freedom, activity and independence.

Hard-won, self-acquired, self-earned property! Do you mean the property of the petty artisan and of the small peasant, a form of property that preceded the bourgeois form? There is no need to abolish that; the development of industry has to a great extent already destroyed it, and is still destroying it daily.

Or do you mean modern bourgeois private property?

But does wage-labour create any property for the labourer? Not a bit. It creates capital, i.e., that kind of property which exploits wage-labour, and which cannot increase except upon condition of begetting a new supply of wage-labour for fresh exploitation. Property, in its present form, is based on the antagonism of capital and wage-labour. Let us examine both sides of this antagonism.

To be a capitalist, is to have not only a purely personal, but a social status in production. Capital is a collective product, and only by the united action of many members, nay, in the last resort, only by the united action of all members of society, can it be set in motion.

Capital is therefore not a personal, it is a social, power.

When, therefore, capital is converted into common property, into the property of all members of society, personal property is not thereby transformed into social property. It is only the social character of the property that is changed. It loses its class character.

Let us now take wage-labour.

The average price of wage-labour is the minimum wage, i.e., that quantum of the means of subsistence which is absolutely requisite to keep the labourer in bare existence as a labourer. What, therefore, the wage-labourer appropriates by means of his labour, merely suffices to prolong and reproduce a bare existence. We by no means intend to abolish this personal appropriation of the products of labour, an appropriation that is made for the maintenance and reproduction of human life, and that leaves no surplus wherewith to command the labour of others. All that we want to do away with is the miserable character of this appropriation, under which the labourer lives merely to increase capital, and is allowed to live only insofar as the interest of the ruling class requires it.

In bourgeois society, living labour is but a means to increase accumulated labour. In Communist society, accumulated labour is but a means to widen, to enrich, to promote the existence of the labourer.

In bourgeois society, therefore, the past dominates the present; in Communist society, the present dominates the past. In bourgeois society capital is independent and has individuality, while the living person is dependent and has no individuality.

And the abolition of this state of things is called by the bourgeois, abolition of individuality and freedom! And rightly so. The abolition of bourgeois individuality, bourgeois independence, and bourgeois freedom is undoubtedly aimed at.

By freedom is meant, under the present bourgeois conditions of production, free trade, free selling and buying.

But if selling and buying disappears, free selling and buying disappears also. This talk about free selling and buying, and all the other "brave words" of our bourgeoisie about freedom in general, have a meaning, if any, only in contrast with restricted selling and buying, with the fettered traders of the Middle Ages, but have no meaning when opposed to the Communist abolition of buying and selling, of the bourgeois condition of production, and of the bourgeoisie itself.

You are horrified at our intending to do away with private property. But in your existing society, private property is already done away with for nine-tenths of the population; its existence for the few is solely due to its non-existence in the hands of those nine-tenths. You reproach us, therefore, with intending to do away with a form of property, the necessary condition for whose existence is the non-existence of any property for the immense majority of society.

In a word, you reproach us with intending to do away with your property. Precisely so; that is just what we intend.

From the moment when labour can no longer be converted into capital, money, or rent, into a social power capable of being monopolised, i.e., from the moment when individual property can no longer be transformed into bourgeois property, into capital, from that moment, you say, individuality vanishes.

You must, therefore, confess that by "individual" you mean no other person than the bourgeois, than the middle class owner of property. This person must, indeed, be swept out of the way, and made impossible.

Communism deprives no man of the power to appropriate the products of society; all that it does is to deprive him of the power to subjugate the labour of others by means of such appropriation.

It has been objected, that upon the abolition of private property all work will cease, and universal laziness will overtake us.

According to this, bourgeois society ought long ago to have gone to the dogs through sheer idleness; for those of its members who work, acquire nothing, and those who acquire anything, do not work. The whole of this objection is but another expression of the tautology: There can no longer be any wage-labour when there is no longer any capital.

All objections urged against the Communist mode of producing and appropriating material products, have, in the same way, been urged against the Communist modes of producing and appropriating intellectual products. Just as, to the bourgeois, the disappearance of class property is the disappearance of production itself, so the disappearance of class culture is to him identical with the disappearance of all culture.

That culture, the loss of which he laments, is, for the enormous majority, a mere training to act as a machine.

But don't wrangle with us so long as you apply, to our intended abolition of bourgeois property, the standard of your bourgeois notions of freedom, culture, law, etc. Your very ideas are but the outgrowth of the conditions of your bourgeois production and bourgeois property, just as your jurisprudence is but the will of your class made into a law for all, a will whose essential character and direction are determined by the economic conditions of existence of your class.

The selfish misconception that induces you to transform into eternal laws of nature and of reason, the social forms springing from your present mode of production and form of property—historical relations that rise and disappear in the progress of production—this misconception you share with every ruling class that has preceded you. What you see clearly in the case of ancient property, what you admit in the case of feudal property, you are of course forbidden to admit in the case of your own bourgeois form of property.

Abolition of the family! Even the most radical flare up at this infamous proposal of the Communists.

On what foundation is the present family, the bourgeois family, based? On capital, on private gain. In its completely developed form this family exists only among the bourgeoisie. But this state of things finds its complement in the practical absence of the family among the proletarians, and in public prostitution.

The bourgeois family will vanish as a matter of course when its complement vanishes, and both will vanish with the vanishing of capital.

Do you charge us with wanting to stop the exploitation of children by their parents? To this crime we plead guilty.

But, you will say, we destroy the most hallowed of relations, when we replace home education by social.

And your education! Is not that also social, and determined by the social conditions under which you educate, by the intervention of society, direct or indirect, by means of schools, etc.? The Communists have not invented the intervention of society in education; they do but seek to alter the character of that intervention, and to rescue education from the influence of the ruling class.

The bourgeois claptrap about the family and education, about the hallowed co-relation of parent and child, becomes all the more disgusting, the more, by the action of modern industry, all family ties among the proletarians are torn asunder, and their children transformed into simple articles of commerce and instruments of labour.

But you Communists would introduce community of women, screams the whole bourgeoisie in chorus.

The bourgeois sees in his wife a mere instrument of production. He hears that the instruments of production are to be exploited in common, and, naturally, can come to no other conclusion than that the lot of being common to all will likewise fall to the women.

He has not even a suspicion that the real point aimed at is to do away with the status of women as mere instruments of production.

For the rest, nothing is more ridiculous than the virtuous indignation of our bourgeois at the community of women which, they pretend, is to be openly and officially established by the Communists. The Communists have no need to introduce community of women; it has existed almost from time immemorial.

Our bourgeois, not content with having the wives and daughters of their proletarians at their disposal, not to speak of common prostitutes, take the greatest pleasure in seducing each other's wives.

Bourgeois marriage is in reality a system of wives in common and thus, at the most, what the Communists might possibly be reproached with is that they desire to introduce, in substitution for a hypocritically concealed, an openly legalised community of women. For the rest, it is self-evident, that the abolition of the present system of production must bring with it the abolition of the community of women springing from that system, *i.e.,* of prostitution both public and private.

The Communists are further reproached with desiring to abolish countries and nationality.

The workingmen have no country. We cannot take from them what they have not got. Since the proletariat must first of all acquire political supremacy, must rise to be the leading class of the nation, must constitute itself *the* nation, it is, so far, itself national, though not in the bourgeois sense of the word.

National differences and antagonisms between peoples are vanishing gradually from day to day, owing to the development of the bourgeoisie, to freedom of commerce, to the world market, to uniformity in the mode of production and in the conditions of life corresponding thereto.

The supremacy of the proletariat will cause them to vanish still faster. United action, of the leading civilised countries at least, is one of the first conditions for the emancipation of the proletariat.

In proportion as the exploitation of one individual by another is put an end to, the exploitation of one nation by another will also be put an end to. In proportion as the antagonism between classes within the nation vanishes, the hostility of one nation to another will come to an end.

The charges against Communism made from a religious, a philosophical, and, generally, from an ideological standpoint, are not deserving of serious examination.

Does it require deep intuition to comprehend that man's ideas, views, and conceptions, in one word, man's consciousness, changes with every change in the conditions of his material existence, in his social relations and in his social life?

What else does the history of ideas prove, than that intellectual production changes its character in proportion as material production is changed? The ruling ideas of each age have ever been the ideas of its ruling class.

When people speak of ideas that revolutionise society, they do but express the fact that within the old society the elements of a new one have been created, and that the dissolution of the old ideas keeps even pace with the dissolution of the old conditions of existence.

When the ancient world was in its last throes, the ancient religions were overcome by Christianity. When Christian ideas succumbed in the 18th century to rationalist ideas, feudal society fought its death-battle with the then revolutionary bourgeoisie. The ideas of religious liberty and freedom of conscience, merely gave expression to the sway of free competition within the domain of knowledge.

"Undoubtedly," it will be said, "religion, moral, philosophical and juridical ideas have been modified in the course of historical development. But religion, morality, philosophy, political science, and law, constantly survived this change.

"There are, besides, eternal truths, such as Freedom, Justice, etc., that are common to all states of society. But Communism abolishes eternal truths, it abolishes all religion, and all morality, instead of constituting them on a new basis; it therefore acts in contradiction to all past historical experience."

What does this accusation reduce itself to? The history of all past society has consisted in the development of class antagonisms, antagonisms that assumed different forms at different epochs.

But whatever form they may have taken, one fact is common to all past ages, *viz.*, the exploitation of one part of society by the other. No wonder, then, that the social consciousness of past ages, despite all the multiplicity and variety it displays, moves within certain common forms, or general ideas, which cannot completely vanish except with the total disappearance of class antagonisms.

The Communist revolution is the most radical rupture with traditional property relations; no wonder that its development involves the most radical rupture with traditional ideas,

But let us have done with the bourgeois objections to Communism.

We have seen above, that the first step in the revolution by the working class, is to raise the proletariat to the position of ruling class, to establish democracy.

The proletariat will use its political supremacy to wrest, by degrees, all capital from the bourgeoisie, to centralise all instruments of production in the hands of the state, *i.e.,* of the proletariat organised as the ruling class; and to increase the total of productive forces as rapidly as possible.

Of course, in the beginning, this cannot be effected except by means of despotic inroads on the rights of property, and on the conditions of bourgeois production; by means of measures, therefore, which appear economically insufficient and untenable, but which, in the course of the movement, outstrip themselves, necessitate further inroads upon the old social order, and are unavoidable as a means of entirely revolutionising the mode of production.

These measures will of course be different in different countries.

Nevertheless in the most advanced countries, the following will be pretty generally applicable.

1. Abolition of property in land and application of all rents of land to public purposes.

2. A heavy progressive or graduated income tax.

3. Abolition of all right of inheritance.

4. Confiscation of the property of all emigrants and rebels.

5. Centralisation of credit in the hands of the state, by means of a national bank with state capital and an exclusive monopoly.

6. Centralisation of the means of communication and transport in the hands of the state.

7. Extension of factories and instruments of production owned by the state; the bringing into cultivation of waste lands, and the improvement of the soil generally in accordance with a common plan.

8. Equal obligation of all to work. Establishment of industrial armies, especially for agriculture.

9. Combination of agriculture with manufacturing industries; gradual abolition of the distinction between town and country, by a more equable distribution of the population over the country.

10. Free education for all children in public schools. Abolition of child factory labour in its present form. Combination of education with industrial production, etc.

When, in the course of development, class distinctions have disappeared, and all production has been concentrated in the hands of a vast association of the whole nation, the public power will lose its political character. Political power, properly so called, is merely the organised power of one class for oppressing another. If the proletariat during its contest with the bourgeoisie is compelled, by the force of circumstances, to organise itself as a class; if, by means of a revolution, it makes itself the ruling class, and, as such sweeps away by force the old conditions of production, then it will, along with these conditions, have swept away the conditions for the existence of class antagonisms, and of classes generally, and will thereby have abolished its own supremacy as a class.

In place of the old bourgeois society, with its classes and class antagonisms, we shall have an association, in which the free development of each is the condition for the free development of all.

SOCIALIST AND COMMUNIST LITERATURE

REACTIONARY SOCIALISM

Feudal Socialism   Owing to their historical position, it became the vocation of the aristocracies of France and England to write pamphlets against modern bourgeois society. In the French revolution of July, 1830, and in the English reform agitation, these aristocracies again succumbed to the hateful upstart. Thenceforth, a serious political struggle was altogether out of the question. A literary battle alone remained possible. But even in the domain of literature the old cries of the restoration period had become impossible.

In order to arouse sympathy, the aristocracy was obliged to lose sight, apparently, of its own interests, and to formulate its indictment against the bourgeoisie in the interest of the exploited working class alone. Thus the aristocracy took its revenge by singing lampoons against its new master, and whispering in his ears sinister prophecies of coming catastrophe.

In this way arose Feudal Socialism: Half lamentation, half lampoon; half echo of the past, half menace of the future; at times, by its bitter, witty and incisive criticism, striking the bourgeoisie to the very heart's core, but always ludicrous in its effect through total incapacity to comprehend the march of modern history.

The aristocracy, in order to rally the people to them, waved the proletarian almsbag in front for a banner. But the people, as often as it joined them, saw on their hindquarters the old feudal coats of arms, and deserted with loud and irreverent laughter.

One section of the French Legitimists, and "Young England," exhibited this spectacle.

In pointing out that their mode of exploitation was different from that of the bourgeoisie, the feudalists forget that they exploited under circumstances and conditions that were quite different, and that are now antiquated. In showing that, under their rule, the modern proletariat never existed, they forget that the modern bourgeoisie is the necessary offspring of their own form of society.

For the rest, so little do they conceal the reactionary character of their criticism, that their chief accusation against the bourgeoisie amounts to this, that under the bourgeois regime a class is being developed, which is destined to cut up root and branch the old order of society.

What they upbraid the bourgeoisie with is not so much that it creates a proletariat, as that it creates a *revolutionary* proletariat.

In political practice, therefore, they join in all coercive measures against the working class; and in ordinary life, despite their high-falutin phrases, they stoop to pick up the golden apples dropped from the tree of industry, and to barter truth, love, and honour for traffic in wool, beetroot-sugar, and potato spirits.

As the parson has ever gone hand in hand with the landlord, so has Clerical Socialism with Feudal Socialism.

Nothing is easier than to give Christian asceticism a Socialist tinge. Has not Christianity declaimed against private property, against marriage, against the state? Has it not preached in the place of these, charity and poverty, celibacy and mortification of the flesh, monastic life and Mother Church? Christian Socialism is but the holy water with which the priest consecrates the heart-burnings of the aristocrat.

Petty Bourgeois Socialism   The feudal aristocracy was not the only class that was ruined by the bourgeoisie, not the only class whose conditions of existence pined and perished in the atmosphere of modern bourgeois society. The mediæval burgesses and the small peasant proprietors were the precursors of the modern bourgeoisie. In those countries which are but little developed, industrially and commercially, these two classes still vegetate side by side with the rising bourgeoisie.

In countries where modern civilisation has become fully developed, a new class of petty bourgeois has been formed, fluctuating between proletariat and bourgeoisie, and ever renewing itself as a supplementary part of bourgeois society. The individual members of this class, however, are being constantly hurled down into the proletariat by the action of competition, and, as modern industry develops, they even see the moment approaching when they will completely disappear as an independent section of modern society, to be replaced, in manufactures, agriculture and commerce, by overseers, bailiffs and shopmen.

In countries, like France, where the peasants constitute far more than half of the population, it was natural that writers who sided with the proletariat against the bourgeoisie, should use, in their criticism of the bourgeois regime, the standard of the peasant and petty bourgeois, and from the standpoint of these intermediate classes should take up the cudgels for the working class. Thus arose petty bourgeois Socialism. Sismondi was the head of this school, not only in France but also in England.

This school of Socialism dissected with great acuteness the contradictions in the conditions of modern production. It laid bare the hypocritical apologies of economists. It proved, incontrovertibly, the disastrous effects of machinery and division of labour; the concentration of capital and land in a few hands; overproduction and crises; it pointed out the inevitable ruin of the petty bourgeois and peasant, the misery of the proletariat, the anarchy in production, the crying inequalities in the distribution of wealth, the industrial war of extermination between nations, the dissolution of old moral bonds, of the old family relations, of the old nationalities.

In its positive aims, however, this form of Socialism aspires either to restoring the old means of production and of exchange, and with them the old property relations, and the old society, or to cramping the modern means of production and of exchange within the framework of the old property relations that have been, and were bound to be, exploded by those means. In either case, it is both reactionary and utopian.

Its last words are: Corporate guilds for manufacture; patriarchal relations in agriculture.

Ultimately, when stubborn historical facts had dispersed all intoxicating effects of self-deception, this form of Socialism ended in a miserable fit of the blues.

German or "True" Socialism The Socialist and Communist literature of France, a literature that originated under the pressure of a bourgeoisie in power, and that was the expression of the struggle against this power, was introduced into Germany at a time when the bourgeoisie, in that country, had just begun its contest with feudal absolutism.

German philosophers, would-be philosophers, and men of letters eagerly seized on this literature, only forgetting that when these writings immigrated from France into Germany, French social conditions had not immigrated along with them. In contact with German social conditions, this French literature lost all its immediate practical significance, and assumed a purely literary aspect. Thus, to the German philosophers of the 18th century, the demands of the first French Revolution were nothing more than the demands of "Practical Reason" in general, and the utterance of the will of the revolutionary French bourgeoisie signified in their eyes the laws of pure will, of will as it was bound to be, of true human will generally.

The work of the German *literati* consisted solely in bringing the new French ideas into harmony with their ancient philosophical conscience, or rather, in annexing the French ideas without deserting their own philosophic point of view.

This annexation took place in the same way in which a foreign language is appropriated, namely by translation.

It is well known how the monks wrote silly lives of Catholic saints *over* the manuscripts on which the classical works of ancient heathendom had been written. The

German *literati* reversed this process with the profane French literature. They wrote their philosophical nonsense beneath the French original. For instance, beneath the French criticism of the economic functions of money, they wrote "alienation of humanity," and beneath the French criticism of the bourgeois state, they wrote, "dethronement of the category of the general," and so forth.

The introduction of these philosophical phrases at the back of the French historical criticisms they dubbed "Philosophy of Action," "True Socialism," "German Science of Socialism," "Philosophical Foundation of Socialism," and so on.

The French Socialist and Communist literature was thus completely emasculated. And, since it ceased in the hands of the German to express the struggle of one class with the other, he felt conscious of having overcome "French one-sidedness" and of representing, not true requirements, but the requirements of truth; not the interests of the proletariat, but the interests of human nature, of man in general, who belongs to no class, has no reality, who exists only in the misty realm of philosophical phantasy.

This German Socialism, which took its school-boy task so seriously and solemnly, and extolled its poor stock-in-trade in such mountebank fashion, meanwhile gradually lost its pedantic innocence.

The fight of the German and especially of the Prussian bourgeoisie against feudal aristocracy and absolute monarchy, in other words, the liberal movement, became more earnest.

By this, the long-wished-for opportunity was offered to "True" Socialism of confronting the political movement with the Socialist demands, of hurling the traditional anathemas against liberalism, against representative government, against bourgeois competition, bourgeois freedom of the press, bourgeois legislation, bourgeois liberty and equality, and of preaching to the masses that they had nothing to gain, and everything to lose, by this bourgeois movement. German Socialism forgot, in the nick of time, that the French criticism, whose silly echo it was, presupposed the existence of modern bourgeois society, with its corresponding economic conditions of existence, and the political constitution adapted thereto, the very things whose attainment was the object of the pending struggle in Germany.

To the absolute governments, with their following of parsons, professors, country squires and officials, it served as a welcome scarecrow against the threatening bourgeoisie.

It was a sweet finish after the bitter pills of floggings and bullets, with which these same governments, just at that time, dosed the risings of the German working class.

While this "True" Socialism thus served the governments as a weapon for fighting the German bourgeoisie, it, at the same time, directly represented a reactionary interest, the interest of the German Philistines. In Germany the petty bourgeois class, a relic of the 16th century, and since then constantly cropping up again under various forms, is the real social basis of the existing state of things.

To preserve this class, is to preserve the existing state of things in Germany. The industrial and political supremacy of the bourgeoisie threatens it with certain destruction—on the one hand, from the concentration of capital; on the other, from the rise of a revolutionary proletariat. "True" Socialism appeared to kill these two birds with one stone. It spread like an epidemic.

The robe of speculative cobwebs, embroidered with flowers of rhetoric, steeped in the dew of sickly sentiment, this transcendental robe in which the German Socialists wrapped their sorry "eternal truths," all skin and bone, served to increase wonderfully the sale of their goods amongst such a public.

And on its part, German Socialism recognised, more and more, its own calling as the bombastic representative of the petty bourgeois Philistine.

It proclaimed the German nation to be the model nation, and the German petty Philistine to be the typical man. To every villainous meanness of this model man it gave a hidden, higher, socialistic interpretation, the exact contrary of his real character. It went to the extreme length of directly opposing the "brutally destructive" tendency of Communism, and of proclaiming its supreme and impartial contempt of all class struggles. With very few exceptions, all the so-called Socialist and Communist publications that now (1847) circulate in Germany belong to the domain of this foul and enervating literature.

CONSERVATIVE OR
BOURGEOIS SOCIALISM

A part of the bourgeoisie is desirous of redressing social grievances, in order to secure the continued existence of bourgeois society.

To this section belong economists, philanthropists, humanitarians, improvers of the condition of the working class, organisers of charity, members of societies for the prevention of cruelty to animals, temperance fanatics, hole-and-corner reformers of every imaginable kind. This form of Socialism has, moreover, been worked out into complete systems.

We may cite Proudhon's *Philosophy of Poverty* as an example of this form.

The socialistic bourgeois want all the advantages of modern social conditions without the struggles and dangers necessarily resulting therefrom. They desire the existing state of society minus its revolutionary and disintegrating elements. They wish for a bourgeoisie without a proletariat. The bourgeoisie naturally conceives the world in which it is supreme to be the best; and bourgeois Socialism develops this comfortable conception into various more or less complete systems. In requiring the proletariat to carry out such a system, and thereby to march straightway into the social New Jerusalem, it but requires in reality, that the proletariat should remain within the bounds of existing society, but should cast away all its hateful ideas concerning the bourgeoisie.

A second and more practical, but less systematic, form of this Socialism sought to depreciate every revolutionary movement in the eyes of the working class, by showing that no mere political reform, but only a change in the material conditions of existence, in economic relations, could be of any advantage to them. By changes in the material conditions of existence, this form of Socialism, however, by no means understands abolition of the bourgeois relations of production, an abolition that can be effected only by a revolution, but administrative reforms, based on the continued existence of these relations; reforms, therefore, that in no respect affect the relations between capital and labour, but at the best, lessen the cost, and simplify the administrative work of bourgeois government.

Bourgeois Socialism attains adequate expression, when, and only when, it becomes a mere figure of speech.

Free trade: For the benefit of the working class. Protective duties: For the benefit of the working class. Prison reform: For the benefit of the working class. These are the last words and the only seriously meant words of bourgeois Socialism.

It is summed up in the phrase: the bourgeois are bourgeois—for the benefit of the working class.

CRITICAL-UTOPIAN SOCIALISM
AND COMMUNISM

We do not here refer to that literature which, in every great modern revolution, has always given voice to the demands of the proletariat, such as the writings of Babeuf and others.

The first direct attempts of the proletariat to attain its own ends—made in times of universal excitement, when feudal society was being overthrown—necessarily failed, owing to the then undeveloped state of the proletariat, as well as to the absence of the economic conditions for its emancipation, conditions that had yet to be produced, and could be produced by the impending bourgeois epoch alone. The revolutionary literature that accompanied these first movements of the proletariat had necessarily a reactionary character. It inculcated universal asceticism and social levelling in its crudest form.

The Socialist and Communist systems properly so called, those of St. Simon, Fourier, Owen and others, spring into existence in the early undeveloped period, described above, of the struggle between proletariat and bourgeoisie (see Section 1. Bourgeois and Proletarians).

The founders of these systems see, indeed, the class antagonisms, as well as the action of the decomposing elements in the prevailing form of society. But the proletariat, as yet in its infancy, offers to them the spectacle of a class without any historical initiative or any independent political movement.

Since the development of class antagonism keeps even pace with the development of industry, the economic situation, as such Socialists find it, does not as yet offer to them the material conditions for the emancipation of the proletariat. They therefore search after a new social science, after new social laws, that are to create these conditions.

Historical action is to yield to their personal inventive action; historically created conditions of emancipation to phantastic ones; and the gradual, spontaneous class organisation of the proletariat to an organisation of society specially contrived by these inventors. Future history resolves itself, in their eyes, into the propaganda and the practical carrying out of their social plans.

In the formulation of their plans they are conscious of caring chiefly for the interests of the working class, as being the most suffering class. Only from the point of view of being the most suffering class does the proletariat exist for them.

The undeveloped state of the class struggle, as well as their own surroundings, causes Socialists of this kind to consider themselves far superior to all class antagonisms. They want to improve the condition of every member of society, even that of the most favoured. Hence, they habitually appeal to society at large, without distinction of class; nay, by preference, to the ruling class. For how can people, when once they understand their system, fail to see in it the best possible plan of the best possible state of society?

Hence, they reject all political, and especially all revolutionary action; they wish to attain their ends by peaceful means, and endeavour, by small experiments, necessarily doomed to failure, and by the force of example, to pave the way for the new social gospel.

Such phantastic pictures of future society, painted at a time when the proletariat is still in a very undeveloped state and has but a phantastic conception of its own position, correspond with the first instinctive yearnings of that class for a general reconstruction of society.

But these Socialist and Communist writings contain also a critical element. They attack every principle of existing society. Hence they are full of the most valuable materials for the enlightenment of the working class. The practical measures proposed in them—such as the abolition of the distinction between town and country; abolition of the family, of private gain and of the wage-system; the proclamation of social harmony; the conversion of the functions of the state into a mere superintendence of production—all these proposals point solely to the disappearance of class antagonisms which were, at that time, only just cropping up, and which, in these publications, are recognised in their earliest, indistinct and undefined forms only. These proposals, therefore, are of a purely utopian character.

The significance of Critical-Utopian Socialism and Communism bears an inverse relation to historical development. In proportion as the modern class struggle develops and takes definite shape, this phantastic standing apart from the contest, these phantastic attacks on it, lose all practical value and all theoretical justification. Therefore, although the originators of these systems were, in many respects, revolutionary, their disciples have, in every case, formed mere reactionary sects. They hold fast by the original views of their masters, in opposition to the progressive historical development of the proletariat. They, therefore, endeavour, and that consistently, to deaden the class struggle and to reconcile the class antagonisms. They still dream of experimental realisation of their social utopias, of founding isolated *phalanstères,* of establishing "Home Colonies," or setting up a "Little Icaria"—pocket editions of the New Jerusalem—and to realise all these castles in the air, they are compelled to appeal to the feelings and purses of the bourgeois. By degrees they sink into the category of the reactionary conservative Socialists depicted above, differing from these only by more systematic pedantry, and by their fanatical and superstitious belief in the miraculous effects of their social science.

They, therefore, violently oppose all political action on the part of the working class; such action, according to them, can only result from blind unbelief in the new gospel.

The Owenites in England, and the Fourierists in France, respectively, oppose the Chartists and the *Réformistes.*

POSITION OF THE COMMUNISTS IN RELATION TO THE VARIOUS EXISTING OPPOSITION PARTIES

Section 2 has made clear the relations of the Communists to the existing working class parties, such as the Chartists in England and the Agrarian Reformers in America.

The Communists fight for the attainment of the immediate aims, for the enforcement of the momentary interests of the working class; but in the movement of the present, they also represent and take care of the future of that movement. In France the Communists ally themselves with the Social-Democrats, against the conservative and radical bourgeoisie, reserving, however, the right to take up a critical position in regard to phrases and illusions traditionally handed down from the great Revolution.

In Switzerland they support the Radicals, without losing sight of the fact that this party consists of antagonistic elements, partly of Democratic Socialists, in the French sense, partly of radical bourgeois.

In Poland they support the party that insists on an agrarian revolution as the prime condition for national emancipation, that party which fomented the insurrection of Cracow in 1846.

In Germany they fight with the bourgeoisie whenever it acts in a revolutionary way, against the absolute monarchy, the feudal squirearchy, and the petty bourgeoisie.

But they never cease, for a single instant, to instil into the working class the clearest possible recognition of the hostile antagonism between bourgeoisie and proletariat, in order that the German workers may straightway use, as so many weapons against the bourgeoisie, the social and political conditions that the bourgeoisie must necessarily introduce along with its supremacy, and in order that, after the fall of the reactionary classes in Germany, the fight against the bourgeoisie itself may immediately begin.

The Communists turn their attention chiefly to Germany, because that country is on the eve of a bourgeois revolution that is bound to be carried out under more advanced conditions of European civilisation and with a much more developed proletariat than what existed in England in the 17th and in France in the 18th century, and because the bourgeois revolution in Germany will be but the prelude to an immediately following proletarian revolution.

In short, the Communists everywhere support every revolutionary movement against the existing social and political order of things.

In all these movements they bring to the front, as the leading question in each case, the property question, no matter what its degree of development at the time.

Finally, they labour everywhere for the union and agreement of the democratic parties of all countries.

The Communists disdain to conceal their views and aims. They openly declare that their ends can be attained only by the forcible overthrow of all existing social conditions. Let the ruling classes tremble at a Communist revolution. The proletarians have nothing to lose but their chains. They have a world to win.

Workingmen of all countries, unite!

CHAPTER ELEVEN

HAYEK

The encounter between capitalism and socialism has led, through the slow working of the democratic political process, to an economy which is neither capitalist, if capitalism means unrestricted *laissez-faire* and rugged individualism, nor socialist, if socialism means an economy that is owned and operated by the state. The mixed economy welfare state seeks to combine the best of capitalism and socialism—the predominantly private energy in private property with predominantly public responsibility in economic macromanagement and social welfare. The relative strength of these two elements always is in flux.

Development of the welfare state was bound to cause a reaction. In the United States, for example, the national government share of gross national product has increased eightfold since 1929, from 2.5 percent to over 20 percent. There is more spending at state and local levels, as well. To consider the expansion of government in the United States from another perspective, government at all levels spent less than $2 billion per year early in the century, but by the end of the century, this figure had increased one thousandfold. The scope of government, as well as its size, also has enormously increased.

Libertarianism—the movement toward less government—is not, at least according to its best proponents, a conservative reaction to the welfare state and general growth of government, but a liberal or even radical one. Friedrich Hayek (1899–1992), perhaps the foremost philosopher of libertarianism during the twentieth century, summed up differences between conservatism and "true liberalism" (or libertarianism) best in his 1956 foreword to his most well-known book, *The Road to Serfdom* (1944): "Conservatism, though a necessary element in any stable society, is not a social program; in its paternalistic, nationalistic, and power-adoring tendencies it is often closer to socialism than true liberalism; and with its traditionalistic, anti-intellectual, and often mystical propensities it will never, except in short periods of disillusionment, appeal to the young and all those who believe that change is desirable if this world is to become a better place."

Trained as an economist in the Austrian tradition, Hayek emerged at the London School of Economics in 1931 as an opponent of John Maynard Keynes and rival of Harold Laski. At Chicago, he was a colleague of Friedman. In 1974, he received the Nobel Prize in Economics with Gunnar Myrdal. Educated at the University of Vienna and intellectually brought to maturity as an assistant to Austrian economist Ludwig von Mises, Hayek was, with Friedman, the leading academic proponent of less government during the twentieth century.

The historical Austrian school of economics can be traced to the nineteenth century Viennese economist Carl Menger, who, in Hayek's view, was the writer after Smith who most explored the idea, as Smith put it, that man in society "constantly promotes ends which are not part of his intention." For Menger, the question "how it is possible that institutions which serve the common welfare and are most important for its advancement can arise without a common will aiming at their creation" is "the significant, perhaps the most significant, problem of the social sciences."

Mises's contribution to libertarian thought and Hayek's work was fundamental. Mises inaugurated the long-lasting and influential "socialist calculation debate," which raised the question of how production in a socialist economy would be determined. Mises stated the main point beautifully: "The [socialist] director wants to build a house. Now, there are many methods that can be resorted to. Each of them offers . . . certain advantages and disadvantages with regard to the utilization of the future building, and results in a different duration of the building's serviceableness; each of them requires . . . [differing] expenditures of building materials and labor. . . . Which method should the director choose? He cannot reduce to a common denominator the items of various materials and various kinds of labor to be expended. Therefore, he cannot compare them."

Mises's argument was that prices, private property, private management, and private exchange are vital to economic productivity. He wrote in the prescient 1920 "Economic Planning in the Socialist Commonwealth": "There are many socialists who have never come to grips in any way with the problems of economics, and who have made no attempt at all to form for themselves any clear conception of the conditions which determine the character of human society. . . . They have criticized freely enough the economic structure of 'free' society, but have consistently neglected to apply to the economics of the disputed socialist state the same caustic acumen. . . . Economics, as such, figures all too sparsely in the glamorous pictures painted by the Utopians. They invariably explain how, in the cloud-cuckoo lands of their fancy, roast pigeons will in some way fly into the mouths of the comrades, but they omit to show how this miracle is to take place." How should production practically be organized in a socialist economy? It is not enough to point to deficiencies in capitalism.

Hayek was born in the pre–World War I Austro-Hungarian Empire and imbibed much from the society in which he grew up. He emphasized order in his thought. The first requisite for a society is safety and order. Without these, no satisfactory life is possible. He also emphasized hierarchy and class. He took it for granted that some will have more and others less in every society—this is a fact of life. He also may have acquired some of his relative disdain for democracy from his Viennese roots. Finally, he adopted a conception of federation as offering the best form of government for resolving many intersocietal issues. Austria-Hungary was a federation.

World War I was an even greater event at the time than it became in retrospect because the worse horrors and convulsions of World War II made the first world war lose some of its centrality. But for central Europeans who experienced it, such as Hayek, World War I was the defining conflagration in their lives. The world that died with the First World War was the nineteenth century, classical liberal world. Keynes perhaps said it best in *The Economic Consequences of the Peace:* "What an extraordinary episode in the economic progress of man that age was which came to an end in August, 1914! The greater part of the population, it is true, worked hard and lived at a low standard of comfort, yet were, to all appearances, reasonably contented with this lot. But escape was possible, for any man of capacity or character at all exceeding the average, into the middle and upper classes, for whom life offered, at a low cost and with the least trouble, conveniences, comforts, and amenities beyond the compass of the richest and most powerful monarchs of other ages. The inhabitant of London could order by telephone, sipping his morning tea in bed, the various products of the whole earth, in such quantity as he might see fit, and reasonably expect their early delivery upon his doorstep . . . [H]e regarded this state of affairs as normal, certain, and permanent. . . . The projects and politics of militarism and imperialism, of racial and cultural rivalries . . . were little more than the amusements of his daily newspaper, and appeared to exercise almost no influence at all on the ordinary course of social and economic life, the internationalization of which was nearly complete in practice." It was always Hayek's goal in many respects to return to the pre–World War I world—which he thought would be progress, not retrogression.

During the 1920s in Vienna under Mises, Hayek focused on monetary theory, industrial fluctuations, and the economics of socialism. His work in monetary theory and a business cycle is disregarded in mainstream economics today. Far more significant was his participation in the socialist calculation debate, beginning in 1935, and his enunciation in the 1937 "Economics and Knowledge" article of "the division of knowledge." The idea he presents in "Economics and Knowledge" is that knowledge is divided:

> There is . . . a problem of the *division of knowledge* which is quite analogous to, and at least as important as, the problem of the division of labor. But, while the latter has been one of the main subjects of investigation ever since the beginning of our science, the former has been as completely neglected, although it seems to me to be the really central problem of economics as a social science. . . .
>
> [E]conomics has come closer than any other social science to an answer to that central question of all social sciences: How can the combination of fragments of knowledge existing in different minds bring about results which, if they were to be brought about deliberately, would require a knowledge on the part of the directing mind which no single person can possess? . . . [T]he spontaneous actions of individuals will, under conditions which we can define, bring about a distribution of resources which can be understood as if it were made according to a single plan, although nobody has planned it. . . .

He added in a later essay, "The Use of Information in Society": "We must look at the price system as . . . a mechanism for communicating information. . . ."

Hayek is most well known for the 1944 anti-planning book *The Road to Serfdom*. He was concerned that, following World War II, Britain might move headlong into wholesale socialist reconstruction of its society, wherein government would own and run all of the means of production. He insightfully argued that not only is a socialist economy inherently unproductive, it is intrinsically despotic: "Whoever controls all economic activity controls the means for all our ends, and must therefore decide which are to be satisfied and which not. This is really the crux of the matter. Economic control is not merely control of a sector of human life which can be separated from the rest; it is the control of the means for all our ends."

Hayek's essential argument against socialism is not that humanity are not good enough for socialism—that we are not benevolent or other-directed enough—but that we are not intelligent enough. Even in a community of saints, a private market and freely fluctuating prices would be necessary effectively to direct production because of limitations in individual human knowledge.

His next major work following *The Road to Serfdom* was *The Constitution of Liberty* (1960), dedicated to "the unknown civilization that is growing in America." In 1950, Hayek left the London School of Economics for the University of Chicago, where he joined Friedman and others, though Hayek was not a member of the economics department at Chicago (he was on the Committee on Social Thought). *The Constitution of Liberty,* conceived as his *magnum opus,* attempted to flesh out arguments made in only a negative and truncated form in *The Road to Serfdom.* Particularly in the first part of *The Constitution of Liberty,* "The Creative Powers of a Free Civilization," he sought to rebut a century of socialist argument: "As a statement of fact, it just is not true that 'all men are born equal.' . . . From the fact that people are very different it follows that, if we treat them equally, the result must be inequality in their actual position, and that the only way to place them in an equal position would be to treat them differently. Equality before the law and material equality are therefore not only different but are in conflict with each other; and we can achieve either the one or the other, but not both at the same time." Hayek chose equality before the law over material equality.

He applied the same standard to relations between nations as he did within them: "There can be little doubt that the prospect of the poorer, 'undeveloped' countries reaching the present level of the West is very much better than it would have been, had the West not pulled so far ahead. Furthermore, it is better than it would have been, had some world authority . . . seen to it that no part pulled too far ahead of the rest and made sure at each step that the material benefits were distributed evenly throughout the world. If today some nations can in a few decades acquire a level of material comfort that took the West hundreds or thousands of years to achieve, is it not evident that their path has been made easier by the fact that the West was not forced to share its material achievements with the rest—that it was not held back but was able to move far in advance of the others?" He was both a domestic and international inegalitarian.

Among the most difficult concepts Hayek put forward is "spontaneous order." As initially developed in his "Economics and Knowledge" article, the idea of a spontaneous order is in largest part that government cannot so much direct every action—economic or otherwise—in a society, but that the goal of government should be to construct certain framework laws or rules that enable a society's members cooperatively to interact. The goal should be not to tell people what to do, but to create opportunities for them to do what they choose to do. He used as an example in *The Road to Serfdom* the difference between government telling people where to travel and providing roads and traffic rules to allow transportation effectively to occur.

Hayek was not opposed to law—he was not an anarchist. He held, in fact, following Locke, that law creates liberty. Hayek quoted Locke: "The end of the law is, not to abolish or restrain, but to preserve and enlarge freedom. For in all the states of created beings capable of laws, where there is no law there is no freedom. For liberty is to be free from restraint and violence from others; which cannot be where there is no law: and it is not, as we are told, a liberty for every man to do what he lists [wishes]. (For who could be free when every other man's humour might domineer over him?) But a liberty to dispose, and order as he lists, his person, actions, possessions, and his whole property, within the allowance of those laws under which he is, and therein not to be the subject of the arbitrary will of another, but freely follow his own."

Law is the crucial constituent of a freedom. Where there is no law, there can be no freedom. Law creates liberty. Law is not inconsistent with liberty, but is its embodiment.

Hayek sanctioned a considerable positive role for government. He allowed many welfare state provisions of social services by government, including in education, health care, unemployment and retirement insurance, and public charity, among many others. In the area of government provision of social welfare services, his primary concern was that government should not have a monopoly in these areas—that if, for example, there is a government retirement program, there should also be able to be private retirement programs—and that government services should be privatized to the greatest extent possible. He also thought that public charity should be as minimal as possible, and largely restricted to the elderly, infirm, and widows with children. He hoped that most societal welfare functions would be provided voluntarily. While he theoretically allowed a significant welfare state, his practical views were more limited.

He opposed a progressive income tax, though he sanctioned some inheritance taxes. In regard to his opposition to a progressive income tax, he felt that it is both unjust and uneconomical. No individual should have to pay more than the same percentage of his income in taxes than anyone else, and taxing at a greater proportion those who earn more discourages initiative. He greatly was opposed to inflation, and thought inflation perhaps is the most ruinous financial condition that can befall a national economy. He was not, though, a Chicago monetarist of Friedman's school.

Law, Legislation and Liberty (1973–79) was mostly written during the 1960s, but completed during the later 1970s, when Hayek was in his seventies. He enjoyed a resurgence in his later years after he was awarded the Nobel Prize in Economics. *Law, Legislation and Liberty* is a more scholarly presentation of many of the ideas in *The Constitution of Liberty*. He emphasized the importance of law as distinct from governmental direction and moral compulsion, though he did not deemphasize the latter as much as he came later to feel that Mill did. For Hayek, cultural norms in addition to law are completely appropriate, indeed an essential part of an effective society.

In *The Fatal Conceit: The Errors of Socialism* (1988), his final work, Hayek returned to the socialist calculation debate. He was now more concerned to attempt to demonstrate that socialism necessarily is unproductive economically than to provide a case for the beneficial operation of democratic interventionist welfare state capitalism: "The main point of my argument is . . . that the conflict between, on one hand, advocates of the spontaneous extended human order created by a competitive market, and on the other hand those who demand a deliberate arrangement of human interaction by central authority based on collective command over available resources is due to a factual error by the latter about how knowledge of these resources is and can be generated and utilised." It is not that socialism would be ethically undesirable; it is that it factually is not possible: "To follow socialist morality would destroy much of present humankind and impoverish much of the rest." He ultimately was a completely materialist philosopher. The best society and best world is the one in which the material standard of living for all people everywhere is as high as it technologically can be. Libertarianism is a rational philosophy. Hayek concluded *The Constitution of Liberty* with a postscript, "Why I Am Not a Conservative": "Personally, I find that the most objectionable feature of the conservative attitude is its propensity to reject well-substantiated new knowledge because it dislikes some of the consequences which seem to follow from it. . . . "

Hayek emphasized the roles of prices and profits. He remarked in one of the last pieces that he himself prepared for publication, "The Moral Imperative of the Market" (1986): "In 1936 . . . , I suddenly saw . . . that my previous work in different branches of economics had a common root. This insight was that the price system was really an instrument which enabled millions of people to adjust their efforts to events, demands and conditions, of which they had no concrete, direct knowledge. . . . Here my thinking was inspired largely by Ludwig von Mises' conception of the problem of ordering a planned economy. . . . [T]he whole economic order rested on the fact that by using prices as a guide, or as signals, we were led to serve the demands and enlist the powers and capacities of people of whom we knew nothing. . . . Basically, the insight that prices were signals bringing about the . . . co-ordination of . . . efforts . . . became the leading idea behind my work." He held in *The Fatal Conceit:* "Profits are all that most producers need to be able to serve more effectively the needs of men they do not know";

"in the evolution of . . . human activities, profitability works as a signal that guides selection towards what makes man more fruitful. . . ."

During his later years, Hayek was an intellectual inspirer for many in the Reagan and Thatcher governments. He soundly believed Keynes' famous closing lines to *The General Theory:* "The ideas of economists and political philosophers, both when they are right and when they are wrong, are more powerful than is commonly understood. Indeed the world is ruled by little else." To the extent this is true, Hayek's own influence may be evaluated.

Hayek's ultimate goal (beyond a world federation of free nations) was of a world of universal law: "It is only by extending the rules of just conduct to the relations with all other men, and at the same time depriving of their obligatory character those rules which cannot be universally applied, that we can approach a universal order of peace which might integrate all mankind into a single society."

HAYEK

*The Road to Serfdom**

THE ABANDONED ROAD

A programme whose basic thesis is, not that the system of free enterprise for profit has failed in this generation, but that it has not yet been tried.

F. D. Roosevelt.

When the course of civilization takes an unexpected turn, when instead of the continuous progress which we have come to expect, we find ourselves threatened by evils associated by us with past ages of barbarism, we blame naturally anything but ourselves. Have we not all striven according to our best lights, and have not many of our finest minds incessantly worked to make this a better world? Have not all our efforts and hopes been directed towards greater freedom, justice, and prosperity? If the outcome is so different from our aims, if, instead of freedom and prosperity, bondage and misery stare us in the face, is it not clear that sinister forces must have foiled our intentions, that we are the victims of some evil power which must be conquered before we can resume the road to better things? However much we may differ when we name the culprit, whether it is the wicked capitalist or the vicious spirit of a particular nation, the stupidity of our elders, or a social system not yet, although we have struggled against it for half a century, fully overthrown—we all are, or at least were until recently, certain of one thing: that the leading ideas which during the last generation have become common to most people of goodwill and have determined the major changes in

our social life cannot have been wrong. We are ready to accept almost any explanation of the present crisis of our civilization except one: that the present state of the world may be the result of genuine error on our own part, and that the pursuit of some of our most cherished ideals have apparently produced results utterly different from those which we expected.

While all our energies are directed to bringing this war to a victorious conclusion, it is sometimes difficult to remember that even before the war the values for which we are now fighting were threatened here and destroyed elsewhere. Though for the time being the different ideals are represented by hostile nations fighting for their existence, we must not forget that this conflict has grown out of a struggle of ideas within what, not so long ago, was a common European civilization; and that the tendencies which have culminated in the creation of the totalitarian systems were not confined to the countries which have succumbed to them. Though the first task must now be to win the war, to win it will only gain us another opportunity to face the basic problems and to find a way of averting the fate which has overtaken kindred civilizations.

Now, it is somewhat difficult to think of Germany and Italy, or of Russia, not as different worlds, but as products of a development of thought in which we have shared; it is, at least so far as our enemies are concerned, easier and more comforting to think that they are entirely different from us and that what happened there cannot happen here. Yet, the history of these countries in the years before the rise of the totalitarian system showed few features with which we are not familiar. The external conflict is

---

*From Friedrich Hayek, *The Road to Serfdom* (1944). By permission.

a result of a transformation of European thought in which others have moved so much faster as to bring them into irreconcilable conflict with our ideals, but which has not left us unaffected.

That a change of ideas, and the force of human will, have made the world what it is now, though men did not foresee the results, and that no spontaneous change in the facts obliged us thus to adapt our thought, is perhaps particularly difficult for the English to see, just because in this development the English have, fortunately for them, lagged behind most of the European peoples. We still think of the ideals which guide us and have guided us for the past generation, as ideals only to be realized in the future, and are not aware how far in the last twenty-five years they have already transformed, not only the world, but also this country. We still believe that until quite recently we were governed by what are vaguely called nineteenth-century ideas or the principle of *laissez-faire*. Compared with some other countries, and from the point of view of those impatient to speed up the change, there may be some justification for such belief. But although till 1931 this country had followed only slowly on the path on which others had led, even by then we had moved so far that only those whose memory goes back to the years before the last war know what a liberal world has been like.

The crucial point of which people here are still so little aware is, however, not merely the magnitude of the changes which have taken place during the last generation, but the fact that they mean a complete change in the direction of the evolution of our ideas and social order. For at least twenty-five years before the spectre of totalitarianism became a real threat, we had progressively been moving away from the basic ideas on which European civilization has been built. That this movement on which we have entered with such high hopes and ambitions should have brought us face to face with the totalitarian horror has come as a profound shock to this generation, which still refuses to connect the two facts. Yet this development merely confirms the warnings of the fathers of the liberal philosophy which we still profess. We have progressively abandoned that freedom in economic affairs without which personal and political freedom has never existed in the past. Although we had been warned by some of the greatest political thinkers of the nineteenth century, by de Tocqueville and Lord Acton, that socialism means slavery, we have steadily moved in the direction of socialism. And now that we have seen a new form of slavery arise before our eyes, we have so completely forgotten the warning, that it scarcely occurs to us that the two things may be connected.

How sharp a break not only with the recent past but with the whole evolution of western civilization the modern trend towards socialism means, becomes clear if we consider it not merely against the background of the nineteenth century, but in a longer historical perspective. We are rapidly abandoning not the views merely of Cobden and Bright, of Adam Smith and Hume, or even of Locke and Milton, but one of the salient characteristics of western civilization as it has grown from the foundations laid by Christianity and the Greeks and Romans. Not merely nineteenth- and eighteenth-century liberalism, but the basic individualism inherited by us from Erasmus and Montaigne, from Cicero and Tacitus, Pericles and Thucydides is progressively relinquished.

The Nazi leader who described the National-Socialist revolution as a counter-Renaissance spoke more truly than he probably knew. It was the decisive step in the destruction of that civilization which modern man had built up from the age of the Renaissance and which was above all an individualist civilization. Individualism has a bad name today and the term has come to be connected with egotism and selfishness. But the individualism of which we speak in contrast to socialism and all other forms of collectivism has no necessary connection with these. Only gradually in the course of this book shall we be able to make clear the contrast between the two opposing principles. But the essential features of that individualism which, from elements provided by Christianity and the philosophy of classical antiquity, was first fully developed during the Renaissance and has since grown and spread into what we know as western European civilization—the respect for the individual man *qua* man, that is the recognition of his own views and tastes as supreme in his own sphere, however narrowly that may be circumscribed, and the belief that it is desirable that men should develop their own individual gifts and bents. "Freedom" and "liberty" are now words so worn with use and abuse that one must hesitate to employ them to express the ideals for which they stood during that period. Tolerance is, perhaps, the only word which still preserves the full meaning of the principle which during the whole of this period was in the ascendant and which only in recent times has again been in decline, to disappear completely with the rise of the totalitarian state.

The gradual transformation of a rigidly organized hierarchic system into one where men could at least attempt to shape their own life, where man gained the opportunity of knowing and choosing between different forms of life, is closely associated with the growth of commerce. From the commercial cities of Northern Italy the new view of life spread with commerce to the west and north, through France and the southwest of Germany to the Low Countries and the British Isles, taking firm root wherever there was no despotic political power to stifle it. In the Low Countries and Britain it for a long time enjoyed its fullest development and for the first time had an opportunity to grow freely and to become the foundation of the social and political life of these countries. And it was from there that in the late seventeenth and eighteenth centuries it again began to spread in a more fully developed form to the west and east, to the New World and the centre of the European continent where devastating wars and political oppression had largely submerged the earlier beginnings of a similar growth.

During the whole of this modern period of European history the general direction of social development was one of freeing the individual from the ties which had bound him to the customary or prescribed ways in the pursuit of his ordinary activities. The conscious realization that the spontaneous and uncontrolled efforts of individuals were capable of producing a complex order of economic activities could come only after this development had made some progress. The subsequent elaboration of a consistent argument in favor of economic freedom was the outcome of a free growth of economic activity which had been the undesigned and unforeseen by-products of political freedom.

Perhaps the greatest result of the unchaining of individual energies was the marvellous growth of science which followed the march of individual liberty from Italy to England and beyond. That the inventive faculty of man had been no less in earlier periods is shown by the many highly ingenious automatic toys and other mechanical contrivances constructed while industrial technique still remained stationary, and by the development in some industries which, like mining or watchmaking, were not subject to restrictive controls. But the few attempts towards a more extended industrial use of mechanical inventions, some extraordinarily advanced, were promptly suppressed, and the desire for knowledge was stifled, so long as the dominant views were held to be binding for all: the beliefs of the great majority on what was right and proper were allowed to bar the way of the individual innovator. Only since industrial freedom opened the path to the free use of new knowledge, only since everything could be tried—if somebody could be found to back it at his own risk—and, it should be added, as often as not from outside the authorities officially entrusted with the cultivation of learning, has science made the great strides which in the last hundred and fifty years have changed the face of the world.

As is so often true, the nature of our civilization has been seen more clearly by its enemies than by most of its friends: "the perennial western malady, the revolt of the individual against the species," as that nineteenth-century totalitarian, Auguste Comte, has described it, was indeed the force which built our civilization. What the nineteenth century added to the individualism of the preceding period was merely to make all classes conscious of freedom, to develop systematically and continuously what had grown in a haphazard and patchy manner and to spread it from England and Holland over most of the European Continent.

The result of this growth surpassed all expectations. Wherever the barriers to the free exercise of human ingenuity were removed man became rapidly able to satisfy ever-widening ranges of desire. And while the rising standard soon led to the discovery of very dark spots in society, spots which men were no longer willing to tolerate, there was probably no class that did not substantially benefit from the general advance. We cannot do justice to this astonishing growth if we measure it by our present standards, which themselves result from this growth and now make many defects obvious. To appreciate what it meant to those who took part in it we must measure it by the hopes and wishes men held when it began: and there can be no doubt that its success surpassed man's wildest dreams, that by the beginning of the twentieth century the working man in the western world had reached a degree of material comfort, security, and personal independence which a hundred years before had seemed scarcely possible.

What in the future will probably appear the most significant and far-reaching effect of this success is the new sense of power over their own fate, the belief in the unbounded possibilities of improving their own lot, which the success already achieved created among men. With the success grew ambition—and man had every right to be ambitious. What had been an inspiring promise seemed no longer enough, the rate of progress far too slow; and the principles which had made this progress possible in the past came to be regarded more as obstacles to speedier progress, impatiently to be brushed away, than as the conditions for the preservation and development of what had already been achieved.

THE GREAT UTOPIA

What has always made the state a hell on earth has been precisely that man has tried to make it his heaven.

F. Hoelderlin.

That socialism has displaced liberalism as the doctrine held by the great majority of progressives does not simply mean that people had forgotten the warnings of the great liberal thinkers of the past about the consequences of collectivism. It has happened because they were persuaded of the very opposite of what these men had predicted. The extraordinary thing is that the same socialism that was not only early recognized as

the gravest threat to freedom, but quite openly began as a reaction against the liberalism of the French Revolution, gained general acceptance under the flag of liberty. It is rarely remembered now that socialism in its beginnings was frankly authoritarian. The French writers who laid the foundations of modern socialism had no doubt that their ideas could be put into practice only by a strong dictatorial government. To them socialism meant an attempt to "terminate the revolution" by a deliberate reorganization of society on hierarchical lines, and the imposition of a coercive "spiritual power." Where freedom was concerned, the founders of socialism made no bones about their intentions. Freedom of thought they regarded as the root-evil of nineteenth-century society, and the first of modern planners, Saint-Simon even predicted that those who did not obey his proposed planning boards would be "treated as cattle."

Only under the influence of the strong democratic currents preceding the revolution of 1848 did socialism begin to ally itself with the forces of freedom. But it took the new "democratic socialism" a long time to live down the suspicions aroused by its antecedents. Nobody saw more clearly than de Tocqueville that democracy as an essentially individualist institution stood in an irreconcilable conflict with socialism:

Democracy extends the sphere of individual freedom [he said in 1848], socialism restricts it. Democracy attaches all possible value to each man; socialism makes each man a mere agent, a mere number. Democracy and socialism have nothing in common but one word: equality. But notice the difference: while democracy seeks equality in liberty, socialism seeks equality in restraint and servitude.

To allay these suspicions and to harness to its cart the strongest of all political motives, the craving for freedom, socialism began increasingly to make use of the promise of a "new freedom." The coming of socialism was to be the leap from the realm of necessity to the realm of freedom. It was to bring "economic freedom," without which the political freedom already gained was "not worth having." Only socialism was capable of effecting the consummation of the agelong struggle for freedom in which the attainment of political freedom was but a first step.

The subtle change in meaning to which the word freedom was subjected in order that this argument should sound plausible is important. To the great apostles of political freedom the word had meant freedom from coercion, freedom from the arbitrary power of other men, release from the ties which left the individual no choice but obedience to the orders of a superior to whom he was attached. The new freedom promised, however, was to be freedom from necessity, release from the compulsion of the circumstances which inevitably limit the range of choice of all of us, although for some very much more than for others. Before man could be truly free, the "despotism of physical want" had to be broken, the "restraints of the economic system" relaxed.

Freedom in this sense is, of course, merely another name for power or wealth. Yet, although the promises of this new freedom were often coupled with irresponsible promises of a great increase in material wealth in a socialist society, it was not from such an absolute conquest of the niggardliness of nature that economic freedom was expected. What the promise really amounted to was that the great existing disparities in the range of choice of different people were to disappear. The demand for the new freedom was thus only another name for the old demand for an equal distribution of wealth. But the new name gave the socialists another word in common with the liberals and they exploited it to the full. And although the word was used in a different sense by the two groups, few people noticed this and still fewer asked themselves whether the two kinds of freedom promised really could be combined.

There can be no doubt that the promise of greater freedom has become one of the most effective weapons of socialist propaganda and that the belief that socialism would bring freedom is genuine and sincere. But this would only heighten the tragedy if it should prove that what was promised to us as the Road to Freedom was in fact the High Road to Servitude. Unquestionably the promise of more freedom was responsible for luring more and more liberals along the socialist road, for blinding them to the conflict which exists between the basic principles of socialism and liberalism, and for often enabling socialists to usurp the very name of the old party of freedom. Socialism was embraced by the greater part of the intelligentsia as the apparent heir of the liberal tradition: therefore it is not surprising that to them the idea should appear inconceivable of socialism leading to the opposite of liberty.

INDIVIDUALISM AND COLLECTIVISM

The socialists believe in two things which are absolutely different and perhaps even contradictory: freedom and organization.
                                                            Elie Halévy.

Before we can progress with our main problem, an obstacle has yet to be surmounted. A confusion largely responsible for the way in which we are drifting into things which nobody wants must be cleared up.

This confusion concerns nothing less than the concept of socialism itself. It may mean, and is often used to describe, merely the ideals of social justice, greater equality and security which are the ultimate aims of socialism. But it means also the particular method by which most socialists hope to attain these ends and which many competent people regard as the only methods by which they can be fully and quickly attained. In this sense socialism means the abolition of private enterprise, of private ownership of the means of production, and the creation of a system of "planned economy" in which the entrepreneur working for profit is replaced by a central planning body.

There are many people who call themselves socialists although they care only about the first, who fervently believe in those ultimate aims of socialism but neither care nor understand how they can be achieved, and who are merely certain that they must be achieved, whatever the cost. But to nearly all those to whom socialism is not merely a hope but an object of practical politics, the characteristic methods of modern socialism are as essential as the ends themselves. Many people, on the other hand, who value the ultimate ends of socialism no less than the socialists, refuse to support socialism because of the dangers to other values they see in the methods proposed by the socialists. The dispute about socialism has thus become largely a dispute about means and not about ends—although the question whether the different ends of socialism can be simultaneously achieved is also involved.

This would be enough to create confusion. And the confusion has been further increased by the common practice of denying that those who repudiate the means value the ends. But this is not all. The situation is still more complicated by the fact that the same means, the "economic planning" which is the prime instrument of socialist reform, can be used for many other purposes. We must centrally direct economic activity if we want to make the distribution of income conform to current ideas of social justice. "Planning," therefore, is wanted by all those who demand that "production for use" be substituted for production for profit. But such planning is no less indispensable if the distribution of incomes is to be regulated in a way which to us appears to be the opposite of just. Whether we should wish that more of the good things of this world should go to some racial élite, the Nordic men, or the members of a party or an aristocracy, the methods which we shall have to employ are the same as those which could ensure an equalitarian distribution.

It may, perhaps, seem unfair to use the term socialism to describe its methods rather than its aims, to use for a particular method a term which for many people stands for an ultimate ideal. It is probably preferable to describe the methods which can be used for a great variety of ends as collectivism and to regard socialism as a species of that genus. Yet, although to most socialists only one species of collectivism will represent true socialism, it must always be remembered that socialism is a species of collectivism and that therefore everything which is true of collectivism as such must apply also to socialism. Nearly all the points which are disputed between socialists and liberals concern the methods common to all forms of collectivism and not the particular ends for which socialists want to use them; and all the consequences with which we shall be concerned in this book follow from the methods of collectivism irrespective of the ends for which they are used. It must also not be forgotten that socialism is not only by far the most important species of collectivism or "planning"; but that it is socialism which has persuaded liberal-minded people to submit once more to that regimentation of economic life which they had overthrown because, in the words of Adam Smith, it puts governments in a position where "to support themselves they are obliged to be oppressive and tyrannical."

The Constitution of Liberty*

THE DECLINE OF SOCIALISM AND THE RISE OF THE WELFARE STATE

Experience should teach us to be most on our guard to protect liberty when the Government's purposes are beneficent. Men born to freedom are naturally alert to repel invasion of their liberty by evil-minded rulers. The greatest dangers to liberty lurk in insidious encroachment by men of zeal, well meaning but without understanding.

L. Brandeis.

Efforts toward social reform, for something like a century, have been inspired mainly by the ideals of socialism—during part of this period even in countries like the United States which never has had a socialist party of importance. Over the course of these hundred years socialism captured a large part of the intellectual leaders and came to be widely regarded as the ultimate goal toward which society was inevitably moving. This development reached its peak after the second World War, when Britain plunged into her socialist experiment. This seems to have marked the high tide of the socialist advance. Future historians will probably regard the period from the revolution of 1848 to about 1948 as the century of European socialism.

During this period socialism had a fairly precise meaning and a definite program. The common aim of all socialist movements was the nationalization of the "means of production, distribution, and exchange," so that all economic activity might be directed according to a comprehensive plan toward some ideal of social justice. The various socialist schools differed mainly in the political methods by which they intended to bring about the reorganization of society. Marxism and Fabianism differed in that the former was revolutionary and the latter gradualist; but their conceptions of the new society they hoped to create were basically the same. Socialism meant the common ownership of the means of production and their "employment for use, not for profit."

The great change that has occurred during the last decade is that socialism in this strict sense of a particular method of achieving social justice has collapsed. It has not merely lost its intellectual appeal; it has also been abandoned by the masses so unmistakably that socialist parties everywhere are searching for a new program that will insure the active support of their followers. They have not abandoned their ultimate aim, their ideal of social justice. But the methods by which they had hoped to achieve this and for which the name "socialism" had been coined have been discredited. No doubt the name will be transferred to whatever new program the existing socialist parties will adopt. But socialism in the old definite sense is now dead in the western world.

Though such a sweeping statement will still cause some surprise, a survey of the stream of disillusionist literature from socialist sources in all countries and the discussions inside the socialist parties amply confirm it. To those who watch merely the developments inside a single country, the decline of socialism may still seem no more than a temporary setback, the reaction to political defeat. But the international character and the similarity of the developments in the different countries leave no doubt that it is more than that. If, fifteen years ago, doctrinaire socialism appeared as the main danger to liberty, today it would be

---

*From Friedrich Hayek, *The Constitution of Liberty* (1960). By permission.

tilting at windmills to direct one's argument against it. Most of the arguments that were directed at socialism proper can now be heard from within the socialist movements as arguments for a change of program.

Unlike socialism, the conception of the welfare state has no precise meaning. The phrase is sometimes used to describe any state that "concerns" itself in any manner with problems other than those of the maintenance of law and order. But, though a few theorists have demanded that the activities of government should be limited to the maintenance of law and order, such a stand cannot be justified by the principle of liberty. Only the coercive measures of government need be strictly limited. We have already seen that there is undeniably a wide field for non-coercive activities of government and that there is a clear need for financing them by taxation.

Indeed, no government in modern times has ever confined itself to the "individualist minimum" which has occasionally been described, nor has such confinement of governmental activity been advocated by the "orthodox" classical economists. All modern governments have made provision for the indigent, unfortunate, and disabled and have concerned themselves with questions of health and the dissemination of knowledge. There is no reason why the volume of these pure service activities should not increase with the general growth of wealth. There are common needs that can be satisfied only by collective action and which can be thus provided for without restricting individual liberty. It can hardly be denied that, as we grow richer, that minimum of sustenance which the community has always provided for those not able to look after themselves, and which can be provided outside the market, will gradually rise, or that government may, usefully and without doing any harm, assist or even lead in such endeavors. There is little reason why the government should not also play some role, or even take the initiative, in such areas as social insurance and education, or temporarily subsidize certain experimental developments. Our problem here is not so much the aims as the methods of government action.

References are often made to those modest and innocent aims of governmental activity to show how unreasonable is any opposition to the welfare state as such. But, once the rigid position that government should not concern itself at all with such matters is abandoned—a position which is defensible but has little to do with freedom—the defenders of liberty commonly discover that the program of the welfare state comprises a great deal more that is represented as equally legitimate and unobjectionable. If, for instance, they admit that they have no objection to pure-food laws, this is taken to imply that they should not object to any government activity directed toward a desirable end. Those who attempt to delimit the functions of government in terms of aims rather than methods thus regularly find themselves in the position of having to oppose state action which appears to have only desirable consequences or of having to admit that they have no general rule on which to base their objections to measures which, though effective for particular purposes, would in their aggregate effect destroy a free society. Though the position that the state should have nothing to do with matters not related to the maintenance of law and order may seem logical so long as we think of the state solely as a coercive apparatus, we must recognize that, as a service agency, it may assist without harm in the achievement of desirable aims which perhaps could not be achieved otherwise. The reason why many of the new welfare activities of government are a threat to freedom, then, is that, though they are presented as mere service activities, they really constitute an exercise of the coercive powers of government and rest on its claiming exclusive rights in certain fields.

The current situation has greatly altered the task of the defender of liberty and made it much more difficult. So long as the danger came from socialism of the frankly collectivist kind, it was possible to argue that the tenets of the socialists were simply false: that socialism would not achieve what the socialists wanted and that it would produce other consequences which they would not like. We cannot argue similarly against the welfare state, for this term does not designate a definite system. What goes under that name is a conglomerate of so many diverse and even contradictory elements that, while some of them may make a free society more attractive, others are incompatible with it or may at least constitute potential threats to its existence.

We shall see that some of the aims of the welfare state can be realized without detriment to individual liberty, though not necessarily by the methods which seem the most obvious and are therefore most popular; that others can be similarly achieved to a certain extent, though only at a cost much greater than people imagine or would be willing to bear, or only slowly and gradually as wealth increases; and that, finally, there are others—and they are those particularly dear to the hearts of the socialists—that cannot be realized in a society that wants to preserve personal freedom.

There are all kinds of public amenities which it may be in the interest of all members of the community to provide by common effort, such as parks and museums, theaters and facilities for sports—though there are strong reasons why they should be provided by local rather than national authorities. There is then the important issue of security, of protection against risks common to all, where government can often either reduce these risks or assist people to provide against them. Here, however, an important distinction has to be drawn between two conceptions of security: a limited security which can be achieved for all and which is, therefore, no privilege, and absolute security, which in a free society cannot be achieved for all. The first of these is security against severe physical privation, the assurance of a given minimum of sustenance for all; and the second is the assurance of a given standard of life, which is determined by comparing the standard enjoyed by a person or a group with that of others. The distinction, then, is that between the security of an equal minimum income for all and the security of a particular income that a person is thought to deserve. The latter is closely related to the third main ambition that inspires the welfare state: the desire to use the powers of government to insure a more even or more just distribution of goods. Insofar as this means that the coercive powers of government are to be used to insure that particular people get particular things, it requires a kind of discrimination between, and an unequal treatment of, different people which is irreconcilable with a free society. This is the

kind of welfare state that aims at "social justice" and becomes "primarily a redistributor of income." It is bound to lead back to socialism and its coercive and essentially arbitrary methods.

TAXATION

Those who advocated progressive taxation during the latter part of the nineteenth century generally stressed that their aim was only to achieve equality of sacrifice and not a redistribution of income; also they generally held that this aim could justify only a "moderate" degree of progression and that its "excessive" use (as in fifteenth-century Florence, where rates had been pushed up to 50 per cent) was, of course, to be condemned. Though all attempts to supply an objective standard for an appropriate rate of progression failed and though no answer was offered when it was objected that, once the principle was accepted, there would be no assignable limit beyond which progression might not be carried with equal justification, the discussion moved entirely in a context of contemplated rates which made any effect on the distribution of income appear negligible. The suggestion that rates would not stay within these limits was treated as a malicious distortion of the argument, betraying a reprehensible lack of confidence in the wisdom of democratic government.

It was in Germany, then the leader in "social reform," that the advocates of progressive taxation first overcame the resistance and its modern evolution began. In 1891, Prussia introduced a progressive income tax rising from 0.67 to 4 per cent. In vain did Rudolf von Geist, the venerable leader of the then recently consummated movement for the Rechtsstaat, protest in the Diet that this meant the abandonment of the fundamental principle of equality before the law, "of the most sacred principle of equality," which provided the only barrier against encroachment on property. The very smallness of the burden involved in the new schemes made ineffective any attempt to oppose it as a matter of principle.

Though some other Continental countries soon followed Prussia, it took nearly twenty years for the movement to reach the great Anglo-Saxon powers. It was only in 1910 and 1913 that Great Britain and the United States adopted graduated income taxes rising to the then spectacular figures of 8¼ and 7 per cent, respectively. Yet within thirty years these figures had risen to 97½ and 91 per cent.

Thus in the space of a single generation what nearly all the supporters of progressive taxation had for half a century asserted could not happen came to pass. This change in the absolute rates, of course, completely changed the character of the problem, making it different not merely in degree but in kind. All attempt to justify these rates on the basis of capacity to pay was, in consequence, soon abandoned, and the supporters reverted to the original, but long avoided, justification of progression as a means of bringing about a more just distribution of income. It has come to be generally accepted once more that the only ground on which a progressive scale of overall taxation can be defended is the desirability of changing the distribution of income and that this defense cannot be based on any scientific argument but must be recognized as a frankly political postulate, that is, as an attempt to impose upon society a pattern of distribution determined by majority decision.

An explanation of this development that is usually offered is that the great increase in public expenditure in the last forty years could not have been met without resort to steep progression, or at least that, without it, an intolerable burden would have had to be placed on the poor and that, once the necessity of relieving the poor was admitted, some degree of progression was inevitable. On examination, however, the explanation dissolves into pure myth. Not only is the revenue derived from the high rates levied on large incomes, particularly in the highest brackets, so small compared with the total revenue as to make hardly any difference to the burden borne by the rest; but for a long time after the introduction of progression it was not the poorest who benefited from it but entirely the better-off working class and the lower strata of the middle class who provided the largest number of voters. It would probably be true, on the other hand, to say that the illusion that by means of progressive taxation the burden can be shifted substantially onto the shoulders of the wealthy has been the chief reason why taxation has increased as fast as it has done and that, under the influence of this illusion, the masses have come to accept a much heavier load than they would have done otherwise. The only major result of the policy has been the severe limitation of the incomes that could be earned by the most successful and thereby gratification of the envy of the less-well-off.

Law, Legislation and Liberty*

CONSTRUCTION AND EVOLUTION

There are two way of looking at the pattern of human activities which lead to very different conclusions concerning both its explanation and the possibilities of deliberately altering it. Of these, one is based on conceptions which are demonstrably false, yet are so pleasing to human vanity that they have gained great influence and are constantly employed even by people who know that they rest on a fiction, but believe that fiction to be innocuous. The other, although few people will question its basic contentions if they are stated abstractly, leads in some respects to conclusions so unwelcome that few are willing to follow it through to the end.

The first gives us a sense of unlimited power to realize our wishes, while the second leads to the insight that there are limitations to what we can deliberately bring about, and to the recognition that some of our present hopes are delusions. Yet the effect of allowing ourselves to be deluded by the first view has always been that man has actually limited the scope of what he can achieve. For it has always been the recognition of the limits of the possible which has enabled man to make full use of his powers.

The first view holds that human institutions will serve human purposes only if they have been deliberately designed for these purposes, often also that the fact that an institution exists is evidence of its having been created for a purpose, and always that we should so re-design society and its institutions that all our actions will be wholly guided by known purposes. To most people these propositions seem almost self-evident

and to constitute an attitude alone worthy of a thinking being. Yet the belief underlying them, that we owe all beneficial institutions to design, and that only such design has made or can make them useful for our purposes, is largely false.

This view is rooted originally in a deeply ingrained propensity of primitive thought to interpret all regularity to be found in phenomena anthropomorphically, as the result of the design of a thinking mind. But just when man was well on the way to emancipating himself from this naïve conception, it was revived by the support of a powerful philosophy with which the aim of freeing the human mind from false prejudices has become closely associated, and which became the dominant conception of the Age of Reason.

The other view, which has slowly and gradually advanced since antiquity but for a time was almost entirely overwhelmed by the more glamorous constructivist view, was that that orderliness of society which greatly increased the effectiveness of individual action was not due solely to institutions and practices which had been invented or designed for that purpose, but was largely due to a process described at first as 'growth' and later as 'evolution', a process in which practices which had first been adopted for other reasons, or even purely accidentally, were preserved because they enabled the group in which they had arisen to prevail over others. Since its first systematic development in the eighteenth century this view had to struggle not only against the anthropomorphism of primitive thinking but even more against the reinforcement these naïve views had received from the new rationalist philosophy. It was indeed the challenge which this philosophy provided that led to the explicit formulation of the evolutionary view.

---

*From Friedrich Hayek, *Law, Legislation and Liberty* (1973–79). By permission.

THE PERMANENT
LIMITATIONS OF OUR
FACTUAL KNOWLEDGE

The constructivist approach leads to false conclusions because man's actions are largely successful, not merely in the primitive stage but perhaps even more so in civilization, because they are adapted both to the particular facts which he knows and to a great many other facts he does not and cannot know. And this adaptation to the general circumstances that surround him is brought about by his observance of rules which he has not designed and often does not even know explicitly, although he is able to honour them in action. Or, to put this differently, our adaptation to our environment does not consist only, and perhaps not even chiefly, in an insight into the relations between cause and effect, but also in our actions being governed by rules adapted to the kind of world in which we live, that is, to circumstances which we are not aware of and which yet determine the pattern of our successful actions. . . .

What we must ask the reader to keep constantly in mind throughout this book, then, is the fact of the necessary and irremediable ignorance on everyone's part of most of the particular facts which determine the actions of all the several members of human society. This may at first seem to be a fact so obvious and incontestable as hardly to deserve mention, and still less to require proof. Yet the result of not constantly stressing it is that it is only too readily forgotten. This is so mainly because it is a very inconvenient fact which makes both our attempts to explain and our attempts to influence intelligently the processes of society very much more difficult, and which places severe limits on what we can say or do about them. There exists therefore a great temptation, as a first approximation, to begin with the assumption that we know everything needed for full explanation or control. This provisional assumption is often treated as something of little consequence which can later be dropped without much effect on the conclusions. Yet this necessary ignorance of most of the particulars which enter the order of a Great Society is the source of the central problem of all social order and the false assumption by which it is provisionally put aside is mostly never explicitly abandoned but merely conveniently forgotten. The argument then proceeds as if that ignorance did not matter.

THE CONCEPT OF ORDER

The central concept around which the discussion of this book will turn is that of order, and particularly the distinction between two kinds of order which we will provisionally call 'made' and 'grown' orders. Order is an indispensable concept for the discussion of all complex phenomena, in which it must largely play the role the concept of law plays in the analysis of simpler phenomena. There is no adequate term other than 'order' by which we can describe it, although 'system', 'structure' or 'pattern' may occasionally serve instead. The term 'order' has, of course, a long history in the social sciences, but in recent times it has generally been avoided, largely because of the ambiguity of its meaning and its frequent association with authoritarian views. We cannot do without it, however, and shall have to guard against misinterpretation by sharply defining the general sense in which we shall employ it and then clearly distinguishing between the two different ways in which such order can originate.

By 'order' we shall throughout describe *a state of affairs in which a multiplicity of elements of various kinds are so related to each other that we may learn from our acquaintance with some spatial or temporal part of the whole to form correct expectations concerning the rest, or at least expectations which have a good chance of proving correct.* It is clear that every society must in this sense possess an order and that such an order will often exist without having been deliberately created. As has been said by a distinguished social anthropologist, 'that there is some order, consistency and constancy in social life, is obvious. If there were not, none of us would be able to go about our affairs or satisfy our most elementary needs.'

Living as members of society and dependent for the satisfaction of most of our needs on various forms of co-operation with others, we depend for the effective pursuit of our aims clearly on the correspondence of the expectations concerning the actions of others on which our plans are based with what they will really do. This matching of the intentions and expectations that determine the actions of different individuals is the form in which order manifests itself in social life; and it will be the question of how such an order does come about that will be our immediate concern. The first answer to which our anthropomorphic habits of thought almost inevitably lead us is that it must be due to the design of some thinking mind. And because order has been generally interpreted as such a deliberate *arrangement* by somebody, the concept has become unpopular among most friends of liberty and has been favoured mainly by authoritarians. According to this interpretation order in society must rest on a relation of command and obedience, or a hierarchical structure of the whole of society in which the will of superiors, and ultimately of some single supreme authority, determines what each individual must do.

The Fatal Conceit*

WAS SOCIALISM A MISTAKE?

The idea of Socialism is at once grandiose and simple. . . . We may say, in fact, that it is one of the most ambitious creations of the human spirit, . . . so magnificent, so daring, that it has rightly aroused the greatest admiration. If we wish to save the world from barbarism we have to refute Socialism, but we cannot thrust it carelessly aside.

Ludwig von Mises.

This book argues that our civilization depends, not only for its origin but also for its preservation, on what can be precisely described only as the extended order of human cooperation, an order more commonly, if somewhat misleadingly, known as capitalism. To understand our civilization, one must appreciate that the extended order resulted not from human design or intention but spontaneously: it arose from unintentionally conforming to certain traditional and largely *moral* practices, many of which men tend to dislike, whose significance they usually fail to understand, whose validity they cannot prove, and which have nonetheless fairly rapidly spread by means of an evolutionary selection—the comparative increase of population and wealth—of those groups that happened to follow them. The unwitting, reluctant, even painful adoption of these practices kept these groups together, increased their access to valuable information of all sorts, and enabled them to be 'fruitful, and multiply, and replenish the earth, and subdue it' (*Genesis* 1:28). This process is perhaps the least appreciated facet of human evolution.

Socialists take a different view of these matters. They not only differ in their

conclusions, they see the facts differently. That socialists are wrong *about the facts* is crucial to my argument, as it will unfold in the pages that follow. I am prepared to admit that if socialist analyses of the operation of the existing economic order, and of possible alternatives, were factually correct, we might be obliged to ensure that the distribution of incomes conform to certain moral principles, and that this distribution might be possible only by giving a central authority the power to direct the use of available resources, and might presuppose the abolition of individual ownership of means of production. If it were for instance true that central direction of the means of production could effect a collective product of at least the same magnitude as that which we now produce, it would indeed prove a grave moral problem how this could be done justly. This, however, is not the position in which we find ourselves. For there is no known way, other than by the distribution of products in a competitive market, to inform individuals in what direction their several efforts must aim so as to contribute as much as possible to the total product.

The main point of my argument is, then, that the conflict between, on one hand, advocates of the spontaneous extended human order created by a competitive market, and on the other hand those who demand a deliberate arrangement of human interaction by central authority based on collective command over available resources is due to a factual error by the latter about how knowledge of these resources is and can be generated and utilized. As a question of fact, this conflict must be settled by scientific study. Such study shows that, by following the spontaneously generated moral traditions underlying the competitive market order (traditions which do not satisfy the canons or norms of rationality embraced by most socialists), we generate and garner

---

*From Friedrich Hayek, *The Fatal Conceit* (1988). By permission.

greater knowledge and wealth than could ever be obtained or utilized in a centrally-directed economy whose adherents claim to proceed strictly in accordance with 'reason'. Thus socialist aims and programmes are factually impossible to achieve or execute; and they also happen, into the bargain as it were, to be logically impossible.

This is why, contrary to what is often maintained, these matters are not merely ones of differing interests or value judgements. Indeed, the question of how men came to adopt certain values or norms, and what effect these had on the evolution of their civilization, is itself above all a factual one, one that lies at the heart of the present book. The demands of socialism are not moral conclusions derived from the traditions that formed the extended order that made civilization possible. They endeavor to overthrow these traditions by a rationally designed moral system whose appeal depends on the instinctual appeal of its promised consequences. They assume that, since people had been able to *generate* some system of rules coordinating their efforts, they must also be able to *design* an even better and more gratifying system. But if humankind owes its very existence to one particular rule-guided form of conduct of proven effectiveness, it simply does not have the option of choosing another merely for the sake of the apparent pleasantness of its immediately visible effects. The dispute between the market order and socialism is no less than a matter of survival. To follow socialist morality would destroy much of present humankind and impoverish much of the rest.

CHAPTER TWELVE

RAWLS

The rise of democratic interventionist welfare state capitalism proved in the end the greatest movement in government during the twentieth century. Advances of fascism, communism, and socialism, which to many for a time seemed waves of the future, in the end proved ephemeral. In 1900, full-scale democracy as in most of the world now exists—the ability of all adults to vote for governmental leaders—nowhere existed. Government on the scale it now exists nowhere existed. Government intervention in nations' economies as it now exists nowhere existed.

Among twentieth century postwar political thinkers, John Rawls (1921–) attained renown for *A Theory of Justice* (1971), the development of a series of papers written over the previous dozen years. *A Theory of Justice* received great attention when it was published. It received rave reviews in many journals, both for its positive message and importance. The *New York Times Book Review* designated *A Theory of Justice* one of the five most important books of the year on the grounds that "its political implications may change our lives."

Notwithstanding the attention *A Theory of Justice* received upon publication, it has not weathered well. The first critical response to the work was from political theorists of the left, who considered it potentially to allow too many concessions to capitalism, and it never really has been considered by those upon the right.

A Theory of Justice is an abstract work with little discussion of practical political issues. Rawls seeks to reintroduce a social contract theory of the origination of societal justice, building upon the legacy of Locke, Rousseau, and especially Kant. In their final form, Rawls' two principles of societal justice to regulate a community's basic institutions of government, economic system, and family are:

First Principle
Each person is to have an equal right to the most extensive total system of equal basic liberties compatible with a similar system of liberty for all.

Second Principle
Social and economic inequalities are to be arranged so that they are both:
  a) to the greatest benefit of the least advantaged, consistent with the just savings principle, and
  b) attached to offices and positions open to all under conditions of fair equality of opportunity.

Rawls' principles of justice are in lexical or serial order, meaning that the first principle is more important than the second and, more importantly, that equal basic liberties cannot be sacrificed for greater social or economic benefits. Rawls values rights such as freedom of speech and expression, and political participation rights, above economic opportunities.

Within his work, Rawls' second principle of justice has attracted the most attention. Also in part by him referred to as the "difference principle" or "maximin" (maximizing the minimum) rule, the idea can be, and has been, interpreted both in egalitarian and non-egalitarian manners. From an egalitarian perspective, the requirement that social and economic institutions should be to the greatest advantage of the least fortunate might seem to indicate a society in which the goods of social interaction equally are shared.

On the other hand, the more conventional interpretation of Rawls, particularly from Marxians, is that the difference principle legitimizes highly inegalitarian societies if the ruling classes claim that an inegalitarian social order is to the benefit of the least well off, which they almost always have.

Unfortunately, it is difficult to know where Rawls stands on this crucial issue. At one point in the section "The Tendency to Equality" of the first chapter of *A Theory of Justice,* he remarks:

> We may observe that the difference principle gives some weight to the consideration singled out by the principle of redress. This is the principle that undeserved inequalities call for redress; and since inequalities of birth and natural endowment are undeserved, these inequalities are to be somehow compensated for. Thus the principle holds that in order to treat all persons equally, to provide genuine equality of opportunity, society must give more attention to those with fewer native assets and to those born into the less favorable social positions.

He also says, though, in the very next paragraph:

> But the difference principle would allocate resources in education, say, so as to improve the long-term expectation of the least favored. If this end is attained by giving more attention to the better endowed, it is permissible; otherwise not.

The strength of the difference principle is that it is non-contentual. Rawls' position is that the best society is the one in which the least fortunate, over time, have the most, regardless of how this goal is achieved—socialism or capitalism.

Rawls is wrong in *A Theory of Justice* when he maintains that utilitarianism values equality only to "break ties." Utilitarianism's core idea is the moral equality of all humanity—in Bentham's words, "everybody to count for one, nobody for more than one." Mill remarked in his own *Utilitarianism*'s closing chapter, on justice, that the principle of utility "is a mere form of words without rational signification, unless one person's happiness, supposed equal in degree . . . , is counted for exactly as much as another's."

Moreover, utilitarianism is highly egalitarian in its conception of the declining marginal utility of most economic goods. Mill wrote in *Principles of Political Economy:* "The difference to the happiness of the possessor between a moderate independence and five times as much, is insignificant when weighed against the enjoyment that might be given . . . by some other disposal of the four-fifths." One of the great strengths of democratic interventionist welfare state capitalism is the emphasis—though not, of course, total emphasis—it places upon equality. It is important that all have some. There is no natural order within which a small minority should have most while the great masses starve.

The human condition is evolving as the "scarce means of satisfaction" that Rawls assumes as one of the bedrock circumstances of humanity is changing. While some may always have more and others will have less, the real privation that characterized the conditions of so many in even western industrial nations during much of the twentieth century may over time become as uncommon around the globe as it is becoming in western industrial nations. This may influence the ethical force of the difference principle, for it is one thing to advocate for those with less when they genuinely have little than when they have access to a decent material standard of living.

Rawls is also incorrect when he suggests of utilitarianism that "since each desires to protect his interests, . . . no one has a reason to acquiesce in an enduring loss for himself in order to bring about a greater net balance of satisfaction. In the absence of strong and lasting benevolent impulses, a rational man would not accept a basic structure merely because it maximized the algebraic sum of advantages irrespective of its permanent effects on his own . . . interests." There are at least two errors here. First, utilitarianism assumes potentially strong and lasting benevolent impulses; its ethical objective is the greatest happiness of all. Second, in determining the basic institutions of society, individuals do not know, according to Rawls, their place in a society. It is not the case, therefore, that individuals would potentially be choosing to sacrifice their own interests in a utilitarian society for others. All they would know is that in a utilitarian society, there would be the greatest happiness.

Perhaps the most unrealistic aspect of Rawls' conception of the practical world, as distinct from his theoretical vision, are his comments on the family. He holds that the "monogamous family" is a "major social institution," coming, therefore, under the jurisdiction of his two principles of justice. He states that "the principle of fair opportunity can be only imperfectly carried out, at least as long as the institution of the family exists. . . . Is the family to be abolished then? Taken by itself and given a certain primacy, the idea of equality of opportunity inclines in this direction. But within the context of the theory of justice as a whole, there is much less urgency to take this course. . . . We are more ready to dwell upon our good fortune now that . . . differences are made to work to our advantage, rather than to be downcast by how much better off we might have been had we had an equal chance along with others if only all social barriers had been removed."

Rawls briefly considers the possibility of genetic manipulation in *A Theory of Justice:* "I should mention one further question. I have assumed so far that the distribution of natural assets is a fact of nature and that no attempt is made to change it. . . . But to some extent this distribution is bound to be affected by the social system. . . . [I]t is possible to adopt eugenic policies, more or less explicit. . . . It is . . . in the interest of each to have greater natural assets. This enables him to pursue a preferred plan of life. . . . [P]arties want to ensure for their descendants the best genetic endowment. . . . [O]ver time a society is to take steps at least to preserve the general level of natural abilities and to prevent the diffusion of serious defects. . . ."

The primary driving force during the twentieth century has been the growth of scientific knowledge. Humanity's fantastically increasing ability to tame nature, to shape it to our purposes, defines the twentieth century. Particularly in the area of genetic knowledge, the possibilities of purposeful human direction and control of DNA will lead to a new human condition, whatever decisions are made. Knowledge itself creates new circumstances that before have not existed. Having once eaten of the tree of knowledge, humanity cannot remain in the Eden of ignorance. We are entering a new age. As humanity gains the knowledge to mold the further development of life, one should hope that the heritage of Hebrew monotheism, Greek rationalism, and Christian love will guide us.

A Theory of Justice is a rich and compelling work and goes into many topics that here have not been touched upon, including Rawls' highly creative attempt to revive the social contract theory of basic governmental institutions through a philosophical "veil of ignorance." He writes within the current of European political philosophy. The extent to which his own work will become a tributary to this mighty river remains to be seen.

In his later work *Political Liberalism* (1993), Rawls discusses diversity, and the circumstance where a "well-ordered society" does not reflect a democratic polity, an assumption of *A Theory of Justice*. In *Political Liberalism,* he offers one of his few specific examples of a concrete application of his ideas (in this case of political pluralism) when he remarks in an illustrative footnote of the proposition in the main text that "the only comprehensive doctrines that run afoul of public reason are those that cannot support a reasonable balance of political values": "Consider the troubled question of abortion. Suppose first that the society in question is well-ordered and that we are dealing with the normal case of mature adult women. . . . Suppose further that we consider the question in terms of these three important political values: the due respect for human life, the ordered reproduction of political society over time . . . , and finally the equality of women as citizens. . . . Now I believe any reasonable balance of these three values will give a woman a duly qualified right to decide whether or not to end her pregnancy during the first trimester. . . . [A]ny comprehensive doctrine that leads to a balance of political values excluding the duly qualified right in the first trimester is to that extent unreasonable. . . ."

One may agree or disagree with Rawls' position on abortion, but this is not the present point, which is that his position is that it objectively is unreasonable to have a position other than his on abortion, and therefore impermissible, even in a diverse, pluralistic polity, to restrict abortion beyond the position he presents. This outlook of objective reason echoes sentiments he expresses within *A Theory of Justice* upon "generally recognized ways of reasoning" and "ways of reasoning acceptable to all." This conception of reason, and sentiment, is different than that of Hume, who holds in *A Treatise of Human Nature* that "reason is, and ought only to be the slave of the passions," and that "the rules of morality are not the conclusions of our reason"; of Mill, who maintains in *On Liberty* that "if all mankind minus one were of one opinion, and only one person were of the contrary opinion, mankind would be no more justified in silencing that one person, than he, if he had the power, would be justified in silencing mankind"; or of Hayek in *The Constitution of Liberty:* "The freedom that will be used by only one man in a million may be more important to society and more beneficial to the majority than any freedom that we all use."

The essence of a truly liberal position is promotion of genuine diversity. Free speech, the moral equality of all people, the factual diversity of humankind, democracy, the right to rebel, a competitive economic order, and internationalism also characterize the liberal view. As humanity enter a new age, the wisdom as well as errors of great political thinkers undoubtedly will continue to influence and reflect societal institutions and government. From Plato to the present, the roots of the West—Greek rationalism, Hebrew monotheism, and Christian love—have defined western political thought at its best.

RAWLS

*A Theory of Justice**

THE ROLE OF JUSTICE

Justice is the first virtue of social institutions, as truth is of systems of thought. A theory however elegant and economical must be rejected or revised if it is untrue; likewise laws and institutions no matter how efficient and well-arranged must be reformed or abolished if they are unjust. Each person possesses an inviolability founded on justice that even the welfare of society as a whole cannot override. For this reason justice denies that the loss of freedom for some is made right by a greater good shared by others. It does not allow that the sacrifices imposed on a few are outweighed by the larger sum of advantages enjoyed by many. Therefore in a just society the liberties of equal citizenship are taken as settled; the rights secured by justice are not subject to political bargaining or to the calculus of social interests. The only thing that permits us to acquiesce in an erroneous theory is the lack of a better one; analogously, an injustice is tolerable only when it is necessary to avoid an even greater injustice. Being first virtues of human activities, truth and justice are uncompromising.

These propositions seem to express our intuitive conviction of the primacy of justice. No doubt they are expressed too strongly. In any event I wish to inquire whether these contentions or others similar to them are sound, and if so how they can be accounted

---

*Reprinted by permission of the publishers from *A Theory of Justice* by John Rawls, Cambridge, Mass.: The Belknap Press of Harvard University Press. Copyright © 1971 by the President and Fellows of Harvard College.

for. To this end it is necessary to work out a theory of justice in the light of which these assertions can be interpreted and assessed. I shall begin by considering the role of the principles of justice. Let us assume, to fix ideas, that a society is a more or less self-sufficient association of persons who in their relations to one another recognize certain rules of conduct as binding and who for the most part act in accordance with them. Suppose further that these rules specify a system of cooperation designed to advance the good of those taking part in it. Then, although a society is a cooperative venture for mutual advantage, it is typically marked by a conflict as well as by an identity of interests. There is an identity of interests since social cooperation makes possible a better life for all than any would have if each were to live solely by his own efforts. There is a conflict of interests since persons are not indifferent as to how the greater benefits produced by their collaboration are distributed, for in order to pursue their ends they each prefer a larger to a lesser share. A set of principles is required for choosing among the various social arrangements which determine this division of advantages and for underwriting an agreement on the proper distributive shares. These principles are the principles of social justice: They provide a way of assigning rights and duties in the basic institutions of society and they define the appropriate distribution of the benefits and burdens of social cooperation.

Now let us say that a society is well-ordered when it is not only designed to advance the good of its members but when it is also effectively regulated by a public conception of justice. That is, it is a society in which (1) everyone accepts and knows that the others accept the same principles of justice, and (2) the basic social institutions generally satisfy and are generally known to satisfy these principles. In this case while men may put forth excessive demands on one another, they nevertheless acknowledge a common point of view from which their claims may be adjudicated. If men's inclination to self-interest makes their vigilance against one another necessary, their public sense of justice makes their secure association together possible. Among individuals with disparate aims and purposes a shared conception of justice establishes the bonds of civic friendship; the general desire for justice limits the pursuit of other ends. One may think of a public conception of justice as constituting the fundamental charter of a well-ordered human association.

THE SUBJECT OF JUSTICE

Many different kinds of things are said to be just and unjust: not only laws, institutions, and social systems, but also particular actions of many kinds, including decisions, judgments, and imputations. We also call the attitudes and dispositions of persons, and persons themselves, just and unjust. Our topic, however, is that of social justice. For us the primary subject of justice is the basic structure of society, or more exactly, the way in which the major social institutions distribute fundamental rights and duties and determine the division of advantages from social cooperation. By major institutions I understand the political constitution and the principal economic and social arrangements. Thus the legal protection of freedom of thought and liberty of conscience, competitive markets, private property in the means of production, and the monogamous family are examples of major social institutions. Taken together as one scheme, the major institutions define men's rights and duties and influence their life-prospects, what they can expect to be and how well they can hope to do. The basic structure is the primary subject of justice because its effects are so profound and present from the start. The intuitive notion here is that this structure contains various social positions and that men born into different positions have different expectations of life determined, in part, by the political system

as well as by economic and social circumstances. In this way the institutions of society favor certain starting places over others. These are especially deep inequalities. Not only are they pervasive, but they affect men's initial chances in life; yet they cannot possibly be justified by an appeal to the notions of merit or desert. It is these inequalities, presumably inevitable in the basic structure of any society, to which the principles of social justice must in the first instance apply. These principles, then, regulate the choice of a political constitution and the main elements of the economic and social system. The justice of a social scheme depends essentially on how fundamental rights and duties are assigned and on the economic opportunities and social conditions in the various sectors of society.

THE MAIN IDEA OF THE THEORY OF JUSTICE

My aim is to present a conception of justice which generalizes and carries to a higher level of abstraction the familiar theory of the social contract as found, say, in Locke, Rousseau, and Kant. In order to do this we are not to think of the original contract as one to enter a particular society or to set up a particular form of government. Rather, the guiding idea is that the principles of justice for the basic structure of society are the object of the original agreement. They are the principles that free and rational persons concerned to further their own interests would accept in an initial position of equality as defining the fundamental terms of their association. These principles are to regulate all further agreements; they specify the kinds of social cooperation that can be entered into and the forms of government that can be established. This way of regarding the principles of justice I shall call justice as fairness.

Thus we are to imagine that those who engage in social cooperation choose together, in one joint act, the principles which are to assign basic rights and duties and to determine the division of social benefits. Men are to decide in advance how they are to regulate their claims against one another and what is to be the foundation charter of their society. Just as each person must decide by rational reflection what constitutes his good, that is, the system of ends which it is rational for him to pursue, so a group of persons must decide once and for all what is to count among them as just and unjust. The choice which rational men would make in this hypothetical situation of equal liberty, assuming for the present that this choice problem has a solution, determines the principles of justice.

In justice as fairness the original position of equality corresponds to the state of nature in the traditional theory of the social contract. This original position is not, of course, thought of as an actual historical state of affairs, much less as a primitive condition of culture. It is understood as a purely hypothetical situation characterized so as to lead to a certain conception of justice. Among the essential features of this situation is that no one knows his place in society, his class position or social status, nor does any one know his fortune in the distribution of natural assets and abilities, his intelligence, strength, and the like. I shall even assume that the parties do not know their conceptions of the good or their special psychological propensities. The principles of justice are chosen behind a veil of ignorance. This ensures that no one is advantaged or disadvantaged in the choice of principles by the outcome of natural chance or the contingency of social circumstances. Since all are similarly situated and no one is able to design principles to favor his particular condition, the principles of justice are the result of a fair agreement or bargain. For given the circumstances of the original position, the symmetry of everyone's relations to each other, this initial situation is fair between individuals as moral persons, that is, as rational beings with their own ends and capable, I shall assume, of a sense of justice. The original position is, one might say, the appropriate initial status quo, and thus the fundamental agreements reached in it are fair. This explains the propriety of the name "justice as fairness": it conveys the idea that the principles of justice are agreed to in an initial situation that is fair. The name does not mean that the concepts of justice and fairness are the same, any more than the phrase "poetry as metaphor" means that the concepts of poetry and metaphor are the same.

Justice as fairness begins, as I have said, with one of the most general of all choices which persons might make together, namely, with the choice of the first principles of a conception of justice which is to regulate all subsequent criticism and reform of institutions. Then, having chosen a conception of justice, we can suppose that they are to choose a constitution and a legislature to enact laws, and so on, all in accordance with the principles of justice initially agreed upon. Our social situation is just if it is such that by this sequence of hypothetical agreements we would have contracted into the general system of rules which defines it. Moreover, assuming that the original position does determine a set of principles (that is, that a particular conception of justice would be chosen), it will then be true that whenever social institutions satisfy these principles those engaged in them can say to one another that they are cooperating on terms to which they would agree if they were free and equal persons whose relations with respect to one another were fair. They could all view their arrangements as meeting the stipulations which they would acknowledge in an initial situation that embodies widely accepted and reasonable constraints on the choice of principles. The general recognition of this fact would provide the basis for a public acceptance of the corresponding principles of justice. No society can, of course, be a scheme of cooperation which men enter voluntarily in a literal sense; each person finds himself placed at birth in some particular position in some particular society, and the nature of this position materially affects his life prospects. Yet a society satisfying the principles of justice as fairness comes as close as a society can to being a voluntary scheme, for it meets the principles which free and equal persons would assent to under circumstances that are fair. In this sense its members are autonomous and the obligations they recognize self-imposed.

One feature of justice as fairness is to think of the parties in the initial situation as rational and mutually disinterested. This does not mean that the parties are egoists, that is, individuals with only certain kinds of interests, say in wealth, prestige, and domination. But they are conceived as not taking an interest in one another's interests.

They are to presume that even their spiritual aims may be opposed, in the way that the aims of those of different religions may be opposed. Moreover, the concept of rationality must be interpreted as far as possible in the narrow sense, standard in economic theory, of taking the most effective means to given ends. I shall modify this concept to some extent, but one must try to avoid introducing into it any controversial ethical elements. The initial situation must be characterized by stipulations that are widely accepted.

In working out the conception of justice as fairness one main task clearly is to determine which principles of justice would be chosen in the original position. To do this we must describe this situation in some detail and formulate with care the problem of choice which it presents. These matters I shall take up in the immediately succeeding chapters. It may be observed, however, that once the principles of justice are thought of as arising from an original agreement in a situation of equality, it is an open question whether the principle of utility would be acknowledged. Offhand it hardly seems likely that persons who view themselves as equals, entitled to press their claims upon one another, would agree to a principle which may require lesser life prospects for some simply for the sake of a greater sum of advantages enjoyed by others. Since each desires to protect his interests, his capacity to advance his conception of the good, no one has a reason to acquiesce in an enduring loss for himself in order to bring about a greater net balance of satisfaction. In the absence of strong and lasting benevolent impulses, a rational man would not accept a basic structure merely because it maximized the algebraic sum of advantages irrespective of its permanent effects on his own basic rights and interests. Thus it seems that the principle of utility is incompatible with the conception of social cooperation among equals for mutual advantage. It appears to be inconsistent with the idea of reciprocity implicit in the notion of a well-ordered society. Or, at any rate, so I shall argue.

I shall maintain instead that the persons in the initial situation would choose two rather different principles: the first requires equality in the assignment of basic rights and duties, while the second holds that social and economic inequalities, for example inequalities of wealth and authority, are just only if they result in compensating benefits for everyone, and in particular for the least advantaged members of society. These principles rule out justifying institutions on the grounds that the hardships of some are offset by a greater good in the aggregate. It may be expedient but it is not just that some should have less in order that others may prosper. But there is no injustice in the greater benefits earned by a few provided that the situation of persons not so fortunate is thereby improved. The intuitive idea is that since everyone's well-being depends upon a scheme of cooperation without which no one could have a satisfactory life, the division of advantages should be such as to draw forth the willing cooperation of everyone taking part in it, including those less well situated. Yet this can be expected only if reasonable terms are proposed. The two principles mentioned seem to be a fair agreement on the basis of which those better endowed, or more fortunate in their social position, neither of which we can be said to deserve, could expect the willing cooperation of others when some workable scheme is a necessary condition of the welfare of all. Once we decide to look for a conception of justice that nullifies the accidents of natural endowment and the contingencies of social circumstance as counters in quest for political and economic advantage, we are led to these principles. They express the result of leaving aside those aspects of the social world that seem arbitrary from a moral point of view.

Justice as fairness is an example of what I have called a contract theory. Now there may be an objection to the term "contract" and related expressions, but I think it will serve reasonably well. Many words have misleading connotations which at first are likely to confuse. The terms "utility" and "utilitarianism" are surely no exception. They too have unfortunate suggestions which hostile critics have been willing to exploit; yet they are clear enough for those prepared to study utilitarian doctrine. The same should be true of the term "contract" applied to moral theories. As I have mentioned, to understand it one has to keep in mind that it implies a certain level of abstraction. In particular, the content of the relevant agreement is not to enter a given society or to adopt a given form of government, but to accept certain moral principles. Moreover, the undertakings referred to are purely hypothetical: a contract view holds that certain principles would be accepted in a well-defined initial situation.

THE ORIGINAL POSITION AND JUSTIFICATION

I have said that the original position is the appropriate initial status quo which insures that the fundamental agreements reached in it are fair. This fact yields the name "justice as fairness." It is clear, then, that I want to say that one conception of justice is more reasonable than another, or justifiable with respect to it, if rational persons in the initial situation would choose its principles over those of the other for the role of justice. Conceptions of justice are to be ranked by their acceptability to persons so circumstanced. Understood in this way the question of justification is settled by working out a problem of deliberation: we have to ascertain which principles it would be rational to adopt given the contractual situation. This connects the theory of justice with the theory of rational choice.

If this view of the problem of justification is to succeed, we must, of course, describe in some detail the nature of this choice problem. A problem of rational decision has a definite answer only if we know the beliefs and interests of the parties, their relations with respect to one another, the alternatives between which they are to choose, the procedure whereby they make up their minds, and so on. As the circumstances are presented in different ways, correspondingly different principles are accepted. The concept of the original position, as I shall refer to it, is that of the most philosophically favored interpretation of this initial choice situation for the purposes of a theory of justice.

But how are we to decide what is the most favored interpretation? I assume, for one thing, that there is a broad measure of agreement that principles of justice should be chosen under certain conditions. To justify a particular description of the initial situation one shows that it incorporates these commonly shared presumptions. One argues from widely accepted but weak premises to more specific conclusions. Each of the presumptions should by itself be natural and plausible; some of them may seem innocuous or even trivial. The aim of the contract approach is to establish that taken together they impose significant bounds on acceptable principles of justice. The ideal outcome would be that these conditions determine a unique set of principles; but I shall be satisfied if they suffice to rank the main traditional conceptions of social justice.

One should not be misled, then, by the somewhat unusual conditions which characterize the original position. The idea here is simply to make vivid to ourselves the restrictions that it seems reasonable to impose on arguments for principles of justice, and therefore on these principles themselves. Thus it seems reasonable and generally acceptable that no one should be advantaged or disadvantaged by natural fortune or social circumstances in the choice of principles. It also seems widely agreed that it should be impossible to tailor principles to the circumstances of one's own case. We should insure further that particular inclinations and aspirations, and persons' conceptions of their good do not affect the principles adopted. The aim is to rule out those principles that it would be rational to propose for acceptance, however little the chance of success, only if one knew certain things that are irrelevant from the standpoint of justice. For example, if a man knew that he was wealthy, he might find it rational to advance the principle that various taxes for welfare measures be counted unjust; if he knew that he was poor, he would most likely propose the contrary principle. To represent the desired restrictions one imagines a situation in which everyone is deprived of this sort of information. One excludes the knowledge of those contingencies which sets men at odds and allows them to be guided by their prejudices. In this manner the veil of ignorance is arrived at in a natural way. This concept should cause no difficulty if we keep in mind the constraints on arguments that it is meant to express. At any time we can enter the original position, so to speak, simply by following a certain procedure, namely, by arguing for principles of justice in accordance with these restrictions.

It seems reasonable to suppose that the parties in the original position are equal. That is, all have the same rights in the procedure for choosing principles; each can make proposals, submit reasons for their acceptance, and so on. Obviously the purpose of these conditions is to represent equality between human beings as moral persons, as creatures having a conception of their good and capable of a sense of justice. The basis of equality is taken to be similarity in these two respects. Systems of ends are not ranked in value; and each man is presumed to have the requisite ability to understand and to act upon whatever principles are adopted. Together with the veil of ignorance, these conditions define the principles of justice as those which rational persons concerned to advance their interests would consent to as equals when none are known to be advantaged or disadvantaged by social and natural contingencies.

There is, however, another side to justifying a particular description of the original position. This is to see if the principles which would be chosen match our considered convictions of justice or extend them in an acceptable way. We can note whether applying these principles would lead us to make the same judgments about the basic structure of society which we now make intuitively and in which we have the greatest confidence; or whether, in cases where our present judgments are in doubt and given with hesitation, these principles offer a resolution which we can affirm on reflection. There are questions which we feel sure must be answered in a certain way. For example, we are confident that religious intolerance and racial discrimination are unjust. We think that we have examined these things with care and have reached what we believe is an impartial judgment not likely to be distorted by an excessive attention to our own interests. These convictions are provisional fixed points which we presume any conception of justice must fit. But we have much less assurance as to what is the correct distribution of wealth and authority. Here we may be looking for a way to remove our doubts. We can check an interpretation of the initial situation, then, by the capacity of its principles to accommodate our firmest convictions and to provide guidance where guidance is needed.

THE DIFFERENCE PRINCIPLE

To illustrate the difference principle, consider the distribution of income among social classes. Let us suppose that the various income groups correlate with representative individuals by reference to whose expectations we can judge the distribution. Now those starting out as members of the entrepreneurial class in property-owning democracy, say, have a better prospect than those who begin in the class of unskilled laborers. It seems likely that this will be true even when the social injustices which now exist are removed. What, then, can possibly justify this kind of initial inequality in life prospects? According to the difference principle, it is justifiable only if the difference in expectation is to the advantage of the representative man who is worse off, in this case the representative unskilled worker. The inequality in expectation is permissible only if lowering it would make the working class even more worse off. Supposedly, given the rider in the second principle concerning open positions, and the principle of liberty generally, the greater expectations allowed to entrepreneurs encourages them to do things which raise the long-term prospects of laboring class. Their better prospects act as incentives so that the economic process is more efficient, innovation proceeds at a faster pace, and so on. Eventually the resulting material benefits spread throughout the system and to the least advantaged. I shall not consider how far these things are true. The point is that something of this kind must be argued if these inequalities are to be just by the difference principle.

I shall now make a few remarks about this principle. First of all, in applying it, one should distinguish between two cases. The first case is that in which the expectations of the least advantaged are indeed maximized (subject, of course, to the mentioned constraints). No changes in the expectations of those better off can improve the situation of those worst off. The best arrangement obtains, what I shall call a perfectly just scheme. The second case is that in which the expectations of all those better off at least contribute to the welfare of the more unfortunate. That is, if their expectations were decreased, the prospects of the least advantaged would likewise fall. Yet the maximum is not yet achieved. Even higher expectations for the more advantaged would raise the expectations of those in the lowest position. Such a scheme is, I shall say, just throughout, but not the best just arrangement. A scheme is unjust when the higher expectations, one or more of them, are excessive. If these expectations were decreased, the situation of the least favored would be improved. How unjust an arrangement is depends on how excessive the higher expectations are and to what extent they depend upon the violation of the other principles of justice, for example, fair equality of opportunity; but I shall not attempt to measure in any exact way the degrees of injustice. The point to note here is that while the difference principle is, strictly speaking, a maximizing principle, there is a significant distinction between the cases that fall short of the best arrangement. A society should try to avoid the region where the marginal contributions of those better off are negative, since, other things equal, this seems a greater fault than falling short of the best scheme when these contributions are positive. The even larger difference between rich and poor makes the latter even worse off, and this violates the principle of mutual advantage as well as democratic equality.

A further point is this. We saw that the system of natural liberty and the liberal conception attempt to go beyond the principle of efficiency by moderating its scope of operation, by constraining it by certain background institutions and leaving the rest to pure procedural justice. The democratic conception holds that while pure procedural justice may be invoked to some extent at least, the way previous interpretations do, this still leaves too much to social and natural contingency. But it should be noted that the difference principle is compatible with the principle of efficiency. For when the former is fully satisfied, it is indeed impossible to make any one representative mad better off without making another worse off, namely, the least advantaged representative man whose expectations we are to maximize. Thus justice is defined so that it is consistent with efficiency, at least when

the two principles are perfectly fulfilled. Of course, if the basic structure is unjust, these principles will authorize changes that may lower the expectations of some of those better off, and therefore the democratic conception is not consistent with the principle of efficiency if this principle is taken to mean that only changes which improve everyone's prospects are allowed. Justice is prior to efficiency and requires some changes that are not efficient in this sense. Consistency obtains only in the sense that a perfectly just scheme is also efficient.

Next, we may consider a certain complication regarding the meaning of the difference principle. It has been taken for granted that if the principle is satisfied, everyone is benefited. One obvious sense in which this is so is that each man's position is improved with respect to the initial arrangement of equality. But it is clear that nothing depends upon being able to identify this initial arrangement; indeed, how well off men are in this situation plays no essential role in applying the difference principle. We simply maximize the expectations of the least favored position subject to the required constraints. As long as doing this is an improvement for everyone, as we assume it is, the estimated gains from the situation of hypothetical equality are irrelevant, if not largely impossible to ascertain anyway. There may be, however, a further sense in which everyone is advantaged when the difference principle is satisfied, at least if we make certain natural assumptions. Let us suppose that inequalities in expectations are chain-connected: that is, if an advantage has the effect of raising the expectations of the lowest position, it raises the expectations of all positions in between. For example, if the greater expectations for entrepreneurs benefit the unskilled worker, they also benefit the semiskilled. Notice that chain connection says nothing about the case where the least advantaged do not gain, so that it does not mean that all effects move together. Assume further that expectations are close-knit: that is, it is impossible to raise or lower the expectation of any representative man without raising or lowering the expectation of every other representative man, especially that of the least advantaged. There is no loose-jointedness, so to speak, in the way expectations hang together. Now with these assumptions there is a sense in which every-one benefits when the difference principle is satisfied. For the representative man who is better off in any two-way comparison gains by the advantages offered him, and the man who is worse off gains from the contributions which these inequalities make. Of course, these conditions may not hold. But in this case those who are better off should not have a veto over the benefits available for the least favored. We are still to maximize the expectations of those most disadvantaged.

FAIR EQUALITY OF OPPORTUNITY

I should now like to comment upon the second part of the second principle, henceforth to be understood as the liberal principle of fair equality of opportunity. It must not then be confused with the notion of careers open to talents; nor must one forget that since it is tied in with the difference principle its consequences are quite distance from the liberal interpretation of the two principles taken together. In particular, I shall try to show further on that this principle is not subject to the objection that it leads to a meritocratic society. Here I wish to consider a few other points, especially its relation to the idea of pure procedural justice.

First, though, I should note that the reasons for requiring open positions are not solely, or even primarily, those of efficiency. I have not maintained that offices must be open if in fact everyone is to benefit from an arrangement. For it may be possible to improve everyone's situation by assigning certain powers and benefits to positions despite the fact that certain groups are excluded from them. Although access is restricted, perhaps these offices can still attract superior talent and encourage better performance. But the principle of open positions forbids this. It expresses the conviction that if some places were not open on a basis fair to all, those kept out would be right in feeling unjustly treated even though they benefited from the greater efforts of those who were allowed to hold them. They would be justified in their complaint not only because they were excluded from certain external rewards of office such as wealth and privilege, but because they were

debarred from experiencing the realization of self which comes from a skillful and devoted exercise of social duties. They would be deprived of one of the main forms of human good.

Now I have said that the basic structure is the primary subject of justice. This means, as we have seen, that the first distributive problem is the assignment of fundamental rights and duties and the regulation of social and economic inequalities and of the legitimate expectations founded on these. Of course, any ethical theory recognizes the importance of the basic structure as a subject of justice, but not all theories regard its importance in the same way. In justice as fairness society is interpreted as a cooperative venture for mutual advantage. The basic structure is a public system of rules defining a scheme of activities that leads men to act together so as to produce a greater sum of benefits and assigns to each certain recognized claims to a share in the proceeds. What a person does depends upon what the public rules say he will be entitled to, and what a person is entitled to depends on what he does. The distribution which results is arrived at by honoring the claims determined by what persons undertake to do in the light of these legitimate expectations.

THE TENDENCY TO EQUALITY

I wish to conclude this discussion of the two principles by explaining the sense in which they express an egalitarian conception of justice. Also I should like to forestall the objection to the principle of fair opportunity that it leads to a callous meritocratic society. In order to prepare the way for doing this, I note several aspects of the conception of justice that I have set out.

First we may observe that the difference principle gives some weight to the considerations singled out by the principle of redress. This is the principle that undeserved inequalities call for redress; and since inequalities of birth and natural endowment are undeserved, these inequalities are to be somehow compensated for. Thus the principle holds that in order to treat all persons equally, to provide genuine equality of opportunity, society must give more attention to those with fewer native assets and to those born into the less favorable social positions. The idea is to redress the bias of contingencies in the direction of equality. In pursuit of this principle greater resources might be spent on the education of the less rather than the more intelligent, at least over a certain time of life, say the earlier years of school.

Now the principle of redress has not to my knowledge been proposed as the sole criterion of justice, as the single aim of the social order. It is plausible as most such principles are only as a prima facie principle, one that is to be weighed in the balance with others. For example, we are to weigh it against the principle to improve the average standard of life, or to advance the common good. But whatever other principles we hold, the claims of redress are to be taken into account. It is thought to represent one of the elements in our conception of justice. Now the difference principle is not of course the principle of redress. It does not require society to try to even out handicaps as if all were expected to compete on a fair basis in the same race. But the difference principle would allocate resources in education, say, so as to improve the long-term expectation of the least favored. If this end is attained by giving more attention to the better endowed, it is permissible; otherwise not. And in making this decision, the value of education should not be assessed solely in terms of economic efficiency and social welfare. Equally if not more important is the role of education in enabling a person to enjoy the culture of his society and to take part in its affairs, and in this way to provide for each individual a secure sense of his own worth.

Thus although the difference principle is not the same as that of redress, it does achieve some of the intent of the latter principle. It transforms the aims of the basic structure so that the total scheme of institutions no longer emphasizes social efficiency and technocratic values. We see then that the difference principle represents, in effect, an agreement to regard the distribution of natural talents as a common asset and to share in the benefits of this distribution whatever it turns out to be. Those who have been favored by nature, whoever they are, may gain from their good fortune only on terms that improve the situation of those who have lost out. The naturally advantaged are not to gain merely because they are more gifted, but only to cover the costs of training and education and for using their endowments in ways that help the less fortunate as well. No one deserves his greater natural capacity nor merits a more favorable starting place in society. But it does not follow that one should eliminate these distinctions. There is another way to deal with them. The basic structure can be arranged so that these contingencies work for the good of the least fortunate. Thus we are led to the difference principle if we wish to set up the social system so that no one gains or loses from his arbitrary place in the distribution of natural assets or his initial position in society without giving or receiving compensating advantages in return.

In view of these remarks we may reject the contention that the ordering of institutions is always defective because the distribution of natural talents and the contingencies of social circumstance are unjust, and this injustice must inevitably carry over to human arrangements. Occasionally this reflection is offered as an excuse for ignoring injustice, as if the refusal to acquiesce in injustice is on a par with being unable to accept death. The natural distribution is neither just nor unjust; nor is it unjust that persons are born into society at some particular position. These are simply natural facts. What is just and unjust is the way that institutions deal with these facts. Aristocratic and caste societies are unjust because they make these contingencies the ascriptive basis for belonging to more or less enclosed and privileged social classes. The basic structure of these societies incorporates the arbitrariness found in nature. But there is no necessity for men to resign themselves to these contingencies. The social system is not an unchangeable order beyond human control but a pattern of human action. In justice as fairness men agree to share one another's fate. In designing institutions they undertake to avail themselves of the accidents of nature and social circumstance only when doing so is for the common benefit. The two principles are a fair way of meeting the arbitrariness of fortune; and while no doubt imperfect in other ways, the institutions which satisfy these principles are just.

THE PRIORITY OF LIBERTY

Aristotle remarks that it is a peculiarity of men that they possess a sense of the just and the unjust and that their sharing a common understanding of justice makes a polis. Analogously one might say, in view of our discussion, that a common understanding of justice as fairness makes a constitutional democracy. For I have tried to show, after presenting further arguments for the first principle, that the basic liberties of a democratic regime are most firmly secured by this conception of justice. In each case the conclusions reached are familiar. My aim has been to indicate not only that the principles of justice fit our considered judgments but also that they provide the strongest arguments for freedom. By contrast ideological principles permit at best uncertain grounds for liberty, or at least for equal liberty. And liberty of conscience and freedom of thought should not be founded on philosophical or ethical skepticism, nor on indifference to religious and moral interests. The principles of justice define an appropriate path between dogmatism and intolerance on the one side, and a reductionism which regards religion and morality as mere preferences on the other. And since the theory of justice relies upon weak and widely held presumptions, it may win quite general acceptance. Surely our liberties are most firmly based when they are derived from principles that persons fairly situated with respect to one another can agree to if they can agree to anything at all.

I now wish to examine more carefully the meaning of the priority of liberty. I shall not argue here for this priority; instead I wish to clarify its sense in view of the preceding examples, among others. There are several priorities to be distinguished. By the priority of liberty I mean the precedence of the principle of equal liberty over the second principle of justice. The two principles are in lexical order, and therefore the claims of liberty are to be satisfied first. Until this is achieved no other principle comes into play. The priority of the right over the good, or of fair opportunity over the difference principle, is not presently our concern.

As all the previous examples illustrate, the precedence of liberty means that liberty can be restricted only for the sake of liberty itself. There are two sorts of cases. The basic liberties may either be less extensive though still equal, or they may be unequal. If liberty is less extensive, the representative citizen must find this a gain for his freedom on balance; and if liberty is unequal, the freedom of those with the lesser liberty must be better secured. In both instances the justification proceeds by reference to the whole system of the equal liberties. These priority rules have already been noted on a number of occasions.

There is, however, a further distinction that must be made between two kinds of circumstances that justify or excuse a restriction of liberty. First a restriction can derive from the natural limitations and accidents of human life, or from historical and social contingencies. The question of the justice of these constraints does not arise. For example, even in a well-ordered society under favorable circumstances, liberty of thought and conscience is subject to reasonable regulations and the principle of participation is restricted in extent. These constraints issue from the more or less permanent conditions of political life; others are adjustments to the natural features of the human situation, as with the lesser liberty of children. In these cases the problem is to discover the just way to meet certain given limitations.

In the second kind of case, injustice already exists, either in social arrangements or in the conduct of individuals. The question here is what is the just way to answer injustice. This injustice may, of course, have many explanations, and those who act unjustly often do so with the conviction that they pursue a higher cause. The examples of intolerant and of rival sects illustrate this possibility. But men's propensity to injustice is not a permanent aspect of community life; it is greater or less depending in large part on social institutions, and in particular on whether these are just or unjust. A well-ordered society tends to eliminate or at least to control men's inclinations to injustice, and therefore warring and intolerant sects, say, are much less likely to exist, or to be a danger, once such a society is established. How justice requires us to meet injustice is a very different problem from how best to cope with the inevitable limitations and contingencies of human life.

These two kinds of cases raise several questions. It will be recalled that strict compliance is one of the stipulations of the original position; the principles of justice are chosen on the supposition that they will be generally complied with. Any failures are discounted as exceptions. By putting these principles in lexical order, the parties are choosing a conception of justice suitable for favorable conditions and assuming that a just society can in due course be achieved. Arranged in this order, the principles define then a perfectly just scheme; they belong to ideal theory and set up an aim to guide the course of social reform. But even granting the soundness of these principles for this purpose, we must still ask how well they apply to institutions under less than favorable conditions, and whether they provide any guidance for instances of injustice. The principles and their lexical order were not acknowledged with these situations in mind and so it is possible that they no longer hold.

I shall not attempt to give a systematic answer to these questions. The intuitive idea is to split the theory of justice into two parts. The first or ideal part assumes strict compliance and works out the principles that characterize a well-ordered society under favorable circumstances. It develops the conception of a perfectly just basic structure and the corresponding duties and obligations of persons under the fixed constraints of human life. My main concern is with this part of the theory. Nonideal theory, the second part, is worked out after an ideal conception of justice has been chosen; only then do the parties ask which principles to adopt under less happy conditions. This division of the theory has, as I have indicated, two rather different subparts. One consists of the principles for governing adjustments to natural limitations and historical contingencies, and the other of principles for meeting injustice.

Viewing the theory of justice as a whole, the ideal part presents a conception of a just society that we are to achieve if we can. Existing institutions are to be judged in the light of this conception and held to be unjust to the extent that they depart from it without sufficient reason. The lexical ranking of the principles specifies which elements of the ideal are relatively more urgent, and the priority rules this ordering suggests are to be applied to nonideal cases as well. Thus as far as circumstances permit, we have a natural duty to remove any injustices, beginning with the most grievous as identified by the extent of the deviation from perfect justice. Of course, this idea is extremely rough. The measure of departures from the ideal is left importantly to intuition. Still our judgment is guided by the priority indicated by the lexical ordering. If we have a reasonably clear picture of what is just, our considered convictions of justice may fall more closely into line even though we cannot formulate precisely how this greater convergence comes about. Thus while the principles of justice belong to the theory of an ideal state of affairs, they are generally relevant.

The several parts of nonideal theory may be illustrated by various examples, some of which we have discussed. One type of situation is that involving a less extensive liberty. Since there are no inequalities, but all are to have a narrower rather than a wider freedom, the question can be assessed from the perspective of the representative equal citizen. To appeal to the interests of this representative man in applying the principles of justice is to invoke the principle of the common interest. (The common good I think of as certain general conditions that are in an appropriate sense equally to everyone's advantage.) Several of the preceding examples involve a less extensive liberty: the regulation of liberty of conscience and freedom of thought in ways consistent with public order, and the limitation on the scope of majority rule belong to this category. These constraints arise from the permanent conditions of human life and therefore these cases belong to that part of nonideal theory which deals with natural limitations. The two examples of curbing the liberties of the intolerant and of restraining the violence of contending sects, since they involve injustice, belong to the partial compliance part of nonideal theory. In each of these four cases, however, the argument proceeds from the viewpoint of the representative citizen. Following the idea of the lexical ordering, the limitations upon the extent of liberty are for the sake of liberty itself and result in a lesser but still equal freedom.

The second kind of case is that of an unequal liberty. If some have more votes than others, political liberty is unequal, and the same is true if the votes of some are weighted much more heavily, or if a segment of society is without the franchise altogether. In many historical situations a lesser political liberty may have been justified. Perhaps Burke's unrealistic account of representation had an element of validity in the context of eighteenth century society. If so, it reflects the fact that the various liberties are not all on a par, for while at that time unequal political liberty might conceivably have been a permissible adjustment to historical limitations, serfdom and slavery, and religious intolerance, certainly were not. These constraints do not justify the loss of liberty of conscience and the rights defining the integrity of the person. The case for certain political liberties and the rights of fair equality of opportunity is less compelling. As I noted before, it may be reasonable to forgo part of these freedoms when the long-run benefits are great enough to transform a less fortunate society into one where the equal liberties can be fully enjoyed. This is especially true when circumstances are not conducive to the exercise of these rights in any case. Under certain conditions that cannot be at present removed, the value of some liberties may not be so high as to rule out the possibility of compensation to those less fortunate. To accept the lexical ordering of the two principles we are not required to deny that the value of liberty depends upon circumstances. But it does have to be shown that as the general conception of justice is followed social conditions are eventually brought about under which a lesser than equal liberty would no longer be accepted. Unequal liberty is then no longer justified. The lexical order is, so to speak, the inherent long-run equilibrium of a just system. Once the tendency to equality has worked itself out, if not long before, the two principles are to be serially ranked.

In these remarks I have assumed that it is always those with the lesser liberty who must be compensated. We are always to appraise the situation from their point of view (as seen from the constitutional convention or the legislature). Now it is this restriction that makes it practically certain that slavery

and serfdom, in their familiar forms anyway, are tolerable only when they relieve even worse injustices. There may be transition cases where enslavement is better than current practice. For example, suppose that city-states that previously have not taken prisoners of war but have always put captives to death agree by treaty to hold prisoners as slaves instead. Although we cannot allow the institution of slavery on the grounds that the greater gains of some outweigh the losses to others, it may be that under these conditions, since all run the risk of capture in war, this form of slavery is less unjust than present custom. At least the servitude envisaged is not hereditary (let us suppose) and it is accepted by the free citizens of more or less equal city-states. The arrangement seems defensible as an advance on established institutions, if slaves are not treated too severely. In time it will presumably be abandoned altogether, since the exchange of prisoners of war is a still more desirable arrangement, the return of the captured members of the community being preferable to the services of slaves. But none of these considerations, however fanciful, tend in any way to justify hereditary slavery or serfdom by citing natural or historical limitations. Moreover, one cannot at this point appeal to the necessity or at least to the great advantage of these servile arrangements for the higher forms of culture.

The problem of paternalism deserves some discussion here, since it has been mentioned in the argument for equal liberty, and concerns a lesser freedom. In the original position the parties assume that in society they are rational and able to manage their own affairs. Therefore they do not acknowledge any duties to self, since this is unnecessary to further their good. But once the ideal conception is chosen, they will want to insure themselves against the possibility that their powers are undeveloped and they cannot rationally advance their interests, as in the case of children; or that through some misfortune or accident they are unable to make decisions for their good, as in the case of those seriously injured or mentally disturbed. It is also rational for them to protect themselves against their own irrational inclinations by consenting to a scheme of penalties that may give them a sufficient motive to avoid foolish actions and by accepting certain impositions designed to undo the unfortunate consequences of their imprudent behavior. For these cases the parties adopt principles stipulating when others are authorized to act in their behalf and to override their present wishes if necessary; and this they do recognizing that sometimes their capacity to act rationally for their good may fail, or be lacking altogether.

Thus the principles of paternalism are those that the parties would acknowledge in the original position to protect themselves against the weakness and infirmities of their reason and will in society. Others are authorized and sometimes required to act on our behalf and to do what we would do for ourselves if we were rational, this authorization coming into effect only when we cannot look after our own good. Paternalistic decisions are to be guided by the individual's own settled preferences and interests insofar as they are not irrational, or failing a knowledge of these, by the theory of primary goods. As we know less and less about a person, we act for him as we would act for ourselves from the standpoint of the original position. We try to get for him the things he presumably wants whatever else he wants. We must be able to argue that with the development or the recovery of his rational powers the individual in question will accept our decision on his behalf and agree with us that we did the best thing for him.

FOR FURTHER
READING

GENERAL

de Crespigny, Anthony and Kenneth (eds.), *Contemporary Political Philoso-phers* (London, 1975).

Ebenstein, William, *Modern Political Thought: The Great Issues,* 2nd ed. (New York, 1960).

McDonald, Lee, *Western Political Theory* (New York, 1968).

Russell, Bertrand, *A History of Western Philosophy: And Its Connections with Political and Social Circumstances from the Earliest Times to the Present Day* (New York, 1945).

Sabine, George H., and Thomas Thorson, *A History of Political Thought,* 4th ed. (New York, 1973).

Sibley, Mulford, *Political Ideas and Ideologies: A History of Political Thought* (New York, 1970).

Strauss, Leo and Joseph Cropsey (eds.), *History of Political Philosophy,* 3rd ed. (Chicago, 1987).

PLATO

Annas, Julia, *An Introduction to Plato's* Republic (Oxford, 1981).

Bambrough, Renford (ed.), *Plato, Popper and Politics: Some Characteristics to a Modern Controversy* (Cambridge, Engl., 1967).

Barker, Ernest, *Greek Political Theory: Plato and His Predecessors* (London, 1925).

Crombie, I. M., *Plato: The Midwife's Apprentice* (London, 1964).

Crospsey, Joseph, *Plato's World: Man's Place in the Cosmos* (Chicago, 1995).

Farrar, Cynthia, *The Origins of Democratic Thinking* (Cambridge, England, 1988).

Findlay, John, *Plato: The Written and Unwritten Doctrines* (New York, 1974).

Foster, M. B., *The Political Philosophy of Plato and Hegel* (Oxford, 1935).

Guthrie, W. K. C., *A History of Greek Philosophy,* 6 vols. (Cambridge, Engl., 1962–1981).

Klosko, George, *The Development of Plato's Political Theory* (New York, 1986).

Kraut, Richard, *Socrates and the State* (Princeton, 1984).

Popper, Karl, *The Open Society and Its Enemies* (Princeton, 1950).

Stalley, R. F., *An Introduction to Plato's* Laws (Chicago, 1975).

Stone, I. F., *The Trial of Socrates* (New York, 1988).

White, Nicholas, *A Companion to Plato's* Republic (Oxford, 1979).

ARISTOTLE

Ackrill, J. L., *Aristotle the Philosopher* (Oxford, 1981).

Barker, Ernest, *The Political Thought of Plato and Aristotle* (London, 1906).

Barnes, Jonathan, *Aristotle* (Oxford, 1982).

Cherniss, Harold, *Aristotle's Criticism of Plato and the Academy* (Baltimore, 1944).

Jaeger, Werner, *Aristotle: Fundamentals of the History of His Development* (Oxford, 1934).

Johnson, Curtis N., *Aristotle's Theory of the State* (New York, 1990).

Layden, Wolfgang von, *Aristotle on Equality and Justice: His Political Argument* (New York, 1985).

Morrall, John, *Aristotle* (London, 1977).

Mulgan, R. G., *Aristotle's Political Theory* (Oxford, 1977).

Ross, W. D., *Aristotle,* 2nd ed. (London, 1930).

Yack, Bernard, *The Problems of a Political Animal: Community, Justice, and Conflict in Aristotelian Political Thought* (Berkeley, 1993).

ST. AUGUSTINE

Bathory, Peter, *Political Theory as Public Confession; The Social and Political Thought of St. Augustine of Hippo* (New Brunswick, N. J., 1981).

Chabannes, Jacques, *St. Augustine* (Garden City, N. Y., 1962).

Chadwick, Henry, *Augustine* (Oxford, 1986).

Coulton, G. G., *Studies in Medieval Thought* (London, 1940).

Deane, Herbert A., *The Political and Social Ideas of St. Augustine* (New York, 1966).

Figgis, John Neville, *The Political Aspects of St. Augustine's "City of God"* (London, 1921).

Gilson, Étienne, *The Christian Philosophy of Saint Augustine* (New York, 1960).

Keyes, G. L., *Christian Faith and the Interpretation of History: A Study of St. Augustine's Philosophy of History* (Lincoln, Nebr., 1966).

Kirwan, Christopher, *Augustine* (London, 1989).

ST. THOMAS AQUINAS

Borresen, Kari, *Subordination and Equivalence: The Nature and Role of Women in Augustine and Thomas Aquinas* (trans. Charles Talbot, Washington, D. C., 1981).

Bourke, Vernon J., *Aquinas' Search for Wisdom* (Milwaukee, 1964).

Chenu, M. D., *Toward Understanding of Saint Thomas* (New York, 1964).

Copleston, F. C., *Aquinas* (Baltimore, 1955).

Gilby, Thomas, *The Political Thought of Thomas Aquinas* (Chicago, 1958).

Gilson, Étienne, *The Christian Philosophy of St. Thomas Aquinas* (New York, 1956).

Malloy, Michael, *Civil Authority in Medieval Philosophy* (Lanham, Md., 1985).

Maritain, Jacques, *St. Thomas Aquinas* (New York, 1958).

Petitot, L. H., *The Life and Spirit of Thomas Aquinas* (Chicago, 1966).

Tracy, David, *Celebrating the Medieval Heritage* (Chicago, 1978).

MACHIAVELLI

Fleisher, Martin (ed.), *Machiavelli and the Nature of Political Thought* (New York, 1972).

Garver, Eugen, *Machiavelli and the History of Prudence* (Madison, Wis., 1987)

Hulliung, Mark, *Citizen Machiavelli* (Princeton, 1984).

Jensen, De Lamar (ed.), *Machiavelli: Cynic, Patriot, or Political Scientist?* (Boston, 1960).

Mansfield, Harvey, *Machiavelli's New Modes and Orders: A Study of the Discourses on Livy* (Ithaca, N. Y., 1979).

————, *Machiavelli's Virtue* (Chicago, 1996).

Pitkin, Hanna, *Fortune Is a Woman; Gender and Politics in the Thought of Niccolò Machiavelli* (Berkeley, 1984).

Prezzolini, Guiseppe, *Machiavelli* (New York, 1967).

Ridolfi, Roberto, *The Life of Niccolò Machiavelli* (Chicago, 1963).

Strauss, Leo, *Thoughts on Machiavelli* (Glencoe, Ill., 1958).

Whitfield, John H., *Machiavelli* (Oxford, 1947).

HOBBES

Bowle, John, *Hobbes and His Critics* (London, 1951).

Brown, Keith C. (ed.), *Hobbes Studies* (Oxford, 1965).

Coleman, Frank, *Hobbes and America* (Toronto, 1977).

Gauthier, David, *The Logic of Leviathan; The Moral and Political Theory of Thomas Hobbes* (Oxford, 1969).

Goldsmith, M. M., *Hobbes's Science of Politics* (New York, 1966.)

Kraus, Jody S., *The Limits of Hobbesian Contractarianism* (Cambridge, 1993).

Macpherson, C. B., *The Political Theory of Possessive Individualism: Hobbes to Locke* (Oxford, 1962).

Oakeshott, Michael, *Hobbes on Civil Association* (Berkeley, 1975).

Ross, Raph, et al., (eds.), *Thomas Hobbes in His Time* (Minneapolis, 1975).

Strauss, Leo, *The Political Philosophy of Hobbes: Its Basis and Its Genesis* (Oxford, 1936).

Warrender, Howard, *The Political Philosophy of Hobbes: His Theory of Oblig-ation* (Oxford, 1957).

Watkins, J. W. N., *Hobbes's System of Ideas* (London, 1965).

LOCKE

Aaron, R. I., *John Locke,* 2nd ed. (Oxford, 1963).

Ashcroft, Richard, *Revolutionary Politics and Locke's* Two Treatises of Gov-ernment (Princeton, 1986).

Cranston, Maurice, *John Locke: A Biography* (New York, 1957).

Dunn, John, *Locke* (Oxford, 1984).

Gough, J. W., *John Locke's Political Philosophy* (Oxford, 1950).

Grant, Ruth, *John Locke's Liberalism* (Chicago, 1987).

Huyler, Jerome, *Locke in American: The Moral Philosophy of the Founding Era* (Lawrence, 1995).

Laski, Harold J., *Political Thought in England: From Locke to Bentham* (Lon-don, 1920).

Laslett, Peter, introduction to *Two Treatises of Government,* by John Locke (Cambridge, Engl., 1967).

Pangle, Thomas, *The Spirit of Modern Republicanism* (Chicago, 1988).

Schouls, Peter A., *Reasoned Freedom: John Locke and Enlightenment* (Ithaca, 1992).

Seliger, M., *The Liberal Politics of John Locke* (New York, 1969).

Wood, Neal, *The Politics of Locke's Philosophy* (Berkeley, 1983).

Yotlon, John M. (ed.), *John Locke: Problems and Perspectives* (Cambridge, Engl., 1969).

ROUSSEAU

Charvet, John, *The Social Problem in the Philosophy of Rousseau* (Cambridge, Engl., 1974).

Cobban, Alfred, *Rousseau and the Modern State,* 2nd ed. (London, 1964).

Cranston, Maurice, *Jean-Jacques: The Early Life and Work of Jean-Jacques Rousseau* (London, 1982).

————, *The Noble Savage: Jean-Jacques Rousseau* (Chicago, 1991).

Ellenburg, Stephen, *Rousseau's Political Philosophy: An Interpretation from Within* (Ithaca, N. Y., 1976).

Fralin, Richard, *Rousseau and Representation* (New York, 1978).

Gildin, Hilail, *Rousseau's* Social Contract (Chicago, 1983).

Hall, John, *Rousseau* (London, 1973).

Kelly, Christopher, *Rousseau's Exemplary Life:* The Confessions *as Political Philosophy* (Ithaca, N. Y., 1987).

Lemos, Ramn, *Rousseau's Political Philosophy* (Atlanta, 1977).

McDonald, Joan, *Rousseau and the French Revolution* (London, 1965).

Melzer, Arthur M., *The Natural Goodness of Man: On the System of Rous-seau's Thought* (Chicago, 1990).

Miller, Jim, *Rousseau: Dreamer of Democracy* (New Haven, 1984).

Shklar, Judith, *Men and Citizens: A Study of Rousseau's Social Theory* (Cambridge, Mass., 1969).

MILL

Anschutz, R. P., *The Philosophy of J. S. Mill* (Oxford, 1969).

Berger, Fred, *Happiness, Justice and Freedom: The Moral and Political Thought of John Stuart Mill* (Berkeley, 1984).

Berlin, Isaiah, *Four Essays on Liberty* (London, 1969).

Cowling, Maurice, *Mill and Liberalism* (Cambridge, Engl., 1963).

Halliday, R. J., *John Stuart Mill* (London, 1976).

Himmelfarb, Gertrude, *On Liberty and Liberalism: The Strange Case of John Stuart Mill* (New York, 1974).

Packe, Michael St. John, *The Life of John Stuart Mill* (New York, 1954).

Robson, John, *The Improvement of Mankind; The Social and Political Thought of John Stuart Mill* (Toronto, 1968).

Ryan, Alan, *J. S. Mill* (London, 1974).

Schneewind, J. B. (ed.), *Mill: A Collection of Critical Essays* (Garden City, N. Y., 1968).

Semmel, Bernard, *John Stuart Mill and the Pursuit of Virtue* (New Haven, 1984).

Stafford, William, *John Stuart Mill* (London, 1998).

Stephen, Leslie, *The English Utilitarians,* 3 vols. (reprinted, London, 1950).

Ten, C. L., *Mill on Liberty* (Oxford, 1980).

MARX

Appelbaum, Richard, *Karl Marx* (Newbury Park, Calif., 1988).

Avineri, Sholomo, *The Social and Political Thought of Karl Marx* (Cambridge, Engl., 1968).

Berlin, Isaiah, *Karl Marx: His Life and Environment,* 4th ed. (New York, 1978).

Felix, David, *Marx as Politician* (Carbondale, Ill., 1983).

Fromm, Erich, *Marx's Concept of Man* (New York, 1961).

Gordon, David, *Resurrecting Marx: The Analytical Marxists on Freedom, Exploitation, and Justice* (New Brunswick, 1990).

Hook, Sidney, *From Hegel to Marx; Studies in the Intellectual Development of Karl Marx* (Ann Arbor, Mich., 1962).

Hunt, Richard, *The Political Ideas of Marx and Engels,* 2 vols. (Pittsburgh, Pa., 1974).

Lichtheim, George, *Marxism: An Historical and Critical Study,* 2nd ed. (New York, 1965).

Lukes, Steven, *Marxism and Morality* (Oxford, 1985).

Maguire, John, *Marx's Theory of Politics* (Cambridge, Engl., 1978).

McLellan, David, *Karl Marx: His Life and Thought,* 2 vols. (New York, 1973).

Ollman, Bertell, *Alienation: Marx's Conception of Man in Capitalist Society* (Cambridge, Engl., 1971).

Strvik, Dirk (ed.), *Birth of the* Communist Manifesto (New York, 1971).

HAYEK

Barry, Norman, *Hayek's Social and Economic Philosophy* (London, 1979).

Butler, Eamonn, *Hayek: His Contribution to the Political and Economic Thought of Our Time* (London, 1983).

Ebenstein, Alan, *Friedrich Hayek: A Biography* (New York, 2001).

Gamble, Andrew, *Hayek: The Iron Cage of Liberty* (Cambridge, 1996).

Gissurarson, Hannes, *Hayek's Conservative Liberalsim* (New York, 1987).

Gray, John, *Hayek on Liberty,* 3rd ed. (London, 1998).

Hoy, Calvin, *A Philosophy of Individual Freedom: The Political Thought of F. A. Hayek* (Westport, 1984).

Seldon, Arthur (ed.), *Agenda for a Free Society: Essays on Hayek's* The Constitution of Liberty (London, 1961).

Shearmur, Jeremy, *Hayek and After: Hayekian Liberalism as a Research Programme* (London, 1996).

Steele, G. R., *The Economics of Friedrich Hayek* (London, 1993).

Walker, Graham, *The Ethics of F. A. Hayek* (Lanham, 1986).

RAWLS

The American Political Science Review (June 1975; contains seven articles on *A Theory of Justice*).

Barry, Brian, *The Liberal Theory of Justice* (Oxford, 1973).

Blocker, H. G., et al. (eds.), *John Rawls' Theory of Social Justice: An Introduction* (Athens, Ohio, 1980).

Daniels, Norman (ed.), *Reading Rawls* (New York, 1980).

Kukathas, Chandran, and Philip Pettit, *Rawls:* A Theory of Justice *and Its Critics* (Stanford, 1990).

Pogge, Thomas, *Realizing Rawls* (Ithaca, N. Y., 1989).

Rawls, John, *Justice as Fairness: A Restatement* (Cambridge, Mass.: 2001).

Schaefer, David, *Justice or Tyranny? A Critique of John Rawls'* A Theory of Justice (Washington, N. Y., 1979).

Wolff, Robert, *Undersanding Rawls: A Reconstruction and Critique of* A Theory of Justice (Princeton, 1977).